A NEW HISTORY OF IBERIAN FEMINISMS

Edited by Silvia Bermúdez and Roberta Johnson

A New History of Iberian Feminisms is both a chronological history and an analytical discussion of feminist thought throughout the Iberian Peninsula from the eighteenth century to the present day.

The essays in this volume, by a distinguished international group of authors, examine the history of Iberian women and their struggle to achieve full citzenship in a geographically and politically diverse area long immersed in a rigorous Roman Catholic tradition. Presenting a wealth of cutting-edge scholarship as well as research on lost historical texts that have been recently resurrected, *A New History of Iberian Feminisms* reveals that the quest for female equality was very much a part of the political conversation even in the early 1800s, a development that would ultimately give impetus to the feminist wave in the second half of the century.

(Toronto Iberic)

SILVIA BERMÚDEZ is a professor in the Department of Spanish and Portuguese at the University of California-Santa Barbara.

ROBERTA JOHNSON is professor emerita of Spanish at the University of Kansas and adjunct professor of Spanish at the University of Kansas.

A New History of Iberian Feminisms

EDITED BY SILVIA BERMÚDEZ
AND ROBERTA JOHNSON

UNIVERSITY OF TORONTO PRESS
Toronto Buffalo London

Toronto Buffalo London
www.utppublishing.com

ISBN 978-1-4875-0014-6 (cloth)   ISBN 978-1-4875-2008-3 (paper)

Library and Archives Canada Cataloguing in Publication

A new history of Iberian feminisms / edited by Silvia Bermúdez and Roberta Johnson.

(Toronto Iberic ; 35)
Includes bibliographical references and index.
ISBN 978-1-4875-0014-6 (cloth). – ISBN 978-1-4875-2008-3 (paper)

1. Feminism – Iberian Peninsula – History. 2. Women – Iberian Peninsula – History. 3. Iberian Peninsula – History. I. Bermúdez, Silvia, editor II. Johnson, Roberta, 1942–, editor III. Series: Toronto Iberic; 35

HQ1725.7.N49 2018   305.420946   C2017-907097-5

This book has been published with the assistance of the University of California, Santa Barbara.

University of Toronto Press acknowledges the financial assistance to its publishing program of the Canada Council for the Arts and the Ontario Arts Council, an agency of the Government of Ontario.

Canada Council for the Arts   Conseil des Arts du Canada

Funded by the Government of Canada   Financé par le gouvernement du Canada

Contents

Figures

Acknowledgments

We wish to thank our outstanding team of authors whose dedication to the project has been unflagging. We thank the UC Comparative Iberian Studies Working Group annual meetings where the volume took shape. We are also grateful for the wise counsel of our editors Mark Thompson, Anne Laughlin, and Carla DeSantis. Special thanks are owed to Paul Cella for compiling the index. We also thank the Biblioteca Nacional Española for permission to use two images in Christine Arkinstall's chapters on the nineteenth-century Spanish press. Silvia Bermúdez thanks the University of California–Santa Barbara and, in particular, John Majewski, the Michael Douglas Dean of Humanities and Fine Arts, for the financial support provided to publish this volume. She dedicates her part in the volume to all the women of the Iberian Peninsula and, more specifically, to her Catalan mother, Marta Rosell Navalles, who taught her about determination and resilience; and to her sisters, Sonia, Sandra, and Lorena, who taught her about laughter and friendship. Roberta Johnson thanks her many students over the years who have offered a testing ground for ideas and her husband, Ricardo Quinones, for his patience and forbearance. She dedicates her part in the volume to all the women of Iberia who have so bravely fought for a better world for themselves and others.

Abbreviations

ADPC	Associació de Dones Periodistes de Catalunya (Association of Catalonian Women Journalists)
AEHM	Asociación of Estudios Históricos sobre la Mujer (Association of Women's Historical Studies)
AFPP	Associação Feminina Portuguesa para a Paz (Portuguese Women's Association for Peace)
AFUNB	Association of Friends of the United Nations in Barcelona
AGAL	Associaçom Galega da Língua (Galician Language Association)
AGM-ADMG	Asociación Galega da Muller (Galician Association of Women)
AMB/BEA	Asamblea de Mujeres de Bizkaiko Emakumeen Asanblada (Assembly of Women from Viscaya)
ANCHF	Asociación de Comunicación Humana y Ecológica (Association of Human and Ecological Communication)
ANME	Asociación Nacional de Mujeres Españolas (National Association of Spanish Women)
APEM	Associação Portuguesa de Estudos sobre as Mulheres (Portuguese Association of Women's Studies)
CC	Coalición Canaria (The Canary Coalition) de Euskai Basque Workers' Commissions
CCOO	Comisiones Obreras (Worker's Compensation)
CEIG	Centre d'Estudis Interdisciplinaris de Gènere, Universitat de Vic (Centre of Gender Interdisciplinary Studies, University of Vic)
CIMA	Asociación de Mujeres Cineastas y Medios Audiovisuales (Association of Women Film-Makers and Audio-Visual Specialists)

CiU	Convergencia i Unió (Convergence and Union)
CMC	Communist Movement of Catalonia
CNMP	Conselho Nacional das Mulheres Portuguesas (National Council of Portuguese Women)
CNT	Confederación Nacional de Trabajadores (National Workers' Confederation)
EAB	Emakume Abertzale Batza (Society of Nationalist Women)
EAJ/PNV	Eusko Alderdi Jeltzalea/Partido Nacionalista Vasco (Basque Nationalist Party)
ETA	Euskadi Ta Askatasuna (Euskadi and Liberty)
EZI/NV	Eusko Aderdi Jettzalea/Partido Nationalista (Nationalist Party)
FAI	Federación Anarquista Ibérica (Iberian Anarchist Federation)
FEMINAE	University Women's Studies Publishing Project, University of Granada
FIGA	Feministas Independientes Galegas (Independent Galician Feminists)
FLM	Frente de Liberación de las Mujeres (Women's Liberation Front)
FRAP	Frente Revolucionaria Antifascista y Patriota (Revolutionary Anti-Fascist and Patriotic Front)
GIRL	Grupo de Intervencão e Reflexão Lésbica (Lesbian Reflection and Intervention Group)
HOAC	Hermandades Obreras de Acción Católica (Workers' Brotherhoods of Catholic Action)
IIEDG	Institut Interuniversitari d'Estudis de la Dona (Seminar in Women's Studies)
ILGA	International Lesbian, Gay, Bisexual, Trans, and Intersex Association
IM	Instituto de la Mujer (The Institute for Women)
ITOAC	Hermandades Obreros de Acción Católica (Workers' Brotherhoods of Catholic Action)
IUED	Institut Universitari d'Estudis de la DONA (University Institute of Women's Studies)
IUEM	Instituto Universitario de Estudios de la Mujer (University Institute of Women's Studies)
IWY	International Women's Year
JOC	Juventud Obrera Católica (Catholic Workers' Youth)
MACBA	Museu d'Art Contemporari de Barcelona (Barcelona Museum of Contemporary Art)
MAPA	Mulheres a Preparar o Amanhã (Women Preparing Tomorrow)
MAV	Mujeres en las Artes Visuales (Women in the Visual Arts)

MDM	Movimento Democrático de Mulheres (Women's Democratic Movement)
MLF	Movement de Liberátion des Femmes (Women's Liberation Movement)
MPF	Mocidade Portuguesa Feminina (Portuguese Young Women)
MUGACOM	Asociación de Mulleres Galegas na Comunicación (Association of Galician Women in Communication)
NOW	National Organization of Women
OMEN	Obra das Mães pela Educação Nacional (Mothers Working for National Education)
PCE	Partido Comunista Español (Spanish Communist Party)
PNV	Partido Nacionalista Vasco (Basque Nationalist Party)
PIDE/DGS	Polícia Internacional e de Defesa do Estado/Direção-Geral de Segurança (International and State Defense Police/Directorate-General of Security)
PSOE	Partido Socialista Obrero Español (Workers' Socialist Party of Spain)
SEM/EBIM	Seminario de Estudios de la Mujer (Women's Studies Seminar)/Emakumeari Buruzko Ikerketarako Mintegia (Seminar for the Study of Women)
SESM	Seminario do Estudios Sociológicos de la Mujer (Seminar for Women's Sociological Studies)
UGT	Unión General de Trabajadores (Workers' General Union)
UMAR	União de Mulheres Alternativa e Resposta (Women's Union for Choice and Response)
UN	União Nacional (National Union)
UPG	Unión do Poblo Galego (Galician People's Union)
UPNA	Universidad Pública de Navarra (Public University of Navarre)

A NEW HISTORY OF IBERIAN FEMINISMS

Introduction

A New History of Iberian Feminisms is an account of feminist activity and writing in all areas of the Iberian Peninsula – the Basque Provinces, the Castilian-speaking areas, Catalonia, Galicia, and Portugal – from the eighteenth century, when a modern feminism began to argue for the equal treatment of women before the law and in society, to the present.[1] To date feminist thinking and activism in the Iberian Peninsula have been chronicled in narratives that do not take into account the diverse linguistic, political, and cultural milieux in which feminist thought and activity developed there. Analyses of feminist writing from the Iberian geopolitical areas are woven together in a cohesive narrative that considers the interaction between the several territorial feminisms. In consonance with the recent formulations of Iberian Studies, this volume understands the Iberian Peninsula as a multilingual cultural and literary configuration in all its complexity. While *A New History* began as a project within the University of California Iberian Studies research group, the editors have gathered together a number of leading scholars on Iberian feminism from Britain, New Zealand, Portugal, Spain, and the United States, who have written essays for the volume on their areas of expertise. These researchers bring cutting-edge scholarship to the book. For example, now that much nineteenth-century periodical press has been digitized, we include references to many more women's writings from this period. There has also been a noteworthy upsurge in the number of scholars researching and publishing on the fin de siècle period. *A New History* builds on such exciting contemporary research to provide different lenses through which to approach the histories of Iberian feminisms. The feminist agendas of many of the writers covered in the volume have only partially been fulfilled. Hence, many of their concerns remain absolutely current in twenty-first-century society, despite labels such as "postfeminism."

For the most part, the previous histories of feminism in the Iberian Peninsula have concentrated on what took place in Madrid and to a lesser extent in Barcelona, while Portugal is considered as a completely separate entity (if Portugal underwent a "gradual de-Iberianization" [Wheeler 6] from the seventeenth century onward, we are looking to reincorporate the country in a comprehensive view of feminist thinking and activity in the Iberian Peninsula). Geraldine Scanlon's *La polémica feminista en la España contemporánea (1868–1974)* (The feminist polemic in contemporary Spain), published in 1975, is still an important starting point for the history for feminism in Spanish-speaking Iberia, although there are several more recent histories. Scanlon organizes her study chronologically in two parts, the first from 1868 to 1931 and the second from 1931 to 1974. The first part is divided into topics: education, work, legal position, antifeminism, and the feminist movement; the second part focuses on specific periods: the republic, the Civil War, and the "New Spain." *El feminismo en España: Dos siglos de historia* (Feminism in Spain: Two centuries of history), edited by Pilar Folguera (1988b), contains essays by specialists on each of the major periods: the Enlightenment; the nineteenth century (focused only on Concepción Arenal and Emilia Pardo Bazán); the seminal period from 1920 to 1930; the Second Republic and the Civil War; women's response to Francoism; and the transition to democracy (1975–88). The chronologically ordered chapters are complemented by a summary of feminism in Spain from 1953 to 1985; a depiction of democratic-era Spanish feminism from the point of view of those who participated in it by Victoria Sendón de León; and a study of the origins and evolution of the contemporary feminist movement by Geraldine Scanlon. As an exception to histories of feminisms focused mostly on Madrid or Barcelona, we have the six volumes edited by Iris M. Zavala for Anthropos that began in 1993 with the title *Breve historia feminista de la literatura española (en lengua castellana)*, volume 1, *Teoria feminista: Discursos y diferencia*, coedited with M. Diaz-Diocaretz. Volume 6, *Breve historia feminista de la literatura española (en lengua catalana, gallega y vasca)* (2000), coedited with Cristina Dupláa, Mari Jose Olaziregi, María Jesús Farina, and Beatriz Suárez Briones, focuses on other Iberian feminisms. In addition, Zavala also edited *Feminismos, cuerpos, escrituras* in 2000. *Recovering Spain's Feminist Tradition* (2001), edited by Lisa Vollendorf for the Modern Language Association, is a valuable volume that locates the beginnings of Spanish feminism in the Middle Ages; but its essays focus on one or another writer across the ages, and thus it cannot be considered a comprehensive history. The two volumes of the *Feminist Encyclopedia of Spanish Literature* (2002), coedited by Janet Pérez and Maureen Ihrie, are another important source of information but centred only in Spain.

The four volumes of *Historia de las mujeres en España y América Latina* (History of women in Spain and Latin America; 2006, 2008), edited by Isabel Morant and organized by topics – politics, work, education, is the most comprehensive of all the histories of Spanish-speaking women. However, unlike the present volume, it does not attempt to systematically consider feminist activity in the regions and incorporate that activity into Peninsular feminist networks as a whole. As the title indicates, there are sections on Latin America, but essays focused on Latin America (excluding Brazil) occupy the second half of each volume. Thus Latin America is treated separately and not in transatlantic dialogue with the Iberian Peninsula, which for the orientation of *Historia de las mujeres* does not include Portugal. Books on Portuguese feminism, such as Regina Tavares da Silva's *Feminismo em Portugal na voz de mulheres escritoras do inicio do séc XX* (Feminism in Portugal in the voice of female writers from the beginning of the twentieth century), R.M. Ballesteros's *El movimiento feminista portugués: Del despertar republicano a la exclusión salazarista (1909–1947)* (The Portuguese feminist movement: From the Republican dawn to the eradication under Salazar), Andrea Simões's *Gendering Transitions: Women's Movements in the Spanish and Portuguese Transitions to Democracy*, and Teresa Martins de Oliveira's *Equality in Law between Men and Women in the European Community: Portugal* each treat an aspect of twentieth-century Portuguese feminism, but a more historically comprehensive view is called for. Since legal and political systems are central to feminist debates and activity, we cannot ignore the differences in legal arrangements within the Iberian Peninsula.

A New History of Iberian Feminisms takes a different approach from these important starting points. One of the most innovative features of this history is its rethinking of old periodizations. Rather than adhering to century markers or to political history, our periodization follows the ebb and flow of feminist activity, which, of course, is tied to political history but also has a rhythm of its own. The volume is organized chronologically by time periods that conform to shifts in feminist activity and writing: a long eighteenth century (1700–1808); an even longer nineteenth century that includes the early twentieth century (1808–1920); Iberian first-wave feminism (1920–39); the dictatorships (Salazar [1932–68] and Franco [1939–75]); the early democratic era (1970–94); and the most recent period (1994–present). The periods are somewhat elastic in order to accommodate the political histories of both Portugal and Spain. The chronological approach allows scholars with expertise in Iberian feminist writing to consider the networks of feminist activity that developed across the peninsula during the time period they know best. Each chronological segment includes a brief political history that focuses on feminist activity and women's contributions to political structures. The heart of each section is a critical reflection on feminist writing, including feminist journals where appropriate. By "feminist writing" we understand primarily the essay, which, unlike fiction, poetry, or theatre, is usually not mediated through voices other than the author's own. Also by "feminist" writing we mean writing that seeks to uncover the individual and social mechanisms that constrain women's lives and/or writing that proposes alternatives to social, political, or individual circumstances that foster inequality between men and women. Tying the book together are several recurring themes in Spanish feminist thought. Given that Iberian feminism arose as the Portuguese and Spanish Empires flourished, there is an important transatlantic dimension to Iberian feminism from its beginnings to the present (as attested by the protagonism of Argentine writers Alicia Puleo and Silvia Tubert in recent Spanish feminist thought). The notions of equality and difference, which are at the centre of Iberian feminism in the recent democratic era, were already an evident polarization in the eighteenth century, and legal issues have promoted feminist activism across the centuries.

Given that the term "feminism" was not used in its modern understanding until the late nineteenth century, throughout the volume the authors are conscious of Karen Offen's definition: "Feminism is the name given to a comprehensive critical response to the deliberate and systematic subordination of women as a group by men as a group within a given cultural setting" (20). For Offen, the concept of feminism "encompass[es] both a system of ideas and movement for sociopolitical change based on a refusal of male privilege and women's subordination within any given society" (20). Considering the history of Iberian feminism from a geographical as well as a temporal perspective complicates and enriches the story. Again Karen Offen's *European Feminisms 1700–1950: A Political History* serves as a model. A little like the Iberia we are trying to envision, Offen's history views Europe as a whole with significant differences among the individual nations. She includes England, Italy, Hungary, Germany, France, Portugal, Ireland, Spain, and Sweden. The book follows a chronological format by centuries – part 1, eighteenth century; part 2, nineteenth century; part 3, twentieth century – and within each part, Offen addresses themes that allow her to discuss several of the countries. Likewise, most of the parts of *A New History of Iberian Feminisms* include a set of themes within each of the chronological periods. For example, after a historical overview, the eighteenth-century section considers the following topics: "Debates over Women's Abilities and Women's Participation in the Public Sphere"; "Women and 'Civic Motherhood'"; "Feminist Expressions regarding Love and Marriage."

Within each period, the scholars consider to what extent feminist thinkers and activists from the different areas of the Iberian Peninsula developed their ideas according to the requirements of their specific national project, the sources of their thinking and models for their activity (be it from other localities within the Peninsula or from abroad), their reactions to central government policies, and their physical displacement (to the centre or to other locations) for activist, professional, or other reasons. Among these displacements, political exile is an important consideration, particularly in the case of some eighteenth- and early nineteenth-century writers and activists and the victims of twentieth-century dictatorial regimes. These displacements necessarily incorporate Latin America, especially during certain periods, such as the early twentieth century when Peninsular feminists travelled and lectured extensively in the Caribbean, Mexico, and South America, or during the repressive dictatorial periods of the twentieth century. *A New History of Iberian Feminisms* cannot be totally comprehensive; no history can be. However, its goal is to complicate the standard histories of Iberian feminism by bringing this diverse production into focus and understanding its contribution to a complex web of feminist interactions from the eighteenth century, where we locate the beginnings of a modern feminist consciousness in the Peninsula, to the present.[2]

OUTLINE OF THE BOOK

Part I. Iberian Feminism in the Age of Enlightenment (Coordinated by Catherine M. Jaffe and Elizabeth Franklin Lewis)

Chapter 1. Situating Women in the Society of the Old Regime: The Other Spanish Enlightenment (María Victoria López-Cordón Cortezo)

This chapter summarizes the political, social, and cultural context of eighteenth-century Spain and Portugal in which the intellectual debates over the nature and purpose of the sexes took place, as well as the transformations that affected women's lives of the period. The chapter establishes the period's chronological limits, taking as a point of departure the dynastic change that in 1700 enthroned the Bourbons in Spain and as an ending point the Guerra de la Independencia (Peninsular War) in 1808, although it also highlights the century's continuities with the history of Spain and Portugal that both preceded and followed it.

Chapter 2. New Inflections of a Long Polemic: The Debate between the Sexes in Enlightenment Spain (Mónica Bolufer Peruga)

The gender debate has long been considered a constitutive trait of Enlightenment culture. Spain and Portugal were definitely engaged in this debate and contributed substantial ideas and discussion to the question of how to define the difference or equality of the sexes in terms of reason, moral and sentimental inclination, and how to contemplate gender's purpose in the framework of a society that sought to modernize and transform itself. The authors include well-known figures, such as the Benedictine friar and representative of the early Spanish Enlightenment Fray Benito Jerónimo Feijoo, together with women who have only recently entered the canon, such as Josefa Amar y Borbón, and others whose lives and works we are just now beginning to uncover, such as Inés Joyes y Blake.

Chapter 3. Women and "Civic Motherhood" (Elizabeth Franklin Lewis)

Debates over women's abilities and their participation in the public sphere (economic societies, academies, and literary salons) led to one of the most distinguishing aspects of eighteenth-century Spanish feminism: women's civic activity fulfilling a public role as "civic mothers." This chapter examines women's role in the public sphere and the formation and expression of the concept of "civic" motherhood, beginning with a study of two works on women's education – Josefa Amar y Borbón's book on women's education, *Discurso sobre la educación física y moral de las mujeres* (1790), and Inés Joyes y Blake's essay "Apología de las mujeres" (1798).

Chapter 4. From the Traps of Love and the Yoke of Marriage to the Ideal of Friendship: Women Writers in the Eighteenth Century (Catherine M. Jaffe)

Historians and literary scholars have observed how marriage during the eighteenth century in Spain underwent a process of change that, without completely rejecting the traditional structures of matrimony, began to incorporate new models of experience such as the recognition and appreciation of sensibility as an ethical impulse. A new way to think about love and matrimony, one that affirmed love and social equality as the basis for the conjugal relationship, began to appear near the end of the century. A new awareness grew of marriage as an affective relationship based on inclination and mutual respect between a man and a woman.

Chapter 5: "Feminism" in Portugal before 1800 (Vanda Anastácio)

Even today most historians of Portuguese culture do not record any traces of feminist claims in Portugal before the rise of the first suffragist movements. However, the similarity of many of the claims made by early twentieth-century feminists to those uttered by the men and women who spoke out for women's rights, needs, and aspirations in the Early Modern Period allows for a broader understanding of the concept, and for the recuperation of their discourses as proof of the existence of a "feminist consciousness" and as part of the history of feminism. The eighteenth century offers a privileged field of inquiry in this context. At a time when philosophers and rulers were discussing ways of reforming society in order to ensure the well-being of large numbers of people, when the origins and the nature of inequality between men were the subject of an intense and widespread debate, women's nature, women's education, and women's roles became recurrent themes of controversy. However, although the rights reclaimed for women and the discourses used to claim them were very similar to those circulating in other parts of Europe, the ways they were formulated and the channels used to convey them were determined, to a large extent, by the specificities of the Portuguese cultural field.

Chapter 6: The Basque Enlightenment: New Visions of Gender in the Crisis of the Old Regime (Bakarne Altonaga)

The Basque provinces, along with the rest of Europe, experienced regulation of their emotions and their customs in the eighteenth century. In addition to being repressive, this process was fundamentally productive, resulting in the creation of different discourses and spaces of knowledge and power centred around sexual and emotional identity. In this context, the debate over the understanding of sexual difference in the Basque Enlightenment followed similar lines to those of

Enlightened thinkers from other places. However, their contribution holds special interest because their desire to reform relations between the sexes is framed within a society (as was the Basque society at the end of the eighteenth century) whose clergy were faithful followers of conservative Tridentine Catholicism and were powerful agents of control over the bodies and the souls of the faithful, to whom they spoke directly in their native language, *euskera* (Euskara).

Part II. The Long Nineteenth Century (1808–1920) (Coordinated by Christine Arkinstall and Maryellen Bieder)

Chapter 7. Historical Background: From Wars and Revolution to Constitutional Monarchies; Spain's Sporadic Path to Modernity, 1808–1919 (Maryellen Bieder)

Nineteenth-century Iberian political history was turbulent. Both Spain and Portugal sustained civil wars with burgeoning liberal movements arising from them. However, these liberal movements did not necessarily mean greater rights for women. Large areas of the legal systems left matters relating to women up to custom and the Catholic Church. For example, in Spain there were no laws governing marriage (except for what the church dictated) until 1870. Laws concerning adultery (even under the liberal regime from 1820 to 1823) continued to focus on men's honour. Education for girls was not legally addressed until the promulgation of the Ley Moyano in 1857.

Chapter 8. Historical Context of Feminism and Women's Rights in Nineteenth-Century Portugal (João Esteves, translated by Deborah Madden)

As in many other European countries, feminist ideas and a struggle for women's rights emerged in nineteenth-century Portugal. A lengthy process, the movement only gained stability in the late nineteenth and early twentieth centuries. Despite the Liberal Revolution of 1820 and the progression from an absolute monarchy to a constitutional or liberal government, a development that was reflected in the social, economic, and political structure of Portuguese society, women in nineteenth-century Portugal still lacked political rights. Relegated to a position of legal, social, political, and cultural inferiority, women were not acknowledged by the law and were legally subordinate to their fathers and husbands. Furthermore, extremely high rates of illiteracy limited women's already meagre professional opportunities. The advancement of women and their progress from the private sphere to the public domain was gradual, with several advancements and setbacks. The progress is illustrated by the establishment of numerous female-authored and -directed periodical publications, which also included contributions from male journalists, as the so-called women's press flourished from 1820.

Chapter 9. A Feminist Press Gains Ground in Spain, 1822–1866 (Christine Arkinstall)

Despite the small number of literate women, a new periodical press directed at women sprang up in the early nineteenth century to provide a platform for female writers. This chapter charts the emergence of feminist voices in such periodicals from initially scarce, hesitant formulations to increasingly strong pronouncements. Although during the Trienio Liberal (1820–3) the *Periódico de las Damas* (1822) did address questions like women's rights, it is not until the mid-1840s that a more overt feminist ethos can be glimpsed in *El Vergel de Andalucía* and the *Pensil del Bello Sexo*, continued in the early 1850s in *La Mujer* and *Ellas*. The presence of a female monarch undoubtedly had an impact on accepted feminine roles.

Chapter 10. Women Authors in the Romantic Tradition (1841–1884) and Early Feminist Thought (1861–1893) (Maryellen Bieder)

In nineteenth-century Spain several protofeminist and feminist thinker-writers emerged to further define feminist goals in the Iberian Peninsula – Cuban-born Gertrudis Gómez de Avellaneda; Carolina Coronado; Catalan María Josefa Massanés Dalmau (Josepa Massanés i Dalmau); Concepción Arenal, who was born in Galicia and spent many years in Madrid collaborating and working in diverse agencies and social organizations; Emilia Pardo Bazán and Rosalía de Castro, both from Galicia; the pioneering Concepción Gimeno de Flaquer, who networked for twenty-five years with other women in Spain and Spanish America through her magazines for and about women; and near contemporary, the Catalan Dolors Monserdà i Vidal de Macià.

Chapter 11. Forging a Nation for the Female Sex: Equality, Natural Law, and Citizenship in Spanish Feminist Essays, 1881–1920 (Christine Arkinstall)

From the late 1870s women's demands to participate more fully in a fledgling Spanish liberal nation were firmly on the agenda of progressive female intellectuals. Political movements such as republicanism, socialism, and anarchism, Masonic lodges, and freethinking associations and publications were the crucibles for entire cohorts of female writers and their feminist aspirations. Although many wrote within a double militancy shaped by the short-lived Spanish First Republic (1873–4), all negotiated the conservative interlocking icons of the Angel in the House and the *perfecta casada* (perfect married woman) to carve out spaces for enhanced sociopolitical participation. This chapter includes considerations of the contributions to the feminist periodical press by Amalia Domingo Soler, Soledad Gustavo (Teresa Mañé), Ángeles López de Ayala, and Belén Sárraga, and especially highlights Rosario de Acuña's essays.

Chapter 12. First-Wave Feminisms, 1880–1919 (Maryellen Bieder)

The twentieth century increasingly saw more overt statements of feminist goals and more public activities accompanied by less reliance on the prevailing status quo for women. Focusing on Carmen de Burgos as a transitional example of Spanish feminist thought and actions at the turn of the twentieth century, this chapter incorporates writers ending their careers in the first two decades of the new century and subsequently progresses forward to new writers just emerging in the twentieth century. Concepción Gimeno de Flaquer, Emilia Pardo Bazán, and the Catalan writer Carme Karr i Alfonsetti continued to make the argument for feminism, as did Blanca de los Ríos and the Catalan writer Caterina Albert i Paradis (pen name Víctor Català). María Martínez Sierra, Margarita Nelken, Clara Campoamor, and Victoria Kent brought the fresh perspectives of a younger generation and more active participation in transforming Spanish women's condition.

Chapter 13. Crossing Centuries, Crossing Words, 1804–1920: Women, Basque Society, and the Struggle for the Public Sphere (Amaia Álvarez-Uria, Josune Muñoz, and Iratxe Retolaza)

This consideration of Basque feminist thinkers in the long nineteenth century includes four main foci; (1) women's participation in Basque book culture in the early nineteenth century through the figure of Bizenta Mogel, author of *Ipui onak* (1804); (2) Basque women's participation in the incipient Basque press in the nineteenth and early twentieth centuries, especially in the emblematic journals *Euskal Esnalea* (1908–31) and *Euskalerriaren Alde* (1911–31); (3) the introduction of aristocratic women into educational institutions, work in which key figures such as María de Maeztu participated; and (4) the contributions of Basque women such as dramatist Katalina Eleizegi to Basque theatre at the beginning of the twentieth century.

Chapter 14. Redefining the Cultural Periphery from Women's Transatlantic Networks: Spanish and Latin American Women of Letters in the Nineteenth Century (Pura Fernández)

Four authors whose feminist activities spanned the Atlantic – Gertrudis Gómez de Avellaneda; Emilia Serrano, baroness of Wilson; Concepción Gimeno de Flaquer; and Belén Sárraga – will serve as hubs in a network of transatlantic relations that connect with some of the principal figures who fought for women's rights in Latin America (Clorinda Matto, Juana Gorriti, Mercedes Cabello de Carbonera, Eduarda Mansilla). The feminist positions of the writers vary from the so-called moderate feminist of Concepción Gimeno de Flaquer to the combative feminism of Belén Sárraga.

Part III. The Iberian Feminist Movements Gain Strength under Republics (1920–1939) (Coordinated by Roberta Johnson)

Chapter 15. Historical Context in Portugal (Deborah Madden)

Republican forms of government with their equality platforms have long been associated with women achieving political and legal parity. Portugal, which had voted for a republic in 1910, was more advanced in its twentieth-century feminist activity than Spain. Portuguese women were important promoters of the Portuguese Republican movement, as was the case with the Second Spanish Republic elected in 1931. Although women achieved a number of rights under the Portuguese Republic, the right to vote was not one of them. Thus womens' suffrage became a lightning-rod issue in Portugal, as it was in the Anglo-American world.

Chapter 16. Feminist Thought in Portugal, 1900–1926 (Deborah Madden)

The chapter focuses on Carolina Beatriz Ângelo, who wrote articles criticizing the Portuguese monarchy and helped sew the Republican flags that were raised in Lisbon in 1910. She formed the Portuguese Group of Feminist Studies, and the Association of Feminist Propaganda with Ana de Castro Osorio, another important Portuguese feminist and founder in 1907 of the first feminist association, The Portuguese Group of Feminist Studies. In 1911, Ângelo became a major advocate for women's suffrage. She had managed to vote under the original Republican law, which allowed heads of household (not specifying gender) to vote. The fact that Ângelo had managed to vote before the law was changed became international news. She was catapulted to fame, and Portugal was regarded as a pioneering country in terms of granting women's suffrage.

Chapter 17. Historical Background in Spain (Roberta Johnson and Olga Castro)

In the 1920s and 1930s, when Carmen de Burgos published her seminal feminist treatise *La mujer moderna y sus derechos* (1927), another younger generation began to emerge that included Clara Campoamor, Margarita Nelken, Federica Monstseny, Rosa Chacel, Hildegart Rodríguez, and María Zambrano. In the lead-up to the Second Spanish Republic (1931–9), political affiliations became important (e.g., Madrid-based Margarita Nelken was first a Socialist and then a Communist, and Catalonian Montseny was affiliated with the anarchists). For the feminists who were strongly identified with a political party, as for some feminists in the democratic era (1975–present), double militancy is an issue. Their publications straddled class and gender concerns, arguing simultaneously for women's rights, as well as for those of the working class.

Chapter 18. First-Wave Spanish Feminism Takes Flight in Castilian-, Catalan-, and Galician-Speaking Spain (Roberta Johnson and Olga Castro)

As discussed in part 2 and in the previous chapter, Spanish feminism during the 1920s and 1930s was mostly an effort by singular figures – Carmen de Burgos, Margarita Nelken, Federica Montseny, and María Zambrano, among others. But important advances in women's rights were proposed in the Spanish Constitution of 1931. More importantly, Spanish feminists, female intellectuals, and activists relied on difference feminism to open up a space in a conservative, Catholic country such as Spain that, despite the economic, cultural, and political modernization porcessess taking place in the first decades of the twentieth century, continued to centre on motherhood as the essential basis of women's cultural identity.

Chapter 19. Basque Feminist Trajectories in the 1930s: New Women between Change and Continuity (Miren Llona)

The first stirrings of Basque feminism arose in the 1920s during the Second Spanish Republic and in the post-Civil War period as part of the anti-Franco movement. Pre-Civil War Basque feminists, such as Dolores Ibárruri and Polixene Trabudua, worked within the Workers' Movement or the National Basque Party. The chapter identifies the changes that allowed Basque women in the 1930s to develop new attitudes and expectations with respect to the sexual order. The lives of these two women allow us to observe the range of changes that occurred during the Second Republic and the brake on change in women's lives that the outbreak of the Civil War in 1936 occasioned.

Part IV. The Dictatorhips of António de Oliveira Salazar (1926–1974) and Francisco Franco (1939–1975) (Coordinated by Roberta Johnson)

Chapter 20. Historical Overview of Portugal (João Esteves) and Spain (Roberta Johnson)

By 1933 Salazar had assumed full dictatorial powers and had presented the Constitution of the New State and the Colonial Charter, the documents that effectively inaugurated the Fascist dictatorship in Portugal and that were only deposed on 25 April 1974. The dictatorship engaged in a duplicitous discourse on "equal rights" evident in article 5 of the Constitution. In Spain during the Franco regime, women's lives were regulated by the Sección Femenina de Falange that emphasized women's domestic role as housewives and mothers. The women's press underscored women's role as eternally smiling and self-sacrificing.

Chapter 21. Portuguese Feminist Writing during the Estado Novo (Fátima Mariano)

Curiously, during the period after 1947, there were a greater number of women writers – essayists and poets – and activists than ever before, and indeed, a number matched only in the postdictatorial period. This section identifies and discusses the different directions of feminist arguments and woman-centred discourse, and the different types of publication venues they employed. From 1947 to 1972, the year Maria Teresa Horta, Maria Isabel Barreno, and Maria Velho da Costa's *New Portuguese Letters* was published, feminism, as such, was eclipsed, although the number of women prose writers continued to grow and find publication venues. Other writers considered here include Agustina Bessa Luis, who published *Sibila*, and Natália Correia.

Chapter 22. Spanish Feminist Writing during the Franco Regime, 1939–1975 (Roberta Johnson)

Reality did not match the ideal of marriage and motherhood projected by the Sección Femenina de Falange during the Franco regime, and there were any number of women who did not marry (and even some who did) and had careers. However, the open expression of feminist principles – legal, social, and economic equality for women – was limited to the clandestine realm in the early years of the Franco regime. The feminist impulse in which some writers had been educated in the 1920s and 1930s emerged in disguised form in novels and short stories in works by Carmen Laforet and Ana María Matute, among others. Some mildly feminist essays were published in Spain in the periodical press.

Chapter 23. Galician Women under Franco: Resistance, Clandestine Politics, and Poetry as Gendered Symbolic Capital (Silvia Bermúdez)

Despite the dangers and the brutal repression ensuing after 1939, many Galician women continued to be involved in anti-Franco guerrilla activities, acting clandestinely through the difficult 1940s. Leading historical figures such as Enriqueta Otero Blanco, María Araujo Martínez, Rita Amparo López Jean, María Elvira Bao Maceiras, María Barbeito

Cerviño, and others, along with scores of Galician women, not registered in the history books, resisted and fought against the dictatorship through everyday practices combating political repression, poverty, and linguistic harassment. Beginning in the late 1940s, and as heirs to Rosalía de Castro's legacy and within the symbolic status of poetry in Galician culture, three women poets, Pura Vázquez (1918–2006), Luz Pozo Garza (1922–2017), and Xohana Torres (1931), along with other women authors, came to emblematize the gendered politics that simultaneously legitimized and limited women's authorship, not dissimilar to what the canonical figure of Rosalía de Castro endured and much celebrated in 1963 during the centenary festivities of the publication of *Cantares gallegos*.

Chapter 24. The Resurgence of Feminism in Catalonia, 1970–1975 (Mary Nash)

Having been severely repressed under the Franco dictatorship, Catalonia (the last area to fall to Franco's troops in 1939 during the Spanish Civil War) witnessed a particularly strong feminist movement in the predemocratic era of the 1970s. Maria Aurèlia Capmany, the Catalan Simone de Beauvoir, published her widely read and influential *La dona a Catalunya: Consciencia i situació* in 1966, and several Catalan feminist groups were organized through political parties, trade unions, and neighbourhood movements during this late Franco period.

Chapter 25. Basque Women Who Resisted: A Feminist Rereading of the Franco Period (Jone M. Hernández García, María Ruiz Torrado, and Iratxe Retolaza)

Franco's persecution of all the other cultural and linguistic identities in the Spanish territory also impacted the Basque Country due to the censoring of all cultural activities between 1939 and 1951. The year 1939 also marked the exile of leading Basque women, such as Aurora Arnaiz, Dolores Ibárruri (La Pasionaria), María de Maeztu, and Polixene Trabudúa. Taking these historical references as the point of departure, this chapter pays attention to three areas of Basque women's resistance – culture, education, and politics – to Franco's antiwomen and antifeminist policies.

Part V. A New Beginning: The Transition to Democracy and Iberian Second-Wave Feminism (1974/1975–1994/1996) (Coordinated by Silvia Bermúdez)

Chapter 26. Historical Overview (Ana Paula Ferreira, Silvia Bermúdez, and Asunción Bernárdez Rodal)

In 1974 the Portuguese Estado Novo fell, and in 1975 Francisco Franco died, thus ending the long dictatorial periods in twentieth-century Iberia and opening the way for more sustained feminist activity in the Peninsula. Since in Francoist Spain some feminist activity was linked to the clandestine activity of illegal leftist political parties, the double militancy that arose in the 1930s reappeared in the democratic era. By the 1980s in Spain under the Socialist government, state feminism was ushered in with the creation of the Instituto de la Mujer whose mission was to foster equality between men and women. By the end of the decade, feminist activism in the Peninsula turned increasingly academic and theoretical, which has produced a significant corpus of written work.

Chapter 27. Feminisms in Postdictatorial Portugal, 1972–1996 (Ana Paula Ferreira)

From the late 1970s until the 1990s feminism in Portugal can be interpreted along the lines of the *destape* (undressing) in Spain, but with emphasis on sex and empire, sex and the damages of the Colonial War (1961–75), sex and "returnees" from the African colonies, and sex and European integration. Both older feminist women, such as Maria Teresa Horta, Isabel Barreno, and Maria Velho da Cosa, and new writers, such as Olga Gonçalves, Lidia Jorge, and Tolinda Gersão, who emerged in the 1980s, are important figures in this period. Questions considered in this chapter include: (1) How and when did women mobilize again after the 1947 closing of the Conselho Nacional das Mulheres Portuguesas?; (2) What was the background of Maria de Lurdes Pintasilgo, the first female prime minister of Portugal (1979–80), and what brought her down?

Chapter 28. Equality and Difference Feminisms in the Castilian and Catalan Areas of Spain (Roberta Johnson)

In the early 1980s a deep division developed in Spanish-speaking Iberian feminism. Equality feminism, ushered in by Celia Amorós's feminist seminar at the University of Madrid, was closely allied with the Socialist government that established the Instituto de la Mujer in 1982. At about the same time, feminist thinkers in Barcelona, under the influence of Italian difference feminism, began to challenge the notion of equality. The debate played out in journals like *El Viejo Topo*, and although many of the feminist writers who were active in the equality/difference debate have moved on to other feminist topics, the hostilities between the two orientations continue today.

Chapter 29. Women above All: The Autonomous Basque Feminist Movement, 1973–1994 (Nerea Aresti and Maialen Aranguren)

The feminist movement as such in the Basque Country began in the southern part of Euskal Herria at the end of the 1970s. Marking the official beginning were the first I Jornadas Feministas de Euskadi (Basque Feminist Days), which took place in 1977 at the University of the Basque Countries (Universidad del País Vasco, UPV/EHU) in Leioa, Biscay. Other Basque Feminist Days took place in 1984, 1994, and 2008. Over the years the Basque feminist movement has become more and more diversified and complex. Today its activities are carried out in four large arenas: associative, professional, institutional, and academic feminism, which overlap and share points of convergence.

Chapter 30. Galician Feminism in the Democratic Era (María do Cebreiro Rábade Villar)

Since its public inception in 1976, the Galician political feminism has offered a unique version of the feminist debate in southern Europe. This subject is based on an oxymoronic identity that is constituted by two partially opposing notions, "women" and "nation," and the theoretical debate inherent in the oxymoronic condition of Galician feminism, which takes up and adapts the international feminist debate over identity and the knowledge produced by women between 1976 and the 1990s.

Part VI. Iberian Feminisms' Diversity (1996 to the Present) (Coordinated by Silvia Bermúdez)

Chapter 31. Historical Overview (Silvia Bermúdez, Asunción Bernárdez Rodal, and Ana Paula Ferreira)

With democracy in Spain and Portugal well established and feminism having assumed the status of "state feminism" in Spain through the

Instituto de la Mujer and a number of laws assuring women's equality before the law, organized feminism turned its attention to minorities such as lesbians and immigrant women and to other feminist topics such as prostitution. Despite a conservative turn in the Spanish government from 1996 to 2004, most of the legal gains women had made remained in place, even if there was a backlash in the workplace. The return of the conservative Popular Party to the Spanish government (2011 to the present) has meant a revitalization of feminist activism to defend the rights acquired. In Portugal, feminism did not receive state-sponsored support. In fact, the long struggle for the right to abortion did not end until February 2007 when it was finally decriminalized by referendum.

Chapter 32. The Spanish Equality/Difference Debate Continues (Roberta Johnson)

In the mid-1990s the debate between equality and difference feminism in Spain grew bitter. Perhaps the stakes were higher now that the Socialist government was discredited, and the legal reforms and institutions such as the Women's Institute were threatened in the wake of socialism's crumbling hegemony. Difference feminists became more disillusioned over the discrepancy between the theory of gender equality and the reality of women's lives in the day-to-day world. They also mourned a perceived loss of "feminine" qualities in Spanish life: willingness to act as caregivers, the cult of motherhood, and emphasis on home and family life. In the uncertain political climate, difference feminists probably felt more emboldened in their rejection of traditional political engagement. *El Viejo Topo* (The old mole) published in 1994 a special issue on feminism that reveals the deepening divide between equality and difference feminists as they increasingly defined their positions in terms of philosophical alliances. Unlike the 1980 issue of the same journal on femininity and masculinity, now both sides of the schism are equally represented.

Chapter 33. Catalan Feminisms from 1996 to the Present (Mª. Ángeles Cabré)

This chapter pays close attention to the diversity of Catalan feminist positions and its specific manifestations, delineating a trajectory that covers institutional feminism and marks 2015 as an important year with the first female mayor of the city of Barcelona, activist Ana

Colau (b. 1947). Associative and academic feminisms are also dicussed with a detailed presentation of how academic feminisms underscore the substantial role played by the Institut Interuniversitari d'Estudis de Dones i Gènere (IIEDG; Interuniversities Institute in Women and Gender Studies), created by the collaboration of groups of researchers from seven Catalonian universities.

Chapter 34. Galician Feminisms Post-1994 (María do Cebreiro Rábade Villar)

Literature played an important role in advancing nationalist feminist discourse and in regard to the tensions within diverse Galician feminist agendas. This chapter first addresses the conflict between Galicia's conservatives and long-standing nationalist feminists. It particularly considers the years between 1991 and 2005, since Manuel Fraga de Iribarne's Xunta (Galician government) established the Galician Equality Service in 1991, an agency within the Ministry of the Family, Women, and Youth, which was renamed the Ministry of Family, Youth, Sports, and Volunteering in 2004. Literature has also been the battleground of feminist demands and, by creating a cohesive narrative for the community, sparked debates over the prestige of women writers and the reception of their work.

Chapter 35. Multifaceted Feminism: Promoting Diversity in the Twenty-First-Century Basque Country (Jone M. Hernández García)

This chapter traces the evolution of Basque feminism from the end of the twentieth century (decade of 1990) to the present. This is a fertile and complex period in which a confluence of agents and the diversification of practices and discourses occur. The new century marks a new stage in the feminist movement in several ways: (1) the development of an academic feminism; (2) the laying of the foundation for an emerging institutional feminism; and (3) going beyond the base movement to develop views, practices, and discourses (such as the so-called transfeminism) that brings new elements into feminist debates.

Chapter 36. Bodies and Feminist Politics in Basque Society (Mari Luz Esteban)

The chapter analyses the diversity of feminist political bodies and their interrelation. It understands political bodies as the configurations of representations, images, ideas, attitudes, techniques, and carnal conduct carried out consciously or unconsciously from a movement (in this case, the feminist movement). Such political bodies carry with them concrete forms of understanding the subject, gender, and social relations, and at the same time are a means to resist, answer, or modify reality. These bodies are classified in relation to diverse themes, such as health and reproduction, sexuality, work, and violence against women.

Epilogue: Some Remarks on Gender Indifference *and the Eulogy of the* Margins *(Fina Birulés)*

Current feminist debates differ from those on equality and difference of the 1980s and early 1990s. In order to address them, this chapter takes into account some of the changes that have occurred in the past three decades: (1) women's access to eroticism; (2) the modification of the sphere of kinship, especially the efficiency of motherhood thanks to scientific and technical advances; and (3) feminist organizations' decline in the power and capacity for innovation and visibility. Some of the variants and spaces of Spanish feminism have lost their revolutionary nature and have become institutionalized in a kind of "state feminism." As a result, the new generation feels very little attraction to what they consider the "old" feminism.

PART I

Iberian Feminism in the Age of the Enlightenment

COORDINATED BY CATHERINE M. JAFFE AND ELIZABETH FRANKLIN LEWIS

1 Situating Women in the Society of the Old Regime: The Other Spanish Enlightenment

MARÍA VICTORIA LÓPEZ-CORDÓN CORTEZO[1]

The installation of the Bourbons on the Spanish throne after a long international conflict affords the opportunity to consider the role of monarchies in the societies of the Old Regime and their influence on the political and cultural transformation of the kingdom. The Bourbon monarchs assumed their heritage, but they modified it according to their own approach. They were not prisoners of their roles, nor did they govern from their distant palaces; rather, they attempted to make their presence known through their agents and the writers and artists who publicized their actions.

The monarchs were devout Catholics, but they also protected their royal prerogatives, and they did not avoid confrontation with the church. They declared themselves pacifists, but they resorted to war in defence of their interests. If anything differentiated them from their ancestors, it was that, in addition to seeking personal glory, they initiated a politics of collective representation of the Crown identified with the royal family. This emphasis was expressed in great canvases, from Van Loo to Goya, in festivals and theatrical performances, and in the undeniable participation of their queens in political and cultural life (Sancho 2008; López-Cordón 2005a). The new dynasty drove changes in the government, created its own nobility, and promoted cultural renovation and a new type of sociability in which women had great prominence. The dynasty's precipitous end in 1808 should not hide the coherence of its trajectory; its breakdown was the work of a revolutionary context of war and also of internal imbalances that had been manifesting themselves for some time.

A New Plan for the Monarchy

The War of Succession and its coda, the Treaties of Utrecht-Rasttat, radically changed the territorial structure of the Spanish monarchy that ended up reduced to the Iberian Peninsula – minus Portugal – and the Balearic and Canary Islands. The overseas territories remained intact, although with important commercial concessions in favour of England. The war also had another consequence – the substitution of its territorial model of confederation for a centralized model that followed the guidelines of the French experience. The dissolution of the Crown of Aragon, as a historic group proceeding from the Middle Ages, by the decrees of the Nueva Planta (New Plan) was the most profound measure. Through these decrees, the representative institutions of those realms were abolished, public law and the tribunals of justice were modified, and others were introduced, some of Castilian origin and others new. There was no uniform plan, and the assimilation to Castile was only complete in the case of Valencia. Neither the kingdom of Navarre nor the Basque provinces that had supported the Bourbons saw their situation altered, and they preserved their own legal systems.

Beyond the reprisals, the political will existed to change the system of the Hapsburg government that many supporters of Felipe V, and of course, his grandfather, judged ineffective. Thus they carried out institutional changes: the progressive renovation of the small number of leaders, given the rapid ascent of a new nobility of financial or administrative origin and the presence – whether in the form of military men, bureaucrats, or businessmen – of French personnel, who accompanied the king, and of subjects proceeding from the lost territories of Flanders or Italy. Joining them were many foreign Catholics, especially Irish, who came to serve the kings of Spain (López-Cordón 2000). The four monarchs who succeeded each other throughout the eighteenth century (Felipe V, 1700–46; Fernando VI, 1746–59; Carlos III, 1759–88; and Carlos IV, 1788–1808) had quite different personalities and, together with their ministers, left their mark on political affairs. Their queens played an important role in politics (Isabel de Farnesio, second wife of Felipe V; María Luisa de Parma, wife of Carlos IV) and cultural life (Bárbara de Braganza, Portuguese princess and wife of Fernando VI).

Active and Enlightened Minorities

Throughout the eighteenth century, complex processes were developing that were not only political, but also social and ideological. The change of dynasty was political, as was the process that accompanied it. The king became the centre of a system organized around a cabinet of secretaries of state with authority over government matters, but not over territories (Dedieu 2010, 24–9). With some modifications, five ministries prevailed, at whose helm were men distinguished not only by their specific activity but also by certain intellectual concerns, channeled through special interests or through institutional actions promoted by the royal academies or the economic societies. Only two of them belonged to the high nobility, while the rest came from the landed gentry, graduates of one of the universities of the kingdom and accredited by their earlier service (López-Cordón 1996a). There were also those of Italian or Irish origin (Téllez 2010).

At their service, especially during the reign of Carlos II, there arose a new set of administrative personnel hailing from the peripheries of the kingdom with connections in both the administration and in the world of business, for now it was not enough to have merely bureaucratic experience; they also needed knowledge in specific areas, as well as knowledge about how to function in court society. Within two generations, government ministers went from being clerks to being men of the world, devotees of the salons they patronized or members of intellectual circles, dividing their time between service to the king and to the Republic of Letters. Among them were the majority of Enlightened Spanish men, for whom the social prestige conferred by knowledge often drove their professional careers. From these men arose, by the end of the century, the future Liberals (López-Cordón 1996b; Franco Rubio 2000; Imízcoz 2001; Imízcoz and Guerrero 2004; Álvarez Barrientos, Lopez, and Urzainqui 1995).

In the ideological realm, changes had to do with understanding religion and relations with the church. The monarchs were Catholic, but they did not tolerate church interference in matters of temporal order. The *regalistas,* Spaniards who favoured civil authority over church affairs, wanted a national church, and those who opposed Rome were close to French Jansenists, whose doctrines were taking shape in Spain in the second half of the century. The defence of the bishops' prerogatives and their intervention in matrimonial dispensations were among their objectives (Saugnieux 1975; Tomsich 1972). They also defended interior religiosity and criticized traditional religious practices. There were circles, like the *tertulia* (salon) of the Countess of Montijo, in which these ideas were the common denominator and which collaborated with French figures and publications of the same tendency (Demerson 1975). Between 1799 and 1800, upon the death of Pope Pius VI, they managed to initiate the process of disentailment of church goods. There was at the same time a growing offensive against the Inquisition, as much from the coordinates of Enlightened Christianity as from a thinly veiled secularism (López-Cordón 2013a; Herr 1991; Freira Álvarez 2007; Sciuti 2009). Although the suppression was not carried out until 1809 and 1812, by King José I and the Courts of Cádiz, respectively, the arguments brandished then were circulating a quarter-century earlier.

Reforms, changes, individual promotion, intellectual curiosity are words that refer to a social minority, constituted mostly, but not exclusively, of men. Of course the administration and professional careers were closed to women, but not so certain social functions or literary activities that they could practise with differing levels of commitment. Although those who participated in these activities did so out of inclination, there was no lack of women with a certain degree of institutional or quasi-professional commitment, such as the case of women translators. If they were not members of the Republic of Letters, they did form part of *tertulias,* occasionally as hostesses. In the academies or the economic societies, their rarity was so notorious that it had little effect. For example, the Junta de Damas de la Matritense (Ladies' Council of the Royal Economic Society of Madrid), discussed in chapters 2 and 3, was formed as a separate *junta* composed only of women (Negrín 1984; Bolufer 1998; Jaffe and Lewis 2009; Franco Rubio 2009, 351–8).

Cultured, wealthy, and well connected, these women formed part of the game of favours and influence that characterized their society. They were in the anterooms of ministry secretaries soliciting the promotion of a relative or protégé; they were proud of the success of their friends, and they enjoyed displaying their taste by favouring artists or writers. Those who were part of the queen's or princess's household, or who had access to the Royal Palace through a family member, also had a presence at court. Proximity to power – the king or the royal consort – allowed them to frequent spaces of increasing politicization such as the court and the salon. As a consequence, the ladies conspired, took sides, suffered punishments and exile, and, at the end of the century, some began to slip from their Enlightened presuppositions towards an incipient liberalism (López-Cordón 2011, and 2013a).

The trajectories for men and women were not parallel, because these cultured and curious women, with exceptions like Josefa Amar y Borbón, discussed further in chapters 2 and 3, lacked a formal education. They did not have stimuli to persevere in their intentions or the combination of factors necessary to achieve security, as they themselves proclaimed, at times with sincerity and at other times as a tactic. Only a few, among whom were Margarita Hickey or María Rosa Gálvez (also discussed in chapters 2, 3, and 4) managed to connect with other writers and with an audience, which was limited. That it was easier to achieve a certain authority and be considered a woman of the Enlightenment from a privileged social position is clear in the cases of María Francisca de Sales Portocarrero, Countess of Montijo, or María Josefa Alonso Pimentel, Duchess of Osuna. In others, like those of Feliciana Maxent, widowed Countess Gálvez, or of Inés Joyes (discussed in chapters 2, 3, and 4), the women overcame circumstances that allowed them to prove themselves as writers (Palacios Fernández 2002; López-Cordón 2005b and 2005c; Bolufer 2008; Yebes 1955; Demerson 1975). Becoming an Enlightened man was a process that began with an education, was consolidated with personal promotion, and culminated in intellectual recognition. It was not an easy road, but it was full of encouragement, and it was travelled in company. Becoming an Enlightened woman was a decision made on less firm ground; it was an exercise in surmounting deficiencies and misgivings, a test of liberty that yielded satisfactions, and was an end in itself.

A Society in Transformation

In the Old Regime, population growth was a necessity. Its number and density was key for state power, and it was the only way to stimulate demand and thus economic growth in societies that were still poor. However in the eighteenth century, survival continued to depend on variables – high birth and mortality rates and periodic crises that reduced food surpluses – that impeded sustained population growth. The plague had disappeared, but malaria, yellow fever, and smallpox continued to ravage the population. On the Peninsula there were three grave demographic crises: 1706–10, during the War of Succession, across a wide geographic area; at the beginning of the 1760s, with repercussions in the north and centre of the Peninsula; and then in the 1780s, due to smallpox and malaria in the Levantine regions and part of Andalusia and La Mancha. One quarter of newborns died, and the rate of feminine postpartum mortality was correspondingly high, affecting all strata of society. The result was that life expectancy hardly reached thirty years, and families with many children and the same parents were rare. To this must be added the effects of celibacy, not only ecclesiastical but also among lay people, with 12% of men between forty and fifty years old unmarried, and 11.5% for women of the same age. Migratory movements acted as correctors of this trend.

Despite these negative factors, the population in Spain grew from eight million at the beginning of the eighteenth century to almost twelve million during the Peninsular War. This was a similar increment to that found in the rest of Europe, but with a lower median density. The regional contrasts were great, and by the end of the century, the periphery was much more populated than the centre (Fernández Díaz 1993, 265–74). The breakdown by sex and age in the census shows that equal numbers of boys and girls were born, but because of a higher death rate for young males, the population of girls grew slowly after they turned sixteen. The number of unmarried women between the ages of sixteen and twenty-five was greatly superior to that of married women, a situation that would totally change for those between twenty-five and fifty years of age. Widows were more numerous than widowers in any age group, but above all after fifty years old (López-Cordón 1986, 53–63).

The majority of the population lived in small nuclei and only 15% lived in cities or towns of over 10,000 inhabitants. Madrid, the only city of over 100,000 at the beginning of the century, reached 150,000 around 1750 and 190,000 at the end of the century. Barcelona's population was 100,000 in 1787, while Seville had 81,000, Valencia 70,000, and Saragossa 40,000. On the contrary, Santiago, La Coruña, Oviedo, Gijón, Bilbao, and San Sebastián each had fewer than 10,000 inhabitants (Reher 1994). Like the rest of Europe, Spanish society was characterized by inequality. Laws and obligations defined the condition of those who belonged to different social strata. There were more differences within each social order than between one society and another. Thus, the lifestyles of the nobility were similar across Europe because of the dense networks of transnational family relations, among other reasons, while among the poor it was difficult to establish degrees of difference (Trevor-Roper, Russell, and Thompson 1972; Saavedra Fernández 1994).

Spain, as well as Portugal, had a large nobility because its lowest rank, *la hidalguía*, was very wide. Of the total group of nobility, those with titles were a minority that grew during the eighteenth century thanks to the Bourbons' policy of awarding titles to those who served the monarchy; titles could also be bought. Noble rank benefited men as well as women, although men had the right of primogeniture and held entailed estates, by which patrimonial family property passed down to the firstborn male. In Castilian law, women without brothers could have the right of primogeniture and could hold entailed estates, in detriment to collateral male relatives. Their lineage also prevailed if it was superior to that of their husband. Noble women did have limitations, since they could not hold public or municipal positions acquired through inheritance or regal concession; they had to delegate the office to a man. Like all other women, they were subject to paternal or marital authority, but their noble position was a corrective to the limitations of their sex, both in social and personal life (Domínguez Ortiz 1983; Soria 2007; Felices 2013).

The clergy was recognized as a social order only in Catholic states and was, in general, numerous due to the existence of regular clergy. As in other places, an ecclesiastic career supposed privileges and was not incompatible with administration or with politics, and it constituted a route to social promotion. It was true that, in Spain as in the rest of Europe, there was an unwritten rule that high offices stayed in the hands of the nobility. The percentage of clergy decreased throughout the century, reaching 1.6% in the 1790s (Callahan 1989; Candau 1994; Aranda Pérez 2000; Barrio 2010; Artola 2013). The existence of female convents dedicated exclusively to prayer was unique to the Catholic world. The convents were almost all cloistered, the number of nuns was much less than that of monks, and the social rank of those who took vows was higher due to the required dowry. Widows also entered the convent, and sometimes married women, for different circumstances, lived there. Taking the veil allowed women to avoid an undesired or unequal marriage and impeded the dispersal of patrimony, but it also offered women independence from the paternal or fraternal yoke. Depending on the rules of the order, the rigidity of the cloister varied and also the material quality of life. There were differences among strictly cloistered nuns, nuns who led a more active life dedicated to the education of girls or other acts of welfare, and lay sisters. Most nuns were literate, since they had obligations as readers, and some were also writers, like the poet Gertrudis Hore (discussed in chapter 4). There was also social and literary activity in the convents. According to the 1787 census, in Spain there were more than twenty-five thousand religious women (Atienza 2008; Morand 2004).

The great majority of these convents were cloistered and had more or less permissive rules. Very few of them were dedicated to education, for the first teaching order established in Spain was the Company of Mary, which arrived in Barcelona in 1650 and later in Tudela in 1687. By the end of the century, the Barcelona convent had established four schools in Catalonia. The Tudela convent also founded four schools in

Saragossa, Santiago, San Fernando de Cádiz, and Vergara (Urra Olazabal 2007; Ramiro Moya 2012, 93–5, 100–2). Queen Bárbara de Braganza founded the Convent of the Salesas Reales in Madrid in 1748 for the education and residence of young noble women. When the school was opened ten years later, it was run by the Order of the Visitation of Holy Mary, or the Salesian Sisters, who had come from France (Franco Rubio 1994 and 1997). There were also other schools for girls in religious convents, some of which were founded by the Crown both in the court and elsewhere, that were under the protection of religious communities such as the Augustians or Dominicans. In general, since the communities were cloistered, the girls were entrusted to them as caretakers, rather than as real teachers (Nava Rodríguez 1995; Comella Gutiérrez 2012).

More than 80% of the population formed the so-called Third Estate, or the bourgeois and working class, within which peasants constituted the overwhelming majority. The largest group after the peasantry was that of the artisans. Here also there was great diversity, but only in the most dynamic towns and cities did mercantile business generate growing financial activity, such as the appearance of guilds and corporations that regulated production and obtained privileges against the competition. The guilds were masculine, but widows often had authorization to keep their workshop open until a son or family member would come to manage it. Although they did not receive an official apprenticeship, they did end up developing manual or accounting skills that constituted a real asset upon their marriage. The number of artisans increased considerably in the second half of the century, exceeding half a million people in 1797 (Fernández Díaz 1993, 396–400).

Compared to the artisans, the development of industry was weak and very localized. The Valencian silk industry revived, as did briefly the wool industry in Segovia, but the real innovation was the development of the cotton sector in Catalonia beginning in 1760. There was also an ambitious state policy in the Colbertist tradition that established different royal factories dedicated to the manufacture of both luxury goods and products for mass consumption, like tobacco or playing cards, or to procure military supplies. To attend to the wider needs of the consumption of textiles, wool factories were established in the interior of the Peninsula, some of which generated important concentrations of capital and work, and introduced technical advances, but that turned out to be unprofitable. They used a great deal of women's labour, establishing legal and fiscal advantages for the workers and their families, such as exempting their husbands from military service. A quarter of the active local female population worked in some of these factories, with those who worked as spinners in their homes representing an even higher percentage (González Enciso 1980 and 2000).

In Catalonia, agriculture enabled the accumulation of enough capital to begin a process of industrialization through the establishment of factories dedicated to the production of printed fabrics. Cotton came from America, and the textiles made in Catalonia were sold throughout Europe, while Carlos III prohibited the importation of cotton fabrics to avoid competition. This type of establishment also used women's work, although after the 1830s women did not represent the majority of workers. According to data from the Real Compañía de Hilados (Royal Company of Spinning Mills), in 1784 the eighty that existed in Catalonia employed 1,740 women, along with 4,607 men and 2,291 children (Fernández Díaz 1993, 391–419; Thomson 1990, 79–90, and 1994). The most important fortunes of the commercial bourgeoisie were made through trade with the Indies. But there were also some who obtained great benefit by collaborating with the monarchy and the privileged strata through leasing seignieurial rights, tithes, taxes, or supplies, especially military. The importance of the liberal professions and of the group of administrators and their increasing social significance has already been mentioned. They were indispensable to governing and helped to knit together a territory that still lacked cohesion.

Family as the Basis for Everything

For poor and for rich, nobles or plebeians, the family was the axis upon which their lives turned. It was an element of stability, but also of change, because its structure, as well as its life cycle, was transformed throughout the century. The family was defined by consanguinity, but also by residence. It extended beyond a couple and their children, without being identified solely with a patriarchal family founded upon an early marriage for the woman and numerous descendents. That model was in retreat and represented less than 20% of all families. The hegemony of the nuclear or conjugal family was general, as was the existence of a significant percentage of single homes (Reher 1996; Chacón Jiménez 1990 and 2009).

The structure of the family turned upon the married couple, which in the Catholic world was regulated by Canon law, while its economic aspects related to guardianship and punishment for infractions belonged to the civil realm. Marriage was an unequal contract that benefited the husband who held *patria potestad*. This paternal legal authority was exercised over three fields. First, it covered a physically delimited space, such as the dwelling, within which the father made decisions regarding patrimony and family economic activity or strategy. Second, paternal legal authority reached a wider space, regulated by law, that was manifested in contractual obligations and in legal forms of substitution for authority. Finally, paternal authority also extended to a diffuse space, sacralized in a certain sense, of moralization and the transmission of social and religious values (Rodríguez Sánchez 1990).

Although all these aspects existed, they were never rigidly observed; social practice was introducing changes, and there were conflicts caused by the demarcation of the two distinct jurisdictions, ecclesiastical and royal. This is what happened with the question of free consent in marriage established by the Council of Trent, which limited paternal authority, making it recommended but not preceptive. Pope Benedict XIV ratified this disposition in 1741, which caused increasing dissension with the state, since greater communication between the sexes added to the number of unequal marriages based on the "mutual inclination of the bride and groom." Passion was distrusted, as was inconsiderate fortune hunting, and breaches of trust caused the prohibition of alliances between masters and servants or of leaving pensionless a widow who was scandalously younger than her deceased spouse. The intent was to avoid "abuses," to safeguard the patrimony or prestige of lineage, and even to leave the order of succession of the Crown well established. All these reasons explain the Pragmática Sanción (Pragmatic Sanction or Decree) of Carlos III in 1776, through which children under twenty-five could not marry without their parents' consent. In 1803, Carlos IV intervened again in this matter, establishing a more detailed casuistry, which in the case of orphanhood translated authority to the mother or in her absence to the grandparents. This is the context of the polemic regarding freedom of choice in matrimony that writers like Leandro Fernández de Moratín or María Rosa Gálvez presented on stage, and the stance taken on this issue by many Enlightened thinkers, from Cabarrús to Josefa Amar y Borbón (Laina 1993; López-Cordón 1998 and 2007a).

Freedom of consent meant the repeal of the obligations of betrothal, a practice regulated by Castilian law that was still in force in the eighteenth century. Through it the betrothed couple was obliged to marry, contravening the Tridentine dispositions that demanded explicitly stated consent pronounced in the act of matrimony. Unfulfilled promises resulted in dishonour for women or gave rise to illegitimate children, which provoked lawsuits that were substantiated before the royal court, but that could only compensate the injured party economically but not morally. Another problem was the need to request dispensations of consanguinity from ecclesiastical authorities. Having to wait for the concession of the dispensations delayed weddings and gave rise to negotiations between families, leading to unfulfilled promises. Dispensations were a point of friction between the monarchy and the Holy See due to the amount of money that their processing cost Rome. A diplomatic rupture could retard or even paralyse the process of granting the dispensation.

Canon law was equal for everyone, unlike civil law, which governed the economic aspects of matrimony. In Castilian law, spouses each maintained their exclusive property during the marriage, although the husband administered his wife's property and dowry, unless there was an agreement to the contrary. The administration of her property only reverted to the wife upon widowhood. The goods generated during the matrimony were held in common, with the part proportional to each of them at the free disposition of the surviving spouse, who was under obligation to reserve them for their children. In families of the middle ranks or those of scarce means, the profits offered certain resources to the widow and assured her of the maintenance of her home. In addition, sometimes the profits in the form of a dowry were reserved for the widow, with which she had greater chances of remarrying. The dowry's economic significance grew as more property was included, such as the proceeds from wages and salaries realized during the marriage, whether from private sources or from the royal treasury.

This system did not affect the former kingdoms of the crown of Aragon, with the exception of Valencia. In the case of Catalonia, the regulations relative to the patrimony of the wife derived from Roman law and were qualified by provisions contained in the Usatges (Usages of Barcelona) and in some privileges, which supposed that the pattern of separation of goods – with the dowry – was maintained, a practice called the *régimen dotal* was implemented. The same occurred in the kingdom of Aragon or in the Balearic Islands, which also kept their own laws.

In Spain, as in the rest of the Catholic world, only the annulment of a marriage could dissolve the conjugal tie. This did not prevent frequent conflicts, as shown by the petitions for separation and even for divorce, which was how it was referred to at that time. The couple would appear in the vicariate, and, in case of injuries and scandal, they filed a complaint before a civil judge. Although there were also men who complained, the number of women who initiated this process, basing their petitions on unsustainable cohabitation or the disappearance of the consort, is greatly superior. There was also the possibility of an informal divorce without the intervention of any kind of judge, which meant entering an institution, whether a convent or a hospital, in the case of women (such as Gertrudis Hore, discussed in chapter 4); thus women could escape cohabitation or avoid the social and penal consequences of criminal behaviour such as abandonment, cohabitation without being married, or bigamy (Pascua 1998; M. Ortega 1999; López-Cordón 2007a; Costa 2007; Espín López 2010).

Of course the growing consideration for sentiment had repercussions on marital and filial affections and helped to set in motion a new familial modality, but its social reach was limited in the eighteenth century (Bolufer 1998). It is easier to observe that the family was not indifferent to incipient capitalism. In order to take care of their needs, many women ended up occupying themselves with activities demanded by the market, like retail or domestic service. The process of feminization of these activities began in the eighteenth century. In other social groups, the growing appreciation for the intangible legacy that spouses brought in the form of lineage, relations, and sociability had repercussions in their consideration within the family. In this sense, the policy that promoted the education of mothers is not only proof of the instrumentalization of their person in favour of others but also an expression of greater confidence in their capabilities and of the necessity of inserting them in a program of social reform.

The Shadows of Enlightenment

What did Enlightenment reform mean in Spanish history? What was its reach and its legacy? Was it a culture directed from above that hardly took root in the population? These questions have given rise to many debates that now are finally better contextualized, because no unified European model exists, nor did it establish itself in any social body. Of course in Spain, royal protagonism headed the reforms and promoted a cultural change, at times in combined action with ministers, intellectuals, and writers. In any case, the result was an opening to the trends of the period and the wish not only to improve the country but also to educate it. In this action, it is not easy to separate politics and culture or to distinguish it from economics. It was not new that princes or the nobility distinguished themselves by their patronage, but it was an innovation that their taste adopted an exemplary dimension and took shape in both a programmed and an institutionalized form. That the middle ranks became the natural means of diffusion of Enlightenment ideals was coherent, given their growing protagonism. Although lacking the philosophical bias of other Enlightenments, the Spanish Ilustración had enough practical sense to understand that the prestige of science, letters, and arts made them useful not only for uplifting the monarchy but also for strengthening its links to the community over which it reigned.

The Enlightenment defended freedom of thought and also the equality of reason. According to these goals, Enlightened men considered women as useful companions and true friends, and praised their nature as more sensitive and less egotistical than their own. Quite a few Enlightened women felt included in these postulates, but others were more reticent. Thus, as Carla Hesse has pointed out, the terms "women" and "Enlightenment" did not fit together completely, because there was also a trend whose reflections, through coherence with its principles, rejected one of its axioms: the different nature of the two sexes (Hesse 2001). Those who denied the difference between the sexes used the same vocabulary but argued from the evidence of a reality that was understood to be the result of history and not ontology. This was very different from the deceptive sentimental family that was promoted rhetorically and from the polite sociability that held sway in the salons. Feminine voices that were consistent with Enlightened ideology were never numerous in Spain or anywhere else. Although rhetorically Enlightenment ideology was directed at women, its arguments were devised by a public formed by men, and for this reason, rather than asserting unrealizable goals, Enlightened women displayed what was their greatest conquest: the ability to express themselves as subjects. Inquiring readers, they knew that they were equal through reason; but they understood themselves as culturally different, and thus they saw in the ideological currents of their time the opportunity to reconcile both parameters, setting reformers and Enlightened men an unexpected challenge: to measure the progress of a society by the situation women had in it (López-Cordón 2005c, 172–3, 191).

2 New Inflections of a Long Polemic: The Debate between the Sexes in Enlightenment Spain

MÓNICA BOLUFER PERUGA[2]

Spanish Versions of an International Debate

In Spain, as in the rest of Europe, the difference between the sexes was a central controversy in the eighteenth century (Taylor 2005; Kitts 1995; Bolufer 1998 and 2009a; Smith 2006). Reflection over the "nature," capabilities, education, and social function of women was ever present in texts of varied content and style: not only in essays specifically directed to the topic but also in works about political economy, reformist projects, popular medical books, pedagogical manuals, satires, travel narratives, novels, comedies, the periodical press, and even visual culture, including paintings and prints (Molina 2013). The primary focus of these texts was to articulate proper new models of femininity for a modern and Enlightened society; however, patterns of masculinity were also questioned, as new ideals for citizenship and responsible fatherhood were proposed, such as the *hombre de bien* (virtuous man) (Haidt 1998, 157–9; Bolufer 2007). Well-known intellectuals, some associated with government, as well as obscure or anonymous authors, participated in these discussions; likewise, a number of women made their voices heard in a debate that they thought concerned them directly, denouncing typical arguments by male points of view as profoundly biased, even those presented as supposedly "impartial" and "philosophical."

What we might call today "feminist" positions were developed in this crucial controversy, if we understand by "feminism" a critical assessment of women's position and education, an egalitarian (or, at least, more balanced) view of women's and men's intellectual and moral capacities, and a strong emphasis on education as responsible for shaping gendered abilities, inclinations, and subjectivities, and therefore as the key to improving not only women's participation in social and cultural life but also their own self-esteem and perception of their potential. This form of feminism could be and was generally reconciled with an acceptance of a division of social roles and authority according both to gender and rank, as befits the Spanish Enlightenment, which was in general not radical but infused with a reforming, pragmatic spirit (Astigarraga 2014, 16; also López-Cordón, chapter 1 above).

This controversy in Spain formed part of an authentic international debate; many foreign texts (in particular, but not limited to, French texts) were translated, paraphrased, adapted, or cited, among them the article "Femme: morale" (Women: Morals) from the *Encyclopédie ou Dictionnaire raisonné des sciences, des arts et des métiers* (1751–72); passages of *Émile, ou De l'éducation* (*Emile, or On Education*) by Rousseau (1762); the "Essai sur les moeurs, l'esprit et le caractère des femmes" ("Essay on the Customs, Spirit, and Character of Women") by Antoine-Léonard Thomas (1772), which was published in Spanish in 1773 – before the English version of 1774 – along with other manuscript versions throughout the century; or *Vindication of the Rights of Woman* (1792) by Mary Wollstonecraft, reviewed in the *Diario de Madrid*. Throughout the debate, the comparative reference to "Europe" was a constant, since Enlightened modernity in Spain was affected by a profound self-consciousness, a sense of backwardness with respect to those countries, particularly France and England, that since the end of the seventeenth century had overtaken Spain's cultural and political hegemony. The debate over the sexes coincided with a self-critical reflection on the role that the Spanish monarchy aspired to fulfil in Western modernity, incorporating the idea that it should show Spain deserving to be included among "civilized" nations (Bolufer 2009a). Spanish contributions achieved some international renown, although in small measure – notably the "Defensa de las mujeres" ("Defence of Women") by Feijoo (1726), translated to various languages (among them French, English, and Portuguese), and also the contributions of Josefa Amar, of which there were Italian translations, and of Francisco Cabarrús, known through the French press.

Although the majority of texts were published in Madrid, the debate reached all the regions of the Hispanic monarchy, including those of the Peninsula, as well as those of the colonies, from Cádiz, Barcelona, and Bilbao, to Mexico City and Lima (Mo Romero and Rodríguez García 2005; Pérez Cantó and Nogal 2005). Given the distinct regional and local contexts (such as the case of the Basque provinces; see Altonaga, chapter 6 below), these discussions were connected to the intense activities of institutions and circles of sociability (academies, salons, and economic societies) and of newspapers in Madrid, as well as in other cities of Spain and Latin America (from *El Pensador* and *El Censor* to *La Pensadora Gaditana, Diario de Valencia, Semanario Instructivo y Curioso de Salamanca* or *Mercurio Peruano*), while at the same time they participated in the wider context of the European Enlightenment. Feijoo, one of the most influential authors of the polemic, was from Galicia, as was Vicente del Seixo, author of *Discurso filosófico y económico-político sobre la capacidad o incapacidad natural de las mujeres* (Philosophical and political-economic discourse on the natural capacity or incapacity of women; 1801). Josefa Amar and Inés Joyes were both born in Madrid but spent their adult lives in other regions, Saragossa for the former and in the Málaga area for the latter; Joyes, along with Margarita Hickey and Francisca Larrea, had strong family and cultural ties to Ireland (Lewis 2017). In Valladolid in 1792, María Rosario Romero published a translation of the *Lettres péruviennes* by Françoise de Graffigny, which underscored criticism of the condition of women (also discussed in chapter 4 below).

The debates were profoundly connected to the cultural and social changes of the century, described by López-Cordón in the first chapter of this volume – economic growth, the advance of urbanization, social diversification, the development of new more hedonist and secular customs, the accelerated circulation of publications, and increased foreign influence (in particular French, but also English, German, and Italian) in the realm of ideas, as well as in literary and artistic tastes and ways of living. Women took part in the new possibilities of mixed social contact in spaces like the *tertulias* (salons), over some of which presided distinguished aristocratic women like the Marchioness of Sarriá, the Countesses of Montijo, el Carpio, Fuerte-Híjar, or Gálvez, the Duchesses of Alba and Osuna, and others frequented by men and women of local elite and middle classes (Demerson 1975, 101–23; Bolufer 2005b). They also participated in increasing numbers as readers and writers, with the expansion of reading and the emergence of public opinion (Jaffe and Lewis 2009; Bolufer 2011).

From the *Querelle des femmes* to the Enlightenment Debate

The debate was strongly connected to the centuries-long international tradition of the *querelle des femmes*. This pan-European debate had had its version in the Iberian Peninsula since late medieval times, with significant sixteenth- and seventeenth-century contributions, such as those of Oliva Sabuco de Nantes's *Nueva filosofía de la naturaleza del hombre* (*New Philosophy of Human Nature*; 1587), and María de Zayas's *Novelas amorosas y ejemplares* (*Exemplary and Love Novels*; 1637) and *Desengaños amorosos* (*Disenchantments of Love*; 1647). However, the controversy took a distinct turn with the publication in 1726 of the essay "Defensa de las mujeres" ("Defence of Women") by Benito Jerónimo Feijoo (1676–1764) (Bolufer 2005a; Blanco 2010). Feijoo, a Benedictine monk and professor of theology at the Universidad de Oviedo, was adept at connecting with a wide audience by directing his writings to them explicitly and establishing a dialogue with his readers. His collections of essays, *Teatro crítico universal de errores comunes* (Universal critical theatre of common errors; 1726–40) and *Cartas eruditas y curiosas* (Erudite and curious letters; 1742–60), achieved record sales, with numerous reprints and translations into various languages. Specifically, his "Defensa de las mujeres" (discourse XVI of the first volume of the *Teatro crítico*) has been recognized for some time as one of the foundational texts of feminism in Spain. Feijoo contributed to the creation of the myth of being the solitary precursor by presenting his work as a daring renovation of thought and a struggle against prejudice, in this case, against the belief in female inferiority. However, Feijoo himself recognizes his debt to male and female authors that preceded him, in particular to women defenders of equality (such as the French Marie de Gournay or the Venetian Lucrezia Marinelli). Feijoo participated intensely in the intellectual and social polemics of his day and kept a dense network of social and epistolary contacts not only with men but also with some artistocratic and Enlightened women, such as the intellectual Ana Moscoso de Prado and other women with whom he corresponded, directing three of his *Cartas eruditas y curiosas* to three women readers. He dedicated volume 4 of the second edition of the same work to Queen Bárbara de Braganza, the cultured wife of King Fernando VI, presenting her, opportunely, as the best living example of women's intellectual abilities and insisting on the idea that belief in the inferiority of the female sex had no basis and is only the product of ignorance (Franco 2005).

In his essay, Feijoo refutes the typical arguments about the physical, moral, and intellectual inferiority of women based on Galenic medicine and Aristotelian philosophy. His concept of reason as a neutral principle, the same for both sexes, and his idea that male testimonies are not objective, since they act as both judges and reporters, connect with the so-called European "rationalist feminism" from the end of the seventeenth century, represented by, among others, François Poulain de la Barre, whose work Feijoo possibly did not know in a direct form, but with whom he shared some affinities. As a matter of fact, his familiarity with medical theories and debates permitted him to point out that many supposed anatomical and physiological proofs were nothing but ad hoc fabricated evidence meant to justify inequality. In order to explain why equality of intellectual capacities among the sexes has not produced equivalent intellectual achievements, Feijoo underscores the fundamental role of education and signals the deficiencies in women's formation that are responsible for the fact that women, although possessing the same potential as men, do not distinguish themselves with the same frequency as men in the fields of knowledge.

The publication of the "Defensa de las mujeres" provoked a great polemic, which lasted until 1750. The detractors accused Feijoo of altering natural and providential order that justified the subordination of women within the family and society due to their innate inferiority, despite the fact that Feijoo had affirmed that demonstrating equal aptitudes among the sexes did not require equality of functions and power. Among his supporters, there were authoritative voices, such as the celebrated doctor Martín Martínez, who agreed with the lack of any anatomical evidence of intellectual inequality among the sexes (and significantly, two years later in 1728, he would produce a new edition of Oliva Sabuco's *Nueva filosofía,* introducing it with a highly complimentary prologue). Feijoo's immense popularity contributed to the fact that the most classic arguments of misogyny fell to the wayside among Enlightenment circles, where openly supporting the idea of the inferiority of women was less and less accepted. Feijoo's enduring influence is noted in many authors who followed him, as is the case with Inés Joyes, Vicente del Seixo, and Valentín de Foronda (whom Altonaga studies in chapter 6 below).

Rational Equality versus Complementarity

In the second half of the century, as in the rest of Europe, the most common tendency was the configuration of a model of difference, which presented men and women as essentially different and irreducible, claiming that among them there was no hierarchy but rather a natural complementarity. It was argued that men inclined towards action, abstract reflection, and exterior activity, while women tended towards interior life, the world of emotion, and the family, which in the eighteenth century was being redefined in more intimate and sentimental terms. This representation of social organization between the sexes attributed to men and women moral, intellectual, and physical qualities that corresponded with different functions and spaces assigned to each sex. Key to the representation of difference was the emerging culture of sensibility, particularly in sentimental literature and in popular medicine (Bolufer 2016b). Women were charged with educating male sentiments in order to shape civilized society, while, paradoxically, they were intensively trained in this allegedly "natural" inclination. The idea that women – "naturally" chaste, self-contained, and sensitive – should restrain men's passionate excesses and harness them to marriage in order to help them fulfil their public and private duties, is evident in novels, short stories, and comedies. The immense success of these sentimental works among different sorts of audiences greatly helped shape women's (and men's) subjectivities and expectations.

Vicente Seixo proclaimed with typical Enlightened optimism in 1801 that "en el día de hoy, en que las luces de la razón triunfan de la ignorancia en que nuestros abuelos estuvieron sumergidos" (Seixo 1801, 46; today, when the light of reason triumphs over ignorance in which our grandfathers were submerged). Contrasting with the severe, even aggressive, tone with which the inferiority of women had been affirmed in the past, during the Enlightenment, the old *querella* is considered resolved; the hierarchy of the sexes is hardly mentioned, and any tension or conflict disappears if each gender accepts its naturally fixed place. Open misogyny is identified in Enlightened texts as barbarous, belonging to the past, in a time that tended to praise women, making them the main keepers of moral virtues who will spread them to the rest of society.

However, this discourse of the complementarity of the sexes coexisted – sometimes in a more or less tense equilibrium, other times in open conflict – with a tradition that affirmed, in the name of reason, the essential equality of human beings, even while admitting that in society men and women should have different functions and responsibilities. It denied that the natural qualities of women reduced them exclusively to domestic life and limited their intellectual possibilities. This notion was argued by Josefa Amar y Borbón (1749–1833), the most prominent woman defender of gender equality, for whom supposed innate characteristics of femininity or masculinity were actually products of moral, intellectual, and sentimental education that moulded women and men in different ways. Another woman writer, Margarita Hickey (1753–93), wrote in her *Poesías varias*: "que el alma no es hombre / ni mujer, y es fijo // que en entrambos casos / su ser es el mismo" (Hickey 1789, 417–18; The soul, as a spirit, does not have a true sex). Thus the discussion about whether feminine and masculine identities were fixed and immutable facts of nature or the result of the way in which societies organize themselves and evolve historically remained open throughout the century. Within this discussion, educational proposals varied, some seeing women exclusively as mothers and wives, while others gave them expanded social functions, as Elizabeth Lewis discusses below in chapter 3. Paradoxes appear, on occasion, inside the same text, as is the case with the *Discurso filosófico* (Philosophical discourse; 1801) by Vicente del Seixo, which attempts to reconcile, with obvious difficulties, two principles, presenting both the physical and moral equality of the sexes and the delicate and sensitive character of women as evident. In Seixo's opinion, the latter quality predisposes women to a domestic vocation.

The debate about the capacities and inclinations of the sexes and their functions in a new society culminated in the last decades of the century. A key episode of this polemic occurred over the admission of women into the Royal Economic Society of Madrid of Friends of the Country, in which important cultural and political figures of the day participated, such as the jurist and literary scholar Gaspar Melchor de Jovellanos, prosecutor for the Consejo de Castilla Pedro Rodríguez Campomanes, the financeer of French origin Francisco de Cabarrús, and the only woman, the erudite Josefa Amar. Unfolding between 1775 and 1787, the debate had wide resonance in Spanish public opinion, as well as in European opinion.

This debate was intense, as was the one that occurred a few years later, in the distinctly different political context of revolutionary France over women's citizenship. This debate suggested that admitting women to the Royal Economic Society of Madrid would open the doors of an institution that represented the new Enlightened public space, which ultimately implied what the spaces and social responsibilities of men and women should be, practically as well as symbolically (Bolufer 1998, 341–88; Smith 2006, 74–107). The main opponent to admission was Cabarrús, for whom the presence of women in the society, which was tolerable for titled noble women (two aristocrats, María Isidra de Guzmán and María Josefa Pimentel, the Duchess of Osuna, had already been invited), was unacceptable for most women as a matter of course. Cabarrús imagined that, in the normative order, an ideal society in which private and public spaces were perfectly delineated, political life was seen as the exclusive realm of men, while women were expected to create familial harmony as mothers and wives.

Among the defenders of admission into the society was, for example, Campomanes, who espoused a utilitarian view that underscores the practical benefits of associating women with Enlightenment projects and entrusting them with specific tasks that correspond to women's "natural" inclinations and functions. In the minority were those voices that considered this pragmatic criteria as less important, placing more emphasis on "reason," "justice," and "progress." Thus for Josefa Amar and Ignacio López de Ayala, admitting women to the society was the logical consequence of accepting the intellectual and moral equality of the sexes. López de Ayala believed that equality cannot be questioned in a modern Enlightened society, its acceptance a necessary sign of progress, as Condorcet would argue later: "Demos este ejemplo de razón a las naciones de Europa. En toda ella fermenta la filosofía y ha llegado su tiempo" (López de Ayala 1786; Let us give the nations of Europe the example of reason. In it, philosophy is fermented, and its time has arrived). We will see a somewhat similar line, but from a distinctly different personal position and an even more cutting tone, from Josefa Amar.

Actually, the debate did not pit Enlightenment reformers against traditionalists, as the polemic initiated by Feijoo had done decades earlier, but rather it revealed the fissures and discordance among the reformers themselves, representing the tension between two opposite discourses that were both rooted in the philosophical premises of the Enlightenment. On the one hand was the Rousseauian discourse that attributed social and civic responsibility to women defined as exclusively related to their domestic role and presented as a consequence of their peculiar physical, moral, and sentimental nature (see chapter 3 below). On the other hand, another discourse presented access to groups like the Royal Economic Society of Madrid as an unavoidable requirement of the Enlightenment and contemplated formulas of participation for women, following the objectives of reformism that extended beyond the strictly domestic realm to spaces for education and philanthropy, both part of the emerging civil society. The discrepancies over the ways in which this integration should take place, from purely formal admission, to full integration without any sexual distinction, to the formation of their own separate female group, show the difficulties and resistance generated (even among the defenders of admission) by women's public presence as equals to men. The debate was finally resolved by royal decree on 27 August 1787: women should be admitted, but in the form of the Junta de Damas de Honor y Mérito (Ladies' Council of Honour and Merit), separate from and subordinate to the Royal Economic Society of Madrid.

Women Speak Up

One of the first tasks of the Junta de Damas, once formed, was to name as a member the only Spanish woman who had expressed herself publicly during this debate, in recognition of her decisive intervention. Josefa Amar y Borbón (1749–1833) belonged to a family of the lower Aragonese nobility, connected to medicine and law, which supported her talent and provided her an excellent education for a woman of her class and time (López-Cordón 2005c). Although born in Madrid, she moved after marriage to Saragossa, where she kept in contact with Enlightenment and reformist circles, translated various important texts, sought association with the Economic Society of Aragon (to which her husband and many of her friends belonged), and was invited to join the society in 1782 (Sullivan 1992; López-Cordón 2005c, 60–2). From this position, when the polemic over the admission of women was raised in the Royal Economic Society of Madrid, Amar declared her support for it through her "Discurso en defensa del talento de las mujeres y de su aptitud para ejercer el gobierno y otros cargos en que se emplean los hombres" (Defence of women and of their aptitude for governing and other positions in which men are employed; 1786). This vehemently and solidly articulated text centres its defence on the equality of the sexes as an evident principle, even though this principle was still questioned by persisting prejudices. As a consequence, Josefa Amar considered the admission of women to the society an example of justice in an Enlightened period and in an institution that claimed to be on the vanguard of the Enlightenment. However, Amar did not offer a vision that totally accepted the "progress" of civilization in the relations between the sexes. On the contrary, she disagreed with the typical idea that contrasted the "slavery" of women among "savage" or "barbarous" peoples with the harmony among the sexes that supposedly reigned in Europe. She turned the tables in a critical sense, pointing out that the "dependence" in which European women live is as unjust, or more unjust, because it hides oppression beneath the appearance of complementarity. Ultimately, rational equality among the sexes cannot exist as a purely rhetorical position in Josefa Amar's opinion; rather, its full recognition is a necessity of Enlightenment that should be put into practice by the admission of women into intellectual and social spaces with full rights, and into an education that understands their capabilities to be the same as those of men.

Taking this intellectual equality as a given – "El que dude de esta verdad querrá cerrar sus ojos a la luz," (Amar 1994, 69; He who doubts this truth closes his eyes to the truth) – her next work, the *Discurso sobre la educación física y moral de las mujeres* (Discourse on the physical and moral education of women; 1790), offers a pedagogical proposal formulated from a sort of possibilism that does not propose radical changes but rather is ambitious in the ample attention dedicated to women's intellectual formation and in reflections about the meaning of women's education, in contrast to the utilitarianism with which this topic was usually treated. As other contemporary women authors (among them her admired Mme. de Lambert), Josefa Amar presents education as necessary not only for the happiness of the family and for public welfare, but also (and perhaps most importantly) for a woman's own personal satisfaction, distancing herself from the increasing tendency in her day to place women's only objectives in conjugal and maternal love (Lewis 2004, 38–56).

Years later, in 1798, a brief and convincing essay by Inés Joyes (1731–1808) offered a new critical perspective on the model for Enlightened femininity (see also chapter 3 below). Its author was a woman of Irish descent, whose family, established in Madrid, had financial relations with the rest of Europe and connections with influential figures in business and politics. As a wife (and later widow) of a businessman, she led a discreet life in Málaga and Vélez-Málaga, with no known public activity beyond the management of the family business and of her family of nine children. The "Apología de las mujeres" (Apology of women; 1798), her only known work, published at the age of sixty-seven, accompanied her translation of the novel *Rasselas, Prince of Abissinia* (1759) by Samuel Johnson, dedicated to a great lady of the Enlightenment, the Duchess of Osuna. Her central ideas are the profound belief in the moral and intellectual capacity of women and the criticism of inequality in moral norms and social values between women and men. She writes as much to convince men of their unjust treatment of women as to exhort women to abandon their degrading moral and sentimental dependence, instead raising their consciousness of their own dignity. Inés Joyes criticized the education of women in her time and among those of her class, which was based on cultivating appearances and the art of pleasing others, but she also disapproves of short-sighted education that is excessively restrictive and domestic. Although she defended the family as essential for the reform of society, aware that expectations upon contracting marriage are not always realized, she does not present domestic life as the exclusive sentimental achievement for women; rather, she invites them to find other distinct accomplishments based on friendship and the cultivation of reason. Inés Joyes is unusually explicit about a sexual double moral standard, reproaching doctors, pedagogues, and moralists who severely blame women if they do not follow the profile of the abnegated mother, completely consumed in the care of her children, while remaining silent about men's sexual infidelities. She, like Josefa Amar and other authors whose contributions Catherine Jaffe examines in chapter 4 (María Lorenza de los Ríos, María Rosa Gálvez, Gertrudis de Hore), understood that the inequalities that so intensely conditioned women's lives and their own expectations and subjectivity not only were a concern for women's intellectual education and presence in social spaces but also crossed over in a particularly insidious way into the realm of marriage, private life, and sentiments.

Therefore, at the end of the century, some women brought to the debate over the sexes an articulated and profoundly critical focus that expressed their own version of Enlightenment values, distilled from their readings and their lived experience. In their words, it is possible to captivate the essence of a controversy that runs throughout the century, with striking examples, such as the open polemics over the work of Feijoo or over the admission of women into the Royal Economic Society, and others that were more diffuse and omnipresent. There are two key aspects of this Enlightened debate, fundamental in its legacy for the nineteenth century (Bolufer 1998, 399–401; Bolufer and Burguera 2010, 13–23; Burguera 2016). On the one hand, there was the intense consciousness, shared by all Enlightenment thinkers, that the reform of society required a transformation in the models of femininity (and masculinity) and of the guidelines for relations between the sexes. On the other hand were discrepancies over the exact form in which this transformation should be theorized, justified, and realized. At the heart of Enlightenment thought was the struggle between the rationalist tradition of the equality of the sexes and the notion of their duality and essential complementarity (corresponding in turn to a dichotomy between private and public), which, far from being resolved, continued sometimes in the form of an explicit debate, other times more hidden. Occasionally these positions were seen as alternative or exclusive possibilities but sometimes combined with a certain degree of tension, including within the same text or within the thought of the same author. This was one of the crossroads that the Enlightenment would leave open and that men and women who, having been educated in the values of the Enlightenment, would tackle as they lived and directed the transition from the Old Regime to liberalism and romanticism in the following century. In this way, as we read in other chapters of this book about the construction of liberal political and cultural systems and the changing meanings of the concepts of public and private, feminine and masculine, sentiment and reason (studied by Burguera 2012 and 2016; Sierra 2015; Burdiel 2012), we cannot but recognize the profound and ambiguous footprint that the Enlightenment left in all of these debates and in the very origins of modern feminism.

3 Women and "Civic Motherhood"

ELIZABETH FRANKLIN LEWIS

As in the rest of Enlightenment Europe, eighteenth-century reformers in Spain sought to involve women in their plans for the cultural, social, and political transformation of Spain by emphasizing their gendered roles as mothers and wives. However, as Mónica Bolufer points out in the previous chapter, there was great disagreement among reformers over whether women's social influence could be public, or whether it should remain within the domestic sphere.[3] In the controversy over the admittance of women into the Royal Economic Society of Madrid (covered by Bolufer in chapter 2), Francisco Cabarrús argued for a strictly private role for women and for their exclusion from such public institutions as the Royal Economic Society:

> Pero ¿acaso la moda y sus partidarios prevalecerán contra la voz de la naturaleza que sujetó las mugeres a la modestia y al pudor, o contra las relaciones inmutables de todas las sociedades que las impusieran como una obligación civil la fidelidad a sus maridos, elcuidado de sus hijos, y una vida doméstica y retirada? (Cabarrús 1786, 80)

> (Perhaps fashion and its supporters will prevail against the voice of nature that subjected women to modesty and decency, or against the immutable relationships of fidelity to their husbands, the care of their children, and a domestic and secluded life that all societies have imposed on them as their civil obligation?)

For Cabarrús, as for many other Enlightenment men and women, women's role as mothers and wives was important to the state, but it was also to be strictly separated from that of men. However, some men and women thought it was possible for women both to honour their womanly duties and, for a few exceptional women, to perform those duties publicly through their published writings and participation in various reform projects, serving as Spain's "civic mothers": nurturing the poor, encouraging industry and morality in working-class girls, and teaching middle-class women how to be better mothers and educators to their own children, especially their daughters – all for the good of Spain (Bolufer 1998, 371–88; Smith 2006, 161).

The notion of women's "natural" domestic role as residing within the idealized private sphere of the home was popularized by Rousseau's portraits of idealized femininity in the characters of Julie (*La nouvelle Heloise,* 1761) and Sophie (*Émile, ou De l'éducation,* 1762), and this physical as well as moral division of the sexes was accepted in Spain, as elsewhere in Europe, becoming part of the construction of a modern society (Bolufer 1998, 353–60). Still, this separation of the sexes did not necessarily preclude women's social and even political influence. Leslie H. Walker has studied narratives and visual art production by eighteenth-century French men and women, finding in their works on feminine virtue a departure from Rousseau's idealized (and marginalized) Julie, with the development of a "maternal discourse" of female agency (Walker 2008, 16). In eighteenth-century British women's writing about motherhood and women's role in the education of children, especially of girls, Rebecca Davies finds that women "employed the trope of maternity to effectively gain social status for themselves as women" (Davies 2014, 1). As in the cases of France and Britain, women in Spain also worked within and beyond their social roles as both real and symbolic mothers to transcend their supposed confinement to the domestic sphere in order to participate both in their writings and in their actions in a very public "civic motherhood."[4] Here we will examine Spanish women's role in the public sphere, and the formation and their own expression of the concept of "civic" motherhood from the 1780s until the early 1800s, as seen in works on women's education by Josefa Amar y Borbón and Inés Joyes y Blake, in the activities and reports of women's civic organizations like the Junta de Damas (Ladies' Council), and in the writings of playwright and poet María Rosa Gálvez.

Josefa Amar y Borbón was one of the earliest and most forceful voices for women's rights and their social and political inclusion into modern Spanish society (see chapter 2 above), and was also a strong advocate for, and example of, Spanish civic motherhood. As a member of the Royal Aragonese Economic Society in Saragossa, Amar y Borbón distinguished herself publicly not only by her intellectual endeavours (including two translations) but also by her work on a charitable project sponsored by the Aragonese society aimed at working-class girls, the School for Spinning (Pérez Sarrión 2003, 280; Sullivan 1992). Her aforementioned 1786 essay "Discurso en defensa del talento de las mujeres y de su aptitud para ejercer el gobierno y otros cargos en que se emplean los hombres" (Defence of women and of their aptitude for governing and other positions in which men are employed) earned her recognition on the national stage, as she gave a female voice to the controversy over admission of women to the Royal Economic Society of Madrid.[5] Amar describes the problem with women's restriction to domestic spaces, as Cabarrús and others had advocated:

> Saben ellas que no pueden aspirar a ningún empleo, ni recompensa pública; que sus ideas no tienen más extensión que las paredes de una casa, o de un convento. Si esto no es bastante para sofocar el mayor talento del mundo, no sé qué otras trabas pueden buscarse. Lo cierto es, que sería mejor ignorarlo todo, y carecer hasta del conocimiento, que sufrir el estado de esclavitud o dependencia. (Amar 2012, 49)
>
> (Women know that they cannot aspire to employment, nor to any public reward; that their ideas cannot go any further than the walls of their house, or their convent. If this is not enough to suffocate the greatest talent in the world, I don't know what other obstacles they could bring on. What is certain is that it would be better to ignore all of it, and even to lack intelligence, than to suffer the state of slavery or dependence.)

Ultimately, as Bolufer discussed in chapter 2, Amar's call for equal treatment for women through their admission as full members into the society was denied, and instead Amar herself was made an honorary member of the separate women's auxiliary group created in 1787 by King Charles III, the Junta de Damas. In 1790, Amar published a book on female education, the *Discurso sobre la educación física y moral de las mujeres* (Discourse on the physical and moral education of women). In contrast to the bold arguments in favour of women's abilities and advocating for women's political inclusion in Enlightenment Spain, her book on women's education seems to many critics much more measured, even conservative (Sullivan 1993). It is meant as a guidebook for mothers on the physical care of themselves and their children during pregnancy, childbirth, and infancy ("physical" education), as well as a guide for mothers in the education and instruction of their daughters ("moral" education).[6] Amar believes girls should be taught by their mothers and not in the convent, as most middle- and upper-class girls were at the time. Her book gives mothers with the inclination to teach their daughters advice on the curriculum they should follow and an extensive reading list to help further guide them. Still, within the more practical advice to mothers on what to teach and what to read, Amar expresses through her book to and about mothers some important social and political messages in keeping with her earlier defence of women.[7] Education, says Amar, is important for women personally, as well as for their social role as mothers: "lo primero porque puede conducir para hacer más suave y agradable el yugo de matrimonio: lo segundo para desempeñar el respetable cargo de madres de familia; y la tercera por la utilidad y ventaja que resulta de la instrucción en todas las edades de la vida" (Amar 1994, 72; first to make the yoke of matrimony softer, second to carry out the respectable job of being mothers, and third for the utility and advantage that comes from instruction in all the stages of life). Women's education is good for society and for women too, and mothers who take an active role in educating their daughters are making important civic contributions. Yet in this *Discurso*, Amar has gone from decrying women's "state of slavery" in their domestic confinement, as she did in the previous "Defensa," to finding ways for women to live within their spatial and social restrictions and to learn to live with the "yoke of matrimony" (a theme discussed in chapter 4 of this volume).

Less than a decade after Amar's book for women, another mother, Inés Joyes y Blake, published an open letter to her daughters to accompany her translation of Samuel Johnson's novel *Rasselas*. Bolufer has called Joyes's "Apología" (1798) "one of the most lucid and vehement texts on women's condition in eighteenth-century Spain" (Bolufer 2009c, 27; and chapter 2 of this volume). Joyes tells women in her "Apología" that they have an important civic role in the success of societal reform and in Spain's future:

> Tendreis la Gloria de reformar las costumbres haciendo amable la virtud; irá decayendo el lujo: vuestro exemplo hará moderados a los hombres: vuestros maridos os amarán y apreciarán: vuestros hijos os venerán: vuestros hermanos se tendrán por dichosos con vuestro trato: vivireis felices quanto cabe en el mundo, y morireis con la gloria de dexar una posteridad virtuosa. (Joyes 1798, 204)

(You will have the glory of reforming customs making virtue desirable; luxury will decay. Your example will moderate men; your husbands will love and appreciate you; your children will venerate you; your brothers will consider themselves lucky to know you: all of you will live happily, and you will die with the glory of leaving a virtuous posterity.)

Both Josefa Amar y Borbón and Inés Joyes y Blake embraced a public maternal role through their publications, which were meant to inspire action in women to Spain's "virtuous posterity" without overtly contradicting their prescribed gender roles within confined domestic spaces. Other eighteenth-century women took on the role of "civic mothers" through their work with poor women and children, notably the ladies of the Junta de Damas, Spain's first civic organization for women not associated with the church, which was created to resolve the controversy over women's admission into the Royal Economic Society of Madrid (discussed in chapters 1 and 2). While individual women had served in other economic societies elsewhere in Spain, including the aforementioned membership by Josefa Amar y Borbón in the Economic Society of Saragossa, in Madrid this small but nonetheless significant group of well-educated, upper-class women publicly participated in social reform projects.[8] The first group of members in the Ladies' Council consisted of sixteen women, most of them from the nobility. They took on projects given to them by the men of the Royal Economic Society, including running the Madrid foundling hospital, the Inclusa, and the administration of the *escuelas patrióticas* (patriotic schools), which taught trades to working-class boys and girls. They also took on projects of their own, including the running of the Madrid women's prison La Galera, which later was taken over by another women's group (formed of members from the *junta*), the Asociación de Señoras (Women's Association). Each member of the *junta* was expected to attend weekly meetings, to be on committees, perform administrative tasks related to their various projects with women and children, and often to visit and bring supplies to the schools, orphanages, and prisons they supported (Demerson 1975; Martin-Valdepeñas 2010). In addition, each year a member was selected to deliver a public address, which was later published, reporting on her activities in the form of an *elogio de la reyna* (homage to the queen), María Luisa herself an honorary member and principal benefactor of the group (Lewis 2009). In the *elogio de la reyna* delivered by the Countess of Castroterreño María Josefa Gálvez in 1801, the womanly work carried out by both the queen and the Ladies Council as civic mothers is exalted, simultaneously praising Bourbon politics and the success of the group's charitable endeavours. The Countess of Castroterreño praises the queen's "corazón sensible" (sensitive heart) and goes on to describe "la suavidad de sus palabras, el interés con que oye al afligido, la ternura con que le Consuela" (Gálvez y Valenzuela 1801, 10; the softness of her words, the interest with which she hears the afflicted, the tenderness with which she consoles). María Luisa as described by Castroterreño is the epitome of the sensitive maternal figure so exalted by men like Cabarrús. She is also protector and main benefactor of the *junta*'s projects, the Galera women's prison, and the Inclusa foundling hospital, which Castrerreño touts in her speech. The orphans of the Inclusa are especially pitiable because they are motherless: "un infeliz en fin, a quien sin culpa suya nunca es concedido pronunciar ¡ay! el nombre delicioso de madre" (Gálvez y Valenzuela 1801, 23–5; an unhappy being, in the end, who without any blame, is never allowed to say, oh!, the delightful name of mother). Both the queen, and the ladies of the *junta* become figurative mothers who provide instruction to working-class girls, edification to women prisoners, and protection for Madrid's abandoned children.

Poet and dramatist María Rosa Gálvez (see also chapter 4) included a poem in the first volume of her collected works titled "Oda a la beneficencia," which praises the charitable work of the queen, the Countess of Castroterreño (who was her cousin), and the women of the Ladies Council (*Obras poéticas* 1804). In it, Gálvez praises her cousin as a "modelo venturoso" (fortunate model) of feminine virtue. She says of the *junta*: "Allí triunfa mi sexo; la Nobleza / De la corte española / A su Reyna benéfica imitando / La gloria de hacer bien disfruta sola" (Gálvez de Cabrera 1804b, 13; There my sex triumphs; the nobility of the Spanish Court, imitating its beneficent queen, enjoys alone the glory of doing good). The actions of the Ladies Council not only inspired poetry but also sparked the creation of similar groups in other parts of Spain, including Valencia and Málaga, that also saw opportunities in their regions to improve women's education and prison reform, as well as the care of foundlings (Bolufer 1998, 371–88).

María Rosa Gálvez, the Countess of Castroterreño's talented cousin from Málaga, was best known for her plays, fourteen of which were published during her lifetime and seven represented on the Madrid stage (see also chapter 4).[9] The drama *Zinda*, published in volume 3 of her *Obras poéticas* (1804) but never staged, is an interesting example of civic motherhood that combines the qualities of a strong political leader with a fierce maternal protector in the figure of another queen and mother, the historical queen of the Mbungu people of the Congo (1620–63) Nzinga,[10] who fought against the enslavement of her people by the Portuguese. Just as Queen María Luisa was depicted as a benevolent mother and protector of the orphans of Madrid, so too the fictional Queen Zinda is presented as a defender of innocent victims – both of her own son and of her enslaved people. In act 2, after she has witnessed the destruction of her people and the imprisonment of her young son, Zinda contemplates her horrifying situation as both a mother and a queen: "Hijo de mi desgracia, tú del sueño / gozas el blando halago; y yo suspiro, / tiemblo, y me afano a contemplar tu suerte" (Gálvez de Cabera 1804c, 147; Child of my disgrace, you enjoy / the gentle satisfaction of sleep; and I sigh, / tremble, and I endeavour to contemplate your fate). At the end of the play, Queen Zinda is able to defeat the evil Dutch slave trader Vinter and to secure freedom for her son and her people. She too is an ideal model of civic motherhood, a woman of high station who protects and cares for those below her. She declares peace with the Portuguese if they renounce the slave trade, to which the Portuguese commander Pereyra responds: "¡Oh generosa Zinda! En ti se ha visto que la ferocidad cede, y se rinde / A la santa virtud y al heroísmo" (Gálvez de Cabera 1804c, 168; Oh generous Zinda! In you we have seen ferocity cease, and yield / To saintly virtue and to heroism). In *Zinda*, a feeling, yet strong, mother achieves success both for her family and her nation.

While civic motherhood in Spain did not necessarily contradict the Rousseauian model of strictly defined gender roles during the Spanish Enlightenment, a small group of educated Spanish elite women expanded their domestic roles to include the importance of their work not only within the family and the home as educators of their young sons and daughters but also outside the home with poor women and children. The civic motherhood they represented in their writings and actions posited a maternalistic society aimed at incorporating working-class women and children into Enlightenment reforms, thus complementing (and not contradicting) the Enlightenment paternalism that many *ilustrados* saw as necessary to achieve the progress they sought (Alemany 2005). While Spanish Enlightenment women rarely overtly challenged their gendered social roles as mothers, for a brief period some of them did challenge assumptions of male superiority, thereby proving themselves to be able intellectuals and civic leaders too. By the end of the Enlightenment period, one of the last of these civic mothers,

Tomasa Palafox y Portocarrero, the Marquesa de Villafranca, found herself struggling to continue the work of her predecessors, such as the aforementioned Countess of Castroterreño and her own mother, María Francisca de Sales de Portocarrero, the Countess of Montijo (one of the founding members of the *junta* who served as its long-time secretary). As president of the *junta* from 1817 to 1823, coinciding with the rise of liberalism during the Trienio Liberal (1820–3), Palafox and her sister *socias* found that although the new liberal government was taking up their causes through acts like the first Ley General de Beneficencia (General Law of Beneficence; 1822), liberalism was at best ambiguous about women's role in social change (Espigado 2016, 268–70). The future women's active participation in the public arena through their civic motherhood, passed from mother to daughter as Amar and Joyes had promoted, seemed destined to end, or at least pause, with Palafox's generation and Spain's Enlightenment.

4 From the Traps of Love and the Yoke of Marriage to the Ideal of Friendship: Women Writers in the Eighteenth Century

CATHERINE M. JAFFE

Eighteenth-century Spanish women writers reacted to subtle changes in social attitudes that were encouraged by Enlightenment thought, as described in the preceding chapters. They expressed their views on the problems and possibilities for love, marriage, and male and female friendship in their creative works in ways that are both similar to and different from women writers of earlier centuries. Their ability and daring to take up the pen to write, publish, or perform their works testify not only to a fortunate confluence of personal circumstances, such as access to instruction and literary culture, but also to personal tenacity and vocation (López-Cordón 2005b; García Garrosa 2007a; Bolufer 2005b and 2009c; Palacios Fernández 2002; Lewis 2004). In their creative works, women writers echoed, albeit indirectly through their poetic voice or through the characters in their plays, the reservations about women's status in society that were also expressed openly in essays by women writers such as Josefa Amar and Inés Joyes (see chapters 1, 2, and 3). As Lisa Vollendorf has pointed out, following the historian Gerda Lerner's insights, even before the advent of modern feminism in the nineteenth century, it is possible to detect a "feminist consciousness" in writing that voiced resistance to behaviours and institutions that were unfair to women, although the writers were not connected to any organized social movements that we would today identify as feminist (Vollendorf 2001a, 8–10).

As López-Cordón indicates in chapter 1, historians and literary scholars have observed how marriage during the eighteenth century in Spain underwent a process of change that, without completely rejecting the traditional structures of matrimony, began to incorporate new models of experience such as the recognition and appreciation of sensibility as an ethical impulse (García Garrosa 1990 and 2007b; Morant and Bolufer 1998, 123–31). A new way to think about love and matrimony that affirmed both love and social equality as the basis for the conjugal relationship began to appear towards the end of the century. This was no longer passionate, sexual love that had to be controlled by the sacrament of marriage (Morant and Bolufer 1998, 38–54). Rather, in women's creative writing, we see a new awareness of the ideal of marriage as an affective relationship based on inclination and mutual respect between a man and a woman, coupled with the recognition that the basis for marriage could not completely ignore family and economic interests.

The Traps of Love

Eighteenth-century women writers protested women's susceptibility to men's dishonesty in love relationships, as had women writers of earlier centuries, such as María de Zayas y Sotomayor (1590–c1661). In her path-breaking study of eighteenth-century love customs in Spain, novelist and historian Carmen Martín Gaite has shown that male writers often complained of women's coquetry and inconstancy. They also criticized the practice of the *cortejo,* or *chichisveo,* "a gallant relation between a married woman and a gentleman (with precedents in sixteenth-century Spanish court customs and in the French *chevalier servant* and the Italian *cicisbeo*), that spread from the aristocracy to other social ranks in the second half of the century" (Bolufer, 2005b, 495–6). Male writers claimed that the *cortejo,* who accompanied a lady to social events and also in the intimacy of her dressing table, imperilled the prestige of the institution of marriage (Martín Gaite 1987, 139–68, 221–40). Women writers, for their part, criticized the double moral standard to which women were subjected and their powerlessness in the face of men's inconstancy. For example, in *Poesías varias* (1789), Margarita Hickey writes about women's unhappy nature in "Definiendo la infelíz constitución de las mugeres en general" (Defining the unhappy constitution of women in general): "De bienes destituidas, / Víctimas del pundonor, / Censuradas con amor, / Y sin él desatendidas" (Hickey 1789, 216–17; Destitute of goods, / Victims of their sense of honor, / Censored when in love, / And neglected without it [Salgado 2009, 68)]).[11] The poet emphasizes unequal power relations between men and women in matters of love in "Definición de los hombres, en punto al género y manera de su querer quando aman, ó dicen que aman" (Definition of men, in regard to the kind and manner of their love when they love, or say that they love):

"Sirven para dominar, / Se rinden para triunfar" (Hickey 1789, 217–18; They are good for controlling / They surrender to win [Salgado 2009, 81]). Hickey condemns men for asserting superiority to women in her *seguidillas*[12]: "como si el alma / tuviera sexô; / locura rara, / pretender distinciones / el que se iguala" (Hickey 1789, 189–90; As if by chance the soul / Had a sex; / A strange madness, / To assume distinctions / Among equals [Salgado 2009, 69–70]). The poet refers here to the long debate over equality between the sexes that was crystallized in Spain by Feijoo's "Defensa de las mujeres," discussed in chapter 2.

Like early modern women, eighteenth-century women writers employed a wide range of strategies to present themselves as authors, such as brandishing the topoi of humility and modesty, defending the usefulness of their work for other women, publishing anonymously or publishing translations of others' work, sometimes adding their own thoughts in more a veiled fashion in footnotes or in prologues, as did Inés Joyes (Bolufer 2009c; see also Bolufer's discussion of Joyes in chapter 2 and Anastácio's discussion of Portuguese women writers in chapter 5). As had early modern women writers, eighteenth-century women writers invoked the desire for equality and liberty, but the Enlightenment solidified those values in an unprecedented way. What is new in their complaints about women's susceptibility to male behaviour is the semantic range that invokes Enlightenment ideals of equality, liberty, right to happiness, and freedom from oppression, and also their warning to the relatively few educated, Enlightened women to be especially wary. During the years that the poet María Gertrudis de Hore participated in Enlightened circles of sociability in Cádiz prior to entering the convent upon the foundering of her marriage, she warned a young girl, María Rosario Cepeda, who had defended her thesis at the university (1768), in an extraordinary and formulaic exhibition of a women's erudition, to avoid the traps of love: "¿Dónde, Minerva, las Lechuzas tristes?: Guárdate, como digo de Cupido, / Pues su alevoso, su engañoso trato, / Enemigo mortal de los ingenios" (quoted in Morand 2009, 35–6; Where, Minerva, the sad owls?: Beware, as I say, of Cupid, / Since his arrogant and deceiving dealings / Are the mortal enemies of the intelligent). Hore warns the young scholar that famous, accomplished women – Sappho, Medea, Circe – abandoned their studies and their contentment for unhappy love (Lewis 2004, 61–95).

The increasing interaction between men and women in polite society led writers to caution women about its dangers. María Lorenza de los Ríos, Marquesa de Fuerte-Híjar, a member of the Junta de Damas

(Women's Council of the Royal Economic Society of Madrid; see chapters 1–3 and 5) in her one-act play *La sabia indiscreta* (The indiscreet learned lady), warns educated women who interact with men intellectually to beware of the subtle ties of the heart: "Señoras, en este espejo / mirarse, y estar alerta, / que al cabo, si no se tiene / con los varones reserva, / y se frecuenta su trato, / la más sabida la pega" (Fuerte-Híjar 1800b, 243; Ladies, in this mirror / Observe yourselves, and remain alert, / Because in the end, if one is not / Reserved with men / And is often in their company / The wisest woman falls in love [Jaffe 2004, 285–7]). In "Canción: Avisos a una joven que va a salir al mundo" (Song: Advice for a young woman who is going out into the world), the poet Hore warns a young woman entering society that its glitter is deceptive and its values are a temptation to abandon useful work. Especially for the educated woman, she points out, society's praise is deceptive, because she will learn that her education has been not for herself, but rather to make her more desirable to her husband: "Que a su amado apreciable / Más la haga cada día más amable" (quoted in Lewis 2004, 78; That for her esteemed lover / Might make her each day more lovable). Again, in "Bellísima Zagala," Hore warns a young girl leaving the convent to enter society to beware: "Mas vela con cuidado / el alcázar del pecho / porque al corazón libre / no le hagan prisionera" (quoted in Lewis 2004, 81; But carefully watch over / the castle of your breast / so that they cannot make a prisoner / out of a free heart).

These writers reveal a consciousness that women – at least those of their own social rank – were in an unjust position. Hickey warns not only the women of Madrid but also all women everywhere that gender relations are a constant battle: "Sexô hermoso, combatido / sin piedad, con furia tanta, / … os sitian, cercan y asaltan" (Hickey 1789, 227–8; Lovely sex, fought / without pity, and with such fury / … besiege you, surround you, and assault you [quoted in Salgado 2009, 72–3]). The female protagonist of *El Eugenio* by Fuerte-Híjar laments women's emotional susceptibility to men's attentions. She claims that women, rather than being flattered, should have more self-respect: "¡Ah! ¡Infelices mujeres! Si fuéramos más amantes de nosotras mismas, evitaríamos muchas amarguras" (Oh! Unhappy women! If we were better friends to ourselves, we would avoid much bitterness). Women's "necio engreimiento" (foolish pride) makes them victims of men's inconstancy (1.1). The dramatist María Rosa Gálvez, whose plays are also discussed in chapter 3, creates a paradoxical "warrior slave" in her last play, *Las esclavas amazonas* (The Amazon slaves), to protest the impossible status of Enlightened women who could not escape subjugation by men. Gálvez's *El egoista* (The egotist) deals with spousal abuse, and her tragedy *Zinda* deals with women and the African slave trade (Lewis 2004, 107; Establier 2006, 188–9). These writers' imagery of confinement, battle, and defences suggests an acute awareness of women's vulnerability in gender relations that were in transition from the Old Regime's emphasis on the honour code and the separation between men and women in society, to a modern society based on rational equality and shared sociability. As some women gained literacy and a measure of education and were able to share social spaces with men, they voiced more openly their protests of unequal relations (Bolufer 2005b, 480–4; 2009c; López-Cordón 2005b and 2009).

The Yoke of Matrimony

Essayists such as Josefa Amar and Inés Joyes (discussed in chapters 2 and 3) invoked the common metaphor of "the yoke of matrimony" and cogently warned women of the constraints the institution represented for women (Bolufer 2008, 289; Amar y Borbón, 1790, xxxii). López-Cordón draws a parallel between the restrained critique of unequal marriage in Leandro Fernández de Moratín's classic play about female consent, *El sí de las niñas* (Girl's consent; 1806) and the erosion of the authority of the monarchy in Spain immediately before the outbreak of the Peninsular War: "Neither the author's [Moratín's] nor Godoy's detractors were revolutionaries; perhaps for this reason the playwright did not know how to perceive the desire for real liberty felt by many women of his time, and Godoy's critics did not sense the fragility of the system that they wished to reform" (López-Cordón 2007b, 337). There was a perception that marriage as an institution that undergirds society was in trouble by the century's end.

Women writers offered possible solutions – both humorous and ideal – to these problems. The actress Mariana Cabañas proposes in her comic *sainete* (one-act farce), *Las mujeres solas* (Women alone; 1757), how wives can take revenge on husbands for their ill treatment. Antonia, an actress, tells her actress friends that husbands are "tratándonos como esclavas / y teniéndose por dueños" (Cabañas 2007, 210; treating us like slaves / and considering themselves as masters), and claims that unmarried men are no better. One of her friends complains that her husband is so stingy he won't buy her anything, "siendo así que como él / yo también gano el dinero" (2007, 215; even though just like him, / I earn my own money). Antonia proposes to her friends that they use their power as actresses to influence society by making it fashionable to treat their husbands as if they didn't exist. In Gálvez's tragedy *Safo,* the Greek poet rejects marriage altogether (Lewis 2004, 107).

The lack of attention paid to women's education was often identified as the source of many difficulties in marriage. The protagonist of the Basque writer María Rita de Barrenechea's didactic drama *La aya* (The governess; 1780) is saved at the last minute from abduction and an unhappy marriage, which was engineered by a corrupt servant posing as a French governess (Bakarne Altonaga discusses Berrenechea's play *Catalín* in chapter 6). The girl's neglectful mother warns other mothers to care for their daughters' education themselves: "Escarmienten las madres holgazanas con este lance, que seguramente no es el peor que ha sucedido por el abandono" (quoted in García Garrosa 2004, 66; Let lazy mothers draw a lesson from this affair, that surely is not the worst that has occurred when they abandon their duty). In her play *Entre los riesgos de amor, sostenerse con honour: La Laureta* (Amid the risks of love, bear yourself with honour, Laureta; 1800), María Martínez Abello also creates an educated, sensible heroine who saves her own and her family's honour when her seducer, impressed by her virtue and understanding, offers to marry her (Establier 2015, 144).

Hickey, like Cabañas, warns a friend of husbands' tendency towards tyranny: "El amante mas rendido / Es, transformado en marido, / Un insufrible tirano" (Hickey 1789, 216; The most enslaved lover / Is, once a husband / An insufferable tyrant). In her play *El Eugenio,* Fuerte-Híjar presents the ideal of a marriage for love for her protagonist, but also a secondary character's vehement opposition to marriage (Jaffe 2009; Jaffe and Martín-Valdepeñas 2013 and 2015). Máxima, the protagonist Balbina's friend, flatly refuses an offer of marriage from a *petimetre* (fop) and condemns the institution as a yoke that leads to slavery or immoral deceit:

> Sométase enhorabuena la juventud incauta o corrumpida a las cadenas que forman la avaricia y la vanidad, imponiendo a nuestro débil sexo la cruel alternativa de abandonarse o a una horrible esclavitud o a una libertad infame. Esta ley escandalosa sólo puede intimarse a las que por estupidez no son capaces de sentir su peso, o las que las reciben con ánimo de quebrantarla. (3.12)

> (Let incautious or corrupt youth submit to the chains formed by avarice and vanity, imposing on our weak sex the cruel alternative of abandoning ourselves either to a horrible slavery or an infamous liberty. This scandalous law can only be suggested to those women who through stupidity are not capable of feeling its weight, or to those who receive it with the intention of breaking it.)

Like Barrenechea, Fuerte-Híjar presents a critique of acceptable feminine gender roles through a secondary character (chapter 5). The semantic choices of these women writers, drawn from the field of political relations – tyranny, yoke, slavery, chains, subordination – directly oppose the idealization of marriage found in amorous poetry or sentimental drama.

The Ideal of Friendship

As a select class of women gained a measure of education and participated in practices of mixed sociability, such as those discussed in chapters 1 and 2, at times they voiced their aspiration to a new model of friendship between women and between women and men. Hore wrote often of her female friends in the world and in the convent, and exalted an interior space shared with them (Lewis 2004, 75–8). Although Martín Gaite refers to the belief in the impossibility of friendship between women, because as subordinates they would always be rivals for men's attention (1987, 221–40), women writers did express an awareness of friendship between women as a supportive relationship. María Joaquina de Viera y Clavijo, an artist and poet from the Canary Islands, invoked the ideal of female friendship as a model of divine love: "¡Qué dulce es la amistad! / ¡Qué amable, qué tranquila! / Con ella, aquí en la tierra / Los gustos de la gloria se anticipan" (2006, 375; How sweet friendship is! / How good, how calm! / With friendship, here on earth / We anticipate the pleasures of eternal glory). In her one-act play *La sabia indiscreta*, Fuerte-Híjar suggests that the hardest thing for educated women of her day was to find a man who would accept them (Jaffe 2004, 285–7). Her protagonist prefers books to love and discovers an uncomfortable truth: "¿Si a la amistad se mezcla / otro afecto menos puro?" (Fuerte-Híjar 1800b, 235; And if with friendship there is mixed / another, less pure affection?). Fuerte-Hijar also wrote of the consolation of friendship among women. Her characters Balbina and Máxima in *El Eugenio* are estranged because of Balbina's unfounded jealousy, and

Balbina cries, "¡Qué cosa tan desabrida es vagar por la vasta región de los celos sin hallar una amiga de quien fiarse! ... Una buena amiga me desagraviaría de este contratiempo" (2.3; How disagreeable it is to wander in the vast region of jealousy without finding a friend to trust! ... A good friend would help me through this difficult time). When the two are reconciled, Balbina tells her friend, "Abracémonos, mi Máxima, y viva nuestra amistad" (3.7; Let us embrace, my Máxima, and long live our friendship!). At the end of the play, Máxima claims that "la virtud y la amistad" are "dos principios de la verdadera felicidad en todas las relaciones humanas" (3.12; virtue and friendship ... two principles of true happiness in all human relations), including in matrimony.

Daring feminist ideas were also introduced into Spain through translation. In *Cartas de una peruana* (Letters from a Peruvian woman), her translation of Françoise de Graffigny's 1747 novel *Lettres d'une péruvienne*, María Romero Masegosa recounts the Incan heroine Zilia's steadfast (and unpopular) refusal to wed her protector D'Eterville (see chapter 2). Zilia daringly proposes instead a friendship between equals: "Venid, aprendereis á conocer los placéres inocentes y durables; venid á gozarlos conmigo; vos hallareis en mi corazon, en mi amistad, y en mis sentimientos, todo quanto puede subsanar la perdida del amor" (Graffigny 1792, 503; Come, you will learn of innocent and long-lasting pleasures; come to enjoy them with me; you will find in my heart, in my friendship, and in my feelings, all that can make up for the loss of love). Although Romero alters the original to have Zilia convert to Christianity, she does not change the story to have her wed the devoted suitor D'Eterville (Bolufer 2014, 306–16; Smith 2006, 178–96).

These women writers might have read translated works like Graffigny's that proposed new gender relations, or the summary of a French translation of Mary Wollstonecraft's *Vindication of the Rights of Woman* published in the *Diario de Madrid* in 1792.[13] They participated in literary culture through their reading and in *tertulias* (salons), and they perceived the transformative effect education might have on society. They criticized the problems women faced in love and marriage, and they aspired to the Enlightenment ideal of friendship, a relation based on equality, at least within their own social rank. When they wrote about marriage as tyranny and slavery or claimed equality with men, it was against a background of new ideologies that were gradually transforming the political underpinnings of society and social practices (Bolufer 2005b). They presented no unified feminist platform or ideology, as López-Cordón cautions us in chapter 1, and their complaints recalled those of earlier women writers. But the writers discussed here did make clear that they believed their problems were the result of an unfair legal and social system that kept women subordinate to men, while they sensed with wariness the winds that would bring political and social change, whether desired or not.

5 "Feminism" in Portugal before 1800

VANDA ANASTÁCIO

In 1901, Helene Lange, the President of the Bund Deutscher Frauenvereine, sent an official invitation to Carolina Michaëlis de Vasconcelos to participate in the Feminist Congress, which soon would take place in Berlin (Frandsen 1974). Michaëlis de Vasconcelos (1851–1925) was born in Germany but was married to a Portuguese man, and had been living in Oporto for twenty-five years. Her familiarity with Portuguese culture was probably the reason why, according to Lange, she was "the only representative of the women of Spain and Portugal" known to the German feminists (Delille 2001, 45n36). Judging from the contribution Michaëlis sent the same year to be published in the *Handbuch der Frauenbewegung*, Lange's difficulty in obtaining information on Iberian feminism was hardly surprising. According to Michaëlis, "Women's struggle for better social conditions is still entirely unorganized in the Iberian world ... Women submit, without noticeable protest, to the centuries-old tradition of inferiority" (Michaëlis 1901, 424).

Carolina Michaëlis de Vasconcelos's view of Iberian women's situation is symptomatic of the invisibility of the efforts undertaken in this part of Europe to improve women's social condition. It mirrors the idea conveyed even today by most historians of Portuguese culture, who do not find any traces of feminist claims in Portugal before the rise of the first suffragist movements, which is to say, before the appearance of the journal *A Voz Feminina* (The feminine voice) in 1868 and the founding of the Portuguese Republican Party in 1876, followed by the creation, in 1909, of the Liga Republicana das Mulheres Portuguesas (League of Portuguese Republican Women) (Couto-Potache 1982; Esteves 2001). The association of the concept of feminism with the moment when the word "feminism" was employed is certainly at the root of this view.

However, the similarity of many of the claims made by early twentieth-century feminists to those uttered by the men and women who spoke out for women's rights, needs, and aspirations in the Early Modern Period allows for a broader understanding of the concept and for the recuperation of their discourses as proof of the existence of a "feminist consciousness," as part of the history of feminism (Offen 2000; Lerner 1993; Tavares da Silva 1983 and 1998).

The eighteenth century offers a privileged field of inquiry in this context. At a time when philosophers and rulers were discussing ways of reforming society in order to ensure the well-being of large numbers of people, when the origins and the nature of inequality between men were the subject of an intense and widespread debate, women's nature, women's education, and women's roles became recurrent themes of controversy. Portuguese culture was no exception. However, although the rights reclaimed for women and the discourses used to claim them were very similar to those circulating in other parts of Europe, the ways they were formulated and the channels used to convey them were determined, to a large extent, by the specificities of the Portuguese cultural field.

Women and the "Women's Quarrel" in Eighteenth-Century Portugal

Discourses about women in sixteenth- and seventeenth-century Portugal illustrate the basically unequal social and political structure of Early Modern society. As far as contemporary theologians, thinkers, and men of letters were concerned, men and women should not be treated in the same manner, but neither should all women. Class and status prevailed over gender. Queens and princesses, noble, single, widowed, religious, and married women were expected to have different social roles and behaviour, and these categories determined, to a large extent, their degree of autonomy, their opportunities to make choices about their own lives, and their access to such "rights" as education, legal protection, and dignity of treatment (Andrade 1630). Although the basic structure of Portuguese society did not radically change at the turn of the century, women, the behaviour of women, and the social and religious norms regulating women's lives became a widespread subject of discussion from the early 1700s onwards and continued to surface regularly in the discourses circulating in the public arena, in spite of the changes in the balance of power resulting from the succession of four monarchs on the Portuguese throne between 1700 and 1800: João V, José I, Maria I, and João VI.

Evidence of discussions related to the European *querelle des femmes*, or "debate on women," is practically nonexistent in Portugal before the eighteenth century (Kelly 1982, 4–28; Bock and Zimmermann 1997; Viennot and Pellegrin 2012; Anastácio 2015, 49–61). As Tobias Brandenberger points out, misogynous stereotypes of women's flaws and weaknesses can be traced in Portuguese literature at least to the fifteenth century, and so can, to a much lesser degree, complaints about the way women were treated by men; but the dialogical nature of the "debate" is usually lacking. There is no evidence of responses to misogynous discourses by women, or attributed to feminine "voices," which could allow for an exchange of ideas on the subject (Brandenberger 1997, 183–202). The appearance in 1715 of a pamphlet titled *Bondade das mulheres vendicada e malícia dos homens manifesta* (Women's goodness vindicated and men's malice manifested) by a woman who signed herself as Paula da Graça, which rejected the way women were portrayed in a popular versified satire called *Malícia das mulheres* (Women's malice) attributed to Baltasar Dias, was a sign that something was beginning to change (Dias 1659; Graça 1741; d'Armada 2008).

Da Graça uses some of the arguments popularized by the tradition of the "debate on women" – the idea that women are at least as capable of heroism as men, the claim that souls are neither masculine nor feminine (and therefore both sexes are spiritually equal), the view that Adam was as responsible as Eve for original sin, and, especially, the conviction that if women were allowed the same education as men, they would be equally able to participate in intellectual life. This pamphlet started a long debate, which led to a series of other pamphlets until 1812. Another exchange of contradictory views on the subject of women's nature and women's social roles surfaced in 1761 in two *folhetos de cordel* (pamphlets) opposing a man's voice disguised under the pseudonym of "Frei Amador do Desengano" (Friar Lover of Disenchantment) to a female author signing herself as Gertrudes Margarida de Jesus (Moutinho dos Santos 1987). In her *Cartas apologéticas em favor e defensa das mulheres* (Jesus 1761a, 1761b; Apologetical letters in favour of and in defence of women), Gertrudes Margarida contradicts the accusations of women's ignorance, inconstancy, and sinful beauty by using similar weapons, namely, an overwhelming display of erudition, with references taken from contemporary works, including the repertoires of Portuguese and "international" heroines assembled by Diogo Manuel Ayres Azevedo

(*Portugal illustrado pelo sexo feminino*, 1734) and by Damião Froes Perym (*Theatro heroino: Abecedario historico e catalogo das mulheres illustres*, 1736 and 1740). In her text, she translates and incorporates large quotations of Benito Feijoo's "Defensa de las mujeres" (1726; discussed in chapter two) without specifically referring to his name or acknowledging her borrowings (Torres Feijó 2005; Reboredo Marques 2005.

The *folheto de cordel* as the medium of intervention in the discussion on women's roles was used again at the end of the century to support an important feminist claim. When King José I died in 1777 without a male heir, his eldest daughter María inherited the Portuguese throne. This situation caused apprehension in some political circles, and there were rumours about the inadequacy of a woman to act as head of state, particularly after the death in 1786 of María's husband and uncle Pedro III, with whom she had shared the throne, and that of her son and heir Dom José in 1788 (she would be removed from power in 1792 and pronounced incapable of ruling on grounds of madness). Disputes over Queen Maria's legitimacy to rule seem to have motivated the appearance in 1790 of a *folheto de cordel* with the title *Tratado da igualdade dos sexos, ou elogio do merecimento das mulheres oferecido, e dedicado às ilustres senhoras de Portugal por um amigo da razão* (A treatise on the equality of the sexes, or eulogy of women's merit offered and dedicated to the illustrious ladies of Portugal by a friend of reason). This text, signed with the pseudonym "um amigo da razão" (A friend of reason) not only celebrates women's right to education but also defends the legitimacy of the involvement of women in state politics and their ability to exercise power. In his arguments in favour of women, this anonymous author openly quotes Benito Jerónimo Feijoo and also makes use of other sources, recalling a number of heroines taken from the repertoires of Azevedo and Perym, and adding the queen herself to the list. The answer to this pamphlet came some time later in 1822, when the first Portuguese Constitution was approved, and the possibility of women's voting for parliament was discussed in a text signed with the initials R.F.C. and called *Dedução filosófica da desigualdade dos sexos, e de seus direitos políticos por natureza* (A philosophical deduction on the inequality of the sexes and of their political rights by nature). As the title suggests, the author argued that there was a "natural incapacity" imposed upon women by their biology and considered it to be a strong motive for their exclusion from voting.

The brief description of this kind of "pamphlet war," as Regina Tavares da Silva calls it (1986, 50), seems to indicate that, although

Portuguese thinkers do not explicitly mention previous texts of the *querelle des femmes*, they were aware, at least in the eighteenth century, of the arguments, commonplace ideas, and claims used to discuss the subject in other countries at different times. In a similar way, they concentrate their arguments in favour of women on the distinction between what we call today "sex and gender" and insist on the need to separate the features inherent to biology ("feminine nature") from social constructions and prejudices about what men and women should be like and what social roles should be assigned to them. The debates taking place in the *folhetos de cordel* testify to the emergence of feminist discourses in the Portuguese cultural field of the eighteenth century. These discourses echo similar concerns (the equivalent of today's concept of "rights") found in other European areas, to the point that we could speak of transnational communities of interpretation and/or of understanding (Fish 1980, 303–90; Chartier 1992). They insist on the recognition of women's intellectual capacity and their right to advanced education, on the need for dignity of treatment, and most significantly, on women's right to rule.

Discussing Women's Right to Education

The contrasting arguments in favour of, or against, women wielded in the polemics just mentioned had the effect of popularizing the discussion on the place and roles women should have in Portuguese society. It was, however, only part of a larger movement of social change, fostered by a variety of factors. Knowledge of foreign mores and of ideas debated abroad has certainly contributed to this movement, but so have local proposals and policies of reform, and local shifts in power, not to mention the disruption caused in the Portuguese traditional way of life by the Lisbon earthquake of 1755 (Lousada and Brito Henriques, 2007).

The debate on women's intellectual capacity and on women's right to education, for instance, was not confined to the controversies arising in the *cordel*. Education was at the heart of the proposals of reform made by the most prominent thinkers of the time, namely, the philosophers Luís António Verney (1713–92), whose *O verdadeiro método de estudar* (The true method of study) was published in 1746, the doctor António Nunes Ribeiro Sanches (1699–1783), who published in 1760 his *Cartas sobre a educação da mocidade* (Letters on the education of youth) and a separate letter known as *Educação de hua menina até a idade de tomar estado, no reyno de Portugal* (Education of a young girl up to the age of majority in the kingdom of Portugal) (Pina 1968), and the theologian and mathematician Teodoro de Almeida (1722–1804), who designed a program of studies for the first boarding school for young aristocratic women, the Colégio da Visitação (Santos 2002). They all mentioned the need to improve women's education, but their proposals do not assume equal rights for men and women to access knowledge. Although they seemed to favour women's claims to the "right" to education, the conceptions of what female education should consist of expressed by these most celebrated eighteenth-century Portuguese reformers of different backgrounds did not meet the expectations expressed by women in the publications associated with the *querelle des femmes* described above. However, reformers seemed to agree on a number of key ideas. For example, they all considered women's intellectual capacities as similar (if not equal) to men's, they all criticized the traditional ways of bringing up women, and they all insisted on the need to improve their education. But neither the justifications given for educating women nor the kind of knowledge considered adequate for them are in tune with the demands for equal access to high culture put forward by contemporary women's voices.

Portuguese reality in the eighteenth century was very similar to what Karen Offen found in her comparative approach to European feminisms in the same period. Most Enlightened reformers saw motherhood, wifely duties, and religion as the "natural" and adequate roles women should play, regardless of their social ranks, and invoked them as the main reasons for educating women. What seems to have changed from previous times was the emphasis placed on the social implications or, in other words, on the public interest of these roles, and on the impact that educating women could have on society as a whole. When underlining the moralizing influence educated wives could have on the behaviour of husbands, the improvement in the accomplishment of the duties of aristocratic ladies that could come from a better education, or the higher aspirations to virtue that education could help inculcate in nuns, these thinkers were recognizing that women are essential to the functioning of society. However, they were equally concerned with limiting women's access to knowledge on the same grounds.

It is worth keeping in mind that the access to written culture in Portuguese society had been subject to tight surveillance at least since 1539, when the Inquisition became responsible for controlling all texts circulating in the Portuguese Empire. The diffusion of manuscript and printed material continued to concern Portuguese rulers throughout the century. Proof of this situation is that, whenever there was a major change in government (1768, 1787, 1792), a new reform of the censorship system was introduced (Almeida Rodrigues 1980; Rego 1982). Also, between 1762 and 1778, the *Gazeta de Lisboa* (the official periodical press) was forbidden. Discourses on women's education therefore need to be contextualized within the social and mental constraints faced by anyone attempting to intervene in this particular cultural field at this particular moment.

Other "Feminist" Claims

The publications on the discussion of the nature and social roles of men and women, as well as the proposals of reform of women's education, reached a relatively wide audience and raised awareness of these issues. It can even be argued that these discourses had an impact on Portuguese society and led, eventually, to the implementation of policies aimed at changing women's condition.[14] One should stress, however, that prowoman claims made by women remained relatively rare, and that not all discriminating practices denounced throughout the century attracted the same degree of attention on the part of their contemporaries.

This was the case of the plea in favour of what we would call today "women's self-determination," meaning the possibility of women's choosing their own destiny, brought to the public attention by Matias Aires in a philosophical treatise called *Reflexões sobre a vaidade dos homens* (Thoughts on the vanity of men; 1752). Although not of noble origin, Aires studied in Coimbra and Paris, and was familiar with the major works of contemporary philosophers. He maintains that all human actions are inspired by some kind of vanity, speculates about the transience and precariousness of all things human, and asserts that all men are born equal (Aires 2005, par. 79), with the exception of sovereigns. His argumentation is particularly interesting for feminist claims because, while severely criticizing contemporary society, he denounces the dynamics of domination not only between men but also between men and women. He compares gender relations to tyranny and considers the state of subjection in which women were kept comparable to slavery. His main attack is directed to the common practice of cloistering women from an early age in convents, where they are forced to become nuns in order to keep the family fortune undivided, to guarantee better dowries for their sisters, or to ensure larger financial means for their brothers. Matias Aires's blunt denunciation of this practice was also brought up in another *folheto de cordel*, published by João Baptista de Castro in the same year (1752), entitled *Confortaçam para os queixosos* (A consolation for those complaining), which gives voice to a nun, who complains about her destiny. Forced cloistering and arranged marriages can be considered two facets of the same notion that women are incapable of or unsuited for making decisions about their own lives, which justified keeping them in a situation of dependency on masculine tutorship.

The difficulty of recuperating the voices of Portuguese women who made "feminist" claims in the eighteenth century is due not only to the fact that, until recently, historiography was almost exclusively concerned with capturing the dominant masculine voices. It is also the consequence of the various strategies of disguise deployed by the women themselves, who tried to enable their interventions in the intellectual field by keeping a "modest" and "discreet" profile, hiding their identities under pseudonyms or anonymity, or distributing manuscript copies of their texts. Also, because of the strict censorship surveillance of the periodical press (which led, as mentioned, to temporary prohibition), the collaboration of women in newspapers and journals was almost nonexistent in Portugal during this period – another circumstance that contributed to their invisibility. Finally, one important factor conditioning the access of historians to female discourses is the fact that only a very small number of eighteenth-century Portuguese women had their works printed. Nuns can be considered as a special group, for, although controlled by the church hierarchy, and with limited possibilities of openly expressing discontent, they could legitimate their involvement with print with an edifying goal.[15] Educated aristocrats and bourgeois male and female poets preferred to disseminate their poetry in manuscript. With rare exceptions, lay women published anonymously, mostly translations. In eighteenth-century Portugal, printing seemed to have been seen, by authors as well as by the ruling powers, as a decisive means of intervention in the public arena (Anastácio, 2010).

An important exception in this respect is Teresa Margarida da Silva e Orta (who was, incidently, Matias Aires's sister). In 1752, she published, under the pseudonym Dorotheia Engrassia Tavareda Dalmira (an anagram of her name), the novel *Máximas de virtude e formosura* (Maxims of virtue and beauty).[16] The narrative takes place in Ancient Greece and gives the author the opportunity to discuss ideas that focus on two key subjects: the condition, education, and social roles of women; and the principles of good government. Since the main characters in the novel are learned women (Hemirena and Climenea) who defend women's education and the ability of women to rule, while they attack the injustice of women's condition and protest against women's subjection to families who sacrifice them to their own agendas, this text has often been presented, by present-day critics, as feminist. The discourses of the characters abound in maxims that sound like a defence of women's rights, such as, "Nature has endowed men with more strengths and women of more subtlety of the spirit" or "Temos igualdade de almas e o mesmo direito aos conhecimentos necessários" (Silva e Orta 2002, 103, 105; [Men and women] are equal in the soul and have the same right to necessary knowledge).· But in most cases, the proposals in favour of women are accompanied by counterproposals, which limit their scope. For instance, women's education is recommended as a virtuous occupation and as a way to avoid ignorance, but, according to the author, it should not be available to just any woman. Even women of the nobility are not expected to "make profession of science" and do not have "the obligation to be scholarly" (Silva e Orta 2002, 102).

The same ambiguous discourse is adopted when dealing with other "feminist" claims. Parents who, "blinded by avarice," force their daughters into arranged marriages with older, adulterous, idle, violent, or jealous men are criticized, but obedience on the part of the young women forced to marry in such circumstances is praised, as is the goodness of "feminine nature," which is said to allow them to assist and care for even the most despicable husbands (Silva e Orta 2002, 109). While the author attacks the excesses in the repression of women, she does not seem to envisage the possibility of a different order of things. In the narrative, men's dominance over women is even presented as inevitable, because it dates from the very act of Creation.

One finds a similar posture in the discussions held in *Máximas de virtude e formosura* (Maxims of virtue and beauty) about the origins of sovereignty and the principles of good government. There seems to be no ideological space for thinking in egalitarian terms; not only are princes said to be different from other men (even if nature makes them look similar to others; Silva e Orta 2002, 122), but equality is presented as a harmful condition proper to barbarians, whereas inequality, "dependency," and "subjection" are considered fundamental pillars of civilized society (Silva e Orta 2002 203–7). It is as if Teresa Margarida's incapacity to conceive an egalitarian society made it impossible for her to envisage a feminist agenda aiming at equality. Her defence of women is clear but selective, conditioned by the traditional views on privilege and class. The ambiguity of the author's ideological posture may have played a part in the success of the book, which was republished four times at important political moments before the end of the century: in 1752, soon after the beginning of King José's reign; in 1777, when Queen Maria was acclaimed; and in 1790, when there was pressure to remove her from power and replace her with João VI, who became regent in 1792.

The presence of Queen Maria on the Portuguese throne gave women of the upper layers of society the opportunity to hope for an improvement of women's condition and, most especially, for a widening of their field of social and political intervention. The idea of having a woman as a head of state was welcomed by a number of learned women of the upper classes, who saw the occasion as an opportunity for promoting feminist agendas, like the improvement of women's education or the possibility for women to interfere in political decisions. This new state of affairs brought the discussion of the legitimacy of women to rule into the public arena. Teresa de Mello Breyner, Countess of Vimieiro, lent her voice, and her pen, to the defence of the queen's sovereignty in 1781. Soon after the Austrian empress Maria Theresia died, Mello Breyner published a translation of a *Eulogy of the Empress* by Marie-Caroline Murray, which had been published in Belgium the same year. The Portuguese version came out anonymously and corresponded, as Raquel Bello Vazquez points out, to a very specific objective: the legitimation of feminine rule through the proposal of a legitimate model of a contemporary woman monarch (Bello 2005). The endeavour of the Countess of Vimieiro was followed in 1785 by the appearance in print of a new edition of the sixteenth-century treatise by Ruy Gonçalves, *Dos Privilégios e prerrogativas que o sexo feminino tem por direito comum e ordenações do Reino mais que o sexo masculino* (Privileges and prerogatives of women). J.A. Presbit, the court chaplain who was the new editor, dedicated it to the queen and compares his own enterprise to Benito Jerónimo Feijoo's defence of women and makes a statement in favour of the women's ability to rule (Presbit 1785).

In the same year, 1785, the newly founded Royal Academy of Sciences announced an award to be granted to the best tragedy inspired by a Portuguese subject. A jury of academics gave the award to *Osmia*, and when they opened the envelope where the name of the author should have been, they discovered it had been sent anonymously. The correspondence of Teresa de Mello Breyner proves that she was the author of the play, which is, in fact, another attempt at a public defence of women's legitimacy to rule and, implicitly, of the Portuguese queen to act as head of state. The subject is inspired by the legend of Osmia, a Lusitan woman who was raped by a soldier during the Roman invasion of the Iberian Peninsula. She waited for the opportunity to kill him and cut off his head, which she took to her husband; she then killed herself in front of her husband to show that she was forced to commit adultery but did not want to live without honour.

The changes introduced by the Countess of Vimieiro to this plot are significant. In her version, Osmia is of noble origin and was married by Elédia, her tutor, to Ríndaco, a man she does not love, and who does not deserve her. Ríndaco was chosen for her, and she accepted him for reasons of state. She is a brave warrior but is vanquished by the Roman Lélio in the theatre of war, and taken by him as a prisoner. Unlike the legend, Lélio does not rape Osmia but is surprised by her beauty, admires her qualities, and falls in love with her. Osmia is impressed by the qualities of the Roman, who behaves in a respectful and virtuous way, very different from the rough brutal ways of her husband. In a moment when he thinks Ríndaco is dead, Lélio confesses his love to Osmia, but she resists his advances in the name of honour and of her people, although she realizes that she also has feelings for him. When her husband reappears on the scene, he understands that his wife is in love with the praetor and orders her to kill him. Torn between her gratitude to her captor and her duty to obey the command of her husband, Osmia kills herself. When Ríndaco finds out about her death, he succumbs to his pain, jealousy, and anger, and also commits suicide.

The central question of the plot is Osmia's inner fight to control her own feelings and to place her duties towards her husband and her people above her own interests. She can master her own behaviour and resist her passion for Lélio, but she cannot follow Ríndaco's orders to kill someone she admires, who behaves in a virtuous way, and who has honoured her. Although she commits suicide in the end, she is depicted as a strong, exceptional woman who can perform the same tasks as men – and better than most men. In short, in her depiction of ancient Lusitania, Teresa de Mello Breyner creates a utopian country, populated by educated and laborious people, where women are equal to men "without losing the delicate gracefulness of their looks" (Bello 2005, 317). That imaginary country is ruled by a woman of superior birth, talent, and virtue, capable of accepting her destiny (by marrying someone for reasons of state who does not compare to her in exceptionality) and placing the interest of her people above her own. One should note that, although a woman rules in this utopian country and although the men and women who live there are considered as equals, it is still a society based on birth (Osmia is a princess of noble descent), where heads of state have absolute power. Gender equality does not suppose, therefore, the elimination of the traditional class system. Teresa de Mello Breyner favours what we would call today "enlightened despotism," aimed at the progress and well-being of people, albeit in the framework of an absolute monarchy.

"Feminist" Claims in Manuscript

Portuguese society changed after the Lisbon earthquake of 1755. Increasing circulation of "new" Catholic ideological models (such as St Francis of Sales), as well as the policies promoted by the new minister of state affairs, Sebastião José de Carvalho e Melo, who tried to promote in Portugal the social practices he had known during his stay in Great Britain and in Austria, are probably the source of new heterosexual sociabilities that had a strong impact on women's lives. After the earthquake, *assembleias* (assemblies) became fashionable in Lisbon. These were periodic meetings of intellectuals who gathered in an informal atmosphere at the home of a woman, and can be compared to the better-known French salons (Lousada 1995 and 1997, 220–32; Lopes 1989, 41–52). In the Portuguese case, women presiding over these meetings were married and were usually accompanied by their husbands. The practice started in the upper layers of society, but judging from the wave of satires aimed at bourgeois women of small resources and little education who tried to organize the same kind of meetings, it must have spread very quickly and was seen as a threat to the usual norms of the separation of the sexes (Lopes 1989, 22–52; Moutinho 1987).

Assembleias allowed for the constitution of social networks of intellectuals who moved from one circle to another, disseminating their textual output either orally or in writing. They fostered the circulation of a considerable number of manuscript texts, in private or semiprivate circles, under the protection of the elites. Being a habitué of the *assembleias* of a certain lady was seen as a sign of distinction and as a certification of talent. The prestige of a number of male poets who were mentioned with praise by their contemporaries, but who left most of their production in manuscript form, was based upon a reputation acquired in this way.

The existence of these means of dissemination of texts made it possible for some aristocratic and bourgeois women to acquire a reputation as authors in a lay context. Thus they had a nonconflictive means to make their talents known without transgressing the discretion and modesty imposed upon them by social rules.

Leonor de Almeida Portugal, Countess of Oyenhausen and fourth Marchioness of Alorna, refused to publish her poetry during her lifetime. However, her daughters brought her works out in print in 1844, five years after their mother's death. Leonor de Almeida includes in her poetry feminist claims that are not found in other sources. For instance, she makes the plea for equal treatment of women before the law in an epistle inspired by the case of Isabel Clesse, a woman accused of killing her husband and sentenced to death, in Leonor de Almeida's opinion, without a proper trial (Topa 2000; Almeida Portugal 1844, 222–6). Another epistle dedicated to "Alceste" (a pseudonym for her doctor, Inácio Tamagnini, who was also a poet) contains similar accusations of public condemnation of innocent women out of prejudice. In this case, she argues that the use of ancient mythology in poetry by a woman author should not be used as a pretext to consider her less virtuous or less faithful to Christian values. She complains of accusations made against her for writing poetry with allegorical images inspired by antiquity and finishes her poem by noting that in a country in which women are burned at the stake for being witches, it is enough for a woman to speak for herself to be condemned.

The case of the Marchioness of Alorna can serve as a warning for the historian looking for the traces of Portuguese women's thoughts and voices of the past in order to recuperate feminist postures and feminist claims. In eighteenth-century Portuguese society, a considerable number of texts written by women were disseminated in manuscript, the majority of which, unlike those of the Marchioness of Alorna, have been dispersed or lost. Hence, although one does not find anything like an organized movement engaging in collective action in favour of women in eighteenth-century Portugal, it is possible to identify elements announcing the existence of a "feminist consciousness" (Lerner 1993, 17) circulating in the Portuguese cultural field at the time. Proof of a renewal of interest in the feminine question is the surfacing of various debates in the style of the European *querelle des femmes*. As was already mentioned, the arguments used in these controversies are very close to the women's quarrel tradition and show that the agents involved were familiar with the literary sources traditionally evoked in support

Figure 1. Leonor de Almeida Portugal, Countess of Oyenhausen and fourth Marchioness of Alorna. Art Collection, Alamy Stock Photo.

of women. In this context, it is useful to underline the constant reference to a contemporary Iberian source, the "Defensa de las mujeres" by Benito Jerónimo Feijoo. As in other European countries, women's education was an important and recurrent theme of discussion, which involved different agents and raised public awareness to this question throughout the century. The subject attracted the attention of philosophers, pedagogues, and men and women of letters, although the views they expressed on the matter were conditioned by the class distinctions operating in eighteenth-century society. Finally, the fact that there was a queen on the Portuguese throne between 1777 and 1792 brought public attention to the discussion of the nature, legitimacy, and constraints of women's rule.

Women's interventions in defence of their own condition are relatively scarce, and some men joined the women's cause and intervened in the public arena as defenders of women. Also, the number of claims made by women or in favour of women in this period is relatively small: the right to the recognition of women's intellectual capacities; the right to advanced education; the right to self-determination (in the choice of cloister or marriage); the right to rule as head of state; the right to be treated with dignity, in all circumstances and, in particular, before the law.

One should note that the proposals in favour of an improvement in women's condition did not always imply an egalitarian vision of the world. For the Portuguese men and women of this period, class and privilege seem to be at least as important as gender, to the point that one might speak of a kind of "selective feminism," since some of the "rights" reclaimed are seen as exclusively reserved for the women of the elites. In fact, except perhaps for Matias Aires, all the players in the prowoman debate seem to have a compartmentalized vision of society, where there is no ideological space for thinking in egalitarian terms. It is as if the impossibility of imagining forms of government and of social organization different from the class-based system and centralized power of the absolute monarchy conditioned the possibility of dreaming of a different world order.

6 The Basque Enlightenment: New Visions of Gender in the Crisis of the Old Regime

BAKARNE ALTONAGA[17]

The Basque territory of the eighteenth century comprised three different provinces within the Spanish Crown: the Señorío de Vizcaya and the provinces of Guipúzcoa and Álava, commonly known as the Bascongadas. Unlike other regions of the kingdom, during the eighteenth and nineteenth centuries the Basque provinces enjoyed an administrative and economic autonomy that was without comparison in the rest of the Spanish territories, founded on maintaining their traditional laws known as *fueros* (Portillo 1991). As indicated in chapter 1, the provincial legislation that gave the region a unique legal status on many occasions ran up against a desire for centralized power, begun during the first part of the century by the first Bourbon, Felipe V (Muñoz 1995, 136). The need to integrate the Basque provinces into the Spanish monarchy was also supported by various liberal governments that developed throughout the nineteenth century as part of a process that was transforming Spain into a modern state (Rubio 1996, 127). After numerous attempts, the traditional *fueros* were finally abolished in 1876.

Also as noted in chapter 1, Basque society at the end of the eighteenth century was characterized, as in the rest of Europe and Spain, by the crisis in the Old Regime. This was a long process in which traditional political and social structures were not definitively modified until well into the nineteenth century (Montero 2008, 253). Various cultural historians have also maintained that during this period the Basque provinces, as in the rest of Europe, experienced regulation of their emotions and their customs (Valverde 1994, 47; Díaz Freire 2001, 86). It can be added from a Foucauldian perspective that in addition to being repressive, this process was fundamentally productive, resulting in the creation of different discourses and spaces of knowledge and power centred around sexual and emotional identity (Foucault 1984).

In this context, the debate over the understanding of sexual difference in the Basque Enlightenment followed similar lines to those of Enlightened thinkers from other places. However, their contribution holds special interest because their desire to reform relations between the sexes is framed within a society (as was the Basque society at the end of the eighteenth century) whose clergy were faithful followers of conservative Tridentine Catholicism and were powerful agents of control over the bodies and the souls of the faithful, to whom they spoke directly in their native language, *euskera* (Valverde y García-Sanz 1989, 204; Altuna 2003, 18–19). Innovations introduced by the Enlightened Basque nobility did not blur the image of that discursive and social panorama. However, that position coexisted with other popular opinions. The comedy *Catalín* by Rita de Barrenechea reveals the tensions beneath the construction of an Enlightenment-style femininity that existed within a social reality distanced from the main currents of the Enlightenment.

From the middle of the eighteenth century, Basque Enlightenment thinkers introduced some of the most innovative ideas regarding sexual difference. Founded in 1765 by distinguished members of the Basque nobility and led by Xabier María de Munibe e Idiáquez, Count of Peñaflorida, the Basque Royal Society of the Friends of the Nation fomented Enlightenment initiatives in the Basque Country.[18] Many members of the Basque Society were connected with and formed part of the circles of Spanish and French nobility. Their zeal for social reform was immediately evident in their understanding of the role of women. The "friends" of the Basque Society, just as with their Spanish and European counterparts at this time, also participated in the revival of the *querelle des femmes* (see Mónica Bolufer Peruga's chapter 2 above, as well as Bolufer 1998, 29–59). The Marquis of Montehermoso's speech from 1765 titled "Discurso philosophico moral: La muger"[19] (Moral philosophical discourse: Woman) is exemplary. There the marquis states that his supporters, as well as his "enemies," had maligned the "bello sexo" (beautiful sex),"estos [sus enemigos] por la injusticia con que han querido avatirlo, aquellos [sus aduladores] por la impropiedad con que han pretendido distinguirla en asumptos propios del otro sexo" (Munibe 1931, 450; These people [his enemies] unjustly have wanted to take them down, while others [the supporters] have attempted to distinguish them in areas proper to the other sex).

This discourse is distanced from the traditional misogynist rhetoric that the most ultraconservative sectors, such as priests and missionaries, continued to produce. But the Basque Enlightenment thinkers did not go so far as to defend the equality of women's and men's abilities, as Benito Jerónimo Feijoo would (see chapter 2 above). The Basque position common among the Enlightened intelligentsia conceived of femininity as "friendly" and "sensitive," and as complementary to masculinity (Bolufer 1998, 61–115). In this way, they created a discourse that praised women's contribution to public happiness and social progress, but always within the domestic realm. Women should be good wives and sensitive mothers of the future statesmen. They should be, in short, "el asilo de las buenas costumbres y el verdadero principio de la felicidad doméstica del hombre" (RSBAP 1985b, 56; the refuge of good customs and the true basis of domestic happiness for men).

The connection established between the home and sentimental femininity represented a great innovation, since until well into the nineteenth century the Basque clergy promoted an understanding of marriage as a necessary evil, as a cross to bear. A profound misogyny guided its concept of femininity and virginity, and monastic life continued to be the highest level of feminine perfection, as compared to marriage and maternity. As mentioned above, family life in marriage was strongly guided by the clergy, for whom bonds of affection were ruled by obedience and fear – obedience to authority by the father and the husband, and fear of divine punishment. Marital sexuality was strictly aimed at procreation according to the minute instructions of their confessors. These ideas, far from decriminalizing carnal relations between spouses, saw marriage as a dissuasive strategy against the sins of lust (Umerez 2013, 273).

Basque Society questioned this vision of marriage and family life, along with the implicit emotional and sexual regulation (Recarte 1990, 113–30). Through their educational proposals, they tried to create a more appealing image of the duties of wives and to provide a new conception of marital obligations in which women were "participantes con ellos [los hombres] en los cuidados y las delicias de la vida domestica" (RSBAP 1784, 1; participants with them [men] in the cares and delights of domestic life). This idea was demonstrated in one of the group's main initiatives for women's education, the design of a plan for and orders to build a seminary for young ladies in Vitoria –ultimately never established – which would be approved in meetings of the society in 1785. One aspect that for a long time had worried several members, such as

Félix María de Samaniego, was that convent instruction did not prepare young women for their tasks as wives and mothers (Munibe 1775, 2). Rather to the contrary, it left them ignorant of their earthly duties, and it filled them with spiritual, but especially bodily, reserve that prepared them more for the cloisters than for the serious obligations of marriage. The principal function to which this school would be dedicated was the cultivation of natural feminine qualities so that they might leave "señoras llenas de ideas virtuosas, y sólidas, que desempeñen noblemente las obligaciones de madres de familia, de amas de su casa, y de dignas compañeras de los hombres" (RSBAP 1985a, 31; ladies full of virtuous and solid ideas, who nobly enact their obligations as mothers of family, as housewives, and as dignified companions to men].

For Basque Society, "el sistema de costumbres de la Europa" (RSBAP 1784, 1; the system of customs from Europe) required women to be educated in the principles of an attractive and cultivated femininity – as enthusiasts of the theatre, art, and music. A woman should be capable of governing the finances and domestic life of a family, but without great intellectual aspirations, since, as the aforementioned Marqués de Montehermoso argues, "El que la muger aga de la docta, la hace perder lo mas vello de sus gracias" (Munibe 1931, 452; What the woman does as an intellectual causes her to lose the most beautiful of her graces). She maintains a balance between "brazenness" and "sanctimoniousness," and practises a "natural" modesty and an attractive sensibility that, as the friends of the Basque Society stated, would inspire "a los jóvenes de nuestro sexo en la necesidad de cultivar los buenos estudios para merecer su estimación" (RSBAP 1985a, 31; in young men the necessity of cultivating good studies in order to deserve their esteem). Once their natural inclinations – sensibility, compassion, and modesty – are perfected, women would help fulfil Enlightenment ideals, since they would generate an emulating effect among men, who would lay brutish customs aside in order to cultivate their more admirable inclinations, thus preparing themselves to be honourable military leaders or politicians (RSBAP 1784, 2). This is an essential aspect that the Basque Society shared with the rest of Enlightened Europe: the conceptualization of the feminine influence as a civilizing element (Taylor 2012, 83–4). Contact between the sexes through marriage stopped being viewed as a question of sin for Enlightenment discourse and became instead the fundamental pillar of the development of civilization, supported in the belief that social progress needed a feminine complement that would domesticate men and pull them out of barbarism. In this way, by displaying a certain orientalism that was characteristic of many Enlightenment thinkers (Bolufer 2009b, 796), they defended the idea that in the civilized nations, unlike Asian countries, women had within their private realm "un grande influjo en las maiores resoluciones y acaecimientos políticos" (RSBAP 1784, 1; a great influence on the greatest political decisions and events).

Although Basque Enlightenment men generated a discourse that was different from traditional Catholic misogyny, and they proposed new patterns of socialization among the sexes, their laudatory rhetoric of the *bello sexo* (beautiful sex) rested on the assumption of a natural difference between the sexes and a hierarchization of their functions. The definition that Barbara Taylor has offered about eighteenth-century British gallantry helps us to understand this contradiction at the centre of the Basque Enlightenment: "In civilised nations, men enforce their dominion over women via rituals of deference rather than brute coercion – gallantry is the non-violent expression of male ascendancy" (Taylor 2005, 39). In this way, it is important to underscore that even authors like the follower of Feijoo from Álava, Valentín de Foronda, who defended the equality of understanding between men and women on more than one occasion (Foronda 1996, 6–7; 1998, 278), subscribed at the same time to the idea that there is a difference in the natural qualities of women with respect to men. Feminine qualities of beauty, submissiveness, and simplicity are balanced, according to Foronda, by masculine qualities of robustness, constancy, and prudence, which impede women from participating in certain activities "demasiadamente pesadas para recaer sobre los débiles hombros de este hermoso sexo" (Foronda 1996, 7–8; too heavy to fall on the delicate shoulders of this beautiful sex). These opinions abandoned misogynist arguments from Catholic tradition to elaborate a discourse of female inferiority that rested not so much on moral arguments but rather on proposals supported in the new fields of natural science and anatomy (Caine and Sluga 2000, 10).

The Basque Enlightenment participated in the debates of its time over the meaning of sexual difference and femininity, offering new visions.[20] As with Enlightenment thinkers from other contexts, these men gave a more positive assessment of women's social purpose, although always with the understanding of difference in women's nature and social destiny. They exalted the roles of mothers and wives, and proposed new customs for sociability, such as directing *tertulias* (salons) or theatrical and musical events, which certain women of the Basque aristocracy hosted and in which women participated actively (Bagüés 1990, 193).

Nonetheless, we should keep in mind that these new practices formed part of a general context in which other powerful agents, such as the Basque clergy, tried to influence the most humble parts of the population. Through their sermons, they recommended paths of sociability that were in direct opposition to those practised by the Enlightenment elites, and they promoted images of femininity that followed the most outdated misogyny. This can be observed in Joakin Lizarraga's sermon delivered in 1780 and entitled "Praxis vivendi faeminar rustic," in which he commended the value of austerity for country women, arguing: "¿Cuáles son los enemigos del labrador? Las hormigas en el campo, los roedores en el granero y la despensa, y el roedor más malicioso es la mujer de mal estómago y fino diente"[21] (Lizarraga 2004, 208; What are the enemies of the farmer? The ants of the field, the rodents in the granary and the storehouse, and the most malicious rodent is the woman with a bad stomach and a taste for fine food).

The Enlightenment Ideal and Its Tensions: *Catalín* de Rita de Barrenechea

Even if they did not advocate equality between men and women, Basque Enlightenment ideas did generate spaces and topics of debate in which several women participated. This was the case of the playwright from Bilbao Rita de Barrenechea, Marquesa de la Solana and Condesa del Carpio (1757–95), who showed in her works great affinity with Enlightenment ideas. Although she spent a large part of her life in Valladolid, Barcelona, and Madrid – far from her birth city of Bilbao – her Basque family connections were very close. She was also tied to the Royal Economic Society of Madrid, where in 1787 she formed part of the first fourteen female members of Junta de Damas of that organization (see chapters 1–3).

In addition to being an important figure in Enlightenment salons (Urzainqui 2006, xxv), Barrenechea wrote several theatrical works, two of which have been recovered: *Catalín* and *La aya*. Both can be considered part of the genre of the *comedia sentimental* (sentimental comedy), a literary trend that together with the sentimental novel had great success among male and female readers at the end of the eighteenth century (Urzainqui 2006, xxxviii–xxxix). The male and female thinkers who participated in these literary genres, which served as the Enlightenment vanguard for demonstrating and expanding social ideas, believed in the instructive effect that these works could have on the public (García

Garrosa 1990, 39; Sturkenboom 2000, 61; Hunt 2009, 58). Barrenechea's comedies displayed the neoclassic educational spirit, and they inform us, in turn, about the ideal femininity they were trying to transmit. A clear example of this is the play *La aya* (The governess), which Catherine Jaffe discussed in chapter 4.

Both in the context and tone, Barrenechea's works are in complete consonance with the Enlightenment belief in the sensibility and the empathetic capacity of the new modern subject, attributes that were a condition for his or her social and moral progress (Hunt 2009). In a certain way, her work can be considered a contribution to what historiography has called eighteenth-century "sentimentalism" (Reddy 2000; Knott 2009; Bolufer 2016a). A clear example of this phenomenon is *Catalín* (Urzainqui 2006, 38) of 1783, which situates its dramatic action in Portugalete, a town near Bilbao, the author's native city in the Basque Country. This work recreates the circumstances of a family in a traditional Basque setting, a *caserío* (rustic country village) – the main setting of the action of the play – in which the characters represent and demonstrate this Enlightened sentimentalism. It is the story of a young couple, Guitia and Catalín, who love each other and want to get married, but who, for lack of financial means – both are members of a family who has fallen on hard times – cannot fulfil their desires to marry. The problems are resolved thanks to the intervention of a great baron, the main male character, a "father" and "benefactor" (Urzainqui 2006, 9) of the town, beloved by all for his magnanimity and his equanimity. This character embodies the principal values of an Enlightened man – honesty and good judgment. The brief play concludes with the resolution of various conflicts through the triumph of virtue, representing the daily life of a Basque family with an unmistakably Enlightened tone.

Barrenechea's comedy shows us ideal femininity embodied in the character of Catalín, who looks for happiness in marriage. This character represents an emotional femininity, almost to the extreme; throughout the play she oscillates between melancholy and sadness over her inability to marry Guitia, and the happiness of achieving her dream. These emotions manifest themselves in continuous weeping, sighs, and swoonings that in the end reinforce an image of femininity conditioned by bodily fragility and accentuated emotionalism. In addition, Barrenechea indicates tensions caused by this vision of femininity, through the younger sister Marichu, who represents the chatty and impertinent counterpoint to the more contained and reserved Catalín. Marichu on several occasions refuses to follow the domestic model of femininity required of her. When the men leave the house to help Guitia, who is arrested due to a confusion, Marichu asks Catalin: "¿Y nosotras, qué hacemos? ¿Nò vámos también?" (Urzainqui 2006, 40; And us, what do we do? Shouldn't we go too?). Faced with the incredulity of her older sister at such a proposal, Marichu protests: "¿Y por que nò? ¿Quién te ha dicho, que no sabría yo tomar una Escopeta, y matar á quantos se me presentasen?" (Urzainqui 2006, 40; Why not? Who told you that I don't know how to use a shotgun and kill whoever might go after me?). This character expresses the greatest resistance to Enlightened femininity throughout the play, proclaiming, for example, her right to go out into the street after her father: "yo siempre [me quedo] guardando la casa, como si fuera un perro" (Urzainqui 2006, 53; I always stay guarding the house, as if I were a dog). She also replies in this way when she is told to be quiet, and she resists obedience when they oblige her to do her housework. These small "rebellions" are punished sometimes by her father directly: "Calla muchacha, que yá estamos cansados de oírte disparatar; las niñas no hablan mas, que quando las preguntan" (Urzainqui 2006, 11; Be quiet girl, we're tired of hearing your nonsense; girls shouldn't speak except when they are spoken to), or other times by her older sister, who rebukes her on numerous occasions by telling her to obey (Urzainqui 2006, 52). In this sense, Catalín represents a formed and responsible femininity, more conscious of her position in the home; she is the ideal woman to imitate, whereas her sister Marichu represents a young girl in the process of learning proper behaviour and the domestication of her impulses.

However, Marichu's resistances and reactions allow us also to glimpse what we could consider tensions that lie beneath the model of femininity promoted by the Enlightenment, expressed through Marichu's inability to conform to the gender norms assigned to her sex. For this reason, *Catalín* demonstrates both the Enlightenment ideal and its tensions. This work was truly innovative, because it painted the intimacy of a family in harmony with Enlightenment and sentimental ideology, a secularized domesticity, situating it in the Basque social environment in which femininity and family and gender relationships continued to be governed by standards of the traditional sociability of the Old Regime.

The literary work of women like Rita de Barrenechea contributed to Enlightenment-influenced changes, and they demonstrated the tensions that existed over the understanding of gender and of their own cultural context. She was part of the cultured elite that believed the reality of their time required profound reforms for social progress. Basque

Society participated actively in this spirit and confronted the challenge to promote new habits and social practices, among them other ways of understanding femininity and relations between the sexes. However, it is difficult to evaluate the influence that these Enlightened proposals achieved. Basque religious literature, principally written in *euskera* (Euskara), continued to reformulate and adjust its ideas about femininity to new contexts. This indicates that the ideal of Enlightened femininity was not able to displace and prevail over these other views; rather it coexisted with them, contributing developments to the understanding of gender that did not respond to historic linearity.

PART II

The Long Nineteenth Century (1808–1920)

COORDINATED BY CHRISTINE ARKINSTALL AND MARYELLEN BIEDER

7 Historical Background: From Wars and Revolution to Constitutional Monarchies; Spain's Sporadic Path to Modernity, 1808–1919

MARYELLEN BIEDER

The boundaries that mark Spain's long nineteenth century defy "the powerful hold of the decimal system on the historical imagination" (Blackbourn 2012, 301). They also signal that the country's relative political, social, and economic conditions remained unchanged throughout the mid- to late-1800s, without a major rupture until the 1923 dictatorship. The years from 1808 to1919 embrace a gamut of political regimes, from absolute monarchs to the introduction of constitutional monarchy and republic, from a queen and two queen regents to two foreign-born kings and various military regents. The period also endured the violent expressions of differences, from the uprising in response to the Napoleonic invasion and the ensuing War for Independence to three Carlist Wars in opposition to the ascendancy of a woman to the throne. These changes of government produced five constitutions between the 1812 Constitution, delayed for years before its ultimate adoption, and the 1876 Constitution, still in effect in the 1920s. In the infamous year of 1898, with Spain's defeat in El Desastre (The Disaster) of the Cuban or Spanish-American War, the country renounced by treaty its rights to its American and Pacific colonies. The shock resounded as a tragedy for the nation and forced many citizens to face Spain's diminished economic and political power, and to acknowledge its loss of international standing. In the mid to late 1800s, industrialization began to take hold in Spain, especially in Catalonia and the Basque Country. Labour unrest followed, leading to the Semana Trágica (Tragic Week) in Barcelona in 1909, fuelled by confrontations between the Spanish army and the working classes in cities across Catalonia. Remaining on the sidelines of World War I, Spain experienced economic prosperity and avoided the further exacerbation of civil turmoil. Nevertheless, political instability remained, as did frequent changes of government. After the world war, Spain's economy declined as its hold evaporated on markets fomented by war. Shortly after 1919, Spain faced a new conflict, as the recently designated territory of Spanish Morocco rebelled against its status as a Spanish protectorate, declaring the Republic of Rif in 1921. Just over the horizon in 1923, the king responded to a coup d'état by declaring the rebellious general a dictator in an effort to appease Spain's restless military, but thereby ending the country's early experience of constitutional monarchy.

As the long nineteenth century commenced, Napoleon Bonaparte's decision in 1808 to place his brother José Bonaparte on the Spanish throne forced Ferdinand VII, who had plotted to achieve the abdication of his father Carlos IV, to abdicate in turn. Although by and large Spanish *afrancesados* (Francophiles) – the intellectual elite, government bureaucracy, nobility, merchants, and industrialists – supported the newly imposed king, the mass of Spaniards opposed foreign rule and new ideas. Continuing their long-standing opposition to the goals of the French Revolution, they took up arms against him. Francisco Goya's well-known paintings of the *pueblo* (Spanish people, working classes) engaged in guerrilla warfare against the French troops – *The Second of May* and *Third of May of 1808 in Madrid* – powerfully document this bloody confrontation between mismatched forces. The introduction of the Napoleonic Civil Code, which replaced the web of multiple regional and local hereditary laws, was one foreign import with a long-term impact on Spanish jurisprudence, including the unequal treatment of women and men under civil law.

Amid the ensuing War for Independence (1808–14), José I Bonaparte gradually lost control of Southern Spain where Spanish liberals held the Cortes de Cádiz (Cadiz parliament) to draft a constitution for a legislative government, the 1812 Constitution. However, the treaty ending the war designated as king of Spain the son of Carlos IV, Fernando VII, who ruled as the last Bourbon absolute monarch in the *ancien régime* tradition, rejecting the 1812 Constitution and other liberalizing reforms proposed by the Cortes de Cádiz. During the period 1814–20, known as the Sexenio Absolutista (Absolutist Six-Year Period), Fernando VII proved, if anything, even bloodier and crueler than his father: he persecuted liberals, Goya among them, and reinstated the Inquisition that Bonaparte had suppressed, without addressing any of Spain's grave economic problems or intervening while its American colonies sought independence. During the following Trienio Liberal (Liberal

Triennium) of 1820–3, Fernando VII accepted the 1812 Constitution and other Cádiz reforms – while in practice sabotaging them – abolished the Inquisition, and allowed General Riego to take an expeditionary force to secure Spain's control over her Spanish-American colonies. He ultimately invited French troops – known as the Cien mil hijos de San Luis (One Hundred Thousand Sons of St Louis) – to overthrow the constitution and reinstate absolute monarchy. The subsequent Década Ominosa (Ominous Decade) proved even more brutal than the previous years of his reign, and he once again resuscitated the Inquisition.

Near the end of his rule, with no surviving children from four marriages and with a pregnant wife, Fernando VII revoked the Salic Law and reinstated Castile's traditional laws of succession, in the form of the Pragmática Sanción (Pragmatic Sanction), drawn up in 1789 but never signed, which included recognizing the right for a female to succeed to the throne. He died in 1833, leaving his three-year-old daughter Isabel as his heir. First her mother, María Cristina de Borbón, and then General Espartero served as regents until 1843, when thirteen-year-old Isabel II was declared of age and crowned queen. Meanwhile Fernando VII's brother, Carlos, who opposed the succession of his niece, launched a conservative movement, the Carlistas (Carlos sympathizers) that supported his succession and ultimately provoked three civil wars – starting in 1833 and lasting until 1876 – between his supporters and the national army. In the early years of the regency, the definitive abolition of the Inquisition and the state appropriation of fallow church lands began to address problems that had hindered Spain's development for decades by freeing up land for individual development and benefiting middle-class entrepreneurs, as well as the wealthy.

Despite these conflicts, the queen regent (1833–40), initially with the support of the liberals and under the provisions of the 1812 Constitution, led Spain to adopt the 1837 Constitution that abolished the monarchy's tradition of absolutism. The reign of Spain's first constitutional monarch, Isabel II (1843–68), suffered continuing political instability and military coups, as well as a groundswell of condemnation of her private life that alienated much of the population. Over her twenty-six-year rule, she had become increasingly erratic, conservative, and dependent on the army to maintain her on the throne. In 1868, the military rebelled in La Gloriosa (The Glorious Revolution), an uprising that removed Isabel II from power and sent her into exile in Paris. The forced abdication of a second Bourbon monarch in sixty years marked a turning point in Spanish politics.

During the ensuing years, Spain implemented various solutions to its political turmoil, starting with a military regent, General Serrano (1869), and then experimenting with democratic governments: a parliamentary monarchy under an elected king, Amadeo I of Savoy (1870–3); the First Spanish Republic (1873–4); and finally the restoration of constitutional monarchy that continued the Bourbon line with the former queen's barely seventeen-year-old son, Alfonso, who in 1874 was studying at Sandhurst in England. His ascendance to the throne initated the Bourbon Restoration (1875–1931) that laid the foundation for Spain's socioeconomic recuperation after almost seven decades of crises. During his short eleven-year reign, Alfonso XII, who died from tuberculosis before reaching the age of twenty-eight, sought to avoid partisanship and divisiveness, and enjoyed popular support, which included his full implementation of the 1876 Constitution. Two attempts on the king's life (1878 and 1879) and an 1883 military *pronunciamiento* (military rebellion) against the regime did not indicate broad discontent with the restored monarchy as much as the troubled climate of society's unrealized expectations. In David Ringrose's appraisal, Spain saw only "sporadic economic development" from 1840 to 1910. Nevertheless, these were also decades during which the country "installed many of the components of a modern economy" and initiated its belated movement towards modernity (Ringrose 1996, 61). Although the Restoration enjoyed some improvement in economic circumstances, ominous signs of stagnation created resentment of the system over time, due to the increasing power of regional *caciques* (political bosses); the growth of nationalist movements, born in the romantic nationalism of the 1830s, in Catalonia, the Basque provinces, and Galicia; and the formation of labour unions.

Alfonso XII's death also seemed to signal a setback for the future of constitutional monarchy in Spain. His unborn son became monarch at birth, while his widow, María Cristina de Habsburgo, served as queen regent for her son until his 1902 coronation as Alfonso XIII. Not as popular as his father, Alfonso XIII (1886–1931) continued the Bourbon Restoration's constitutional monarchy while experiencing assassination attempts, one of which occurred on his wedding day, and greater political instability that discredited the legislative system. The king further weakened the constitution in the postwar period by intervening personally in government decisions and ignoring parliament, until in 1923 he named General Miguel Primo de Rivera dictator following a military coup d'état, thus ending eighty years of constitutional monarchy.

Over the course of the long nineteenth century, the liberal solution to Spain's ever-mounting national debt was *desamortización* (disentailment or sale of church or public lands), the sale by the state of lands that previously could not be sold, mortgaged, or transferred. This real estate embraced church lands, the real property owned by monasteries and convents or secular priests; lands held by the nobility; and communal lands belonging to villages. Spain had enacted such laws from the late 1700s into the early nineteenth century, but in 1835–6 royal decrees brought the full scope of disentailment to bear as a way to pay off the national debt. José I Bonaparte had already suppressed the religious orders, acquiring their property for the state. The later liberal promoters of this land-redistribution legislation, prominently Juan Álvarez Mendizábal (1836–7) and others in later decades, sought to foment Spain's underdeveloped bourgeoisie by making land available to citizens with money, including peasants with sufficient cash to acquire land for the first time, although in practice mainly the wealthy benefited from the land sale by augmenting their holdings. Furthermore, since the Catholic Church owned more land than any other entity until the 1830s, the Spanish government had to negotiate the effects of the disentailment of church property, reaching an agreement with the Vatican in 1851. This concordat, which lasted sixty years until 1911, stipulated: "In return for the Vatican's recognition of the sale of church property the Spanish government would impose religious orthodoxy (Roman Catholicism), give the Church full control of the nation's education, and subsidise the Spanish clergy" (Davies 1998, 16). By placing education under the power of the church, successive governments avoided meeting the needs of female students.

Nevertheless, in 1857 the Ley Moyano de Instrucción Pública (Law of Public Instruction) authorized centralized, obligatory, secular primary education for all Spanish boys and girls, without cost for those unable to pay. At the same time, it accorded the church the right to have its religious teaching communities of both sexes offer primary and secondary education. Furthermore, it recognized the church's right to monitor the ideological purity – doctrinal purity and the purity of faith and customs – and the religious education of public and private schools, as a logical extension of the 1851 concordat with Rome. The Asociación para la Enseñanza de la Mujer (Association for Women's Education), founded in 1870, extended postprimary education to females for the first time by establishing secondary schools and training colleges for women throughout Spain. Since 1872 a small number of women had, with difficulty, studied careers at Spanish universities by special dispensation (Flecha 1996). Emilia Pardo Bazán caustically remarked of women's university education in Spain that rarely and only in a limited number of professions were women permitted to put their university education to good use to assure themselves an independent life or to pursue their vocation for itself (1981b, 101). In 1910, Spain allowed universities to admit women students to degree programs on the same terms as men.

Throughout the second half of the long nineteenth century, Spain saw growing industrialization that led to labour discontent, especially in response to the expansion of the Catalan textile industries. These demonstrations took the form of labour congresses, such as the Congress of the Anarchist Labour Confederation in 1870, and the formation of major labour organizations that continue to play a key role in Spanish politics: the Spanish Socialist Workers Party (PSOE) in Madrid in 1879; and in 1888 the first congress in Barcelona of the General Union of Workers (UGT), the PSOE's labour organization. The events of Barcelona's 1909 Tragic Week brought Socialists, anarchists, and Republicans into confrontation with the government in response to the calling-up of reserve troops for the Second Rif War in Spain's colony of Morocco. In 1916 and 1917, general strikes occurred in response to the loss of Spanish troops in the Moroccan war. At this time, the Spanish labour movements that would play such central roles in ensuing decades took shape: the Anarchist-Syndicalist Confederation; the National Confederation of Workers (CNT), an anarchist-syndicalist confederation formed in Barcelona in 1918; the Spanish Communist Party (PCE) in 1921; and the Iberian Anarchist Federation (FAI) in 1927. The success of the Socialist leader Pablo Iglesias and the growth of the syndicated workers' organizations began to "frighten the church, state, and military factions, setting the stage for [civil] war" (Mangini 1995, 16).

A further important advance in the articulation of Spanish cultures and politics was the approval in 1914 by the Spanish government of the Catalan Mancomunitat (Commonwealth), which granted the Catalan provinces the right to form themselves into a federation with purely administrative functions. Across the long nineteenth century in Catalonia, but principally beginning in the 1830s, a profound cultural revival, La Renaixença (Renaissance), fostered increased desire for political and economic autonomy on a par with its superior cultural status. As the first act of recognition by the Spanish state of the existence and unity of Catalonia since the year 1714, the Mancomunitat had immense symbolic significance, representing an initial step in the direction of a long-desired (two hundred years) independent government. It rapidly created social, educational, industrial, and agricultural infrastructure, and enhanced the prestige of the Catalan language and culture. It introduced the standardization of Catalan writing and pronunciation, moving it from a fragmented oral language to a uniform written one viable throughout Catalonia. However, Miguel Primo de Rivera's dictatorship outlawed the Mancomunitat ten years later.

During the Bourbon Restoration, the metallurgical industries in the Basque provinces, like Catalonia's textile industries, prospered and benefited especially from the tremendous increase in demand and inflated prices during World War I, which resulted in mushrooming profits and rising employment. On the downside, domestic prices rose more than wages, producing a loss in buying power for the households that had enjoyed full employment before the boom. The start of the world war proved "un momento clave" (González Calbet 2007, 81; a key moment) in the history of Spanish feminisms. Soaring prices, along with increased demand from abroad for Catalan and Basque industrial products, thrust lower-middle-class Spanish women into the labour market for the first time (81–2). Thus the war brought the "first impetus for modern feminist reform in Spain," as labour agitation continued and more women entered the workforce to produce goods for the nations at war (Davies 1998, 101). These economic changes shifted the balance of feminists in these areas of Spain from aristocratic and bourgeois women to working-class women. As women's participation in the industrial workforce forged a new axis in Spain's spectrum of feminisms, while also making possible women's involvement in labour movements, it eventually resulted in a "double militancy" that merged women's left-wing political activism with their feminist agenda (Davies 1999, 177). In the subsequent decades, women's engagement in factory work opened the way for further types of technology-related employment, such as telegraph and telephone operators, work initially only available to men. Galicia, in contrast, failed to undergo an economic regeneration to offset its century of sending emigrants to Cuba and the American colonies for economic survival. However, in the late nineteenth century, it experienced, as had Catalonia and the Basque provinces, a cultural and linguistic movement, the Rexurdimento (Renaissance), which brought a degree of validation for its culture and language, especially within Galicia. Chapters 10 and 12 address significant Galician and Catalan women authors, while chapter 13 charts the gradually increasing participation of Basque female writers in the long nineteenth century.

By 1919, with the rest of Europe recovering from World War I, Spain had entered a period of prolonged instability under Alfonso XIII that ultimately culminated in his 1929 abdication. Alongside the political tensions and labour unrest that unsettled the country, Spain's nascent women's movement had taken shape. The first generation of women to espouse the ideals and goals associated internationally with feminism had already died or were reaching the end of their careers. A new more politically active generation was taking the call for the vindication of women to the public in more visible forms. The year 1918 saw the first major women's organization in Spain emerge, the Asociación Nacional de Mujeres Españolas (ANME; National Association of Spanish Women). Despite its conservative pedigree, ANME supported reforming Spain's Civil Code and granting women greater educational and professional opportunities, while nevertheless hewing to the orthodoxy that motherhood is every woman's mission and promulgating a patriotic "love of the mother-land, which is one and indivisible" (Davies 1998, 101). ANME's contradictory mix of reformist and reactionary discourses mirrored similar contradictions in much Spanish feminist thought in the last decades of the long nineteenth century. From 1920 through the twentieth century, the panorama of Spanish feminism – its response to the Woman Question – would change radically, reaching its apogee before swinging violently to the other extreme, but always retaining traces of the thought expressed by its early nineteenth-century proponents.

8 Historical Context of Feminism and Women's Rights in Nineteenth-Century Portugal

JOÃO ESTEVES, TRANSLATED BY DEBORAH MADDEN

As in many other European countries, there was an emergence of feminist ideas and a struggle for women's rights in nineteenth-century Portugal. A lengthy process, the movement only gained importance in the late nineteenth and early twentieth century. Despite the Liberal Revolution of 1820 and the transition from an absolute monarchy to a constitutional or liberal government, a development that was reflected in the social, economic, and political structure of Portuguese society, women in nineteenth-century Portugal still lacked any political rights, subordinate to their fathers and husbands. Furthermore, extremely high rates of illiteracy limited women's already meagre professional opportunities.

The advancement of women and their progress from the private sphere to the public domain was gradual, with several advancements and setbacks. The developments are illustrated by the establishment of numerous female-authored and -directed periodical publications, which also included contributions from male journalists, as the so-called women's press flourished from 1820. According to Ivone Leal, between 1822 (*Gazeta das Damas* [Ladies' Gazette]) and 1899 (*Ave Azul* [Bluebird]), seventy-seven newspapers were published: forty-one based in Lisbon and nineteen based in Porto, with others throughout Portugal; two in Coimbra, two in Elvas, one in Albergaria-a-Velha, one in Beja, one in Braga, one in Funchal, and one in Viseu (Leal 1992c, 14–18).

Two central issues of interest were women's education and women's subordinate social position. The majority of discourse pertaining to these areas came to the fore in the latter half of the nineteenth century, with the writers Antónia Pusich (1805–83), Francisca Wood, Guiomar Torrezão (1844–98), Maria Amália Vaz de Carvalho (1847–1921),

Carolina Michaëlis de Vasconcelos (1851–1925), Angelina Vidal (1853–1917), Alice Pestana (1860–1929), and Alice Moderno (1867–1946).

Poet, novelist, playwright, and journalist Antónia Gertrudes Pusich was born in Cabo Verde and travelled to Brazil. Like her father, she was opposed to the new political order that followed the Liberal Revolution of 1820, and she was the first woman in nineteenth-century Portugal to support herself by writing and fighting for the social and cultural emancipation of women. One example of her work is the pamphlet she published in 1848 entitled *Galeria das senhoras na câmara dos senhores deputados, ou as minhas observações* (The women's gallery in the chamber, or My observations). The piece was a response to those who had ridiculed the women who had attended Portuguese political debates, and highlighted the discrimination and injustices directed towards women. The first woman to found and run a newspaper in Portugal, she set up three publications: *A Assembleia Literária* (1849–50); followed by *A Beneficência* (1852–5); and lastly, *A Cruzada* (1858). Pusich also advocated women's access to education, and the first periodical founded, *A Assembleia Literária*, was described in that same paper as a "jornal de intrução" (3 [18 August 1849]: 1; educational newspaper). The publication had forty-one editions, with both female and male collaborators, where she advocated the education of girls as a way for the economic independence of women.

Francisca de Assis Martins Wood was a contemporary of Antónia Pusich and a writer known for her progressive stance. Born in Lisbon and married to William Thorold Wood, she spent many years in England. Returning to Portugal after thirty-five years, she and her husband founded and directed two newspapers. The first was *A Voz Feminina* (Woman's Voice; January 1868–9), a publication dedicated to the social and intellectual development of women; the second publication was *O Progresso* (Progress; July–December 1869), which Ivone Leal deems the first feminist newspaper to emerge in Europe (1992c, 71). In both newspapers, Francisca Wood came across as a progressive intellectual who, along with the collaborators and readership, sought to dismantle the ideas of frivolousness and ignorance associated with the female sex. Wood believed that Portugal's backwardness stemmed from the restricted availability and low standards of education for girls and women, which resulted in their limited possibilities and a disinterest in public activity. Equality and justice were paramount to both publications: *A Voz Feminina* printed the phrase "A mulher livre ao lado do homem livre" (The free woman next to the free man) on its first page, while *O Progresso* had the slogan "La justice soit faite, coûte que coûte" (Justice at any cost).

As well as defending the intellectual, economic, professional, and political emancipation of both sexes, rooted in the belief that intelligence was an attribute of women and men alike, the newspapers published documents pertaining to women's rights, suffrage, and professional careers, while informing readers of the progress that women were making in other countries. The articles found in these publications introduced the ideas of activists such as Victor Hugo, Jules Ferry, Charles Lemonier, Jules Simon, Garibaldi, and the philosopher Stuart Mill and his book *The Subjugation of Women*, as such beliefs were publicized, promoted, and deliberated. Two decades after the ideas of Antónia Pusich came to light, Francisca Wood was among a group of prefeminists in Europe and the United States of America. While Francisca Wood's press activity and ideology did not flourish in a conservative Portuguese society, her work did constitute a step in the right direction. Wood's work allowed women access to the public sphere, anticipating the Republican and nineteenth-century feminists who would follow her.

Guiomar Delfina de Noronha Torrezão was a journalist, writer, essayist, and poet. Educated in line with the values of the period, she did not receive a formal education in an academic institute. Like many of her female predecessors, however, she forged her way in society by writing, translating, and publishing articles in the press. She began this work as a means of supporting herself when she was young, despite making limited earnings. Like many of her contemporaries, Torrezão was the recipient of criticism, attacks, and slander, and introduced a female-authored periodical. Torrezão's contribution to women's press was *Almanque das Senhoras* (Women's Almanac), the publication that she founded, maintained, and directed for twenty-nine years from 1871 to 1898. In addition to garnering literary recognition, Torrezão used the publication as a means of expressing her views on the position of Portuguese women, gathering the collaboration of hundreds of writers – including those from the islands and colonies, both Spanish and Brazilian names. The question of women's intellectual capability was a common topic. Although she was an advocate for women's education, Torrezão did not classify herself as a feminist, and she satirized its ambition for equality between women and men in the play *Educação moderna* (1894). Furthermore, no references to feminism appeared in *Almanque das Senhoras* while Torrezão was overseeing the publication, even in articles written by contributors who did support feminism.

From 1900, under the literary direction of Júlia de Gusmão (1900–10) and Maria O'Neill (1911–25), the feminist question began to have a scope in *Almanque das Senhoras*. The publication reported on the feminist movement in Paris, the international congresses of women, and biographical details of feminists or emancipated women in other countries. The direction Torrezão's publication took, therefore, illustrates that while Guiomar Torrezão may not have been an avowed feminist, she did pave the way for future feminists.

Guiomar Torrezão was a cosmopolitan who brought together the Portuguese intelligentsia and various French writers, both female and male, such as Alexandre Dumas and Victor Hugo. She contributed to dozens of other newspapers, pamphlets, and noteworthy publications, and authored biographical summaries of women from the seventeenth to the nineteenth centuries. Torrezão's rousing literary and press publications made her the only woman among the founding partners of the Associação dos Jornalistas e Escritores Portugueses (Association of Portuguese Journalists and Writers; 1880) and a member of the Sociedade de Geografia da França (Society of the Geography of France).

Angelina Casimira do Carmo Vidal was a writer who valiantly advocated Socialist, Republican, and workers' movements, and produced a range of literary works. She fought for the recognition and emancipation of women, and maintained that clericalism, the monarchy, and the bourgeoisie were responsible for women's limited civil rights and lack of education. A democrat and free-thinker, she was impoverished and was frequently supported by working-class members of the tobacco industry. A literary woman, she supported herself through writing: working as a translator, a short-story writer, essayist, teacher, lecturer, poet, playwright, and, above all, a journalist, particularly for the publication *A Voz do Operário* (The Worker's Voice). In spite of these activities, she never classed herself as a feminist, nor did she express any sympathy for the growing movement that resulted in her losing ground as a public speaker and publicist. Her concerns, stemming from her Republican ideals and social outlook, were based on poverty and the neglect of working-class women, in relation to their educational opportunities and conditions that inhibited their ability to raise children to become upstanding citizens. Her vision of women's education was founded in conservative ideas pertaining to the traditional roles of women.

Alice Evelina Pestana Coelho, a contemporary of Angelina Vidal, seven years younger, was a writer, translator, and teacher who moved to Madrid in 1901 following her marriage to Pedro Blanco Suarez, a

Spanish teacher. A leading figure at a time when women's emancipation was making promising progress, Pestana is associated with the establishment of the feminist and pacifist movements in Portugal at the turn of the twentieth century. After having completed a typical bourgeoisie education, Pestana went on to attend the Liceu Nacional de Lisboa (National High School of Lisbon), studying foreign languages and basic skills with female tutors. In the Liceu, she perfected her Portuguese, French, and English – the language in which she wrote her first texts – and developed an understanding of physics, chemistry, and natural history, while also studying classic and contemporary writers. She contributed to various newspaper publications, always writing under pseudonyms – Caiel, the most well-known – and devoted many of her writings to the position of women and their educational opportunities.

In addition to publishing prolifically, both fiction (short stories, novels, and plays) and her reflections on education, Alice Pestana was an advocate of pacifism. She became the first president of the Liga Portuguesa da Paz (Portuguese League of Peace), founded in 1899, a subsidiary organization of the Sociedade Altruísta (Altruist Society), whose slogan was "Verdade, Justiça, e Bondade" (Truth, Justice, and Righteousness). More so than other female writers, both her predecessors and contemporaries, Pestana used her literature as a means of reflecting her modern vision of girls' education, which encompassed the social recognition of women, the battle against common stereotypes, social commitment, and her pacifist and feminist ideals. For Pestana, as was written in *La femme et la paix: appel aux mères portugaises* (Women and peace: A call to Portuguese mothers; 1898), feminism was about the advancement of women, their economic, psychological, and emotional liberation.

Although the publications had varying levels of relevance and influence, women's periodicals were a means of spreading initiatives. Reaching an upper-class female readership, the publications publically named female benefactors, educators, teachers, writers, bourgeois women, and aristocratic women who were, sometimes indirectly, associated with recognizing the inferiority of Portuguese women and the need for reform. By valuing activities related to women's education, training for traditional roles, and the formation of the first professional groups of women, these women sought to improve the position of women in Portuguese society. The aim of these publications was to transform the traditional image of women by awarding recognition to women who, not always intentionally, countered stereotypes of women and left their homes in order to enter the public sphere.

Through the written word, female journalists were breaking the long-established silence and submission of Portuguese women. They navigated the difficulties that public exposure caused, and facilitated new opportunities and possibilities for women – albeit sometimes in a conciliatory manner – in a Portuguese society dominated by patriarchy. According to Ana Maria Costa Lopes, the female-authored press of the nineteenth century, although still heavily influenced by the conservative intelligentsia of the era, "permitiu establacer um 'dialógo' entre os dois sexos, um fio mágico que facultou a saída das mulheres da penumbra" (Costa Lopes 2005, 257; established a "dialogue" between the two sexes, a magical link that facilitated women's emergence from the shadows). This dialogue promoted the struggle against discrimination, intolerance, and oppression through social and cultural developments, against the backdrop of the ever-changing times and conflicts. The periodicals also contributed to the transformation of the image of women from "frivolous" beings to "thinking" beings, becoming seen in this way by both women themselves and others. The opinions of nineteenth-century male authors, for instance, ranged from contempt, to disregard, to begrudging recognition – views rooted in and influenced by the misogynist and reactionary discourses of the time.

At the same time, the literary salons for women at the end of the nineteenth century also played an influential role in the intellectual development and advancement of women in Portuguese society. Salons were places where female writers would meet to spend time together and recite their works, and where educated women would debate literature; topics for discussion included the female condition, the rights of women, feminism (Esteves 2001), and the participants were empowered by their role as writers. To some extent, the seeds of feminist momentum in Portugal were developed in these informal meetings. It was not by chance that female writers introduced the feminist question to Portuguese society. Driven by an increasing volume of news coming from abroad, mostly from the USA and England, Portuguese women were in personal and professional communication with Spanish and French activists, such as Concepción Arenal (1820–93), Concepción Gimeno de Flaquer (1850–1919), Carmen de Burgos y Seguí (1867–1932), and Jeanne Oddo-Deflou. These international collaborations heightened their awareness of the feminist phenomenon on a worldwide scale and highlighted the backwardness of Portugal in comparison to other countries.

Against the backdrop of an increasing consciousness of the international struggle for women's emancipation in Portugal, the terms "feminism" and "feminist" came into usage. Although there are historical examples of the terms being used in Portugal, it was Joaquim Pedro de Oliveira Martins who employed the words for the first time in the Portuguese press. In July 1888, he references the terms in the articles "Homens e mulheres" (Men and women) and "Feminismo" (Feminism), both published in *Réporter* (Reporter) (Oliveira Martins 1924, 159–66). Oliveira's articles were published at a time when the formation of the feminist movement in Portugal was gaining momentum, until Portuguese feminism finally began to materialize in the final decade of the nineteenth century.

In September 1896, a German woman named Luise Ey (1854–1936) spoke on the position of Portuguese women at the Congresso Feminista Internacional de Berlim (International Feminist Congress in Berlin). A pianist, teacher, translator, and writer, she had taught at girls' schools in Germany and France before taking up a position at a German school in Porto. While there, she became friends with Carolina Michaëlis de Vasconcelos (1851–1925) and José Joaquim Rodriques de Freitas (1840–96). Ey's commitment to women's rights developed while working in Portugal and after her return to Germany to care for her mother. Having maintained a physical and cultural connection to Portugal for several decades, she presented "Memória acerca da mulher portuguesa" (History of the Portuguese woman) at the congress.

In the address, Ey cited statistics to illustrate the relative backwardness of education in Portugal. Observing the overwhelming percentage of illiterate women and the limited number of girls receiving an education, in both schools and private classes, she denounced the dire lack of public education for girls, in reference to the absence of both state regulations and provisions for providing schooling. According to Ana de Castro Osório (1872–1935), she spoke "brilhantemente como representante das mulheres portuguesas" (brilliantly as a representative for Portuguese women) and her speech "foi-lhe logo pedido e publicado na íntegra por um dos mais importantes jornais de Berlim, coisa excepcional, porque da maior parte apenas eram feitos os resumos" (Castro Osório 1907, 2; was then requested and published in full in one of the most important newspapers in Berlin, an exceptional thing given that the majority of the other reports merely provided summaries). Despite praise from Castro Osório, a pioneer of the feminist movement in the early twentieth century, Ey's views were met with enraged responses in the Portuguese press (Vilas-Boas 1990 334–7; Tavares da Silva 198?, 580). In answer to the criticism, Michaëlis de Vasconcelos published an article entitled "O Congresso Feminista de Berlim" in four parts, in which she defended Ey and her speech (Michaëlis 1896). Controversy about feminism was escalating in Portugal.

The debates intensified as the final year of the nineteenth century bore witness to significant commentaries on feminism in the press. In 1899, Alice Pestana (1860–1929) outlined her stance on feminism in the newspaper *Vanguarda,* signed under the pseudonym Cil (Pestana 1899b).[1] In the same year, Beatriz Pinheiro de Lemos (1872–1922) and Carlos de Lemos released one of the first contentious pieces in *Ave Azul* (Bluebird; 1899–1900), the magazine they both directed in Viseu, consisting of a series of texts that focused on the debates about the position of women, women's education, and the problematic notion of feminism (Pinheiro 1899a). For Beatriz Pinheiro, the purpose of feminism was "pôr a mulher em condições de viver dignamente na sociedade, por meio do seu trabalho, sem precisar dum homem que a mantenha" (Pinheiro 1899b, 500; allowing a woman to live with dignity in society, by working for a living, without needing a man to keep her). Pinheiro implored women to fight "[para] que reivindiquem os seus direitos, que façam por conquistar a igualdade civil e política, que sejam nos bancos das Escolas as dignas rivais dos mais inteligentes e dos mais estudiosos" (Pinheiro 1899b, 324; so that they reclaim their rights, achieve civil and political equality, and at school are worthy rivals of the most intelligent and studious pupils). She also considered economic independence a fundamental right, which she believed would only be achieved by allowing women a comprehensive education. Pinheiro was also an ardent believer in women's contribution to the establishment of world peace and was a supporter of the Liga Portuguesa da Paz (Portuguese League for Peace), which was founded on 18 May 1899 by Alice Pestana, the group's president.

The final year of the nineteenth century also saw a future president of the First Republic, Bernardino Machado (1851–1944), asked to discuss women's rights. Machado was invited by the Countess of Aberdeen to deliver an address in June about the protection of women and minors in Portugal. The event was to be held while the International Congress of Women was taking place in London. In the end, Machado did not attend, due to unforeseen circumstances. The request illustrates how the question of women's rights in Portugal was becoming increasingly prevalent as the nineteenth century drew to a close.

With the turn of the century, reflections on issues pertaining to women's rights and feminism were strengthened as more and more women supported the movement. In September 1902, the periodical *O Primeiro de Janeiro* (The first of January) published six articles by Carolina Michaëlis de Vasconcelos. An educated, well-read German philologist, Michaëlis de Vasconcelos's text was translated from the original German with the broad title "O movimento feminista em Portugal" (The feminist movement in Portugal). In the piece, she detailed the situation of women in Portugal and Spain, and maintained that, given the high levels of illiteracy among Iberian women, "a questão feminista, na península hispânica, é atualmente uma simples questão de instrução" (Michaëlis 2002, 26; the feminist question, in the Hispanic peninsula, is actually a simple question of education).

From the very beginning of the essay, Michaëlis de Vasconcelos argues that there is no organized feminist movement in Iberia, and that women have barely begun to reclaim their rights:

> O combate das massas femininas em vista de melhores condições sociais está inteiramente por organizar no mundo peninsular. Elas não têm reclamada, por ora, a equiparação nos direitos civis dos dois sexos, e não pensam sequer em direitos de ordem mais elevada, como seja o do sufrágio. É perfeitamente nula a sua influência no campo político. ...
>
> As mulheres submetem-se, sem protesto sensível, à tradição secular da inferioridade. ... [F]altam revistas, e escasseiam as corporações femininas. Nos congressos internacionais não consta que até agora tenha aparecido delegado algum representando ligas ou associações de mulheres portuguesas e brasileiras, espanholas, ou do Sul da América. (Michaëlis 2002, 21–2)

> (The struggle for better social conditions by the female masses is yet to be organized in the Peninsula. Women have not reclaimed, for now, equal civil rights for both sexes and have not even begun to consider more aspirational developments such as suffrage. Their influence in the political sphere is absolutely nonexistent. ...
>
> Women submit themselves, without just protest, to the long-standing tradition of inferiority. ... There are no magazines; and barely any women's organizations. In international congresses, up to now no representatives

from women's leagues or associations of women from Portugal, Brazil, Spain, or South America have been present.)

Here, Michaëlis de Vasconcelos summarizes the limitations that feminism faced during the long nineteenth century. In 1905, Ana de Castro Osório published the book *Às mulheres portuguesas* (To Portuguese women), considered "the manifest of the Portuguese feminist movement" (Tavares da Silva 1998, 286). The words "feminism" and "feminist" gained importance in the Republican press, which understood feminism as a fair fight for women's rights, and feminist associations were founded from 1906 on. Educators, teachers, doctors, publicists, and writers – Albertina Paraíso, Alice Pestana, Ana de Castro Osório, Aureliana Teixeira Bastos, Beatriz Pinheiro de Lemos, Cláudia de Campos, Domitila de Carvalho, Maria Veleda, Olga Morais Sarmento da Silveira – were considered the first ambassadors of Portuguese feminism. An organized feminist movement did begin to materialize, orchestrated by and directed at female members of the elite, although it was limited by extreme rates of illiteracy among women and girls. Relatively moderate, the feminist movement avoided excessively advanced ideas and never managed to reach a significant number of women. The transition period from the monarchy to the Republic, which followed the 1910 Revolution, did, however, have some influence, as did the Republican political leaders at a time when the feminist movement in Portugal finally gathered some momentum.

9 A Feminist Press Gains Ground in Spain, 1822–1866

CHRISTINE ARKINSTALL

Nineteenth-century feminist periodicals did not emerge in a vacuum of feminist thought. Most female founders and contributors were highly conscious of continuing Enlightenment legacies, enacting liberal principles in all spheres, and strengthening the foundations of early nineteenth-century liberal politics. Many women's periodicals, however, performed a delicate balancing act, often cloaking feminist declarations with a veneer of conformity to the normative feminine ideals of subservience and modesty encapsulated in the Angel in the House paradigm. This chapter and chapter 11 foreground the diversity of feminist narratives in Spain's nineteenth and early twentieth centuries within a discursive system constantly in tension with "textual strategies, genres, and social constraints" (Kirkpatrick 2011, 232). Rather than tread terrain covered by other scholars,[2] this chapter probes the messages that female-authored essays promoted in key feminist periodicals from the mid-1840s until the 1868 Liberal Revolution. Although Guiliana di Febo pinpoints 1870 as initiating the feminist debate in Spain (Cabrera 1988, 33), this debate, as my discussion will highlight, was already evident from the 1840s onward.

The essay, traditionally considered a masculine genre for conceptual matters, relies on logic and reasoning, but it also possesses more "feminine properties in its flexible, dialogic, and open-ended structure" (Glenn and Mazquiarán 1998a, 1–3). Because reason has conventionally been identified with the masculine, and emotion and empathy with the feminine, nineteenth-century female writers who appropriated the essay to advance feminist claims positioned themselves in the realms of reason and an Enlightenment culture that premised the equality of all human beings due to their innate capacity for reason. The essay, however, is not bereft of emotion. As María-Ángeles Durán reminds us, one of its forms, the manifesto, draws on a collective pain and anger to propose ideas, values, and actions that contest dominant paradigms (1993, 17–19, 28–9). For Spanish feminist Margarita Pérez de Celis, "la discusión razonada" (1857, xiv; reasoned discussion) was the powerful weapon of her age.

An early precursor was María del Carmen Silva's 1811 epistolary defence of her husband, Pedro Pascasio Fernández Sardinó, editor of the Cádiz periodical *El Robespierre Español* (The Spanish Robespierre), accused of antipatriotism during the War of Independence. Silva, who assumed the editorship of the publication during her husband's imprisonment and took his case to the Supreme Council of the Indies, signed with her own name. She demonstrated a skilful command of legal discourse, inheritance laws, the situation of women, and the obligations of Spanish citizens.[3] Her letters reveal how a woman could have a political voice in a public forum by using a culturally sanctioned relational capacity to authorize it.

During the liberal *trienio* (three-year period), from January to June 1822, the Madrid weekly *El Periódico de las Damas* (The periodical for ladies) brought together a community of bourgeois female readers and writers. Although León Amarita authored most articles (Hartzenbusch 1894, 37), they foreground women's rights, education, and contribution to the nation, and celebrate noteworthy female writers, leaders, and warriors.[4] What is unusual in a women's periodical are articles on political governance intended to educate them for the liberal cause (Kirkpatrick 1991, 78). Female readers themselves contributed *charadas* (word puzzles) and letters, signed with initials or pseudonyms. Although considered entertainment, the *charadas* were also intellectual exercises in coded content.

In 1844, the year that Espartero's regency was succeeded by moderate liberals, who upheld conservative order as their governing principle (Carr 1982, 227–36), José Zorrilla's *Don Juan Tenorio* exalted a similar conservatism in the submissive femininity of Doña Inés, a dove taught to eat from the palms "del dueño que la ha criado / en doméstico vergel"(2002, vv. 1464–5; of the master who has raised her in a domestic garden). One year on, in an area of Spain associated with revolution in the early 1840s, a different kind of garden appeared in the form of *El Vergel de Andalucía* (The garden of Andalusia; 19 October–31 December 1845). A Córdoba weekly whose ten Sunday issues with consecutive pagination had exclusively female subscribers and a majority of female contributors, it replaced the Sevillan *El Vergel* (The orchard), whose male contributors wrote for the fair sex, or "bello secso" (*sic*). The concept of husbanded land encapsulated in the word *vergel*, a garden or orchard, also connotes, however, a more open space of luxuriant diversity. Exceeding the limits of the garden, or *pensil*, which informed the titles of the so-called *Pensiles* published between 1845 and 1859, *vergel* challenges an overly ordered environment to situate itself between domestication and wilderness. This liminal position characterizes the writings of its female contributors, who couch their demands for emancipation through nature imagery culturally identified with women and used to mark them as essentially inferior to men.

"Nature," however, is already culturally inscribed (Pateman 1989, 125). Images of cultivation, for instance, were key in Rousseau's development in *The Social Contract* of concepts of ownership, while John Stuart Mill used horticultural metaphors to pursue notions of social development and organization (Gatens 1991, 15, 30). I maintain that while women's recourse to a rhetoric of nature outwardly conforms to traditional feminine conventions, it can also be used to argue for women's rights by addressing principles of natural law. Affirming the innate equality of all human beings discovered through reason, natural law upholds the principle of sovereign power as opposed to regimes of military force (*imperium*) and subjection of others (*dominium*). Privileging consent in personal and collective relationships, it defends human rights applicable to all: the sovereign individual's right to self-preservation (Hobbes), to freedom of conscience (Spinoza), and freedom of property (Locke) (Kriegel 2002, 15–20). Historically, feminists have used natural law to counter a discrimination founded on women's supposedly natural, and negatively inflected, differences from men (Young 1998, 420). This approach holds in Spanish feminist writings during the nineteenth century and beyond.

From the outset, the main essayist in *El Vergel de Andalucía*, La Adalia, affirms that while nature has given women a free heart, men have obtained women's domination and absolute tutelage through humiliating them (no. 1, 4). Hence the periodical constantly foregrounds emancipatory thought, going beyond what Inmaculada Jiménez Morell calls a moderate feminism (1992, 74) to insist on achieving women's equality, their natural right: "No es nuestro objeto avasallar al hombre, pero sí colocarnos a su nivel, que es nuestro verdadero lugar" (no. 3, 25; We do not aim to subjugate men but to position ourselves at their level, which is our rightful place). One of the principal means of doing so is through poetry, the genre most identified with and open to women. Natural imagery, especially pertaining to flowers, channels a fierce critique of women's situation, as in Carolina Coronado's poem "Las extremeñas" (Women of Extremadura), which likens the deprivation that women's intellect suffers to a flower's violent uprooting from an original soil (no. 1, 7).[5] Many of *El Vergel de Andalucía*'s contributors formed part of a network of female friendship and solidarity termed an *Hermandad Lírica* (Manzano 1969, 7; poetic sisterhood). This virtual organization bonded through writing not only reflects culturally sanctioned close relationships among women. It also constitutes a literary platform for collective action linked to Democrat and progressive Republican circles (Burguera 2011, 63, 72), and a form of associationism, important for developing sociopolitical engagement and vital in natural law for humankind's "self-preservation and self-determination" (Kriegel 2002, 24). Later in the century, as discussed in chapter 11, these intellectual associations would result in the first feminist-oriented associations in Spain.

El Vergel de Andalucía's daring in vindicating women's independence and emancipation is affirmed in La Adalia's lead article in issue 4, which uses political discourse to situate women's demands as a political matter (see figure 2). Despite men's "inmensa monarquía" (27; immense monarchy), "absoluto imperio" (absolute domination), and "universal despojo" (universal dispossession) of women, they might perceive the tone of women's claims as "subversivo" (subversive) and "sedicioso" (seditious). Nevertheless, she asserts, her fellow female contributors' thought receives validation from the Enlightenment spirit of regeneration and principles of natural law, which combat centuries of vested interests and an obsolete, imported legislation (28), namely, the Napoleonic Code. The avant-garde ethos of *El Vergel de Andalucía* can be calibrated by contrasting it with the contemporary Madrid weekly, *El Pensil del Bello Sexo* (The garden of the fair sex; 23 November 1845–25 January 1846). Over ten issues its two main contributors, literary director Miguel Ángel Príncipe and Ramón de Satorres, defend conservative values. Contrasting with *El Vergel*'s feminist use of natural law, Satorres deploys its premises to justify women's domestic containment and maintains apocalyptically that equality will denaturalize women and set the world adrift.[6]

The year 1851 is a significant date for the birth of two important feminist periodicals: the Madrid weeklies *Ellas* (Those women; 1 September–30 November 1851) and *La Mujer* (Woman; mid-1851–17 October

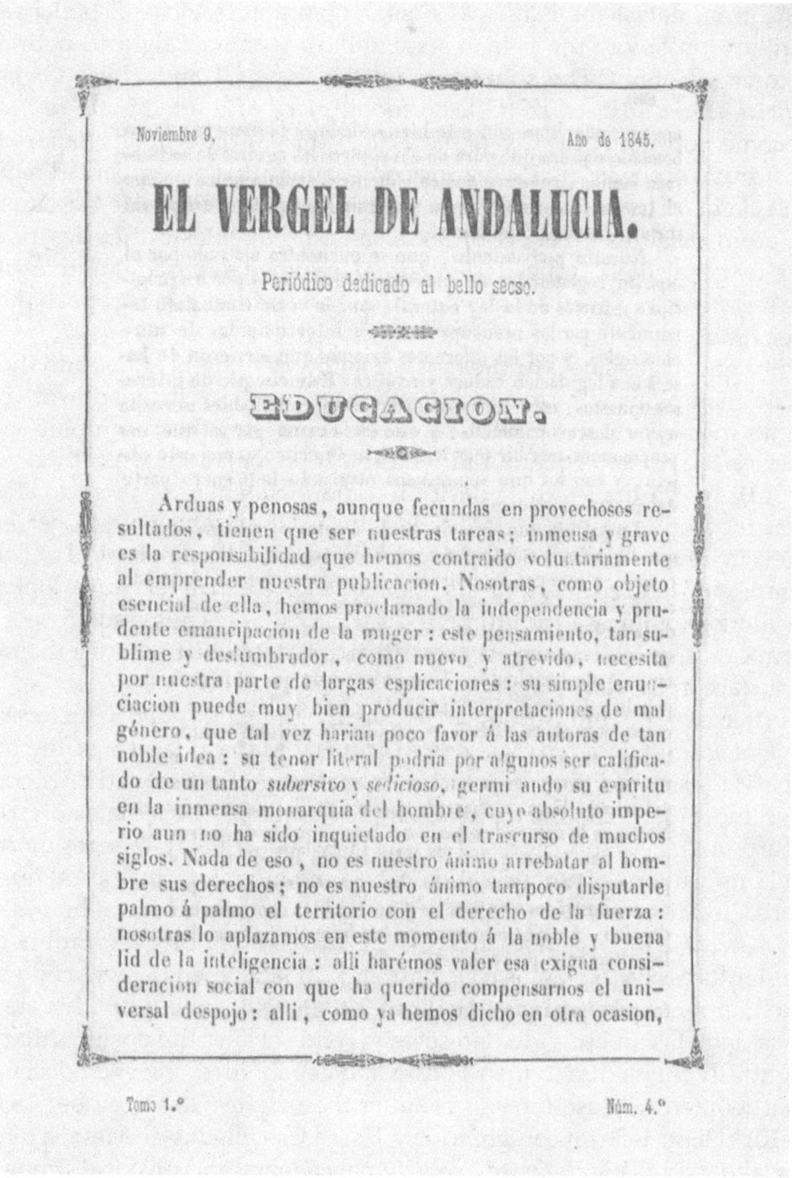

Noviembre 9. Año de 1845.

EL VERGEL DE ANDALUCIA.

Periódico dedicado al bello secso.

EDUCACION.

Arduas y penosas, aunque fecundas en provechosos resultados, tienen que ser nuestras tareas; inmensa y grave es la responsabilidad que hemos contraido voluntariamente al emprender nuestra publicacion. Nosotras, como objeto esencial de ella, hemos proclamado la independencia y prudente emancipacion de la muger: este pensamiento, tan sublime y deslumbrador, como nuevo y atrevido, necesita por nuestra parte de largas esplicaciones: su simple enunciacion puede muy bien producir interpretaciones de mal género, que tal vez harian poco favor á las autoras de tan noble idea: su tenor literal podria por algunos ser calificado de un tanto *subersivo* y *sedicioso*, germinando su espíritu en la inmensa monarquia del hombre, cuyo absoluto imperio aun no ha sido inquietado en el trascurso de muchos siglos. Nada de eso, no es nuestro ánimo arrebatar al hombre sus derechos; no es nuestro ánimo tampoco disputarle palmo á palmo el territorio con el derecho de la fuerza: nosotras lo aplazamos en este momento á la noble y buena lid de la inteligencia: alli harémos valer esa exigua consideracion social con que ha querido compensarnos el universal despojo: alli, como ya hemos dicho en otra ocasion,

Tomo 1.° Núm. 4.°

Figure 2. First page of "Educación" by La Adalia, *El Vergel de Andalucía* 4 (9 November 1845): 27. By kind permission of the Biblioteca Nacional de España, microfilm no. 783<1>(1).

1852). A catalyst for *Ellas* was French abolitionist Victor Schœlcher's vindication before the French Assembly of women's right to petition (Elorza 1975, 52). The subtitle of *Ellas* in issues 1 and 2 was *Órgano Oficial del Sexo Femenino* (Official mouthpiece of the feminine sex), to become subsequently *Gaceta del Bello Sexo* (Gazette of the fair sex), indicative of the kind of semantic compromise that accompanied feminist claims. The first issue opens with editor Alicia Pérez de Gascuna's "Cuatro palabras" (Four words), a sarcastic manifesto that describes the fear that their "cruzada femenina" (women's crusade) and "grito de regeneración" (call for regeneration) have aroused in European men (see figure 3).

She envisages a new future that her fellow daughters of Eve and their male champions will create and challenges men's exclusive power and rights in intellectual and public spheres. Tempering this confrontational piece is the editorial board's addendum, "Otra palabrita" (Another wee word), which denies their desire for complete emancipation, to state that they only wish to defend and educate themselves.[7] Such oscillations in tone and negotiation of societal restrictions were typical of contemporary feminist periodicals (Espigado 2008, 25), a facet overlooked in Elorza's appraisal of the periodical (1975, 52). Thus issue 5 sees a temporary swing towards conservative content, while feminist themes resurface in the following one.

After issue 10, the periodical became the *Gaceta del Bello Sexo: Revista de Literatura, Educación, Novedades, Teatros y Modas* (Gazette of the fair sex: Magazine of literature, education, novelties, theatre, and fashion; 8 December 1851–23 January 1852). In its first issue, the female editorial board, in "A las suscritoras" (To our lady subscribers), reneges on the full implications of emancipation proclaimed in *Ellas*'s inaugural number, defending women's rights but within familial and social boundaries (*Gaceta* 1 [8 December 1851]: 1–2). In issue 2, however, Emilia de Tamarit's essay "Nosotras a los hombres" (We women to men) contests such limits. Claiming individuality for women ("como individuo de la sociedad" [as an individual in society]) and seeking the position that is rightfully theirs due to their nature and capabilities, she even declares that women will use force to conquer their rights (15 December 1851: 9–10).[8] Her article on contemporary Teresa Castellanos de Mesa, a fencing and gymnastics teacher, exalts female agency and physical strength in traditionally male spheres (*Gaceta* 2 [15 December 1851]: 12–13). In another, "De la autoridad marital" (On the husband's authority), she denounces men's perception of women as disposable chattels to assert

Año I. Madrid 1.° de Setiembre de 1851 N 1.°

ELLAS,

ÓRGANO OFICIAL

DEL SEXO FEMENINO.

CUATRO PALABRAS.

—

La Europa entera se ha estremecido al solo preludio de nuestra cruzada femenina; todos los paises han escuchado atónitos el grito de regeneracion dado por nosotras, y el prospecto de ELLAS ha producido una confusion general, siendo un enigma que nadie alcanza á comprender ni á descifrar.

Alarmados los hombres, considerando la gran probabilidad del término prodigioso de esta empresa, han prorumpido en lastimeros clamores, y una fuerte sacudida, causada por el primer susto de la gran masa masculina, ha puesto en peligro á todo el orbe cristiano.

Ellos han temblado! el pavor se ha recogido en sus corazones, y nuestro triunfo parece afianzarse de esta manera. Bello se presenta el horizonte del porvenir, hijas de Eva. ¡Sús! ¡A reñir sin tregua ni descanso!

¡*Ellos!* ¿qué significa esta palabra? ¿Acaso querrá manifestar un poder absoluto, una facultad universal, un derecho indisputable á la dominacion de las criaturas? ¿Acaso hemos podido creer que solo *ellos* son capaces de figurar en el mundo intelectual, de ejercer la autoridad sobre todas las cosas y de mantener bajo su esclusiva dependencia cuantos elementos constituyen las sociedades?

¡Cuán lejos estamos de pensar de ese modo! Nos creemos con facultades mas estensas de las que se nos señalan; nos juzgamos aptas para mucho, y hé aquí porque no hemos vacilado en escribir, dando á luz un periódico para nosotras, donde se ventilen todas las cuestiones que hasta el dia hayan permanecido entre el polvo del olvido. Dispuestas nos hallamos á sostener la dignidad que nos compete, y ¡ay de los que, olvidándose del decoro ó de la prudencia puedan llegar á acrecentar nuestro mal humor! Difícilmente conseguirán de nosotras el perdon de sus escesos, porque intolerantes por represalias, no hemos de dejar títere con cabeza ni rincon por husmear.

Preparaos, vosotros los que blasonais de atrevidos y asaz desmandados, disponeos á sufrir, con la verguenza consiguiente, la burla que os vamos á hacer; no os quedarán ánimos de reproducir vuestras tentativas en contra de nuestro sexo. Corridos y confusos os rendireis en la pelea á merced de los funestos golpes de nuestra espada vencedora.

Como toda regla admite sus escepciones, aun cuando la de nuestra enseña pueda ser mas ó menos general, tiene tambien las suyas. Cobijados bajo nuestra bandera un puñado de hombres de buen humor, galantes y justicieros, no han vacilado en auxiliarnos con sus luces y conocimientos contribuyendo á la mayor variedad de las páginas de nuestro periódico: con estos no usaremos por lo tanto del rigor prescrito para los demás y por el contrario los trataremos cual corresponde á la hidalguía de sus corazones. En el mismo caso se encuentran los que prestándonos un apoyo con su suscricion cooperan de este modo á llevar adelante nuestro gran pensamiento. Somos imparciales y queremos dar á cada uno lo que le corresponde.

Como vereis por este primer número, no adoptamos el tono lastimero y compungido, tan comun en estos tiempos de progreso literario; todo lo contrario, usando del mejor humor y con la risa siempre en los labios pretendemos que no

Figure 3. First page of "Cuatro palabras" by Alicia Pérez de Gascuna, *Ellas* 1, Year 1 (1 September 1851): 1. By kind permission of the Biblioteca Nacional de España, microfilm 2621<1>.

that the rights and duties of husband and wife must be equal and reciprocal (*Gaceta* 4 [30 December 1851]: 26).[9]

These diverging positions indicate two different feminisms constantly debated in the feminist press, which Karen Offen terms relational and individualist. Heralding the twentieth-century feminism of difference, the first "emphasized women's rights as women (defined principally by their childbearing and/or nurturing capacities) in relation to men. ... and made claims on the commonwealth on the basis of these contributions." The second, evident in de Tamarit's stance and dominant in Anglo-American feminisms, sought female autonomy based on equal rights (Offen 1988, 136, 143). Regarding *La Mujer*, extant issues comprise numbers 32 to 52 in year 1, and all twelve – numbers 1 to 12 – in year 2. Most contributors were female and used the essay for feminist goals that, unlike the more radical and often secular agendas evident in chapter 11 below, did not appear to challenge head-on the Catholic Church's pronouncements on women's sociocultural place.[10] The periodical's stated purpose ranges from more modest pretensions, such as providing a space for all opinions (33 [14 March1852]: 1), being useful to the female sex (38 [18 April 1852]: 1), and fostering morality (39 [25 April 1852]: 3), to the evidently feminist agenda of aiding women's emancipation (44 [30 May 1852]: 2), protecting them from misogyny (46 [13 June 1852]: 1), and staunchly defending their rights (52 [25 July 1852]: 1). Thus the periodical's title, *Woman*, arguably designates not an essentialist position, but what Durán calls a political strategy that seeks women's precarious unity in the face of their fragmentation and isolation (1993, 32).[11]

This feminist ethos is always present in the mainly unsigned lead articles, which emphasize women's equality with and even superiority to men, and their capacity for literary immortality and entry into the public sphere.[12] Throughout, great women in politics, science, literature, and religion are upheld as examples to emulate and proof that women's inferior position in nineteenth-century society is not natural but socially produced.[13] Behind early feminists' stress on the development of women's capacity lay the demand for the rights that should accompany that capacity. As Geneviève Fraisse asserts, "Tiene derechos la persona a la que se le reconoce una 'capacidad'" (2003, 89; A person has rights because their "capacity" has been recognized). Developing one's capacity was another way for feminists then to assert what Offen refers to as the "freedom to become ... a project for autonomous behavior that, by ignoring socially constructed norms or goals, refuses to acknowledge limitation by them"(1988, 146).

In issue 46 of *La Mujer*, the lead article, "La mujer a través de los siglos" (13 June 1852, 1–2; Woman through the centuries), creates a female genealogy of heroism, leadership, and talent to vindicate the call for equality, stating that men have never wished to acknowledge the perfect balance ("equilibrio") of the two sexes (2). Contradicting the affirmation that women seek a "fantástica emancipación" (illusory emancipation), the text demands that men recognize women's rights for the latter's regeneration (2). The awareness that such a declaration challenged the limits of the culturally admissible is apparent in the concluding remark: "Pero dejemos esto, que probablemente nos conduciría más allá de los límites que nos hemos trazado y que convienen a la índole de nuestro periódico" (2; But let's leave this aside, as it would probably lead us beyond the limits that we have marked out and that are appropriate to our kind of periodical).

Other lead articles in *La Mujer* indirectly broach equal citizenship rights for women by debating if they are capable of governing and military prowess. Continuing Josefa Amar y Borbón's argument in her 1786 "Discurso en defensa del talento de las mugeres, y de su aptitud para el gobierno y otros cargos en que se emplean los hombres" (Speech in defence of women's talent and their aptitude for government and other positions held by men) and Gertrudis Gómez de Avellaneda's 1845 essay, "Capacidad de las mujeres para el gobierno" (Capacity of women for government),[14] the topic also represents in serious terms the premises of a long, anonymous satirical treatise, *Gobierno representativo y constitucional del bello sexo español* (Representative, constitutional government of the Spanish fair sex; Madrid, 1841). Refuting muscular strength as the justification for political superiority, *La Mujer*'s lead essay in issue 50, "Si las mujeres son capaces de gobernar" (11 July 1852, 1–2; Whether women are capable of governing), premises political virtue on prudence and magnanimity, qualities equally present in women and men (2). In issue 51, "Si las mujeres son susceptibles de las virtudes militares" (18 July 1852, 1–3; Whether women may possess military virtues) draws on Enlightenment thinker Benito Jerónimo Feijoo to affirm women's capacity to serve as military, political, and religious leaders on the basis of reason, scientific knowledge, and historical fact (1–2). By using the discourses of family and nature proper to a conventional femininity to articulate the link between the ability to govern and military virtue – "[porque] pudiéramos asegurar con verdad que es hijo legítimo del primero; ... ¿qué cosa más natural que decir si son susceptibles de las virtudes militares?" (which we could truly assure is the legitimate offspring of the first; ... what could be more natural than to ask if women are susceptible to military virtues?) – the writer apparently upholds sociocultural norms while simultaneously challenging them. Indeed, she signals, the attributes most aligned with femininity – the emotions and sensibility – are those that make heroes and conquerors, insisting that divine design has given the hearts of both sexes the same composition (1–2). In so doing, the essay echoes arguments proferred by early modern European feminists, which were exemplified in Spain by María de Zayas (1590–1661) (see Vollendorf 2001b, 64–5).

In the second year of *La Mujer*, which saw a change in its subtitle, the lead essays continue the tactic of writing on matters ostensibly aligned with a normative femininity to argue for women's ability to participate equally with men in intellectual, political, legal, and religious spheres. Anna Caballé likens such manoeuvres to acts of resistance by a marginalized subject who seeks openings in the constraining sociocultural systems that she inhabits (2013, 16). Thus in the lead essay in *La Mujer*'s issue 8, the conventional importance of women's virtue is used as a screen to justify their access to male-dominated spheres like the priesthood and judiciary, unlike Arenal's writings discussed in chapter 10 below. Families are compared with small nations, whose happiness depends on women's good domestic government and impacts on that of nation states, making women's virtue more important than men's (19 September 1852, 1–2). Citing women virtuous in science, literature, and art, several of whom taught in universities, the writer authorizes her argument through the Enlightenment values of reason and scientific fact: "Fundándonos en razones y en hechos" (2; Basing our statements on reason and facts).

The importance of marriage by choice in a society in which women's legitimate roles were those of wife and mother stands out in Rogelia León's essay, "El porvenir" (*La Mujer* 7 [12 September 1852]: 1–3; The future). Given that, under men's laws, marriage equates to slavery for women, León attempts to resolve the impasse between women's alleged but nonexistent free agency and their real subjection by arguing that if women enter into marriage voluntarily, legal bondage ceases to be such: "Dejad al alma la verdadera elección de unos lazos en los cuales quedáis esclavas, porque así lo ha dispuesto el hombre ... El yugo voluntario no es yugo"(3; Leave to the soul the true choice of ties that will make you slaves, because man has thus determined it ... Voluntary yokes are not yokes).[15] On the one hand, León's words foretell Carole Pateman's contention that "the presumed consent of a woman, in a free marriage contract, to her subordinate status gives a voluntarist gloss to an essentially ascribed status of 'wife'" (1989, 218). However, on the other hand, as Wendy Jones indicates, consensual marriage implies a "contractual subjectivity for women ... ultimately incompatible with women's subjection" (2005, 5).

An excellent example of how these feminists effected their veiled critique is María Verdejo y Durán's essay, "Talento, ciencia y gloria" (*La Mujer* 11 [10 October 1852]: 1–3; Talent, science, and glory), where positive adjectives characterize women's heads and negative ones, men's: "¿Y qué argumento lógico pudieran tampoco aducir los hombres para probar que las cabezas adornadas de sedosas trenzas y ondulantes rizos no pueden estar tan bien organizadas como esas orgullosas testas donde campean mutiladas melenas, cerradas barbas y retorcidos bigotes?" (2; What logical argument could men adduce to prove that heads adorned with silken braids and undulating curls cannot be as well organized as those proud heads where mutilated manes, impenetrable beards, and twisted moustaches run riot?). The supposedly good organization of men's heads, or *testas*, a Latinate word that connotes the male sexual organs, is contradicted by the qualities of pride, mutilation, intransigence, and deformity present in the descriptions of their hair, beards, and moustaches. The essay insists on women's rights as individuals to cultivate their talents – not just to benefit the family but also to escape from their domestic objectification and invisibility as "un mueble inútil y desapercibido" (2; a useless, overlooked piece of furniture) and achieve immortality through their genius.

From 1856 to 1859, Cádiz was the crucible for a series of feminist-oriented periodicals that scholars term the *Pensiles*, influenced by Republican thought and Charles Fourier's utopian socialism.[16] *El Pensil Gaditano* (The Cádiz garden) emerged in 1856, when the Moderates returned to power after a two-year Progressive government. In the one extant issue, the lead article by M. P. de C. (Margarita Pérez de Celis), "La mujer en la sociedad" (6 [16 February 1857]: 1–2; Woman in society), initially argues for women's education so that they might fulfil their duties as educators within the home (1). This more conventional message, however, then challenges the status quo: education becomes the means for not only women's awareness of their duties but also their exercise of "indisputables derechos" (indisputable rights), given that women, the author contends, have excelled in the Vatican and in war (2). Men's resistance to women's emancipation is attributed to their refusal to share power (2).

In January 1857, the year that the Moyano Law made primary education compulsory for girls,[17] Pérez de Celis and María Josefa Zapata founded *El Pensil de Iberia* (The garden of Iberia), published thrice monthly. The two extant numbers, its last, are from 20 and 30 September 1857. In the first, issue 26, all contributions bar two are by women. The lead article is Zapata's translation of Fourierist Alphonse Toussenel's *El mundo de los pájaros* (The world of birds; 1853–5), followed by Pérez de Celis's essay, "Cuadros de costumbres contemporáneos: Lucha de amor y deber, II" (Contemporary vignettes of customs: The struggle between love and duty, II), which both continue in issue 27. The periodical also advertises Rosa Marina's essay in book form, *La mujer y la sociedad* (Woman and society), free to subscribers, to which I turn shortly.

On 10 October 1857, this *Pensil* became *El Nuevo Pensil de Iberia* (The new garden of Iberia) to initiate a more openly feminist agenda, contrasting with the hesitant declarations in Barcelona's *La Floresta*. Essays from male champions, such as José González Alegre y Álvarez and Joaquín Fiol, lent authoritative weight to female writers' claims and demonstrate, as Margarita Nelken would affirm in 1922 in *La condición social de la mujer*, "el *porqué* visto a través de los beneficios que la emancipación de la mujer ha de reportar, no sólo a ella, sino a toda la humanidad" (19 [emphasis in original]; why the emancipation of women is beneficial not only for women, but also for all of humanity).[18] In the last available issue, Antonio Quiles's article, "La mujer no es inferior al hombre (Continuación)" (Woman is not inferior to man: Continuation), upholds women's equal right to participate in science and cultivate their intelligence so as to become once again "la paloma portadora de la buena nueva" (*El Nuevo Pensil* 42 [10 December 1858]: 6; the dove that bears great tidings): words that herald Pérez de Celis's iconoclastic 1866 periodical, *La Buena Nueva* (Great tidings).

El Nuevo Pensil published a good number of translations of male Fourierist thinkers, such as again Zapata's translation of Toussenel's *El mundo de los pájaros*, which cites Victor Considerant's theories in support of writing gender equality into the French Constitution (24 [30 May 1858]: 1). The periodical also featured a translation of Juan Czinski's "El porvenir de las mujeres" (Women's future), which had first entered Spain in 1841.[19] A eulogy of cooperative socialism, Czinski's text defended the theory of passionate attraction, based on natural law, and advocated women's freedom of choice in marriage (21 [30 April 1858]: 5–6). These translations perform a mediating function by granting authority to contentious feminist claims through authoritative male thinkers. The final incarnation of the Cádiz *Pensiles* was *El Pensil de Iberia: Revista Universal Contemporánea* (The garden of Iberia: Contemporary universal magazine; 10 April–10 August 1859), published three times a month after an initial period prohibited by censorship (see "A nuestros lectores," no. 1, 1; To our readers). A key work in the first five issues was José Bartorelo's annotated translation of the North American spiritualist A.J. Davis's "Derechos y misión de la mujer" (Woman's rights and mission). Although Davis supports two separate gendered spheres (2 [20 April 1859]: 1–2), she vindicates women's assertion of their natural rights (3 [30 April 1859]: 4) and presents their dignification and freedom within a narrative of progress and republicanism (5 [20 May 1859]: 3). Also prevalent in *El Pensil de Iberia* is a critique of the rich and the exaltation of the working classes, as in Zapata's essay, "El pueblo se ilustra y se moraliza" (12 [30 July 1859]: 4; The people educate themselves and grow morally).

Issues 1, 2, 3, 5, and 6 feature Marina's "Leyendas morales" (Moral legends), in which Jesus as the authorizing narrative voice defends associationism, blames men for women's prostitution within and outside marriage, advocates political unity, and criticizes a legal system that permits husbands to imprison their wives in lunatic asylums. The biblical imagery that Marina, Zapata, and Pérez de Celis systematically deploy indicates how mid-nineteenth-century feminists drew on Christian premises of gender equality to advance their agendas in a language familiar to female Catholic readers, in what Espigado Tocino calls an "instrumentalización del mensaje evangélico como medio de subversion social" (2008, 26; instrumentalization of evangelical discourse for social subversion), which looks ahead to Concepción Gimeno's *Evangelios de la mujer* (1900; Gospel truths about women), discussed in chapter 12. While Spanish feminisms have had to contend with the Catholic Church as an institution (Ugarte 1998, 62), the Catholic faith was enshrined in constitutions to underpin premises of Spanish citizenship. Thus religious teachings could authorize feminist thought and claims for greater sociopolitical rights, which in turn worked to shift the patriarchal premises of Catholicism and exclusionary concepts regarding membership of the nation.

This dynamic feminist environment produced one of the most advanced treatises of Spain's nineteenth century: Marina's extraordinarily modern *La mujer y la sociedad* (1857).[20] Pérez de Celis's prologue defends women's claims to equal duties, rights, and education so as to become socially independent to then turn to the desirability of women's legal emancipation (1857, v–vii). She considers that while absolute equality is incompatible with nature, that concept protests against arbitrary inequalities established by force against nature, justice, and religion (ix–xi). Affirming that women should enjoy the same civic and political rights as men, she strongly endorses Marina's ideas by stating that they are divinely supported (xv–xvi).[21]

Marina positions herself as the mouthpiece of reason against reactionary philosophers, statesmen, and politicians who have not advanced what is rightfully women's due (Marina 1857, 1–4). Indeed, she makes women's inadequate education and rights a political matter that impacts on government institutions and the struggle for liberty, regeneration, and social progress (4–6). Anticipating Concepción Arenal's 1861 essay, "La mujer del porvenir" (Irizarry 1998; The woman of the future), Marina frames her claims as a question of justice (1857, 17, 28), deploying legal language – "Yo probaré que" (8; I will prove that) – and emphasizing historical proof: "He dicho que los hechos y la historia justifican mis asertos. Hé aquí la prueba" (11; I have said that the facts and history justify my asseverations. I have here the proof). She inserts women into the sphere of production on asserting that they contribute directly and indirectly to national wealth (10). Refuting Gall's theories on the correlation of intelligence with skull size, she uses historical and contemporary examples to affirm women's equal intelligence, superior sensitivity and imagination, political acumen, and right to aspire to all careers (11–14).

Like Pérez de Celis's later article "Injusticia social" (*El Nuevo Pensil de Iberia* 7 [10 December 1857]: 1–3; Social injustice), Marina states that women should be able to earn an honourable living in all commercial and manufacturing establishments, where men have taken over work that was formerly women's to become effeminate and denaturalized (19–20). Stressing the compatibility of marriage with women's exercise of their intellectual and physical capabilities in employment, she contends that the couple's combined income produces greater marital wellbeing (22–5). Negating that her ideas are utopian, she represents women's cause as a war to which educated writers must contribute with their publications to achieve independence, dignity, and rights for all (31).

The last of the Fourierist-inspired feminist periodicals of this period was *La Buena Nueva* (Cádiz, 15 December 1865–15 April 1866), directed by Zapata and with regular contributions from Pérez de Celis and

Bartorelo. Ten issues appeared before financial problems and censorship closed the publication down.[22] In keeping with Fourierist principles of universal harmony, the periodical demonstrated a strong freethinking and pacifist stance,[23] and both Bartorelo and Zapata translated Fourier's works. As in the *Nuevo Pensil de Iberia*, Christian figures were adapted for feminist purposes, but most essays were written by male champions of feminist causes, such as Juan Mañé y Flaquer, who even urges that women be paid more than men (23 January 1866, 7–8). The only feminist essay by a woman is Zapata's "A la civilización del siglo XIX" (30 January 1866, 1–2; To nineteenth-century civilization), where she demands justice for an enslaved female sex in the name of humanity's quest for fraternal love. Like Marina, she calls on female writers to assist in achieving women's equality, because the former have been freed from the pernicious fanaticism of society's education through a second education procured through their genius and learning from nature.[24] Citing from the book of Genesis, Zapata affirms woman's equality by calling her "varona por ser de la misma esencia que el varón" (2; a female man, of the same composition as the male), and declares both sexes "iguales en el régimen de su ministerio" (2; equal in their ministry or respective governance). Hence *La Buena Nueva* continues Cádiz's proud feminist tradition that takes its bearings from Beatriz Cienfuegos's 1763 *La Pensadora Gaditana* (The female thinker of Cádiz).

10 Women Authors in the Romantic Tradition (1841–1884) and Early Feminist Thought (1861–1893)

MARYELLEN BIEDER

Nineteenth-century Spain saw multiple political transformations and the promulgation of different constitutions that stipulated increased or reduced individual freedoms for men and, on rare occasions, for women. These redefinitions of the nation allowed some women to rethink the place and opportunities for their gender in Spain. When Napoleon overthrew the Spanish monarchy in 1808, he imposed the Napoleonic Civil Code, with its own provisions regarding the treatment of women, many of which ran counter to the prevailing laws and practices in different regions of the country. The Napoleonic Code outlived José I Bonaparte and held sway in Spain throughout the nineteenth century and much of the twentieth, with the exception of the First and Second Republics.

Contrary to Arkinstall's findings in chapters 9 and 11, Adolfo González Posada (1860–1944), a law professor and prolific author of books on jurisprudence, suffrage, Spain, and Hispanic America, reached a negative conclusion about Spain's progress on women's issues in his 1899 book *Feminismo* (Feminism):

> No hay una polémica seria sobre cuestiones feministas y ... no existen grupos feministas bien organizados con un programa de reformas prácticas. Los escritores y los políticos han demostrado poco interés por el tema y las manifestaciones del feminismo, o al menos los acontecimientos reseñables que denoten un interés por la posición de las mujeres son escasos. (1899, 191–3)

> (There is no serious polemic on feminist questions, and there are no well-organized feminist groups with a program of practical reforms. Writers

and politicians have shown little interest in the topic and manifestations of feminism, or at least there are few events being reviewed that denote an interest in the position of women.)

Yet Geraldine Scanlon states affirmatively that at the beginning of the 1900s feminism was a hot topic, "cada vez más frecuente en los artículos periodísticos y conferencias públicas" (1986, 4; an ever more frequent subject in newspaper articles and public lectures). Nevertheless, it was not until the end of the new century's second decade that women began to form "grupos feministas que plantearon programas de reforma coherentes" (Scanlon 1986, 5; feminist groups that drew up coherent programs for reform). While both these authors employ the term "feminism" to identify the parameters of Spain's Woman Question – as it was internationally known in Posada's day – much pro-women writing and activity eschewed it, while of course those opposed to any change in the pattern of women's role in the home and family condemned it freely and often satirically. Writing in her 1902 column in a Barcelona magazine, Emilia Pardo Bazán looked favourably on feminism, finding consolation and hope in "el hecho de que ninguna persona culta e imparcial que examine despacio la situación de la mujer ante la ley y la costumbre, deja de manifestar en ese sentido que se llama feminista y que no debiera llamarse más que humano" (Herrero 2010–11, 61; the fact that no cultured and impartial person who carefully examines the situation of women before the law and social custom fails to proclaim that, in that sense, s/he is a "feminist" and should only be called human). But by 1919 and writing for a Buenos Aires newspaper, she raised the "problem" of feminism among both genders and decried the reactions against it. In her youth, she had judged it impossible for feminism to take root in Spain; men mocked it and made jokes about it. Women fled from it, and their attitude became an obstacle to those females who sought change: "Las mujeres … ¡ah las mujeres! se crispaban, se escandalizaban y se deshacían en protestas de sumisión a la autoridad viril … eran las peores enemigas de las que pensábamos en reivindicarnos derechos" (Smith 2006, 699; Women … Ah, women! Women flinched, were scandalized, burst into elaborate protests of their submission to male authority. Women were the worst [female] enemies of those of us who sought to claim our rights). Thus the negative connotations that "feminism" had accrued hindered its widespread acceptance by Spanish women, while also thwarting public identification with it by women otherwise committed, in one degree or another, to what had become throughout Europe core social and gender issues on the women's agenda. The question of staking out one's own individual position on social and gender issues versus committing oneself to a movement, already widely ridiculed in Spain, surely determined the stance of early, perhaps protofeminist Spanish women intellectuals.

Spain's nineteenth-century female thinkers on women's issues formulated in various ways the situation facing middle-class women who desired to find work or have a career. Emilia Pardo Bazán defined their only, if improbable, options as queen or *estanquera* (a woman licensed by the government to sell government-controlled tobacco products and stamps in an official kiosk), adding later, as legislation permitted, telegraphers and telephone operators (1981c, 41). As Concepción Arenal stipulated, the government admited that women have the aptitude to be kiosk vendors or queens but not to carry out other options: "Que pretendiese ocupar los puestos intermedios, sería absurdo" (1974b, 102; That she attempt to occupy intermediary positions [between the two extremes] would be absurd). Nevertheless, she identifies elementary-school teacher as another job available to women and considers them perfect for the priesthood. She highlights the irony that although the church may declare a woman a saint or a martyr, man "la cree indigna de llenar las funciones del sacerdocio" (102; believes her unworthy of fulfilling the functions of the priesthood). Arenal sides here with logic, not with social acceptance: "La lógica aquí sería escándalo, impiedad" (102; Here logic would be a scandal, ungodliness). Pardo Bazán considered women's suitability for the priesthood a "radicalísimo concepto de la igualdad de los sexos" (1981a, 178; very radical concept of the equality of the sexes). She added with cynicism that however few the professions open to women, "más contadas aún las mujeres de la clase media que se resuelven a ejercerlas" (1981c, 49–50; even fewer are the middle-class women resolved to undertake them).

These two protofeminists, among others, assigned the major share of the blame for middle-class women's absence from income-earning work to the poor or nonexistent education available to women. Inevitably Spain's educational system "limita a la mujer, la estrecha y reduce, haciéndola más pequeña aún que el tamaño natural, y manteniéndola en perpetua infancia" (Pardo Bazán 1981c, 51; limits a woman, narrows and reduces her, making her smaller than natural size, and keeping her in perpetual infancy). Arenal concludes that the Spanish woman's economic condition is "deplorable, y, si no fuera triste, sería ridículo oír hablar de su *emancipación*, cuando el estómago la sujeta a todo género de esclavitudes" (1895, 66 [emphasis in original]; deplorable, and, if it weren't sad, it would be ridiculous to hear her *emancipation* spoken of, when her stomach subjects her to all manner of slaveries). Catherine Davies summarizes Arenal's ironic assertions in *La mujer del porvenir* on "the absurdities of the so-called rational thought of men with respect to women: a woman can be the Mother of God but not a priest; Queen but not a customs official; she is a child in Civil Law, but a man's equal in Criminal Law; she may gain professional qualifications, but may not practice the profession" (Arenal 1974b, 101–5; Davies 1998, 38). Philanthropy was a middle-class woman's alternative to marriage or the convent, one to which the widowed Arenal dedicated herself: "La única otra actividad que se le permitía a una mujer de clase media era la filantropía" (Scanlon 1986, 62; The only other activity that was allowed the middle-class woman was philanthropy); that is, associating with others of her class for ostensibly beneficent purposes, especially in church-run organizations. Carmen Simón Palmer asserts that "no oculta Arenal nunca sus creencias religiosas" (2014, 5; Arenal never hid her religious beliefs) and that she insisted on "la necesidad del culto" (2014, 5; the need for worship).

Against this backdrop, it comes as no surprise that few of the women who began to publish in the waning years of Spain's romantic literary revolution identified as feminists, although many made occasional declarations that anticipate the movement for women's emancipation. As Susan Kirkpatrick has eloquently argued, the romantic exaltation of the individual and its personal expression of intimate emotions opened a way for women to voice their subjectivity and share it with others – initially with other women but ultimately a mixed-gender reading public: "Women's intervention as poets in mid-nineteenth-century print culture thus played a role in creating a kind of evolving verbal mirror in which literate nineteenth-century Spanish women came to see themselves as subjectively inhabiting a given social identity. Thus formed, the feminine poetic tradition functioned as part of a complex discourse that regulated women's self-representation throughout the rest of the century (2011, 231–2). With "the evolving differentiation of the print market and the emergence of new techniques of distribution," after 1850 print products for women took a radical shift away from poetry – much of it written by and addressed to women – to serial fiction and conduct manuals for women (232).

From the collated biographies of almost three thousand women authors who published in the nineteenth-century, Simón Palmer has concluded that most were married, middle-class women whose fathers pursued careers in one of the liberal professions or had links to politics (1991, xi). This pedigree explains the exceptional access to and level of education of many women authors, although others could only find space to read and write by hiding from their family. A significant number had a family connection to published authors (Simón Palmer 1991, xi). Each of the following four women authors – Cecilia Böhl von Faber, Gertrudis Gómez de Avellaneda, Carolina Coronado, and Rosalía de Castro – at times under exceptional circumstances, received a remarkable level of education for their times and enjoyed reading widely in literature, with an access to private libraries uncommon among middle-class or upper-middle-class girls. The result of their individualized, even autodidactic, education enabled each one to create, write, and often gain a place for her verse and prose in Spain's mainstream literary publications.

The first nineteenth-century woman to reach a wide reading public with her prose both in Spain and abroad, Cecilia Böhl von Faber or Böhl de Faber (1796–1877), was also the major Spanish woman author of that century consistently to mask her name with a male pseudonym, "Fernán Caballero."[25] Her fiction pursued a moral social agenda and tended to punish female characters for their deviations from proper societal norms or deploy a mature female character as the spokesperson for Böhl's model of womanhood. Her opposition to allowing her name to appear in print, which replicated her father's negative attitude to women who wrote and made their works public, faltered under economic duress. Following the death of her second husband, a socially and economically well-placed marquis, whose estate passed on his death to his heir from a first marriage – together with the financial disaster brought about by her profligate third husband, which led to his suicide – Böhl sought to remedy her penury by submitting works for publication in Spanish, starting in 1859. She had been producing these manuscripts for decades, apparently without any intention of publishing them, especially during the more tranquil Andalusian years of her second marriage. She wrote in French and German, the languages in which she had received her education.

Kirkpatrick maintains, referring to the protagonist of Böhl's best-known novel, *La Gaviota* (*The Sea Gull*), that Böhl "is and must be read as antifeminist and antiliberal, even though she was the only one of the Spanish women writers of her time who cast a woman in the Romantic role of the artist-hero" (1989, 275). Antifeminist in her writings and dependent, like other women authors, on male patronage to launch her career, Böhl nevertheless embodied for other aspiring female writers the value of a superior education and a sustained dedication to her career. Her situation bares one of the truths of nineteenth-century life in Spain for unmarried, disadvantageously married, or widowed women: the lack of an alternative to destitution. Her decision to launch herself in public, albeit under a pen name, underscores one of the prime reasons why an upper- or middle-class woman faced the opprobrium of displaying her name on her publications: to provide economically for herself and perhaps her husband. Böhl was more a feminist in her life than in her oeuvre. Concepción Gimeno de Flaquer may well have financially supported both herself and her husband from the earnings of the periodicals and books she published, as was certainly true of other writers such as María del Pilar Sinués de Marco and probably Josefa Pujol de Collado. In other cases, the situation of women who wrote remained dire. Turning on its head the trope of the poverty of writing women, later in the century upper-middle-class Pardo Bazán aspired to live exclusively from her earnings as an author, transposing what for Böhl was stark necessity into a declaration of feminist independence and equality (Pardo Bazán 2013, 114).

The upper-class Cuban-born colonial Gertrudis Gómez de Avellaneda (1814–73) immigrated with her family to Spain in the mid-1830s, at the height of the country's romantic literary movement in poetry and theatre. She published poetry, drama, and fiction in the late romantic mode throughout the reign of Isabel II. Her first novel, *Sab* (1841), named for the black male slave protagonist, dramatizes a cross-class and cross-race romance set in Cuba; it became the first antislavery novel in Spanish. Her passionate writing and her intense projection of female subjectivity draw her close to achieving the defining characteristics of (male) romanticism and allow her to create an authentic female romantic voice. Kirkpatrick clearly elucidates Avellaneda's relationship to the movement: "What distinguishes [her] cultivation of Romantic subjectivity from that of her leading male contemporaries is her focus on relations between subjects rather than on the relation of subject to object" (1989, 173). In making a woman the subject of romantic experience in *Sab* and applying the "heroic Romantic paradigm" to a woman in the novel *Dos mujeres* (1843; Two women), Avellaneda opens a space within Spanish romanticism for women to express themselves and dialogue with another subject (Kirkpatrick 1989, 147, 164). Kirkpatrick similarly asserts that Avellaneda breaks with the romantic tradition by transforming its paradigms into "instruments of critique" in her fiction, inserting a feminist dimension when she "vents in disguised form anger and frustration about the oppression of women" (1989, 283). Sab enacts another fundamental theme of male-authored romanticism, "the Promethean impulse toward revolt" (Kirkpatrick 1989, 153). As Kirkpatrick highlights, beyond Avellaneda's incorporation of romantic paradigms, language, and themes into her work, she inverts "the conventional moral lessons concerning love and marriage" in another gesture towards a feminist agenda (1989, 164).

In both her life and writing, Avellaneda defended a woman's rights and sought enhanced opportunities for herself in the public arena as a writer and contributor to periodicals. Her life, to a greater extent than her thought, advanced possibilities for women in Spain; however, as happened to other female authors who ventured into the public arena, she also suffered for what was for the times her excessive visibility and notoriety. Her private life – twice widowed, a child out of wedlock, lovers – would have condemned a Spanish woman writing later in the century. Nevertheless, Avellaneda received many accolades and wide admiration among the literati. Her feminist ideas emerge in the plotting and discourse of her fictional works. In her autobiographical writings and in her correspondence, she acknowledges women's need for equal rights. In the male cultural circles of belles-lettres, she sought election to a seat in Spain's prestigious Real Academia Española de la Lengua (Spanish Royal Academy of Language) and suffered the rejection, based on her gender, as a personal humiliation, although the academy would not elect its first female member until 1979. Despite the generational difference between Böhl and Avellaneda, the lives of the two women overlapped, and they experienced at least epistolary contact and a degree of mutual admiration.

Carolina Coronado (1820–1911) began publishing as a provincial poet from the remote region of Extremadura in the more liberal early years of Isabel's reign. As the century progressed and as her social position evolved – she married the United States diplomat Horace Perry and had children – she became more conventional and circumscribed in her writing, until she eventually abandoned poetry and fiction. Nevertheless, Kirkpatrick signals the early 1840s as a key moment in Spanish poetry and celebrates the "unprecedented publications of three volumes of poetry by women authors between 1841 and 1843" (2011, 229) – Coronado, Gómez de Avellaneda, and Josefa Massanés. Some of Coronado's occasional verse pithily elaborates feminist themes of freedoms denied and the creation of a liberating sisterhood of women writers, as seen in chapter 9.

The poem "Libertad" (Freedom), written from Coronado's hometown of Almendralejo, Badajoz in 1846, upon the promulgation of a new constitution granting additional rights to men, speaks directly to women: "Dicen, compañeras, que hay libertad para el pueblo" (Valis 1991a, 389; They say, sisters, that there is freedom for the people).[26] She continues in a more ironic vein, identifying the problem as "el yugo de nuestro sexo" (the yoke our gender bears):

¡Libertad! ¿qué nos importa?
¿qué ganamos, qué tendremos?
¿un encierro por tribuna
y una aguja por derecho?

(Freedom! what does it matter to us? / what do we gain, what will we attain? / an enclosure for a podium / and a needle as our right?)

The conclusion's brutal honesty characterizes the position of women in mid-century Spain:

Pero, os digo, compañeras,
que la ley es solo de ellos,
que las hembras no se cuentan
ni hay Nación para este sexo. (Valis 1991a, 390)

(But I tell you, sisters, / that the law is only for them [men], / that women do not count / nor is there a nation for this gender.)

In "La flor del agua" (The waterlily) and "Cantad, hermosas" (Sing, pretty women), as Kirkpatrick has theorized, Coronado breaks with the isolated romantic individual and anticipates collective feminist agency, in this case through a strategy of facing down the opposition to women poets with the collective strength of a "lyrical sisterhood" (1989, 79–87). The water lily figures the tactic that enables a single plant, its roots invisible under the water, to survive in a difficult habitat by intertwining its roots with those of other lilies, modelling what aspiring young women poets can also achieve by supporting and encouraging each other:

Y cual ella más felices
desde hoy serán nuestras vidas
si con las almas unidas,
vivimos, las dos así. (Valis 1991a, 519)

(And like her [the flower] our lives will be happier from today if the two of us live with our souls united in this way.)

Thus Coronado attempted to convey "the alienating effects of cultural objectification of women," as Kirkpatrick writes of another poem (1989, 228). Although Coronado did not explicitly formulate a feminist agenda as such, or even identify herself as a feminist, some of her verse and her forging of a lyrical sisterhood did set the groundwork for positions adopted by later women, such as Gimeno de Flaquer. Coronado's very long life kept her contemporaneous with successive generations of women writers, albeit for the last decades from her home in Portugal, to which, upon her husband's death, she retreated accompanied by his body.

Another solitary poet, this time from the distant province of Galicia where she remained almost her entire life, Rosalía de Castro (1837–85) wrote both verse and epistolary prose calling for women's rights within a lingering, sentimental, late romantic paradigm of the solitary, isolated individual. In a somewhat sociological tenor, Castro evoked lyrically both the male economic émigré forced by poverty to abandon his homeland for Cuba or South America and the single or married woman left behind to fend for herself in Galicia. Castro penned her first volume of poetry, *Cantares gallegos* (*New Songs* [poems]; 1863), in the Galician language. It inaugurated modern Galician literature, being "the first collection of Galician lyrical poems published since the Medieval *Cancioneros* [songbooks]" (Davies 1998, 63). Curiously, she dedicated the book to Fernán Caballero, whose recently launched publications sought to immortalize the culture and spirit of rural Andalusia, as Castro envisioned doing for Galicia. While Castro kept house for her growing family in Galicia, her husband, a journalist, sometime national civil servant, and primary advocate for the revival of Galician culture, marketed her poetry in Madrid and fostered her reputation outside her native region. Helena Miguélez-Carballeira characterized her life as continuous itinerancy between locations in Madrid and Galicia, frequent childbirth, and "fitful creative processes" (2014, 178).

In addition to three novels, Castro also wrote another volume of poetry in Galician, *Follas novas* (*New Leaves*; 1880), as well as stories, and one last poetry collection in Spanish, *Las orillas del Sar* (*On the Edge of the River Sar*; 1884).[27] Her last two poetry volumes received financial publication support from Galician émigrés living in Havana and Buenos Aires, for whom she was the poetic voice of the poor and dispossessed of their homeland. Beyond the Galician diaspora readership,

Castro's poetry also resonated within Spain and figures in the national literary canon as "the precursor of twentieth-century poetry in Spain" (Davies 1998, 67).

Castro's 1858 essay "Lieders," published in Galicia during or after her brief residence in Madrid and before her marriage to Manuel Murguía, is widely considered the first feminist statement published in Galicia. Written early in her career, it echoes familiar romantic tropes, even recalling the romantic poet par excellence José de Espronceda's iconic "Canción del pirata" ("Pirate's Song"). However, it voices a passionately felt declaration that, while slavery is a woman's patrimony, at the same time her freedom resides within herself:

> Sólo cantos de independencia y libertad han balbucido mis labios, aun alrededor hubiese sentido, desde la cuna ya, el ruido de las cadenas que debían aprisionarme para siempre, porque el patrimonio de la mujer son los grillos de la esclavitud.
>
> Yo, sin embargo, soy libre, libre como los pájaros, como las brisas; como los árabes en el desierto, como el pirata en el mar.
>
> ...
>
> Yo soy libre. Nada puede contener la marcha de mis pensamientos, y ellos son la ley que rige mi destino. (Castro 1996a, 469–70)

> (My lips have only stammered out songs of independence and freedom, although I had felt all around me since the cradle the sound of the chains that should imprison me forever, because the shackles of slavery are woman's patrimony.
>
> Nevertheless, I am free, free as the birds, as the breezes; like the Arabs in the desert, the pirate on the sea.
>
> ...
>
> I am free. Nothing can restrain the movement of my thoughts, and they are the law that rules my destiny.)

A second essay in Spanish, "Las literatas: Carta a Eduarda" ("The Bluestockings: Letter"), appeared in Galicia in 1865 and evinces a damning awareness of the consequences for a woman of exhibiting her name in the public sphere. The epistle warns Eduarda, a fictitious would-be author, of her inevitable future if she perseveres as *una mujer literata* (a woman writer) or *poetisa* (woman poet), both derogatory terms at the time: "Los hombres miran a las literatas peor que mirarían al diablo, y éste es un nuevo escollo que debes temer tú que no tienes dote"

(Castro 1996b, 475; Men view writing women as worse than they would the devil, and this is a new obstacle that you should fear, you who have no dowry). In linking the economics of marriage – the career awaiting most women from families with adequate financial means – with the desire to write, Castro perhaps makes her most overtly feminist statement about the inequality, mistreatment, and backlash meted out to women who inserted themselves into the public arena, thereby putting their reputations and marital prospects on the line.[28] An important cultural movement, the Galician Rexurdimento (Renaissance), began to take shape with the 1861 Xogos Florais (Floral Games; originally medieval literary contests) and Castro's 1863 *Cantares Gallegos*, and fostered Galicia's growing nationalism: "The success of the Rexurdimento in the 1860s and 1870s ... created a solid basis for the expression of modern Galician culture and identity" (Hooper and Puga Moruxa 2011, 6–7). As the site of tensions between feuding cultural camps, Castro has become today "un auténtico fetiche" (González Fernández and Rábade Villar 2012, 11n3; an authentic fetish) that bears the burden of figuring Galician culture.

Two other well-known writers from Galicia were more overt feminists and, while their lifespans overlapped with Castro's, they predominantly grounded their early literary lives in Madrid: Arenal, over fifteen years Castro's elder; and Pardo Bazán, almost fifteen years younger than Castro. Since Castro died relatively young, both women outlived her. Other less well-known Galician women authors, among them Emilia Calé y Torres de Quintero (1837–1908), Filomena Dato Muruais (1856–1926), and Sofía Casanova (1862–1958), were contemporaneous with Castro. The first two women remained in Galicia throughout their lives. Casanova lived her married life abroad and increasingly espoused a feminist agenda; through her correspondence with other women writers, she created a network of mutual support (see Hooper 2008). While both Arenal and Pardo Bazán recognized the value of Castro's poetry, their own intellectual world centred largely on Madrid, although Pardo Bazán split her year between Madrid and Galicia, and the widowed Arenal lived principally in Asturias and finally Galicia.[29] Despite their continued contact with Galicia, neither woman devoted sustained attention to its culture or to transforming oral *gallego* into a written language of high culture, as was already happening in Catalonia with the Catalan language and in the Basque provinces with Euskara (see chapter 13).

Hence Castro remained a unique case: a writer who, in unpromising circumstances, forged a greatly valued poetic idiom and from her virtual isolation furthered Galician culture and its language. She came to embody the possible emergence of a vibrant and respected Galician culture – a mark of Galicia's advance towards enlightenment thinking – that might help lift a desperately poor region out of its marginalization within Spain. This political agenda, fostered by her husband even after her death, with its implications for the broader Spanish nation, dominated the reception of her work and largely silenced her latent feminism.

Barcelona produced its own flourishing women's culture with periodicals, philanthropic and educational organizations, and church sponsorship and women's associations. Each of the leading women's advocates in both Madrid and Barcelona edited her own feminine or feminist magazine (see chapter 5). Because of Catalonia's growing industrialization and the emergence of labour organizations, the concerns of the working class, especially labouring women, were more evident and of great concern to middle-class feminists in Barcelona. Among the most visible names to collaborate in the creation of Catalan feminism were Ángeles López de Ayala (see chapter 5), Josefa Massanés Dalmau, and Dolors Monserdà de Macià. The latter two women, from different generations, contributed fundamentally to the development of Catalan nationalism and "Catholic feminism" through their writings, promoting education for women and conservative feminism within the context of the church. A contemporary of Gómez de Avellaneda, Massanés differed from her in her lifestyle and subject matter. Two generations later, Dolors Monserdà de Macià, a few years younger than Castro and older than Pardo Bazán, shared with the latter contacts in the press and membership in sociopolitical organizations, such as La Unión Iberoamericana (The Ibero-American Union).

Close in age to Gómez de Avellaneda, Josefa Massanés Dalmau, in Catalan "Josepa Massanés i Dalmau" (1811–87), lived principally in Barcelona where she wrote poetry, plays, and essays in Spanish until 1859, when she adopted Catalan as the language of her creative expression. As did most women in the mid-nineteenth century, she initiated her literary career by writing poetry that appeared earlier than that of her contemporary Avellaneda, or Coronado, although it garnered less visibility outside Barcelona, where her work received tributes. Catalonia's Jocs Florals (Floral Games), resuscitated in 1859, named her queen in 1862. In the "Discurso preliminar" (Opening remarks) to her 1841 collection of poems, *Poesías*, she defends public education for women and invokes their "intellectual emancipation" (Kirkpatrick 1989, 281). She participated in the newly revived Jocs Florals and began to contribute literary pieces in Catalan to Barcelona newspapers and magazines. Starting in 1869, she actively addressed what was emerging as one of the pillars of Spanish feminism: the necessity of a solid education for women at all levels. She opened a school for daughters of Barcelona's upper-middle class, trading on her literary fame and pressured by the need to support her family after her military husband lost his position following the 1868 Revolution. A contributor to important women's periodicals in Madrid and Barcelona, Massanés was the leading representative of conservative, morally grounded feminism in Barcelona at midcentury. She seems to embody Scanlon's apposite observation that "fueron las mujeres de Cataluña, región de un considerable desarrollo comercial e industrial, las que se distinguieron constantemente en el siglo XIX por su seriedad, sentido práctico, y por su intervención en los asuntos de negocios y en la vida pública" (Scanlon 1986, 6; it was the women from Catalonia, a region with considerable commercial and industrial development, who constantly distinguished themselves in the nineteenth century for their seriousness, their practical sense, and for their participation in business matters and public life).

More than thirty years later, another Barcelona author, Dolors Monserdà de Macià, or Dolors Monserdà i Vidal de Macià (1845–1919), a leading figure in the first generation of the women's movement in Catalonia, whom Maria Aurèlia Capmany described as "the Right's social conscience" (1973, 33), gave voice to the conservative feminism of the Barcelona middle class in the last half of the long nineteenth century. A near contemporary of Rosario de Acuña, Pardo Bazán, and Gimeno de Flaquer, Monserdà started writing poetry, plays, and essays in Catalan after 1875. The recipient of awards for her poetry in several of the Jocs Florals, she broke tradition with her appointment as their first female president in 1909. As a journalist, she coedited the Barcelona periodical *La Ilustración de la Mujer* (The enlightenment of women) from 1883 to 1885 (see chapter 11) and later contributed to the newspaper *La Renaixença* (The renaissance) and the magazine *Feminal* (For women; 1907–17), edited by Carme Karr, a feminist from a younger generation (see chapter 11). As a playwright, Monserdà had at least two plays staged, but their public success aroused her husband's opposition.[30] She continued to write on urban women's moral, social, and economic conditions, identifying the need for moral reform in social and marital relations (Bieder 1994b, 246). She opined that the role of the bourgeois woman was to protect working-class women through individual and collective initiatives that reinforced their moral behaviour and kept them from adopting the radical ideas propagated by the labour movements. After 1890, she dramatized her feminist thought in novels that culminated in her best-known work, *La fabricanta* (The woman factory owner; 1904), which centred on a middle-class woman's making a place for herself in an industrial family in Barcelona. The protagonist models bourgeois capitalism, but with her factory's financial future assured, the same set of values forces her to abandon the hard work in which "la seva veu i el seu vot hi eren sempre imprescindibles" (Carbonell 1997, 26; her word and her vote were always indispensable), and to accept the totally passive role for middle-class women of bourgeois well-being that displays her newly established wealth.

Moral in orientation, Monserdà's work adopted a realist model within a religious framework. After her husband's death in 1899, she engaged more controversial social questions, among them women's participation in events of the 1909 Setmana Tràgica (Tragic Week). Witness to the changing philosophy about women's roles in society, she wrote some of the earliest treatises on Catalan feminism: *El feminisme a Catalunya* (Catalan feminism; 1907) and *Estudi feminista, orientacions per la dona catalana* (A feminist study, suggestions for the Catalan woman; 1909). Honouring the tradition that shaped her, at the end of her life she wrote a biography of Massanés, *Biografía de Mª Josepa Massanés i Dalmau* (1917).

The Galician intellectual Concepción Arenal (1820–93) is known in Spain today as an "escritora española pionera" (pioneer Spanish woman writer) in the nineteenth-century feminist movement and "la madre del feminismo español" ("Concepción Arenal" 2015; the mother of Spanish feminism). Her aspirations for women differed from those of later Spanish feminists; but her activities and thought were distinctly advanced for her day, and her personal life embodied many aspects of a liberated woman, both before and after she was widowed. She acquired a level of education that very few Spanish women of her day attained. The paradigmatic episode of her life still resonates with critics today – her dressing in men's clothing in order to attend lectures in the University of Madrid Law School in an era long before the university admitted female students or allowed women to attend classes. Unfortunately, as María José Lacalzada maintains, no evidence for this classroom cross-dressing exists, although it is firmly entrenched in popular culture as Arenal's defining act (2012, 71–2). Arenal formulated her ideas so intelligently, both in person and in her writing across a range of subjects, that many people believed her to have obtained some level of university education. In either case, she used her legal knowledge, whether autodidactic or classroom imparted, to argue for the rights of the oppressed and the marginalized, including prisoners and working-class women. Pardo Bazán reports another episode that gave Arenal direct access to exclusively male public culture, again featuring men's clothing: "El traje masculino que la eminente pensadora vistió en su juventud y con el cual se la veía todas las noches en el café del *Iris*, dedicada a escuchar la instructiva conversación de los literatos y hombres políticos" (1981a, 183; The masculine dress that the eminent thinker wore in her youth and with which she was seen every evening in the Iris Café, intent on listening to the instructive conversation of [male] literary figures and politicians). Arenal similarly rejected conventional marriage; she and her husband considered themselves equal partners, who both provided for their family through their writings (Kirkpatrick 1989, 280).

The three major works in Arenal's vast output – *La mujer del porvenir* (The woman of the future), *La mujer de su casa* (The woman of her house), and *El estado actual de la mujer en España* (The current state of women in Spain) – develop her position on the situation of Spanish women, their characteristics, and society's opinion of them. She also published books on women's education, women's work, social and political equality, and the social inequality between men and women, among many other topics. In Arenal's verdict, her tomes were "libros impresos, pero no leídos" (Pardo Bazán 1981a, 186; books that were printed, but not read). Nevertheless, she achieved a broader social vision and garnered greater credibility and respect than any other contemporary woman. She was also very much a woman of her time in positing conformity, rather than radical social reform, within the parameters of the law. Her critiques of Spanish society addressed its vision of women and their morality, and argued forcefully for the need to improve women's education, with special attention to the working classes.

The great social question of women, as Arenal called feminism, was only one of her many social engagements that centred on the moral state and educational opportunities for women leading to their employment, self-respect, and possible self-sufficiency. Lacalzada characterizes Arenal's mind as "ilustrado-liberal con sensibilidad cristiana reformista" (enlightened-liberal with a reformist Christian sensibility) and specifies three areas to which she productively contributed: radical humanism, organic liberalism, and Christian ecumenism (2012, 483). Following the early death of her husband in 1857, Arenal worked for prison reform and women's education for all classes, as did her Catalan contemporary, Massanés. Appointed Visitor of the Women's Prison in La Coruña, Galicia, in 1863, Arenal, one of the earliest women to hold a government position, was removed two years later. However, the Spanish government later named her the first female national Inspector of Women's Prisons (1868–73). Over the years, she assiduously contributed to newspapers and journals, laying out her position on issues in a prolific stream of articles, especially as cofounder, with the Condesa de Espoz y Mina, and editor of the long-running journal *La Voz de la Caridad* (The voice of charity) from 1871 until her death. As did many women writers in the long nineteenth century, Arenal founded and edited a journal that communicated her thinking on women. In Lacalzada's view, Arenal's intellectual, political, and social ties linked her to an older generation, where she found her early supporters among those who had fought for a liberal revolution against absolutism and religious obscurantism (2012, 427). She and Gómez de Avellaneda, for example, shared a mutual admiration, now largely forgotten, that led the latter to contribute financially to several of Arenal's causes and leave a legacy for another in her will (Simón Palmer 2014, 3, 5).

In her book *La mujer del porvenir* (1868, written in 1861), Arenal approached the woman question by attempting to "desvanecer los errores que existen con respecto a la mujer" (1974b, 105; dispel the errors that exist about women). Seeking to imbue women with a sense of their own worth, "trataba con su libro de despertar la conciencia de dignidad en la mujer, como persona" (Lacalzada 2012, 233; with her book she tried to awaken a woman's consciousness of personal dignity as a person). Arenal understood the necessity of inculcating women's self-respect and of preparing them to contribute morally and financially to the family and the community. She grounded her book on the premise of the equality of men and women, while nevertheless proclaiming women's moral superiority: "No es posible desconocer la superioridad moral de la mujer" (Arenal 1974b, 116, 184; It is impossible not to recognize women's moral superiority).[31] Since civil laws considered a married woman a minor and, if not married, "le niegan muchos de los derechos concedidos al hombre" (1974b, 104; they deny her many of the rights given to men), she favours granting all civil rights to women. She also supports admitting women to "todas las profesiones y oficios que no repugnen a su natural dulzura" (185; all professions and trades that are not repugnant to her natural gentleness), but she firmly opposes the exercise of authority by women (162). Thus she stipulates the exclusion of women from judgeships, which might "provocar una lucha continua entre su deber y su corazón" (161; provoke a continual struggle between her duty and her heart); the military, "tan antipática a su natural sensibilidad y compasión" (161; so opposed to her intrinsic sensitivity and compassion); and politics or any form of political activity, because of its militant nature (164). Despite promoting women's education and employment opportunities, she defines "woman's mission" as peace and her role as to aid those who suffer (164). In sum, Arenal does not defend women's emancipation and neatly sidesteps the issue by professing that the concept lacks a clear definition (185).

Arenal's later book, *La mujer de su casa* (1883), reformulates her theories about women and society, laying bare "la evolución y transformación de sus ideas" (Pardo Bazán 1981a, 185; the evolution and transformation of her ideas). She announces a fundamental change in her thinking: "Debemos declarar que hoy no abrigamos aquel íntimo convencimiento de la igualdad de inteligencia de los dos sexos" (Arenal 1974c, 269; We must declare that today we do not hold that personal conviction of the equality of intelligence of the two sexes). The positive force of the new book comes from its resounding attack on the feminine ideal widely espoused in her day, the Angel of the House or, in Arenal's phrase, *la mujer de su casa*. She wryly states that the model of female perfection in a feudal castle is absolutely wrongheaded for a citizen of a modern nation, "que es o tiene la pretensión de ser libre, y que necesita libertad" (1974c, 199–200; who is or desires to be free and who needs freedom). The false ideal of the woman of her house "señala el bien donde no está"(1974c, 202; identifies goodness where it is not).

Pardo Bazán summarized Arenal's thinking about women in her essay written when the author died, "Concepción Arenal y sus ideas acerca de la mujer": "Tiene por objeto reclamar la acción directa de la mujer en la sociedad, reconociendo que no debe hallarse privada de derechos políticos, y que hasta en la guerra, y no en los hospitales, sino en el terreno estratégico, donde brilla el genio militar puede prestar servicios tan eminentes" (1981a, 189; It has as its object to demand direct action for women in society, recognizing that they should not find themselves deprived of political rights, and that even in war, and not in hospitals but in the strategic arena, where military genius shines, they can provide such eminent services).

Scanlon opines that Arenal's two books, together with Sofía Tartilán's *Páginas para la educación popular* (1877; Pages on popular education) constitute "la denuncia más clara de la educación tradicional de la mujer" (1986, 22–3; the clearest denunciation of traditional women's education). Like many other spokeswomen of her day, Arenal placed education for women leading to individual freedom and employment ahead of other feminist vindications, seeking to release women from their indentured roles in the family, from the authority of institutions, and from debt. Scanlon argues that conditions in Spain did not produce a demand for educated women, did not require their presence in the workforce, and lacked the requisite economic pressure to provide even a basic education for women (1986, 5). When Arenal lauds the consecrated ideal of womanhood, which requires preparing women to be good mothers, she incorporates a twist into her argument, touting the equal need to prepare men for fatherhood, an egalitarian concept that Pardo Bazán judges "un punto de vista tan nuevo como profundo" (1981a, 193; a viewpoint as new as it is profound). Throughout Arenal's life, women's emancipation continued to lie beyond the outer limits of her feminist thinking.

In 1884 Edward Stanton's international anthology *The Woman Question in Europe: A Series of Original Essays* invited Arenal's report on the present situation of Spanish women. The Spanish version of her essay "Estado actual de la mujer en España" appeared in 1895, following her death, in the prestigious Madrid cultural review *La España Moderna* (Modern Spain). Arenal speaks forthrightly against the clergy, whom she characterizes as generally ignorant: "No quiere la mujer instruida, y por inclinación, por instinto o por cálculo, es mejor auxiliar para mantenerla en la ignorancia que para instruirla" (1895, 69; They do not want women educated, and by inclination, by instinct, or by calculation, they are better at helping to keep her in ignorance than at educating her). When Arenal critiques the words of St Paul, frequently cited to justify denying an education to women, she finds it necessary first to establish her religious credentials as a respectful Catholic. After affirming that no one has more "cariño y respeto y entusiasmo" (affection, respect, and enthusiasm) for the Apostle than she, she pointedly comments that things have changed in nearly two millennia, and that his "preceptos y consejos respecto a la mujer fueron un progreso en su época, pero se quedan atrás en la nuestra" (1895, 74; precepts and counsel regarding women represented progress in his era, but they are outdated in ours). She makes no reference to the church's control of education in Spain, but she contends that religion has "escasa influencia moral en la mujer española" (1895, 68; little moral influence on Spanish women) and is often an obstacle to her improvement, rather than a positive force. Lacalzada opines that Arenal thought and acted for herself, hence "no vivía precisamente sometida a las directrices ortodoxas" (2012, 24; did not live exactly in submission to orthodox directives).

One of Arenal's strengths was her willingness to reconsider her position and acknowledge changes in her thinking. She worked for new forms of employment for petit bourgeois women and for entry into the professions for bourgeois women, but she drew the line at a woman occupying a judgeship, which seemed too conflictive a role for women. Ultimately, however, she changed her opinion and confessed to having given too much attention to "los prejuicios convencionales" (Scanlon 1986, 75; commonplace prejudices). Pardo Bazán expressed admiration for her compatriot but referenced her "curiosa evolución" (curious evolution) and pinpointed the weaknesses in her evaluation of women: "La exclusión de ciertas profesiones, como la judicatura; la negación de ciertos derechos, los derechos políticos, eran cosas, no pensadas, sino sentidas, lirismos de un corazón que, sin advertirlo, soñaba todavía a la mujer con aureola, nimbo y vara de azucenas en la mano" (1981a, 185; The exclusion of certain professions, like the judiciary; the denial of certain rights, political rights, were things not thought through but felt, lyricisms of a heart that, without realizing it, dreamed of woman with an aureole, halo, and spray of lilies in her hand). She further distanced herself from Arenal's attitude towards marriage, recognizing a similar idealization and viewing her as "una apologista y una idealizadora de la institución del matrimonio" (1981a, 131; an apologist and idealizer of the institution of marriage). Since their personal experience of marriage differed markedly, Pardo Bazán recorded somewhat satirically that for Arenal marriage was "una institución admirable, perfectible" (an admirable, perfectible institution), although she may have come to agree with Arenal that this was possible "cuando se realiza entre dos seres iguales en cultura" (183; when it takes place between two people with a comparable cultural formation).

The belief in women's moral superiority was an article of faith in early Spanish protofeminisms of different stripes and a cornerstone of the philosophy of most early Spanish women with feminist aspirations.

Moral superiority garnered women social approbation and granted them their only advantage over men, one which endorsed their right to speak out and seek change. Arenal did not abandon the basic tenet of treatises on women that defined motherhood as their mission in life; at the same time, she insisted on improving and extending education for women to pave a more fulfilling and economically sound future for them.

The turmoil that engulfed Spain following the 1868 Revolution resulted in multiple short-lived political regimes, followed by the Bourbon Restoration, and left insurmountable political, class, and regional divisions to fester, as chapter 7 details. Pardo Bazán laid the responsibility for Spain's contemporary social and legal practices regarding women on the historical context that shaped their current position: "En efecto, la burguesía, que hizo las revoluciones políticas, no las hizo sino para el varón: ... antes de ellas [la mujer] no era tan inferior al hombre" (2010a, 262; Effectively, the bourgeoisie, who launched the political revolutions, did so only for men: ... before the revolutions [women] were not as inferior to men). At the same time, she also confirmed that it was men in the first place who sought the feminist movement's "reivindicación de los derechos de la mujer" (261; vindication of the rights of women), men being the gender with political and economic power. The 1870s onward were not, however, a propitious climate in which to promulgate or implement a feminist agenda. As middle-class society imposed more self-regulation, it became less open to new ideas and practices. In 1902, Pardo Bazán held the middle classes responsible for the failure of feminism to take root in Spain, opining that if the project were left to the bourgeoisie, the slavery of women would remain in place (262). Why has the (male) bourgeoisie deprived women of their political rights, and even many civil rights, she queries. Why this obstinance, when women are a basically conservative part of society and hence present no threat to the bourgeois status quo (262)?

Nevertheless, feminist thought slowly came into its own in two interrelated forms in the last three decades of the long century: One, a conservative, Catholic-inflected (high) bourgeois feminism grounded in religion, social cohesion, and moral integrity, together with a mission to improve the social, moral, and economic conditions of working-class women. The other, a liberal bourgeois feminism that broke with or ignored the impediments of Catholicism in seeking legal and economic rights for all women, regardless of class or social consequences in a conformist society. Small numbers of both men and women, especially intellectuals, adopted this second approach, although as Arenal sternly remarked, espousing this view in public and actually putting it into practice in one's own life were not necessarily synonymous (1895, 75). The generation of women who emerged in print by the late 1870s defined themselves in one of these categories. Although Arenal died in 1893, many of the younger generation of more overt feminists lived to the end of the long nineteenth century, some becoming more liberal over time, or, in the case of Pardo Bazán, more open and forthright about their feminism. By the early 1900s, a third generation of women began to apply their intellectual activity and feminist commitments to social action, taking Spanish feminism in a new direction (see chapter 12).

11 Forging a Nation for the Female Sex: Equality, Natural Law, and Citizenship in Spanish Feminist Essays, 1881–1920

CHRISTINE ARKINSTALL

Late nineteenth- and early twentieth-century Barcelona and Valencia were undoubtedly major crucibles for progressive feminist writings and activities. Factors that contributed to this strong awareness of feminist issues were Catalonia's history of independence claims; its distinctive legal system, which gave women greater property rights than elsewhere in Spain; rapid industrialization; and the marked presence of an educated, urban, liberal middle class aligned with freethinking and working-class movements.[32] While chapters 10 and 12 address significant Catalan feminist writers, this essay focuses on feminist periodicals founded in Barcelona and Valencia, their principal themes, and their links with international feminisms. It also examines articles published in the freethinking press in the 1880s by one of Spain's foremost intellectuals, Rosario de Acuña, and her use of natural law to further feminist claims. The themes that emerge in these specific periodicals – whose female contributors came from many parts of Spain – and in Acuña's essays demonstrate that their concerns converge with the broader mosaic of feminist thought in Spain outlined thus far, but now with more daring pretensions and forceful arguments for women's greater involvement in the public sphere and the nation's affairs.

One of the most fascinating periodicals of feminist slant in the early Restoration period was Barcelona's fortnightly *La Ilustración de la Mujer* (The enlightenment of woman; 1 June 1883–15 May 1884), which Josefa Pujol de Collado edited with Gertrudis Gómez de Avellaneda and Dolores Monserdà de Macià under the literary direction of Nicolás Díaz de Benjumea. Far more avant-garde than its earlier Madrid counterpart of the same title, its twenty-four issues with consecutive pagination published contributions from fifteen female and twenty male writers.[33] The editorials are of particular interest for gauging the temperature of feminist claims. While only two are signed – the very first by "La Redacción" (The editorial board) and another by Díaz de Benjumea – their invariably daring defence of female equality and rights suggests that they were written by the periodical's three female editors.

The first such essay, "Nuestro programa" (Our program), sets out the publication's mission: to defend women's right to the development of their reason. While the justification given is woman's role in the family and society, and the need to provide her with the means of earning her living should she be left a widow, the article also defends women's right of access to all professions. Here the principle of women's right to work not only affirms an individualist feminism sanctioned under the mantle of their relationships with others. Enlightened education also constituted a vital step in women's pursuit of citizenship, because "both egalitarianism and liberalism entertain, from their inception, an explicit connection between citizenship and the ability to engage in publicly defined labouring relations" (Gatens 1991, 25). The constant theme of women's education in the periodical demonstrates its greater presence in liberal public awareness influenced by Krausist thought and the successive measures taken in the 1870s and 1880s to establish for women schools of commerce and postal services, and hold librarian courses and pedagogical conferences (Caballé 2013, 120–2). The essay refutes woman's alleged intellectual inferiority, because history has shown that women can surpass men in all spheres, and negates that educating women will denaturalize them. Affirming that the mission of the press is to contribute to women's social redemption, the piece avers that now that the French Revolution has proclaimed men's rights, it must also affirm women's.[34]

Romantic idealizations of woman are rejected in several lead articles. In an early call for female suffrage, "O votos o rejas" (Either votes or barred windows), negates that the movement for women's emancipation is a utopia or madness by calling on historical evidence and common sense to affirm the contrary. The ideals of angel and sylph, the author maintains, are rooted in a cultural imaginary derived from urban modernity rather than from class-informed realities.[35] A later essay, "La inteligencia y el corazón" (Intelligence and the heart), rejects woman as romantic angel because she upholds an unnatural cultural division between "feminine" sentiment and "masculine" thought. Noble hearts can only develop from highly educated minds.[36] A frequent theme is the privileging of nurture over nature in the construction of femininity and masculinity. Hence "La mano izquierda" (The left hand) describes women's cultural inferiority in terms of the repudiated left hand that must be rehabilitated for both hands to function equally well: "Justamente en el período en que la mujer reclama sus derechos, se presenta la mano izquierda haciendo valer los suyos ... a intervenir en los actos de la vida, proclamándose para esto tan capaz como su compañera" (Just when women are claiming their rights, the left hand comes forward ... to intervene in life's actions, asserting that it is as able as its companion).[37] Likewise "Las preocupaciones" (Concerns) vindicates women's equal intellectual capacity and criticizes regressive laws responsible for their inadequate education and the misconception that they are unsuited to certain realms of knowledge. In a statement that resembles Acuña's ethos, the essay declares that education will give women back their "naturaleza íntegra" (whole nature).[38]

Several essays address head on the subject of domestic work and the need to uncouple it from woman's culturally assigned roles. "Mujeres hacendosas" (Industrious women) indicates that, with the invention of the machine, educated women should relinquish mechanical household tasks and dedicate themselves to work more fitting to intelligent individuals.[39] "Puerilidades" (Childish acts) even advocates for equal distribution of work in the home, so that women have time to educate themselves and understand their mission in society: "También el hombre debe ocuparse en aquellos trabajos que por capricho y no por razón fundada se han pensado de la exclusiva competencia de la mujer" (Men must also participate in those tasks that, due to whim and not well-founded reasons, have been thought exclusive to women).[40]

The role of women in marriage is another focus of attention. "El santo matrimonio" (Holy matrimony) refutes the pagan and romantic concepts of woman as slave and goddess respectively in favour of a rational, enlightened female companion who will regenerate marriage and counter its current disrepute.[41] In "¡La compañera!" (The female companion), the reduction of marriage to an economic affair and the ideal of the ignorant *perfecta casada* (perfect spouse) enslaved to her husband are rejected to support women's equal intellectual cultivation, the "neutral sphere" where gender differences disappear. At present, the essay denounces, marriage is a business company in which the wife is the "socia durmiente" (sleeping partner) and "en la parte civil ... una especie de nulidad" (a civil nonentity): women do not possess the same juridical rights as their husbands to effect contracts, nor do they have the same freedom as their partner to work and move in the public sphere.[42] By taking to its furthest consequences the concept of marriage as an unequal economic contract, the argument shifts marriage from the private sphere to the public arena.

Lead essays also constantly compare Spain with more progressive countries so as to counter prejudice with statistical proof. Thus, on debating women's right to participate in all professions, "El justo medio" (A happy medium) praises England for admitting women to careers in pharmacy and the public service, and censures the Spanish government for considering that only men make up the state. Other nations show how women's participation in male-dominated professions is not incompatible with their decorum. Indeed, the article claims, eliminating men's monopoly on professions will guarantee a nation's moral fibre.[43]

Especially noteworthy is the regular reporting on activities in Spain and Europe that support women's rights and indicate a burgeoning female associationism. Thus "¡Adelante!" (Onward!) privileges the forthcoming Congreso Femenino Nacional (National Women's Conference) in Palma de Mallorca and lauds women's efforts to advance their emancipation through associationism, which enables them to overcome their isolation and a normative modesty to assert their rights. The conference's manifesto demonstrates, the article opines, that Spanish women also possess foreign women's "ánimo viril" (virile character) and argues for the compatibility of femininity with feminism: "Se puede ser hermosa y tener seso, y sobre todo, cuidar de sus derechos y hacer valer su personalidad, para salir de la categoría de mueble de adorno, animal de recreo o bestia de carga, que es a lo que viene a parar ... la mujer que se anula política y civilmente" (A woman can be beautiful and still have brains, and above all, look after her rights and assert her talents, so as no longer to occupy the category of ornamental furniture, recreational animal, or beast of burden, which is the fate of ... the woman annulled in political and civil terms).[44]

Like María del Pilar Sinués's earlier *Galería de mujeres célebres* (Gallery of famous women; 1864–9), each issue of *La Ilustración* featured a "Galería de mujeres notables," dedicated to national and international nineteenth-century female writers (nine), stage artists (twelve), a doctor, and a traveller. While Benjumea writes most, after his death on 8 March 1884 Pujol de Collado pens several. When aristocratic writers are featured, such as Princess María de la Paz Borbón and Paulina Isabel of Rumania ("Carmen Silva"), attention focuses on the former's literary talents and on the latter's support of women's emancipation.[45]

Especially interesting is the piece on Pujol de Collado herself ("Evelio del Monte"), who began to write under her own name when she became editor of Barcelona's *El Parthenón* (The Parthenon). Renowned for her Hellenism and welcomed into the Academia Gaditana de Buenas Letras (Cádiz Academy of Letters), she wrote a *Galería de mujeres ilustres* (Gallery of learned women) on Greek and Roman women and many novels, and directed the weekly *Flores y Perlas* (Flowers and pearls).[46] Many of these biographical notes stress that writing is not incompatible with an exemplary femininity. Thus María Josefa Massanés (see also chapter 10) is "tan consumada en el manejo de la aguja como en el de la pluma" (as skilled in using her needle as her pen); María Mendoza de Vives is not only a "distinguida poetisa" (distinguished poet) but also an "amante esposa y cariñosa madre" (loving spouse and affectionate mother); and Elisa Curado ("Elisa Caodur"), the Portuguese campaigner for women's rights and founder in 1883 of the periodical *A Mulher* (Woman), is an award-winning writer and model daughter, mother, and wife.[47]

Minority, antihegemonic movements such as freethinking, freemasonry, republicanism, spiritism, socialism, and anarchism also brought great impetus to feminist claims in Restoration Spain. Many of the women who wrote on feminist themes came together in the associations and circles linked to these movements and disseminated their ideas in freethinking periodicals.[48] One of the longest running was Barcelona's spiritist, anticlerical weekly with consecutive pagination, *La Luz del Porvenir* (The light of the future; 1879–94). Founded and edited by Amalia Domingo Soler, *La Luz* served as a crucible for female contributors to debate women's part in a progressive society and was a worthy inheritor of the heterodox ideas that *La Buena Nueva* had promulgated just prior to the 1868 Revolution.[49] As a point of comparison with Barcelona's *La Ilustración de la Mujer* and Acuña's ideas, I examine essays published from 1884 to 1888.

An important strand, equally present in *La Ilustración*, was the denial of the incompatibility of "masculine" reason with "feminine" emotion. These gendered, hierarchical concepts are challenged in Cándida Sanz de Castellví's essay "Paralelo entre el claustro y el hogar" (Comparison between the cloister and the home), which stresses the interdependence of sensibility and ideas.[50] Just as feeling is vital for nourishing ideas, so too is knowledge essential for developing noble sentiments in the daughter, wife, and mother (15–16). Deploying socialist language, the article casts the home as the "gran taller de su progreso" (16; great workshop for women's progress) and the wife and mother as "una de las principales obreras de la civilización" (16; one of civilization's foremost workers). Domestic work and reproduction are valued similarly to work in the public sphere of production to contest the inequality in the private/public division and reframe conventional paradigms. Palmira G.'s "La misión de la mujer" (Woman's mission) likewise affirms that like man, woman is both "sentimental y racional" (255; sentimental and rational) and should be his equal, a "co-redentor social" (co-redeemer of society) and "corredentora de su hogar" (coredeemer of the home). Again the essay underlines how gender and class are intertwined on comparing man's domestic confinement of woman to the relationship between lord and serf.[51] An alternative opinion, representative of the inclusive nature of the periodical, is that of Dolores Navas, who considers that women's authority lies in their superior sensitivity.[52]

Unlike *La Ilustración de la Mujer*, however, female-authored essays in *La Luz* did not reject the figure of the Angel in the House but insistently reworked this conservative symbol to give her a greatly extended sphere of influence and underscore the inseparability of home from nation. Thus in "Necesidad apremiante" (Urgent necessity), Domingo Soler asserts that the secularly educated woman is "el ángel del hogar, y es la que influye poderosamente en las costumbres y en la prosperidad de las naciones" (114; the Angel in the House and she who exerts a powerful influence on customs and the prosperity of nations).[53] Isabel Peña from Cádiz affirms a similarly transcendental purpose in "La mujer" (Woman): education transforms woman from "ángel del hogar" (191; Angel in the House) into the "gran obrero de la reforma social" (great worker of social reform). The adaptation of religious discourse to feminist aspirations is stressed in the pronouncement that the highly educated woman effects "la regeneración del mundo" (192; the world's regeneration) as "digna sacerdotisa del hogar" (worthy priestess of the home).[54] Likewise in "La mujer en los tiempos modernos" (Woman in modern times), Pujol de Collado affirms that women's work within the domestic sphere affects all humanity.[55] Such pronouncements echo the discourse that other contemporary European and North American feminists were promulgating, namely, that women's moral gifts and duties, honed in the home, would be especially beneficial in the political world (Okin 1998, 123).

In 1896, the same year that Domingo Soler exclaimed that "el movimiento feminista iniciado en las postrimerías del siglo XIX augura para el siglo XX una verdadera revolución social" (the feminist movement inaugurated in the fin de siècle promises a true social revolution in the twentieth century),[56] Belén Sárraga and Amalia Carvia, in collaboration with Catalonia's foremost feminist Ángeles López de Ayala (Sánchez Ferré 1998, 6), established another influential freethinking periodical, *La Conciencia Libre* (Freedom of conscience), which regularly published feminist columns until its demise in 1907.[57] Their contemporary, anarchist Teresa Mañé ("Soledad Gustavo"), published alongside them in *Las Dominicales del Libre Pensamiento* (The Sunday periodical for free thought), while also typical of the increasingly strong feminist voices in fin de siècle Spain was Concepción Sáiz de Otero's 1897 essay "El feminismo en España" (Feminism in Spain) (see Sáiz de Otero 1998).[58]

Significantly, the late 1880s saw established the first feminist-oriented associations. In 1889, López de Ayala, Domingo Soler, and anarchist Teresa Claramunt founded Barcelona's Sociedad Autónoma de Mujeres (Autonomous Society for Women), which in 1898 became the Sociedad Progresiva Femenina (Progressive Women's Society). Engaged with international feminist organizations and conferences from the mid-1890s and active till at least 1919, this organization, under López de Ayala's leadership, had the greatest impact of all Spanish freethinking feminist bodies (Ramos 1999, 104).[59] Its mouthpieces were the periodicals that López de Ayala founded and directed: *El Gladiador: Órgano de la "Sociedad Progresiva Femenina"* (The gladiator: Mouthpiece for the Progressive Women's Society; 1906–9), *El Libertador: Periódico Defensor de la Mujer y Órgano Nacional del Libre-Pensamiento* (The liberator: Periodical in defence of woman and national mouthpiece for freethinking; 1910–14), and *El Gladiador del Librepensamiento: Órgano de la Federación Librepensadora de Barcelona y otros Pueblos Adheridos* (The gladiator for freethinking: Mouthpiece of the freethinking federation of Barcelona and other associated towns; 1914–20). In 1897, Sárraga and Ana Carvia y Bernal followed suit on founding the Asociación General Femenina (Association for All Women) in Valencia, which soon had branches in Catalonia and Andalusia. These associations anticipated by several decades the establishment in Madrid in April 1918 of the Asociación Nacional de Mujeres Españolas (ANME; National Association of Spanish Women].[60] Other feminist associations briefly active in Barcelona and Madrid were the more middle-class Damas Radicales (Radical ladies; 1909) and the Damas Rojas (Red ladies; 1909–11). Associated with the Radical Republican Party and with strong working-class participation, the latter was cofounded by Consuelo Álvarez ("Violeta," 1866–1957), who collaborated closely with Burgos (see Moral 2007).

While Mary Nash cautions against linking fin de siècle Spanish feminisms exclusively to female suffrage (1994, 153–63), a telling indication that female suffrage was on feminist agendas before the turn of the century was Sárraga's substantial essay, "La mujer ante el progreso social" (Woman and social progress), published in *La Luz* in 1895.[61] Attacking a legal system that does not protect women's natural rights, Sárraga upholds secular education as key to women's reclaiming their rights and eventually their status as full citizens through universal suffrage.[62] Demand for female suffrage was behind the most important feminist meeting of the Restoration period: the demonstration that López de Ayala organized in Barcelona on 10 July 1910 – and in which some twenty thousand Catalan women of all classes participated – to call for the revision of article 11 of the Constitution (Ramos 1999, 106; Méndez 1922, 389). In May 1917, she organized another major feminist demonstration, for which Acuña wrote a powerful speech in support of the "feminist problem" and envisaged a future matriarchy in the wake of World War I's carnage.[63]

Although all the periodicals that López de Ayala headed carried feminist contributions, such content increased markedly in *El Gladiador del Librepensamiento*, partially due to the influence of World War I (see González Calbet 1988, 51). One important article, "¿Más privilegios?" (More privileges?), which López de Ayala published in October 1919, highlights divisions within Spanish feminisms over whether female suffrage should be universal or restricted to educated women. López de Ayala stresses that the premises of reason and equality demand universal female suffrage, even if it initially undermines the freethinking cause. This issue had already surfaced in October 1906, when Burgos had publicly supported restricting suffrage to educated women (Fagoaga 1985, 93–100, 117), and foreshadows the contrasting positions that Clara Campoamor and Margarita Nelken would defend in 1931.[64]

Publishing on aligned themes was one of the most influential feminist writers in fin de siècle Spain, Rosario de Acuña, who inspired López de Ayala and a host of contemporary feminists.[65] Essays of hers that appeared between 1881 and 1888 with publishing houses and periodicals throughout Spain (Madrid, Barcelona, Alicante, and Oviedo) privilege two key issues in relation to women that constituted leitmotifs in nineteenth-century Spanish feminist thought: natural law and the debate regarding emancipation versus liberation.[66] In her 1881 article, "Algo sobre la mujer (apuntes)" (Something on women: notes), Acuña affirms natural law on stating that both sexes were originally perfect and equal. Social engineering, however, may well be responsible for apparent inequalities in skull size and has relegated women to the passivity of irrational beings (2008b, 167–8). Her discussion here recalls Mary Wollstonecraft's contention, as Moira Gatens puts it, that "essentially all human beings start from the same point, all are equally capable of reason, and ... the apparent differences between people and between the sexes are the result of environment and education" (Gatens 1991, 23). Acuña's equation of femininity with passivity also resonates with what Helene Eisenberg sees as a constant threat for women: their "backsliding into 'being,' or female passivity" (quoted in Offen 1988, 149). For Acuña, the further from nature woman becomes, the less equal and rational she is.

Moreover, given that women are already naturally free, in a rhetorical flourish Acuña denies that they are enslaved: "¿Qué es emancipación para quien se tiene por libre? Un mito irrisorio. ... solamente al esclavo se le puede manumitir, y nosotras nunca lo fuimos" (2008b, 169, 179; What is emancipation for those who consider themselves free? An illusory myth. ... only slaves can be freed and we women were never slaves).[67] In what appears to be a regressive statement, Acuña maintains that emancipation will reduce women's unconditional power of influence over men and affirms that women must first develop self-esteem before they can emancipate themselves (173, 178–9).[68] Acuña's fluctuation here between denying the need for emancipation and affirming it parallels the confusion between these terms in French society from 1830 onward, as Geneviève Fraisse highlights. Liberation, bound up with abolitionist discourse, refers to freeing a slave and denotes a political vision, whereas emancipation, used for a minor, is primarily a legal term and refers to equality (Fraisse 2003, 45).

Emancipation is again highlighted in Acuña's 1887 essay "A las mujeres del siglo XIX" (To nineteenth-century women), dedicated to the female contributors of *Las Dominicales del Libre Pensamiento*.[69] There she stresses that the Catholic Church has made women slaves and that freedom is their redemption (2007b, 1227, 1230). Like previously cited female contributors to Barcelona's *La Ilustración* and *La Luz*, Acuña undoes the binary of masculine reason and feminine emotion to tell her female reader that "tan necesario es que tu cerebro *piense* como que *sienta* el corazón masculino" (1233 [emphasis in original]; it is as necessary for your brain to *think* as it is for the male heart to *feel*). The nineteenth century, which recognizes nature's supreme laws, including those of physics and chemistry, has raised women from beast to angel and is the time of women's emancipation (1230, 1240). Acuña apparently not only upholds the immaculate Angel in the House figure but also politicizes her as patrician, thus arguing for a feminization of Spain's masculine nation: "Esta España masculina puede ser inspirada por vuestros sentimientos ... sed las patricias sin mancilla dentro de vuestro hogar" (1237; This masculine Spain can draw inspiration from your sentiments ... be patricians without taint within your homes).[70] She calls on her freethinking sisters to fight with their pens in the "seno" (1239; breast/heart) of society, in an implicit analogy between writing and breastfeeding, culture and motherhood. By seeking to feminize society and politics, Acuña's arguments intersect with similar debates among French feminists such as Hubertine Auclert, who in 1885 sought to "regender" her militaristic nation through the notion of the "motherly state" (Offen 1988, 142).

Natural law returns to the fore in Acuña's 1888 essay "Consecuencias de la degeneración femenina" (Consequences of women's degeneration), first delivered, like many of her pieces, to the Madrid Fomento de las Artes (Promotion of the Arts) in oral form. This prior oral delivery is especially important not only to reach as wide a female audience as possible in a period of high illiteracy levels among women but also because, as Durán indicates, oral messages had great impact, and even more so, I affirm, when delivered by a woman at public gatherings (1993, 23).[71] Given that nature and equality are synonymous, Acuña argues that nature, on endowing the unborn child with "la virtualidad de los dos sexos" (2008c, 512; the virtuality of both sexes), considers sexual determination of secondary importance and leaves it till last in the fetus's development. Social practices, however, violate nature by making woman deformed, inept, ill, ignorant, and cunning (511–14). In fact, Acuña eschews the socially produced *mujercita* (little woman) to replace that term with "entidad femenina"(feminine entity): a vigorous, intellectually wealthy creation of nature (518). Here she arguably challenges Rousseau's notion of man's exclusive "double birth" into nature and then culture (Gatens 1991, 12–13) by stating that woman must be resurrected from a socially induced death and reborn into an enhanced nature through science, philosophy, and morality (Acuña 2008c, 531). Women, she insists, have to effect progressive change for themselves rather than through male champions, given that changes resulting from men's actions will only underline further women's alleged inferiority and inability to act autonomously (515–16).

In another 1888 essay, "Discurso pronunciado en el acto de la instalación de la logia femenina Hijas del Progreso" (Speech on the inauguration of the women's lodge, Daughters of Progress), again first delivered orally, Acuña reiterates that laws, religion, and customs mould women's souls into the "raquíticos destinos de la sierva" (2008d, 563; stunted destinies of the slave). Women's culturally induced idolization of men transforms marriage from a contract between two responsible consciences and free wills into a relationship of servitude and changes women's souls from active to passive (568–73). Given that nature did not limit women's rational faculties, Acuña affirms that they can and must think, refuting the notion that women are bad daughters, wives, and mothers if they exercise rationality. She exhorts women to surrender their will to nature so as to conquer her laws and know her processes. Women's mission is to be not only wives and mothers but also "patricias" (citizens) and members of humanity (577–81). Society's transformation begins by women forging self-esteem, which exceeds an exclusive heterosexual love to expand love's influence into all realms of society (566–70). Hence Acuña arguably attempts to reconcile individualist and relational feminisms, in that while women's emancipation constitutes a personal revolution, it inevitably affects women's broader relationships within the civic and public spheres.

12 First-Wave Feminisms, 1880–1919

MARYELLEN BIEDER

Spain experienced an enhanced interest in feminism during the last decades of the long nineteenth century, which led to a passionate debate about the exact nature of the feminist movement (Scanlon 1986, 197). In his 1899 *Feminismo*, Adolfo González Posada acknowledged that it represented one of the greatest revolutions taking shape in the nineteenth century, defining it as requiring "el cambio de la condición política, doméstica, económica, educativa y moral de la mujer" (1899, 8; change in woman's political, domestic, economic, educational, and moral condition). His analysis of the forms that feminisms took in Spain remained viable into the 1900s: radical, conservative, and Catholic feminisms (1899, 19, 29–32, 38–9). Geraldine Scanlon warns that Spanish feminism never coalesced into a coherent, functional whole, lacking "un desarrollo libre e independiente; fue arrastrado, quizá inevitablemente, al conflicto más general entre la izquierda y la derecha" (1986, 199; a free and independent development; it was dragged, perhaps inevitably, into the more general conflict between left and right). Margarita Nelken reached a similar understanding about Socialist feminism and Catholic feminism, considering them antagonists and, consequently, "un derivado del problema que agita todo el espíritu del país" (1922, 13; a by-product of the problem that destabilizes the whole spirit of the country). Nevertheless, she concluded that feminism "parece haber triunfado ya en idea en nuestro país" (156; seems to have now triumphed as an idea in our country).

The principal Spanish women associated with feminist issues mostly adhered to the conservative model that espoused some rights for women and emphasized the significance to society at large of their unique childbearing and nurturing roles. Many of these conservative feminists were also Catholic feminists, including Gertrudis Gómez de Avellaneda and Concepción Gimeno de Flaquer. Catholic feminism linked women's emancipation with religion (Hibbs-Lissorgues 2008, 335), while radical feminism centred on the thought and action of an individual.[72] Margarita Nelken opined sardonically that Catholic feminism attempted to immobilize Spanish women in the name of defending religious ideals not under attack in contemporary society. For her, it constituted another form of conservative feminism, one that sought to protect women from "las nuevas corrientes" (new currents), always in conjunction with "alguna obra benéfica o educativa" (some beneficent or educational work). Catholic feminism, she asserted, represented "el mayor enemigo en cuanto pueda significar en España evolución y progreso" (1922, 208–9; the greatest enemy as regards everything that signifies evolution and progress in Spain). Barcelona feminists such as Josefa Massanés Dalmau and Dolors Monserdà i Masià forged strong ties to the church, beneficent organizations, and educational activities.

Some of the major feminist voices from the late 1800s continued to resound in the early 1900s as they entered the last decades of their careers: Gimeno de Flaquer (1850–1919) in the first decade of the 1900s, Emilia Pardo Bazán (1851–1921) and Rosario de Acuña (1850–1923)[73] throughout the first two decades. In a younger generation, Carmen de Burgos (1867–1936) launched her career in 1900, as did the Catalan writers Carme Karr d'Alaforetto i Alfonsetti (1865–1943) and Caterina Albert i Paradís (1869–1966). Both generations contributed their thoughts and actions to the creation of a new model for women. Blanca de los Ríos (1859–1956), a close friend of Pardo Bazán, remained a productive scholar and author; although not given to feminist pronouncements, she enlarged the space in literary studies for women scholars. Eva Infanzón Canel (1857–1932), widow of her journalist husband since 1889, continued to live primarily in Cuba and South America where she exemplified feminism's goal of self-sufficiency by earning her livelihood by founding and editing a series of magazines. Pardo Bazán and Acuña remained advocates for radical or individualist feminism, while other women, principal among them Gimeno de Flaquer, gathered around them supporters and fellow female writers, as well as male acolytes, building a moderate feminist band whose numbers reinforced the beliefs of the whole.

The early 1900s witnessed the slow transformation of the Woman Question from wishful-thinking articles in women's magazines and public statements in lectures and books into public displays of action in support of a collective sociopolitical agenda on women. At the core of many of these muted manifestations on controversial issues, such as divorce or women's suffrage, was the journalist Burgos, whose professional pseudonym and trademark "Colombine" accompanied her full name. Pardo Bazán, Gimeno, and later Burgos all strove to position themselves within international feminism not only by reading the periodical press but through travel and attendance at international conferences. They all kept abreast of developments in feminism in England, Italy, the United States, and, especially for Pardo Bazán, France. The contrast between those countries and the situation in Spain served as a stimulus to increased public visibility, especially for the more action-oriented Burgos. Of great significance in the development of feminism in Spain is the fact that illiteracy among women diminished from 90.9% in 1860 to 74.7% in 1900 (Flecha 1996, 65), although in Madrid and Barcelona it was probably closer to 50% by 1900.[74] By 1920 40.5% of Spanish women could read and write (Botrel 1987, 110).

Many of the women who espoused some form of feminist thought closely identified themselves with Catholicism, which provided an affidavit of their moral character. Some like Burgos did so more ambivalently than others, while Acuña repudiated the church. Scanlon signals a core factor in Catholicism's role of retarding the spread of feminism in Spain, due to "la debilidad de la Ilustración española y a la subsiguiente hostilidad de un estrecho conservadurismo católico hacia las doctrinas igualitarias de la Revolución" (Scanlon 1986, 6; to the weakness of the Spanish Enlightenment and the subsequent hostility of a narrow-minded Catholic conservatism to the egalitarian doctrines of the [French] Revolution). She further stresses the extent to which the church delayed development of Spanish feminism because of its preponderant role both as a social institution and through its influence in politics, economics and education (6–7).

Between 1888 and 1921, Spain's most prominent exemplar of radical feminism and its only late nineteenth-century's canonical female author, Emilia Pardo Bazán, positioned women's writing and feminist thought within Spain's literary mainstream, where her works figured alongside those of her prestigious male colleagues. An unwavering proponent of equality feminism, in both her life and her plethora of publications, underlies her pursuit of equal opportunity and treatment on all fronts. Her specifically feminist proclamations are infrequent until the 1890s, because she tended not to separate her entrenched belief in the necessary equality of the sexes from her other writings. Although a practising Catholic and ally of the church in action and in print, especially when under attack, she was also a radical feminist, although she did not espouse divorce or, until very late, the vote for women. Having published a biography of St Francis of Assisi and at some point taken vows as a Third Order Franciscan, she exhibited exceptional religious credentials that allowed her room to deviate from the norm for women in other areas and stake her position in the male-dominated territories of culture and literature. Separated from her husband, in general amicably, she lived with her parents and her children in Madrid, partaking fully of the intellectual, social, and cultural scene, while residing with them in Galicia during the summer and fall.

On commission in 1889, Pardo Bazán penned a series of four essays on "La mujer española" ("The Women of Spain") for the British magazine *The Fortnightly Review*, dividing her treatment into three sections by class: aristocracy, middle class, and *el pueblo* (the working class). Although she originally resisted releasing the essays in Spain, fearing the reading public would find her analysis too unflattering, the Spanish version appeared in the Madrid cultural magazine *La España Moderna* (Modern Spain) the following year. In it she made a harsh allegation about the dismal to nonexistent education for women in Spain: the inevitable result of its shameful educational system. Her speech for the 1892 Congreso Pedagógico (Pedagogical Congress) critiques the goals of the education currently available to women: "No puede, en rigor, la educación general de la mujer, llamarse tal *educación*, sino *doma*, pues se propone por fin la obediencia, la pasividad y la sumisión" (1892, 92; The general education of women cannot, strictly speaking, call itself *education*, but *a breaking in*, since it proposes as its goal obedience, passivity, and submission).

Pardo Bazán's 1886 "Apuntes autobiográficos" (Autobiographical notes) directly addressed the difficulty facing women who desire an education and must acquire it through their own efforts, as she did:

> Apenas pueden los hombres formarse idea de lo difícil que es para una mujer adquirir cultura autodidáctica y llenar los claros de su educación. Los varones, desde que pueden andar y hablar, concurren a las escuelas de instrucción primaria; luego al Instituto, a la Academia, a la Universidad, sin darse punto de reposo, engrana los estudios. ... Todo ventajas, y para la mujer, obstáculos todos. (1886, 38)

> (Men can scarcely form an idea of how difficult it is for a woman to acquire self-taught culture and fill in the blanks in their education. From the moment they can walk and talk, men attend primary school, then the institute, the university, without taking a break, [which] ingrains studies. ... It is all advantages [for men], and for women, all obstacles.)

Literature, as she defined it, however, set no boundaries for women: "En el reino de las letras no hay ... *lado de las mujeres y lado de los hombres*" (1890, x [emphasis in original]; In the kingdom of letters [belles lettres] there is no ... *women's side* and *men's side*), a conviction that guided her actions with greater or lesser success. Pardo Bazán's feminism centred on achieving equal opportunity and education for women and a woman's right to support herself economically, something she herself strove to do with great pride. She proclaimed in an 1889 letter: "Me he propuesto vivir exclusivamente del trabajo literario, sin recibir nada de mis padres" (Pardo Bazán 2013, 114; I have resolved to live exclusively from literary work, without receiving anything from my parents). Her declaration of emancipation relies on her own actions: "En suma he de ser yo misma quien me emancipe" (Pardo Bazán 2013, 119; In short, it is I who will emancipate myself). As Pardo Bazán frequently declared, she learned her unshakeable belief in the necessary equality of the sexes from her father: "Mi padre era muy feminista y me educó en una amplia libertad de conciencia" (*El Caballero Audaz* 1914, 8; My father was very feminist, and he educated me in a broad freedom of conscience). From him she learned to ignore the strictures that, in his words, men, being egotists, placed on women: "Di que es mentira porque no puede haber dos morales para los dos sexos" (*El Caballero Audaz* 1914, 8–9; Say it is a lie because there cannot be two moralities for the two sexes).

Pardo Bazán's deep respect for her father may have shaped her admiration for leading (male) intellectuals, authors, and politicians and led her to expect friendships among equals. She might not agree with Francisco Giner de los Ríos and Emilio Castelar, among others, on all issues, but she valued their friendship and their defence of the rights of women. Her ability to operate on an intellectual plane and recognize common ground with men with whom she could discuss or debate the burning issues of the day carried greater weight for her than her aristocratic connections, her *haute bourgeoisie* social life, or her adherence to and defence of aspects of Catholic dogma, although she was no blind defender of the church or its clergy. Pardo Bazán explicitly defined her concept of feminism when she declared that the famous university professor and liberal educator Giner de los Ríos was "resueltamente feminista" (resolutely feminist): "Todo lo que atañía al mejoramiento de la condición de la mujer le interesaba en el más alto grado" (1915, 273; Everything that had to do with the improvement in women's condition interested him to the highest degree). He fully espoused equal rights for all humanity, without distinction between the sexes (274).

Her attempts to introduce Spanish women to contemporary feminist thought with her careful selection of titles for her Biblioteca de la Mujer (Women's library) series, which did not attract a readership, resulted in disillusionment. Susan Kirkpatrick confirms that "for a vanguard figure, Pardo Bazán was in many ways too far out in front of the mass of Spanish women, as she herself conceded" (2011, 237). In a 1913 letter to a Galician newspaper editor, Pardo Bazán admitted her bitter disappointment over women's lack of interest in gaining an education or thinking for themselves:

> He visto, sin género de duda, que aquí a nadie le preocupan gran cosa tales cuestiones, y a la mujer, aún menos. Cuando, por caso insólito, la mujer española se mezcla en política, pide varias cosas asaz distintas, pero ninguna que directamente, como tal mujer, le interese y convenga. Aquí no hay sufragistas, ni mansas ni bravas. (1962, 279–81)
>
> (I have seen, without the slightest doubt, that here nobody cares much for such questions, and women, even less. When, in a rare case, a Spanish woman gets involved in politics, she asks for various and very different things, but none that directly, as a woman, is of interest to her or in her own interest. Here there are no suffragists, neither tame nor wild.)

Pardo Bazán's most intense feminist activity, the shaping of her radical feminism, transpired between 1889 and 1892, a period that documents her professionalization as a "woman of letters" through the enhanced recognition and prestige derived from her increased contributions to major newspapers and cultural magazines (González Herrán 2008). These densely active years culminated in her becoming "emancipada y autónoma" (González Herrán 2008, 346; emancipated and autonomous.) She was already singlehandedly writing the contents of and would continue to publish monthly for a total of three years her *Nuevo Teatro Critíco* (New critical theatre), a literary and cultural magazine addressed to Spain's intellectuals and which Kirkpatrick considers "a feminist magazine" (2011, 237). By the 1890s, she actively engaged in furthering "important modernizing cultural institutions," collaborating with a financier to found Spain's "leading intellectual journal of her time," *La España Moderna* (237; Modern Spain).

The key corollary of Pardo Bazán's fundamental, life-long belief in the equality of the sexes challenged the prevailing attitude in Spanish society that mandated a woman's relative destiny, a dependency that she attributed to the "instinto colectivo del varón" (1981b, 77; men's collective instinct). She formulated the thesis of women's "destino relativo, subordinado del ajeno" (88; relative destiny, subordinated to that of another [person]) that runs throughout her address to the 1892 Pedagogical Congress on "La educación del hombre y la de la mujer: Las relaciones y diferencias" (The education of men and that of women: Their relationships and differences). Education, she maintains, is the only method for liberating women from subordination to male authority figures, since at present a woman's existence does not revolve around her own life but rather her husband's and her children's, and if they do not exist, then it revolves around "la de la entidad abstracta género masculino" (75; that of the abstract entity [called] male gender). Only education can teach women to reorient the axis of their life to achieve "la dignidad y felicidad propia" (75; their own dignity and happiness). Pardo Bazán assigns the historical emancipation of women's consciousness, including the affirmation of their personality, "su libertad moral" (their moral freedom), and "la libertad práctica" (their practical freedom) to Christianity's emancipation of women "en el interior santuario de la conciencia" (83–4; in the internal sanctuary of their consciousness). Despite this theoretical long-standing freedom, society still imposes a woman's reproductive identity on her life, which "determina y limita las restantes funciones de su actividad humana, quitando a su destino toda significación individual, y no dejándole sino la que puede tener relativamente al destino del varón" (75; determines and limits the remaining functions of her human activity, eliminating from her destiny all individual meaning, and only leaving her that meaning relative to man's destiny). In another essay, Pardo Bazán fundamentally disagrees with the dominance that the discourse on reproductive functions wields in women's lives to the extent that she extends exercise of "libertad individual indiscutible" (Pardo Bazán 1981e, 159; indisputable individual freedom) to the absolute right to celibacy and sterility, that is, a woman's infertility.

The session at the Pedagogical Congress chaired by Pardo Bazán voted two conclusions: (1) It recognized that a woman has her own destiny, that her first duty is to herself, and consequently that she has the same right to an education as men; and (2) It called for immediately granting women free access to "la enseñanza oficial"' (formal state-controlled education) and allowing her to "ejercer las carreras y desempeñar los puestos a que le den opción sus estudios y títulos académicos ganados en buena lid" (1981b, 100; practise the careers and carry out the positions for which her studies and academic titles, competitively and honourably earned, have prepared her). In a personal note, Pardo Bazán defends coeducation, which the church opposes, adding "predico con el ejemplo" (102; I preach by example) – her elder daughter attends a coeducational high school.

In her 1901 speech at the Juegos Florales (Floral games) in Orense, Galicia, Pardo Bazán dialogues with Carolina Coronado's ironic denunciation in her poem "Libertad" that "there is no nation for this sex" by tentatively affirming women's place in the nation: "La patria existe o debe existir para nosotras" (2010b, 314; The nation exists or should exist for us [women]). After critiquing the absence of political rights for women, "a pesar de ser hembra el Jefe de Estado" (314; despite a female being head of state), she asserts: "Hoy nuestra patria necesita de todos, hasta de la mujer, y la mujer necesita valer a la patria, porque la mujer, mantenida a larga distancia de la cultura, ha sido el áncora de peso incalculable que nos aferró a la tradición mal entendida y funesta" (315; Today our country needs everyone, even women, and women need to give value to the country, because women, kept at a long distance from culture, have been the anchor of incalculable weight that bound us to a misunderstood and disastrous tradition).

One of the first feminist vindications enacted by Pardo Bazán, and subsequently by Burgos and de los Ríos, was to enrol in 1905 in Madrid's premier cultural institution, the Ateneo Científico, Literario y Artístico (Scientific, Literary, and Artistic Atheneum), when it first admitted women as members on an equal basis with men. Pardo Bazán valued the intellectual parity that membership implied: "Soy la primera mujer que pisa oficialmente el Ateneo ... y esto es para mí una de las mayores satisfacciones que he recibido" (El Abate 1905, 7; I am the first woman to enter the Atheneum in an official capacity ... and this is for me one of the greatest satisfactions that I have received). The newspaper *La Época* responded to the event by recognizing that "la inteligencia no tiene sexo" ("La señora Pardo Bazán" 1905; intelligence has no sexual identity). Before becoming a member, she had already served as professor in the Ateneo's School of Higher Studies ("Emilia Pardo

Bazán" 1897). In 1914, she still remained both the first and only woman to do so (*El Caballero Audaz* 1914, 9).

Although Pardo Bazán did not actively attract a sisterhood of followers in her wake, as Coronado advised other women poets to do and as Gimeno did, she consciously took advantage of her visibility to further the position of other women with exceptional talent and a similar drive for excellence.[75] Within a year of joining the Ateneo, she stood as candidate to the presidency of the Literature Section. She wrote to Blanca de los Ríos extolling the gain that this step entailed, not only for herself, but for all women: "Me va a robar mucho tiempo si lo logro ... pero ¿y *la mujer*? Este será un paso, una conquista ... " (2016b [letter dated 3 November 1905; emphasis in original]; It is going to rob much of my time if I succeed ... but, and *women*? This will be a step [forward], a conquest). When she loses the vote in the first round, she considers the result a victory, convinced of her ultimate success: "este triunfo que es un triunfo de la mujer" (2016c; This triumph is a triumph for women). Similarly, when the prestigious Real Academia Española de la Lengua (Spanish Royal Academy of Language) denied her election as a member, she adopted a disinterested position in print: "Si a título de ambición personal no debo insistir ni postular para la Academia, en nombre de mi sexo creo que hasta tengo el deber de sostener, en el terreno platónico, la aptitud legal de las mujeres 'que lo merezcan' para sentarse en aquel sillón, mientras haya Academias en el mundo" (1891, 64–5; If in the name of personal ambition I should not insist [on my candidacy] nor propose [anyone] for the academy, in the name of my sex I believe that I even have the duty to defend, on a platonic basis, the legal aptitude of women 'who deserve it' to sit in that seat, as long as there are academies in the world).

In a 1911 interview with Pardo Bazán, Burgos lauds her as "esa mujer superior, de talento positivo, que supo en época hostil a la educación femenina demostrar su valor y su esfuerzo; esa polígrafa ilustre, honra nuestro sexo" (1911a; that superior woman who used her talents well, who in an era hostile to women's education knew how to demonstrate her valour and her efforts; that illustrious polygraph honours our sex). Burgos records Pardo Bazán's position on feminism: "Entusiasta de la cultura de la mujer, partidaria de que se le concedan todos sus derechos y convencida de que éstos han de ser los hombres los que nos los han de otorgar" (1911a; An enthusiast of women's culture, in favour of [women] being granted all their rights and convinced that it has to be men who bestow these [rights] on us). On the central platform of Spanish feminism, Burgos reports that Pardo Bazán's "alto criterio conoce de [educación] ha de venir la salvación del pueblo" (1911a; superior criterion recognizes that the salvation of the people/nation has to derive from education).

In her 1914 interview with *El Caballero Audaz*, Pardo Bazán openly avowed her feminism with few qualifiers: "Yo soy una radical feminista: creo que todos los derechos que tiene el hombre, debe tenerlo la mujer" (*El Caballero Audaz* 1914, 9; I am a radical feminist: I believe that all the rights that the man has a woman should have), limited only by their compatibility with women's physical nature. Furthermore, she espies a value to the nation in feminism's program, declaring that "hay una relación directísimo entre los derechos y privilegios concedidos a la mujer y el estado de cultura de las naciones" (1914, 9; there is a very direct relationship between the rights and privileges accorded women and every nation's cultural level). She is, however, less than optimistic about the future of feminism in Spain, although lauding past achievements. The sticking point, as she perceived it, was women themselves: women must want to move forward, and they require some aid from men. Opportunities already exist to attend university and pursue a career; only the female students are wanting.[76] In Spain, "el estancamiento del feminismo, depende de las costumbres, que son encogidas, ñoñas" (*El Caballero Audaz* 1914, 9; the stagnation of feminism depends on its customs, which are shrivelled and insipid).

In a 1917 newspaper article, Pardo Bazán humorously ridicules the nineteenth-century commonplace that it was a woman's primary function to darn socks, revelling in a memory that rejuvenated her, since the invention of knitting machines has demolished this "radical criterion" (1917). Feminism, she states, came late to Spain and in 1917 has not yet found "franco ambiente de simpatía; y menos que en nadie, en las mismas mujeres" (1917; an open sympathetic milieu; and less than in anyone else, in women themselves). She declares herself "poco propagandista y menos predicadora" (very little given to propagandizing and even less to preaching) and admits to not being an activist like Pankhurst, although she respects "esa señora de ánimo singular" (1917; that woman of singular spirit). Nevertheless, she contends that feminism continues "su ciclo, cada día con mayor empuje" (1917; its cycle, every day with greater force) and acknowledges with "sorpresa grata" (pleasant surprise) that advances for women have occurred in just a few years, even if "no aquí" (not here), but in Europe and Asia (1917).

Elsewhere, Pardo Bazán heralded feminism as "la única gran conquista de la humanidad (la más trascendental, de fijo, en sus resultados y en su alcance) que se habrá obtenido pacíficamente, sin costar una lágrima ni una gota de sangre" (Zavala 1993, 101; humanity's only great conquest – the most transcendent in its results and in its reach – that has been obtained peacefully, without costing a single tear or drop of blood). One critic has signalled the "combatividad y audacia" (Núñez Paredes 1992, 313; combativeness and audacity) with which Pardo Bazán adopted radical postures in defending women's rights. In her 1914 interview, she articulated her role as exemplar: "Mi obra para abrir las puertas españolas al feminismo, ha sido solamente personal: dando el ejemplo de hacer todo aquello que puedo, de lo que está prohibido a la mujer" (*El Caballero Audaz* 1914, 9; My work to open Spanish doors to feminism has been exclusively personal: giving an example of doing all those things that I can of what is prohibited to women). Her hortatory observation synthesizes pride, hope, disillusionment, and arrogance: "No cabe duda, que si muchas mujeres siguieron mi ejemplo, el feminismo en España sería un hecho" (*El Caballero Audaz* 1914, 9; Without a doubt, if many women followed my example, feminism in Spain would be a fact).

Pardo Bazán's contemporary Concepción Gimeno de Flaquer was a prolific journalist, who also published novels, volumes of essays, a few short stories, didactic handbooks for women, and travelogues; she also edited magazines, lectured on and for women, and advocated for women and women's issues. In many ways, Pardo Bazán's alter ego, Gimeno became Spain's best-known representative of conservative or "moderate feminism" at the turn of the century. In contrast to the individualist feminism of Arenal and Pardo Bazán, Gimeno sought to forge a transatlantic community of like-minded women that supported her views and her activities. She also exemplified Catholic feminism in her conformist creed of upholding social and moral conventions. The as-yet unmarried Gimeno initiated her writing career in 1877 with *La mujer española: Estudios acerca de su educación y sus facultades intelectuales* (The Spanish woman: Studies about her education and her intellectual faculties), which thrust her onto the Madrid literary scene ostensibly at the precocious age of twenty-four. Raised in Saragossa, she presented herself in Madrid as exceptionally young and pretty, to judge from her photograph and male-authored reviews, when in fact she was probably twenty-seven (almost of legal age). As was common in Carolina Coronado's day and still prevalent among less well-known women authors, Gimeno's first book carried a prologue by an established man of letters that validated its worth. She had already authored a serialized novel, *Victorina o heroísmo del corazón* ([Victorina or heroism of the heart; 1873) and founded and edited a Madrid periodical, *La Ilustración de la Mujer* ([The enlightenment of women; 1873–5). She continued to construct autobiographies that omitted years from her age, a not uncommon practice, since society permitted young women with intellectual pretensions a degree of indiscretion condemned in older or married women authors.

Gimeno and other neo-Catholic women relied on the teachings of the French bishop Félix Dupanloup and his writings, principally *La femme studieuse* (The Studious Woman; 1868), which lauded the biblical "strong woman," to affirm the orthodoxy of women's aspirations. Dupanloup's intended audience were upper-class women whose forays into education he guided, as his subtitle clarified: some advice to Christian women who live in the world, about the intellectual work appropriate for them (Sarazin 1995, 11). Dupanloup encouraged women's education in order to improve society and family life, not to emancipate women but for them to fulfil better their obligations as daughters, wives, and mothers. In this sense, Gimeno became a popularizer across the Spanish middle class, spreading Dupanloup's extremely limited message about women's opportunities in society.

Similar to many other authors of her generation, upon marriage Gimeno appended her husband's last name, Flaquer, to her own to manifest publicly her marital state and social respectability in fulfilment of the paradigm of the ideal woman. A new biography of Gimeno tellingly asserts that despite invoking her husband's name to establish her identity, "tuvo monedero, habitación y vida propia" (Pintos 2016, 11; she had a purse, a room, and her own life). Not having children put Gimeno in a difficult position by calling into question her embodiment of the Angel of the Hearth ideal, leading her to overcompensate for this lack. As Carmen Servén Díez specifies, Gimeno differed from Pardo Bazán in "la permanente glosa que [Gimeno] hace de la madre y su tono expositivo mucho más cauto y suave" (2013, 403; the permanent commentary that she makes on the mother figure and her much more cautious and gentle expository tone); that is, she upholds women's relative destiny or dependency on others. Through her periodicals and travels, she attracted a growing transatlantic circle of admiring readers who espoused, as she did, a conservative feminism, interspersed with advocacy for more radical positions.

In 1883 Gimeno and her husband moved to Mexico City, where she launched and edited the biweekly illustrated magazine *El Álbum de la*

Mujer (The women's album; 1883–90). Upon returning to Spain she continued as editor of the periodical under the title *El Álbum Ibero Americano* (The Ibero-American album; 1890–1910).[77] Gimeno's magazines combined information, history, news, literature for and by women, and high culture images, as well as photographs of contemporary Spanish and American authors, all set within a moral framework. Lou Charnon-Deutsch has called attention to the contribution that the new illustrated magazines for women made in their consumption of visual culture in the last decades of the century, when such magazines "became more affordable for the middle classes" (2011, 193). Gimeno's two albums stood midway between the lush, profusely illustrated high-end magazines that Charnon-Deutsch analyses and the low-circulation, run-of-the-mill women's magazines. She purchased photographs of famous places and people, especially women, and solicited others from her contemporaries, giving her readers a degree of visual cultural literacy and a knowledge of women in history. Guardians of women's virtue, as Charnon-Deutsch notes, treated illustrated magazines ambiguously: "Reading periodicals, however, was considered a modern, and therefore frivolous, activity, something the arbiters of feminine conduct advised Spanish women to avoid even as magazines were increasing their appeal to women" (2011, 195).

As well as composing novels with female protagonists facing moral dilemmas, Gimeno devoted herself to writing and lecturing about the position of women in society, emphasizing the importance of education – *Ventajas de instruir a la mujer y sus aptitudes para instruirse* (Advantages of teaching women and her aptitud for instruction; 1895) – and publishing her lectures on "La mujer intelectual" (The intellectual woman; 1903); "El problema feminista" (The feminist problem [a lecture at the Ateneo]; 1901); and "Iniciativas de la mujer en higiene moral social" (Women's initiatives in social moral hygiene; 1908), a lecture before the Spanish Hygiene Society. She also dedicated volumes to women's moral role and behaviour in society: *La mujer juzgada ante el hombre* (Women judged before men; 1882) and *La mujer juzgada por la mujer* (Women judged by women; 1882). As Burgos did, Gimeno also produced self-help manuals for middle-class women, such as *En el salón y el tocador* (In the drawing room and the boudoir; 1899), a likely source of income for both authors.

Gimeno attracted a very different following from Arenal and Pardo Bazán. Her mutually supportive readers grant primacy to their social standing and would not risk a social scandal or their condemnation by society – or even the church – as Pardo Bazán and Burgos did at times. She kept them in the know on social, cultural, literary, and some political issues in Spain and abroad, and her words, social appearances, and self-presentation constituted the model of feminism that few of them imitated. Pura Fernández notes Gimeno's dictum in an 1891 article that women should take the greatest pleasure in extolling the "esclarecidos talentos" (distinguished talents) of other women (2015b, 12), as she and her female followers assuredly did. Gimeno's high level of visibility, offset by her unimpeachable social contacts – including the women of the royal family – never violated middle-class social conventions. Nevertheless, she enacted some of the very feminist vindications she initially rejected in her writings, including supporting herself through earned income as a journalist, a career masked to some degree by the accompaniment of her husband's name, and her public appearances, such as lectures at the Ateneo, that made her an object of the public gaze. Her persona differed significantly from those of Arenal and Pardo Bazán, and she lacked their unshakeable belief in and the dramatization of the equality of the sexes. Reviewers tended to refer to her beauty (many of her volumes carry her photograph), discretion, and modesty in laudatory dedications: "La animosa y bella dama, la afamada y discreta escritora y la dama distinguida" (The spirited and beautiful lady, the renowned and modest woman writer, and the distinguished lady; *E.* 1901, 447). In 1893, she denounced women's reputation as the "weaker sex" and exalted their moral strength, comparable to men's, declaring in terms that defined her world and echoed her preoccupation with women's self-image: "El heroísmo, el genio y el alma no tienen edad ni sexo" ("No hay sexo débil" 17, quoted in Servén 2013, 398; Heroism, temperament, and soul have no age or sex). When she advocated emancipation, she qualified her endorsement: "emancipación, pero únicamente en las esferas de la inteligencia" (179; emancipation, but only in the spheres of intelligence).

Feminist and religious discourses merge in much of Gimeno's prose, as when she defines a woman as the "sacerdotisa del hogar" (priestess of the home) and in her volume *Evangelios de la mujer* (1900; Gospel truths about women). In "La mujer intelectual," she figures women in religious language: "La mujer moderna, *sacerdotisa* de las ideas redentoras, apóstol de la regeneración, tiene una maternidad moral, ilimitada e infinita" (1900, 10; The modern woman, *priestess* of redemptive ideas, apostle of regeneration, has a moral, unlimited, and infinite maternity). The mother figure, including the Virgin Mary, occupies a central place in many collections of her essays on women both past and present, foreign and Spanish: *Madres de hombres célebres* (Mothers of celebrated men; 1884); an 1891 Ateneo lecture on women in the French Revolution; Latin women (1904); women of royal blood (1907); and the Virgin Mother (1907). The tradition of compiling genealogies of famous women has its Spanish origins in Padre Benito Jerónimo Feijoo's 1726 "Defensa de la mujer" ("Defence of Women") in his Enlightenment-inspired, multi-volumed *Teatro crítico universal* (*Universal Critical Theater*). By inserting herself into the practice of disseminating recognition of overachieving women, Gimeno foments admiration for them and generates greater aspirations and increased reverence for motherhood in middle-class women.[78] María José Lacalzada pinpoints the weight given to the mother in Gimeno's feminist thinking (2005, 380). By privileging the role of mother as educator of the family, Gimeno upholds what Pardo Bazán decries as the relative destiny of women. She relegates Pardo Bazán's central tenet, the need for a woman's self-realization, to inferior status and rejects Pardo Bazán's priority of a woman "como persona independiente del estado civil, fundamental para la ruptura de la sociedad patriarcal" (Lacalzada 2005, 383; as a person independent of her civil state, fundamental for the rupture of patriarchal society).

In her 1900 *Evangelios de la mujer*, Gimeno propounded a feminist ideal of marriage: "Anhelan los feministas que el matrimonio sea la asociación de dos seres *conscientes, libres e iguales*; exigen la misma ley *moral, civil y económica* para los dos sexos" (Lacalzada 2005, 369 [emphasis in original]; Feminists desire marriage to be the association of two *conscious, free, and equal* beings; they require the same *moral, civil, and economic* law for the two sexes), with the result that woman will no longer be "civilmente menor, moralmente esclava" (369; legally underage, morally a slave). She also supported changing civil law so that women could serve as witnesses in court and guardians of minor children. Her platform expanded to "la emancipación intelectual y económica" (Lacalzada 2005, 369; intellectual and economic emancipation), the freedoms she herself exercised. Rather than giving a woman the vote or the possibility of election to political office, Gimeno preferred to maintain her role designed to "inspire a los legisladores la reforma de [las leyes]" (1900; inspire male legislators to reform [the laws]). By 1901 she began to subscribe in a limited way to feminist goals. Solange Hibbs-Lissorges clarifies that between 1901 and 1908 Gimeno propounded "una reflexión más comprometida de la realidad jurídico-social y política de su época" (2006, 133, quoted in Servén 2013, 411n1; a more committed reflection on the juridical, social, and political reality of her era). Servén attributes to Gimeno a "reclamación temprana del voto femenino" (410; early call for the female vote). Indeed, in a 1905 article on "El sufragio femenino" (Feminine suffrage), Gimeno accepted that "universal suffrage" was meaningless unless women also voted, but she remained firmly opposed to their accepting political positions. By 1907 she openly defended the vote for women, always with the caveat of avoiding women's masculinization and consequently praising "la tradicional feminidad de luchadoras por la causa de la mujer" (Servén 2013, 410; the traditional femininity of women who fight for the cause of women).

Gimeno ultimately echoed the feminist positions championed by Arenal and Pardo Bazán, but always set within her moral parameters. Given to bold declarative sentences, she followed her declarations by wording that nuanced, contradicted, or reshaped the ostensible position just staked out. Her writings comingled feminist discourse with a feminine discourse that was alien to Arenal and Pardo Bazán, except perhaps when a social context demanded it (Bieder 1990). In her role of journalist and novelist, she kept Spanish women abreast of advances in other countries and familiarized them with feminist discourses, but without challenging their comfort zone. Arenal and Pardo Bazán each forged her own intellectual position, including her Catholic belief; their religion was a strength, not an impediment to confronting feminist issues. Unless she was a figurehead for her husband's journalistic enterprises targeting women readers, which does not seem to be the case, Gimeno in fact was a successful entrepreneur and acute businesswoman.

Both Servén and Hibbs-Lissorgues recognize the central pillars of Gimeno's feminism as the defence of education for women, the regeneration of Spanish society, and improved conditions for women (Servén 2013, 405; Hibbs-Lissorgues 2006, 4–5). As late as her 1903 Ateneo lecture on "El problema feminista" (The feminist problem), Gimeno understood that for her audience feminism was still a problem, not a solution, and she similarly rejected the vote for women. By 1908, however, in "Iniciativas de la mujer en higiene moral social," she seemed to favour the limited suffrage under consideration in the Senate and urged men to reform the laws that condemn women to remain eternally legal minors. Servén cites an 1897 article, "Conversaciones privadas con las damas" (Private conversations with the ladies), which illustrates the duplicitous manoeuvres of Gimeno's feminism to configure itself to suit her audience: "No me parece mal que ante el hombre nos lamentemos *eternamente* de la falta de igualdad de *derechos*, pero creedme, no nos conviene adquirirlos" (Servén 2013, 407 [emphasis in original]; It doesn't seem a bad idea to me that in front of men we *eternally* regret the lack of equal *rights*, but believe me, it is not in our interest to acquire them). Nevertheless, her positions did evolve, although always within a religious framework and without accepting women's intervention in politics. For Gimeno, the woman's sphere was always the domestic sphere, although in certain cases she acknowledged the importance of women's economic independence.

At one time or another Gimeno advocated all the goals on the feminist agenda but in such a way that she did not alienate her base readership or alter her feminine model of morality, beauty, good taste, and social conformity. Hibbs-Lissorgues insightfully concludes that Gimeno's moralizing and religious focus "neutraliza a menudo la modernidad de su obra y de su reflexión" (frequently neutralizes the modernity of her work and her reflection), yielding instead "un reformismo social conservador" (a conservative social reformism) or "un regeneracionismo cristiano" (a Christian regenerationism) (2006, 7).

At the end of 1909, the long-running *El Álbum Ibero Americano* ceased publication, and a year later Gimeno abandoned her home in Spain, perhaps no longer earning an adequate income or attracting sufficient support for her magazine and books. Beginning with her Mexican contacts, Gimeno had emerged as the principal Spanish conduit for women's rights in Spanish America, where she had "bastante repercusión para la emancipación de las mujeres americanas" (Ezama 2015, 236; impacted significantly on the emancipation of [Spanish] American women). Ultimately, she networked for nearly forty years with women in Spain, Mexico, and South America, building personal relationships and enlarging her circle of feminists (see also chapter 14). Activating her wide network of women, in early 1911 Gimeno initiated a tour of South American countries, which ended a decade later with her death in Buenos Aires (Pintos 2016, 202–3). Her recently located death notice characterizes her as an "indefatigable publicista" (indefatigable publicist) and signals her "vocación de propagandista" (vocation as a propagandist), presumably while advocating her feminism ("Muerte" 1919).[79] Lacalzada concludes that Gimeno created a respected place for herself that allowed her ideas to spread as they matured along with social and political conditions in Spain (2005, 383). By 1909 Burgos was orchestrating the agenda of new generations of feminist activists, shifting the spotlight from Gimeno and her diminished cohort of moderate, Catholic feminists.

Carmen de Burgos is the key figure to emerge in Spanish feminist thought and action in the 1900s as the voice of "el pensamiento progresista radical" (Núñez Rey 2005, 21; radical progressive thought). Her feminist vision and agenda infuse her prolific output of novellas, lectures, books, travelogues, handbooks for women, and newspaper articles. From her first book, *Ensayos literarios* (1900; Literary essays), her feminist sympathies are evident, even though in its prologue she rejects the "feminismo exagerado que se ha despertado en nuestros días" (exaggerated feminism that has awoken in our time) and "esa promiscuidad feminista" (that feminist promiscuity) that obliterates the different missions for men and women, a position she would soon abandon (quoted in Núñez Rey 2005, 79–80). Nevertheless, her goal of effecting "una labor regeneradora" (Núñez Rey 2005, 80; a work of regeneration) is unmistakable. Her beliefs about women take shape in the essay "La educación de la mujer" (The education of women), in which she makes her one and only defence of the social value of religion (1900, 81–2). Concepción Núñez Rey avers that the essay's feminist ideas, grounded in "un modelo de mujer desarrollada plenamente por la educación para su propia dignificación" (2005, 84; a model of woman fully developed by education for her own self-worth), conveyed in its day "una subversión del orden social" (84; a subversion of the social order), much as Pardo Bazán's vindication of women's self-worth had.[80]

Married and with a young daughter, Burgos earned her teaching certificate and in 1901 moved with her child from Almería to Madrid. Abandoning her husband, at age thirty-three she obtained her first teaching position. As well as a Normal School teacher, Burgos became the first woman in Spain to earn a salary writing for a newspaper on a regular basis. In her first decades as a journalist, she was perhaps the most visible and most widely read woman in Spain. As part of her teaching obligations, in 1904 she compiled articles from her newspaper column and issued a pedagogical study, *La protección y la higiene de los niños* (The protection and hygiene of children), which explored Spain's high rate of infant mortality.[81]

By the end of 1919, Burgos had published almost forty novellas, twenty short stories, and twenty-five book translations, a further source of income for her. She also launched her own cultural magazine, *Revista Crítica* (Critical review), which survived from 1908 to 1909 (Ena 2013, 102–3). The last decades of the long nineteenth century increasingly witnessed more overt statements of feminist goals of equality accompanied by public actions, as reliance on the prevailing status quo for women dwindled, exemplified by Burgos's own trajectory. Government travel grants funded educational trips to expand her knowledge of educational systems abroad, transforming Burgos into an inveterate traveller who disseminated her impressions first as articles and then in book form. In this way, she learned first-hand about women in other cultures and evolved an international and transatlantic perspective. Her frequent travels around Europe, especially to Paris, and her travel grant to South America resulted in newspaper articles and then books. In 1906, she lectured in Rome at the Italian Press Association on "La mujer en España" (The woman in Spain) and in 1911 in Bilbao on the "Misión social de la mujer" (Social mission of women). Her newspaper *El Heraldo de Madrid* sent her to Morocco in 1909 as Spain's first woman war correspondent and reproduced her columns from the front.

Núñez Rey states baldly a characteristic of all Burgos's treatises: "Carmen condiciona sus palabras al tipo de auditorio" (2005, 160; Carmen modifies her words to suit her audience). Hence, in her well-received 1906 lecture in Rome, she opposed female suffrage on the grounds that it would "poner un arma peligroso en manos de un niño" (Núñez Rey 2005, 160; put a dangerous weapon in the hands of a child), whereas her own actions reveal her support for the suffrage campaign.[82] Speaking to Bilbao's liberal cultural and social society El Sitio (The Siege), Burgos gave her first major address that covered the present state of women in Spain. She pressed for the improvement of women's education and derided the current inferior state of women's weak preparation for employment. Nevertheless, she called for women's equality on all fronts. Núñez Rey summarizes the speech:

> Sus ideas apoyan un modelo ilustrado y tolerante que repercute en la organización de la familia, donde los esposos son compañeros. Apuesta a favor del matrimonio civil y del divorcio, y resueltamente ve con tolerancia el amor libre. Repasa después la situación de la mujer en el código civil. (2005, 285)
>
> (Her ideas uphold an enlightened and tolerant model that resonates in the organization of the family, where the spouses are companions. She backs civil marriage and divorce, and resolutely views free love with tolerance. She then reviews the situation of women in the Civil Code.)

Burgos drew on her international experience to make her case for reform of the legal status of women and reshaping society's understanding of the place and value of women.

In newspapers and fiction, Burgos challenged the strictures in law and custom that circumscribed women's existence and severely limited their options. She represented herself as both a paragon of female attributes, modelling and distributing socially sanctioned advice for Spanish women, while at the same time confronting the status quo, often in outrageous, virtually unthinkable terms. Burgos also increasingly used her press platform to disseminate resistance to the conventional limitations on women's participation in the social sphere, as well as on their self-determination. At the same time, her job as the woman's columnist for a newspaper paid her to conjure up the image of a more conformist modern woman to lure women readers seeking confirmation and enhancement of their beliefs and practices. Thus contradictory discourses lingered as a hallmark of her multiple careers and readerships.

Burgos's survey of opinions on the legalization of *divorcio* (legal separation), launched in 1904 from her Madrid newspaper *Diario Universal*, confirms that few major public figures, especially women, willingly committed themselves in print on the subject.[83] She reported and tallied the responses, reprinting them later as a book. Burgos grounded her rationale in favour of *divorcio* in the conditions surrounding marriage: "Quiero a la mujer independiente, para que no se case por necesidad; para que tenga derecho a elegir, para que sea consciente de sus actos" (1911b, 17; I want a woman to be independent, so she does not marry out of necessity; so that she has the right to choose, so that she is conscious of her actions). For her, *divorcio* was the logical reparation for a bad marriage and the only way to protect the wife. At the time, *divorcio* signified a legal separation that restored a woman's control over her own body and over any monies remaining from the wealth she brought to the marriage, which a husband had the legal authority to administer. It did not dissolve a marriage or allow either party to remarry (see Louis 2005, 26). Thus Burgos broke the silence on controversial topics, making public such previously taboo issues. Her bold strategies doubtless sold newspapers, but they also confronted literate Spaniards with the consequence and possible solutions to serious social problems.

In 1908, when Parliament considered a limited vote for women, Burgos declared openly: "Encarno espíritu feminista, respiro espíritu liberal ...; pero liberal de veras; de esos que defienden el voto de la mujer o lo discuten con razones" (1908; I am the spirit of feminism incarnate, I breathe the liberal spirit ...; but truly liberal; one of those that defend the vote for women or debate it with reasoned arguments).[84] She anchored her argument on equity between women and men: "La mujer, responsable como el hombre de sus actos en la sociedad, debe tener, como él, el derecho de luchar por sus opiniones y también en el mejoramiento de la vida pública y la vida privada" (1908; Woman, responsible as is man for her actions in society, should have, like him, the right to fight for her opinions and also for the betterment of public and private life). Although on this occasion Congress rejected allowing women a restricted vote, Burgos sought a way to convey a positive outcome by touting this defeat as a first step towards the triumph of female suffrage in Spain (1908). Paloma Castañeda affirms that from this moment on, Burgos will use "todos los medios a su alcance para divulgar sus ideas y contactará con las sufragistas británicas para darles su apoyo y solidarizarse con su causa" (1994, 121; all means at her disposal to spread her ideas and will contact the British suffragettes to give them her support and express her solidarity with their cause). In 1921, as president of the Cruzada de Mujeres Españolas (Spanish Women's Crusade), she led a demonstration through the streets near the Congress demanding voting rights for women, among other equal rights, and delivered a signed manifesto to the Congress (Guallart 2011, 139).

Through such events, small groups of Spanish women began to transform their thinking into public action. In publicizing both divorce and female suffrage, Burgos manifested a lack of respect for and adherence to the Catholic Church, a cornerstone of middle-class Spanish women's existence and the public expression of their moral character. Thus in her own life choices, Burgos helped liberate Spanish feminism from the control of Spain's dominant institution and realized many of the goals that international feminism espoused. Separated from her husband, who died in 1906, Burgos, as a widow, regained many freedoms lost to her upon marriage, including the sole control over her person and her income. She modelled one woman's active resistance to a failed marriage by subsequently surmounting the challenge of having no source of income, no education or job skills, no control over any assets in her name, and little societal support for remedying her circumstances (several of her siblings accompanied her in Madrid). In her life, her writings, and her activism, Burgos was a living poster for her brand of Spanish feminism (Bieder 2017).

As did Madrid and some of Spain's smaller cities, Barcelona produced its own flourishing women's culture with periodicals, philanthropic and educational organizations, and church sponsorship of women's associations. The best-known women's advocates in both Madrid and Barcelona each edited her own magazine (see chapter 11). Because of

Catalonia's growing industrialization and the emergence of labour organizations, the concerns of the working class, especially labouring women, were more evident and of greater concern to middle-class feminists in Barcelona. In Catalonia, two women of the same generation approached feminism in very different ways: Carme Karr, a very visible, upper-class Barcelona feminist; and Caterina Albert, a reclusive literary innovator with feminist tendencies. Among the most high-profile collaborators in the creation of Catalan feminism in conjunction with Catalan nationalism, their reputation resounded throughout Spain's literature and journalism as well. Both were close contemporaries of Madrid-based authors de los Ríos and especially Burgos, who like Karr engaged in the newly emerging feminist activism.

Born into the Barcelona *haute bourgeoisie*, Carme Karr d'Alaforetto i Alfonsetti had an Italian mother and a French father who was France's vice consul; the popular French novelist Alphonse Karr was her uncle. A well-known public figure, she moved in highly educated, intellectual, and international circles, being proficient in Catalan, Spanish, French, and German. Barcelona considered her "una erudita y una activa defensora de la renaciente cultura catalana" (Sánchez Dueñas 2014; an erudite woman and an active [female] defender of renascent Catalan culture) and "una de las cinco personas más sabias de Cataluña en el ámbito de las humanidades" (ibid; one of the five most learned people in Catalonia in the humanities). Karr dedicated her career to the defence of Catalan nationalism, feminism, women's education, culture, and women's greater employment opportunities. Nationalism and feminism coincided in the woman as "depositaria y transmisora" (depository and transmitter) of national identity (Simón Palmer 2013, 294). She mainly wrote articles published in magazines in Barcelona and also elsewhere in Spain, in which she emphasized women's education, employment, and legal rights. In various Barcelona periodicals, she defended women's suffrage, argued for equal right for women, and championed women's access to the liberal professions in order to become self-supporting. Her contributions to Catalan music, both as a musicologist and a composer, were greatly admired, bringing her added fame and prestige. Carmen Simón Palmer characterizes her as a conservative but reformist feminist and a defender of women's education (2013, 303).

Karr began her public career by writing articles for weekly magazines, starting with the modernist *Joventut* (Youth), under a series of pseudonyms. When she signed her own name to publications, like

Pardo Bazán and Burgos she did not append her husband's last name. Between 1906 and 1918, she published short fiction, novels, and theatre, as well as musical compositions. In her novellas, Karr depicted contemporary middle-class society with irony, satirizing women characters that represented types she condemned and engaging in the "biting demythification" of male characters ("Carme Karr" 2015). She also founded and edited the Catalan-language magazine for women, *Feminal* (For women; 1907–17), a long-running monthly literary supplement to the weekly *La Ilustració Catalana*. Her magazine reflected her own model of feminism, and her initial editorial informed her readers she would communicate everything useful, pleasing, and interesting "en l'actual moment artistich, industrial i social" ("Carme Karr" 2015; in the present artistic, industrial, and social moment). Monserdà and Massanés both contributed to *Feminal*; its Madrid correspondent was Burgos. Nevertheless, a profile of the magazine avers that it contains few opinions or declarations of principles (Segura and Selva 1984, 258). Karr's ideas evolved over time, and in 1915 *Feminal* incorporated a section on Catalan feminists. Unlike most women's magazines, it had lavish illustrations, including many photographs, as did Gimeno's *Álbum Ibero Americano*, making it more similar to a mainstream commercial publication.

In 1910 Karr became the first woman to lecture in the Ateneu Barcelonès (Barcelona Atheneum), with a short course on feminism and women's rights that highlighted the need for equal education for men and women, and promoted professional schools as a way to increase options for women outside the home (Simón Palmer 2013, 303). Attesting to their popularity, these lectures, entitled "Cultura femenina" (Women's culture), also appeared in the weekly magazine *La Cataluña* and then the same year in book form as *Cultura femenina: Estudi i orientacions* (Feminine culture: studies and directions). In 1916, Karr and other feminists, including Monserdà, gave a lecture course in the Ateneu Barcelonès on "Educación femenina" (Feminine education), which similarly became a book. In 1913, she established a school, La Llar (The Hearth), to promote extension courses for the further education of women professors and students. Taking Madrid's Residencia de Estudiantes (Student Residence [for men]) as a model, Karr founded La Llar two years before the inauguration of Madrid's Residencia de Señoritas (Young Women's Residence). In 1915, she organized and served as president of a pacifist society, the Comité Femenino Pacifista de Cataluña (Feminine Pacifist Committee of Catalonia), which became the basis for the 1921 association Acción Femenina (Feminine Action). Karr lived throughout the Second Spanish Republic, the Civil War, and into the Franco regime. After that war, she turned to writing children's fiction, as did other women authors seeking an income in the Franco era.

Caterina Albert i Paradís, perhaps the most widely known Catalan woman author in her lifetime and one of the early Catalan modernists, wrote exclusively in her native language. She lived much of her life in her rural hometown, returning there in her last years, but after 1904 she maintained an apartment in Barcelona. Her submission to the 1898 Jocs Florals of a dramatic monologue in a woman's voice, "L'infanticida" (Infanticide), provoked a scandal, due to the inappropriate, but protofeminist, subject for a woman of her day. Thereafter, Albert published under the male-inflected pseudonym with nationalist Catalan overtones "Víctor Català," even though the public knew her identity. Despite her seeming cultural isolation, she kept abreast of literary trends and also studied painting, both of which impacted on her startlingly naturalist, modernist, and at times poetic prose in novels, plays, and short stories. She also maintained a vast correspondence with other authors, both women and men. To some degree reminiscent of Rosalía de Castro, she remained "peripheral to the literary world" and did not write for women's periodicals or enter debates about the woman question (Bieder 1994a, 33). Her first work appeared in print at age thirty-two in 1900, the same year as Burgos's, and within two years she had released three volumes: dramatic monologues, poetry, and rural short stories. The novel *Solitut* (Solitude; 1905) remains her most admired work, with its underlying feminism conveyed through its narrative focus on the female protagonist's suffering and quest for liberation, against a stark background of male domination and aggression. In her most productive period, 1901–7, her fiction furthered the evolution of Catalan Modernism. By 1907 Albert had written almost her entire output, except *Un film (3.000 metres)* (A film: 3000 metres; 1920), but new works kept appearing over the next decades, rather like Cecilia Böhl von Faber's delayed release of fiction written many years earlier. Named president of the Jocs Florals in 1917, Albert became a member of the Acadèmia de la Llengua Catalana (Academy of the Catalan Language) in 1915, while the Barcelona Reial Acadèmia de Bones Lletres (Royal Academy of Belles Lettres) elected her its first female member in 1923. In the 1970s, recently emerged Hispanic feminist criticism rediscovered Albert; it has kept *Solitut* in its canon ever since.

13 Crossing Centuries, Crossing Words (1804–1920): Women, Basque Society, and the Struggle for the Public Sphere

AMAIA ALVAREZ-URIA, JOSUNE MUÑOZ, AND IRATXE RETOLAZA

It is well known that from the 1920s and 1930s the number of women who participated in Basque public life increased. Nevertheless, it was the nineteenth century that saw the first signs of such participation, due to the gradual rise in women's literacy and education. In that context, cultural movements and educational institutions emerged, to which cultural and pedagogical factors contributed substantially towards encouraging women's activities in the public sphere and in forming public opinion. In this chapter, we analyse the beginnings of this gradual insertion of women into that space, from the beginning of the nineteenth century to the early twentieth century.

In the early nineteenth century, the work of the Biscayan Bizenta Mogel (1782–1854) is noteworthy, given that she was the first woman to publish a book in Basque.[85] Entitled *Ipui onak* (Good tales; 1804), her work was a collection of adaptations of classical fables by Aesop and Phaedrus. This publication was extraordinary in that social context for several reasons. First, after the Council of Trent (1545), Christian teachings rigorously regulated women's presence in the public sphere, and the fallout from their exclusion conditioned society and culture in the eighteenth and nineteenth centuries in the Basque Country, or Euskal Herria (Madariaga 2014, 524). Second, with respect to the Basque language, the progressive deterioration that it suffered in the seventeenth and eighteenth centuries increased in the nineteenth, especially among men, due not only to their education in Castilian Spanish but also to employment and military reasons that obliged them to learn Castilian. Moreover, Castilian Spanish was the only means of engaging with different administrative layers, such as the education system. In this sense, language became a tool for social discrimination. Given that at the end of the eighteenth century and beginning of the nineteenth most women still spoke only Basque (Madariaga 2014, 393–401), many suffered a dual discrimination: exclusion from the public sphere and linguistic marginalization. Last, Basque public institutions occasionally published in Basque, but due to the high cost of such publications, they did not award or promote subventions. Hence during the eighteenth and nineteenth centuries, it was very difficult to publish in Basque. The institution that did most to promote the Basque language was the Catholic Church for doctrinal reasons, and especially the Jesuits, until they were expelled from Spain in 1767. Thus, according to Joan Mari Torrealdai (1997, 93), until the twentieth century most books written in Basque were linked to Catholic teaching. In this context, *Ipui onak* is quite extraordinary, because a woman positions herself in the public sphere and overcomes several social restrictions: she publishes in Basque on a nonreligious topic (although with a moralistic purpose); she vindicates female authorship in the work's prologue; and she inaugurates the fable in Basque, which becomes a model and cultural point of reference for other nineteenth-century writers of fables.

Although unprecedented, Bizenta Mogel is, however, a paradigmatic figure, because she is representative of a group of upper-class women educated at home, whereas for the majority of Basque women a formal intellectual education was out of the question.[86] In her domestic environment, Mogel mastered Basque, French, and Castilian and read the works of classics, such as Virgil, Aesop, and Phaedrus (Olaziregi 2003, 208). Nevertheless, she was fully aware that, because she was a woman, private and public education limited her knowledge to those realms imposed on her gender: maternity, charity, domesticity, and care of others. As is evident in her prologue, she was conscious of the fact that her participation in the field of letters would be challenged:

> Badakit, enzunaz beste gabe, neskatx gazte baten izena dagoela itxatsirik liburutxo onen aurrean, jardungo dutela siñuka ez gutxik, diotela beren artean ... besten bearrak artu nai ditudala neretzat: ez dagokiola neskatxa bati bururik ausitze liburugiñen: asko duela gorua, naiz jostorratza zuzen erabiltzea ... Nola nik siniserazoko diet askori, euskeratu ditudala erdaldun jakitunak argiratu dituzten ipuiak? Nolako arrotasuna berri latiñezko itzkuntzarekin liburu onen asmoa agertzea? Orretarako bear litzake jakitea euskera, gaztelania, eta latinezko iru izkuntzak. Zein gauza sinisgaitza neskatxa bategan! (Mogel 1963, 37)

> (I know that merely on hearing that the name printed on the cover of this book is that of a young woman, many will pull a face, thinking ... that I intend to usurp men's work; that it is not right for a woman to worry her pretty little head about writing books: that she has enough to do with knowing how to spin and sew ... How am I going to convince many that I have adapted for the purposes of the Basque language tales published by learned foreigners? To do this, it would be necessary to know three languages: Basque, Castilian, and Latin. Incredible for a woman!)

As so often occurred in the history of women's literature, a female writer uses the prologue, a space of affirmation, to denounce the educational norm that restricted women to learning to read (and not always to write), sew, embroider, and so on.

Bizenta Mogel's work inaugurates a century characterized by the slow but unstoppable incorporation of women into the educational system, both as pupils and teachers.[87] During the second half of the century, female literacy rates increased slightly. Moreover, according to the 1860 census, the female literacy rate in three Basque provinces was higher than 20% (Álava, 28.9%; Navarre, 21%; Biscay, 21.7%), which in turn was greater than the state average of 11.9% (Sarasúa 2002, 285). In these provinces, mixed education was more common (in Álava, in 84.5% of all schools; in Navarre, 69.4%; and in Biscay, 68.8%), which demonstrates the link between literacy rates and mixed schooling (Sarasúa 2002, 285–6). The low literacy rate among women is due to not only the fact that fewer attended school but also the type of education that Mogel had denounced: "A model of womanhood dedicated to work within the domestic sphere, a moral and economic model that had conditioned girls' education for centuries, was easily integrated into the new liberal programme of public education that was gradually established in the nineteenth century" (Sarasúa 2002, 296).

Throughout this century, European states aimed to establish, protect, and control children's education (Escolano 1982, 55). In this context, the state's powers to intervene increased so as to establish institutions to form teachers (López Atxurra 1995, 56). As a result, the Normal Schools flourished in much of the Western world. However, in the Spanish state this process was slower, to the extent that in the second half of the century deficiencies in education were considered one of the most serious problems (Sarasúa 2002, 283). Among the measures taken to redress this situation was the founding of the Normal Schools. Although initially Normal Schools for male teachers were established, children's education was gradually left to women due to men's lack of vocation and the interest shown by many lower-middle-class women in this profession. Hence, Normal Schools for female teachers were progressively established in Pamplona (1847–1930), the first in the Spanish state; in Vitoria (1856–1904); in San Sebastián (1899–1930); and in Bilbao (1902–30) (López Atxurra 1995, 5–8). After the expansion of these schools, elementary schools and high schools for female teachers were also founded. These centres were crucial for women's education and their incorporation into the labour market. Nevertheless, as evident in their 1914 curricula, each course offered a specific subject for women, such as sewing, embroidery and dressmaking, dressmaking and housework, and domestic economy (Escolano 1982, 68).

School education was not the only space to which women gained access in this period. Others, like Juana Witney (also Whitney), opened academies that taught not only languages but also general culture (Brancas 1998, 85–6). Witney's own daughter, prominent educator and activist María de Maeztu, later taught in her mother's academy. After completing her education in the School for Female Teachers, Maeztu ran the adult night schools in Bilbao, as well as the nursery in Cortes Street (1909–12), and became a model in the field of education. Thus, she gave lectures in the Instituto Vizcaíno (1904) and was a speaker at the pedagogical conferences with Miguel de Unamuno.

This entire process of forming literate Spanish women and educating them would prove even more complex for the Basque language, for various reasons. On the one hand, the intermittent Carlist conflicts, to which chapter 1 refers, meant that different literacy projects were delayed. On the other hand, the Law of Public Education (1857), better known as the Moyano Law, would be crucial because it stipulated that the central government appoint all teachers. Henceforth, the central government, provincial councils, and town councils would contest the jurisdictions and contracts that would allow an educational system in Basque to become established.

Given that teaching in Castilian in public schools was compulsory, and that male and female teachers taught in Basque as they saw fit, education in the Basque language did not increase until the second decade of the twentieth century. The ambitious, successful project of the town schools in the Basque provinces would play an important role in the eventual development of education in the Basque language (Arrien 1987, 629–30). As the first attempt to teach completely in Basque in public schools and an unprecedented effort to achieve bilingual literacy, this project would not be repeated until the later transition to democracy (1977–81). Female teachers were vital in the transition to education in the Basque language. Nationalist Basque women, who saw their mission as disseminating the Basque language and culture, wanted to ensure that both the Basque language and the Catholic faith were taught in public schools, and drove the education of female teachers in this nationalist, Catholic, and Basque vein.[88] Such outstanding women as Julene Azpeitia, Consuelo Gallastegui, Polixene Trabudua, and Elvira Zipritia were all dedicated to this endeavour. Their participation was made even more necessary by the enormous scarcity of pedagogical materials in Basque in the early twentieth century (Pérez, Ezkurdia, and Bilbao 2012, 59–62).[89]

Likewise, in this fin de siècle period, cultural magazines published articles on education, which formed one of the foremost topics of public debate. These magazines became great allies of women, because there they could articulate their opinion on educational matters. Thus, from 1906 nationalist Basque women participated in the public sphere, especially in the press (Rekalde 2012, 32; Retolaza 2012, 110–14). Many of the foremost magazines of the day contained sections reserved for female writers who addressed female readers – magazines such as *Napartarra, Euzkadi, Euskal Erria,* and *Euskalerriaren Alde* (Díaz Noci 1992, 57; Nuñez Betelu 2001, 53–77). Although it was common for female authors to use a pseudonym and for their real identity not to be known, these spaces in the press were crucial for women to set out their written opinion in the public sphere and to produce a community of female readers. Furthermore, some of these sections gradually became less restrictive, and female writers tackled more general topics addressed to the wider reading public. Arising from these reflections in the press was the articulation of the need to form an organization of nationalist women (Ugalde 1993, 58), which became the organization of Emakume Abertzale Batza (1922–3, 1931–6).

Within the public sphere, theatre was the predominant literary genre between 1876 and 1935 (Torrealdai 1997, 119), functioning as an important tool for political propaganda. Two tendencies stand out in relation to this boom: nationalist theatre written in Castilian in Bilbao and theatre written in Basque in San Sebastián. Both modalities were greatly influenced by Sabino Arana's nationalist discourse. Hegemonic in fin de siècle Basque culture, its foundations were the pillars of God, race, language, Basque laws, and history. As a result of this ideology, nationalist theatre produced dichotomous visions – old/modern, rural/

urban, Basque/Spanish. Works by Basque female dramatists identify with a theatre written in Basque that is clearly nationalistic. In order to justify women's participation in writing theatre, one such dramatist, Tene Mujika, differentiated between politics and patriotism, linking the former with reason and the masculine, and the latter with love and the feminine (Mujika 1923, 9–11).

Among the theatre groups that performed women's works, it is necessary to highlight San Sebastián's School of Declamation, which Toribio Altzaga directed between 1915 and 1936. This group took modern Basque theatre to the highest level. Noteworthy among its contributions to Basque culture is women's participation, from acting to directing, because until then women had not participated in Basque theatre. Due to this impetus, female dramatists began to enter their works in literary competitions, and several were awarded prizes, published, and even performed. In this context, the first female actors and directors, such as Pepita Aramendi, Felisa Areitioaurtena, Miren Nekane Arrizabalaga, Maria Arizmendi, and Janamari Malharin, performed on Basque stages and in the public sphere.

Three dramatists in particular stand out: Karmele Errasti, Tene Mujika, and Katalina Eleizegi. The first two followed Arana's teachings to the letter, and hence their works disseminated Catholic practices (charity and prayer) and transmitted the Basque culture and language. Errasti (Bilbao 1885–Pau 1954), the director of Emakume Abertzale Batza, wrote *Oleskari biyak* (1915), a comedy that moralizes on the need to choose an appropriate husband for the Basque nation's prosperity (Nuñez-Betelu 2001, 93). In contrast, Tene Mujika (Deba 1888–1981) wrote the children's play *Nekane* (1922), which conveyed Catholic values, such as charity. Her two later dramas, *Gogo oñazeak* (1934) and *Gabon* (1935), were awarded prizes and published.

The situation changed slightly with the works of teacher and dramatist Katalina Eleizegi Maiz (Donostia 1889–Lizarra 1963), because they show ways of being a Basque woman that differ from those hegemonic representations of femininity (Álvarez-Uria 2011, 263–4). Due to the quality of her works and the success with which they met when performed, she was called the "euskal antzerki modernoaren ama" (Cano 1997, 1–2; mother of modern theatre). Before the Spanish Civil War, the following works were published and performed: *Garbiñe* (1916), *Loreti* (1917), *Gaine* (1929), and *Jatsu* (1934). Alongside traditional nationalist women, Eleizegi's works give a voice to modern, frivolous, coquettish women, or to marginal figures such as witches or transgender women (Álvarez-Uria 2011, 268).

By the beginning of the twentieth century, women's constant efforts in convents, nuns' schools, private homes, Sunday schools, and small rural schools had increased literacy rates, which would further grow after the establishment of the Normal Schools for Female Teachers. In a century in which university doors were closed to women, this kind of education was the only way of gaining access to work that might give them a degree of economic independence. Evidently, the increase in women's literacy and education during the nineteenth century was crucial for enabling a greater number of Basque women to participate in the public sphere and in cultural, social, and political movements, as the teachers, journalists, writers, and artists mentioned in this chapter did.

14 Redefining the Cultural Periphery from Women's Transatlantic Networks: Spanish and Latin American Women of Letters in the Nineteenth Century

PURA FERNÁNDEZ[90]

The nineteenth century is the century of Western nationalisms and their borders, and at the same time, of migrations, journeys, and such isochronous cultural movements as romanticism, realism, or naturalism, which, like shock waves, seem to standardize a supranational literary physiognomy. Side by side with literatures deeply rooted in local histories, there also exist what Ottmar Ette calls "literaturas sin residencia" (2012, 14; literatures without a home). Derived from mobile maps of literary Hispanism, their poetics clarify the need to pass from a purely spatial history to a history of movement in transatlantic space (Ette 2012, 21).

Cultural elites have often been linked to the political history of Latin America since its independence movements, and their path can be traced in Carlos Altamirano and Jorge Myers's grand project *Historia de los intelectuales en América Latina* (History of the intellectuals in Latin America). In these volumes, however, the newly emerging figure of the woman of letters is excluded, because "hasta avanzado el siglo XIX esa esfera de la cultura intelectual estuvo bajo el poder de los varones" (Altamirano and Myers 2008, 15; well into the nineteenth century that particular space in intellectual culture was under the control of men). This exclusion removes from scholarly consideration such authors as Soledad Acosta, Juana Manuela Gorriti, Clorinda Matto, Mercedes Cabello, and Juana Manso, writers who participated actively in the political, social, educational, and literary life of various republics, handed down an extensive, varied discursive corpus, and contributed to the formation of the imaginaries woven by each nation's systems of cultural representation. To continue cementing this idea of the exceptional nature of women of letters – whose sociocultural experiences defy the institutional paradigms developed in national literary historiographies – presupposes the rejection of a noncanonical corpus that is essential for the analysis of contemporary cultural history.

Something similar happened with contemporaneous Spanish women writers of the Isabeline period (1843–68), such as Pilar Sinués de Marco, Faustina Sáez de Melgar, Cecilia Böhl de Faber, and the Spanish-Cuban Gertrudis Gómez de Avellaneda. As promoters of a moralizing novel of domesticity and contributors to a dense network of periodicals that entered subtly, yet powerfully, into private homes and collections of fiction destined to shape new generations, these female writers gradually lost historiographic visibility due to the masculinization of the literary canon imposed by the predominance of realism and naturalism in literature (Sánchez Llama 1999, 282–3).

In this context of the exclusion of the feminine from the public stage and from political and cultural action, due to women's condition as subordinate individuals, it would have been possible to think about a parallel sisterhood that would not only attempt to reorganize gender categories in the social sphere through prudent negotiation but also encourage the emergence of another parallel, transnational cultural canon that could coexist with the current exclusively masculine canon and not necessarily have to pit itself against it. Is it possible for this Republic of Letters to offer women a framework of identity more in tune with a soft concept of citizenship and with a broader, more flexible concept of nation in geographic and symbolic terms, in accordance with Joseph Nye's soft-power model (Nye 2004)? Female patriotic love, devoid of the imaginary forged in a warrior tradition reliant on military education and experience, and of direct political action, was formalized by means of affective attributes that were channelled into the moral formation of future citizens in bourgeois domestic space. In Spain, such a process began with the liberal political agenda following the death of Fernando VII (1833) and in so-called Spanish America with its independence movements.

The poem "Libertad," written by Spaniard Carolina Coronado in 1846, synthesizes women's feeling of exclusion from structures of social organization and the liberal revolutionary agenda. At the same time, it maps a path of action, directed at other women writers of her generation: "Pero, os digo, compañeras, / Que la ley es sola de ellos, / Que las hembras no se cuentan / Ni hay nación para este sexo" (Coronado 1991, 390; But I tell you, my [women] friends, / That the law is only for men, / That women do not count / Nor does our gender have a nation). Her 1845 poem "Cantad hermosas" (Sing, beauties) underpins Susan Kirkpatrick's thesis regarding the existence of an "hermandad lírica" (1990; lyrical sisterhood), which found in romantic verse a way of expressing female subjectivity and self-vindication, and found in literature a public arena for performances coded as *respectable* feminism (Burguera 2012).

Gertrudis Gómez de Avellaneda made her mark by demanding validation of a female genealogy that would contradict the sexual essentialism codified by Enlightenment thought and adopted by revolutionary liberalism to justify the existence of two states of nature – one for the masculine gender and the other for the feminine – which became the basis for the differentiated social spaces that violated the essential trait of human nature: equality (Albin 2007, 165). In her 1845 article "Capacidad de las mujeres para el gobierno" (Ability of women to govern), Gómez de Avellaneda called on historical evidence to show that women had played acknowledged leading roles throughout Spain's history, as part not of a quaint exceptionality but rather of a rich genealogy rendered invisible by the emphasis on two women of the church who wrote women's protoliterature in Castilian Spanish: St Teresa and Sor Juana Inés de la Cruz.

The construction of a supranational, transcultural feminine Parnassus through the creation of biographies, anthologies, and excerpts about illustrious women – with special attention to women writers – was a constant undertaking for nineteenth-century women, who would trace the path of their precursors in numerous volumes and periodicals on both sides of the Atlantic. These biographical sketches, which resembled the hagiographic paradigm of exemplarity, would stimulate a self-reflexive process in those women who, by describing the example of another female writer, are at the same time voicing their own desire for glory and expressing their experience on their path to professional self-affirmation, without overly risking their socially required humility and modesty (Fernández 2011, 164).

Nations are built on the basis of varied, contingent, and arbitrary forms of identification, and, as Homi K. Bhabha maintains (2010), from their margins. Transnational practices, beginning with the interaction of groups, social collectives, or institutions, "*a pesar del* Estado-nación" (*in spite of* the nation-state), its borders, and ideologies, denaturalize the nation as a *hegemonic* way of organizing space, as well as of revealing the importance of "structures of feeling" that bind people to geographic units greater or smaller than the nation (Peyrou and Martykánová 2014,

14). As Mabel Moraña points out, the theories that begin to emerge with the so-called affective turn posit affection as "una forma desterritorializada, fluctuante e impersonal de energía que circula a través de lo social sin someterse a normas ni reconocer fronteras" (2012, 323; a deterritorialized, fluctuating, and impersonal form of energy that circulates throughout the social sphere without yielding to norms or recognizing frontiers). Recent studies support the performative capacity of literary texts to provoke emotions, as well as the political use potentially made of such reactions (Ahmed 2004; Delgado, Fernández, and Labanyi 2016). Thus, relational practices among those members of a Republic of Letters who share a marginalized, unsanctioned position within that republic, like the stereotypical, satirized community of *literatas* (lady scribblers), can be analysed beginning with their feeling of belonging to a community based on the feelings of those who fight for inclusion in the republic. This seems to be the mindset of Peruvian author Clorinda Matto on her 1908 trip to Spain, following the banquet that her writing sisters offered in her honour in Madrid. At this homage, she reveals that "la emoción que me domina es suprema" (Matto 1909, 319; a supreme emotion overwhelms me), and "pienso en esta propensión de enraizar que tiene el corazón humano dondequiera que siente clima de afectos sinceros" (319; I think of that propensity of the human heart to put down roots wherever it finds a climate of sincere affection). Upon returning from her journey across Europe, Matto highlights the strength of a common linguistic homeland as she again crosses the Spanish frontier at Irún and feels "las fruiciones de familia" (1909, 311; the joys of family) in a shared language: "No hay lazo más fuerte, vínculo más estrecho que el del idioma" (311; There is no stronger tie, no tighter bond than language). The homeland of emotions that Matto mentions refers to a web of relationships, formed across time, countries, and continents, among those who are called sisters in (and of) letters (Matto 1909, 323–5). The Weberian category of emotional community can be productive in analysing social groups with similar or shared forms of emotional expression, which create very solid social ties, particularly in adverse situations.

Matto's famous literary gatherings, and those of Argentinian author Juana Manuela Gorriti and of Spanish women in Madrid, such as Emilia Pardo Bazán or Concepción Gimeno de Flaquer, became transatlantic meeting points for women's letters, linked by their common language and similar religious and cultural roots. Their literary formation and similar social class unite these women writers, who found shelter within a program of morality and civilization that took its bearings from the cultural prestige of Europe and the ideal of progress and emancipation in the United States to forge a paradigm of female Latin modernity, as Gimeno de Flaquer proposed (Fernández 2011, 163). Gimeno's Christian-based protofeminism, already present in her first book, *La mujer española: Estudios acerca de su educación y sus facultades intelectuales* (1877; The Spanish woman: Studies on her education and intellectual faculties), and her later works, *Evangelios de la mujer* (1900; Gospel truths about women) and *Una Eva moderna* (1909; A modern Eve), significantly dedicated to Matto, evolves from the systematic defence of women's education and right to work into a pioneering call for female suffrage (Pintos 2016).

The nineteenth-century press, which experienced an extraordinary increase in the number of publications specifically aimed at women, channelled the authoring desires of many women writers and permitted the creation of virtual networks for sharing not only cultural but also political aspirations. Especially relevant for women's transatlantic networks are those publications founded in countries that are not the countries of origin of their women editors, such as those periodicals launched by Spaniards Emilia Serrano de Wilson (*El Semanario del Pacífico* [The Pacific weekly], Lima, 1877–8) and by Gimeno de Flaquer (*El Álbum de la Mujer* [Album for women], México, 1883–90; which would later become *El Álbum Ibero Americano* [The Ibero-American album], Madrid, 1890–1909); the Colombian Soledad Acosta (*La Revista Americana* [The American magazine], Lima; *La Mujer* [Woman], 1878–81); the Peruvian Matto (*Búcaro Americano* [American vase], Buenos Aires, 1896–1908); the Mexican Laura Méndez de Cuenca (*Revista Hispano Americana* [Hispanic-American magazine], San Francisco, 1895–6); or the Argentinean Juana Manuela Gorriti (*La Alborada del Plata* [*River Plate Sunrise*], Buenos Aires, 1877–8, 1880).

Oliva López Sánchez explores how the structuring role of emotions in Mexico in the second half of the nineteenth century serves to conquer spaces for women's participation in civic and public spheres (2010, 14–15). The implementation of emotional capital as a sociocultural category that makes negotiation possible contributed to the consolidation of female social agency, especially through the women's press, as can be seen in progressive journals like *Violetas del Anáhuac* (Anáhuac violets; 1887–9) and *La mujer mexicana* (The Mexican woman; 1904–6). Women writers exhibited a supranational accord that is both moral and aesthetic when they based their natural destiny on administering affection to form and educate citizens, as well as on philanthropy and social welfare.

Women like the aforementioned Spaniards and Latin Americans moved from place to place because of political, family, professional, and/or economic reasons. They repeatedly travelled to other countries and stayed at various destinations, often for extended periods of time. At any given time, the definition of who is a *transmigrante* (transmigrant, transnational migrant) is a matter of point of view: "individuos que mantienen fuertes lazos con sus países de origen al tiempo que se integran en países de acogida; que construyen 'campos sociales' que vinculan origen y destino; que mantienen relaciones múltiples (familiares, económicas, sociales, políticas, organizativas) que trascienden fronteras" (Peyrou and Martykánová 2014, 15; individuals who maintain strong ties with their country of origin at the same time as they become integrated into the countries that receive them; who construct 'social fields' that link origin and destination; who maintain multiple relationships – family, economic, social, political, organizational – that transcend frontiers). Along this trajectory, the networks established with the spouses of political leaders stand out, as in the case of Carmen Romero Rubio, wife of Mexican President Porfirio Díaz, of whom her biographer, the learned Laureana Wright, writes in 1887: "Una mujer hizo que se realizara la Independencia de México; ¿por qué otra no haría que se consumara su perfeccionamiento civil?" (López Sánchez 2010, 13; A woman made Mexican independence happen; why wouldn't another woman bring about its civil perfection?).

It is this process of perfecting civil society that is promoted as the ideal professional pathway for women writers and intellectuals. Its corollary, formulas of associationism based on ideological relationships – whether explicit or not – can explain the transcendence and intensity of international networks centred on women like Serrano, Gimeno de Flaquer, or Belén Sárraga, who travelled internationally and established direct contact with the principal heads of state of various American nations (Fernández 2011, 168–9). It was due to her affiliation with freemasonry that Serrano, who dedicated *Americanos célebres* (Famous American men; 1886–8) to Porfirio Díaz, was received with all honours in San Salvador at the request of the president of the Republic, also a Mason. The national press reproduced some of her articles, and the Department of Public Instruction authorized her texts in national schools. A similar occurrence took place in Peru, as Serrano relates in *América y sus mujeres* (1890; America and its women), dedicated to one of her patronesses, the wife of the president of Venezuela, Jacinta Parejo de Crespo.

The ideals that Serrano defends centre on women's education informed by Enlightenment values as the only avenue for their emancipation and the international prestige of nations. This is the message that she transmits in her travels through Ecuador, El Salvador, the Dominican Republic, Peru, Chile, Venezuela, and so forth. Her works demonstrate an in-depth knowledge of the journalistic networks of the countries she visits and reveal the very welcoming attitude of the press towards peripatetic women writers and their works. Serrano immediately reports on such experiences in her following books, exemplary in their mission of pan-American cultural diplomacy, given that Serrano compliments all, whether she is referring to the polemical Mercedes Cabello or Matto, or the obscure Ecuadorian poets. The sympathetic linkage of gender, race, and class stems from the rejection of the stereotype of the *criolla* (a Latin American woman of European descent) as an indolent lady attended to by "cholas, indias o negritas" (Serrano 1890, 32; women of mixed race, American Indian women, or black women). In Serrano's text, the American *hermana* (sister) submits herself to a process of Europeanization that removes her from the legacy of pre-Hispanic civilizations as a savage, degraded woman, which only has mystery and charm for anthropologists and historians (1890, 246). Such an argument is also present in Soledad Acosta's essays on the model of the writing patriot of *raza española* (Spanish lineage) (Fernández 2011, 164–5). As for Gimeno de Flaquer, she constantly seeks out discursive spaces on both sides of the Atlantic to make cultures intelligible through their differences and similarities, beginning with historical paradigms of women that may anticipate encounters between European modernity and local American customs (see Vialette 2015).

In this brief essay, I do not claim to obviate or disregard the undeniable differences that contextualize the trajectories of Spanish and Latin American women writers, and thus argue for their sisterly homogenization. Rather, I wish to indicate the need for a critical dialogue based on these women's experiences of transatlantic cultural contact as they sought entry into a Republic of Letters on the periphery of international centres of literary prestige, and from their positioning as writers on the very margins of that periphery.

PART III

The Iberian Feminist Movements Gain Strength under Republics, 1910–1939

COORDINATED BY ROBERTA JOHNSON

15 Historical Context in Portugal

DEBORAH MADDEN

Following the fall of the constitutional monarchy in 1910, Portugal established the First Republic (1910–26) and would become the third country behind France and Switzerland to maintain a long-standing Republican government. The inauguration of the First Republic brought about a range of reforms that afforded Portuguese women personal, legal, and professional freedoms. Offering a window of opportunity between the nineteenth century and the dictatorship that imposed social and legal restrictions on women, the sixteen-year Republic saw the lives of Portuguese women change significantly.

The Republican government was supported by Portuguese feminists, an affiliation that can be explained by the establishment's defence of the rights and freedoms of women. The Constituição Portuguesa de 1911 of the First Republic facilitated a wave of feminist reforms. The legislation outlined equal legal rights for both sexes (Art. 3.2), stripped the Catholic Church of the power it had held over Portugal by defending religious freedom (Arts. 3.5, 3.6, 3.7, 3.8), and explicitly defended freedom of speech (Art. 3.13). The stage was therefore set for monumental changes in the lives of Portuguese women, as the feminist movement was gaining ground. The fundamental aims of feminist action and thought in early twentieth-century Portugal were the implementation of divorce legislation, women's right to education, and, the most divisive of all, the right to vote.

Divorce was one of the first reforms on the agenda of the First Republic, introduced just one month after its establishment in 1910. The legislation was at the forefront of marital reform in Iberia, as divorce in Spain would not be legalized until twenty-one years later in 1931 under the Second Republic. The law itself was liberal, permitting no-fault divorce by mutual consent (Art. 3) and treating women and men as equally responsible in cases of adultery (Arts. 4.1, 4.2) and abandonment (Art. 4.5). Divorce was introduced as part of a set of laws known as the Leis da Família (Family laws), legislation which, in line with the secular leanings of the Republic, also made civil marriages obligatory.

The introduction of the divorce law was more symbolic than pragmatic; it exemplified the social reforms of the Republic yet was rarely employed. For instance, from the limited statistics available, Douglas L. Wheeler cites a mere 341 divorces recorded in Lisbon during the first six months following the introduction of the legislation. Wheeler uses this figure to highlight the minimal impact the law appears to have had (1978, 284). Remarkably, the divorce law was not immediately overturned with the establishment of the dictatorship and would remain intact until it was restricted to non-Catholics under the concordat of 1940, before being abolished entirely in 1966 (Phillips 1991, 221).

Equal educational opportunities for women were high on the agenda of Portuguese feminists in the early twentieth century. The first school for girls, the Escola Maria Pia (Cordeiro 2012, 33), was opened in 1906 in Lisbon; however, illiteracy rates for women continued to soar, recorded at 80% in 1911 (Belo 1989, 164). The topic of women's education became a central aspect of feminist debates and congresses throughout the early twentieth century, and initiatives were introduced during the First Republic to allow women access to education. The Constituição Portuguesa de 1911 introduced compulsory primary education, without limiting the legislation's application to male students (Art. 3.11), while coeducation remained a source of contention. Coeducation was eventually achieved in 1920 thanks to the campaigning efforts of women's groups, but women graduates would not be permitted to teach in boys' schools until 1926, the final year of the Republic (Guimarães 1987, 24). Increasing numbers of women achieved secondary and university educations during this period, as Elina Guimarães, a vocal advocate for women's rights in twentieth-century Portugal, explains in *Portuguese Women Past and Present* (1987). Guimarães indicates that girls were actively encouraged by their parents to study, as it was considered a valuable and useful activity endeavour (1987, 20).

The question of women's suffrage in twentieth-century Portuguese history is complex. Despite the many advancements afforded to women under the First Republic, the government resisted the right to vote. While the Republic had voted against women's suffrage in 1911, one valiant woman, Carolina Beatriz Ângelo, exploited the vague wording of the legislation. Taking the phrasing of the law in its most literal sense, Beatriz Ângelo registered to vote on the basis that she was literate, she was the legal head of her family as a widow and mother, and was over the age of twenty-one (Mariano 2011, 159, 270; Sadlier 1989, 117). Although her initial attempts to register were rejected, Beatriz Ângelo won her right to vote through a legal appeal and became the first Portuguese woman, and the first woman in the history of Southern Europe, to vote in an election. In response, the Republic changed the wording of the legislation to specify that only literate male heads of household were eligible to vote, in changes passed on 3 July 1913 (Rebelo 2008, 47).

The opposition to women's suffrage under the First Republic, an establishment that enhanced the social and legal standing of Portuguese women, may seem perplexing – particularly so when one considers that women's right to vote was introduced by the Second Republic in Spain. The most convincing reason for the refusal of the First Republic to allow women the vote is that the Republican government feared the influence that the Catholic Church had on women and was concerned that it would implore them to vote for conservative parties (Esteves 1998, 74; Gallagher 1983, 23; Robinson 1979, 36; Sadlier 1989, 119). The Catholic Church and its opposition to the feminist movement can thus be seen to have inhibited progress during the First Republic, albeit in an indirect manner. Lobbying, however, continued throughout the 1920s. In January 1920, for instance, the socialist Ramada Curto proposed women's suffrage to parliament, while Aurora de Castro e Gouveia defended women's right to vote in 1924 at the I Congresso Feminista e de Educação (First Conference on Feminism and Education) (Reynolds de Souza 2013, 37–8). A pamphlet entitled *Reivindicações sociais e políticas da mulher portuguesa na república* (Social and political demands of Portuguese women in the Republic) was also published in 1921 by Aurora de Castro Gouveia. It defended the Republic's record on women's rights and predicted that women's suffrage would soon be granted (Esteves Pereira 2006, 196). All efforts to allow women the vote during the First Republic were, however, fruitless.

Portuguese women would not have the right to vote for the remaining years of the First Republic, a right that was eventually won with the strategic decision of the dictatorship in 1931. In response to Spanish women's recently established suffrage, Portuguese women were granted the vote with certain restrictions. Following the example set by Miguel Primo de Rivera in Spain, women aged twenty-one and over who had a university or secondary school education and who were the head of the household were eligible to vote (Cova 2014, 65). The decision to afford women the vote was rooted in the belief that women were inherently conservative due to their relationship with the Catholic Church (Sadlier 1989, 119). Representing a calculated means of placating women under a dictatorship, then, the right to vote in Portugal did not constitute a victory for the feminist movement, nor can it be counted among the achievements of the First Republic.

The success of the feminist movement in the years preceding and during the First Republic may be gauged by the number of women's groups that emerged. Factions such as the Secção Feminista da Liga Portuguesa da Paz (Feminist Section of the Portuguese League for Peace; 1906), the Grupo Português de Estudos Feministas (Portuguese Group of Feminist Studies; 1907), the Associação de Propaganda Feminista (Association of Feminist Propaganda; 1911), the União das Mulheres Socialistas (Union of Socialist Women; 1912), and the Comissão Feminina "Pela Pátria" (Women's Commission for the Nation; 1914) (Mariano 2011, 273–9) illustrate the range of women's organizations in Portugal in the early decades of the twentieth century.

One of the most influential organizations was the Liga Republicana das Mulheres Portuguesas (Republican League of Portuguese Women).[1] Established by Ana de Castro Osório and Adelaide Cabete in 1909, the league was closely linked to the Partido Republicano (Republican Party). Ana de Castro Osório was one of the most influential feminist theorists and activists in early twentieth-century Portugal, while Adelaide Cabete was a primary school teacher and later a doctor, who was part of a group that famously hoisted a Republican flag to celebrate the founding of the First Republic (Samara 2007, 105). The two founders were both admitted to Masonic lodges in 1907, highlighting the link between republicanism, feminism, and freemasonry in early twentieth-century Portugal (Wank-Nolasco 1995, 27).

The aims of the league were described as follows: "orientar, educar e instruir, nos princípios democráticos, a mulher portuguesa ... tornando-a um indivíduo autónomo e consciente; fazer propaganda cívica, inspirandose no ideal republicano e democrático" (quoted in Tavares da Silva 1983, 877; to guide, educate and instruct Portuguese women, in our democratic principles; turning them into independent and aware individuals; to make civic propaganda, inspired by the Republican and democratic ideal). The group called for education for women, the right to divorce, equality within the family, economic independence for women, women's suffrage, and amendments to the Civil Code of 1867. While the implementation of the 1910 divorce law was seen as a victory for the league, the sustained pressure it placed on the government to introduce women's suffrage was ultimately unsuccessful. The conflict over the right of educated women to vote ultimately led to internal splits, which in turn led to the league's eventual dissolution in 1912.

Adelaide Cabete later founded the Conselho Nacional das Mulheres Portuguesas (CNMP; National Council of Portuguese Women) in 1914.

An independent apolitical association and branch of the International Council of Women, the council defended women's rights from a range of perspectives and launched the magazine *Alma Feminina* (Women's soul). Darlene Sadlier deems this group "the most important and longest sustained organization in the history of Portuguese feminism" (1989, 118). The 1920s, an exciting decade for feminism in Portugal, was also an active period for the CNMP. The council organized two feminist congresses in 1924 and 1928. The date of the second conference is significant, as it was following the establishment of the dictatorship in 1926, indicating the CNMP's continued presence under the regime until its forced closure in 1947. The topics discussed at these gatherings were coeducation and the right to vote (Cova 2014, 65), the latter a particularly pressing topic for the group. The organization's magazine *Alma Feminina*, for instance, made continued calls for women's suffrage in the 1920s in its pages (see, for instance, *Alma Feminina* 7 and 8 [July 1921]; *Alma Feminina* 1 and 2 [January and February 1922]). The sustained, albeit unsuccessful, pressure of the group indicates how the First Republic was seen as a period of action among Portuguese feminists – a time when feminist reform could be realized.

A political climate felicitous for women's emancipation can also be said of the years following the outbreak of the First World War, a conflict that spurred another factor of Portuguese feminists. The First World War facilitated feminist movements throughout Europe, as women became obliged to take up the professional and personal roles previously reserved for men. Portugal was no exception to this trend, and the Cruzada das Mulheres Portuguesas (Crusade of Portuguese Women) was founded after the outbreak of the war. The establishment of the organization has been attributed to both Ana de Castro Osório in 1917 (Guimarães 1987, 22; Rebelo 2008, 47; Sadlier 1989, 119) and Elzira Dantas Machado, the wife of the then president of the Republic, Bernardino Machado, in 1916 (Machado Rosa 2013, 213; Mariano 2011, 279). The organization sought volunteers to support soldiers and their families in response to a call from the Portuguese government for female volunteers to become nurses. In her personal reflections on the feminist movement in Portugal, Elina Guimarães observes that, while the group was not "especially feminist," the organization did give women an opportunity to take part in public life (1987, 22). Above all, this organization exemplifies how pacifist causes became the natural ally of many female activists in the early twentieth century, and how national and international upheaval aided and shaped women's emancipation at a time when feminists were beginning to have their voices.

16 Feminist Thought in Portugal, 1900–1926

DEBORAH MADDEN

Women's access to education was a fundamental component of feminist thought in late nineteenth- and early twentieth-century Portugal. As João Esteves indicates in chapter 8, Maria Amália Vaz de Carvalho was a pioneering figure in Portuguese women's access to education, despite her reservations about other aspects of the feminist movement. A poet, writer, and literary critic, Vaz de Carvalho was instrumental in the development of women's education in nineteenth- and early twentieth-century Portugal. With her husband, Vaz de Carvalho wrote an educational manual that was approved by the Conselho Superior de Instrução Pública (Higher Council for Public Education) (Flores, Duarte, and Moreira 2009, 190), and would have a girls' school named after her in Lisbon. For Vaz de Carvalho, education was key to the image she envisaged of a modern Portuguese woman, as she explains in *As nossas filhas: Cartas ás mães* (Our daughters: Letters to mothers): "O maior inimigo de todo o desenvolvimento moral e intelectual da mulher portuguesa é o meio social que a cerca e oprime, impondo-lhe as suas leis absurdas" (1904, 255; The greatest enemy of the moral and intellectual development of the Portuguese woman is the social environment that surrounds her and oppresses her, imposing absurd laws upon her).

For Vaz de Carvalho, a backward, oppressive society was responsible for inhibiting the intellectual development of Portuguese women. The author of several other nonfictional texts in the nineteenth and early twentieth century, she published *Coisas d'agora* (Things of the here and now) in 1912. The work details her observations of recent social and political activity, with chapters including "O congresso e a educação da mulher" (The congress and women's education; 1909); "A mulher na democracia" (The woman in democracy; 1911); "Evolução do feminismo (Entre dois romances)" (Evolution of feminism – Between two novels; 1910; the novels in question are Jane Austen's *Emma* and Charlotte Brontë's *Jane Eyre*); and "Por terras de Portugal e Espanha" (Through the lands of Portugal and Spain; 1911). The latter two chapters use literature as a means of documenting social activity, focusing on the feminist movement in the former, while the final chapter laments the lack of a unified literary history in Spain and Portugal.

One aim of this edited collection on Iberian feminism is to reincorporate Portugal into a comprehensive overview of feminist activity and thinking in Iberia. The most salient link between the feminist movements in early twentieth-century Portugal and Spain is the professional and personal collaboration of Ana de Castro Osório and Carmen de Burgos. The life and works of Castro Osório remind us that feminist thought in Portugal is best understood in conjunction with an appreciation for the developments in Spain, since highlighting the links and similarities can develop our overall understanding of the feminist movement in Iberia and the shared experiences of Iberian women.

Ana de Castro Osório was a vocal supporter of women's personal and political emancipation in early twentieth-century Portugal. One of the leading female figures during the First Republic, Castro Osório was a committed Republican and dedicated her life to implementing her theories on women's liberation. In 1905, five years before the introduction of the Republic, Castro Osório produced the first feminist manifesto in Portugal, *Às mulheres portuguesas* (To the Portuguese women). Castro Osório defends her own understanding of what it means to be a feminist, in response to the prevalent antifeminist discourse in early twentieth-century Portugal:

> Ser feminista não é querer as mulheres umas insexuais, umas masculinas de caricatura, como alguns cuidam; mas sim desejá-las criaturas de inteligencia e de razão, educadas util e praticamente de modo a vêrem-se ao abrigo de qualquer dependencia, sempre amarfanhante para a dignidade humana" (1905, 24)
>
> (To be a feminist is not to want desexualized women, masculinized caricatures, as concerns some people; rather it is to desire that women are intelligent, reasoning beings, educated usefully and practically so they are saved from any dependency, which is always an obstacle to human dignity.)

Continuing with her desire to reclaim the idea of feminism from negative depictions, Castro Osório also acknowledges in the text the extreme reactions the word "feminism" elicits:

> Feminismo: É ainda em Portugal uma palavra de que os homens se riem ou se indignam, consonante o temperamento, e de que a maioria das proprias mulheres córam, coitadas, como de falta grave cometida por algumas colegas, mas'de que ellas não são responsaveis, louvado Deus! ...
>
> E, no entanto, nada mais justo, nada mais rasoavel, do que este caminhar seguro, embora lento, do espirito feminino para a sua autononomia. (1905, 11)

> (Feminism: In Portugal, the word still makes men laugh or incenses them, depending on their temperament, and makes the majority of women blush, the poor things, because of the grave crime committed by some of their fellow women, for that which they are not responsible, praise be to God! ...
>
> It is, however, nothing fairer, nothing more reasonable, than this steady, albeit slow, path of the female spirit towards its autonomy.)

The manifesto defends women's emancipation from a range of perspectives, argues for increased educational and professional opportunities, critiques the legal subordination of Portuguese women, particularly married women, under the Civil Code of 1867, and draws on the author's knowledge of the rights and expectations of women in other European countries. Directing her message to women of all social classes and to both women and men, Castro Osório used her manifesto as a means of uniting the Portuguese nation.

In line with other Portuguese feminist thinkers of the early twentieth century, education was key to Castro Osório's envisaged feminist revolution. Drawing on the recent scientific discourse that discussed women's biological capabilities, Castro Osório defends women's right to an education, arguing that intellect is not determined by biological sex: "Está provado pela sciencia que intelectualmente não ha sexos privilegiados" (1905, 15 [emphasis in original]; It is proven by science that there is no intellectually superior sex). Uneducated women, in Castro Osório's view, inhibited not only women's progress but also the development of the Portuguese nation as a whole. As it stood, women were not contributing to Portuguese society as they could, as "insuficientemente são educadas para serem as companheiras e as mães do homem moderno" (1905, 6; they are not sufficiently educated to be the partners and mothers of the modern man). Education for women would also be beneficial to Portuguese men and children, as they would make more suitable partners for twentieth-century Portuguese men, and educated mothers would raise enlightened children. A positive result of feminist reform, Castro Osório believed, would be the development of women into "criaturas conscientes e autónomas, companheiras e aliadas do homem, as verdadeiras educadoras de seus filhos" (1905, 81; aware and autonomous creatures, partners and allies of men, the true educators of their children).

As indicated in chapter three, Carmen de Burgos saw Portugal as a haven for feminist ideas in the early twentieth century; Ana de Castro Osório, on the other hand, laments the difficulties faced by Spanish women in comparison to their Portuguese counterparts in *Às mulheres portuguesas*. Defending Spanish women from common criticisms, Castro Osório empathizes with their predicament:

> Ha quem afirme, e tenha isso como consolação, que a hespanhola é muito mais futil e vaidosa, muito mais ignorante e inutil. Não temos dados para establecer o confronto, mas o que é certo é que nada nos devem consolar tais opiniões. Se são verdadeiras, pesa-nos que haja um paiz na Europa no qual a mulher, ainda mais do que no nosso, se esqueça de que deve ser a companheira e auxiliar do homem, sua igual e sua amiga. (1905, 196)
>
> (There are those that believe, and take it as some consolation, that Spanish women are more frivolous and vain, much more ignorant and useless. We have no proof to confirm this criticism, but we certainly should not take solace from such opinions. If they are true, it should disturb us that there is a country in Europe in which women, even more so than in our own country, forget that they should be man's partner and supporter, his equal and his friend.)

Here Castro Osório reiterates her argument that women's emancipation would allow women to support men, illustrating how a restructure of the female/male dynamic underpins her feminism. In 1911, Castro Osório released a nonfictional text about divorce, *A mulher no casamento e no divórcio* (Women in marriage and divorce), echoing Burgos's *El divorcio en España* (Divorce in Spain) of 1904. In the work, Castro Osório commends the Republic for its hasty introduction of divorce legislation, noting how such reforms were only possible under a Republican government. The text celebrates how the legislation is imposed upon women and men equally, and takes the opportunity to criticize the treatment of women under the Civil Code of 1867. In Castro Osório's view, the divorce law "é uma das que mais profundamente revolvem a estructura social, modificando a familia" (1911, 7; is one of the laws that most significantly reforms social structure, changing the family).

A further parallel between Castro Osório and Burgos is fiction, as both women used literature as a means of promoting their feminist ideals. Castro Osório wrote tales for children and published several novels throughout the early decades of the twentieth century. Common themes in her works are Portuguese nationalism, religion, and the rights of women. There are also explicit references to the legal situation of women that echo Burgos's oeuvre. The novel *O direito da mãe: Novela* (A mother's right: Novel; 1925), for instance, critiques marriage and divorce legislation, as well as the limited legal rights of mothers after a marriage breakdown, while *Mundo novo* (New world; n.d.) examines the social and legal constraints of marriage, draws on feminist ideology, and critiques the rights of women under the 1867 Civil Code.

The term "feminism" has long been contentious in Iberian popular culture, as can be seen in Castro Osório's attempts to explain her own understanding of the concept. Often (mis)interpreted as an inverse form of patriarchy, several other feminists in early twentieth-century Portugal sought to rectify misunderstandings and misconceptions by detailing their own feminist beliefs. Emília de Sousa Costa, a leading figure in Portugal's feminist movement, is one such example. An activist, journalist, translator, and writer, sometimes writing under the pseudonym "Maria Valverde," Sousa Costa was a vocal advocate of women's right to education. She was one of the founders of Caixa de Auxílio a Estudantes Pobres do Sexo Feminino (Support Fund for Poor Female Students) (Esteves 1998, 189), acting as the organization's president. Among Sousa Costa's numerous nonfictional publications are her Portuguese translation of *Aos professores e às professoras* (To the male and female teachers; 1914); *Maria Amália Vaz de Carvalho* (1934), a homage to one of the first advocates for women's education in Portugal; and *A mulher educadora* (The female educator; 1945) on the topic of education. Sousa Costa also authored several fictional pieces that engaged with the question of women's education (see Nogueira, 2013).

Sousa Costa details her own understanding of feminism in her publication *Ideais antigas de mulher moderna* (Old ideas about the modern woman) from 1923. Here, Sousa Costa explains:

> o feminismo, que não é, não pode, nem deve ser mais que a nobilitação da mulher, a sua reabilitação de criatura humana, como um factor social equivalente ao homem, pela sua inteligência, para a maior parte das pessoas, mesmo das mais cultas do nosso país, é a pretensão criminosa da mulher a igualar o sexo masculino em defeitos e em vícios, o esquecimento da tarefa que a natureza lhe impõe no lar e na família. ... Em Portugal, o feminismo, tal como êle deve ser compreendido, é religião de duas dúzias de mulheres conscientes, que de coração magoado vão assistindo à crescente perversão de costumes, à dissolução dos laços de família. (1923, 121, 122)

> (feminism, is not, cannot and should not be more than recognizing women, acknowledging them as human beings, as a social being equal to men, due to their intelligence, for the majority of people, including some of the most educated of our country, feminism is the outrageous idea of women being equal to men in terms of their failings and vices, forgetting their natural role within the home and family. ... In Portugal, feminism, as it should be understood, is a doctrine of two dozen conscientious women with heavy hearts who are witnessing the increasing perversion of customs, the dissolution of family ties.)

Championing the equal status of women and men, particularly in terms of their intelligence, Sousa Costa argues that the aim of feminism is to give women equal social status to men, and she distances herself from strains of feminist thought that strip women of their feminine qualities. A woman's position within the private sphere and the family was, for Sousa Costa, commendable. In this sense, her feminist beliefs were relatively modest, particularly when compared with those of Ana de Castro Osório. In her thorough, illuminating review of feminist women in early twentieth-century Portugal, Maria Regina Tavares da Silva classes Sousa Costa as a "defensora de um feminismo moderado" (1983, 880; defender of a moderate feminism). Sousa Costa's argument for women's working rights, for instance, relies on the assumption that women tend to work outside the home only when they have no other option. The extent to which Sousa Costa's views were strategic – hoping to achieve reform more quickly by not being overly ambitious and extreme – is debatable, and Tavares da Silva acknowledges that Sousa Costa's brand of moderate feminism was, above all, "profundamente realista" (1983, 880; deeply realist). In essence, her commitment to advocating women's access to education does include her among the forward-looking women who developed and contributed to feminist thought in early twentieth-century Portugal.

A subdued take on feminism is not unusual among the so-called feminists of early twentieth-century Portugal. Another leading figure, Virgínia de Castro e Almeida, is also noted for her seemingly tame expectations. Margarida Esteves Pereira remarks that Castro e Almeida's *A mulher: História da mulher, a mulher moderna – Educação* (Woman: History of women, the modern women – Education), from 1913, "might appear, at best, paradoxical" (2006, 187) when it states that women should aspire to love, motherhood, and education. As we have seen in relation to women's suffrage, the term "paradoxical" could be applied to many aspects of the Portuguese feminist movement. As Esteves Pereira continues, Castro e Almeida's views are "very suggestive of the type of ideological contradictions that pervade women's writing on [feminism] and, especially, the writings of the first Portuguese women who, nevertheless, justly claim the epithet of feminists" (2006, 187–8).

Although contradictions may be par for the course when examining feminism in early twentieth-century Portugal, many of the leading feminist figures did, indeed, explicitly outline their own interpretation of the concept and accept the label of "feminist." Castro e Almeida, like Sousa Costa, clarified her own understanding of feminism. A translator and writer of children's stories, she represented Portugal in Paris at the Comissão de Cooperação Intelectual (Commission of Intellectual Cooperation), and she was the first Portuguese woman to play a leading role in the cinematic industry, founding Fortuna Films in 1922 (Mariano 2011, 268). Castro e Almeida reclaimed the term "feminism" and disassociated her own beliefs from negative connotations of the movement:

> Não sou feminista na accepção errada que frequentamente se dá a esta palavra tornando-a synonimo de violência, de aspirações absurdas ou ridiculas.
>
> No feminismo, como no socialismo, como em todas as grandes crenças ... ha os exaltafos, os fanaticos, os incomprehensivos, os que vão além do sonho ...
>
> O feminismo não é uma força que se levanta contra o homem; é a voz da mulher instruida, forte, equilibrada e pura, que aspira nobremente a um lugar ao lado do seu companheiro para compartir as suas odores, os seus trabalhos, os seus cuidades e as suas alegrias.

> O feminismo quer que o homem deixe de considerar a mulher como agente exclusivo de prazer, como serva, como utensílio, como objecto de luxo; quer fazer da mulher a igual de homem e não a usurpadora dos seus direitos. (1913, 19–21)
>
> (I am not a feminist according to the incorrect understanding that is frequently attributed to a word becoming synonymous with violence, with absurd or ridiculous aspirations.
>
> In feminism, as in socialism, as in all large belief systems … there are the extremists, the fanatics, the ignorant, those that go beyond the call of duty …
>
> Feminism is not a force that rises up against men; it is the voice of women who are educated, strong, balanced, and pure, who nobly aspire to a place alongside their partner to share their hates, their work, their concerns, and their happiness.
>
> Feminism wants men to stop seeing women as a means of pleasure, servants, as a tool, as an object of luxury; it wants to make women equal to men without usurping on their rights.)

Putting her emphasis on equality and drawing on Castro Osório's argument that feminism would make women more suitable partners for men, Castro e Almeida believed the fundamental aim of feminism was to make men view women as equals.

In the same text, Castro e Almeida considers the feminist movement(s) in Portugal and Spain. Illustrating the links that arose naturally as a result of geographical proximity, she laments the influence of the Catholic Church and cultural expectations imposed on Iberian women. Castro e Almeida considers the progress, or lack thereof, in Portugal and Spain:

> Nos paizes latinos o movimento feminista não tem a força nem a gravidade que acabamos de observar nos outros.
>
> Na Hespanha e em Portugal o feminismo é apenas embryonario. Neste rápido esboço de analyse ao desenvolvimento da questão da mulher em varios paizes, nem vale a pena falar do que sobre o assumpto se passa na peninsula.
>
> Ainda ha bem pouco a triste iniciativa de um numero elevadissimo de senhoras hespanholas manifestando-se contra a lei que subtrahia a escola primaria ao ensino religioso obrigatorio, nos dá a prova concludente do

abrazo d'aquelle paiz no sentido da libertação da mulher. O catholicismo, sob a sua forma mais nociva, – o jesuitismo, – domina poderosamente o sexo feminino.

Emquanto essa força não fôr vencida, a mulher, escrava do padre, será um elemento de atrazo e de desmoralisação. (1913, 204, 206)

(In the Latin countries, the feminist movement does not have the force or the strength that we have observed in other countries.

In Spain and Portugal feminism is barely embryonic. In this brief overview of the question of how women have developed in various countries, it is not worth talking about what is happening on the Peninsula.

Even until quite recently there are still relatively few examples of the sorrowful initiative of a huge number of Spanish women who protested against the law that removed primary schooling from obligatory religious education, giving us conclusive evidence of the support in the country for women's liberation. Catholicism, in its most harmful form – Jesuitism – powerfully controls the female sex.

As long as this force remains undefeated, women, slaves of the priest, will be an element of backwardness and demoralization.)

Castro e Almeida observes how, in comparison to other countries, feminism in Spain and Portugal was underdeveloped and inherently weak. She commends Spanish women for their activity, and condemns the power of the Catholic Church in Iberia and its impact on the feminist movements. If the shared aims and activities of Ana de Castro Osório and Carmen de Burgos epitomize the successes of the feminist movements during the Republics in early twentieth-century Iberia, then the influence of the Catholic Church in both Spain and Portugal encapsulates one reason for the eventual decline of feminist ideals in both countries. The progress made by feminist movements in early twentieth-century Iberia was systematically dismantled during two long-standing dictatorships, and the Catholic Church was instrumental in the formation of these regimes' views on women.

17 Historical Background in Spain

ROBERTA JOHNSON AND OLGA CASTRO

The first and second decades of the twentieth century were important turning points in Portuguese and Spanish feminism, because Republican movements gave feminism a significant boost. Republican forms of government, with their equality platforms, have long been associated with women achieving political and legal parity. Portugal, which had voted a Republic in 1910, was more advanced in its feminist activity than Spain. As was the case with the Second Spanish Republic elected in 1931, women were important promoters of the Portuguese Republican movement. Carolina Beatriz Ângelo wrote articles criticizing the monarchy and helped sew the Republican flags that were raised in Lisbon in 1910. She formed the Portuguese Group of Feminist Studies and the Association of Feminist Propaganda with Ana de Castro Osorio, another important Portuguese feminist and founder of the first feminist association, The Portuguese Group of Feminist Studies, in 1907. Ângelo earned a degree in medicine at age twenty-four and in 1905 published *As mulheres portuguesas*. In 1911, she became a major advocate for women's suffrage. She had managed to vote under the original Republican law, which allowed heads of household (not specifying gender) to vote; because Ângelo successfully voted under the old law, the law was then changed to read "men" only as heads of household. The fact that Ângelo had managed to vote before the law was changed became international news. She was catapulted to fame, and Portugal was regarded as a pioneering country in terms of granting women's suffrage.

The atmosphere of women's liberation and debate on women's status in Portugal had an important impact on Spanish feminist Carmen de Burgos. Burgos, a mother estranged from her Andalusian husband and working in Madrid – where she had a long-standing affair with Ramón Gómez de la Serna – found in Portugal a refuge from the hostile eye of Spanish society trained on her unconventional lifestyle. Maryellen Bieder has chronicled the shift in Burgos's feminist position from an early difference feminism that denied women the vote to an equality feminist stance that did include franchise in the 1920s (Bieder 2001). However, it is important to remember that in 1919 Burgos travelled to Portugal as a newspaper correspondent and interviewed a number of people about the Republic. One of the articles she wrote about her encounters in Portugal includes the following passage: "Se siente un gran optimismo contemplando esta labor sana, fructífera, tan distina de ... otros países. Crear trabajo, estudiar las condiciones sociales, moralizar y educar, preparando un futuro más equilibrado y más feliz, esa es la obra admirable de las mujeres de Portugal" (Starcevic 1976, 58; One feels a great optimism contemplating this healthy, fruitful work, which is so different from ... other countries. Creating work, studying social conditions, moralizing and educating, preparing a happier and more equal future that is the admirable work of the Portuguese women).

Burgos's novelette *La flor de la playa* (1920) captures the dichotomy between the Spanish and Portuguese ambience and laws regarding women in early twentieth-century Spain and Portugal. A young working-class Madrid couple that has been dating for three years, putting off marriage to sometime in the future when they will have saved enough money for a proper wedding, decides to vacation together in Portugal. They pretend to be husband and wife, and take a room together in a beachside hotel. They follow all the social prescriptions for a middle-class married couple – she wears a hat, something she did not do as a working-class woman in Spain, and neither of them dons a bathing suit or actually goes to the beach, because respectable middle-class people do not disrobe in public. Both the man and the woman grow bored with this lifestyle, and the couple breaks up when they return to Madrid, fully aware that they will continue to live single lives and not marry (at least not marry each other). Portugal is thus portrayed as a more liberal country, where people have the opportunity to try out the kind of intimacy marriage supposes, before it is too late.

The First World War, which fuelled the Spanish economy and saw a swelling in the ranks of women in the Spanish workplace, had ended in 1918. As Spanish women were being forced back into the home at the end of the war, their discontent grew, as did their willingness to follow their Anglo-Saxon sisters' lead in openly feminist manifestations. Key

Spanish feminist books appeared around this date: Margarita Nelken's *La condición social de la mujer en España* (Women's social condition in Spain; 1919 or 1920); María (Gregorio) Martínez Sierra's *Cartas a las mujeres de España* (Letters to the women of Spain; 1920); and Graciano Martínez's conservative, Catholic, albeit decidedly feminist *El libro de la mujer española: Hacia un feminismo cuasi dogmático* (The book of the Spanish woman: Towards a quasi-dogmatic feminism; 1921). Women's organizations proliferated in Spain in the 1920s. The first feminist organization, the firmly middle-class and moderate Asociación Nacional de Mujeres Españolas (ANME; National Association of Spanish Women), had been founded in 1918; its associated journals *El Pensamiento Femenino* (Feminine thought) and *La Voz de la Mujer* (Women's voice) are from 1917 and 1918. Its political arm, Acción Política Femenina Independiente (Independent Feminine Political Action) would not appear until 1934. The independent feminist journal *Mundo Femenino* (Feminine world), reporting on feminist activities, began publication in 1921. The women's intellectual association the Lyceum Club came into existence in 1926. In the 1920s, Georg Simmel, Gregorio Marañón, and José Ortega y Gasset circulated "scientific" theories in Spain about the relative merits of male and female roles based on biology that some feminist thinkers, such as Carmen de Burgos and Rosa Chacel, challenged in fiction and essays.

Spanish dictator Miguel Primo de Rivera's regime (1923–30) saw some tepid prowomen legislation: laws protecting women's work, facilitating women's university education, and opening to women certain jobs in municipal governments. Under the dictatorship, which was allowed by the weak monarch Alfonso XIII, Republican sentiment grew in Spain. As we saw in the case of Portugal, Republicanism and feminism went hand in hand. In 1930, Primo de Rivera stepped down; Republicans won municipal elections in 1931, and Alfonso XIII, seeing the handwriting on the wall, went into exile, making way for the proclamation of the Second Spanish Republic on 14 April 1931. Solidifying the identification between women's status and Republicanism was the fact that many referred to the new Republic as *la niña bonita* (the pretty girl; see figure 4).

Under the Republic, both women and the territories – the Basque Country, Catalonia, Galicia – made significant legal gains. Importantly, feminist and territorial or peripheral nationalist movements grew together during this period. If feminism teamed up with the antislavery movement in the United States, in the Spanish territories it joined

Figure 4. *La república española*. Postcard. Madrid, 1931. ©With permission from the Centro Documental de la Memoria Histórica. Ministerio de Educación, Cultura y Deporte.

forces with nationalist (sometimes separatist) movements in the Basque Country, Catalonia, and Galicia. Although the territories were under the jurisdiction of Spanish national law, each area saw feminist organizations develop according to its local characteristics. In Galicia, for example, women had long worked in its primarily rural economy; in addition, Galician men's high rate of immigration to the New World for economic reasons placed more economic and other responsibilities on women's shoulders. Galician nationalist organizations that would accommodate such prowomen activities included cultural societies, such as Irmandades da Fala (Galician Language Societies; founded in 1916), Xeración Nós (The Us Generation; founded in 1920), and also the political party Partido Galeguista (Pro-Galician Party; founded in 1931). The growth of a distinctive Galician female consciousness is intimately related to the emergence of a cultural and political nationalist consciousness. Showing that they were committed both to nationalism and to creating a space for women, the Partido Galeguista and the Irmandades da Fala both added a feminine section, which was not independent. Noa Rios Bergantinhos concludes that in reality these cultural and political associations created these spaces with electoral designs, not because they were interested in women's wellbeing, but because men had emigrated, and women were in charge of educating the children (Rios Bergantinhos 2001, 37, 56). Thus they wanted to indoctrinate women to transmit the nationalist message to their families. These developments in Galicia were quite different from the relationship between nationalism and feminism in the Basque National Party (with the women's branch, Emakunde Abertzale Barza) and the Catalan Lliga Catalana (and its Secció de la Dona), as these two groups worked quite independently from the main party to address women's issues from a feminist perspective, thus achieving much more visibility at a state level. This different visibility may explain why the national feminist organization ANME was aware of the Basque and Catalan organizations, but not of the Galician one. Despite the linking of Basque, Catalonian, and Galician feminism (or protofeminism) and the nationalist movements in the three areas, women's demands were ignored by their male counterparts, and women were excluded from the nationalist publications of the era.

Spanish Enlightenment writings by Benito Jerónimo Feijoo and Josefa Amar y Borbón, among others, had raised Spanish consciousness about women's nature and abilities, and this consciousness, albeit transformed by romanticism's idealization of women, maintained a public presence in Republican circles during the constitutional and liberal periods of the early nineteenth century. Education continued to be a primary concern for feminists in the lead-up to the Second Spanish Republic. The Residencia Femenina (Women's residence; directed by María de Maeztu) was founded in 1915 as a parallel to the masculine Residencia de Estudiantes (Student residence). Increased women's literacy fostered the creation of a number of feminist publications. In 1925, the feminist journal *Feminal* began publishing a series of articles on the injustices in the Civil Code and proposed a number of changes. For example, article 438 stated that the penalty for a husband who killed his adulterous wife and her lover was exile to another province, while adulterous husbands were not subject to any penalties as long as they were discreet. The Constitution of 1931 righted these inequities by declaring that all citizens were equal before the law. Article 2 of the 1931 document declares that "todos los españoles son iguales ante la ley" (*Constituciones* 1998, 157; all Spaniards are equal before the law), and article 25 enumerates the areas of equality, including sexual equality: "No podrán ser fundamento de privilegio: la naturaleza, la filiación, el sexo, la clase social, la riqueza, las ideas políticas ni las creencias religiosas" (161; Nature, family, sex, social class, wealth, political ideas, or religious beliefs cannot be the foundation of privilege). Article 43 of the 1931 Constitution further stipulates that "el matrimonio se funda en la igualdad de derechos para ambos sexos y podrá disolverse por mutuo deseo o petición de cualquiera de los cónyuges" (163; marriage is based on equal rights for both sexes and can be dissolved by mutual wish or petition of either one of the partners). Divorce was legalized in article 43 of the Constitution, but the women's vote had to await separate legislation that was hotly debated in Parliament, creating the strange paradox that women could be elected to Parliament (three were: Margarita Nelken, Clara Campoamor, and Victoria Kent), although they themselves could not vote. The debate split feminist deputies; Margarita Nelken, who feared women's conservative tendencies under the influence of the clergy and male members of their families, was opposed to women's franchise, and Clara Campoamor eloquently defended women's right to vote. The legislation passed by a narrow margin, and the law went into effect in 1932 in time for women to vote in the 1933 elections. The balance in Parliament was tipped to the more conservative factions. In fact, many have blamed the women's vote for this shift, but such blame has never been scientifically established.

In addition to the nationalist organizations' providing feminism an organizational space in Spain, workers' associations (beginning in the 1870s) also offered a ready-made structure for women to air their concerns. This situation gave the Spanish feminist movement a different class composition from that of other countries where feminist activism was primarily a middle-class phenomenon. In Spain, each social class had its own feminists and feminism with their own agendas. In some cases, as with anarchist Federica Montseny in Barcelona, a would-be feminist preferred to think of him- or herself as furthering a human agenda, rather than a strictly feminist program. Catalonia, one of the most industrialized areas of Spain and thus home to more developed middle and working classes, saw the rise of both middle-class and proletarian feminisms.

The years before the Spanish Civil War, which broke out on 18 July 1936, greatly slowed the advance of strictly women's concerns, whether on the Republican or the Nationalist (conservative) side. In 1934, with the establishment of the Sección Femenina as part of the Fascist Party, the Falange, the progressive agenda for women set by the Republic had already begun to fade. The polarization between Republican feminists and Nationalist antifeminists deepened after the Civil War began. The tendency to organize begun in the 1920s accelerated, and the war years (1936–9) saw a number of women's organizations come into existence, among them: the Unió de Dones de Catalunya (Union of Catalan Women), of Communist orientation; Mujeres Libres (Free Women), primarily anarchist; and youth organizations such as Unión de Muchachas of Madrid and Aliança (Girls of Madrid) and Nacional de la Dona Jove of Barcelona (National of Young Women of Barcelona), both founded in 1937. Strong female leaders like Basque Communist Dolores Ibárruri and Catalan anarchist Federica Montseny rose to national prominence, giving speeches calling for women's right to work, equal salaries, paternity investigations, divorce, abortion, and the abolition of sexual discrimination in the professions.

During the Civil War, women once again occupied work positions formerly held by men who had joined the war effort. Women on both sides of the conflict worked behind the lines to keep the fighting men clothed, fed, and attended to medically. In the early days of the war, some women on the Republican side took up arms and joined the militias to fight alongside men, but as the Republican forces became more organized, women were forced into the rear-guard support position. Most of the women active in the Republican war effort were affiliated with Communists or anarchists. In 1936, the journal *Mujeres* was founded; it was linked to the Communists but in theory allowed for all (leftist) points of view. For example, anarchist Lucía Sánchez Saornil wrote in the journal that she hoped women's participation in politics would erase the rivalries between factions. However, this turned out to be a vain hope, as the better organized Communists took over the Republican war effort and actively persecuted the anarchists.

Mujeres Libres (Free Women) was an organization founded in Madrid and Barcelona shortly before the outbreak of the Civil War.

Although its agenda seems quite feminist in purpose, it did not identify with the notion of feminism per se and did not limit itself to demanding social and political rights for women, work, or economic parity with men. Under the leadership of Lucía Sánchez Saornil, Dr Amparo Poch y Gascón, and journalist Mercedes Comaposada, they published the namesake journal *Mujeres Libres,* which also focused on psychological independence for women, the advocacy of a female identity, personal autonomy, and self-esteem, in moves that remind one of arguments forged some years earlier by María Martínez Sierra. The founding of *Mujeres Libres* was a reaction to anarchist men's exclusion of women in their organizations and activities and to their desire to keep women within the domestic sphere. The organization served the dual purpose of feminism and anarchism, and established a precedent for the dual militancy that typified Republican and Civil War era feminism in Spain.

18 First-Wave Spanish Feminism Takes Flight in Castilian-, Catalan-, and Galician-Speaking Spain

ROBERTA JOHNSON AND OLGA CASTRO

Throughout the nineteenth and earlier twentieth centuries, Spanish feminism consisted mostly of an effort by singular figures – Concepción Arenal, Emilia Pardo Bazán, Concepción Gimeno de Flaquer, and Carmen de Burgos. Margarita Nelken's *La condición social de la mujer en España* and María (Gregorio) Martínez Sierra's *Cartas a las mujeres de España* reflected the very different orientations that Spanish feminist thinking took in the early twentieth century, marking the beginning of a more organized feminism in Spain. Martínez Sierra's book reminds us that in considering the history of Spanish feminism we cannot overlook the presence of the Catholic Church and the fact that the church fathers recognized that if they were to remain relevant in Spanish women's lives, they had to move with the times and find ways to reconcile the church with women's agendas for their lives in the modern world. As a Socialist, Margarita Nelken's basic premise in *La condición social* is that "el verdadero problema feminista es un problema económico" (1922, 75; the real feminist problem is economic); thus she concentrates on the topic of work rather than the law, devoting only a chapter to Spanish women's legal situation. Nelken clearly favours the working-class woman who engages in paid employment, deeming the middle-class woman (probably the most important audience for Burgos and Martínez Sierra) a "*peso muerto de la nación*" (1922, 56 [emphasis in original]; dead weight on the nation). Although Nelken does occasionally employ biological data to bolster her arguments (brain size, for example), for the most part her evidence for fostering women's work is social. One of Nelken's most important contributions to the history of Spanish feminist theory is her complete coordination of the categories of gender and class. Nelken found it impossible to consider women's issues apart from social class; she believed that feminism in Spain was inextricably intertwined with class affiliations. According to Mary Lee Bretz, "the conflict between gender and class and the complex interactions between these two categories, which sometimes overlap and sometimes compete with each other, constitute a major focus of *The social condition of women in Spain*, informed by feminist and socialist concerns and addressed to women readers and to workers, the text struggles to create bonds between these two groups without conflating them" (Bretz 1998, 106). Nelken believed that working-class women, who were already equal to men in that they worked, were naturally feminists. A working-class woman has a "mentalidad más sana y espontánea, ignorante de los prejuicios y de los convencionalismos, se encuentra, implícitamente, al mismo nivel social que su hermano o su marido" (1922, 36; a healthier and more spontaneous mentality; she is implicitly on the same social level as her brother or her husband because she is unaware of social prejudices and conventions); thus her battle is limited to fighting for equal salaries and obtaining protective legislation and workers' unions that will put her on equal footing with male workers.

Nelken's analysis of the middle-class woman, which occupies an entire chapter of *La condición social de la mujer en España*, follows a Marxist line in its foundations in economics: "La cuestión feminista en España es ... una cuestión puramente económica" (1922, 49; The feminist question in Spain is ... purely economic). She avers that economics bedevil the middle-class woman most of all, because she has to find a husband to support her; her expected lifestyle is a true economic burden on the middle-class married man. The upper-class woman of means has little difficulty finding a husband, or if she does not find one, she can support herself. In the working class, since money is not an issue, there is greater freedom when choosing a marriage partner, and in fact marriage benefits a working man, because a wife can save him a lot of money on household work and paid sex. Nelken points out that middle-class women in some other countries do work and bring money into the household, but that is not the norm in Spain. She insinuates that marriage for middle-class women is a form of prostitution, since women's work is so disparaged and ill paid that women's only options are to sell their bodies to strangers or to a husband: "La única diferencia es que, en el matrimonio, el agarradero es definitivo y que, una vez conseguido el comprador, la mujer no se preocupa ya, en compensación, de seguirle agradando" (1922, 51; The only difference is that in marriage the hold is definitive, and once a buyer has been found, the woman no longer feels it necessary to continue pleasing him as a compensation). Nelken concludes her chapter on middle-class women with the above-cited epithet about their being a dead weight on the nation, but she adds that at the same time they are "lo que hay en ella más enérgico y más valiente" (56; what is most energetic and brave in the nation). She believed that middle-class women had a steeper hill to climb because they were combating prejudices, "un ambiente mezquino" (a mean-spirited ambience) that created a real obstacle course in the march towards liberation: "Su libertad de trabajo va siempre precedida de una emancipación moral, penosísima las más de las veces; de ahí la necesidad de la lucha, la solidaridad intuitiva con las que, en otros países, supieron ya unirse a éstas, de imitarlas" (36; Their freedom to work is always preceded by an often painful moral emancipation; thus the need for struggle, an intuitive solidarity with women in other countries who have already achieved this emancipation and to imitate them).

María (Gregorio) Martínez Sierra, who wrote under her husband Gregorio's name as a kind of pseudonym, focuses more on the middle-class woman as already a being in her own right, but who has been denied social and legal equality. Antonina Rodrigo, quoting María Martínez Sierra's speech "De feminismo," reminds us that "María Lejárraga cifraba el *sentido* y la *aspiración* del feminismo en la igualdad, en la creencia de que 'no hay libertad donde el deber no ata por igual a los dos que soportan el yugo'" (Rodrigo 1994, 125 [emphasis in original]; María Lejárraga located the *sense* and *aspiration* of feminism in equality, in the belief that 'there is no liberty where duty does not equally apply to those who bear the yoke'"). Martínez Sierra further maintains that the law recognizes women as equals in the realm of responsibilities and punishments, but not when it comes to rights (1916, 16). Martínez Sierra recurs to the oldest Spanish traditions to buttress her arguments in favour of equal rights for women before the law: "leyes visigodos, fundamento de nuestro 'españolismo,' y díganme ustedes lo que encuentren en ellas. Individualismo absoluto e igualdad perfecta en derechos y deberes para el hombre y la mujer; todas las restricciones antifeministas, señores españolizantes, nos han venido de extranjís" (1920, 131; Visigothic laws, foundational to our "Spanishness," and tell me what you find in them. Absolute individualism and perfect equality in laws and duties for women and men; all the antifeminist restrictions, pro-Spanish gentlemen, have come to us from foreign lands). Although she does not mention Rousseau, she in fact follows one of his basic precepts in the social contract when she states that "no hay libertad donde no hay igualdad" (1920, 26; there is no liberty where there is no equality). She does, however, cite John Stuart Mill on the necessity of "igualdad absoluta" (1920, 84; absolute equality).

Like María Martínez Sierra, Clara Campoamor argues for complete equality between men and women. According to Mary Nash, Campoamor maintains "una clara postura teórica de signo igualitario" (1994, 171; a clear theoretical posture of egalitarian stripe). Nash further asserts that

> ni siquiera el proceso de Modernización económica, cultural y política en las primeras décadas del siglo XX que conllevó una reformulación modernizadora de un nuevo prototipo femenino – la "Mujer Nueva" o "Mujer Moderna" – cambió el eje constitutivo del discurso tradicional de la domesticidad ya que la maternidad seguía representando la base esencial de la identidad cultural femenina. (1994, 162)

> (not even the process of economic, cultural, and political modernization in the first decades of the twentieth century that saw a modernizing reformulation of a new feminine prototype – the "New Woman" or the "Modern Woman" – changed the constitutive axis of the traditional discourse of domesticity since maternity continued to represent the essential basis of women's cultural identity.)

However, Nash believes that difference feminism opened a space for feminism in a conservative, Catholic country, which eventually led to a discussion of women's equal rights: "El discurso de la domesticidad amparó en términos políticos la noción de una ciudadanía diferenciada por género, es decir, una ciudadanía política para los varones y una ciudadanía social para las mujeres" (1994, 163; The discourse of domesticity supported in political terms the notion of a citizenship differentiated by gender, that is to say, a political citizenship for males and a social citizenship for women).

Having been elected to parliament in 1931, Campoamor worked tirelessly in favour of women's franchise. Her sharp reasoning surely had an impact on the favourable vote achieved in Parliament in 1932. She points out the faulty logic of a draft version of the equality clause in the Constitution, which stated that "no podrán ser fundamento de privilegio jurídico el nacimiento, la clase social, la riqueza, las ideas políticas y las creencias religiosas. Se reconoce *en principio*, la igualdad de derechos de los sexos" (2006, 43 [emphasis in original]; social class, wealth, political ideas, and religious beliefs cannot be a foundation of juridical hereditary privilege. *In principle*, equal rights between the sexes are recognized). Campoamor further notes that these two sentences contradict each other. The first one grants equality to all, although the equality of the sexes is left to the second sentence, which grants equal rights to the sexes in principle. She believed that sex should be included in the first sentence and that the second sentence should be eliminated. Campoamor scolds her male colleagues for the "in principle" rider to sexual equality before the law:

> Esta declaración constituía una burda ficción de la igualdad que la mujer tenía derecho a esperar de la Constitución republicana. Era la eterna cicatería masculina, la reminiscencia de su vanidosa tutela, incapaz de abordar lealmente el problema de la dignificación de la mujer y de resolverlo totalitariamente, cuando se veía en trance de no poder desconocerlo, una reminiscencia de diosecillo dispensador de la ley, la justicia o la merced, que en trance de desprenderse de algo que constituyó su plena y absoluta soberanía, le duele hacerlo totalmente y aspira a hacerlo poco a poco, concesión a concesión, en la graciosa y galante avenencia a la eterna demanda, a la obligada súplica femenina. (2006, 45)

> (This declaration constituted a gross fiction of equality that the woman had the right to expect from the Republican Constitution. It was the eternal male miserliness, a reminder of his vain tutelage, his incapacity to faithfully broach the problem of dignifying women and to totally resolve it when he saw himself unable to ignore it, a hold-over of the little god, dispenser of the law, justice, and mercy. When in the process of giving up something that constituted his full and absolute sovereignty, it pains him to do it completely, and he aspires to do it little by little, concession by concession, in the graceful and gallant deal with the eternal demand, the obliging feminine plea.)

Campoamor achieved her goal of making sex an equal condition for equality before the law in article 25 of the 1931 Constitution, the final version of which read that nature, application, sex, social class, wealth, political ideas, or religious beliefs were not grounds for judicial privilege. Campoamor also prevailed in other sexual equality clauses, such as the right of women to be elected to office, women's right to vote, the right of married women to retain their nationality, the right to investigate paternity, marriage based on equality of the sexes, and the right to divorce. She mentions, however, that a clause was attempted that would allow women to ask for divorce without giving a cause. Most members of Parliament did not favour this amendment, and out of expediency Campoamor went along with leaving the divorce provision as it was (with the "show cause" provision). She personally favoured the amendment, because it was "acorde con un principio humano de ayuda preferente a seres desiguales" (2006, 49; in accord with the human principle of giving preference to unequal beings), a version of our contemporary notion of affirmative action.

If Nelken's major feminist essay *La condición social* centres on social class and work, Carmen de Burgos's *La mujer moderna y sus derechos* (1927; Modern woman and her rights), published some eight years later, focuses on women's legal standing, an aspect of feminism that levels the playing field for all social classes, at least in theory, if not in practice. Even though equal rights before the law might suppose no need to consider differences in social class, in her introductory history of feminism, Burgos does recognize class distinctions in some parts of her book. In outlining the various types of feminism in her first chapter, the first two categories are "El feminismo obrero" (Workers' feminism) and "El feminismo burgués" (Bourgeois feminism), which appear before "El feminismo mundano" (Worldly feminism), "El feminismo profesional" (Professional feminism), "El feminismo cristiano" (Christian feminism), "El feminismo revolucionario" (Revolutionary feminism), and "El feminismo independiente" (Independent feminism) (Burgos 1927, 66). Burgos points out that feminism first arose among women of the lower classes ("mujeres del pueblo") because they were the most affected by economic problems, especially in the cities. Following an argument already present in Margarita Nelken's *La condición social*, Burgos declares that the middle class lagged behind in raising the feminist flag due to its resistance to work, an important focus of feminist activity. She points out that vanity precluded acceptance of middle-class women's working. Middle-class daughters, she notes, were brought up idle and given to luxurious ostentation. If the head of the household died, the women in the family were suddenly thrown into a penury from which they could not escape via work.

Burgos's rational style of argument, her cool level-headedness, and ability to go straight to the heart of the matter with incontrovertible evidence align her with the long rational equality feminist tradition that began in Spain with Benito Jerónimo Feijoo (informed, as Monica

Bolufer argues [1998]), by seventeenth-century radical Enlightenment thinker Francois Poulain de la Barre), and that has more recently inspired Celia Amorós's Enlightenment (or Equality) Feminists of the post-Franco era (who also base their thinking on the seventeenth-century Cartesian Poulain de la Barre).[2] In the fourth chapter of *La mujer moderna y sus derechos*, Burgos mentions what Descartes's rationalism offers feminism: "Descartes no acepta por verdadero más que lo que muestra la razón, y al querer demoler prejuicios sirve la causa femenina" (1927, 111; Descartes does not accept as true anything except what reason can demonstrate, and in attempting to erase prejudices, he served the female cause). She points out, long before 1980s equality feminism did, that Descartes's disciple François Poulain de la Barre "pide en *Educación de las Damas* y en *Igualdad de sexos*, todos los derechos de la mujer" (111; in *Women's Education* and *Equality of the Sexes* asks for all rights for women).

Although Burgos argues for legal parity ("La base está en las leyes, en la proclamación de la 'Igualdad de derechos'" [1927, 60; The basis is in the laws, in the proclamation of the "Equality of rights"]), as Anja Louis and Maryellen Bieder note (Louis 2005; Bieder 2001), her arguments sometimes slip over into a difference feminist position when the point she is making seems to benefit from such a manoeuvre. For example, on the page following the above quotation in which Burgos calls for legal equality, she declares that feminism never meant "un deseo de inversión de sexos o de funciones, y mucho menos la aspiración a la igualdad, que hace imposible la naturaleza" (61; a desire for the inversion of the sexes or of their functions, and much less the aspiration of equality, which nature makes impossible). However, here, as elsewhere, Burgos seems to distinguish between biology and the law. In chapter 2 of *La mujer moderna*, for instance, she undermines the biological arguments for inequality tendered by Gregorio Marañón, Otto Weininger, and Paul Julius Moebius.[3] Bieder and Louis also note that Burgos's feminist stance evolved over time, beginning closer to difference feminism and ending closer to equality feminism. Even in Burgos's last feminist work, *La mujer moderna y sus derechos*, her position is subtle, complex, and ultimately pragmatic. She may have most in common with postfeminist Spanish thinkers such as Carmen Alborch and Lucía Extebarria, who try to supersede the narrow confines of both equality and difference feminism to defend women's right to be both feminine and feminist. However, despite Burgos's often original and eclectic positions on some feminist issues, her style of argumentation places her firmly in the Enlightenment equality feminist camp. She had in common with eighteenth-century thinkers the love of intellectual conversation afforded by the *salón* or *tertulia,* a regular gathering of people for intellectual conversation. In fact, she hosted her own *tertulia* for many years, and the quality of her reasoning indicates someone who is used to marshalling evidence to make a point. Often in *La mujer moderna y sus derechos,* her expository style reminds one of Feijoo, who argued against received wisdom, correcting what he understood as errors in previous knowledge.

No other Spanish feminist thinker in Burgos's own generation, which includes María Martínez Sierra and Margarita Nelken, argues for their feminist program from a strictly legal point of view. Such an approach in the Spanish feminist canon will have to wait for Lidia Falcón, some thirty-five years later in 1962. Standing on a legal platform provides Burgos with solid evidence of inequities that can be easily remedied through legislative means. Social customs on which Martínez Sierra (in her early work) and Nelken dwell, often carried out in the privacy of homes and which Burgos also discusses, are much more difficult to control and change. Given that laws concern all social classes equally, compared with Margarita Nelken's *La condición social de la mujer en España* (1922), Burgos's focus is much less class oriented. Nelken's one chapter on women's legal situation focuses almost entirely on marriage, and like Burgos, she argues for legal parity within that institution.

Carmen de Burgos joined a long line of Spanish feminist thinkers, including Father Feijoo, Concepción Arenal, and Emilia Pardo Bazán, in arguing for women's right to work outside the home. Concepción Arenal and Emilia Pardo Bazán had in common with Father Feijoo that their early lives unfolded in Galicia, an area of Spain where women had always worked, especially in highly visible agricultural fields. According to María Aurèlia Capmany,

> Sin duda alguna el comportamiento de la mujer gallega del pueblo, que ellas conocían profundamente, no les dejaba lugar a dudas sobre las facultades ante el trabajo de ambos sexos. Es notorio que tanto en Concepción Arenal, como en la condesa de Pardo Bazán jamás se plantea la duda sobre las facultades de la mujer para trabajar, para estudiar, para intervenir en la vida pública de la nación. (Nelken 1922, 12 ["Prólogo"])

> (Surely their intimate knowledge of Galician village women's behaviour left them no doubt as to the ability to work in both the sexes. Notoriously,

> neither Concepción Arenal nor the Countess Pardo Bazán ever doubted women's ability to work, to study, to intervene in the public life of the nation.)

Concepción Arenal points to the example of North America, which was built on work that in turn underpins equality (1974a, 203–4). As Carmen de Burgos will do almost seventy years later, Arenal affirms women's "right to work"; from the principle of equality, society, Arenal avers, cannot deny women the ability to exercise their faculties (1895, 88). She confidently states that women can "ejercer toda profesión u oficio que no exija mucha fuerza física y para la que no perjudique la ternura de su corazón" (1974b, 79; exercise any profession or trade that does not demand much physical force and which does not harm the tenderness of her heart). Arenal immediately retracts the statement about physical stamina, recalling the back-breaking work women undertake in the agricultural sector (something she would have observed at close hand in Galicia and Asturias).

If charity work is central to Concepción Arenal's strategy for getting women out of the domestic sphere and also figures importantly in Margarita Nelken's discussion of women and work (although Nelken would rather shore up women's opportunities for paid work), Burgos avoids the topic altogether, presumably because charity work does not fit within her legal approach to women's situation. Two other points on which Burgos and Nelken disagreed are the role of religion in women's lives and women's franchise. Nelken believed religion to be a pernicious influence, while Burgos tried to find ways to accommodate at least Christianity into her feminist vision, noting Christ's positive attitude towards women. Nelken did not believe that Spanish women were, on the whole, prepared to vote, while Burgos, like Campoamor, did. This divergence signals a fundamental philosophical difference between Burgos and Nelken. Burgos argues that the law can effect social change, while Nelken believed that social change must occur first and the law affirm that change a posteriori.

Class is another area in which Burgos's feminist theory differs from that of her near contemporary Nelken. As is evident in Capdevila-Argüelles's assessment, by the early twentieth century the term used to refer to the middle class has shifted to "bourgeois" (2008), a practice already evident in Nelken's and Burgos's respective books *La condición social de la mujer* and *La mujer moderna y sus derechos*, in which they distinguish between the bourgeois woman and the working-class woman.

Burgos does address the aristocracy, calling its feminism "mundano" (2007; worldly). Aristocratic women, she believes, took advantage of feminism, not to fight for work and responsibility but rather to escape from forced seclusion. Aristocratic women wanted to be able to leave the house or travel alone and take part in sports, activities that were considered men's realm. Theirs was an emancipation via gesture – wearing make-up, hair styles, and clothes of their own choosing. Burgos considers these aristocratic feminist manifestations more authentic than the traditional aristocratic women's activities, such as charity work and social clubs. Burgos rues the fact that the different facets of feminism (many of them with class origins) are often at cross-purposes when women should be working together for the common good. This fragmentation and infighting repeats itself in the late twentieth- and early twenty-first-century democratic era in Spain, now along ideological grounds rather than on class distinctions.

A biological essentialism that conceptualizes women as mothers opens a public space for a "ciudadanía diferenciada que ignora el principio de la igualdad y de la individualidad" (Burgos 2007, 163; differentiated citizenship that overlooks the principle of equality and individuality) and allows for emancipating political projects "desde el reconocimiento de la diferencia de roles de género" (from the viewpoint of recognizing differences in gender roles). Once this transition was effected, women began to question the notion of separate spheres and to claim a role in the public arena. As mentioned at the beginning of this essay, Maryellen Bieder has chronicled the shift in Burgos's feminism over time from one of difference to equality by the time of her 1927 *La mujer moderna y sus derechos*. For example, in her early feminist essays and speeches, Burgos did not favour women's participation in politics, and she argued against the vote for women: "Eventually ... Burgos was swayed by the Portuguese feminists Elzira Dantas and Ana de Castro that the time had come to demand the vote for women. In 1921, Burgos organized the first public demonstration to demand that Parliament take up the issue. Later, as president of the Liga Internacional de Mujeres Ibéricas ... she continued her fight for unrestricted voting rights that culminated in the 1931 vote" (Bieder 2001, 215n5). Burgos often called upon the kind of observation and logic that reminds us of Feijoo and Arenal, who take certain truths to be self-evident: "Es un hecho evidente que las mujeres que ejercitan la fuerza superan a los hombres que lo trabajan o se dedican a deportes" (Burgos 1927, 37; It is evident that women who employ force are superior to men who employ it or who practise sports). In *La mujer moderna y sus derechos*, Burgos advocates absolute legal parity between men and women. However, unlike Poulain de la Barre, who argued for absolute equality in all spheres of life, Burgos falls somewhere between the absolute equality of Poulain de la Barre and the limited equality of Locke and Feijoo. She argues for equality before the law but not in daily life. For example, although Burgos believed that "el espíritu de nuestras leyes ha sido de igualdad" (1927, 166; the spirit of our laws has been of equality), her idea of equality in relationships between men and women is more idealistic than legalistic: "Sólo el amor, que supera a toda ley, establece la igualdad entre los cónyugues y mantiene el hogar indisoluble" (161; Only love, which is above all law, establishes equality between married people and maintains an indisoluble home).

Thus Burgos distinguishes between legal parity and biological and social equality. When it comes to work, however, her concept of equality is more absolute. Burgos believed that if women's work is the same as men's, women should receive the same pay, and that there should not be any inequality in working conditions: "Lo indispensable es la igualdad; la llamada protección perjudica a la mujer más que sus mismos enemigos" (1927, 141; Equality is indispensable; so-called protection damages women more than their enemies). True feminism, she believes, does not want privileges. Co-opting naturalistic arguments about a woman's biology determining her destiny, Burgos argues that inequality is not natural; therefore feminism wishes to re-establish the natural order. Inequality in the home, she believes, "prejudica a la familia toda" (1927, 200; damages the entire family). Like Arenal, she points out that "en cuanto a obligaciones sí somos iguales. La mujer paga las mismas contribuciones que los hombres. ... ¡En Derecho penal las leyes son muy generosas para conceder la igualdad!" (212, 243; as for obligations, we *are* equal. Women pay the same taxes as men. ... In penal law, they are very generous in awarding us equality!). Unfortunately, Carmen de Burgos died in 1932 of a long-standing heart condition, so we do not know what role she might have played on the Republican side of the Civil War.

Burgos's Catalan counterpart, anarchist feminist Federica Montseny (daughter of anarchists Soledad Gustavo and Federico Urales, both of whom were politically motivated writers) did play a significant role both during the Republic and the Civil War. Francisco Largo Caballero's government named Montseny to the post of minister of Health and Social Assistance in 1936; thus she became the first woman to hold a ministerial post in Europe, although she lost her post months later at the onset of the Civil War. She is reported to have been an impressive orator capable of motivating crowds, and she often did so after the Civil War broke out. Montseny is a good example of "double militancy," since her loyalties lay both in anarchism (a particularly strong movement among working-class Catalans in industrially developed Catalonia) and feminism. In essays and fictional works, she argued for humanity above all, not privileging women's issues over those of other oppressed groups (such as male workers). As Geraldine Scanlon writes, "Las mujeres anarquistas habían criticado siempre al movimiento feminista no sólo porque representaba a reducidos intereses de clase, sino porque creían que la emancipación era algo que tenían que lograr los dos sexos luchando juntos" (1986, 305; Anarchist women had always criticized the feminist movement not only because it represented narrow class interests, but because they believed that emancipation was something that the two sexes had to achieve by fighting together). Some statements Montseny made in her articles might place her in the line of difference feminists. For example, she argued that women possessed a "collective force of a sex, sacrificing themselves, struggling as do the women workers in munitions factories in Spain, defying death during many hours of the day" (quoted in Ackelsberg 1991, 127).

Along with Carmen de Burgos, another pioneer of "corporal feminism" was Galician painter Maruja Mallo, one of the few Galician-born feminists of the Spanish Silver Age (1920s and 1930s). Although Mallo was not a self-declared feminist, nor did she work for specific feminist reforms as Carmen de Burgos, Margarita Nelken, María Martínez Sierra, and Clara Campoamor did with activities and writing, she projected a feminist stance through her extravagant appearance and "performances." As an extraordinary painter, Mallo was a true "member" of the Generation of '27, which included Jorge Guillén (poet), Pedro Salinos (poet and literary theorist), Federico García Lorca (poet and artist), Rafael Alberti (poet and artist), Concha Méndez (poet), Luis Buñuel (film maker), and Salvador Dalí (painter), although she is rarely mentioned in their company. Mallo manifested her feminism primarily in her painting subject matter (often showing women working or engaging in recreation) and in her personal demeanour. She frequently dressed and was photographed in outlandish outfits that made clear she did not conform to the reigning social norms for women. As Shirley Mangini González notes,

> Mallo era insólita por muchas razones, y una de las más importantes era su aparente confianza en sí misma como artista, esa seguridad que se puede dar en los genios, pero rara vez se da, especialmente en una mujer y, además una provinciana. Era una persona de acción, capaz de llevar consigo a los otros, de convencerles de que su percepción del mundo era la acertada, la única. ... Rompió las leyes fosilizadas que todavía estaban obligadas a seguir las mujeres; salía sin carabina y todavía peor, salía acompañada por hombres" (2001, 120, 121).
>
> (Mallo was outlandish for a number of reasons, one of the most important being her apparent confidence in herself as an artist, this security that is common in geniuses but rarely seen in a woman, especially a woman from the provinces. She was a person of action, cabable of carrying others along with her, of convincing them that her view of the world was the right, the only, one. ... She broke the fossilized rules that women were still obliged to follow; she went out without a chaperone, and, even worse, she went out accompanied by men.)

Thus Mallo was a precursor of the "corporal" feminism that Spanish feminists adopted during the repressive Franco regime (e.g., see the comments on Carmen Laforet's rebellious hair style in chapter 28) and in the so-called postfeminist era of the 1990s (see the analysis of Carmen Alborch's and Lucía Etxebarria's feminist statements via hair and clothing styles in chapter 32).

Other Galician feminists of the 1920s and 1930s who followed more recognized forms of feminism – writing and overt activism – include educators such as María Barbeito Cerviño (1880 –1970), the first to implement the Montessori method in Galicia and a fierce advocate of women's rights; and journalists such as Sofía Casanova (1861–1958), who wrote articles on women and feminism in the 1920s (see Hooper 2008, 185–208 for a comprehensive list of her articles), and María Luz Morales (1898–1980), the director of the prestigious Catalan newspaper *La Vanguardia* from July 1936 to February 1937 (see Rios Bergantinhos 2001, 141–2 and Marco 1993, 161–3 for an analysis of her journalistic writings). Although Morales's professional life unfolded in Catalonia, she was closely linked to the political and cultural movements that favoured Galician culture. As a member of the Asociación de Escritoras e Escritores en Lingua Galega (Association of Galician Writers) and of the Partido Galeguista (Pro-Galician Party), she visibly positioned herself in favour of the first Statute of Autonomy for Galicia. Likewise, as secretary of Mulleres Galeguistas (Pro-Galician Women) during the Spanish Civil War (1936–9), she repeatedly declared her feminist affiliations. In her Galician and Castilian journalistic writings, she showed this twofold political consciousness about the feminist and Galician nationalist cause. An illustrative example is her article "Galega, ¡para i-escoita!" (Galician woman, stop and listen!), in which she denounced the pressure on women – and especially, on educated women – to conform to gender roles and abandon their own language.

Also significant is the contribution of Corona González, the most prolific woman author in the Galician nationalist journal *A Nosa Terra* between 1926 and 1930, at a time when women were almost banned from these publications (see Rios Bergantinhos 2001, 136–9 and Marco 1993, 185–8 for a selection of her political writings). A travelled woman – some of her writings were sent from London, Weymouth, Paris, and Rio de Janeiro – González was exposed to avant-garde feminist ideas. Most of her writings concerned three topics: the existing hypocrisy about women's issues such as prostitution, arranged marriages, and labour exploitation; the situation of Galician women who were victims of the massive emigration of the time; and, most especially, the need for an education for women. In her column "Pr'os pais que tein fillas" (González 1927; To parents/fathers who have daughters), she energically criticized fathers who have sons and daughters but only worry about providing education for their sons, which has disastrous results. Instead, she claims that it is necessary to provide opportunities for their sisters: "É necesario insinarlle a traballar, pra ser independente, e facerlle comprender que non é necesario o casamento, nen ser monxa, pra ser feliz n'este mundo" (10; It is necessary to teach her how to do a job, so that she can be independent; it is also necessary to make her understand that she does not need to get married or to become a nun in order to be happy in this world).

These are among the Galician women who, during the first three decades of the twentieth century, actively participated "na polémica feminista do Estado Español" (Blanco 1986, 147; the feminist polemic of the Spanish state [see chapter 23 for further discussion of these authors during the Franco regime]). All of them defended political suffrage for women, including Galician-born activist María Vinyals (1875–1940?) who authored key texts such as "El voto de la mujer" (Women's vote; 1906) and "Sobre el voto femenino" (On women's vote; 1931). A remarkable exception is the antifeminist Francisca Herrera Garrido

(1869–1950), who maintained an antisuffragist stance and a conservative and very religious view of women's role in society, as shown in her essay "A muller galega" (The Galician woman) published in 1921 in the Galician nationalist journal *Nós*. The essay is considered to be "o primero achegamento ensaístico á muller galega desde unha perpsectiva á vez galega e feminina" (Blanco 1986, 148; the first essayistic approach to Galician women from a perspective simultaneously Galician and feminine) in a nationalist journal. Her popularity within (masculine) nationalist circles could have favoured Herrera Garrido's becoming, in March 1945, the first woman ever invited to be a member of the Real Academia Galega (RAG; Royal Galician Academy), although she died five years later, before she could take up her seat (see chapter 23 n8 for further explanations). Also worth mentioning is the fact that very early on (in the third issue), the feminist journal *Festa da Palabra Silenciada* (Celebration of the silenced word), launched in 1986 and discussed in chapter 30 of this volume, paid homage to Herrera Garrido. These contradicting views on women's suffrage and women's liberation demonstrate that within the complex Galician reality of the time, a Marxist liberal *galeguismo* (pro-Galician stance) coexisted with traditional and conservative views on gender.

19 Basque Feminist Trajectories in the 1930s: New Women between Change and Continuity

MIREN LLONA

During the conservative phase of the Second Spanish Republic (1933–6), two Basque women were imprisoned in Bilbao in 1933. Polixene Trabudúa, a propagandist for the Partido Nacionalista Vasco (PNV; Basque Nationalist Party), was jailed for the radical nature of her speeches in favour of Basque independence from the Spanish state; and Dolores Ibárruri, "La Pasionaria" (The passionate woman), director of the Spanish Communist Party, was accused of hiding comrades sought by the police. These imprisonments are symptomatic of the changes occurring with respect to sexual and gender order in the Basque Country (and Spain in general) in the 1920s and 1930s. The reach of these transformations had more to do with women's experience in militancy and activism in diverse social and political organizations than with the surge of a structured and influential feminist movement. During the 1920s and 1930s, the collective female experience in spaces previously off-limits for women encouraged a social apprenticeship that allowed for questioning of gender roles in a feminist sense. Nonetheless, the model of the "new woman" that arose after the First World War was viewed by Basque (and Spanish) society as a threat to the social and natural order. The foreshadowing of women's emancipation planted a seed of increasing social unease that was combated with increased emphasis on sexual difference and on motherhood. Thus, women's public and political activity was often carried out under the guise of the mother figure. In this way, many women were able to carry out activities in the social and political arena in the 1930s. The motherhood role gave them the opportunity to break through the sexual and gender order, to resignify women's public image, and to reformulate their individual and collective expectations.

In the Basque Country, middle-class Catholic women like Polixene Trabudúa, advocate of Basque nationalism, walked a fine line between the past, in which middle-class respectability demanded enclosure in a female domesticity, and the present, in which notions like "female moral superiority" fortified women who went out into the public sphere in order to influence and "domesticate" it. This contrast was a constant source of conflicts and contradictions in conservative, Catholic parties and also within the Partido Nacionalista Vasco (PNV). The Basque Nationalist Party tried timidly to foment the collaboration of women in the nation-building project, but it had problems when trying to define the limits of female activism by the so-called *emakumes* (Basque women) in their ranks. This behaviour is evident when Trabudúa was released from prison. The PNV organized a large public act on 5 February 1933 at the jai alai stadium in Bilbao and called it Homage to the Basque Mother. The political activity of the young propagandist women could only be accepted by the party within the rhetoric of the mother country. The same rhetoric also holds in the case of Galicia. Its political activity, if seen by the organizers and by the public as innovative, in practice contributed to reinforcing the limits that Basque nationalism imposed on women's activity.

Trabudúa, in a later reflection on her participation in the Homage to the Basque Mother, recovered the transgressive meaning of the act: "We were not mothers. ... It was a kind of camouflage of the real meaning of this homage; it was an homage to audacious women, to valiant women, to participative women, to women who fought alongside men" (Llona 2002, 198). With the conquest of new areas of action, the new Basque nationalist women contributed to redefining the prevailing gender barriers. They, and Trabudúa, modernized the public image of women in the 1930s. However, during the Spanish Civil War, the need to renew legitimation of the Basque state, as well as the organization of the front and rearguard on solid gender grounds, provoked a brutal reaction to the timid advances and a reinforcement of social maternity as the only legitimate female public action. In order to achieve victory, harmony in gender relations took priority over women's emancipation.

The trajectory of Dolores Ibárruri in her audacious acts within the Communist Party and as a representative to Congress transmitted a more transgressive image that broke with established gender norms. Ibárruri's conversion into a mass political leader resulted in her separation from Julián Ruiz, her husband and father of her children. It also occasioned her abandoning her home in a Basque mining town and her moving to Madrid. Ibárruri placed her militant activism above her family obligations as a wife and mother. In the 1930s, Ibárruri became a woman emancipated from conventional ties, whose political and personal decisions had a more masculine than maternal imprint. In Ibárruri's life trajectory, it is paradoxical to see her act first as a woman who was above the prejudices that limited female activism during those years, and the later exaltation of her public persona as a mother, which was fomented by her and by the party. To a certain extent, clinging to the legitimizing power of the mother figure was politically valuable, especially in the context of the Civil War, as we will see; but above all, it was a means to build a smoke screen around her experience that did not fit what was conventionally meant as feminine and maternal and was, in fact, closer to the stereotype of "the new woman," with gender-bender characteristics more associated with virility (Llona 2016).

Her political career was an extraordinary event in the deeply masculinist Communist political culture between the two World Wars. During the Second Spanish Republic, Ibárruri formed part of the Central Committee of the Communist Party, becoming the oldest member of the Executive Committee of the party and the only woman to be elected to the Communist International in 1935. Once the Spanish Civil War began in the summer of 1936, Ibárruri exhorted women to fight alongside the men and to create militia units within the Fifth Regiment: "Youth, on your feet for the fight! Heroic women, women of the people, remember the heroism of the Asturian women; fight alongside the men to defend the bread and tranquility of our threatened children!" (Ibárruri 1936, 4). In Ibárruri's thought, the identification of the workers' revolution with women's emancipation was a stimulus to encourage women to participate in the fight to save the Republic. However, as Mary Nash has pointed out, the exaltation of the militia woman as a symbol of popular mobilization was brief. By October 1936, militia women were ordered from the fronts (1999, 104). Taking the place of militia women was the image of the "combative mother," dedicated to the war cause from the rearguard. At this moment, the image of Ibárruri as the great mother emerged forcefully. Gina Herrmann suggests that a fusion of "the mother country" and "the mother Pasionaria" turned out to be one of the most effective Republican propaganda weapons of the Civil War (1998, 196). The emergence of La Pasionaria as a heroic mother constituted a new patriotic symbol and contributed to providing national identity and legitimacy to the Republican cause but at the same time weakened the ambiguous and transgressive nature of her image. The feminization of the Pasionaria consolidated the heroic role of Republican men in defence of the nation, reaffirmed their masculinity as combatants, but also played a conservative role from a gender perspective in the restructuring of the rearguard during the Civil War and women's role in it.

The cases of Trabudúa and Ibárruri during the Basque and Spanish 1920s and 1930s indicate how difficult it was for women to negotiate the public sphere, which was considered a male prerogative. The rhetoric of motherhood contributed to women's transitioning into public space, but it was a double-edged sword. It gave women sufficient legitimacy to constitute themselves as public figures and to transgress established norms, but at the same time it turned out to be a formula for reorienting and short-circuiting transgressive attitudes and liberating feminist activism.

PART IV

The Dictatorships of António de Oliveira de Salazar (1926–1974) and Francisco Franco (1939–1975)

COORDINATED BY ROBERTA JOHNSON

20 Historical Overview of Portugal and Spain

JOÃO ESTEVES AND ROBERTA JOHNSON

With the fall of the First Republic on 28 May 1926, the situation of Portuguese women suffered a major setback in terms of their rights and the way in which they were treated within the family and the public domain. During the Republic, the Divorce Law and the Family Laws of 1910 had mitigated many of the rules of the Civil Code of 1867 and the Penal Code of 1886 that subordinated married women to their husbands and abolished legislation that differentiated between the sexes. With the establishment of the Ditadura Militar (Military Dictatorship) that gave way to the Estado Novo (New State), both openly antifeminist regimes, women's rights in Portugal took a step backwards. The regimes advocated women's returning to the home and married women's subordination to their husbands, and celebrated the roles of wife and mother. Up until the end of the regime in 1974, therefore, the lives of women were limited by oppressive regulations. Numerous restrictions were imposed, with some variation throughout the forty-eight years of the dictatorship.

The Constitution of 1933 defined the political rights of women and their status in the family, at work, and in society. The charter based its legislation on the natural differences between the sexes for the "bem da família" (good of the family) and did not provide all citizens with equality before the law. It was only in 1971 when the fifth article was altered, albeit slightly, that this situation changed. Although the Constitution repeated the phrase that all citizens were equal, except for "quanto às mulheres, as diferenças resultantes da sua natureza" (women as a result of their natural differences), it dropped the clause that explicitly referenced the good of the family. The Código do Processo Civil (Civil Procedure Code) of 1939 maintained that men were head of the family, bestowed upon husbands jurisdiction in all aspects of married life, and granted husbands the power to obligate their wives to return to the marital home, a stipulation that was only removed in 1967.

In 1940, the Divorce Law introduced by the First Republic in 1910 was modified. Through a concordat between the Holy See and the Portuguese state, Catholic marriages could no longer be legally dissolved. Female primary-school teachers had to request permission in order to marry, while women in other professions could not marry at all. Nurses at Hospitais Civis, for instance, could not marry until 1962, nor could female telephone operators of the Anglo-Portuguese Telephone Company, a restriction not overturned until 1939. The law also applied to female staff at the Ministério dos Negócios Estrangeiros (Ministry of Foreign Affairs) and to female airhostesses working for Transportes Aéreos Portugueses (TAP; Portuguese Air Transports) until 1974. Women were not permitted to have legal or diplomatic careers, and married women, who were completely subjugated, could not travel out of the country without their husband's consent, a stipulation not abolished until 1969. Furthermore, married women required their husband's permission to work, publish books, enter contracts, own property, or have bank accounts. It was only in 1967 that the new Civil Code removed the stipulation that sought spousal consent for married women to have professional careers, work in public service, publish books, or manage financial affairs. Husbands maintained the right to open their wives' correspondence until 1974, the year the dictatorship ended, as, in many cases, married couples were known by the husband's surnames, given their status as "head of the family."

One area in which women's rights did make progress during the dictatorship, however, was the right to vote. As of 1934, women aged twenty-one and over who were either single and earned their own income or married women and had received a high-school level education or paid property taxes became eligible to vote and stand for election in the National Assembly and the Corperative Chamber. In the elections held on 16 December of that year, when women finally had the right to vote after the failed aspirations of the suffragettes of the First Republic, three women were elected. Domitila Hormizinda Miranda de Carvalho, a doctor and teacher (1871–1966), Maria Cândida Parreira Bragança, a lawyer (1877–1942), and Maria Baptista dos Santos Guardiola, a teacher (1895–1987) became the first female deputies of the National Assembly, as chosen by António de Oliveira Salazar (1889–1970), the president of the Council of Ministers, and became the first female deputies in the National Assembly, joining the União Nacional (UN; National Union), the only political party under the regime. Clemency Dupin Seabra (1874–1936) and Maria José de Abreu Couto de Amorim Novais (1896–1982) both became Procuradoras à Câmara Corperativa (Esteves 2015, 11–12). Such a development did not mean, as Salazar told the newspaper *O Século* (The century) on 19 November 1934, that "ter-se o Estado ou elas próprias convertido, agora, ao feminismo" (Reynolds 1986, 429; the state or the women in question had converted to feminism). Therefore, although women's right to vote was amended during the dictatorship, it would not be until 1974 that Portugal introduced universal suffrage.

The conservative, authoritarian, and repressive nature of the new regime did not immediately seek to dismantle the Conselho Nacional das Mulheres Portuguesas (CNMP; National Council of Portuguese Women). The only feminist organization from the First Republic still in operation under the regime, the council held the II Congresso Feminista e de Educação (Second Congress on Feminism and Education) in June 1928 (Esteves 2013a). Many supporters of the Republic did not attend the event as they were in exile, and it was less well attended than the CNMP event held just four years earlier. Sixteen theses were presented, eleven authored by women, while Elina Guimarães (1904–91) (Ribeiro et al. 2004) presided over the opening ceremony of the congress, and Elisa Soriano, a doctor and president of Juventude Universitária Feminina Espanhola (Young Female Spanish University Students), was the international guest of honour.

During the congress, Manuela Palma Carlos (1906–94), a student of the Faculty of Letters (Faculdade de Letras), and teacher Deolinda Lopes Vieira (1888–1993) raised the issue of coeducation in the addresses "Coeducação" (7th thesis, 25 June 1928; Coeducation) and "Escola única" (8th thesis, 26 June 1928; Single-sex schooling). The theses corresponded with the recent legislation introduced by the Ditadura Militar (Military Dictatorship), the precursor to the Estado Novo, which restricted primary-school education through Decree No. 13791 of 16 June 1927. For feminists, it was considered abnormal to separate children, as both sexes would reap the benefits of coeducation. Although many primary and secondary schools did have coeducation, it never materialized fully due to logistical problems. Julia Franco, the first woman appointed as an interim school inspector during the First Republic, also spoke at the congress. She presented "A mulher como valor social" (12th thesis, 25 June 1928; Women as social value), a speech that discussed how boys' and girls' different educations harm girls. Franco argued that their education prevented girls from developing their capabilities and deprived them of adequate training that would prepare them for work. Aurora Teixeira de Castro (1891–1931), the second Portuguese woman to obtain a law degree, practise as a lawyer, and serve as the first female notary, also spoke at the congress. She presented the thesis "Reivindicações feministas" (10th thesis, 25 June 1928; Feminist demands), which examined the developments since the last CNMP congress four years earlier and noted how, silenced and ignored by the state, it was imperative that women continue to protest and fight. The writer Maria O'Neill raised the issue of "O voto às mulheres" (9th thesis, 25 June 1928; The vote for women), criticizing attempts to justify the fact women had not been granted suffrage, while Elina Guimarães presented the thesis "Da situação da mulher profissional no casamento" (5th thesis, 27 June 1928; The situation of professional women in marriage), which denounced the fact that women could not work without the consent of their husbands, except as lawyers and saleswomen.

The congress ended on the 28 June with a closing session dedicated to Paz Universal (World Peace) chaired by Madeleine Frondoni Lacombe (1857–1936), an advocate for pacifism. In the same month that the congress was held, feminists and Republicans from the CNMP, including Adelaide Cabete (1867–1935), Elina Guimarães, and Vitória Pais Freire de Andrade Madeira (1883–1930), led a national movement in support of victims of the Ditadura Militar, such as prisoners, deportees, and political exiles, in an initiative organized by the Republican newspaper *O Rebate* (Fight back).

The 1920s – a decade that had started out as very promising for the feminist movement in Portugal – ended with founder and president of the CNMP and gynecologist Adelaide Cabete's departure for Angola. The 1930s began with an event in Lisbon entitled Exposição da Obra Feminina Antiga e Moderna de Carácter Literário, Artístico e Científico (Exhibition of Modern and Ancient Female Literary, Artistic, and Scientific Work). The initiative was organized by the journalist and writer Maria Lamas (1893–1983), with support from the newspaper *O Século* (The century). A cultural event dedicated to the diverse artistic, literary, and scientific heritage produced by women from the Renaissance to the current day, the exhibition sought to unite women from all regions of the country working in different professions – from labourers to intellectuals – and was well attended. The section dedicated to women's writing presented hundreds of varied works and themes – from literature to manuals – and it was noteworthy that many of the texts were written by women associated with the construction of the feminist movement or by those who had directly collaborated and introduced initiatives.

The 1930s were particularly difficult for Portuguese feminism, which was already in a precarious position. It was a complex period for the CNMP due to unclear objectives and concerns over the council's survival under the regime. The number of activists was scarce, the organization's publication *Alma Feminina* (Woman's soul) was released sporadically, and pacifist initiatives decreased (Wank-Nolasco 1995, 116–18). In addition to the ideological propaganda, which advocated that women should be confined to the home and family, devoting themselves to housework, child rearing, the harmony of the family, and defending moral values – all for the good of Portugal (Cova and Costa Pinto 1997) – two organizations emerged called Obra das Mães pela Educação Nacional (OMEN, 1936; Work of Mothers for National Education) and Mocidade Portuguesa Feminina (MPF, 1937; Portuguese Young Women), both established by the Estado Novo (New State) (Flunser 2000, 95, 195). OMEN, which women could join voluntarily, aimed to educate women within the family by preparing them for their maternal, domestic, and social role with the aid of social assistants and teachers. The MPF, on the other hand, had compulsory membership. Sessions by the organization were run mainly in female high schools in cities, and instilled in girls moral values believed to be inherent to the female sex, based on the triad of God, country, and family (Deus, Pátria, e Família). The CNMP did continue to operate in line with its feminist values until the mid-1940s, although its impact and prominence were limited.

Between 1945 and 1947, coinciding with the postwar era and the victory of the Allied forces, the CNMP resumed a more combative stance. It developed a more political dimension and entered its final stage as an organization, a time that proved to be a dynamic period for the council. Maria Lamas was elected president, and a new directing body with dozens of members was announced (Esteves 2013b, 881). The revival of the council resulted in an increase in membership, as hundreds of women joined – many of them recent graduates from the Universities of Lisbon, Porto, and Coimbra – as well as in the establishment of offices in numerous cities and provinces that sought to combat female illiteracy and the professional, economic, and cultural position of women from all walks of life. In December 1946, the publication associated with the group, *Alma Feminina*, which had run from 1917, became *A Mulher* (Woman), which ran from 1946 to 1947. The struggle for women's suffrage was central to the magazine (Gorjão 1994, 48–55), and a project calling for the expansion of voting rights was presented to the National Assembly, well received by the chamber, and recorded in the minutes.

The final achievement of the CNMP occurred in January 1947 when the council organized the *Exposição de Livros Escritos por Mulheres* (Exhibition of Books Written by Women) at the Sociedade Nacional de Belas Artes (National Society of Fine Arts). There was a display of three thousand books written by authors from all over the world, with texts from twenty-nine countries,[1] as the event highlighted women's achievements in the fields of literature and science through forums and film screenings. Following the success of the event and the growing influence of the CNMP among women, illustrated by the gradual increase of subscriptions from all over the country and the influence of the council's civil programs, the organization was banned by the Estado Novo on 28 June 1947. After thirty-three years of uninterrupted activity in support of women and their needs, the CNMP was no more, a decision that was undoubtedly linked to the participation of the council leaders and its members in opposition to the ruling regime.

As an organization, the CNMP underwent great change, from the group established by Adelaide Cabete to the council directed by Maria Lamas, due to the differing historical circumstances. Many women joined the CNMP in order to express their opposition, implicitly and explicitly, to the Salazar dictatorship, taking advantage of its legal status, working alongside progressive and influential women and, for the first time, working-class women. The CNMP, which had been established as a feminist organization, albeit under the influence of Republican feminism, was officially apolitical and nonpartisan. It was perceived, however, as an anti-Fascist organization, which ultimately led to its downfall. The legacy of the CNMP is twofold. In what may be considered the first phase of the council, when under Cabete's lead, the CNMP drew together feminist, Republican, and Freemason beliefs. The latter phase, on the other hand, under the charge of Lamas, mobilized and inspired anti-Fascist women; that is to say, Portuguese feminists banded together to confront the political situation they faced. Under Cabete, the council stood in opposition to the monarchy, advocating republicanism, as it was believed that a Republican establishment would be more favourable to women. Forty years later, however, the objective of the league was to stand united in opposition to the dictatorship that suppressed women's rights and aspirations. In both cases, feminism lost ground to the politicization of the Republican women's organizations.

In late 1935, the period when the CNMP was at its weakest, the Associação Feminina Portuguesa para a Paz (AFPP; Portuguese Women's Association for Peace) was founded, the first feminist organization without Republican or Masonic influences. Significantly more politicized by the anti-Fascist, anti-Nazi, and anti-Salazar struggle, the association counted among its members women who were known for their opposition to the dictatorship. The association sought to continue the work developed by the CNMP, with many of the council's former members, and the publication *Boletim* (Bulletin), which continued to promote the emancipation of women. The organization's bylaws were approved by the Civil Government of Lisbon on 8 February 1936, as the AFPP sought to promote conferences, exhibitions, film screenings, and the organization of a library in order to advance world peace.[2] Centres were established in Lisbon, Porto, Coimbra, and Figueira da Foz, as the group's focus extended beyond pacifism. The final phase of the association, before it was banned in 1952, also shared many objectives with the CNMP. The delegation of Porto (Serralheiro 2011, 167–74) was a particularly potent source of the energy that came to be associated with the AFPP and its hundreds of members in the struggle against the dictatorship.

Although Portuguese female pacifism underwent many transformations in the four decades of its ideology, it constituted a privileged space for upper-class women to participate in social causes and, based on its principles, contributed to the construction and recognition of women's citizenship in a national and international context. While women's political participation in relation to the monarchy, the Republic, and opposition to Salazar was only feasible for a temporary period, given changes in the political landscape, pacifism was a constant. Even when it was less tangible and more innocuous, pacifism was a consistent creed that facilitated women's entry into the public sphere and was an important manner of providing women with a civic and political education, freeing them from the repressive authorities. With the prohibition of the two associations, the members sought to unite the opposition movements in order to find a platform for their views. Examples of this phenomenon are found in the election campaign for the presidency of Norton de Matos in 1949, when the Comissão Eleitoral Feminina de

Apoio à Candidatura (Women's Electoral Commission of Support for Candidacy) was set up, and the electoral campaign for Humberto Delgado in 1958. In both cases, interventions in defence of women's rights were made. Although its prominence was limited, aggravated by censorship and the repressive regime, there was an increase in the number of women seeking to make their presence felt in the public and political sphere. Leadership roles were, however, reserved for men.

In the late 1950s, Graal emerged, the International Movement of Christian Women, which began in the Netherlands in 1921 and arrived in Portugal in 1957. The organization was aimed at the personal development and education of women of all social backgrounds, although it focused its work on women from the countryside (Tavares 2000 and 2013, 113). In the following decade, the Comissão Democrática Eleitoral de Mulheres (Women's Democratic Electoral Commission) was established in 1968, which gave way to the formation of the Movimento Democrático de Mulheres (MDM; Democratic Movement of Women) in 1969, an anti-Fascist organization that opposed the dictatorship. The group campaigned against the colonial war and supported political prisoners and women's rights, with particular reference to the right to vote, legal equality, equal pay, access to all professions, combating the cost of living, access to family planning, and denouncing the exploitation of the female body. Despite such views, the commission is not usually considered a feminist organization.

The forty-eight-year dictatorship overturned much of the feminist progress in Portugal that had begun to prosper in the nineteenth century and severed the international ties the feminist movement in Portugal had developed. From the second half of the twentieth century, the struggle against the dictatorship took precedence over women's rights (Tavares 2011), as had happened in the final stages of the monarchy when the feminist movement became secondary to the need to strengthen the Republican movement and establish the First Republic. Women's organizations did, however, in one form or another, facilitate women's access to the public domain. Subject to numerous stops, starts, and upsets, and often undervalued in historical accounts, these groups did manage to leave their mark, explicitly or more subtly, on the struggle for women's emancipation in twentieth-century Portugal.

Spain's feminist movement of the 1920s and early 1930s suffered a similar fate in 1939 with the conservative National Movement under the leadership of Francisco Franco, who won the Civil War; Spanish women's legal and actual situation took a giant leap backwards.

Many of the measures regarding the family and women reverted to the Napoleonic Code installed in 1889. Women's work was redefined as domestic and bound to the home, and women's work outside the home (especially for married women) was discouraged in every way possible and rigorously controlled by laws. Women were prohibited from taking nocturnal jobs, and they were encouraged to leave jobs they held and return home (after 1942 married women were required to leave their jobs and were to receive a dowry from the state). To help out with any household income lost by women leaving jobs, the state provided a subsidy for families with more than a certain number of children. The wages of married women who did work could be paid directly to their husbands. Women were barred outright from some professions, such as chief administrator in state jobs (including the telephone company), diplomat, work inspector, notary, functionary in departments of justice, state lawyer, state police, or state administration of the stock market. Even a politically and religiously conservative thinker like Mercedes Formica, who herself had received a law degree, could see the impossible nature of this legislation given the economic realities of post-Civil War Spain. In a review of Simone de Beauvoir's *Le Deuxième sexe* (*The Second Sex*) – a work whose distribution in Spain was prohibited by the church until after Franco died – Formica proclaimed that "ya nadie puede plantear en conciencia, si una mujer debe o no trabajar. La española de este momento tiene que trabajar, se enfrenta con este imperativo, inesquivable en nuestro medio, aunque precisamente nuestro medio, por paradoja, no se caracterice por facilitar el trabajo de la mujer" (Simone de Beauvoir, *Le deuxième sexe: les faits et les mythes* [Paris: Gallimard, 1949], 1:268–9, quoted in Ruiz 2007, 50; Now no one can ethically dictate whether or not a woman works. The Spanish woman today has to work; she faces this unavoidable imperative in our situation, although paradoxically it is precisely our situation that does not facilitate women's working).

Although the militant feminism of the 1920s and 1930s that built on the work of nineteenth-century pioneers such as Concepción Arenal, Emilia Pardo Bazán, Concepción Gimeno de Flaquer, and Rosario Acuña had to wait until the 1960s to make the beginnings of a come-back, the earliest nineteenth-century feminist thinker, Concepción Arenal was not forgotten in the Franco era, perhaps due to her Catholicism and relatively conservative approach to feminism. It is also true that the Franco-era writings on Arenal do not emphasize her feminist essays. For example, Juan Antonio Cabezas's *Concepción*

Arenal o el sentido romántico de la justicia (1942; Concepción Arenal or the romantic sense of justice) is essentially a biography detailing how Arenal's life intertwined with that of liberal romantics of her age. Cabezas does not mention Arenal's *La mujer del porvenir* (The woman of the future) until page 216 where he states that "no es el de Concepción un feminismo histérico, influido por las teorías que ya vienen incubando en el extranjero. Su feminismo es un 'feminismo aceptable' como lo califica el padre Alarcón" (Cabezas 1942, 216; Concepción's feminism is not hysterical, influenced by theories that were being incubated in foreign countries. Her feminism is an "acceptable feminism" as Father Alarcón classifies it), and on page 220, Cabezas refutes some of Arenal's feminist precepts. Other Franco-era books on Arenal include Manuel Casas Fernández's *Concepción Arenal en su aspecto pedagógico* (Concepción Arenal in her pedagógical aspect; 1954) and Jesús Fabio Fernández's *Las ideas sociales de Concepción Arenal* (The social ideas of Concepción Arenal; 1960).

Arenal, however, was the only earlier Spanish feminist to survive Francoist censorship of feminist writings. All the propaganda promoted by the state and the Sección Femenina de Falange (Feminine Section of the Phalange Party) marshalled its forces against feminism, associating it with drug addiction and other social evils of modern society. Most of the militant feminists of the Republican era were exiled (María Martínez Sierra, Margarita Nelken, Victoria Kent) or dead (Carmen de Burgos), and the written works of feminists like Carmen de Burgos were banned. It took many years before the story of predictatorial feminism began to be pieced back together again. If Carmen de Burgos's publications had not been banned during the forty-year Franco regime, she would have been an important link to Lidia Falcón's work on women's legal situation in Spain in her 1963 *Los derechos civiles de la mujer* (Women's civil rights) and *Los derechos laborales de la mujer* (Women's work rights; 1963) and her better known *Mujer y sociedad* (Women and society; 1969). And both thinkers should have been an important resource for the equality feminists who took up the rationalist banner in the 1980s. In her *La razón feminista* (*Feminist Reason*) from 1981, Lidia Falcón confidently states that Simon de Beauvoir's *The Second Sex* from 1949 was "la primera denuncia de la condición del segundo sexo en el siglo XX" (Johnson and Zubiaurre 2012, 408; the first critique of the second sex's condition in the twentieth century). But what about Carmen de Burgos, Margarita Nelken, María Martínez Sierra, Clara Campoamor, Hildegart, and other Spanish feminist thinkers of the Silver Age? Catalonian author and journalist Carmen Alcalde, who cofounded *Vindicatión Feminista* with Lidia Falcón, admits that

> quedamos un poco cortas. No supimos ver de verdad todos los valores que hubo en los años veinticinco, treinta y trenta y cinco, y en la Guerra, la gente de un valor extraordinario como Victoria Kent y Margarita Nelken o digamos "La Pasionaria", que ya es mito, y Federica Montseny y una cantidad de gente anónima con unos esfuerzos tan grandes y tan pioneras que verdaderamente no se puede decir que no hubo feminismo, tal como se dijo en este libro [referring to her *El feminismo ibérico*, coauthored with María Aurelia Campany and published in 1970]. (Levine and Waldman 1979, 27–8)
>
> (we were left a little short. We could not see the truth of all the values that existed in the years 1925, 1930, 1935, and during the war, people of extraordinary worth such as Victoria Kent and Margarita Nelken, or let's say "La Pasionaria," who is now a myth, and Federica Montseny, and a large number of anonymous people with enormous, pioneering effort, that really one cannot say that there wasn't feminism as they say in this book.)

During the Franco dictatorship, the Sección Femenina de Falange gained even greater ascendancy over women's lives, and any woman who wanted to study, travel, or work had to prove that she had fulfilled her service in the Sección Femenina, which consisted of taking classes in sewing, cooking, childcare, and fulfilling the role of housewife and mother. One of the basic tenets of the new state was to strengthen the family in the Christian tradition; thus the state wanted to ensure that men's salaries were sufficient to allow women to stay home. In order to encourage large families, the state provided subsidies to married couples with more than two children (excluding illegitimate children). Women were barred from a number of professions, but they were allowed to take jobs as teachers, one of the worst paid professions. Other laws eliminated coeducation in primary and secondary schools. Civil marriage and divorce, legalized under the Republic, were once again rendered illegal. The laws regarding adultery from the pre-Republican era were reinstated, and severe penalties for abortion were instituted, a law only revoked in 1985, when abortion was permitted in very limited circumstances. Prostitution was not declared illegal until 1956. Women were allowed to vote in the national referendum of 1947 on the law of succession, which excluded women from ascending the throne.

Despite the regime's efforts to keep foreign feminist writing from entering Spain, Simone de Beauvoir's *Le Deuxième sexe* (1947) was known in Spain from smuggled copies in French and a Spanish translation, which appeared in Argentina in 1948. By the 1960s, when the most repressive years (1940s and early 1950s) of the dictatorship were over, Lidia Falcón could openly publish feminist books such as *Los derechos civiles de la mujer* and *Los derechos laborales de la mujer*, although it is not clear that anyone paid much attention to them. Some minimal legislative reforms were introduced in 1958 and 1961, inspired by a shortage of labour in Spain. For example, a 1961 law stipulated that women had the same rights as men to exercise "toda clase de actividades políticas, profesionales, sin más limitaciones que las establecidas en la presente ley" (quoted in Scanlon 1986, 346; all kinds of political and professional activities without any limitations beyond those established by the present law). The final clause essentially negated the positive effect of the first clause, but a door had opened, even if not very far.

Receiving more attention and having a significant impact on the timid revival of feminism in Spain was Betty Friedan's *The Feminine Mystique* (1963), published in Spanish in 1965 as *La mística de la feminidad*. Even though strict censorship kept much openly feminist writing from being published, feminist writers found outlets in fiction. Carmen Laforet's *Nada* (Nothing; 1945) and *La mujer nueva* (The new woman; 1955), and Ana María Matute's *Primera memoria* (First memory; 1960) are good examples of the diversion of feminism into fiction. All the female characters in Laforet's novel *Nada* work or study at the university, while the lead male characters are ne'er-do-wells. Carmen Martín Gaite calls female novelistic protagonists that refuse to fit the stereotypical female prototype of the Franco years "chicas raras" (1987; odd girls). Well situated, socially prominent, aristocratic women such as María Lafitte, Countess of Campo Alange and Lilí Álvarez were able to publish feminist works as early as 1948, and writers such as Rosa Chacel and María Zambrano, who had written feminist works during the Republican era, continued their feminist writing in exile. The countercultural movement that developed in the rest of the West in the 1960s also arrived in Spain, the way having been paved for American influence in Spain by the establishment of US military bases in Spain in 1953. Franco's government found in tourism the cash cow it needed to keep the Spanish economy afloat. The hordes of tourists arriving in Spain from the US and other European countries in the 1950s and 1960s introduced new lifestyles into tradition-bound Spain.

In 1965, the first feminist organization under the Franco dictatorship, the Movimiento Democrático de Mujeres (MDM; Women's Democratic Movement), linked to the illegal, underground Communist Party, was founded. The MDM emphasized work as central to women's lives. As early as 1953, bourgeois feminism had made an appearance in the guise of the Sociedad Española de Mujeres Universitarias (Spanish Society of University Women), whose audience was clearly very limited. In 1962, the women's research group El Seminario de Estudios Sociológicos de la Mujer (SESME; The Women's Sociological Studies Seminar) – including Lilí Álvarez (the Countess Campo Alange), Concepción Borreguero, Elena Catena, Consuelo de la Gándara, María Jiménez Bermejo, Carmen Pérez Seonae, María Salas, and Pura Salas – began a program of research, which resulted in several published books. As in Republican-era Spanish feminism, a divide developed between working-class feminists and bourgeois/aristocratic feminists. Thus the feminism that flourished in Spain immediately after Franco's death in 1975 did not spring from a vacuum and continued to manifest the class divide.

21 Portuguese Feminist Writing during the Estado Novo

FÁTIMA MARIANO

Among the female voices that stood out in defence of women's emancipation during the military dictatorship (1926–33) and the early stage of the Estado Novo (1933–74) are Elina Guimarães (1904–91) and Maria Lamas (1893–1983). Both heiresses of Republican feminism, they were activists in the Conselho Nacional das Mulheres Portuguesas (CNMP; National Council of Portuguese Women) and the Associação Feminina Portuguesa para a Paz (Female Portuguese Association for Peace). They fought for equal rights between men and women by writing articles in newspapers and magazines at a time when the authoritarian regime limited the freedom of the press and speech, arguing for women's return to the home. After all, as Elina Guimarães argued, "escrever é lutar" (Guimarães, 1975, 203; to write is to fight).

Elina Guimarães's feminism was already evident when as a child she refused to recite the poem "A minha boneca" (My doll) that the writer Júlio Dantas (1876–1962), a friend of her father, had dedicated to her: "Só uma coisa me contrista / Quando lhe vou dar lição / Diz que quer ser sufragista / E andar de saia-calção" (AA.VV. 2004, 16; Only one thing grieved me / When I'll give her a lesson / She says she wants to be a suffragist / and wear skirt-shorts). Guimarães always manifested her feminism and criticized those who considered feminism a "destructive doctrine," a "subversive freak":

> O que pretende o feminismo?
>
> Apenas isto: valorizar a mulher, permitindo-lhe, em primeiro lugar, pela educação e instrução, o pleno desenvolvimento das suas capacidades naturais e assegurando-lhe depois na sociedade o lugar que pelo seu mérito mereça. (Guimarães quoted in AA.VV. 2004, 56)

> (What does feminism want?
> Only this: to value women, allowing them, first, through education and instruction, the full development of their natural abilities and assuring them of the place they deserve in society according to their merits.)

Before finishing law school in 1926, Elina Guimarães joined the CNMP and was invited to lead its Legal Section. Together with other women with legal degrees, she was one of the most active promoters of so-called juridical feminism, "nome que afoitadamente podemos dar aquela corrente doutrinária que impõe e preconiza a igualdade dos sexos perante a lei" (Guimarães quoted in AA.VV. 2004, 37; name that one can give to that doctrinal current that imposed and advocated gender equality before the law).

Her writing focused almost exclusively on feminism and on the laws and court decisions relating to women in order to explain their using a common language or to criticize them. Guimarães regretted that Portuguese women were ignorant of the laws that concerned them: "Os homens, tendo vida social mais intensa sabem, pelo menos, que a lei existe, e procuram informar-se quando as circunstâncias o exigem. As mulheres até isso ignoram" (AA.VV. 2004, 38; Men, having a more intensive social life, at least know that law exists and seek to inform themselves when circumstances require. Until now, women are ignorant). She went on to say:

> Quando ingressei nas lides feministas, as mulheres não tinham direito nenhum político. Além disso, dentro da família, a sua situação era tal que o marido podia, sem consultar a esposa, vender todo o mobiliário da casa, ou internar no estrangeiro o filho de ambos impedindo depois a mãe de o ir visitar. (73)

> (When I joined the feminist labours, women had no political rights. Moreover, in the family, their situation was such that their husbands could, without consulting them, sell the furniture in the house or intern their son abroad, preventing his mother from visiting him.)

These were the reasons for embracing legal feminism that "modificando a legislação de harmonia com a nova situação criada à mulher era … o executor do feminismo 'tout court'" (AA.VV. 2004, 57; modifying the law in harmony with the new situation created for women was the performer of feminism "tout court").

Unlike Elina Guimarães, Maria Lamas never considered herself a feminist: "De um modo geral, estou fora do problema do feminismo, porque não o compreendo nem o sinto como a maioria das mulheres. Não me interessa, por exemplo, a luta pela conquista dos direitos políticos, pois só a "política humana" merece a minha atenção de mulher."(Fiadeiro 2003, 98; In general, I am not involved in feminism, because I do not understand it nor do I feel it like most women do. For example, I am not interested in the struggle to gain political rights, because only "human politics" deserves my attention as a woman). However, all her action was devoted to reporting the problems faced by Potuguese women and dignifying their role in the family, at work, in politics, and in society.

Maria Lamas was what might be called a "practical feminist." She did not write about the ties that bound Portuguese women to a life of submission and minority, urging them to free themselves. From a very young age, she herself gave the example by breaking with the stereotypes of the time. At seventeen years of age, she married Teófilo José Pignolet Ribeiro da Fonseca (1886–1972), with whom she had two daughters. They divorced nine years later. Much as Carmen de Burgos had done in 1901, when she was twenty-five years old, divorced and with two young daughters, Lamas left Torres Novas (where she has born) with her family and set off for Lisbon. In 1921, she married journalist Alfredo da Cunha Lamas (1877–1953), sixteen years her senior and also divorced; he had a daughter with Lamas. The couple separated in 1936.

Maria Lamas began her career as a journalist and writer in the 1920s. She worked in the Agência Americana de Notícias (American News Agency), collaborated with children's journals, and was the director of *Modas e Bordados* (Fashion and embroidery), a supplement of *O Século* (The century) for nearly twenty years. She promoted various cultural events, such as the Exposição da Obra Feminina Antiga e Moderna de Carácter Literário, Artístico e Científico (Exhibition of Modern and Ancient Female Literary, Artistic, and Scientific Work), and directed the CNMP between 1945 and 1947, when the association was closed by the government. In 1947, she was also fired from *Modas e Bordados*.

In 1948, unemployed and without the responsibilities of the CNMP, Maria Lamas launched a new personal and journalistic project. For two years, she travelled throughout the country "by train, bus, ox cart, on foot, by donkey" (Fiadeiro 2003, 141) to personally contact Portuguese women and "tell how they lived, and dreamed and struggled and suffered" (Lamas 1948, 6). The result was *As mulheres do meu país* (1948; My country's women), a "live and sincere documentary" and "an expression of brotherly solidarity" (Lamas, 1948, 6) towards Portuguese women. The book denounces the difficulties facing peasant women, factory workers, and bourgeois women and identifies common problems. It also reveals how the traditions and the inequalities consecrated in law contribute to perpetuating their condition of women subjugated to men's will. Although the author does not consider herself a feminist, *As mulheres do meu país* is, in fact, an important feminist manifesto.

In the book, Maria Lamas does not concern herself only with public and political power, but she challenges women themselves to take action. She criticizes women's lack of aspirations, "sintoma alarmante de ignorância, desinteresse e derrota" (Lamas 1948, 5; an alarming symptom of ignorance, disinterest, and defeat) and their indifference to national and international political issues and to their own problems. She regrets the absence of an institution, without doctrinal concerns, that worked for female dignity and suggests that it is better for women to fulfil their destiny as man's life mate, and as a mother "fight side by side, without absurd divisions" (Lamas 1948, 474). However, she has hope that young girls will find "the way that leads to a future without surprises or humiliations" (948, 469). More than a live portrait of the "humble and care-free lives" of Portuguese women, Maria Lamas wanted the book to shake off "the indifference" with which the Portuguese regarded "female problems," leading them to action: "Se ... alguém estender a mão, firmemente, às grandes sacrificadas, vítimas milenárias de erros milenários, que, apesar de tudo, continuam a ser as obreiras da vida, bem pequenos foram, afinal, os incalculáveis esforços, fadigas e obstáculos vencidos, que a sua publicação representa ..." (Lamas 1948, 6; If ... someone reached out firmly to those great women who were sacrificed – millenary victims of millenary errors – who, after all, continue to be the small workers of life, after all, the incalculable efforts, strains, and obstacles overcome, whom this publication represents ...).

As Catarina Inverno underlines, "A produção feminina, como qualquer outra, não deve fugir ao cânone ideário instituído e é por muitos entendida também como veículo de propaganda e propagação dos princípios, nomeadamente de ordem social, que alicerçam o regime" (Inverno 2010, 52; Female production, like any other, should not escape the established canon of ideas and is widely understood also as a vehicle for propaganda and for spreading principles, including social order, which underpins the scheme). However, from the 1950s onward there was a proliferation of female authorship, although the work is not necessarily feminist: "protagonizados por mulheres jovens, activas e independentes, que tão bem demonstram o papel que lhes coube na sociedade do pós-guerra" (Almeida 2006, 31; protagonized by young, active, and independent women, who demonstrate well the roll that was assigned them in postwar society). Few, however, consider themselves feminists. As Manuela Tavares avers, "O valor negativo que o termo 'feminismo' transportava e o 'medo' que inspirava em muitos sectores da sociedade, e mesmo em muitas mulheres, levava a que muitas enjeitassem ser apelidadas de 'feministas'" (Tavares 2011, 248; The negative value that the term "feminism" conveyed and the "fear" that it inspired in many sectors of society, and even in many women, meant that many could be called "feminist").

Like Maria Lamas, Natalia Correia (1923–93) never considered herself a feminist (at least in the classic sense of the term), despite sharing with feminists "princípios, ideias, urgências e lutas frontais. Refutando injustiças sexistas, discriminações, mordaças, passividades e obediências impostas desde o berço" (Correia 2003, 15; principles, ideas, emergency and direct struggles. Refuting sexist injustices, discriminations, gags, passivity, and obedience imposed from the cradle), as Maria Teresa Horta recalls. Correia always rejected the existence of a "female problem" because she didn't believe there were issues that concern only women, only those that concern society as a whole. For her, feminism was merely a "tabela de valores arbitrários onde o anseio dignificante de emancipação caminhava a par de ambições da mais precária moral" (Correia 2003, 119; table of arbitrary values where the dignifying yearning for emancipation coincided with ambitions of precarious morality).

She did not understand why feminists insisted on the achievement of civil and political rights when they would not be of any use if women did not first achieve economic freedom:

> Só tomando parte activa na vida económica do país é que a mulher pode com ciência pronunciar-se sobre os problemas constitucionais. Só no pleno uso da sua independência económica pode adquirir conhecimentos e cultura prática que a habilitem a intervir na orientação política e organização social. ... A independência feminina só pode ser conquistada através do trabalho. (2003, 121–2)

(Only by taking an active part in the economic life of the country can women speak knowledgably about constitutional issues. Only in the full use of their economic independence can they acquire the knowledge and practical culture that enable them to intervene in political orientation and social organization. ... Women's independence can only be achieved through work.)

In relation to a demonstration by activists of NOW (National Organization of Women), she writes:

O que me maça nestas feministas é o seu feminismo, a sua estúpida fixação aos problemas femininos debatidos em palavrosas assembleias e gritados em marchas que arvoram pendões de guerra contra o homem. O que me aflige nestas feministas é o seu racismo estreito de curto alcance que disputa posições em vez de arrasar as estruturas que impedem a transformação do mundo num lugar habitável por homens e mulheres. Procedem como se quisessem o mundo para elas tal como os homens quiseram o mundo para eles. Imitam o erro no que demonstram a tristíssima falta de imaginação de errar por conta própria! (2003, 196)

(What bothers me in these feminists is their feminism, its stupid attachment to female problems discussed in wordy meetings and shouted in marches flying banners proclaiming war against men. What distresses me in these feminists is their close-range racism that disputes positions rather than razing the structures that prevent the transformation of the world into an inhabitable place for men and women. They act as if they wanted the world to treat them as men. They imitate the error of demonstrating a very sad lack of imagination to make mistakes on their own.)

Natália Correia believed there would come a "fase de conciliação, de harmonia, de combinação ... das categorias características do pensar e do sentir masculino com a mundovisão da mulher" (Sousa et al. 2004, 66; time of conciliation, of harmony, of a combination ... of characteristic categories of male thinking and feeling with a female world view). Her idea was not only to establish a balance but also to ensure the pacification of the world. After all, woman "gives life but does not like to take it," and she is "allergic to the idea of war and conflict" (2004, 45). Natália Correia was one of the most persecuted feminine writers during the Estado Novo, and several of her books were seized. In 1966, her book *Antologia de poesia portuguesa erótica e satírica* (Anthology of Portuguese Erotic and Satiric Poetry) was seized by the censorship services. She was accused of abuse of freedom of the press and sentenced to three years in prison; the sentence was suspended.

Censorship kept the Portuguese in ignorance of what was happening in their own country and abroad: "Textos e publicações abertas a novos valores e concepções sobre os direitos das mulheres, sexualidades, vivências e lutas de outros povos não tinham entrada em Portugal a não ser pela via de uma ou outra deslocação pessoal a Paris, cidade onde se podiam sentir alguns ventos de mudança" (Tavares 2011, 123; Texts and publications open to new values and ideas about women's rights, sexuality, experiences, and these struggles elsewhere were not allowed in Portugal except from those who personally travelled to Paris, where one could feel some winds of change). Unlike Spain, books such as *The Second Sex* by Simone de Beauvoir and *The Feminine Mystique* by Betty Friedan only began to be sold in Portugal after the revolution of 25 April 1974. In April 1972, *Novas cartas portuguesas* (*New Portuguese Letters*), written by Maria Isabel Barreno (1939–2016), Maria Teresa Horta (b. 1937), and Maria Velho da Costa (b. 1938) and published by Natália Correia's publishing company, Estúdios Cor (Colour Studios), revolutionized feminine and feminist literature in Portugal. The work contained a strong political component and challenged social and sexual roles assigned to women. Inspired by the book *Lettres portugaises* (published anonymously by Claude Barbim in 1669), *Novas cartas portuguesas*, denouncing the laws and customs relating to women, is a translation of five letters that the Portuguese nun Sorór Mariana Alcoforado, who lived cloistered in the convent of Beja, wrote to a French officer.

As the authors point out, even more disturbing than the bonds imposed by tradition and law was women's lack of awareness of the existence of those bonds. After all,

> a mulher vota, é universitária, emprega-se; a mulher bebe, a mulher fuma, a mulher concorre a concursos de beleza, a mulher usa mini-maxi-saia, "hot-pants," "tampax," diz "estou menstruada" à frente de homens; a mulher toma a pílula, rapa os pêlos das pernas e de debaixo dos braços, põe biquíni; a mulher sai à noite sozinha, vai para a cama com o namorado; a mulher dorme nua, a mulher entende, já sabe o que querem dizer certas palavras, tais como: orgasmo, pénis, vagina, esperma, testículos, erecção, frigidez, clitóris, masturbação, vulva. As mulheres entre elas, na

intimidade das retretes da repartições públicas onde estão empregadas, nos recreios dos liceus, nas universidades, nos quartos, nas salas, à porta fechada, até já contam anedotas obscenas, certos pormenores íntimos de cama e em segredo tomam certas liberdades de linguagem, e assim se modernizam, se libertam, se promovem ... E o homem exulta, irmãs, e ajuda a mulher nesta farsa, neste engodo de, nesta falsa e vergonhosa "libertação" onde cada vez mais presa (e agora de si própria), a mulher é apanhada nas malhas de uma sociedade que a usa, a domina, a escraviza, a conduz, a utiliza, a manuseia, a consome. (Barreno, Horta and Velho da Costa 1974, 285–6)

(The woman votes, attends a university, is employed; the woman drinks; the woman smokes; the woman participates in beauty contests; the woman uses mini-maxi-skirts, "hot pants," "tampax"; says, "I am menstruating" in front of men; women take the pill, shave their legs and underarms, wear bikinis; women go out at night alone, go to bed with their boyfriends; women sleep naked, and they know what certain words mean, such as orgasm, penis, vagina, sperm, testicles, erection, frigidity, clitoris, masturbation, vulva. They tell obscene anecdotes, reveal certain intimate details, and secretly take certain freedoms with language in the privacy of public bathrooms of the buildings where they work, in the schoolyards of high schools and universities, in bedrooms, in living rooms, behind closed doors, and in that way they modernize; they free themselves; they promote themselves ... Men exult, sisters, and help women in this farce, this con game, this false and shameful "liberation" that increasingly preys on them (and now they on themselves); the women are caught in the mesh of a society that uses them, that dominates them, that enslaves them, that guides them, that makes use of them, that handles them, that consumes them.)

Although using the epistolary, a literary genre traditionally associated with women, the three Marias (as they were known worldwide) broke with women's writing style. *Novas cartas portuguesas* is also a transgressive book because the authors venture into a genre usually reserved for men – eroticism – and for resenting women as a subject of action, a being that has sexual desire and delights – and as an object – whose body only serves to please men. In most of the erotic books published, "il n'y a [vait] pas des femmes libres, il y a[vait] des femmes livrées aux hommes" (Barreno, Horta and Velho da Costa 1974, 264; there were not liberated women; there were women liberated from men). As Maria de Lourdes Pintasilgo writes in the prepreface, the audacity lies in that women were "a inverter a situação sujeito/objecto universalmente adquirida (ao apropriarem-se de situações até hoje só ditas por homens) (Barreno, Horta, and Velho da Costa 1974, 214, xxviii; to reverse the universally acquired situation subject/object – the appropriating situations today only spoken by men). Also for that reason, *Novas cartas portuguesas* was considered a pornographic book.

The innovative character of *Novas cartas portuguesas* is also evident in the way the three writers assume their authorship. The book is both an individual – each one of the authors freely wrote a set of letters – and a collective project – authorship of the letters is assumed by the three together, and it is not known even today who wrote which letter. The book presents itself as the revolutionary outcry of a young woman who has the courage to break the stereotypes created of her sex, to shake the foundations of a sexist and patriarchal society, and who refuses to keep silent and submit:

> O caminho da nova mulher é traçado graças à palavra que denuncia, desmonta o conformismo, configurando um discurso incómodo no sentido que subverte e aborda questões ou temáticas até aí reservadas à esfera do masculino – nomeadamente o amor, o prazer e o desejo sexual. Até esse momento não tinha sido concedida à mulher liberdade para pensar ou falar de si – isto justificando-se com o facto do sexo feminino ser encarado apenas como um objecto que era desfrutado pelo seu dono. (Martins 2004, 130)
>
> (The way of the new woman is drawn through language that denounces and destroys conformity, configuring an uncomfortable discourse in the sense that it subverts and addresses issues or themes hitherto reserved for the male sphere – namely love, leisure, and sexual desire. Until that time, women did not have the freedom to think or talk about themselves – that is, justifying themselves before the fact that the female sex is regarded only as an object to be enjoyed by its owner.)

Novas cartas portuguesas was considered subversive and was seized by the PIDE/DGS (political police); its three authors were prosecuted for abuse of freedom of the press and an attack on public morals, incurring a penalty of up to two years in prison. The case generated a wave of indignation and protest. Several intellectual and feminist organizations appealed to the Portuguese embassies and wrote manifestos defending the three Marias. The judicial process ended abruptly after the revolution of 25 April 1974, and the charges against the authors were dropped.

22 Spanish Feminist Writing during the Franco Regime, 1939–1975

ROBERTA JOHNSON

María Zambrano and Rosa Chacel, who wrote feminist essays during the Republican and Civil War eras, after the war penned important feminist works during their exile in the New World – Chacel in Brazil and Argentina, and Zambrano in Cuba and Puerto Rico. Chacel wrote and published an expanded book-length version of her "Esquema de los problemas prácticas y actuales del amor" titled *Saturnal* (1972), the writing of which was funded by the Guggenheim Foundation. *Saturnal* indicates a thorough knowledge of Virginia Woolf's writing (Chacel calls Woolf a "gran artista y pésima teorizadodra" [Chacel 1972, 50; great artist and very bad theoretician]), Simone de Beauvoir's *Le Deuxième sexe*, and the Countess Campo Alange's *La guerra secreta de los sexos* (The secret war of the sexes). Chacel disagrees with these feminist writers, and she especially refutes de Beauvoir's notion of woman as "other." She objects to the use of the neuter *lo otro* (that which is other), a concept that the Countess of Campo Alange found particularly useful. However, Campo Alange and Chacel agree in their opposition to José Ortega y Gasset's conception of women, especially his notion that the female soul allows for much less diversity of attention than the male soul (Laffitte 1948, 120). And like Chacel, Campo Alange argues for women to forge a new self from the interior: "la formación espiritual de la mujer tiene ... que llegar hasta ella por medios autodidácticos" (Laffitte 1948, 111; the woman must forge her own spiritual formation). Campo Alange presages a new being in which the feminine and the masculine meld: "La humanidad ha sido privada de una equitativa y armónica participación de las dos tendencias que Dios creó en el hombre y en la mujer. Y no cabe posible equilibrio social dentro de una fórmula unilateral" (Laffitte 1948, 159; Humanity has been deprived of an equitable and harmonious participation from the two tendencies that God created in the man and the woman. And there is no possible social equilibrium within a unilateral formula).

In Cuban exile in 1940, Zambrano gave some lectures on women that resonate with contemporary difference feminism, which sharply distinguishes between the sexes. In these lectures, Zambrano argues that men have exercised an extreme individualism that has brought the world to a crisis point, while women have not yet gained the status of individual. The characteristics of individual life that elude women are solitude and liberty. Again, Zambrano borrows Max Scheler's notion of spirit (or creation) to differentiate men from women. According to Zambrano, men create (enter intellectual, objectifying life) from the beginning, while women remain closer to nature and thus never experience the terrible metaphysical solitude of which philosophy is born. Men combine raw instinct with spirit, while women's captive, reclusive, hermetic soul maintains in contact with the body. In "Eloísa o la existencia de la mujer" (Heloise or the existence of women; 1945), Zambrano identifies Heloise as having found a way to free herself from women's traditional captivity while continuing to be a soul, or a specifically feminine being-in-the-world. According to Zambrano, Heloise dared to exist (Zambrano 1995).

In 1967, Zambrano published one last work, *La tumba de Antígona* (Antigone's tomb), on a major female figure. The Antigone theme was not new to Zambrano; in 1948 while still in Cuba, she wrote "Delirio de Antígona" (Antigone's delirium), which is a forerunner of the later play. In both works, Zambrano radically modifies Sophocles's version: Antigone, rather than committing suicide in her tomb, lives on and gains a significant voice that the Greek dramatist denied her. Both of Zambrano's versions can be interpreted in either a political or philosophical way, but the 1967 version more fully develops each strand. Antigone (with her classical garb and political role) can be seen as an allegory of the Second Spanish Republic, holding out hope of redemption from the defeat at Francisco Franco's hands, despite crushing odds to the contrary. The Greek Civil War between the brothers Eteocles and Polinices and the tyrant Creon are easily read as Spain's situation (Civil War and dictatorship) between 1939 and 1967. In philosophical terms, Zambrano positions Antigone at the dawn of consciousness, poised in a space between the deep, sacred interior reaches (the tomb) and the luminous exterior of full self-consciousness. Images of light and darkness alternate as Antigone carries on dialogues with each of the characters that play a role in her life – her sister Ismene, her mother Jocasta, her father Oedipus, her brothers Eteocles and Polinices, King Creon, and the harpy. The conclusion of the play is open-ended. Unnamed characters approach Antigone to lead her from her tomb towards an unknown future.

In 1961 in Franco's Spain, the Countess Campo Alange had already written about women as myth and as a human being (*La mujer como mito y como ser humano*, 1949). Coming out of the same philosophical climate as did María Zambrano, the Countess's analysis refutes Ortega's ideas about women even more overtly than does his "disciple" Zambrano. Campo Alange thoroughly undermines Ortega's notion that different periods in human history are "feminine" or "masculine." However, she follows in Ortega's footsteps in dissecting the tenor of her own times in Spain. Towards the end of the essay, she notes that "en España la independencia femenina tiene unas características *sui generis*" (Laffitte 1948, 53; in Spain female independence has some sui generis traits). In Spain, she avers, women did not have to conquer independence as did the suffragettes in England; independence was simply handed to Spanish women, and Spanish women merely received it. In a sentence that has a decidedly Sartrean ring, Campo Alange declares that "la mujer española se encontró un día – por así decirlo – condenada a la libertad" (53; Spanish women found themselves – in a manner of speaking – condemned to freedom]. She adds that since Spanish women are inclined towards passivity, the transformation was only exterior and not interior. It took them a while to internalize this freedom, which required a certain amount of self-discipline, interest in working, and a sense of responsibility. In 1961, Campo Alange also believed that Spanish women had not yet achieved these characteristics that would make them truly liberated.

Lilí Álvarez, Campo Alange's friend and collaborator on feminist projects with SESME (Sociedad para Estudios Sociológicos de la Mujer Española [Society for Sociological Studies of Spanish Women]), published a highly original and very Spanish book titled *Feminismo y espiritualidad* (Feminism and spirituality) in 1964. Álvarez was a deeply religious woman who lived a free life as an independently wealthy aristocrat with a noble title. Because she was born of a couple that was not legally married, her parents raised her outside of Spain, where she became a leading female sports figure. When she retired from the sports world, she lived in Spain and turned to feminist and spiritual activities (e.g., she mentored Carmen Laforet in her spiritual journey in the early 1950s; both women also had a feminist view of the world in common). Álvarez's essay "Feminismo y masculinismo," included in her book *Feminismo y espiritualidad*, attempts to forge a middle road between biological and sociological explanations for the differences between the sexes. Álvarez asserts that the members of the male sex are "masculinistas constitucionales" (Johnson and Zubiaurre 2012, 341; constitutionally masculinist), but that natural inclination is reinforced by the social customs in which they are raised from the earliest age. Álvarez further observes that women are also naturally inclined and socially conditioned to passively accept their lot, citing female factory workers who had recently signed a contract to receive 20% less pay for the same work that men do.

Interestingly, if paid work for women was viewed as a major goal by nineteenth- and early twentieth-century Spanish feminists, in the Franco era such work became suspect. By 1966, when Maria Aurèlia Capmany wrote *La dona a Catalunya* (Woman in Catalonia), there was definitely a new air of liberation in Spain; in this climate, her chapter on work titled "El treball, una nova esclavitud?" (Work, a new slavery?) sounds a note of alarm. Capmany repeats arguments we have seen in earlier Spanish feminist thinkers, noting that women have always worked "en els camps, s'ha esdernegat rentant i traginant coves de roba, ha portat tota mena de pesos, ha filat, ha teixit, ha fet cèramica, ha anat a vendre als mercats. ... Naturalment sense contracte de treball" (Capmany 1973, 171; in the fields, they have to exert themselves washing and carrying loads of clothes, transporting all kinds of weights; they have spun, have knitted, have done ceramics, have gone to sell in the markets . ... Naturally without a work contract). Capmany quotes Lidia Falcón's *Los derechos laborales de la mujer* (1964), who in turn quotes Gregorio Marañón on women's capacity for specific kinds of work, such as teaching, medicine, laboratory and office work – anything that requires patience, manual dexterity, and attention to detail. Capmany differs with Marañón because he limits his observations to middle-class women, who are a small percentage of women in Spain. She also points out that Spanish law does not distinguish between salaries for men and salaries for women, but in reality there are significant discrepancies. If Lidia Falcón considers women as a social class, Capmany contemplates womanhood as a profession in "De profesión mujer" (Profession: woman).

Although Lidia Falcón dedicates sections of *Mujer y sociedad* (Women and society) to women's work, especially to the legal restraints on women's ability to work during the Franco era, she does not believe, as did some prewar feminist thinkers, that work and economic independence will achieve true female liberation. Work is not central to Falcón's existential conception of women's independent state. She believes that if women achieve a sense of themselves as women, economic liberation will follow. She does not believe that women have been economically oppressed, because they have never held wealth (if they do, it is because their fathers or husbands allow it): "Ella es un personaje, un ser oprimido, lo mismo economicamente que sexualmente, que personalmente. ... porque no ha tenido nunca poder económico, no ha tenido tampoco el poder politico. La mujer se liberará como ser humano, más tiene que liberarse en una sociedad en que no haya distinciones de clases" (Falcón 1973, 72; She is a puppet, an oppressed being, economically, sexually, and personally. ... because she has never had economic power, nor has she had political power. The woman will become free as a human being, but she has to become free in a society without class distinctions). Catalonian essayist, novelist, and political activist Eva Forest also argues that work in and of itself is not necessarily liberating: "El trabajo por sí solo no libera a nadie. Aunque estuvieran en igualdad de condiciones con el hombre, tampoco liberaría el trabajo" (Levine and Waldman 1979, 102; Work in and of itself does not free anyone. Even if it were carried out in equal conditions to men's, work would not be liberating). She even speaks of work in some societies (clearly including Spain) as a type of slavery for both men and women, although she believes women suffer a double oppression if they work outside the home, because their work at home continues to be the same. According to Forest, in order for work to be liberating, it must be appropriate and satisfying.

A Chilean-born translator and feminist book promoter in Barcelona, Mireia Bofill also addresses whether or not work is liberating. She notes that women of around thirty years of age grow tired of staying home and develop a desire to work. Bofill believes that these women are exploited "porque esta mujer ve el trabajo como una liberación, no lo ve como la explotación por parte de la empresa donde trabaja" (Levine and Waldman 1979, 45; because these women see work as a liberation; they do not see it as exploitation by the company where they work). Bofill finds this situation accrues especially in more intellectual work, while Carnen Alcalde points out that working-class women, who should be the most conscious of women's oppression, are too busy working to be conscious of anything, much less do anything about their oppression (Levine and Waldman 1979, 32). Journalist Elisa Lamas approaches women's working from the point of view of the married woman. She notes that it is extremely rare for a Spanish man to consider women as complete human beings who are capable of anything beyond taking care of the home and children, and Spanish men are unwilling to share household responsibilities. She also observes that when it comes to studying for a career, if funds are limited, what funds there are go towards educating the male children, leaving the female children out. If women do manage to get a degree in order to enter a profession (e.g., law or engineering), employers will invariably select the male candidate over the female. A woman candidate for a position has to be ten times better than the male candidate to be a serious contender. Lamas also points out that in manual labour employment, where there is supposed to be equal pay for equal work, factory owners get around this rule by basing pay on production rates. Women who work double workdays at home and in the factory are often unable to produce as much as men who are more rested. In 1974, Lamas accurately predicted that were the political system to change, because women do work and under such lamentable conditions, the latent women's movement would emerge in full force (Levine and Waldman 1979, 110–21). When dictator Francisco Franco finally died in November 1975, that is exactly what happened.

Franco-era feminist thinkers who were aligned with the revolutionary left looked to the Soviet Union and to China for models. Mireia Bofill, for example, found that under Stalin the Soviet Union sent women back to the home and the family in order to advance economically by means of adopting some capitalist tendencies. In a way, her argument recognizes Lidia Falcón's desire to incorporate women's work in the home and the family into the national economy, although she gives such an economic appropriation of home and family a negative cast. Bofill notes that China is less rigid ideologically about women's place in the workforce than the Stalinist Soviet Union, and she is especially attracted to a model she found in a book by French feminist Claudie Broyelle, who describes small industries that women have founded in their neighbourhoods, allowing them to engage in employment outside the home while remaining close to home (Levine and Waldman 1979, 39–50). In a system with some similarities to María Martínez Sierra's utopian society (see part 3), these industries sponsor day-care centres for children and teams of people who clean houses and do other household chores for those women who work in the local industries.

Day care is an especially crucial service for women who work, and according to Bofill day care occasioned an entire movement in the late Franco era, because the state was doing little about it. The Franco government did encourage industries to offer child care, but this approach (according to Bofill) had the negative side effect of making women workers more dependent upon the companies they worked for and less able to negotiate with them. Bofill greatly prefers government supported day-care centres in the neighbourhoods rather than factory-sponsored childcare at the plant (Levine and Waldman 1979, 39–50). Lidia Falcón assures that the Franco government, despite its overt policies on women remaining in the home, will make it possible for women to work: "Las utilizarán para trabajar porque ya se sabe que trabajan, y bien, y que son un sostén de la economía de cualquier país, muy importante. Y para que trabajen, les pondrán guarderías infantiles para que lleven los niños" (Levine and Waldman 1979, 76; They will use them to work because they know they work, and well, and that they are an important support to the economy of any country. And so they establish childcare centres for the children so that they will work).

Echoing Margarita Nelken's concerns about middle-class women from the 1920s, Carmen Rodríguez brings up the question of the married middle-class woman who does not necessarily have to work in order to survive (eat, have shelter, etc.), but who feels an existential need to work: "Lo que yo deseaba era sentirme útil para mí misma y para los demás" (Levine and Waldman 1979, 136; What I wanted was to feel useful to myself and to others). Her children were now in school, and she had hired help for the household chores. Rodríguez herself saw her options as either becoming a typical bourgeois woman who goes to the hairdresser, makes social calls, and goes shopping, or staying home and becoming neurotic (she feared the latter would be her fate). She did find a job at a magazine, which was not satisfying because the editors gave her all the tasks no one else wanted to do. She worked long hours and arrived home tired, which created problems with her husband. The experience was consciousness raising for her and for those around her. Everyone finally realized that she was working because she had a vital need to do so. When the magazine she worked for had to cut back on personnel, she was the first to be let go, but she fought the decision in the courts and eventually moved up to the world of television journalism, where she was able to devise some programs on women's issues. Rodríguez once again echoes Margarita Nelken (without acknowledging her, probably because she had not had the opportunity to read *La condición social de la mujer en España*) in stating that middle-class men are exploited (her word is "enslaved"), because they have to work very hard to support their wives (who do not work) and their families.

Maria Aurèlia Capmany (1973, "Prologue") reveals how important it was to her to have come across Margarita Nelken's book *La condición social de la mujer en España* from 1919 when she was writing *La dona a Catalunya* in 1965. In the early years of the Franco regime, books of this type were completely erased from public memory. Capmany was surprised to realize that many of the feminist issues Nelken had addressed in *La condición social de la mujer en España* had still not been resolved: "Margarita Nelken hablaba con una prosa dúctil y eficaz, con un absoluto rigor dialéctico, con un propósito de inserción en la circunstancia histórica que resultaba – ¡desgraciadamente! – terriblemente actual en 1965, como – ¡por nuestros pecados! – en 1975" (Capmany 1973, 17; Margarita Nelken spoke with a flexible and effective prose, with an absolute dialectic rigour, mindful of her historical circumstances, which unfortunately turned out to be terribly appropriate in 1965 as it was –to our disgrace – in 1975. Capmany calls it an aggressive book that denounces the tame Spanish feminism to date and argues for inserting women's issues into the general social revolution being agitated; she also argues that the social revolution cannot take place without addressing women's concerns. Capmany especially appreciates Nelken's analysis of Spanish women's situation according to their social classes. Capmany also provides a useful summary of public reaction to Nelken's book. Capmany calls her book's reception "violent" (1973, 18). Conservative newspapers panned it, while more liberal reviewers defendoit. The minister of Public Instruction allowed an indictment to go forward against a normal school teacher who assigned the book to her students.

Two books significant to the Spanish feminist movement burst on the scene when dictator Francisco Franco died in 1975: historian of Spanish feminism Geraldine Scanlon's *La polémica feminista en la España contemporánea* (The feminist controversy in contemporary Spain; still the only history of Spanish feminist thought) and Amalia Martín Gamero's *Antología del feminismo* (Anthology of feminism). Martín Gamero's life is emblematic of a number of women who had lived as children during the Second Spanish Republic and as independent adult women during the Franco regime. After beginning her education at the coeducational Instituto Escuela in Madrid, during the Civil War, as the child of prominent Republicans (her grandfather was university professor and early feminist Adolfo Posada), Martín Gamero was sent to England to continue her education at an all-girls school. It was a shock to her to move from a liberal coeducational institution to the single-sex school in Britain. However, there she learned English, which made it possible for her to develop a career abroad in the book trade. Martín Gamero never married and survived quite well as a single, professional woman in Franco's Spain; her ability with languages certainly helped her professional opportunities, opportunities she might not have enjoyed if she had been limited to working in Spain. Her facility with English also aided her in composing her anthology of feminist writers, which includes María de Zayas y Sotomayor, Sor Juana Inés de la Cruz, Abigail Smith Adams, Mary Wollstonecraft, Elizabeth Cady Stanton, Susan B. Anthony, George Sand, Gertrudis Gómez de Avellaneda, Concepción Arenal, Emilia Pardo Bazán, and Virginia Woolf, among many others. Scanlan's and Martín Gamero's books, which follow so closely on the heels of the dicator's death, indicate that by 1975 Spanish feminist thought was already a recognizable and organizable body of work.

23 Galician Women under Franco: Resistance, Clandestine Politics, and Poetry as Gendered Symbolic Capital

SILVIA BERMÚDEZ

If the desire to empower women and women's emancipation were some of the pillars in the creation of a more just and fair society during the years of the Spanish Second Republic, the Franco period set back all those processes and achievements. Seeking the ideological and moral re-education of women, the Franco regime used coercion and indoctrination through the implementation of an extensive discriminatory legislation and the support of the church (Martins Rodríguez 2010). In the immediate aftermath of the war, Francoist repression forcefully focused its attention on a specific group of forward-thinking women that had been active in the public sphere through civic and political acts (Martins Rodríguez 2011, 95). The systematic repression that ensued, which also included the prohibition and persecution of the linguistic and cultural manifestations of the Basque Country, Catalonia, and Galicia, did not crush the will of some defiant Galician women despite their being jailed or exiled, although they paid a heavy price for their acts.[3] In other cases, the experience of interior exile – the "experience [of] disaffection from the majority even while dwelling in its midst" (Ilie 1980, 2) – did not quell their opposition to the dictatorship; they managed to resist through everyday acts and survival strategies in the midst of their misery and suffering, and the horror of living under the Franco regime. This chapter focuses first on leading Galician women who resisted Franco's subjugating machinery – the Sección Femenina (Feminine Section) and laws rendering women at the mercy of the state and the men in their lives – by defending their gender identity, their Galicia-ness, and their leftist political positions, as well as equality between men and women.[4] It then addresses some of the clandestine politics carried out under Francoism in regard to women's concerns.

And last but not least, it considers Rosalía de Castro's legacy in authors Pura Vázquez (1919–2006), Luz Pozo Garza (1922–2017), and Xohana Torres (b. 1931), and the 1963 centenary celebrations of the publication of Castro's *Cantares gallegos*, which as Ramón Piñeiro states in his *Olladas no futuro* (2007; Gazes into the future) marked "o verdadeiro punto de partida do noso renacemento cultural" (193; the true starting point of our cultural renaissance). The chapter concludes by calling attention to the work by playwright and activist María Xosé Queizán (b. 1939), a central figure in the development of Galician feminism in the 1970s.

Despite the dangers and the brutal repression that ensued with the 1936 uprising, many Galician women continued to be involved in anti-Franco guerrilla activities after 1939, acting clandestinely through the difficult 1940s. And while many of these women remain anonymous because of the circumstances, we do have examples of two leading combatants in the anti-Franco guerrillas in Galicia, Enriqueta Otero Blanco (1902–89) and María Araújo Martínez (1904–89). In regard to the anonymous women of this period, Anna Amorós i Pons, in "Unha homenaxe as mulleres das nosas vidas" (2012; A homage to the women in our lives) explains that the journal *Andaina*'s section titled "Lembranzas dunha época" (Memories of a period) was created to attest to all the Galician women that are not registered in history books, newspaper articles, or the media, but who through everyday practices resisted and fought against the lengthy dictatorship, particularly during the times "caracterizados polo estancamento económico, pola escaseza alimentaria, pola represión política, pola pobreza cultural, polo fustrigamento lingüístico, polo elevado índice de analfabetismo e polo medo" (49; characterized by economic stagnation, food scarcity, political repression, cultural poverty, linguistic harassment, high illiteracy rate, and fear). Enriqueta Otero Blanco, a teacher and secretary to Dolores Ibárruri during the Civil War, was an activist committed to women's incorporation into all areas of social life. As a fierce combatant, she tirelessly organized and promoted the resistance from the moment she escaped the Ventas Prison (Madrid) on 27 March 1939 and joined the *maquis* (anti-Franco guerrilla) until her capture in Lugo on 16 February 1946. Tortured and sentenced to death, Otero Blanco's sentence was commuted thanks to an international campaign. She then spent nineteen years in various prisons throughout Spain, finally returning to Galicia in 1965. Otero Blanco represents "como nadie las penurias y las luchas de las mujeres gallegas en la larga dictadura" (Martins Rodríguez 2011, 115; like nobody else the hardship and struggles of Galician women during the long dictatorship).

The author of political and cultural articles, as well as opinion pieces and poetry, Otero Blanco's work is now collected as *Letras armadas: As vidas de Enriqueta Otero Blanco* (2005; Armed letters: The lives of Enriqueta Otero Blanco) by Ángel Rodríguez Gallardo.[5] The publication is a result of the "recovery of the historical memory" of the years of the Second Republic, the armed conflict, and the Franco period that, in Galicia's case, can be traced back to 1963, the year Galicia celebrated the centenary of the publication of *Cantares gallegos* – whose publication date of 17 May was declared Día das Letras Galegas by the Real Academia Galega (RAG; Royal Galician Academy) that same year.[6] Also in 1963 the renowned Ceramic Sargadelos Group created the editorial house Ediciós do Castro with the explicit purpose of recovering Galicia's historical memory (see Quintás Pérez 2015, 518). One such example was the publication in 1986 of *Testimonio de la Guerra Civil* (1986; Testimony of the Civil War) by Isabel Ríos Lazcano (1907–97). Also a committed Communist, Ríos Lazcano was jailed from 1936 to 1943, after the commutation of her death sentence on 31 December 1936, the same day her husband, Manuel Calvelo, was put to death. In 1946, Ríos Lazcano emigrated to Argentina where she returned to her Communist militancy, joining the Federación de Sociedades Galegas (Federation of Galician Societies), actively participating in the committee on women and culture (García López, "Isabel Ríos").

María Araújo Martínez, known as "María a guerrilleira" (María the guerrilla fighter), identified herself as Galician and Cuban, having immigrated as a two year old with her family to Havana (Cuba), as did thousands of Galicians at the turn of the twentieth century. In Cuba, Araújo married a Galician, and both engaged in the struggle of the proletariat and Cuban communism before returning to Galicia in 1927. She worked at a cannery and became the leader of the Sindicato de Conserveras (Union of Women in Canneries) as member of the Communist Party of Spain. In this capacity, she fought for equal pay for women (García López, "María Araujo"). In 1936, with the beginning of the Civil War, Araújo and her husband went into hiding. She became a combatant against the Franco's forces in Galicia, being jailed until 1944, when, thanks to the good offices of the Cuban consul, María Araújo was allowed to travel to Havana. In Cuba, she began a new life working in many capacities to support the anti-Batista movement. With the triumph of the Cuban Revolution in 1959, Araújo dedicated herself to the success of the revolution and was recognized for her extensive contributions by Fidel Castro in 1975 (García López, "María Araujo").

Other leading Galician women who occupied important positions during the Second Spanish Republic also emblematize the resistance against the Franco regime, despite their being forced into exterior or interior exile. Respectively, this is the situation, for example, of Rita Amparo López Jean (1885–1942) and María Elvira Bao Maceiras (1890–1971), both teachers, steadfast Galicianists, and central figures in A Coruña's Agrupación Republicana Femenina (Republican Feminine Association). This association was constituted in A Coruña on 13 April 1933 and, according to their by-laws, was dedicated to defending social justice and democracy, the Second Spanish Republic and its Constitution, and women's rights, while also committing to work for securing the women's rights yet to be recognized (Pereira Martínez 1998, 280). Within the events organized by the Agrupación Republicana Femenina, the teacher and educationist María Barbeito Cerviño (1880–1970) gave the influential lecture "La mujer, antes, ahora y después" (Women, before, now, and afterwards) on 19 May 1934.

Amparo López Jean, a defender of women's rights, was also a member of both the Irmandades da Fala (Brotherhood of Language) and the historic Partido Galeguista (Pro-Galician Party). She was forced into exile in France, where she died in 1942 (Pereira Martínez 1998, 271). Her husband, Bernardino Varela, and Bao Maceiras were the original members of the Irmandades da Fala and were active in the Partido Galeguista. Elvira Bao Maceiras was jailed for a few months after the 1936 uprising that led to the Civil War, and she was permanently banned from public education after 1939. She resisted by creating her own private school in 1945 at home in A Coruña. Her daughter Elvira Varela Bao (b. 1926) and Luz Fandiño (b. 1931), both Galician activists, are recognized for their resistance to Francoism in "Galicia: Memoria histórica de las mujeres con las que el franquismo no pudo" (Coordinadora Feminista 2012; Galicia: Historical memory of the women that Francoism could not break).

On the literary front, the number of Galician-language women authors, particularly novelists and playwrights, publishing during the Franco years "remains consistently small until the 1980s" (García-Liñeira 2015, 186). It was as heirs to Rosalía de Castro's legacy and within the iconic status of poetry in Galician culture that three women authors Pura Vázquez, Luz Pozo Garza, and Xohana Torres afforded the Galician nation indispensable symbolic capital. Another poet, María Mariño Carou (1907–67) was acclaimed as the "new Rosalía" by Uxío Novoneyra (1930–99), her friend, mentor, and editor, for the 1963 poetic collection *Palabra no tempo* (García-Liñeira 2015, 212). And while the 1963 centenary sought to commemorate Rosalía de Castro's life and works, in honour of the publication of her *Cantares gallegos* in 1863, the celebration provided the ideal stage for promoting contemporary writing in the Galician language with a particular interest in sponsoring women authors.[7] The desire to further women authors writing in Galician exposes the gendered politics that simultaneously legitimized and limited women's authorship – not dissimilar to what the canonical figure of Rosalía de Castro endured.

Returning to the first of the three poets, Pura Vázquez, the author of over thirty books in Galician and Spanish, wrote *Íntimas* (Intimates) in 1952, her first poetic collection entirely in Galician, followed by *A saudade i outros poemas* (Nostalgia and other poems) in 1963, a collection dominated by the Galician's feeling of nostalgia (*saudade*). However, as early as 1943 Vázquez had included nine poems in Galician in her *Peregrino de amor* (Pilgrim of love). In 1955, she immigrated to Caracas, leaving behind a well-known public literary life that saw her active in the 1940s and 1950s not only in Galicia but also in Madrid. In Galicia, she was considered the heir to Rosalía de Castro for her 1948 volume *En torno a la voz* (Surrounding the voice), with its constant references to the Galician landscape. A year earlier, in 1947, she had already been proposed as a corresponding member of the Real Academia Galega (RAG; The Royal Galician Academy), having being elected in 1949.

For her part, Luz Pozo Garza, as one of the paradigmatic authors delineating the poetic pathways and genealogies to be followed, began her trajectory in 1949 with the publication of *Ánfora* (Amphora), written in Spanish (González Hernández 2004, 68). Pozo Garza describes the impact of her first book as follows: "[It] takes as its protagonist a nymph or goddess who is identified with my own life. It is a bold feminine expression in a society which was prudish and closed to the expression of eroticism" (Nogueira 2009b, 208). In 1952, she published *O paxaro na boca* (The bird in the mouth), her first poetic collection in Galician, and with *Códice calixtino* (1986; Calixtine Codex) – required reading for over a decade at the high-school level – and *Prometo a flor de loto* (1992; I promise the lotus flower) she secured entry to the Royal Galician Academy in 1996. As the first woman writer to join such a prestigious institution, with an acceptance speech titled "Diálogos con Rosalía" (Dialogues with Rosalía) Pozo Garza cemented a major symbolic moment in Galician letters (Bermúdez 2002).[8]

Two leading women authors placed gender front and centre in rewriting feminine myths – as does Xohana Torres with Penelope – and by offering alternative models to those valued by the patriarchal system as does María Xosé Queizán (Nogueira 2009a, 98–101). In 1956, on Radio Ferrol, Torres launched her first radio program titled "Teresa," specifically geared to women. In 1965, on the radio station La Voz de Vigo, she directed "Raíz e Tempo" (Root and time), the first cultural program in Galician since the Civil War. She began her work as a monolingual Galician writer in the journal *Aturuxo* (1953) and published her first poetic collection *Do sulco* (1957; Groove), thus marking innovative trends in Galician poetry since the 1950s. During the 1960s, she was fully engaged in theatre and was promoted by the Grupo Galaxia "as *the* female poet in Galician," displacing both Pura Vázquez and Luz Pozo Garza from their central positions (García-Liñeira 2015, 176). Torres was also elected to the Royal Galician Academy in 2001; her acceptance speech was titled "Eu tamén navegar" (I also sail), the title of her canonical poem from her poetic collection *Tempo de ría* (1992; Estuary time) and an important slogan for feminist writers publishing in the 1990s. Both texts offer an active and daring Penelope, who instead of passively waiting, affirms her agency by reclaiming the right to "also sail."

In the late 1950s, María Xosé Queizán, a pivotal figure within Galician and Spanish feminisms, became highly active in the public sphere. In 1959, Queizán created the Teatro de Arte y Ensayo de la Asociación de la Prensa de Vigo (The Art and Essay Theatre Group of Vigo's Press Association). From 1967 to 1968, she founded and directed the Teatro Popular Galego (Popular Galician Theatre). And in 1977, in the midst of the Transición (transition to democracy), she published her essay *A muller en Galicia* (1977; Women in Galicia). The publications of these authors, along with the some of their activities, ranging from the late 1940s to the early 1970s, opened the doors for the strong presence of Galician women poets and authors – some unequivocally identified as feminists – that will come to define Galician letters in the 1980s, 1990s, and up to the present.

24 The Resurgence of Feminism in Catalonia, 1970–1975

MARY NASH

The feminist, lesbian, Catalan activist, and prominent poet Maria Mercè Marçal (1952–98) identified three key fundamentals in her identity as a rebel in her poem "Divisa" published in her book *Cau de llunes* that was awarded the prestigious Carles Riba prize for poetry in 1976: "A l'atzar agraeixo tres dons: haver nascut dona, / De classe baixa i nació oprimida. / I el trébol atzur de ser tres voltes rebel (1977; To chance I am thankful for three favours: born a woman, of lower class and an oppressed nation. And the azure shamrock of three times a rebel). This poem became a manifesto for many Catalan feminists and speaks to the multiple ingredients of Catalan feminism in the late Franco period and the transition to democracy.

As has been noted in other chapters of this book, the systematic repression of women and the abolition of equal rights, citizenship, and freedom characterized the Franco dictatorship. The repressive machinery of the regime attempted to relegate women to enforced domesticity under male surveillance. Moreover, in the case of Catalonia, the authoritarian state was heightened by Franco's systematic repression of Catalan culture and language. On abolishing the Autonomous Statute (1932) that had established the Catalan language as co-official with Castilian, language and rights to Catalan culture were banned, and the Spanish language – the language of the empire – prescribed as compulsory in education, media, and culture, relegated Catalan to the private sphere; Catalan was severely repressed.

The feminist revival of the early 1970s was a response to the confiscation of Catalan women's political, social, civil, and cultural rights. Feminists challenged the patriarchal order of the Franco regime and advocated egalitarian gender values. The feminist agenda of many

Catalans also encompassed the recuperation of the women's rights as established under the Generalitat during the democratic Second Republic. Usually the historical landmark for the emergence of the new feminism of the 1970s refers to the Jornades Catalanes de la Dona (Catalan Conference on Women) held in Barcelona in May 1976. However, by paying closer attention to the history of women's activism during the early 1970s, a picture emerges that provides insights not only to understanding the disruption of traditional male dominance and the gender order of the Franco dictatorship but also to the grounding of Catalan feminism, which by the mid-1970s thrived as a influential social movement. As such, Catalan feminism was a pluralistic movement at the intersection of political opposition to Franco within the clandestine political parties, the lay Catholic social-reform movements, social activism in the peripheral working-class neighbourhoods, student rebellion at Catalan high schools and universities, and cultural resistance in Catalan through song, poetry, visual media, together with the recuperation of the memory of historical feminism.

Women hailed "from the eternal night of Francoism," in the words of activist Empar Pineda, an exceptional figure as a strong female leader of the radical left-wing party Communist Movement of Catalonia (CMC) (Interview by Mary Nash, Barcelona, 10 February 2005). They were shrouded in the long "dark years" of the Franco dictatorship, as evoked in the testimony of poet and feminist Mari Chordà, who later inaugurated the renowned feminist bar, La Sal (Interview by Mary Nash, Barcelona, 19 May 2005). This generation of young women had been educated in submission and servitude. However, far from conforming to national Catholic and Francoist gender codes, they experienced such empowerment that it led them to develop a collective feminist identity and engage in public debates and clandestine actions in defence of women's rights. Most were politically committed to the fight against the Franco regime and advocated social justice. However, they shaped a new feminist consciousness that eventually led to a collective identity and agenda as feminists.

Women's rebellion was inspired to some extent by the writings of feminists such as Simone de Beauvoir, Betty Friedan, Lidia Falcón, and Maria Aurèlia Capmany known as the Catalan Beauvoir. The latter's pioneer work *La dona a Catalunya: Consciencia i situació* (1966) became very popular and greatly influenced the conversion of young readers to feminism. Many found a vocabulary that described their own personal experience, as Elvira Altès excitedly revealed: "I found myself reading

Maria Aurèlia Capmany … I found all the words to say everything that happened to me, everything I felt, all the rebellion that I had not been able to channel. And it was fantastic, a great discovery, and I converted to feminism" (Interview by Mary Nash, Barcelona, 5 July 2005). However, as a transclass social movement, the development of feminism was triggered by political practice and lived experience. Feminist psychologist Victoria Sau described Francoism as a black shadow that covered everything (Interview by Mary Nash, Barcelona, 11 February 2005). The imposition of a biological and national Catholic mandate of obligatory maternity, large families, and reclusion to the home affected women's options to education, employment, or social activity. Young women suffered continuous deprivations, and by the early 1970s differential gender conduct led them to be more aware of their discrimination. Girls were obliged to do housework. In contrast to their brothers, they had to cook, make the beds, and sew their brothers' socks, as Carme Alcalde, a feminist journalist later to become the director of the influential journal *Vindicación Feminista* (Feminist vindication) condemned (Tuñón 1977). Engineer and social activist Carolina Costa, who came from an affluent family of Catalan Republicans who had spent several years in exile, by age eleven had already rebelled against the privileges of her brothers as she "had to wash the dishes and make the beds on Sundays when her brothers went to play football" (Interview by Mary Nash, Barcelona, 22 July 2005). Even revolutionary young men never dreamed of doing housework. While living in a commune in 1974, Núria Cornet, journalist and later member of the resurgent anarchist feminist organization Mujeres Libres, invented short slogans supposedly by Marx, such as "Share the housework," which she put on the kitchen walls as an inducement to her radical housemates (Interview by Mary Nash, Barcelona, 22 September 2005).

Young women began to rebel against enforced submission, thus challenging the victimist lifestyle of suffocating domesticity led by their mothers. Ana Mercadé, from a liberal family background, left home to gain economic independence and greater freedom from her father. As a left-winger associated with the radical left-wing Partido de Trabajo (Work Party), she later became a notable feminist leader as head of one of the major feminist organizations, the Catalan Association of Women. She based part of her feminist agenda on the recuperation of Catalan women's rights under the Second Republic, such as free abortion.

The demand for freedom to choose their education and a professional career motivated women's challenges to the dominant patriarchal family and gender conventions that restricted female life options. Many young women had to study careers considered more suitable for females, and for a number of students, such as Laura Tremosa, who was a pioneer in the Faculty of Industrial Engineering, attending the university meant everyday sexual harassment both by students and professors. Personal experiences of deprivation and discrimination common to women opened an initial feeling of rebellion against their status as a woman. The trigger to move from individual rebellion to collective conflict was the creation of small groups of feminist self-awareness that identified female oppression and challenged Francoist gender models. One of the first groups began to meet at Maria José Rague's home in Barcelona in June 1970. Just back from Berkeley, Rague had published a book on women's liberation in the US. In 1975, Laura Tremosa's home became a site for feminist consciousness when she opened it to clandestine weekly meetings of forty to fifty women to discuss their daily life, everyday problems, and to engage with feminist readings. From a first stage of resistance to the dictatorship, feminists went on to express a new discourse that confronted Francoist female arquetypes of domesticity and the mandate of compulsory prolific motherhood.

Ongoing discussion in the consciousness-raising groups (CRG) led to establishing a collective identity as feminists. They were also one of the sites for the founding of an organized feminist movement. The feminist organization Asociación de Comunicación Humana y Ecología (ANCHE; Association for Human Communication and Ecology) was created on 21 November 1975, a day after Franco's death, by Laura Tremosa, Núria Pompeia, Amparo Moreno, and Mireia Bofill, among others who attended Tremosa's CRG. ANCHE was named without any reference to feminism as a strategy to avoid police repression. Its goal was to create a new path for feminism with a unitary democratic autonomous women's liberation movement.

The informal CRGs grounded the Catalan women's liberation movement on the core notion that the personal is political. Enforced silence and repression were overcome through the dynamics of communication and affinity, which allowed many women to speak for the first time in decades without moral coercion or restrictions on such taboo issues as female sexuality or dissatisfaction with motherhood and marriage. Educated in the incontestable belief that sexuality is associated with sin or the dangers of intercourse, this group exchange of views and information on birth control was crucial to their feminist awareness. The consideration of sexuality as pleasure unrelated to procreation became a significant revolution. As a safe site for women to meet, the CRGs became spaces to recover dignity, solidarity, the centrality of women's experience, and the first words to express this collectively as women's liberation.

Of course it is true that political militancy in the clandestine movement against Franco was also a decisive scenario for female consciousness. Many feminists were active militants in political parties, trade unions, and in the neighbourhood movements advocating social justice for the working classes. A number of feminists were also active participants in the Assembly of Catalonia created in 1971 to lead a unitary political and social organization to achieve democratic freedom, amnesty for political prisoners, and the restitution of the Catalan institutions under the 1932 Statute. Feminist activists such as lawyer Magda Oranich represented democratic lawyers and reported on their activities, on political prisoners, laws, and Francoist repression, while Laura Tremosa represented the College of Engineers. In 1973, a number of women were imprisoned because of their activism in the assembly, among them prominent lawyers such Montserrat Avilés, Magda Oranich, Asunción Sallés, and engineer Laura Tremosa.

Most anti-Francoist activists were left-wing militants in a range of Communist and radical revolutionary parties. The political left and the unions did not have a feminist agenda, nor did they subscribe to gender equality. Many left-wing activists in political and social protests acquired a feminist consciousness through their growing awareness of their subsidiary role and lack of recognition by progressive male militants. The Communist run Democratic Movement of Women had claimed equal labour rights for women since the mid-1960s; however, left-wing women and syndicalists did not have a decisive impact in challenging male hegemony until the emergence of more critical feminist voices in the early 1970's, such as syndicalist and radical leftist CMC militant Núria Casals who was elected as a delegate for the unitary democratic candidature of Comisiones Obreras trade union for metallurgy workers in the spring of 1975. She went on to play a decisive role in the establishment of a women's secretariat in this union.

Women also developed a very active role in the social protests of neighbourhood associations during the early 1970s. They defended their rights and the welfare of their working-class community. They occupied the streets and marched to demand basic public services such as schools, markets, health services, paved streets, street and traffic lights, adequate sewage systems, and appropriate housing conditions.

Although they did not speak then in a feminist voice, they also organized to defend women's rights, and it is remarkable that nineteen women's neighbourhood groups (*vocalias de dones*) participated at the Catalan Conference on Women in May 1976.

The first initiatives of organized Catalan feminism emerged in response to the official Francoist agenda of the International Women's Year (IWY). In early 1975, a unitary women's movement was created under the aegis of the Association of Friends of the United Nations in Barcelona (AFUNB). Anna Balletbò and Carmen Alcalde were convened by the AFUNB to develop an alternative activity for the IWY. With the contribution of Ana Maria Vela as president, a Women's Department was created in the AFUNB, which provided the legal cover to promote initiatives on women's rights. A clandestine assembly celebrated in February 1975 was attended by more than two hundred women. A declaration was later circulated criticizing Franco's appropriation of the International Woman's Year as a paternalist act. It established five crucial feminist demands: "Total change of the legislation that typifies women in a role of dependence within society; Reassessment of the educational system that qualifies women as inferior and subordinate; Right to birth control; Elimination of discriminatory situations within the labor market; Creation of the necessary community services for women, until now unjustly marginalized to perform housework, so they can be liberated and attain their social and professional fulfillment" (Grups de dones, de diverses procedències, diverses entitats no governamentals de Barcelona, fan pública la següent declaració a L'OPINIÓ PÚBLICA; private archive). The declaration included a critique of sexism in society and the manipulation of the female image for political or commercial goals while demanding equal rights for women. It also comprised the usual political demands for amnesty, the abolition of the death penalty, and democratic rights. This feminist manifesto anticipated many of the debates and demands expressed six months later in May 1976 at the Catalan Conference on Women.

In May 1975, the Fifth Conference of Young Lawyers of Catalonia and Baleares celebrated in Barcelona claimed women's legal and political rights and the elimination of all discrimination against women. Among other demands, it advocated the elimination of the crime of adultery, the principle of equality of the spouses in marriage, and the suppression of honour as a mitigating circumstance in all the articles of the Penal Code. It also demanded the right to birth control, the suppression of all prohibitions relating to contraception, and the legalization of abortion. In the workplace, the proposals focused on wage equality, the creation of kindergartens, equal rights for domestic service, and equal benefits between men and women. In the framework of Spanish universities, women's studies was first institutionalized at the University of Barcelona in October 1975 with the pioneer course "Feminist movements in the contemporary Spain" taught by Mary Nash, while the Associació de Dones Universitàries per a l'Estudi del Problema de la Dona (Association of University Women for the Study of the Problem of Woman), led by Trinidad Sánchez Pacheco, promoted debates on women and equality.

The Women's Department of the AFUNB proposed the celebration of a legal feminist conference. The organizing secretariat avoided any specific leadership and was comprised of Carmen Alcalde, Anna Balletbò, Mireia Bofill, Dolors Calvet, Rosa Grisó de Sala Ponsati, Anna Mercadé, Amparo Moreno, Magda Oranich, Ana Maria Vela, and Laura Tremosa. As a unitary platform, it included a wide range of committed independent feminists and Socialist, Communist, and Christian Democrat political militants. Thirty-nine years after the first feminist conference held in Civil War Barcelona in 1937 and six months after the death of Franco, almost four thousand women attended the four-day feminist conference at the University of Barcelona (27–30 May 1976). The success of this organized feminist movement speaks to the groundwork achieved by Catalan feminism during the final stages of the Franco regime.

25 Basque Women Who Resisted: A Feminist Rereading of the Franco Period

JONE M. HERNÁNDEZ GARCÍA, MARÍA RUIZ TORRADO, AND IRATXE RETOLAZA

Among the Basque women who had to flee from Franco's Spain after the Spanish Civil War were Aurora Arnaiz, Dolores Ibarruri (La Pasionaria), María de Maeztu, and Polixene Trabudua, all known for their cultural, social, and/or political activities during the Second Spanish Republic. Some also actively defended women's rights. Here we analyse three areas of Basque women's resistance to the antiwomen and antifeminist measures of the Franco dictatorship in the areas of culture, education, and politics, spheres in which Basque women had been gaining notable protagonism and in which their presence was appreciable, although not without some controversy.

The Second Republic witnessed a significant development of Basque culture, the basis of which had begun to be established in the late nineteenth century with the appearance of what is known as Euskal Pizkundea (Basque Renaissance), a broad sociocultural movement whose objective was to foment Basque language and culture.[9] A number of important initiatives were undertaken between 1876 and 1938, particularly with regard to women who at that time demonstrated a determination to participate in the public sphere. In fact, the long process that marked the development of a Basque cultural field (Apalategi 2005) fomented the social relevance of nationalist women, as well as their political protagonism (Aldekoa 2004, 110; Rekalde 2012). However, the project was truncated by the military uprising in 1936. From that moment on, the Franco regime promoted and installed linguistic centralism anchored in Castilian, prohibiting and persecuting any other linguistic and cultural manifestations in Spain. In order to inculcate Francoist ideology and undermine anti-Franco positions, the authorities applied censorship to all cultural activities from 1939 to 1951.

Prohibiting *euskera* (Euskara; the Basque language) and Basque culture made it almost impossible to promote the Basque language and culture (Torrealdai 1998).

After decades of repression and silence, there was a small opening up within the cultural arena under the second phase of Francoism that allowed for the appearance of different cultural initiatives, some of which stemmed from the prewar cultural tradition. Women's participation in prewar theatre, for example, was crucial (Álvarez-Uria 2011; Cano 1997), and Maria Dolores Agirre even received the post of instructor in the Euskal Iztundea (Basque Declamation School) in Donostia in 1932. Agirre reorganized the school in the decades of the 1950s, inaugurating the second phase of this theatrical institution (1953–81) (Auzmendi 2002, 11–22; Urkizu 2000, 639). During the decades of the 1950s and 1960s, Euskal Iztundea's activity was intense, representing adaptations of classical works, as well as works by Basque authors, almost all traditionalist and moralist in nature. Women participated as directors and actresses, and in addition authored prize-winning plays. Among them Mayi Elissagaray, who published in the journal *Gure Herria* (Our people) (Sudupe 2011, 67–9), stands out, as does María Dolores Agirre, who published in the journal *Egan* (Flying) (Auzmendi 2002).

In these pedagogical and moral works, the dramatists promoted the prototype of a nationalist woman with a Catholic ideology. Nonetheless, and in spite of representing traditional themes and ideologies, Euskal Iztundea participated in the cultural resistance because its labour was fundamental to the transmission and conservation of *euskera*. This situation created a strange paradox – Basque women were traditionalists in their thought and discourse, but modern in their practices. This paradigm became a model for action that, in spite of the contradictions and tensions it generated, legitimized female activity in the public sphere (Llona 2002, 252). Other cultural initiatives, however, were the consequence of a cultural and generational renewal that embodied a new radicalized cultural and political sensibility that questioned the nationalist tradition: "The solid moral pillars that anchored the traditional national ideology as well as *Euskal Pizkundea*, its cultural project during the Republic, recede before the agnosticism, atheism, neopaganism, nihilism, existentialism, and aestheticism that were spreading among the new Basque literary writers" (Aldekoa 2004, 150). These cultural movements were situated among the European countercultural, anticapitalist measures, and Basque anti-Franco cultural practices (Oronoz 2012, 36–43). In this process of renovation, the creation of the Donostian

Jarrai (Carry On; 1958–69) was key; it brought experimental theatre to the town squares of Euskal Herria, adapting vanguard works in *euskera* (Aguirre 2006, 368).

Several actresses, such as Arantxa Gurmendi (b. 1944), were trained in this theatre group; Gurmendi also participated directly in the translation of theatre texts (López Aguirre 2015, 9–21).[10] All the members of Jarrai participated in the journal *Zeruko Argia* (Light of the sky), which published cultural chronicles, through which this group had a great deal of influence. Gurmendi covered the musical chronicles and advocated for rock in *euskera*, which was unthinkable at that time. In the decade of the 1970s, independent theatre groups proliferated, which were "una alternativa socio-político-cultural contra la estructura dominante en la España de los años setenta" (Aguirre 2006, 344; a socio-political-cultural alternative to the dominant structure of Spain in the 1970s). Although women's presence in these groups was not large, in some cases women were the principal promoters of the groups. Such was the case of Elena Armengod de Bekereke (Balido), Maribel Belasegi de Orain (Ahora), and Pilar López de Eterno (Paraíso) (Aguirre 2006, 362). In addition, the independent theatre represented diverse types of women that did not correspond to the domestic feminine ideal promoted by the Franco regime.

In this cultural transformation, the musical project Es Dok Amairu (There are not thirteen; 1965–72) promoted the new Basque song and collective spectacles that combined music, poetry, theatre, and even dance (Oronoz 2012). Well-known popular singers like Lourdes Iriondo and Arantxa Gurmendi stood out. Until 1969, Gurmendi played Euskal Herria theatres and discoteques with Biurriak, her Basque rock band, rendering versions of songs by the Beatles, the Rolling Stones, and Manfred Mann (López Aguirre 2015, 9). In that era, the band was known for its rock aesthetic, distancing itself from the more distinct aesthetic tendency of Ez Dok Amairu (There Aren't Thirteen). Gurmendi was "la neska de minifalda y enorme desparpajo que, en los históricos festivales de Ez Dok Amairu, rompía con el climax de seriedad de aquellas manifestaciones de auto afirmación de la cultura vasca" (López Aguirre 2015, 9; the miniskirted chick with great abandon who in the historic Ez Dok Arairu festivals broke with the culminating seriousness of those manifestations of Basque culture's self-affirmation).[11]

With the rise of the new song, the figure of the popular singer gained strength, and this context framed the trajectories of singers like Estitxu and Maite Idirin. In addition, anti-Fascist festivals proliferated, in which women like Jeni Prieto of the folk group Lantzale (Obrero; Worker) participated (López Aguirre 2015, 41–9). In a period in which freedom of expression was limited, popular singers and anti-Fascist festivals became society's mouthpieces (Eskisabel 2012, 19). Thus women's participation in this ambience was very important, since women arose as spokespeople in the public arena for the collective population. The need for women's roles and voices facilitated the incorporation of women into theatre and music, but the participants in these collectives did not take on the role passively; they were active agents in cultural modernization. As for literature, in the decades of the 1950s and 1960s, women authors devoted themselves to didactic and pedagogical genres like theatre and children's literature. Marijane Minaberri was central to the modernization of children's literature. She wrote poetry and drama for children that was distributed by publishers and journals coordinated by the popular movement that favoured a Basque education. Not until the 1970s did several female authors come to the fore in the Basque literary field. The poetic voice of Amaia Lasa embodied the self-affirmation of a feminine consciousness that recognized and condemned the social limits placed on women (Izagirre 2012, 25–6; Aldekoa 2004, 183–4). Arantxa Urretabizkaia's contributions were involved with the editorial house Lur (Land), founded in 1969 by Gabriel Aresti. In the 1970s, Urretabizkaia published poems and translations, and collaborated on the journal *Zeruko Argia*. Many of the women who participated in these cultural activities also actively collaborated in the articulation of the feminist movement during the Transition (1975–9). Although with much less public frequency, women participated in oral improvisation, or *bertsolarismo.* These performances took place not only in private spaces in which oral culture was very present among women (*bertsos*, i.e., stories, songs), but also some participated in the *bertsolarismo* that took place in public plazas. Women even won some public contests, as was the case of Inaxia Etxabe and Sister Justina Aldalur, who respectively won first and second prizes in a contest held by the Franciscans in 1956 (Larrañaga 2000, 404–5). Francoist persecution and censorship made it extremely difficult to publish think pieces that criticized the regime's ideology. Thus writers, thinkers, and intellectuals of the era scarcely cultivated the essay, and in order to express their ideas they employed other genres such as journalism and poetry. For example, Angela Figuuera Aymerich (Bilbao 1902–Madrid 1984) wrote poetry in Castilian from the end of the 1940s onward, in which her emphasis shifted from the existential to the social, paying special attention to women's social role.

The educational field was another important axis of social and cultural resistance to the Franco dictatorship. In the same way that school constituted an important tool for the spread of Francoist ideology, in the Basque territory it was also a site of criticism and transgression. Thus phenomena like the recovery of the Basque language and culture in post-Franco Spain could not be understood without the figure of the *andereños*, or Basque women schoolteachers. Idoia Fernández refers to these women as a key element in the nationalist resurgence in the 1950s (Fernández 1994, 38–9). Two factors favoured the schoolteachers' significant role. First, during the first half of the twentieth century, women's dedication to teaching did not provoke controversy (Llona 2002). In fact, teaching had become a professional option for women with intellectual interests, as well as for middle-class women who had to work and who saw in teaching a means to make use of the knowledge they had acquired as "educated young women" (Llona 2002, 72–3). As Miren Llona points out, teaching was considered "una prolongación natural de los atributos femeninos (Llona 2002, 77; the natural extension of feminine attributes). Secondly, the fact that the educational function women had assumed was connected to socialization carried out in private contributed to the appearance that Francoist repression against women who worked in this area was less severe (Fernández 1994).

In any case, what the different careers reveal is that attempts to revitalize the Basque language and culture from the end of the nineteenth century, including the years of Francoism, cannot be understood except through the participation of many women who, in their role as teachers and taking advantage of the possibilities for public access that this profession gave them, extended their influence and their sociopolitical practice to other spheres like culture or politics (Fernández 1994; Llona 2002; Ugalde 1993). And those who were not teachers formed part of the networks they created – networks that, according to Fernández, were pillars of a kind of microsociety (1994, 80), which, among other things, was determined to resist the mandates imposed by the Franco regime. Today the feminist dimension of what Fernández (following Jaxinto F. Setién) has defined as a movement of the *andereños* (Fernández 1994, 161) still remains to be studied. Doubtless, it is work that would be worthwhile because it would help build bridges between women who fought for public access at the turn of the twentieth century and who finally emerged with a clear feminist consciousness in the years after Francoism, a consciousness that, in principle, Basque women lacked in the twentieth century.

If Basque women were condemned to anything it was to be mothers (Llona 2002) – mothers called to support their families and the central element of Basque social organization, the *baserri* (farm house). In Basque culture, women are fundamentally associated with the space of the house (Aretxaga 1988). Thus the house and principally the *baserri* are considered the heart of Basqueness, as well as the language and other elements related to the Basque cultural imaginary like architecture, landscape, the oral tradition, etc. Begoña Aretxaga (1988) has underscored the relationship between *etxea* and *herria* (house and people, the latter understood in terms of nation). The ties between these two concepts were interpreted and made manifest in very different ways in the cases of men and women. While support and defence of the family and home were demanded of women "from inside" and "towards inside," attending above all to the affective and socialization dimensions, the sphere of men's work was projected towards the exterior, where it acquired a clear social and political dimension, often incarnated in the figure of the *gudari* (soldier) called to defend the father's house (*aitaren etxea*).[12] Aretxaga points out the centrality of the house; her careful analysis from a gender perspective allows anyone who examines Basque culture the necessary tools to decipher the role of Basque women, a mandate that necessarily involves conflict and questioning.

The creation in 1922 of Emakume Abertzale Batza (EAB; Society of Nationalist Women) was a serious and organized incursion of women into the public and political spheres. Some of the women were literally mothers, but others were, above all, social mothers or mothers of the country (Llona 2002, 231). Their function in the political arena was to take the roles traditionally assigned to them in the home and family into the public sphere. As Mercedes Ugalde has amply demonstrated, thousands of women got personally or collectively involved in conserving all that nationalism of the period considered characteristic of Basque identity, especially the Basque language (Ugalde 1993, 198). With the idea that women could develop different public functions, traditional nationalism distinguished two types of political participation: the so-called patriotic action and political action (Llona 2002). Women were included in the first of these, while the second was the exclusive arena of men. According to Ugalde, the means by which patriotic action was carried out was in political propaganda, social welfare, the religious and affective, and the cultural and educational (Ugalde 1993). Above and beyond formal education, many *andereños* worked in the realm of informal education, developing a number of activities related to literature, theatre, dance, music, or manual arts. According to Fernández, the influence of these women reached thousands upon thousands of children. Later Francoism suppressed this activity but did not manage to eliminate it altogether. Thus, as Fernández (1994) points out, it is possible to think that the networks forged among women participating in this intense patriotic activity did not disappear under the dictatorship, but remained active. One constant element is the emergence of the *etxe-eskolak* (home schools) established in the decade of the 1950s and promoted by the well-known *emakume* Elvira Zipitria.

Zipitria had founded the first *ikastola* (Basque school) in Donostia during the Second Republic, but she had to go into exile at the beginning of the Civil War.[13] When she returned, she began to give classes to Donostian children by going to their homes, and in 1946 she created the first home school in the same city (Euskal Herriko Ikastolak and Euskaltzaindia 2010, 26). Houses were rehabilitated as school centres where the kitchens functioned as classrooms. They replicated the use made in the *baserri*, or country house, of the table around which the family sat at meals (Fernández 1994, 81). The experience was so successful that, in time, more centres of this kind opened up, extending their activity to adults interested in learning *euskera* or becoming literate in the language. Gradually more home schools appeared in different townships in Gipuzkcoa and later in Biscay under the leadership of Xabier Peña and María Ángeles Garai, an *andereño* who knew this kind of experience thanks to Zipritia herself in the first home school created in Bilbao in 1957 (Euskal Herriko Ikastolak and Euskaltzaindia 2010, 40). In 1966 in Bilbao, the *ikastola* Resurección María de Azkue was inaugurated, the first home school officially recognized in Biscay and in whose founding women like Juliana Berrojalbiz and Tere Rotaetxe participated. In these same years, *ikastolas* were established in different townships of Euskal Herria, above all in the southern areas. Many women participated in this process, not only as *andereños* but also as leaders involved in administration. Progressively, the *ikastola* movement gained social and even political and economic prominence. According to Fernández, all of this activity had an important impact on transforming the educational milieu; school was no longer viewed as a prolongation of the maternal function (Fernández 1994, 157), while at the same time, men began to enter the educational profession, a circumstance that fomented the academicist nature of school (Fernández 1994, 161) and that, along with other factors, generated quite a bit of tension in the heart of the educational community (Fernández 1994).

Women in the Socio-Political Arena: The Struggle against Francoism

The extremely repressive nature of the Franco dictatorship, which was maintained from the beginning until the end of the dictatorship, could not silence the movements in opposition to the regime that, with more or less intensity, maintained their activity at all times. Many Basque women were active in the anti-Franco organizations and movements in defence of their most fundamental rights, and, of course in their daily activities they also carried out a variety of more individual and unplanned resistance practices (Altuna 2015). These activities and practices were the basis for the appearance of the feminist movement and consciousness the 1970s (Andrieu 1988, 91). Unfortunately, given the circumstances of the moment, these women remain anonymous.

Many women had already played an important role in the fight against the Nationalists during the Civil War. In the postwar, and despite the harsh repression and the danger that their acts implied, some women continued to be combatants. They acted clandestinely as a link between prison and the exterior, helping political prisoners and their families. They also hid people who were sought by the regime, and they distributed anti-Franco publications. There is no doubt that those were truly difficult years for the opposition and that it was not easy to organize, but despite all the obstacles, they managed to do it. As an example, we note the cases of Bittori Etxeberria, Delia Lauroba, Itziar Mujika, and Teresa Verdes, who were associated with the Eusko Alderdi Jeltzalea/ Partido Nacionalista Vasco (EZJ/PNV; Basque Nationalist Party) and in some cases also with Emakume Abertzale Batza (EAB). All of these women had a remarkable participation in a secret network of support for the Basque government in exile. They helped political prisoners and their families, and they carried out espionage, gaining information of interest to the Spanish state. Today we know of their activities, because in 1940 the women were arrested and imprisoned (Chueca 2012).

The nationalist women were not the only ones to participate in the anti-Franco struggle. Also having an important role was the Association of Anti-Fascist Women (AMA), of which Dolores Ibarruri was the principal organizer. This association was a collective tied especially to Communist women, but it also included women of other political ideologies. Organized in small clandestine groups, their purpose was to obtain and distribute information and to help political prisoners. There were groups of anti-Fascist women in Biscay, Gipuzkoa, and Nafarroa. As a sample of this activity, we quote a letter that reflects their efforts. It refers to the organized nationalist women and a group of nuns who were not supporters of the regime:

> In the Basque Country there are groups of anti-Fascist women in all the towns of manufacturing and mining belt. There are also groups of *Emakumes* with which we have strong ties, and we help each other in our work. In some towns we work with the organization of nationalist women. Here it has not been difficult to organize groups of anti-Franco women, because Basque women have always been active in the struggle. There is a convent whose nuns help us a great deal because the Mother Superior says that they will never forget what the Falangists did to the Basque priests and because they think that helping the people to fight against their tyrants is the obligation of every Catholic. The most active women in our organization are in the mining area; we must not forget that the miners are those that suffer most and live in the most poverty. In Guipúzcoa we also work hard, above all in San Sebastián. But we are not satisfied; we think we can and must do more and we will do it. We publish a little newspaper on a small ditto machine but it is possible that soon we can publish it on a press. We also work to help the prisoners and their families by making sweaters and embroidering. Meanwhile, greet the anti-Fascist women of Spain from the anti-Fascist women of Euzkadi. Mirenchu. (Radio España Independiente 23 October 1943, quoted in Romeu 2002)

The Basque women continued mobilizing in support of the political prisoners and carrying out campaigns for amnesty until the end of the Franco regime. However, after the second half of the 1940s, other important centres of opposition arose, in which women also had a notable role. Little by little, both the workers' and student movements became more and more relevant, and within them women were mobilized in a clear and visible way, especially in workers' strikes, which were very important in the Basque Country. Basque women went out into the street to demand higher salaries and to protest the inflation of prices and the higher cost of living. Although the dictatorship remained strong, and the opposition was weak, at no time did they cease their activities.

In the 1970s, now within the frame of the second Francoism, a new political left arose, and in this context there appeared new organizations and collectives against the regime. In the area of the workers' struggle, among many others, we particularly note groups like the Comisiones Obreras de Euskadi (CCOO de Euskadi; The Workers Commissions of the Basque Country), Hermandades Obreras de Acción Católica (HOAC; Workers' Catholic Action Associations), and Juventud Obrera Católica (JOC; Workers' Catholic Youth). In the nationalist realm, above all the appearance of an armed group, Euskadi Ta Askatasuma (ETA; Euskadi and Liberty), is notable. Anti-Franco opposition was increasing and involved more and more people – male and female workers, students, Socialist activists, Communists and anarchists, nationalists, progressive Christians, etc. The protests were more and more numerous, and of course the numbers of women that participated in them grew (Solé and Díaz 2014, 71). Basque women continued to mobilize for amnesty for political prisoners and for better labour conditions and the end of repression. Some, like Dolores Ibarruri (from exile), also defended the need for women to be united and organized for the struggle. Ibarruri spoke thus on 8 March 1960:[14]

> Todavía sin libertades, es difícil la celebración de este día. Mas decir difícil no es decir imposible. Y nuestras mujeres como en las huelgas y protestas nacionales contra la Dictadura, encontrarán la forma de celebrar el 8 de marzo, de expresar sus anhelos y sus esperanzas en una mañana de paz y de democracia . ... Queridos amigos y camaradas, al saludaros con el alma hacemos votos porque el 8 de marzo de 1960 sea el punto de partida de un nuevo esfuerzo de reagrupamiento y en la organización de las mujeres para que España vuelva a ser un país democrático, soberano e independiente ¡Viva el 8 de marzo! (Radio España Independiente 8 de marzo de 1960, quoted in Romeu 2002)
>
> (Still without liberties, it is difficult to celebrate this day. However, to say difficult is not to say impossible. And our women, as in the national strikes and protests against the dictatorship, will find a way to celebrate the eighth of March, to express their desires and hopes for a future of peace and democracy. ... Dear friends and comrades, upon greeting you with my soul, I do so with vows to make 8 March 1960 a point of departure for a new effort to regroup and organize women to make Spain a democratic, sovereign, and independent country. Long live 8 March!)

Thus, the birth of the Movimiento Democrático de Mujeres (MDM; Democratic Movement of Women) was celebrated in 1965. Of clear sociopolitical and feminist intent, the organization arose in Madrid, but it immediately had a Basque delegation, comprised mainly of women from the industrial areas of Bizkaia (Epelde, Aranguren, and Retolaza 2015, 64). Although it was created by Communist women, it was fairly pluralistic and attracted women from diverse political ideologies. They worked clandestinely, articulating an anti-Francoist struggle and the struggle for women's liberation (Moreno 1988; Pardo 1988).

In addition, there were a number of meeting places for women in the period, such as centres for popular culture, groups tied to the church, neighbourhood associations, and parents' groups. Even though they did not yet have a political orientation, they were frequently places of consciousness raising and of reflection in which women began to organize due to their concerns (Epelde, Aranguren, and Retolaza 2015, 69–70). When faced with any kind of political opposition, the response of the dictatorship was more and more repressive. As a result, in the Basque Country there were violent encounters with the police, and a state of emergency was declared several times. Arrests and torture were habitual, which generated a climate of great tension and at the same time resulted in greater numbers of demonstrations and strikes.

Thus in the 1970s, the numbers of women in the ranks of the opposition to the Franco regime grew concomitantly. Basque women were prominent in sit-downs demanding amnesty for political prisoners; they also protested in the streets to denounce the speculation on basic food prices; and they occupied spaces to denounce the contamination of their towns and cities (Epelde, Aranguren, and Retolaza 2015, 64). Especially important were the protests against the Burgos trial[15] and the attempts to stop the death sentences of José Antonio Garmendia, Ángel Otaegi, and Juan Paredes Manot ("Txiki").[16] Among these protests, the convocation of the Mouvement de Libération des Femmes (MLF; Women's Liberation Movement) stands out. It organized a Marcha de Mujeres (Women's March) to the border between France and Spain on 5 October 1975, in which some one thousand women united to denounce the executions (Epelde, Aranguren, and Retolaza 2015, 49). Thus bridges were built and ties strengthened between women and feminists on both sides of the border, as evidenced in the final act of the march in which the Basque popular singer Maite Idirin sang "Amaren etxea" (The mother's house), reinscribing the aforementioned poem by

Gabriel Aresti. The situation had become impossible for the regime. So, at the end of 1975, after Franco's death and the end of the dictatorship as such, a new political and social scenario opened up.

In the popular and cultural movements of the 1960s and 1970s, Basque women activists and anti-Francoists coincided, although they did not always accept the roles that these collectives assigned them. On many occasions, they met and collaborated in order to denounce the discrimination they suffered in various anti-Franco venues. The complicity that was generated among the women of these groups established the bases of a social network that gave rise to the organization of the autonomous feminist movement during the political transition. This same idea of a network has been stressed in the section above devoted to women's presence in the educational arena, since, following Fernández's hypothesis (1994), the initiation of the Basque school under the Franco dictatorship would not have been possible without a social network and the communication that existed between women. A network had been in place in the prewar era, fundamentally around the movement of the *emakumes*, an especially relevant women's collective for its wide presence in the territory and for the diversity of its spheres of action.

From education to culture, passing through propaganda, the *emakumes* represent as no other collective does the paradox in which Basque women have lived for a long time. They are prisoners of a mandate that converts them into protagonists of not only the defence of tradition but also the practice – performance – of which gives them a feminist consciousness "capaz de convertirse en acción política desafiante del orden establecido" (Llona 2002, 79; capable of converting it into a political action that defies the established order). A consciousness is attributed to women who, according to Llona, "valoran la acción de las mujeres y confían en su capacidad transformadora, elementos ambos que, en definitiva constituyen la piedra de toque del feminismo" (Llona 2002, 205; value the action of women and have faith in their power to transform, both elements that definitely constitute the touchstone of feminism). This view allows us to carry out a contextualized reading of the acts of resistance advocated by Basque women during the Franco dictatorship and to reinterpret them as resistance and even rebellion and insubordination to gender norms, an attitude that in time will appear embodied in the body politic of Basque feminism.

PART V

A New Beginning: The Transition to Democracy and Iberian Second-Wave Feminism (1974/1975–1994/1996)

COORDINATED BY SILVIA BERMÚDEZ

26 Historical Overview

ANA PAULA FERREIRA, SILVIA BERMÚDEZ, AND ASUNCIÓN BERNÁRDEZ RODAL

In 1974, the Portuguese Estado Novo fell, and in 1975 Francisco Franco died, thus ending the long dictatorial periods in twentieth-century Iberia and opening the way for more sustained feminist activity in the Peninsula. Before then, and beginning in 1972, Portuguese society experienced such numerous and radical changes that ideologies of gender connected to times of dictatorship, fascism, and colonialism were presumably eradicated or, at least, weakened. However, after the momentary scandal of an experimental feminist literary tract published during Marcello Caetano's dictatorship following Salazar's death and notably titled *Novas cartas portuguesas* (*New Portuguese Letters*), little more disturbed the norms of gender in "Europe's garden planted by the sea."[1] In Spain, the actual transition to decentralization and democracy is said to have begun in December 1973 when ETA's Operación Ogro (Operation Ogre) succeeded in assassinating Franco's prime minister (and personal confidant) Admiral Luis Carrero Blanco (Paniagua 2009). Also in 1973, a small group of leftist intellectual women joined the University Women's Association to strengthen and transform the association from within to begin advocating for the legalization of divorce and contraceptives (Rigaudias 2009, 2). By disrupting Franco's succession plans, Operation Ogre marked the beginning of the end of the lengthy dictatorship.

The year 1973 also marked an important development in the liberation of Spanish women with the founding in Madrid of the first Asociación de Mujeres Separadas (Association of Separated Women), which worked to repeal articles of the Francoist Criminal Code governing adultery and concubinage, categories still used then to subject women to their husbands' control. The leading role of lawyer Ana María Pérez del Campo (b. 1936), an expert on matrimonial law, was instrumental in the creation of the Association of Separated Women, as well as in the drafting of the 1981 Spanish Divorce Law. Further evidence of the disruption of Franco's legacy emerged when under the United Nations' naming of 1975 as the International Women's Year, underground feminist organizations celebrated 8 March 1975 against the guidelines and events programmed by the regime's Sección Femenina (Feminine Section). A full-blown feminist activity was carried out in early December of that year with the hosting in Madrid of the Primeras Jornadas Nacionales por la Liberación de la Mujer (First National Conference for the Liberation of Women; see Asociación "Mujeres en la Transición Democrática" 1999). One of the direct results of the conference was the creation of the Frente de Liberación de la Mujer (FLM; Women's Liberation Front) consisting of two hundred activists. Many of them would come to play an important role in Spain's public sphere, such as, among others, philosopher Celia Amorós, whose work is discussed in chapter two; and feminist historian Gloria Nielfa (b. 1947), the cofounder of the Instituto de Investigaciones Feministas (Feminist Research Institute) of the Universidad Complutense de Madrid, which began operating in the academic year 1988–9, although it had been developing activities since 1983. As a pioneer of sexual and reproductive rights in Spain, gynecologist and author Elena Arnedo (1941–2015) had an important role in the development of the Centros de Planificación Familiar (Family-Planning Centres) since the later years of the Franco regime; she became the first president of the Asociación de Planificación Familiar (Family-Planning Association) in Madrid in 1983.[2]

Several feminist milestones took place across the Spanish territory one year after Francisco Franco's death on 21 November 1975. Between 27 and 30 May 1976, the Jornades Catalanes de la Dona (Catalan Conference on Women), to which Mary Nash refers in her contribution to this volume (chapter 24), took place at the University of Barcelona with four thousand women in attendance (Pàmies 1976, 105; Nash 2007, 89–137). A number of important claims regarding sexuality, contraception, and abortion were voiced at the conference, thus establishing "personal and reproductive rights of women as basic components of a new democratic political culture" (Nash 2011, 298). On 1 July 1976, the pioneer journal *Vindicación Feminista*, published until October 1978, was launched in Barcelona by Lidia Falcón (b. Madrid 1935) and Carmen Alcalde (b. Girona 1936). After the arrest of eleven women in the town of Basauri (Basque Country) on 9 September 1976 for participating in abortion practices, women's associations and feminist organizations mobilized and worked tirelessly first in Bilbao and then throughout the Spanish territory to demand their freedom on the key feminist issue of abortion rights. The year 1976 came to a close on 24 November with the first feminist demonstration in Madrid since 1936, including banners stating, "Mujer, lucha por tu liberación. En defensa de tus derechos" (Woman, fight for your liberation. In defence of your rights).

The democratic elections followed in 1977, and that same year Lidia Falcón founded the Organización Feminista Revolucionaria (Revolutionary Feminist Organization) through which she created the Feminist Party (Johnson and Zubiaurre 2012, 405). The following year, Spaniards experienced the referendum and enactment of the 1978 Spanish Constitution, which was opposed by many feminist groups and associations since women were left out of the formulation and writing of the document produced by the so-called Fathers of the Constitution. In addition, as enacted, the Constitution prolonged women's oppression (see Coordinadora Feminista de Barcelona 1978). Two months before the Constitution was signed by King Juan Carlos I on 27 December 1978, the Librería de Mujeres y Centro de Encuentro (Women's Bookstore and Meeting Place), as it was named then, opened in Madrid in mid-October 1978. The bookstore, now just Librería de Mujeres (Women's Bookstore) continues to operate at the same location with renewed purpose in furthering feminist positions (www.libreriamujeres.com).

Meanwhile in Portugal, an initial moment of hope emerged with the institutionalization of women's rights to equality in the period following the 25 April 1974 military coup that deposed the Fascist dictatorship in place since 1933, thus ending five centuries of colonialism. For some, that hope attached itself to the economic prosperity that was temporarily brought about as a result of Spain's and Portugal's official entry into the European Community in 1986. However, as the decrease in the number of feminist groups indicates, disappointment (or, simply, indifference) set in during the consolidation of the laissez-faire liberal democracy that was sustained by the unilateral and politically centred Socialist government elected in 1996. At the same time and in tune with what was going on elsewhere, the waning of uniformly defined feminist issues was accompanied by the rise of difference feminism, with those arguing for the rights of gay, lesbian, and transgender people attaining some public voice.[3]

Considering the apparent absence of Portuguese feminism from the period following World War II until the recent present, historian and feminist activist Manuela Tavares wonders whether the struggle against the Fascist New State that had ruled Portugal since 1933 "eclipsed" from historical memory not only the robust feminism of the early twentieth century but also that which surfaced after the democratic revolution of 25 April 1974 (Tavares 2011, 23). The virtual invisibility of feminism and, particularly, of feminist thought in democratic Portugal in contrast to elsewhere in Europe and in other areas of the Iberian Peninsula needs to be examined more carefully with attention to context, especially in relation to a difficult history of late colonialism that culminated in colonial wars mandating the conscription of all young men between 1961 and the early months of 1974.

During this period, Portuguese emigration increased exponentially, especially men fleeing clandestinely to France. Thus, feminist concerns were integrated into or overpowered by anti-Fascist struggles in which the opposition to the war and the colonialism it tried to sustain gained an enormous emotional urgency. Between 1974 and 1975, women's issues in Portugal were coopted by those of a people undergoing abrupt change in most areas of life as a consequence of more than half million Portuguese, their descendants, and African nationals arriving in Portugal from the former colonies of Angola, Mozambique, Guiné-Bissau, Cape Verde, São Tomé, and Principe. Finding these migrants places to live and integrating them, along with their pain, resentment, and relative destitution, into the rather small and poor Portuguese society is still an unsung success story. It takes place virtually at the same time that women acting on behalf of "the people" took hold of factories, organized strikes, seized vacant homes, and demanded the reform of public service institutions (Tavares 2000, 29). Such revolutionary gestures, at least in part prompted by the radicalization of the military leftist government until its defeat in November 1975 by liberal forces within the military, may not have improved women's lot, but they were the popular and spontaneous counterpart of women's groups mobilized at the time.

The first was the Movimento de Libertação das Mulheres (Women's Liberation Movement), modelled after its French counterpart, which had also emerged in the context of a postcolonial metropolitan society.[4] It was organized immediately after the coup d'état and prompted by the solidarity manifested by feminists from other countries with the legal case involving the so-called Three Marias – Maria Teresa Horta (b. 1937), Maria Isabel Barreno (1939–2016), and Maria Velho da Costa (b. 1938), the coauthors of *Novas cartas portuguesas* (Barreno, Horta, and Velho da Costa 1974; *New Portuguese Letters*, 1994). Less than a month after it was released, *Novas cartas portuguesas* was taken off the market and banned by the government of Marcello Caetano, who, succeeded António de Oliveira Salazarin in 1968. The authors refused to identify the authorship of each of the texts constituting the book; specifically, in question were the passages centred on feminine eroticism. The three women were thus jointly charged with obscenity and abuse of the freedom of the press. The legal proceedings captured national and international attention. The involvement of feminists from England, the United States, and France, among others, in the case known as that of "The Three Marias" called international attention to the Fascist dictatorship still reigning in Portugal. It also prompted the mobilization of the first radical feminist group, the Movimento de Libertação das Mulheres (Women's Liberation movement).

The Portuguese Women's Liberation Movement brought together women of diverse socioeconomic, professional, and educational backgrounds to challenge the patriarchal basis of society as a common source of gender discrimination and violence against women. It petitioned for legislation on equality of rights and for the alteration of the Civil Code. In January 1975, the group organized a rally in Lisbon's central square park, Parque Eduardo VII, where symbols of oppression and violence against women were burned (e.g., pornography, the Portuguese Civil Code, sex toys, etc.). It is unlikely that the rally was successful in raising feminist public consciousness and ending "the dictatorship of men," but the infamous confrontation reported by the media, according to which more than one thousand men opposed the feminists with physical and verbal violence, has become the sad legend of second-wave feminism in Portugal.

The United Nations' naming of 1975 as the International Women's Year and its subsequent proclamation of the Decade of Women (1975–85) had important consequences on the entire Iberian Peninsula. In Spain, it spurred the above-mentioned Primeras Jornadas Nacionales por la Liberación de la Mujer (First National Conference for the Liberation of Women) in Madrid, attended by over five hundred women with delegates representing nineteen provinces from across the Spanish nation. In Portugal, both events are likely to have encouraged the newly elected civilian democratic government to attend to equal rights for men and women. Still during the dictatorship, in 1970, the Ministry of Work and Welfare had charged a work group with creating a national plan for the integration of women into all aspects of social and economic development. It was presided over by Maria de Lurdes Pintasilgo (1930–2004), an industrial chemical engineer with a strong record of leadership in the areas of women's rights and social justice. Projects initiated then were taken up by what was renamed in 1975 the Comissão da Condição Feminina (Commission on the Status of Women), and Maria de Lurdes Pintasilgo was once again appointed to preside over it.[5] The commission was instrumental in passing new legislation on behalf of women's rights in the areas of labour, health, and social welfare; and it became the main source of public events and editorial initiatives that aimed to study, raise consciousness, and change the status of women. By 1976, under the first popularly elected democratic government in Portugal, the new Constitution declared men and women to be equal. And two years later, the Civil Code, the bulk of which still dated to 1867, was amended to give wives the same rights as husbands in family life.

In the case of Spain, and following the chronology established by María Ángeles Durán and María Teresa Gallego, the history of the first ten years of the feminist movement during the transition to democracy has been divided into three stages beginning in 1975 (Johnson and Zubiaurre 2012, 399). Accordingly, during phase one, which lasted from 1975 to 1979, the movement was created, organized, and expanded; in phase two from 1979 to 1982, the movement became fiercely divided due to infighting regarding positions and objectives; and in phase three from 1982 to 1985, organized feminism became fragmented into hundreds of minicollectives and organizations across the country. During this phase, state agencies, both at the level of the Autonomous Communities and the nation, engaged with feminist agendas (Durán and Gallego 1986, 207). In fact, the 1978 Constitution, by decentralizing power and recognizing Spain as a kingdom constituted of seventeen Autonomous Communities, with the so-called Historical Nationalities – the Basque Country, Catalonia, and Galicia – enjoying particular privileges in light of their status during the Second Republic (1931–6/9), allowed for the implementation of, in many instances, feminist policies. For example, the Autonomous Communities had almost absolute control over important areas such as health and education, of particular interest to feminists for establishing new policies. The governments of each particular Autonomous Community became "the main political reference for many feminists" (Valiente 2003, 44). This phenomenon explains the development of women's policy agencies throughout the Spanish territory, but in particular in Andalusia, Catalonia, Galicia, and the Basque Country from 1983 until 1996 when the Socialist era came to an end.

A year after the beginning of Socialist Felipe González's four terms in office (1982–96), Spanish state feminism was ushered in with the creation in 1983 of the Instituto de la Mujer (IM; Institute for Women), whose mission was to foster equality between men and women. Also during the 1980s, the Spanish legislature passed laws legalizing divorce (1981) and limited abortion (1985).[6] The enactment of these two laws was a major victory for feminist collectives and organizations since it meant curtailing the Catholic Church's extraordinary power over Spanish life. Specific feminist "equality policies that impact gender relations and challenge patriarchal practices" (Ortbals 2008, 94) were facilitated during the 1980s and 1990s so that each Comunidad Autonómica (Autonomous Community) could develop and establish equality plans and inform and educate women of their rights (Threlfall, Cousins, and Valiente 2005; Ortbals 2008). The 1980s also saw the publication of foundational feminists essays such as, among others, Lidia Falcón's two volumes of *La razón feminista* (1981 and 1982, respectively; *Feminist Reason*). Victoria Sendón de León (b. Alicante 1948) also published *Sobre diosas, amazonas y vestales: Utopias para un feminismo radical* (About godesses, amazons, and vestals: Utopias for a radical feminism) in 1981, while Montserrat Roig (Barcelona 1946–91) published *El feminismo* (Feminism) in 1985. In the academic year 1988–9, the Instituto de Investigaciones Feministas (Feminist Research Institute) of the Universidad Complutense de Madrid (Complutense University of Madrid) began their interdisciplinary and interfaculty activities (see www.ucm.es/investigacionesfeministas/). The origins of the Feminist Research Institute date back to 1983, when a group of female students and professors from the Third Cycle in the humanities and social sciences began meeting regularly to discuss feminist studies under the leadership of Professor Mª Carmen García-Nieto from the Department of Contemporary History.

In Portugal, the struggle for equal rights in all domains of social, professional, and personal experience, with particular attention to rights over the body, sexuality and reproduction, was common in the agendas of several women's groups that emerged in the late 1970s and throughout the 1980s. One of these was the União das Mulheres Anti-fascistas e Revolucionárias (Union of Anti-Fascist and Revolutionary Women), renamed in 1989 União de Mulheres Alternativa e Resposta (Women's Union for Choice and Response). It has been known since then by the acronym UMAR. Combining feminism and Marxism, the group fought for equality between the sexes, free childcare for working women, the right to occupy and take legal, contractual possession of empty homes; and universal literacy. UMAR caught more public attention, however, due to its struggle for the availability of legal and free contraception, the decriminalization and legalization of abortion, the prosecution of domestic violence, and the extinction of prostitution and trafficking of women. The same orientation and many of the same goals were shared by other second-wave feminist groups that coalesced in urban centres, such as the Grupo Autónomo das Mulheres do Porto (Autonomous Group of Oporto Women) and the Mulheres da Associação Académica de Coimbra (Women of the University of Coimbra Academic Association). The battle of these groups against both sexism and capitalism is well documented in the articles and data included in their respective newsletters, *Situação da Mulher* (Women's condition) and *Boletim da Mulher* (Women's bulletin).

In the 1980s, a number of women's groups undertook initiatives in consciousness raising among wider and more diverse populations than a minority sensitive to feminist messages in urban centres. An important group founded in 1980 and having representation in fifteen of Portugal's eighteen districts was a national women's network, or REDE. Their work was pivotal in raising consciousness about the political nature of private life, with the goal of leading women to recognize and fight against their status as an oppressed group. According to Maria de Lurdes Pintasilgo, their main instigator and inspirational force, the mere thought of women forming a network and transforming themselves and transforming other women represented a menace to the established gender order (Tavares 2011, 316).

Such was not the case with the agents of MAPA, the acronym for Mulheres a Preparar o Amanhã (Women Preparing Tomorrow), Catholic secular women's groups connected to the international Graal, or Grail, who worked in informal educational and consciousness-raising projects in rural areas with women of different classes. In regard to Pintasilgo, the nonnegligible support she had as an independent candidate for president in the 1986 elections and her subsequent defeat at the polls arguably brought to a halt the hopes harboured by at least a feminist elite that the success of the young Portuguese democracy depended upon the directive of social justice that was at the core of feminist agendas.

By contrast, at about the same time – the second half of the 1980s – the state-supported Comissão da Condição Feminina (Commission on

Women's Condition) was strengthened and achieved greater visibility with the affiliation of several women's groups. The Commission's Advisory Council, formalized in 1979, secured government funding for seminars in women's rights and other educational and consciousness-raising projects organized by nongovernment women's groups. This led to a greater degree of institutionalization of feminist activities, discouraging broader grass-roots feminist initiatives (Tavares, 2011, 347).[7] In 1987, the UMAR feminist group founded a Platform of Action for Equality to confront the government with the need to attend to women's rights that surpassed equality agendas (Bento 1998, 86).

One area in which Portuguese state feminism did not get involved was the struggle for and the debates surrounding the legalization of abortion, which brought together several women's groups since the second half of the 1970s. While for some it was a matter of choice and control over the woman's own body, for the more radical feminists (e.g., those belonging to or sympathizers of the Portuguese Women's Liberation Movement [Movimento de Libertação das Mulheres]) the fight for abortion also meant the defiance of the patriarchal ideology of maternity as women's destiny (Tavares, 2011, 277). In addition to abortion, the 1980s witnessed growing feminist concerns against domestic violence, including sexual violation, and the continuing inequality of salaries between men and women workers, the latter being paid roughly two-thirds of what men were paid. The connection between economics and women's bodies clearly pointed to the source of women's oppression, as, for example, Maria Isabel Barreno argued (Tavares, 2011, 308–9).

Mobilization against the depiction of stereotypical images of women in advertising and mass media grew exponentially in Portugal since the second half of the 1980s, as feminists called for formal education to change the gender ideologies that children traditionally learn at home. In this context, a critical feminist psychology movement emerged, arguably the most important development in Portuguese feminism at a time when academic women were beginning to claim the field of women's studies; it would take a decade at least for the first graduate degree to be awarded (Saavedra 2010, 66).

In Spain, the 1990s saw the furthering of the two major theoretical schools developed in the 1980s: equality feminism centred in Madrid and difference feminism centred in Barcelona. Milagros Rivera (b. Bilbao 1947) is considered one of the leading thinkers of Spanish difference feminism for works such as, among others, *Nombrar el mundo en femenino: Pensamiento de las mujeres y teoría feminista* (To name the world in feminine: Women's thoughts and feminist theory; first edition 1994, second 1998) and *El fraude de la igualdad* (1997; The fraud of equality). Philosopher Amelia Valcárcel (b. Madrid 1950) first advanced her notion of feminism as a political theory in *Sexo y filosofía* (Sex and philosophy; 1991), which was followed by *Del miedo a la igualdad* (On the fear of equality; 1993). It is within this flurry of intellectual exchanges and debates that in 1991 the editorial powerhouse Cátedra launched the series Feminismos (Feminisms) cofounded by Professors Giulia Colaizzi and Isabel Morant, both from the Universitat d'Valencia (University of Valencia). Colaizzi's impact on Spanish feminisms cannot be overstated, since her 1990 volume *Feminismo y teoría del discurso* (Feminism and discourse theory), published by Cátedra inaugurates studies on the politics of representation, gender, and sexualities in Spain.

The November 1992 assassination of Lucrecia Pérez, a black Dominican woman who had briefly worked as a maid in Madrid, brought to light the connection between migration and women's inequality in 1990s Spain. As Carmen Gregorio Gil argues, "If we had to search for the single face to represent immigration in Spain it will have to be that of a woman from the South" (quoted in Bermúdez 2001, 188). Both aspects are highlighted by director Iciar Bollaín in her 1999 film *Flores de otro mundo*. A cinematographic appeal for interracial and cultural coexistence centred on the lives and differing experiences in a rural community of Patricia, a Dominican immigrant, Milady, a young Cuban woman, and Marirrosi, a middle-aged divorced woman from Bilbao. There are, however, problems since the film does reify traditional gender roles and religious homogeneity (see Ballesteros 2005 on how Bollaín's film subverts hegemonic representations of the sexualized immigrant; Martin-Márquez 2002).

Finally, the 1990s are also the decade when feminist and gender-studies centres and research groups were institutionalized in universities across the Spanish nation. Precursors to all were created in the 1980s in Andalusia, a leading Autonomous Community regarding the implementation of equal rights: first in 1985 with the creation of the Asociación de Estudios Históricos sobre la Mujer (AEHM; Association of Women's Historical Studies) at the University of Malaga; then in 1989 with the launching of the Instituto Andaluz de la Mujer (The Andalusian Institute of Women).The Instituto Universitario de Investigación de Estudios de las Mujeres y de Género (University Institute for Research on Women and Gender Studies) at the University of Granada, which originated in the academic year 1984–5 as the Seminario de Estudios de la Mujer (Women's Studies Seminar) and became the Institute for Research on Women and Gender Studies in the academic year 1995–6, created one of the first university publishing projects in women's studies in 1989: the FEMINAE collection. In 1990, they launched the first PhD in Women's Studies at state-sponsored universities.

Among other leading centres are the Institut Universitari d'Estudis de la Dona (IUED; University Institute of Women's Studies) at University of Valencia initiated in 1991 and officially formalized by the Valencian government's decree in 1994. The IUED has offered a PhD program on gender since 1992 and is also responsible for publishing the series Quaderns Feministes. In addition, the Instituto Universitario de Estudios de la Mujer (IUEM; The Institute of Women's Studies) of the Autonomous University of Madrid was established by royal decree in March 1993. The institute derives its strength from the Seminario de Estudios de la Mujer (Seminar on Women's Studies) created in 1979. In 1994, the Centre Dona i Literatura (The Centre for Women and Literature) was founded by Àngels Carabí and Marta Segarra within the Facultat de Filologia (College of Letters) at the University of Barcelona. The centre began its activities in 1990 as the Seminar of Literature Written by Women, and it is recognized as a Consolidated Research Group Creació i Pensament de les Dones (CiPD; Women's Creation and Thought) financed by the Generalitat de Catalunya. The centre edits *Lectora: Revista de dones i textualitat* (Journal of women and textuality) and the series Mujeres y culturas (Women and cultures) published by Icaria Editorial in Barcelona. Other such centres are the University of Salamanca's Centro de Estudios de la Mujer (Centre for Women's Studies), born as such in 2002, but originated in 1997 when a group of female professors from diverse academic fields created the Seminario de Estudios de La Mujer (Women's Studies Seminar); subsequently, some of these professors then launched the doctoral program Estudios sobre las Mujeres y Relaciones de Género, Bienio 1998–2000 (Women's Studies and Gender Relations 1998–2000). All of these initiatives indicate that feminism in the Iberian Peninsula, after much activism, turned increasingly academic and theoretical.

27 Feminisms in Postdictatorial Portugal, 1972–1996

ANA PAULA FERREIRA

In one of the many poetic celebrations of the 25 April 1974 coup d'état that toppled the Portuguese dictatorship, the writer, journalist, and feminist activist Maria Teresa Horta identifies one of the most prized and yet equivocal gifts brought about by what became known as the Carnations Revolution:[8] "Deu-nos Abril / o gesto e a palavra / fala de nós / por dentro da raíz/ ... / O povo somos: / mulheres do meu país" (Horta 1977, 106; April gave us / the gesture and the word / it speaks of us / from within its root / ... / We are the people: women of my country).[9] The suggestion is that it was women, as subjects of their own voices, who launched the liberating call for what erupted two years later as an all-male military feat of historical accomplishment.

Two fundamental intertextual citations can be identified in the verses quoted, inviting the reader to connect the fall of the Fascist-colonialist government to the fractured, silenced history of feminism in twentieth-century Portugal. The first is the reference to "Abril." It was precisely in April 1972 that a decisive challenge to authoritarianism, patriarchy, sexism, colonialism, and fascism erupted in the form of a hybrid, experimental literary text titled *Novas cartas portuguesas* (*New Portuguese Letters*). Weaving together poetry, philosophy, sociology, cultural history, and politics, it is the most important document of second-wave feminism in Portugal. It was published by a press owned by the prolific poet, writer, and social activist Natália Correia (1923–93), known for her polemic stands against Enlightenment reason; for her philosophical, experimental modernist works; for her feminist scholarship; and for her public celebration of the "matrix structure" ruling all life.[10]

A second reference in Horta's poem, "mulheres do meu país" (women of my country), conjures an earlier feminist text that probably few people still remembered at the time of the 1974 Revolution: *As mulheres do meu país* (Lamas 1948; The women of my country).[11] Maria Lamas (1893–1985) had published this book first in instalments and in 1950 in a volume of large dimensions. This collection of ethnographic essays, profusely illustrated with her and others' photos, is a homage to the multiple and diverse contributions that women of various regions and classes, on the continent as well as on the islands of Madeira and Azores, were making to Portuguese society, particularly in the areas of economics and culture, despite the multiple hardships imposed by motherhood. The author wrote the essays in a gesture of defiance against the shutting down by Salazar's dictatorship of the Concelho Nacional das Mulheres Portuguesas (National Council of Portuguese Women), months after she organized a highly visible international Exhibit of Women's Books in 6–12 January 1947.[12] It was met with silence as part of the imposed silence on its author, whose increasing association throughout the 1950s with the democratic opposition made her persona non grata to the regime. After several imprisonments, she went into exile in Paris from 1962 to 1969. Not necessarily identifying herself as a feminist, Maria Lamas stood for the democratic values of emancipation and justice for all people. Symbolically joining the Portuguese Communist Party in her eighties, she herself would likely proclaim Maria Teresa Horta's "O povo somos" (We are the people). Between first- and second-wave feminism and owing to both, decades of fighting against fascism and colonialism and the revolution that followed, "women" become thus toppled into "people," continuing to silence and making invisible feminisms per se.[13]

Not unlike what happens with feminists elsewhere, it is mainly through artistic, philosophical, and political engagements with language that a number of Portuguese women attempt to break down that silence. Three notable cases in point are the *Novas cartas portuguesas* (*New Portuguese Letters*), banned from circulation until after the 25 April 1974 Revolution; the feminist interventions of each of its authors, Maria Isabel Barreno's essays serving as a good example; and the political and moral philosophy of Maria de Lurdes Pintasilgo. The following summarizes their respective contributions to feminist thought in postdictatorial Portugal.

Although Maria Teresa Horta, Maria Isabel Barreno, and Maria Velho da Costa had already published important feminist works by the time they agreed to write a collective book, it is *Novas cartas portuguesas* that comes to be identified with second-wave feminism – if not feminism tout court – in postdictatorship Portugal. Despite the common stress placed on sexuality as a radically political issue, the various letters, poems, narratives, and essays comprising the volume stage a debate between feminist positions, challenging not only the expectation of a coherent, somewhat unitary argument but also the notion of sisterhood. At the time, this notion was already beginning to be questioned as a given based on supposedly common, transnational women's experiences and not on particular historical and political conjunctures (cf. Mohanty 2003, 24).

Novas cartas portuguesas exposes the cultural, historical, and ideological basis of women's oppression, as well as their own complicity with that oppression. By appropriating and subverting the story of the seventeenth-century nun Mariana Alcoforado, epistolary subject and supposed author of the seventeenth-century *Lettres portugaises*, the authors create a flexible poetic frame for an adventure in writing that blurs the distinction between genres and registers of enunciation. Wavering between the personal and intimate and the public, the expository and the theoretical, the national and transnational, most texts within the volume shed light on the mutual interdependency of all forms of colonialism and violence, beginning with that of women by men. References to the colonial wars still being fought in the African continent, to immigration, to the hard lives of workers, and to the authoritarian regime are ubiquitous throughout the volume. The liberation that it calls for is connected to the sexual body but cannot be reduced to it. The work ultimately appeals to the broader social, cultural, and political transformation that would enable the reinvention of human love outside restrictive gender codes and outside the cycle of consumption. Letter 3 puts it thus: "Chegará tempo de amor, em que dois se amem, sem que uso ou utilidade mútua se vejam e procurem, mas, apenas prazer, prazer só, no dar e receber?" (Barreno, Horta, and Velho da Costa 1980, 112; Will there ever come a time for love, when two people love each other without either of them seeking to use or exploit the other, seeking only pleasure, the pleasure of giving and receiving?").

Frequently associated with motherhood, that ethics of generosity has, however, contributed to women's invisibility and oppression. Although surfaced in the feminist tour de force that was *New Portuguese Letters* (Barreno, Horta, and Velho da Costa 1994), the argument is developed in more detail in Maria Isabel Barreno's *A morte da mãe* (The mother's death), published in 1979. The author's most important nonfictional work, it is comprised of short narrative pieces drawing from myth, philosophy, and history. They offer a vast reflection on the ways in which women's identities are systematically controlled by ancestral cultural practices and beliefs, leading to the erasure of the mother in Western culture.

Between 1983 and 2001, Barreno deploys the short story within a more or less fantastic mode to reflect upon the discursive, iterative, construction of gender following the binary and hierarchical logic that commands Western thought.[14] In the prize-winning *Os sensos incomuns* (The uncommon senses; 1993), the third of five collections published during this period, Barreno calls attention to the violence enacted by banal commonplaces that are used every day. The short fourteen texts of the volume invite the reader to reflect upon words, concepts, narratives, and beliefs that, as evinced when put to the test in a fictional text, are easily reversible in both their enunciation and effects. In the same systematic, yet playful and poetic, way in which Barreno earlier deconstructed the myth of motherhood in Western culture, each story sheds light on the "jogo de palavras" (word play) to which amount most cultural beliefs (Barreno 1989, 98). Therein results what may be understood in terms of a queering that defies any fixed interpretation while metafictionally performing, or "making gender," against the binary heterosexist logic that commands the very making of sense (Ferreira 2011).

Partaking of the anti-Cartesian philosophical position and intellectual sources that animate Barreno's thought, but at the same time experienced by training and profession in scientific and technical discourse, Maria de Lurdes Pintasilgo (1930–2004) is arguably the most important and internationally visible Portuguese feminist of the period. An industrial chemical engineer, in 1957 she became one of the founders in Portugal of the international Christian women's movement, Grail, thus beginning a career of leadership in the area of women's rights and social justice on a global scale (Joaquim 2010, 78–9). While consistently advocating for equal rights in all areas of life, she valorized the difference of women's culture as part of a larger social and political project of defending the right to difference of all human beings (Joaquim 2010, 79–80).

Both promoting and practising a moving, fluid thinking "entre sabers" (between-knowledges), Pintasilgo famously refused fixed answers to societal problems, leading the poet and public intellectual Natália Correia to praise her as an "engenheira de utopias" (in Tavares

2011, 358; engineer of utopias). For the majority, however, that arguably utopian thinking was slandered and, at best, criticized for lacking an accepted (i.e., "masculine") political rationality (in Joaquim 2010, 80).[15] Her appointment as prime minister for three months in 1979, during the transitional government of António Ramalho Eanes, was apparently tolerated. However, her defeat at the polls when running for president of the republic as an independent, in 1986, speaks volumes for how ineffective the 25 April 1974 Revolution had been in moving gender ideologies – and dichotomous, reductive, boxed thinking in general. In her election manifesto, Pintasilgo not only professed political independence but also emphatically rejected the idea that the first civil president of the new democratic republic should belong to any party (Pintasilgo 1986, 4). Given more than one decade of military governments and the deep political polarizations in the country at the time, Pintasilgo's stand was surely dissonant, along with other points of her political agenda. These included the call for decentralization, participatory democracy, modernization – though not without the conscientious defence of national traditions; and she also called for the creation of a new political culture that fostered economic development while protecting all aspects of democracy (5–6).

Although she steered away from any language connected to specifically feminist goals, Pintasilgo's electoral agenda for the presidency in 1986 could be subtitled, in hindsight, "Portugal: Daring to Be Different." This was the title of her article in the collection, *Sisterhood Is Global: The International Women's Movement Anthology*, edited by Robin Morgan in 1984. Her brief, critical exposé of women's struggle in Portugal in view of the much talked about exceptionality that had been her appointment as a woman prime minister in 1979 coheres with a number of talks and works she published throughout the 1980s and early 1990s on new feminisms.[16] The "difference" that she dares for feminism not only in Portugal but also globally is one that refuses to take legislature on equal rights as the end point of a struggle that encompasses the whole of society. "Statistics and laws," she asserts, "reassure certain souls. But the question I am asked – about the general situation of women and a female Prime Minister – belongs to another realm" (Pintasilgo 1984, 572). That realm is that of culture, something that Pintasilgo's thought shared with the new social movements of the 1990s: beyond the agenda of legal and civic rights, much still needs to be done to reassert the right of women to education, to informed and empowering suffrage, and to one's sexuality (see Amaral and Macedo 2005, 27).[17]

28 Equality and Difference Feminisms in the Castilian and Catalan Areas of Spain

ROBERTA JOHNSON

The notion of equality is a leading principle in Spain's 1978 Constitution. Article 1.1 of the document reads, "España se constituye en un Estado social y democrático de Derecho, que propugna como valores superiores de su ordenamiento jurídico la libertad, la justicia, la igualdad y el pluralismo político" (*Constituciones* 1998, 213; Spain is constituted of a social and democratic state of law that proclaims freedom, justice, equality, and political pluralism as superior values in the judicial realm). Article 14 specifically mentions gender equality along with that of other possible subordinating designations: "Los españoles son iguales ante la ley, sin que pueda prevalecer discriminación alguna por razón de nacimiento, raza, sexo, religión, opinión o cualquier otra condición o circunstancia personal o social" (Constituciones 215; Spaniards are equal before the law; there can be no discrimination on the basis of race, sex, religion, opinion, or any other personal or social condition or circumstance). The 1978 Constitution also stipulates the equality of husband and wife in articles 32 and 39. While the other equalities – race, religion, opinion – were not controversial, the concept of gender equality has became the centre of a heated debate between so-called equality feminists and difference feminists, a debate that began before the Constitution was promulgated and that continues even today. The debate arose despite the fact that the gender equality clauses were included in the Constitution thanks largely to the feminist movement that had begun developing underground in the late Franco era and that became public immediately upon the dictator's death on 20 November 1975, when a feminist congress was held in Madrid on 6 December 1975. Many contemporary feminist thinkers are academic women whose strong philosophical backgrounds inform their arguments about equality, although some have found means of popularizing their views as well.

Spanish "equality feminists" believe that women must continue to work for a parity with men that remains elusive despite the Constitution and for specific laws guaranteeing equality in institutions such as marriage and the work place. For equality feminists, women's reality – less accessibility to work, unequal wages, more responsibilities at home even if they work full-time outside the home, restricted abortion rights, domestic violence – differs significantly from their equal legal status. Philosophically, equality feminists locate their roots in the eighteenth century, when the concept of social equality culminated in the French Revolution. Some equality feminists call themselves *feministas ilustradas*, or Enlightenment feminists, after eighteenth-century philosophers such as François Poullain de la Barre who argued for women's equality with men. Their philosophical method privileges reason or the logos as the only sure path to a more just world for women. Equality feminists also recur to Descartes, Rousseau, and Kant in their rational arguments about the role of the state and/or society in the life of individual human beings. Thus equality feminists place significant emphasis on official social institutions and the law as the means to achieve parity between the sexes. In terms of their historical roots in the Spanish feminist tradition, equality feminists in Constitutional Spain, such as Amelia Valcárcel and Celia Amorós, have continued the work of pre-Franco-era feminist thinkers like Margarita Nelken (*La condición social de la mujer en España*, 1922; first published in 1919) and Carmen de Burgos (*La mujer moderna y sus derechos*, 1927), although they do not necessarily acknowledge their Spanish forebears.

Difference feminists such as Victoria Sendón de León and Milagros Rivera, on the other hand, are more interested in women's interior realm; from a feminocentric position, they identify distinctly female qualities, which, if nurtured within a female hierarchy, would, they believe, contribute measurably to the betterment of women's lives and society as a whole. They argue strenuously against the notion of equality, which, they argue, accepts patriarchal values. Spanish difference feminists reject political action for securing rights. Philosophically, difference feminists often draw on more recent French and Italian feminists such as Luce Irigaray, Carla Lonzi, and Luisa Muraro, who posit a feminine self, a women's mode of existence that differs from male being in the world. Interestingly, Spanish difference feminists, especially Milagros Rivera, have discovered an ally in the work of exiled Republican philosopher María Zambrano. While Zambrano's articles on women published in 1928 in the left-leaning *El liberal* and her early long essay *Horizonte del liberalismo* (1930) could make her a source for equality feminists, her 1934 "Hacia un saber sobre el alma" and much of her writing in exile point towards her move to the interior realm, the "soul," which coincides with difference feminism's notion of *partir de sí* (departing from oneself).[18]

As we have seen in earlier chapters of this volume, contemporary Spanish difference feminism is heir to the long tradition of Spanish difference feminism that Mary Nash traces. Much of the discourse and many official policies about women during the Franco regime restored legal and social conditions for women that were the norm in the nineteenth and early twentieth centuries. These policies could be understood as paving the way for democratic era Spanish difference feminism in the same way that, according to Nash, nineteenth-century domesticity discourse fostered the development of difference feminism at the same time that Spanish feminist thought had begun to change that discourse (Nash 1994). This is not to say that contemporary Spanish difference feminism is a politically conservative body of theory, but its having taken such firm root on Spanish soil can be attributed at least in part to its encountering fertile conditions there. As I indicated, the notions of gender equality and difference arose in Spanish feminist thinking before the Constitution of 1978 set forth the general precepts for equality in articles 1.1 and 9.2, but the Constitution marks an important watershed in the debate and reminds us of its political significance.

Although Durán and Gallego – as does leading equality feminist Celia Amorós (1986) and others – located the open hostility between equality and difference feminists at the general meeting of the feminist movement held in Granada in May 1979, Anny Brooksbank Jones believes the schism was already evident by the time the Constitution was voted in 1978.[19] According to Brooksbank Jones, the constitutional vote itself was an occasion for differences of opinion to assert themselves:

> Radical feminists who saw party politics as irredeemably patriarchal tended to reject the [Constitution] as "machista," while most dual activists gave it qualified support. As the detailed and painstaking incorporation of constitutional principles into law got under way, however, earlier levels of concerted activism and mobilization proved impossible to sustain. Outside of the parties too the promised coexistence began to look increasingly unrealistic, as the loss of focus encouraged the proliferation of single activist groups and a corresponding dispersal of energies. (1997, 10)

Brooksbank Jones notes, however, that at the Granada Jornadas Feministas in 1979 "the familiar distinction between single and dual activism [was] redrawn around the axes of equality and difference" (Brooksbank Jones 1997, 11).[20] According to Durán and Gallego, at the Granada Conference, Spanish feminists had not yet theorized the concepts of equality and difference as they would in the 1980s and 1990s:

> There was never any attempt to arrive at a real theoretical analysis of either of these two concepts. Broadly speaking, the idea of equality was adopted by the section of double militancy that advocated the formation of a political platform demanding women's rights and liberties for women and eliminating all the barriers encountered by women. The women who advocated "difference" feminism were involved with the radical groups [those not allied with political parties who wanted to make feminist concerns a first priority beyond more general party platforms]. (1986, 213)

Because democratic era Spanish feminism had its beginnings during the late Franco regime, when many feminists were double militants who belonged either to the underground Communist or Socialist Parties, feminism in early democratic Spain worked mainly through party antidictatorial, prodemocratic (or sociodemocratic) activism.[21] Thus Spanish feminist theory of the post-Franco era continued to be informed by political ideology, although as Brooksbank Jones, following Monica Threlfall, observes, "Spanish feminists seeking political legitimacy were hampered by the absence of a strong feminist tradition, the lack of a democratic culture sympathetic to the idea of equal rights, and the disinclination of many progressive women to return to sex-segregated activities after the years of Catholic-run, single-sex schooling" (Brooksbank Jones 1997, 7).[22] The stridency of the debate and the sui generis nature of the divide between Spanish difference and equality feminists, unique to Western feminisms, can only be understood in the context of Spanish women having to overcome forty years of institutionalized proscriptions for women under the Franco regime and its virulent repression of the Republican era's advances towards women's legal equality. The postdictatorship Spanish feminist movement's beginnings in the underground leftist resistance to the Franco regime have made an indelible mark on both equality and difference feminism. Significantly, the venue for airing the debate at several key points was the leftist journal *El Viejo Topo*, first with a special section titled "Masculino/Femenino" in 1980, just as the recently legitimized Partido Socialista Obrero Español (PSOE; Spanish Workers' Socialist Party) was ascending in the political landscape (leading to its victory in the 1982 elections) and again in the mid-1990s when corruption scandals ended Socialist political hegemony.

As indicated earlier, difference feminists reject institutionalized politics. Mercedes de Grado notes that

> el ideario feminista de la diferencia originó una réplica en las filas de las militantes de corte socialista, que evolucionan en sus posiciones y empiezan a abogar por un feminismo de la igualdad que contrarreste la reinvindicación de la diferencia. Sin embargo, estos dos tipos de feminismo van perdiendo progresivamente contacto con el feminismo como movimiento de masa. (2004, 30)
>
> (feminist difference ideology provoked a response from Socialist militants, whose positions evolved and begin to advocate for an equality feminism that countered difference feminism's position. However, these two types of feminism were progressively losing contact with feminism as a mass movement.)

Although difference feminist ideas had circulated in Spain in the 1970s,[23] and a difference feminist group (LA MAR) existed briefly in 1977–8, the 1980 special issue of *El Viejo Topo* on masculinity and femininity is rather one-sided in its presentation of equality and difference feminism. The three feminist articles by Empar Pineda, Amelia Valcárcel, and Celia Amorós all defend equality in one way or another; difference feminism is not directly represented by a thinker identified with the position.

The difference feminists against whom the Spanish thinkers write are foreign. Empar Pineda's article "¿El mito de la femininidad cabalga de nuevo?" (The femininity myth rides again?) challenges Carla Lonzi's difference feminism with arguments from Simone de Beauvoir's *El segundo sexo* (*The Second Sex*) against biological destiny and for a socially constructed feminine identity that relegates women to the domestic sphere. Pineda goes beyond what she considers mere equality before the law to propose "profundas transformaciones ... para que la igualdad plena sea posible" (1980, 19; profound transformations ... for full equality to be possible). She claims not to suggest that women become like men, but rather that men also be freed from the social constraints placed upon them. These transformations include the elimination of the patriarchal family, the socialization of domestic work, and a complete restructuring of individual and collective consciousness to overcome "la ideología y la dominación machistas" (19; *machista* ideology and domination).

In the second part of her article, Pineda attempts to balance her view and to understand those who find positive value in what are traditionally considered feminine traits in order to "autoafirmarse" (Pineda 1980, 19; reaffirm themselves). She describes the position based on reason, now called "equality feminism," as just another branch of difference feminism. She argues that equality feminism maintains the division masculine/feminine by proposing women adopt a masculine mode of thinking, which ends up creating the same division between the sexes maintained by difference feminism. The latter opposes a men's mode of thought based on reason to a women's style of thinking centred on "la intuición, el sentimiento, las vivencias" (22; intuition, sentiment, living). Pineda places her own position outside these polarities, which she believes dangerously allow for the reassertion of "posiciones pseudocientífcas" (23; pseudoscientific positions). She is especially averse to difference feminist emphasis on women's bodies and women's sensual pleasure. Her alternative to difference feminists' search for a women's space is a common space for men and women: "el del trabajo social, el de la acción, el de la ciencia, el del arte y la poesía, el de la economía, el de las relaciones afectivas, el de la política … Querer ocupar este terreno es reinvindicar la igualdad. Que es lo que reivindico" (24; social work, that of action, science, art and poetry, economy, affective relations, politics ... Wishing to occupy this terrain is to vindicate equality. Which is what I vindicate).

Amelia Valcárcel's article "El derecho al mal" ventures an even more subversive approach than Pineda's in defence of equality. She affirms women's right to be just as "immoral" as men. Unlike Pineda's, however, Valcárcel's position does not disparage rational thought. She rebels against thinkers such as Herbert Marcuse, who suggest women serve as models for social and ethical behaviour in a reformation of society towards a benevolent utopia beyond reason: "Se espera que las mujeres, sistemáticamente alejadas del Logos, tengan, por esta secular costumbre un discurso diverso en el que se pueda confiar" (Valcárcel 1980, 28; One hopes that women, systematically removed from the logos, have for this secular custom a diverse discourse that one can trust). Valcárcel is repelled by extreme feminists who propose a utopian destruction of all that is associated with women, especially reproduction of the species: "La utopia, puede ser, más que una guía, un cul de sac" (28; Utopia can be a cul-de-sac rather than a guide); thus she posits equality as the only concept that can grapple effectively with women's situation. If women cannot convert men to good behaviour, then women should adopt male values, eliminating the traditional values of chastity, sweetness, and nature. This line of thinking raised the ire of difference feminists who maintain that equality feminism is just another version of patriarchy.

Even though Valcárcel's essay is cast in an ironic tone, at this juncture the tenor of the equality/difference debate is still fairly cordial. Celia Amorós situates herself in a conciliatory position between Valcárcel and difference feminism. She politely poses the questions:

> ¿Cómo debería orientarse en la lucha el movimiento feminista? ¿Sería posible que tuviera la idea de igualdad con el hombre como criterio regulador de su teoría y de su práctica? ¿O debe afirmarse ante todo como voluntad de diferencia de lo femenino, como propuesta de alternativa de valores formulada a partir de la especificidad de la experiencia y la inserción en el mundo de las mujeres? (Amorós 1996,132)
>
> (How should the feminist movement position itself within the struggle? Would it be possible for it to have the idea of equality with men as a regulating criterion in its theory and practice? Or should it affirm itself above all as the difference of the feminine, as a proposed alternative value on the basis of specific experiences and the insertion in women's world?)

Her more moderate position (as compared to Valcárcel's) takes into account the difficulty of defining femininity. She notes the challenge of separating the truly feminine from what is now called "feminine" after centuries of oppression and marginalization.

Amorós draws on Giulia Adinolfi's notion of "subcultura femenina" (female subculture) as an important means of distinguishing between essentialist biological determinants and what is socially constructed.[24] Amorós worries that the discourse of difference feminism is set on a path of self-destruction, if its values – "la dulzura, la ternura, y la emocionalidad" (1985c, 134; sweetness, tenderness, and emotionality) – cannot become universal and transcendent in the way male values have throughout history. She points out that the values associated with the feminine realm were invented by men. In addition, she finds difference discourse too ambiguous and suggests that

> el discurso ilustrado de la igualdad tiene la ventaja indudable de librarse de las ambigüedades, de ser directamente incisivo e irrenunciablemente reivindicativo, de tener un punto de referencia polémico claro al manejar en la discusión términos precisos como los de superioridad e inferioridad para establecer las impugnaciones de las definiciones patriarcales. (1985c, 140–1)

> (the Illustration discourse of equality has the undoubtable advantage of being free of ambiguities, to be directly incisive and irreversibly vindicative, of having a clear polemic reference in the discussion of precise terms such as superiority and inferiority and for establishing counters to patriarchal definitions.)

She immediately recognizes that such a statement could be taken as an oversimplification and asserts that freedom from ambiguity does not mean freedom from complexity, since "el contenido mismo de la igualdad es un cajón de sastre tan confuso como ambiguo es el de la diferencia" (142; the content itself of such equality is just as confused and ambiguous a jumble as difference feminism). At the end of her essay, she attempts to find a way to validate both difference and equality. Quoting Hegel as saying that the road to the spirit is a "rodeo," she postulates the road to women's liberation as a "rodeo de los rodeos" in which theorists will have to move beyond difference and equality to draw on both discourses as they are modified by practical experience (142). Such a route was not taken, although several Spanish feminist theorists (Justa Montero and Marina Subirats, among others) have attempted to negotiate this middle road since the mid-1990s. In the meantime, the division between equality and difference feminists deepened and grew more hostile as difference feminist theory began to be cultivated by autochthonous Spanish thinkers.

Victoria Sendón de León's *Sobre diosas, amazonas y vestales: Utopías para un feminismo radical* (On goddesses, Amazons, and vestals: Utopias for a radical feminism), published in 1981, is characterized by the utopian nature of much difference feminist thinking. Sendón de León's book signals a break in the more tempered discussion of difference and equality that had taken place to date. Sendón de León lashes out at rational logic, one of the main tools of equality feminism: "No me preguntéis qué es el feminismo. Las respuestas me horrorizan y también las preguntas que desde otra percepción de la realidad nunca llegaría siquiera a formularse. El afán de respuesta no es más que una mediocre pretensión de reducir la experiencia a un tipo de conocimiento restringido a la razón lógica" (quoted in de Grado 2004, 40; Don't ask me what feminism is. The answers horrify me and also the questions that from another perception of reality would never be formulated. The desire for an answer is nothing more than the mediocre attempt to reduce experience to a kind of knowledge circumscribed by logical reason). Further on, she throws the notion of equality on the trash heap with provocative, vitriolic language:

> Nos ronda el fantasma de un mito o el mito de un fantasma: la igualdad … ¿Iguales en qué? … Quiero la diferencia. *Me repugna profundamente la igualdad.* … ¿A qué igualdad se refiere? … No me vale esa falacia de que la igualdad es requisito para la libertad. La libertad no crece en putrefactas aguas pantanosas. (*Sobre diosas* 112–14, quoted in de Grado 2004, 43 [de Grados's emphasis)
>
> (The phantom of a myth or the myth of a phantom – equality – encircles us. ... Equal to what? ... I want difference. *I am profoundly repulsed by equality.* ... To what equality are they referring? ... I am not convinced by this fallacy that equality is required for liberty. Liberty does not grow in rotten, swampy waters.)

The following year (1982), Amorós continued her conciliatory approach. In "Feminismos ilustrados y feminismos helenísticos" (1985b; Enlightenment and Hellenistic feminisms), she casts difference feminism as ambiguous and equality feminism (or *el feminismo ilustrado*) as confused: "Los contenidos de tal discurso de la igualdad distan de ser cartesianamente claros y distintos" (Amorós 1985c, 157; The contents of the so-called equality discourse is far from being the Cartesian clear and distinct discourse). However, she now assumes a somewhat more aggressive stance vis-à-vis difference feminism, which she says, perhaps in reaction to Sendón de León's attack on equality feminism, "recoge resonancias ancestrales, caras a la sensibilidad romántica como lo abismático, lo misterioso, lo incontrolable, lo insondable" (148; draws on ancestral resonances, a romantic sensibility like the abysmal, the mysterious, the uncontrollable, the unfathomable). She also allies difference feminism with ancient philosophies such as Cynicism,

Epicureanism, and Stoicism. Even though she believes difference feminist theory falls into impasses that echo those of some ancient philosophies, she does accept difference feminists' notion of self-affirmation, which can provide the oppressed with mechanisms to combat their marginalization.

The year 1983 saw the founding of the Instituto de la Mujer (Women's Institute) by the recently elected Spanish Socialist Party – a seminal event in the development of Constitutional-era Spanish feminism. The express purpose of the Instituto was to promote women's equality. Equality, as defined in the Constitution, figures prominently in its mission statement: "El Instituto de la Mujer es un organismo autónomo dependiente del Ministerio de Igualdad, a través de la Secretaría General de Políticas de Igualdad" (The Women's Institute is an autonomous organism dependent on the Ministry of Equality, through the Secretariat General of Equality Politics).[25] The purpose of the Instituto was described as to promote and encourage the conditions that would make social equality between the sexes possible, as well as the participation of women in political, cultural, economic, and social life. Thus it was an organism of the central government that promoted the politics of equality between women and men. Its rationale specifically noted that its principles were tied to the 1978 Constitution whose promulgation took for granted the recognition of legal equality between men and women as one of the principle inspirations of the judicial order. In a clause that appeared to recognize some difference feminists' arguments about the problems of legislation as a sole avenue to women having a proper place in all spheres of life, the statement recognizes that equality cannot be achieved by legislative means alone. It notes that all obstacles should be removed so that women could participate in culture, work, and political and social life. All the references to equality and the Instituto's presumed independence from the government (at the time dominated by the Socialist Party) did not inspire difference feminists' confidence.[26]

In 1986, Celia Amorós, repeating some of the ideas of the 1982 lecture about parallels between difference feminism – which she calls a "curiosa combinación de elementos ideológicos" (1986, 53; curious combination of ideological elements) – and dead-end classical philosophies, names Sendón overtly. Taking the high road and avoiding Sendón de León's stridency, Amorós calls Sendón's book *Sobre diosas, amazonas y vestales* "vibrante" (vibrant) and "una reelaboración relativamente original" (1986, 52; a relatively original re-elaboration) of difference feminism. Amorós then deconstructs Sendón's central ideas. She notes that while

Sendón argues against the rational logos as a patriarchal invention, she proposes the very Cartesian "autoconciencia feminista transparente y directa que saltaría por encima de mediaciones definitorias de la propia cultura patriarcal ... para que la mujer se autorreconociera 'a partir de sí misma' en ese cuerpo marcado" (1986, 53; direct and transparent feminist self-consciousness over and above definitive mediations of patriarchal culture itself ... so that women could recognize themselves 'from their own viewpoint' in their own bodies).

Thus early democratic-era feminist thought in Spain, although focused on the equality/difference polemic, developed a unique theoretical orientation that would carry it through the 1990s to the present time (see chapter 32 below for the continuation of the debate). The feminist activist period that erupted after the dictator's death in 1975 on the Iberian Peninsula in the 1980s and beyond joined the burgeoning nationalist movements in the several territories, as we shall see in the chapters on the Basque Country and Galicia in this part.

29 Women above All: The Autonomous Basque Feminist Movement, 1973–1994

NEREA ARESTI AND MAIALEN ARANGUREN

Recent historiography has challenged the idea that the transition from the Franco dictatorship to parliamentary democracy was just a project conceived by political elites, or that it was the natural outcome of socioeconomic development, calling attention instead to the role of social movements in this process (Molinero and Ysàs 2015; Domènech 2008; Marín, Molinero, and Ysàs, 2001). During the mid-1970s, the first feminist groups organized and those called "assemblies of women" flourished in Spain, and this feminist movement became a main political actor of the political transition (Moreno 2012, 100; Verdugo 2010; Threlfall 2009; Aguado 2007, 173). However, this autonomous feminist movement was much more than a struggle against the Franco regime. Above all, it was a process by which a new political actor emerged that placed its aspirations and demands for the radical transformation of gender relations at its centre, relations that were especially unjust and oppressive in the European context of the 1970s. In this chapter, we will bring light to the formation and evolution of this political subject.

We argue that the new political subject – feminist women – was solidly and firmly constituted, as had been the normative category "women" during the Franco regime. Actually, it was this identitarian fortress inherited from the past that was transformed into rebellion, bringing together feminist wills. The essentialist nature of this early democratic-era feminism was later questioned from within and from outside its organizations, and it was progressively overcome. In a certain sense, the story of this movement is the history of the progressive fracture of the political subject as the diversity and differences between women were being recognized. And this fracture would years later be related to the crisis in the movement itself.

In the mid 1970s, many Basque feminists organized themselves autonomously from the so-called Asambleas Feministas de Euskadi (Basque Feminist Assemblies). The assemblies were provincial in nature and drew under their umbrella numerous groups and different feminist currents, adopting a nonhierarchical, horizontal structure, in which decisions were made by a show of hands. As the activist Begoña Zabala has demonstrated, what characterized these organizations was not their political platforms or their agreement about the advisability of militating in political parties and mixed gender unions (Zabala 2008, 22). Above all, what united those feminists was the conviction that it was necessary to organize "as women" autonomously with respect to other political forces and institutions, vindicating the centrality of their gender condition in their life experiences and in their political action.

Three great assembly meetings in 1977, 1984, and 1994 marked the evolution of autonomous Basque feminism. These three political and emotional events structure the three sections of this chapter. The first stage was marked by the rupture with the Franco legacy and by the solidity and strength of the feminist subject. During the 1980s, an organizational consolidation occurred, and feminism even adopted the form of a "political culture" (Nash 2011), in a context in which the Socialist governments and its institutions were carried out or, rather, took over some of the feminist demands. The growing diversification of the struggles and the recognition of plurality and the differences among women were characteristic of this second phase. This tendency culminated in the 1990s. The 1994 conference was remembered, as the feminist Tere Maldonado said, as the "conference of diversity" (Maldonado 1994, 52). It also signalled a moment of crisis and the search for a new meaning for the feminist struggle.

The First Steps

As the historian Pamela Radcliff has affirmed, "Transitions represent special moments in which the rules of the game are questioned and redefined" (Radcliff 2007, 345). In the specific case we are considering here, the first feminist campaigns were linked to the anti-Franco struggle in defence of political liberties. Thus at the same time that a significant part of society was demanding amnesty for political prisoners (Aguilar 1997), the feminists vindicated amnesty for women condemned for so-called women's crimes – adultery, prostitution, and abortion. They railed against laws that criminalized women who did not "correctly fulfill their role" (Asamblea de Mujeres de Vizcaya [AMV]) and who dared to decide about their own bodies. In this framework of exigencies, they also demanded the repeal of the Law of Social Danger applied to prostitutes. And they rejected the 1978 Constitution, which governs today, considering it *machista* and antidemocratic.

The defence of what was called "the right to one's own body" constituted the fundamental axis of the feminist agenda during the transition. From the beginnings, they affirmed that women's oppression always passes through their bodies. As the historian Mary Nash has pointed out, they conferred great political value on the female body from the idea that the personal is political (Nash 2012, 363). In fact, this pronouncement sums up the feminist view of the world in those years; feminists affirmed that matters that had heretofore remained hidden in the private realm were political matters of the first order.

When faced with maternity as a required female destiny, the feminist movement proposed a radically different conception, which was summarized in the slogan "sexuality is not maternity." Desired maternity and the right to use contraceptives and abortion were central demands. In October 1978, the Franco-era law that penalized the sale, distribution, and promotion of contraceptive methods was struck down. This measure was perceived as a great triumph and as a "first step toward establishing the struggle for liberation on equal terms" ("Anticonceptivos" 1977, 26). However, without any doubt, the most important concrete objective of the Basque feminist movement in those years was abortion, a practice punished with prison by law. As the feminists pointed out, illegality did not impede its practice. On the contrary, the ending of a pregnancy was carried out in horrific conditions that caused more than three thousand deaths per year. The campaign against some abortion judgments involving eleven women in the Biscayan town of Basauri in 1976 became a symbol of the fight for the right to abortions in the entire country. The wave of feminist solidarity reached towns and cities. The Provincial Audience of Bilbao pardoned ten of the eleven condemned women in 1982 and asked for a particular pardon for the woman who had performed the abortions.[27] The triumph of the feminist campaign gave a boost and legitimacy to the movement it had not previously enjoyed.

The I Jornadas de la Mujer de Euskadi (First Conference of Basque Women) served as a platform for feminist organization in this first phase. There they debated the principal feminist agenda items and traced lines of action for the immediate future. In spite of the fact that some women's groups had been created earlier, we can confirm that those meetings were foundational for a movement that aspired to overcome political differences among feminists. In spite of that will, the question of militancy, of whether or not feminists should or should not participate in political projects with men, generated a lively debate that was on the verge of destroying the climate of unity. In broad strokes, there were three tendencies. Those who defended double militancy, whose view rested on a Marxist theoretical framework, carried out a critical reading of Marxism and rejected the idea that women's liberation would come about as an immediate consequence of the implantation of a Socialist society. Thus, the double militants, who shared their work in the assemblies and in the extraparliamentary parties (above all Trotskyites and Maoists) believed that women suffered exploitation as a sex that needed "its own, specific treatment" (Mujeres del EMK de la AMV 1977). In second place, so-called radical or independent feminism rejected double militancy. The group Lanbroa, which later abandoned the assemblies in order to form its own organization, was the most important representative of this tendency. Lanbroa defended a feminist theory that combined the application of Marxism to the contradiction of gender (suggesting that women were a social class) with notions that were characteristic of difference feminism. This third tendency, difference feminism, was in the minority in the Basque Country.

Despite these differences, the idea of feminist unity was especially powerful in the Basque Country. The women who attended the first meetings of 1977 agreed that, in the patriarchal system, all women suffered a common oppression exercised by the opposite sex. Domestic work and the figure of the housewife were central to their discourse, defining the position of all women and eclipsing the differences among them. This constructed unity favoured the development of a relatively strong and compact feminism that covered up important weaknesses that came to light during the 1980s.

The 1980s: Consolidation and Diversification

In 1984, seven years after the first meeting, the Second Basque Feminist Meeting took place and assessed the movement's situation. On this occasion, organization of women's assemblies was consolidated, and the intense work that had been achieved was emphasized. The unity of feminism continued to constitute a value to maintain over and above differences. (Arantza et al. and AMV 1986, 267; Asamblea de Mujeres de Álava 1986). In a parallel fashion, during those years it became evident that the themes of political action had been diversifying. Along with the already mentioned struggles against legislation inherited from Francoism, work had been done in the area of *machista* violence, antimilitarism, pornography, knowledge production and education, health, and relations with political power.

It is also important to point out that feminist organizations tied to the radical Basque nationalist movement and organized in the heart of the parties of *izquierda abertzale* (*abertzale* left) participated in the 1984 meetings. These organizations believed that women suffered a triple oppression – as women, as working class, and as Basques. They postulated that feminism constituted one of the axes that should contribute to the construction of a Socialist, independent, and nonpatriarchal *Euskal Herria* (Basque Country) (*Aizan!* 1986); they were not in favour of organizing autonomously in mixed parties. Without a doubt, the nationalist question produced tensions and generated debates in the assemblies, which, on occasion, appeared to threaten to destroy the movement. Nonetheless, again, a deeply rooted notion of unity resisted these frictions and allowed for the coexistence of different views on the national question.

Among the many campaigns carried out in this second period, perhaps the struggle against sexist aggression was the centrepiece of the feminist agenda. In the face of socially dominant views, the definition of this violence as a structural phenomenon inherent in patriarchal society (Grupo "Mujer y violencia" 1986) and related to power and education in values of inequality achieved a significant social echo. Doubtless, the reform of the Penal Code in 1989, long demanded by feminists, was one of its most important triumphs. In the reformed code, aggression against women came to be called "crimes against sexual freedom" and important steps were taken in both the characterization of this violence and help for its victims, even if it is true that soon the serious limitations to change became evident (Comisión Antiagresiones 1991). On the other hand, in the early 1980s, the autonomous Basque feminist movement joined in the intense antimilitary and pacifist debates and struggles. For the feminists, the struggle for peace and antimilitarism should not be limited to opposing wars, NATO, and the arms race, but should include "peace without oppression" in all areas of life and the construction of a new society based in egalitarian relations.

Not only were the ideologies more and more diverse; the feminist political subject began showing its different faces. In the first half of the 1980s, groups of young women formed to work on specific problems that differentiated them from women of the previous generation. In the I Encuentro de Mujeres Jóvenes (First Meeting of Young Women), which took place in 1986, those attending denounced society's "insisting on our continuing as much as possible in our mothers' footsteps," although they affirmed that "we are all women, and we are all on the same side of the barricade" (Grupo de Mujeres Jóvenes de la AMV 1985, 15). In addition, lesbians further added other identity markers to the feminist subject. In the I Encuentros de Lesbianas (First Lesbian Meetings), those present debated whether they should form part of the assemblies as a specific group or if, on the contrary, this specificity required them to organize themselves independently (*I Encuentro de Lesbianas de Euskadi* 1983). During the 1980s, the journal *Sorginak*, published by the Basque lesbian collectives, complained that feminism had concerned itself solely with problems of interest to heterosexual women, such as abortion and divorce. In the face of silence and marginalization, the women attending the Lesbian Meetings declared that love between women "existed and resisted" inside and outside feminism (Comisiones y Colectivos de Lesbianas de Euskadi 1986).

Crisis and Transformation of the Autonomous Feminist Movement

The situation at the end of the 1980s and beginnings of the 1990s revealed the success of the autonomous Basque feminist movement and the crisis this movement was undergoing. This apparent contradiction was, in reality, the two sides of the same coin. If the historian Joan W. Scott called attention to the paradox of the effects of reaffirming the sexual difference of historical feminism (Scott 1996), it was the paradox of the dissolving effect of the feminist subject produced by the success of their demands. The conquest of certain equality measures had weakened the subject constructed on an ironclad otherness. The Basque feminist movement thus faced the challenge of reconstructing the necessarily contingent and diverse political subject.

This process of crisis and change was reflected in both activism and discourse. On the one hand, organized feminism seemed to be deprived of its raison d'être in that a substantial number of its issues had been taken over by state institutions. The takeover bowed to feminist pressure. The struggle against sexual aggression, the fight for contraceptives and abortions, the elimination of some of the laws inherited from the Franco regime, and even a rhetoric that had been the exclusive patrimony of the feminist movement were in large part absorbed by the central power (Aresti, Llona, and Díaz Freire 1994, 76). The creation of Emakunde, the Basque Women's Institute, by the Basque government in 1988 was clear evidence of the phenomenon. The consolidation of so-called academic feminism also shared a role in the movement's progressive loss of social protagonism. Over the years, the most active centre of the feminist debates shifted from the streets to the university.[28] And if this were not enough, the advances in equality made new generations of women believe that activist feminism was passé or simply unnecessary.

From the point of view of political action, these were difficult years. At times, the situation was viewed pessimistically, even with desperation. Ana Palomo, a "militant" in the Asamblea de Mujeres de Gipuzkoa (Assembly of Guipuzkoan Women), said in 1993 that "en este momento… el debate es escaso, la organización caótica y las acciones puntuales y casi sin fuerza (por no decir sin ganas)" (Palomo 1993, 14; at the present time ... there is little debate, the organization is chaotic, and the actions are knee-jerk and without force – not to say, without will). In this context, the key dates on the feminist calendar acquired a growing protagonism in detriment to the campaigns for concrete measures that, for decades, had achieved a great social repercussion. So, 8 March (International Women's Day), 28 June (International Day of LGTB Pride), and 25 November (International Day for the Elimination of Violence against Women) came to structure a large part of feminist activity. From the Asamblea de Bizkaia you could hear the lament that all had been reduced to 8 March, "just as the unions celebrate May 1" (Rodríguez and Bila 1993, 1). Even worse, these celebrations acquired a certain official character that undermined their ability to mobilize.

In 1994, once again the meetings served as a point of encounter and reflection. In the III Jornadas Feministas de Euskal Herria (Third Basque Feminist Meetings), the problems, the concerns, and efforts were laid out in order to find alternatives at this critical time. As is logical, the question of political power was the centre of the debate. Another point of contention was the concept of "gender," which had been adopted by feminist activists in their theoretical reflections. And above all, as mentioned above, those meetings would be remembered as the meetings on the diversity among women and the plurality of feminism. The spaces and the organizations had multiplied, which in one way or another, worked to better the position of women in gender relations. The meaning of feminism was, or should be, plural. New contexts created new challenges: recognizing diversity; renouncing monolithic identities, redefining the significance of unity, and not losing the critical profile and the capacity to transform. Even today, well into the twenty-first century, this reconstruction on new parameters continues to be Spain's and the Basques' main feminist challenge.

30 Galician Feminism in the Democratic Era

MARÍA DO CEBREIRO RÁBADE VILLAR

To understand the history of Galician feminism in the 1970s, we must consider it within the context of the political struggle for regional political autonomy prior to democracy, especially since feminism is an internationalist movement, and the local political agenda was not always sensitive to the demands of gender activism.[29] In order to calibrate the true social impact of feminism in Galicia during the early transition, three levels of analysis are needed that correspond to the existence of different methods of geocultural analysis. First, a method is required that takes into account the change in political and judicial model for the Spanish nation-state, which would take place in what is now called the "political regime of 1978." Second, another method should be implemented that considers the appearance in Galicia of a system of parties, some of which – in particular the specifically nationalist – had operated clandestinely during the preceding decades and which during the 1970s were transitioning into becoming official. And third, a process should be considered within the local or municipal arena that was less decentralized and unhierarchical than the previous two processes and more related to activism, since it is at this level that decisive campaigns on feminist concerns such as divorce and the elimination of penalties for adultery were initiated.

The first of these processes invites us to consider the interchange between the centre and the margins of the state, assuming two premises: (1) The social and cultural history of the peripheries is not only the history of the mechanisms and practices of resistance to hegemony but also the history of those mechanisms by which the centre assures itself a place in the periphery. (2) The way that the central organizations delegate power to the periphery end up giving way to an intercultural dialogue in accordance with the hypothesis of Spain's weak nationalization; this gives the lie to the idea of a monolithic nation-state, impervious to exterior cultural dynamics.

The way in which Iberian feminisms are integrated into a network of centre-periphery relationships, employing party and union structures as means to advance their agendas, still requires further analysis. For now I note merely the presence of divisions central to gender activism, which belong to unions and state political parties that operate as centralized state entities but, in terms of operators on a national or local scale, should be understood as a means to delegate from the centre to the margins or as mechanisms of political or cultural decentralization. In Galicia, this is the case of the Asamblea de Mulleres da Cruña (Assembly of Women of Coruña) integrated into the Comisiones Obreras (CC.OO.; Workers' Commissions), or the Unión Popular de Mujeres de Galicia del FRAP (Frente Revolucionario Antifascista y Patriota; Popular Union of Galician Women of the Anti-Fascist and Patriotic Revolutionary Front), an anti-Fascist resistance group tied to the Communist Party, which broke up in 1979.

The dialogue of feminist movements with nationalist parties of the period was not free of tensions. The tie of feminism to Galician nationalism has been clarifyingly studied by scholars such as Olga Castro (2011) and Helena Miguélez Carballeira (2013), but in the first issue of the journal *A Saia* (The skirt), Margarita Ledo Andión, the history-making director of the Unión do Pobo Galego (UPG; Union of the Galician People) and refounder of the newspaper *A Nosa Terra* in the contemporary period devoted an openly critical article to analysing the relationship between "a prensa nacionalista e a muller" (Ledo 1982, 3; the nationalist press and women). Among other things, Ledo Andión affirmed that it was impossible to maintain that *A Nosa Terra* "resista unha lectura feminista ou mesmo que supere os estereotipos reductores asignados á muller, estereotipos como as merecentes liñas dedicadas 'á patriótica e meritísima labor que veñen realizando as patriotas señoritas e os entusiastas irmáns'" (Ledo 1982; resists a feminist reading or that it overcomes reductive stereotypes assigned to women, stereotypes like the deserved lines devoted to the patriotic and meritorious work that the patriotic young ladies and the enthusiastic sisters are carrying out).

It was within the premises of associationism that gender activism developed firmly and sustainedly from the middle of the 1970s, with groups such as Mulleres Progresistas (Progressive Women), Grupos de Mulleres da Universidade (University Women's Groups), Mulheres

Livres de Santiago (Free Women of Santiago; an anarchist collective), or Mulleres Rurais (Rural Women), in addition to such notable collectives as the coordinator of feminist groups E.E. Galicia AGM-ADMG (Asociación Galega da Muller-Asociación Democrática da Muller Galega [Association of Galician women-Democratic Association of Galician Women]).[30] However, perhaps the most active associations were Coordinadora Galega de Asociacións Legais da Muller (Galician Coordinator of Women's Legal Associations) and the Asociación Democrática da Muller Galega (ADMG; Democratic Association of Galician Women). This associationist movement, which was especially active in Vigo, was in the ensuing years to translate into various initiatives of cultural action.[31] The fruit it bore was the surge of publications such as the above-mentioned journal *A Saia* and *A Festa da Palabra Silenciada* (The celebration of the silenced word), both centred on the group Feministas Independentes Galegas (FIGA; Independent Galician Feminists). The *festa* (celebration) endeavour involved "an intense project of analysis and reclamation of gendered and nationalist subjectivities" (Roseman 1997, 44). The first attempts at studying feminism, such as the ones carried out by the association Alecrín de Vigo, can be linked to the above-mentioned initiatives (Dopico and López 2010).

The 1980s in Galicia are marked by the cultural policies resulting from the installation of autonomous governments after the approval of the Statute of Galicia (1981), the Carta magna regulating the Galician community including the public administration of the Galician language and culture.[32] In terms of feminist movements, one of the outstanding achievements of the decade was the incorporation (very timid, as we will see) of Galician women writers into the school curriculum for contemporary Galician literature. This incorporation is evidenced by poet Luz Pozo Garza's book *Códice calixtino* (1986; Calixtine Codex), which was required reading at the beginning of the following decade for those middle-school students who had chosen to take the optional course on contemporary Galician literature for their university-entrance exams.

The process of progressive institutionalization of feminism nonetheless has its counterpoint in the emergence of subversive (even countercultural) initiatives that oppose the hegemonic forms of cultural action. One such initiative was the publication of the journal *Andaina*, founded in 1983 with the objective (as per the declaration in its first issue) of "dar voz ao movemento feminista de Galicia e a todas as mulleres e que queiran colaborar ou utilizar estas páxinas para expoñer as súas ideas e proxectos" ("¿Por qué?" 1983b; giving voice to the Galician feminist movement and to all the women who want to collaborate or use these pages to put forth their ideas and projects). On the first page of the first issue, there appears a small clause, conceived almost as an advertisement, signed by the "Comisión de lesbianas de la A.G.M. de Santiago de Compostela" (Commission of Lesbians of the AGM of Santiago), in which lesbian women are encouraged to collaborate in the journal, brandishing the "necesidade de organización e loita das mulleres lesbianas dende dentro do movemento feminista no que estamos arraizadas" ("Lesbianismo" 1983a; need for lesbian women to organize within the feminist movement in which we are rooted).

The 1980s also mark the beginnings of feminist criticism, understood as a practice connected to educational institutions at the mid or upper levels, in which the incorporation of feminism into the public political agenda would have to wait until the following decades.[33] The abovementioned publications like *A Festa da Palabra Silenciada* were an important platform for exercising a criticism that, in the words of Alfonso Reyes (1944), we could call *judicial* (judiciary), in that it was based on the valorizationof certain authors, tendencies, and books from the immediate present. This process, without a doubt, contributed to the dissemination and canonization of activist authors of the time such as Ana Romaní, Pilar Pallarés, and Xohana Torres, among others.

In the face of this model of media criticism, tuned as it was into the register of the culture of the time, feminist academic criticism could begin to project itself into the delayed analysis of the Galician literary tradition. Carmen Blanco (b. 1954), writer, cultural activist, and pioneer in feminist literary studies in Galicia, incarnated the possibility of these kinds of studies with her 1995 publications *Nais, damas, prostitutas e feirantas* (1995a; Mothers, ladies, prostitutes and marketers) and *Mulleres e independencia* (1995b; Women and independence), among others. Besides taking up the systematic analysis of sexuality in the Galician academic arena (Blanco 2006), the author was important to the establishment of a solid tradition of feminist analysis of the work of Rosalía de Castro. Of course, in the 1980s, the models of media and academic criticism often coincided, and Rosalía de Castro is an eloquent example of the phenomenon. It is no coincidence that *A Festa da Palabra Silenciada*, cofounded by María Xosé Queizán, among other leading authors, devoted its entire second issue of 1985 to this author. The influence of this second analytic line will be evident in some of the contributions to the *Actas del I Congreso Internacional sobre a obra de Rosalía de Castro no seu tempo* (Proceedings of the first international congress on the works of

Rosalía de Castro in her times), proceedings from a conference that took place in the same year to commemorate the centenary of the author's death and which stands out for its resulting studies by authors such as Pilar García Negro.

The academic trajectory of Carmen Blanco is also relevant to the critical tendency based on the analysis of misogyny in Galician literature. Her conception of the representation of women in the narrative of Álvaro Cunqueiro, one of the most canonical authors of contemporary Galician and Spanish literature, brought feminist criticism to the centre of academic discourses. This model of reception on the part of Galician-feminist analysis makes clear the polemic nature of counter-hegemonic readings of patriarchal texts, a problem exemplified some years later with even greater media coverage with the book that María Xosé Queizán devoted to misogyny in the Galician Rexurdimento poet Eduardo Pondal (Queizán 1998).

The application of a gynocritical focus to a historical corpus incurs certain risks, perhaps the least of which is historical anachronism and the greatest is the critical indistinction between reality and fiction. Blanco's and Queizán's readings could be disputed on the grounds that the objective of an author like Cunqueiro, a well-known cultivator of fantastic literature who is especially attentive to the specific rules governing literary fiction, is not to create a model for the Galician woman but to try to capture some of the keys to Galician rural society that, in spite of what is often said, is not necessarily a matriarchal society. As for Pondal's misogyny, we should ask if it is not undergirded by a consideration of poetic texts as nonfiction whenever the poet forges a Galician literature with a bellicose background, inspired by models such as the classic epic or Celtic culture and poetry.

The processes taking place in the 1990s need to be contexulized within the political, social, and cultural developments brought by the years that Manuel Fraga Iribarne (1922–2012), Franco's secretary of Information and Tourism (1962–9), was president of Galicia's Xunta (Galician Government; 1991–2005). It was under Fraga that the Galician Equality Service was established in 1991, an agency within the Ministry of the Family, Women, and Youth, which was renamed the Ministry of Family, Youth, Sports, and Volunteering in 2004.

On the literary front, the repertorial novelty of the 1990s was the entrance of explicit eroticism and pornography.[34] I will spend some time on this matter because, as Miguélez-Carballeira (2013) demonstrates in her analysis of the contemporary erotic short story, it allows us to illustrate aptly the unstable alliances between the processes of women's access to power and the purposes of linguistic and cultural normalization in the peripheries of the Peninsula.

The process of explicitly promoting publications on eroticism and pornography cannot be understood without taking into account the opening of a market, at times called "captive," that arises in aid of autonomic normalization policies and that converts Galician literature into a timid commercial logic. The emergence of the editorial press Edicións Xerais de Galicia, at present directed by Manuel Bragado, should be read as an attempt to create a large field of cultural production from a private business initiative in the Galician language. With this same purpose, in 1991 the editor Víctor Fernández Freixanes charged a series of writers to produce erotic stories.

The project yielded two volumes, *Contos eróticos: Eles* and *Contos eróticos: Elas* (Fernández 1992; Erotic stories: Men and Erotic stories: Women), whose more or less explicit objectives were: (1) to cover a "vacancy" that the editorial agents perceived in the Galician system, a vacancy always conceived in relation to the repertorial regime of other more institutionalized forms; and (2) to foment the incorporation of women writers into the literary market. Nevertheless, Miguélez-Carballeira has shown that at least two names in the volume *Contos eróticos: Elas* are in fact male authors, a notable error in the equal representation that the publisher itself had promoted (2013, 184–5). Besides, Miguélez-Carballeira pointed out that the general thematic orientation of the books and the abundance of scenes of physical violence and sexual vexation do not serve the dignification and normalization of the presence of women in literature (2013, 184–5). In addition, there is a sense of domineering – if not openly paternalistic demeanour – in the erotic stories.

Despite the incorporaton of Galician culture into a timid commercial logic in the early years of the democracy, the normalizing goals activated by autonomic institutions continued to prevail. Proof is the leading role assumed by the publishing house Galaxia, whose purpose was decidedly more culture oriented than that of Xerais, and whose relations with the institutional and preautonomic apparatus (e.g., the Real Academia Gallega [Galician Royal Academy] or the Fundación Rosalía de Castro [Rosalía de Castro Foundation]) had given ample proof of its deep involvement in the Galician cultural fabric. Situated in an intellectual field in between a conversion of literary wealth into a product for consumption and its conversion into a patrimony by cultural institutions, feminism also saw itself obliged to take a position.

And the strong impulse of normalizing politics that began in the 1980s ended up strongly affecting the feminist actions at the end of the last century and beginning of the present. Proof of the displacement of feminist action towards the arena of institutional representation is the reactionary nature of many of the tactics and strategies carried out in recent years, such as the manifesto *O xogo das cadeiras* (The game of the hips) that came as an answer to the small representation of women in the Real Academia Gallega; or the celebration on the part of the collective A Sega of a Día das Galegas nas Letras (Galician Women of Letters Day), a pun that tries to invert the official Día das Letras Galegas (Galician Letters Day) in order to make women's literary activity more visible. But the end-of-the-century dynamics, like its dependence on the institutional initiatives and the media and market treatments, will be addressed in greater detail in chapter 34.

PART VI

Iberian Feminisms' Diversity: 1996 to the Present

COORDINATED BY SILVIA BERMÚDEZ

31 Historical Overview

SILVIA BERMÚDEZ, ASUNCIÓN BERNÁRDEZ RODAL, AND ANA PAULA FERREIRA

The year 1996 signals major political transitions in the Iberian Peninsula. In Portugal, and ten years into becoming a member of the European Economic Community, as the European Union was called then, a presidential election brought to government a Socialist candidate, Jorge Sampaio, backed by the first noncoalition government since 1976. In tune with the Socialist and social-democratic governments elsewhere in Europe, Portugal entered an era of political stability that did much to restore public confidence.[1] In Spain, the ruling Socialist Worker's Party (PSOE), plagued by numerous corruption scandals, lost the 1996 General Elections to the Popular Party (PP). This marks the end of Felipe González's era (he had served as prime minister for thirteen and a half years). From 1996 to 2004, the Popular Party's José María Aznar was Spain's prime minister. Unable to reach a majority in 1996, Aznar had to make a pact with the Catalan Nationalist Party Convergencia i Unió (CiU; Convergence and Union), the Partido Nacionalista Vasco (PNV; Basque Nationalist Party), and the Coalición Canaria (CC; The Canary Coalition, i.e., the Canary Islands Nationalist Party). The complex and divisive political landscape was echoed within Spanish feminisms by the fierce opposition between equality and difference feminists as attested both by the special issue on feminisms published by *El Viejo Topo* in 1994 and by the 1996 publication of the Spanish version of *El final del patriarcado* (Librería de Mujeres de Milán 1996; The end of the patriarchy), also in *El Viejo Topo*. The antagonism has not abated and continues to the present time.

The issue of equality for women in Spain at the national level was taken over by the Instituto de la Mujer (IM; Institute for Women), which between 1993 and 2006 published the Second, Third, and Fourth Plans for Women's Equal Opportunity. The Segundo Plan para la Igualdad de Oportunidades de las Mujeres 1993–5 (Second Plan for the Equal Opportunity of Women) describes 172 specific actions to achieve said equality and was introduced at the 1995 United Nations Fourth World Conference on Women, held in Beijing. The Tercer Plan para la Igualdad de Oportunidades de las Mujeres 1997–2000 (Third Plan for Equal Opportunity of Women) sought to abide by the commitments pledged at the United Nations Fourth World Conference on Women, discussed later in this introduction. The Cuarto Plan para la Igualdad de Oportunidades de las Mujeres 2003–6 (Fourth Plan for Equal Opportunity of Women) sought to underscore the transversality of gender while still promoting equal opportunities. A turning point in equality policies in Spain took place on 22 March 2007, when the Organic Law 3/2007 (Ley Orgánica) for the effective equality of women and men was approved. The law establishes that the Spanish government shall periodically adopt a Strategic Plan for Equal Opportunities, which will include measures to achieve the objective of equality between women and men, thus eliminating discrimination.

In the meantime in Portugal, under the government of Jorge Sampaio, numerous projects in building renovations, new construction, and public works, including the extension of Lisbon's Metro, created an unprecedented number of jobs, bringing in immigrants and a renewed climate of economic prosperity. Besides preparing the country to take its turn as "European Capital of Culture" in 1996, the construction frenzy was connected to the celebration of the Five Hundredth Anniversary of the Portuguese Discoveries. The 1998 World's Exhibit, Expo, was the major highlight; their memory also graced the interior of one of the largest shopping centres in Portugal, Centro Comercial Colombo (Columbus Shopping Centre), opened in 1997, right in front of the old Benfica soccer stadium.[2] Legislation in defence of women's rights evolved slowly amidst fantasies of a new, no-longer marginal European identity, while celebrating a glorious oceanic past – the violence of which was glossed over.[3] Slower yet were changes in thinking about sacrosanct ideologies of gender, sexuality, and reproduction. In 2016, the gap between laws and behaviours, not only in private but also in public life, is a reminder of what feminism has and has not accomplished in the last twenty years.

In 1995, one year before the election that opened the door to the unbridled development of a neoliberal economy in Portugal, the Fourth World Conference on Women organized by the United Nations took place in Beijing. Portugal was one of 189 countries represented at the event that set the agenda for subsequent legislation on equal rights. A thirty-eight-point Declaration of Principles pointed to the commitment by all the goverments present in Beijing to implement a "Platform for Action, ensuring that a gender perspective is reflected in all [their] policies and programmes" (United Nations 1995, 5). Defined as "an agenda for women's empowerment" (7), the platform lists twelve areas of concern in the struggle for equality of rights in different areas of life. Following this directive, in 1997 the Portuguese Constitution (created in 1976) was revised to include the first National Plan for Equality, which included equal access of opportunity to political positions by men and women; subsequent plans were added, the last of which will be in place until 2017 ("Report Beijing+20 Portugal" 2014, 2). Despite the creation of organizations such as the Aliança para a Democracia Paritária (Alliance for Parity Democracy), validating and politically grounding the differences between men and women, it was not until 2006 that the Law of Parity was introduced in the Constitution (Tavares 2011, 407–8). Parity assures equality by gender quotas, or what is normally considered "positive discrimination" (Baum and Espírito-Santo 2012, 323). The law requires electoral lists to contain a minimum of 33% of each, men and women, for the National Parliament, the European Parliament, and local governments (Baum and Espírito-Santo 2012, 3; see also Sanches 2015, 4). Despite the scepticism with which the law was initially met, by 2015 parity had been reached in the number of women elected to the National Parliament (Rodrigues 2015).

With the exception of education, where the number of women that completed bachelor and doctoral degrees as of 2012 is notable – 61% and 53%, respectively – other areas outlined in Beijing's Platform for Action have been less forthcoming ("Report Beijing+20 Portugal" 2014, 20–1). The increase in the number of women in leadership positions in the public and business sectors has been minimal, and the disparity in salaries between men and women continues to be high, with women earning roughly 80.5% of what men earn performing the same jobs (44). Labour sociologist Sara Falcão Casaca notes that this disparity is one of the highest, with Portugal ranking 97 among 142 countries (in Sanches 2015, 10).

Portugal's main government institution dedicated to women's rights, originally named Comissão da Condição Feminina (Committee on the Feminine Condition) in 1976, became in 1991 the Comissão para a Igualdade e para os Direitos das Mulheres (Committee for the Equality and Rights of Women). The new name reflected the new orientation towards the construction of equality in all sectors of society, a step forward in relation to the earlier denouncement of and defence against gender discrimination. Because the commission, since its beginning, was heavily involved in the collecting, dissemination, and publication of informative and scholarly works about women, it reportedly was involved in the creation of the Portuguese Association for Women's Studies by sociologist Virgínia Ferreira in 1991. From 1997 on, in the context of the constitutional revision calling for the state's responsibility in securing, protecting, and promoting gender equality as part of a global effort, the committee became active in tackling social problems, calling for education, legislation, and prompt, decentralized intervention. Important measures include the attempt to eradicate gender stereotypes through educational efforts and, especially, to eradicate violence against women, including trafficking (Silva n.d.). Tellingly, the committee, as a government institution that champions gender equality, has not taken stands on sexual and reproductive rights, including lesbianism and abortion. From the mid-1980s to the present, the latter has been the most disputed area of women's rights in Portugal; even after abortion was legalized in 2007, its defence was left primarily to some women's movements (Monteiro 2012, 593).

Four issues – domestic violence, abortion rights, gender equality, and lesbian and queer identities – took centre stage in both Portugal and Spain from the mid-1990s through the first two decades of the twenty-first century. As for domestic violence in Portugal, in 1979 journalist Maria Antónia Palla published *Só acontece aos outros* (It only happens to other people), a collection of stories about violence against women, young girls, and children that originally appeared between 1970 and 1979 in the weekly *Século Ilustrado*. At the time, the topic of domestic violence was only beginning to surface in public discourse as a serious, systematic social problem. The circuit of shame, silence, and invisibility of both victims and perpetrators began to be broken in 1995 as a result of the first survey about violence against women conducted in Portugal.[4] It found that 52.2% of women were victims of at least one act of violence (in Sanches 2015, 3). From this disclosure – and as if no one knew about it before the survey – a succession of legal measures was taken to combat domestic violence and offer shelter and protection to its victims. Since 2000, domestic violence has been considered a public crime; and to ensure that the law was upheld in rural areas, by 2004 the Republican National Guard began to set up special units throughout the country to receive and act on complaints (Sanches 2015, 3–5). In 2013, Portugal was one of the first member countries to ratify the European Union's "Convention on preventing violence against women and combating domestic violence," an agreement made in Istanbul, Turkey in 2011 (Sanches 2015, 9; see also Council of Europe 2016). Advances in national legislature and European or global government treaties did little to alter the fact that in 2014 the problem of violence against women was as conspicuous as ever in Portugal. Among the findings of the studies conducted by the European Institute for Gender Equality is that one in ten women aged fifteen and over had been the victim of some form of sexual violence, and one in twenty women reported having been raped. Also, slightly above one in five women was the victim of violence by her partner or former partner; and more than forty women were killed by their partners (in Sanches 2015, 9, 11, 12). The problem continues to be connected to lack of education and consciousness raising about violence as the most dramatic form of gender inequality.

In 1998 in Spain, and following in the footsteps of the World Health Organization that declared domestic violence a priority for health services, the first Plan de Acción contra la Violencia Doméstica (Action Plan against Domestic Violence) was established by the then Ministry of Health and Consumers – currently Ministry of Health, Social Services, and Equality. In 1999, Ángeles Álvarez Álvarez, feminist activist and important political figure in the Socialist Worker's Party, published the *Guía para mujeres maltratadas* (The guide for battered women), edited by the Consejo de Mujeres de la Comunidad de Madrid (The Women's Council of the Community of Madrid). With over ten editions, the guide is a pioneering work offering a comprehensive look at the social ill that is violence against women, foreshadowing the Ley Orgánica 1/2004 de Medidas de Protección Integral contra la Violencia de Género (Organic Law 1/2004 on Comprehensive Protection against Gender Violence). Álvarez is also instrumental in the creation of the Foro de Madrid contra la Violencia de Género (Madrid Forum against Gender Violence), which in 2001 became the Red Estatal de Organizaciones Feministas contra la Violencia de Género (State Network of Feminist Organizations against Gender Violence).[5]

In 2004, the Socialist Party won the general elections once again, and Prime Minister José Luis Rodríguez Zapatero named a cabinet that for the first time in Spain's history had an equal number of male and female ministers: eight, with a woman, Carme Chacón (b. 1971), as secretary of defence. It was thanks to Rodríguez Zapatero's newly minted government that feminism achieved a major victory in December 2004 with the passing of the first-ever Spanish law against gender-based violence. The Ley Orgánica 1/2004 de Medidas de Protección Integral Contra la Violencia de Género (Organic Law 1/2004 on Comprehensive Protection against Gender Violence) was enacted in January 2005.[6] Despite its comprehensive nature, the law has not diminished violent behaviour against women, including feminicide (Bermúdez 2015, 148). Still, Silvia Bermúdez considers that the Law against Gender Violence remains the most radical attempt to combat the problem of domestic violence in Spain. Attending to the relationship between art and reality, Spanish cinema has paid attention to intimate-partner abuse in films such as Javier Balaguer's *Sólo mía* (2001; Only mine) and Icíar Bollaín's award-winning *Te doy mis ojos* (2003; I give you my eyes), cowritten by Bollaín and screenwriter Alicia Luna. Both Bollaín and Luna, also committed to abortion rights, participated in the documentary *Yo decido: El Tren de la Libertad* (2014; I decide: The Freedom Train), the result of collective work that included over eighty women from the Spanish-film industry documenting the 1 February 2014 demonstrations in Madrid against the Popular Party's desire to restrict abortion laws in Spain.[7]

The so-called Abortion Law of 1985 – Organic Law 9/1985, adopted on 5 July 1985 – legalized abortion in three cases: serious risk to physical or mental health of the pregnant woman; rape; and malformations or defects, physical or mental, in the fetus. The law remained unchanged until its broadening in 2010 with the promulgation of the Organic Law 2/2010 of sexual and reproductive health and abortion. The reform was supported by the ruling party of Spain at that time, the Spanish Socialist Workers Party (PSOE) led by José Luis Rodríguez Zapatero, and allowed for the termination of pregnancies up to fourteen weeks along, or up to twenty-two weeks in cases of fetal abnormalities or danger to the mother's life. The 2010 reform drew much criticism from the Popular Party, the Catholic Church, and antiabortion groups. The change of this legislation became part of the Popular Party's election program in 2011 and, to make good on their promise, in December 2013, the Popular Party's government headed by Prime Minister Mariano Rajoy approved a draft bill fiercely challenged by opposition parties and feminist and women's groups across Spain. To combat the government plans to roll back access to abortion in the country to the times of the Franco dictatorship, the Tren de la Libertad (Freedom Train) protest was instrumental in getting tens of thousands of Spaniards to Madrid on 1 February 2014. Central to the gathering of protesters from all walks of life, all ages, and from the entire Spanish territory were feminist groups and women's associations from Gijón – the Tertulia Feminista Les Comadres (Feminist Gathering the Sistahs) – and the organization Mujeres por la Igualdad de Barredos (Women for Equality from Barredos), both cities in Asturias, where the Freedom Train movement initiated. Similar marches were scheduled all over Spain with such success that a few months later Mariano Rajoy's government abandoned its plan to limit abortion access.[8]

In Portugal, in the context of disenchantment with laws of gender equality promulgated in the 1976 Constitution, rights of sexuality and reproduction incrementally gained visibility in the public sphere since the 1990s. The delay was due not only to the traditional difficulty that the Left had in dealing with sexuality but also to the very concept of equality inherited from second-wave feminism. While lesbian feminism surfaced alongside those claiming rights for gay, bisexual, and transgendered people, the struggle for the legalization of abortion was long and difficult. In 1975, Maria Teresa Horta, Célia Metrass, and Helena Sá Medeiros, activists of the Movimento de Libertação das Mulheres (Movement for the Liberation of Women), published *O aborto: Direito ao nosso corpo* (Abortion: The right to our body). The authors were inspired, as was also the case with other radical feminists in the 1960s and 1970s, by Simone de Beauvoir's famous formula "A libertação da mulher começa no ventre" (Tavares 2011, 456; Woman's liberation begins in the womb). In that same year, 1975, an international gathering on abortion took place in Portugal by initiative of English and French feminist movements, which lent their support to the Portuguese Movement of Women's Liberation. Feminists of many other countries took part in the discussions and workshops, but few of them were from Portugal (Tavares 2011, 457). It was not until 1984 that a very limited abortion law went into effect; it did not take into consideration those who were neither raped nor whose life or that of the fetus was in danger. Clandestine abortions thus continued, some ending tragically or in scandalous legal cases, which captured media attention, especially after a 1998 referendum in which the abortion law was voted down.[9]

Among several interventions in the early 2000s by national and international doctors, nurses, and other professionals connected with women's reproductive health, the best known is the visit to Portugal in 2004 of the Dutch nonprofit proabortion organization Women on Waves. Founded in 1999 by Dr Rebecca Gomberts, this organization distributes information and support on abortions in a boat clinic that remains in international waters offshore from countries where abortions are illegal or difficult to obtain ("Who Are We" n.d.). The fact that the Portuguese government did not allow the boat to enter Portuguese waters even for maintenance, forcing the boat to go to Galicia, in Spain, was well covered by national and international media and mobilized numerous protests in favour of decriminalization (Tavares 2011, 421–5; Monteiro 2012, 598).

After the rise to power in 2005 of José Socrates, the new leader of the Socialist Party, another referendum was introduced in favour of abortion. It finally passed in 2007, but for gestation of no longer than ten weeks. This change arose thanks to what Manuela Tavares characterizes as the new interpretative frame, which was able to mobilize many of those who had opposed abortion earlier (2011). Rather than a matter of women's choice, the "yes" to abortion hinged upon women's health and the many problems connected to clandestine abortions (Monteiro 2012). It is telling that within one year of the legalization of abortion in Portugal, on 15 July 2008, the major Lisbon newspaper *Público* reported that "almost five hundred women secured abortions in Spain" (Gomes 2008).[10] Like what had happened in Spain, a conservative turn in the Portuguese legislature took place in July 2015 and required women wanting an abortion to receive psychological counselling. Duarte Vilar, the executive director of the Family Planning Association, considered this measure an affront to women's rights, which suggested that women were incapable of making a decision on their own (in Sanches 2015, 4).

The LGBT (Lesbian, Gay, Bisexual, and Transexual) movement emerged in Portugal in the late 1990s and with it the open struggle for the rights of lesbians. Earlier in the decade, a number of lesbian journals and groups emerged. Among the latter was the Associação Clube Safo (Sappho Club Association), founded in 1996 and officially established as an association in 2002; and GIRL (Grupo Intervenção e Reflexão Lésbica [Lesbian Reflection and Intervention Group), founded within the International Lesbian and Gay Rights organization (ILGA) in Portugal in 1998. Clube Safo, still active, is the most important lesbian organization in Portugal, being the first in which its members assumed their identities publicly. Its official newsletter, *Zona Livre* (Free zone), published between 1997 and 2007, is available online, at the website of Clube Safo (Ferreira 2014, 63–5). Subsequently, Eduarda Ferreira former president of the association and one of its most active members, founded with other women an online Discussion Group of Lesbian Issues, known by the acronym LES; in 2010, the group began publishing the first lesbian scholarly journal in Portugal (Ferreira 2014 53, 66–7).

In discussing the emergence of the lesbian movement in Portugal, Manuela Tavares underlines the importance that mixed feminist groups had in the struggle for rights of sexuality, including lesbian rights (Tavares 2011, 845–91). Alongside the decriminalization of homosexuality in 1982 and the inclusion in the Portuguese Constitution of a clause for nondiscrimination based on sexual orientation, several important advances in rights of sexuality point to a broader nexus of solidarity than allowed by mobilization along strict lesbian experiences or identity claims.[11] In 2000, at the World March of Women that took place in Lisbon, a lesbian manifesto was presented, demanding the recognition of lesbians as people with full rights of – among others – abortion, civil union, maternity, artificial insemination, and adoption (Tavares and Magalhães 2015, 105). This was followed in 2002 by the first Jornadas Lésbicas (Lesbian Workshops), which took place in association with the Institute of Applied Psychology in Lisbon (Tavares 2011, 482). Although infamously five years later than in Spain, same-sex marriage was finally allowed in Portugal in 2010; it took yet another six years for same-sex couples to be allowed to adopt children (Esselink 2016). The fact that the conservative president, Aníbal Cavaco Silva – who had also not supported same-sex marriage and had previously banned adoption rights for homosexuals – was forced to sign the new bill by a majority vote in Parliament bespeaks the increasing support for LBGT rights by not only the Parliamentary Left but also, arguably, by a relatively wider sector of Portuguese society that – conservatisms and Catholicisms apart – shared long, tacitly silenced histories of homosexuality in Portugal. Their account is captured by São José Almeida in *Homossexuais no Estado Novo* (Homosexuals in the New State), published in 2010.

As stated earlier, the furthering of gender equality took place in Spain in 2007 when Parliament, led by the Spanish Socialist Workers Party and with José Luis Rodríguez Zapatero serving as prime minister since April 2004, approved the Ley Orgánica para la Igualdad Efectiva de Mujeres y Hombres (Organic Law for the Effective Equality of Women and Men). In light of said law, the Institute for Women devised two more plans: Plan Estratégico de Igualdad de Oportunidades entre Mujeres y Hombres 2008–2011 (Strategic Plan for the the Equality of Opportunity between Women and Men 2008–2011) and the Plan Estratégico de Igualdad de Oportunidades entre Mujeres y Hombres 2014–2016 (Strategic Plan for the Equality of Opportunity between Women and Men 2014–2016). Promoting the cause of equality, and as a political victory for Catalan feminists, the Generalitat of Catalonia on July 2015 enacted Law 17/2015 "Of the Effective Equality Women and Men."

Since the late 1990s, several feminists thinkers began exploring the connections between feminism and queer theory. One such author is Galician feminist and scholar Beatriz Suárez Briones as per her leading 1998 article "Sobre hombres y márgenes: Relaciones entre el feminismo y la teoría queer" (About men and margins: Relations between feminism and queer theory). To define, defend, and delve into lesbian/gay/bisexual/transsexual identities, many Spanish gays, lesbians, transsexuals, feminist activists, and/or thinkers have produced important studies at the turn of the twenty-first century, for example: Beatriz Preciado's 2002 *Manifiesto contrasexual* (2011; Contrasexual manifesto; now Paul B. Preciado after transitioning); Beatriz Suárez Briones's *Sextualidades: Teorías literarias feministas* (2003; "Sextualities": Feminist literary theories); Susana López Penedo's *El laberinto queer: La identidad en tiempos de liberalismo* (2008; The queer labyrinth: Identity in times of liberalism); Gracia Trujillo's *Deseo y resistencia (1977–2007): Treinta años de movilizacion lesbiana en el estado español* (2009; Desire and resistence, 1977–2007: Thirty years of lesbian mobilization in the Spanish state); and the 2014 volume edited by Suárez Briones titled *Feminismos lesbianos y queer: Representación, visibilidad y política* (2014; Queer and lesbian feminisms: Representation, visibility, and politics).[12] Equality for the LGBT communities was finally achieved in Spain in 2005 with the Same-Sex Marriage Law (which took effect in on 3 July 2005) establishing both that same-sex marriages had the same status as heterosexual marriages and that lesbian and gay couples can adopt children.

Accompanying the rise of women finishing bachelor and graduate degrees in Portuguese universities, women's studies programs have surfaced in Portugal since the 1990s. The founding in 1991 of the Associação Portuguesa de Estudos sobre as Mulheres (Portuguese Association of Women's Studies) was pivotal in that regard, encouraging the founding in 1995 of the first degree-granting program in women's studies (Moutinho dos Santos 1987, 15; Tavares 2011, 23). Perhaps it is not surprising that such a progressive initiative took place at the Lisbon campus of Universidade Aberta (Open University), devoted to distance education since 1988. Its master's degree in women's studies, completely online, continues to be offered alongside other graduate degrees in women's studies that have subsequently been offered, for example, at the New University of Lisbon, at the University of Oporto, and integrated into the program in American studies at the University of Coimbra. Together with the official journal of the APEM (Associação Portuguesa de Estudos sobre as Mulheres [Portuguese Association of Women's Studies]), which began publication in 1999, the journal *Faces de Eva*, part of the Centre for Women's Studies, a research unit of the Universidade Nova de Lisboa, are presently the most important academic journals in this ever-changing interdisciplinary field.

Research centres, research collaboratives, and academic conferences focusing in whole or in part on gender or women's studies have been numerous since the 1990s, naturalizing feminist critical perspectives and adding to the knowledge production related to women in Portuguese history, culture, and society. The work of historians in particular has been substantial, thanks to scholars such as Irene Flunser Pimentel, Ana Vicente, Cecília Barreira, Irene Vaquinhas, Helena Neves, Inês Paulo Brasão, among many others. Mention should also be made of the successful and productive conferences held at Fundação Calouste Gulbenkian in 1994, O Rosto Feminino da Expansão Portuguesa (The Feminine Face of Portuguese Expansion); in 2004, the commemoration of the Eightieth Anniversary of the First Feminist and Education Congress of 1924; and the Feminist Congress 2008, that brought academics and activists together, not only making visible the diversity of feminist standpoints but also legitimizing those that have been historically ghettoized and invisible, as is the case with lesbian feminism.

The creation of the Universidade Feminista (Feminist University) in 2013 by a group of alumnae of the first MA in gender studies offered by Universidade Aberta represents an important moment of transition and also solidification of the feminist activities generated by the women's group União de Mulheres Alternativa e Resposta (UMAR; Womens's Union for Choice and Response) since the late 1970s.[13] The publication in 2015 of the collection of essays *Percursos feministas: Desafiar os tempos* (Feminist trajectories: Challenging the times), composed of the papers presented at the Feminist University's forums, presents a broad panorama of generational perspectives on social, cultural, and political issues bearing on women's evolving efforts to "mudar a vida" (change life), the action slogan lending unity and direction to the volume.

Whether related or not to the growing interest in women's studies in Portugal, a considerable number of literary works have been published recuperating the historical memory of women and of feminist activity from the oblivion to which the Fascist period dictated them. Among the many writers inspired by the historical recuperative current, Lídia Jorge (b. 1946) in particular has, since 1980, chronicled in twelve novels and four volumes of short stories the role of women in Portuguese society since the last years of fascism and the so-called Colonial War in Africa (Mozambique in this case) through the transition to democracy and post-European integration economic liberalism. Among many other titles, her novel *O vento assobiando nas gruas* (2002; The wind whistling in the cranes) can be considered exemplary on both aesthetic and ideological registers of Jorge's testimonial. It is a markedly ironic and at times darkly humorous rendition of just how much the colonial past survives in the present and cries out to be heard in the trigenerational, dissonant, haunting chorus of women's voices. Isabela Figueiredo (b. Mozambique 1963) is perhaps the author who has most poignantly captured one of those voices – that of the daughters of those who moved to an African colony between the 1950s and 1960s – in *Caderno de memórias coloniais* (2009; *Notebook of Colonial Memories*), originally published on the author's blog *O Mundo Perfeito* (The perfect world). For Figueiredo and other women repatriates from the colonies and their descendants (e.g., Dulce Maria Cardoso, in her novel *O retorno* [*The Return*; 2011]), the memory of the mother remains an appendage to the overwhelming need to identify Portuguese colonialism with the father.

It is the generation of the mothers, of women like Lídia Jorge, who can arguably better capture the complex histories of those who still went unheard in the debates surrounding domestic violence, the right to abortion, and to nonheteronormative sexual identities and expression. Cases in point, respectively, are Lídia Jorge's stories "O marido" (The husband), published in 1997 in the collection by the same title (Jorge 2011); and "As três mulheres sagradas" (The three sacred women), published in 2012 in *O belo adormecido* (Jorge 1997). In relation to the right of women to love each other in whatever register and intensity the need for human love may call for, acclaimed feminist poet and scholar Ana Luísa Amaral's *Ara* (2013; Altar) is a suggestive poetic narrative worthy of mention, as is the rather more discursive and long *O sexo inútil* (Zanatti 2016; The useless sex), composed of hundreds of letters, e-mails, and documents collected by acclaimed actress and openly lesbian writer Ana Zanatti.

On the literary front, in Spain there has been a rediscovering/remembering of the mother in novels written by women and published since 2000. The revaluing of the mother figure can be understood as a way of extracting her "from the sea of anonymity and the shroud of mystery that enveloped her during Franco's dictatorship" (Schumm 2015, 249).[14] The diverse range of authors and novels include, among others, Cristina Cerezales's *De oca a oca* (2000; From spot to spot); Rosa Montero's *El corazón del Tártaro* (2001; The Heart of Tartar); María de la Pau Janer's *Las mujeres que hay en mí* (2002; The women inside of me); Carme Reira's *La mitad del alma* (2003; Half of the soul); Lucía Etxebarria's *Un milagro en equilibrio* (2004; A balanced miracle); Soledad Puértolas's *Historia de un abrigo* (2005; History of a coat); and Julia Montejo's *Violetas para Olivia* (2011; Violets for Olivia). Two of the authors, Puértolas and Cerezales, have also written memoirs about their own mothers, *Con mi madre* (2001; With my mother) and *Música blanca* (2009; White music), respectively. In other novels, the mother's influence is significant to the stories narrated but not the only focus, as in the case of Esther Tusquets's *Correspondencia privada* (2001; Private correspondence); Dulce Chacón's *La voz dormida* (2002; The sleeping voice), Cristina Cerezales's *Por el camino de las grullas* (2006; By the way of the cranes); Ángeles Caso's *Contra el viento* (2010; Against the wind); and María Dueñas's *El tiempo entre costuras* (2009; *The Time in Between*).

Along with these novels, we are witnessing the emergence of what Marina Bettaglio terms "maternal chronicles" (2015, 228; i.e., a varied set of autobiographical texts examining the experience of mothering) that include, among others, Lucía Extebarria's aforementioned text, Care Santos's *Supermami: Mil maneras de ser una mamá feliz* (2009; Supermommmy: A thousand ways of being a happy mother); Inmaculada Gilaberte's *Equilibristas: Entre la maternidad y la profesión* (2009; Acrobats: Between motherhood and career); and Isabel García-Zarza's *Diario de una madre imperfecta* (2010; Diary of an imperfect mother). The impact of the re-emergence of pronatalist discourses in Spain is best exemplified by celebrity top model Bimba Bosé's recent memoir, *Y de repente soy madre* (2013; And suddenly I am a mother), in which she narrates her transformation from all-around bad girl in her younger years to a now devoted mother committed to the "natural" upbringing – home birthing, breastfeeding, ecological diapers – that her economic and social status affords her. Bimba is the granddaughter of famed Italian actress Lucia Bosé and renowned bullfighter Luis Miguel González Luca, known as Dominguín, and the niece of famous performer Miguel Bosé. Thus the impact of her views on motherhood and the "natural" movement reach millions of Spaniards who follow celebrities through all media outlets.

Some feminists perceive these chronicles as indicative of the postfeminist turn in twenty-first century Spain (Bettaglio 2015), and others such as Beatriz Gimeno go further by presenting an antimaternal stance in her February 2014 post "Construyendo un discurso antimaternal" (2014; Constructing an antimaternal discourse). Gimeno's articles prompted an intellectual "mommy war" in feminist circles, which, as Bettaglio explains, expose the contradictions of professional women and feminists being caught between postfeminism and neoliberalism' often walking" a fine line between *seeming* to dismantle patriarchal tradition and inadvertently *bolstering* it" (Bettaglio 2015, 214; emphasis in original).

Twenty-first-century Spanish feminisms cannot be understood without two distinct important contributions. On the one hand, the impact by thinkers Silvia Tubert (1942–2014) and Alicia H. Puleo (b. 1952), both born in Argentina but residing and producing their major works in Spain since the 1980s. On the other hand, the powerful use of social media by what we could now begin to identify as Fourth Wave feminists working from, among other social media sites, the well-visited podcast *Sangre Fucsia* (Fuchsia blood), launched in 2013 in Madrid and which can be accessed free online on-demand (see sangrefucsia.wordpress.com), and the digital *Pikara magazine*, founded in 2010 in Euskadi by journalists Itziar Abad, June Fernández Casete, Lucía Martínez Odriozola, and Maite Asensio (see chapter 35). In regard to Tubert and Puleo, we have Tubert's influential work connecting feminism and psychoanalysis in *Deseo y representación: Convergencias de psicoanálisis y teoría feminista* (2001; Desire and representation: Convergences of psychoanalysis and feminism) and in *Del sexo al género: Los equívocos de un concepto* (2003; From sex to gender: The equivocation of a concept). Puleo investigates the relations between feminism and ecological ethics (Johnson and Zubiaurre 2012, 679). See, among others, Puleo's coedition of *Mujeres y ecología: Historia, pensamiento, sociedad* (2004; Women and ecology: History, thought, society) with María Luisa Cavana and Cristina Segura, and her groundbreaking *Ecofeminismo para otro mundo posible* (2011; Ecofeminism for another possible world).

Many virtual communities are currently disseminating feminist theories and practices and labour equality through social media sites, such as *Iguálate/Orientación sociolaboral con perspectiva de género* (Equalize yourself/Sociolaboral Training with a gender perspective) by the Federación de Mujeres Progresistas (Federation of Progressive Women; see www.igualate.org). In addition, there is the work by Carmen G. de la Cueva (b. 1986, Seville), founder of *La Tribu de Frida*, launched in 2014 along with the feminist journal *Blusa*, this one in collaboration with Sara Herrera Peralta (see http://latribu.info/feminismos/blusa/). Carmen G. de la Cueva is also the author of *Mamá, quiero ser feminista* (2016; Mamma, I want to be a feminist), where she narrates how after "discovering" feminist authors such as Virgina Woolf and Carmen Conde, and feminism's empowering dynamics, she committed herself to advocate feminisms from the fields of cultural production. The pivotal work of *Pikara magazine* to transform the social sphere was recognized in 2017 by the Provincial Council of Bizkaia with the award of the annual Zirgari Prize for Equality, in the category of Empowerment and Change of Values.

32 The Spanish Equality/Difference Debate Continues

ROBERTA JOHNSON

In the mid-1990s, the debate between equality and difference feminism in Spain grew bitter. Perhaps the stakes were higher now that the Socialist government was discredited, and the legal reforms and institutions such as the Women's Institute were threatened in the wake of socialism's crumbling hegemony. Difference feminists became more disillusioned over the discrepancy between the theory of gender equality and the reality of women's lives in the day-to-day world. They also mourned a perceived loss of "feminine" qualities in Spanish life – willingness to act as caregivers, the cult of motherhood, and emphasis on home and family life. In the uncertain political climate, difference feminists probably felt more emboldened in their rejection of traditional political engagement. *El Viejo Topo* (The old mole) published a special issue on feminism in 1994 that reveals the deepening divide between equality and difference feminists as they increasingly defined their positions in terms of philosophical alliances. Unlike the 1980 issue of the same journal on femininity and masculinity, now both sides of the schism are equally represented.

In her essay "Partir de sí" (Rivera 1994; To begin from oneself) for the special issue of *El Viejo Topo*, Milagros Rivera prefers the expression "práçtica política de la diferencia" (political practice of difference) to "feminismo de la diferencia" (difference feminism). According to Rivera, such "practice" does not demand rights, quotas, or power within the patriarchal order, nor does it measure itself against patriarchal values (31); therefore, the opposite of equality feminism is "desigualdad, no diferencia" (31; inequality, not difference). Rivera exhorts feminists to think the unthinkable and say the unsayable, "mirar el mundo entero y decirlo con palabras nacidas de una política que no cancele el cuerpo femenino" (31–2; to look at the whole world and say it with words born of a politics that do not cancel women's bodies). Rivera invokes a new symbolic order that echoes ideas put forth by French feminist thinkers Luce Irigaray and Hélène Cixous, as well as those of the Italian Milan Book Store and Verona Diotima groups. She especially relies on Luisa Muraro's *El orden simbólico de la madre* (The symbolic order of the mother), although she brings the concept of the symbolic order of the mother closer to home by comparing it to María Zambrano's notion of poetic reason, a link she develops further in *El fraude de la igualdad* (Rivera 1997; The fraud of equality).

Central to achieving the new order in which women intervene freely in the world is the concept of "partir de si, el partir de lo que tenemos, que es principalmente la experiencia femenina personal" (Rivera 1994, 53; beginning with oneself, to begin with what we have, which is mainly a personal, female experience). "Partir de sí" allows for a "first-person politics" that accords ample space to female personal experience, which, Rivera believes, structuralism and certain postmodern authors thoroughly devalued. (As I note below, Spanish equality feminism is also averse to postmodernism.) A politics in the first person frees women from living a partial reality, an existence limited by the masculine sex. Thus Rivera is against affirmative action, because a first-person politics does not enter into dialogue with the system of democratic representation. In first person politics, the key strategy is the mediation of another woman or women whose authority the woman recognizes; the woman-to-woman relationship allows her to realize herself, to signify, and thus opens the way to a female liberty that modifies existing power relations in society. The first of these relations is the relation with the mother, the mother who taught the woman to speak, guaranteeing a concordance between words and things.

Celia Amorós's searing answer to the concept of the symbolic order of the mother appeared in 1998:

> ¿A quién beneficia este nuevo tratado de paz entre los sexos, cuyos términos, esta vez, han sido definidos por las propias mujeres, sin que se sepa qué batalla han ganado, a menos que sea la victoria "simbólica"? ¿No habremos cambiado nuestra participación en el derecho a la primogenitura – ¡oh, qué concepto tan patriarcal! – por un plato de simbólicas lentejas? Simbólicas, desde luego, porque no sé cómo se va a paliar la feminización de la pobreza desde la política de la "diferencia sexual." (1985a, 133)

> (Who does a new peace treaty between the sexes benefit, the terms of which have been defined by women themselves without out knowing what battle they have won, unless it is a "symbolic" victory? Haven't we exchanged our participation in the right of primogeniture – oh, what a patriarchal concept! – for a symbolic dish of lentils? Yes, symbolic, because I don't know how we can rectify the feminization of poverty from the politics of "sexual difference.")

The more heated polemic between equality and difference feminists had been brewing since 1996 when *El Viejo Topo* published the Spanish version of *El final del patriarcado* (Librería de Mujeres de Milán 1996; The end of patriarchy), the same year it was edited in Italian by the Milan Women's Book Store. Not only do difference feminists theorize a symbolic order of the mother, but now they also declare that patriarchy as the source of female identity has ended. Celia Amorós expresses dismay at the optimistic title of the work, which at first she thought meant that systematic male domination over women's collective lives had ceased, in spite of all the evidence to the contrary – the persistent feminization of poverty, rampant violence against women, the notable inequality in the distribution of domestic duties, the segregation of work on the basis of sex, and women's lack of access to positions of responsibility. Amorós was disappointed to discover that instead of talking about matters relating to women's concrete lives, "estamos hablando de lo simbólico, nada menos que de 'la política de lo simbólico'" (1996, 64; we are talking about the symbolic, nothing less than "the politics of the symbolic"). Thus patriarchy has been banished by "un efecto de conjuro que emanaría de la actitud despectivo de quienes han llegado a la verdadera 'toma de conciencia'" (64; an effect of a conjuring that would arise from the scornful attitude of those who have arrived at the real "coming into consciousness"). One can easily detect the aversion to postmodern philosophy in this interpretation of the linguistic orientation of a symbolic order.

In the declaration of the end of patriarchy, Amorós hears familiar Heideggerian echoes of the end of the reign of the subject, "con sus pretensiones fundamentantes y sus designios objetivadores y manipuladores de un ente que ha perdido el aroma y el halo del ser en un mundo desencantado" (1996, 64; with its fundamental pretentions and the objectifying and manipulative designs of an entity that has lost the aroma and halo of a being in a disenchanted world). Amorós dismantles one by one all the happy present and future circumstances difference feminists describe. For example, the Milan group quotes the cheery statistic that Italian women (and probably Spanish women a close second) count the highest number of women working simultaneously inside and outside the home, in order to prove that traditional domestic roles no longer constrain women's lives and have ceased to be a barrier to their having paid employment. Amorós considers that the Milan group presents this statistic as some kind of "armonía preestablecida" (64; pre-established harmony). She notes that this positive interpretation of the double workday for women inspires in her an "hermeneútica de la sospecha" (1996, 64; hermeneutics of suspicion). Amorós (67) categorizes as a new stoicism or something akin to a slave mentality difference feminists' view that abstract law cannot take into consideration the complexity involved in decisions women must make and that women should just ignore the patriarchy and forge something different based on their inner urges. Directly addressing the difference feminists as "inefables anunciadoras del fin del patriarcado" (ineffable announcers of the end of patriarchy), she retorts that "los muertos que ustedes matan gozan de muy buena salud" (67; the dead that you are killing off enjoy very good health). She further argues that the positions taken by difference feminists intentionally or unintentionally reinforce rightist political positions.

The combative tone of the equality/difference exchange of the 1990s was perhaps self-conflagratory, although Milagros Rivera attempted to revive the smoldering embers in her acidly titled *El fraude de la igualdad* of 1997. While *El fraude de la igualdad*, like Rivera's article for the 1994 *El Viejo Topo* special issue, relies on concepts such as the symbolic order of the mother borrowed from Luce Irigaray and Luisa Muraro, she now more fully integrates ideas inspired by María Zambrano. She invokes Zambrano's statement from her 1945 essay "Eloisa o la vida de la mujer" (Heloise or the life a women), that "'la vida de la mujer es *la vida del alma.'* ... Vida misteriosa de las entrañas, que se consume sin alcanzar la objetividad ..." (Rivera 1997, 79–80; "the life of women is *the life of the soul."* ... Mysterious life of the entrails, that is consumed before it reaches objectivity ...), to reinforce the notion of "partir de sí," which she believes the concept of equality erases. Like Zambrano, Rivera elaborates on the importance of language in forging the female or, in Zambrano's terms, poetic realm in the symbolic order of the mother: "la capacidad de transformación de la palabra aprendida de la madre ... la fluidez de la lengua que ella [la madre] enseña, la fortuna mudable del azar que abre la vida a la necesidad de relacionarse con los demás, sin cuya percepción y escucha no hay ni sociedad ni palabra" (1997, 17, 31–2; the word's capacity to transform learned from the mother ... the fluidity of the tongue that the mother teaches, the mutable fortune of chance that opens life to the necessity of relating to others, without whose perception and ear there is no society or word). On this point, she quotes Zambrano's *España, sueño y verdad* (Spain, dream, and reality): "'Y la peña se hace así entraña maternal, alma' ... 'El alma virginal de la palabra. Allí se da a ver algo propio de la palabra: ser como agua allí donde la realidad es como piedra'" (Rivera 1997, 31; "And the rock thus becomes maternal heart, soul" ... "The virginal soul of the word. There something that belongs to language: being like water there where reality is like a rock"]. Also coinciding with Zambrano, Rivera is suspicious of emphasizing language at the expense of the corporal. Here Rivera parts company with French and Italian difference feminists who follow Lacan in privileging language as the ultimate reality. Rivera believes that the body and language are inseparable –"o sea, unidos equilibradamente" (1997, 97; or, united in equilibrium). She critiques Luisa Muraro for separating the soul and the body, "cuidando en este caso el estudio de la lengua y descuidando el del cuerpo, lo cual desequilibra esa unidad que ... es la obra y el gran don de la madre" (95; protecting the study of language to the exclusion of the body, which throws that unity out of balance ... it is the work and the great gift of the mother).

The year 1998 marked a turning point in the equality/difference stand-off in Spanish feminist theory of the democratic era. In that year, Marina Subirats published *Con diferencia* (1998; With difference), an attempt to reconcile the two positions, and Cristina Caruncho and Purificación Mayobre edited the essay collection in Galician *Entre a igualdad e a diferencia* (1998; Between equality and difference). The attempt to find ways around the seeming impasse was already evident in the 1994 special issue of *El Viejo Topo*. There Justa Montero asserted that a pragmatic feminism must overcome the philosophical differences of the several Spanish feminist groups in order to continue to make concrete gains for women in the real world. Montero argues for a common philosophical position that blends important elements of equality and difference feminisms. She points out that all egalitarian suppositions implicitly or explicitly begin by recognizing difference, since what is being called for is equal consideration for those who do not enjoy it, precisely because they are not identical: "Hemos entendido la lucha por la igualdad de derechos, que durante estos años ha desarollado el movimiento feminista, unida la reafirmación de nuestra identidad como mujeres y la autonomía de las mujeres" (Montero 1994, 40; We have understood the fight for equality of rights, which during these years the feminist movment has developed, united to the reaffirmation of our identity as women and the autonomy of women). Montero rejects the idea, implied by both equality and difference feminists, that equality means assuming a traditionally masculine identity, "una falsa analogía entre igualdad e identidad" (41; a false analogy between equality and identity).

Marina Subirats, once director of the Instituto de la Mujer (IM; Women's Institute), suggests eliminating genders from our thinking and replacing all references to "hombres y mujeres" (men and women) with "'individuos' de experiencia diferenciada, y diferenciada en tanto que individuos, no en tanto que seres pertenecientes a un género" (1998, 25; "individuals" with different experiences, and differentiated as individuals rather than as beings belonging to a gender).[15] Subirats (1998) goes beyond the legal issues and arguments that normally limit equality-feminist thinking and programs to include interior transformations, and unlike difference feminists, she points out the need for both men and women to reshape their consciousness. She affirms that in order for every human being to achieve status as an individual, there must be absolute parity in all of life's arenas, not just in the public sphere. Equality feminism's focus on legal parity has a hard time reaching into the private sphere where such matters as shared domestic duties are negotiated, immune from the long arm of the law. In this area, perhaps the difference feminists have an edge in their concentration on fortifying women's inner selves.

Political theorist Alicia Miyares's *Democracia feminista* (2003; Feminist democracy) returns us to the key concepts of liberty and equality set forth in the 1978 Constitution. Miyares proposes a feminist democracy to replace the two basic Western democratic models – liberal democracy and social democracy. She believes neither of the models provides women access to equality. Liberalism cannot take women into account because its notion of the person is based on property holding, and Marxism does not consider women a social class.[16] Miyares attempts to reconcile liberty and equality by asserting that, for a political feminism, a defence of equality must also be the defence of liberty, and that all equality is liberty, while all inequality is a deficit of liberty (2003, 154). Her reconciliation, however (again echoing an unacknowledged Rousseau), tips in favour of equality over liberty: "El cambio institucional que facilita la cohesion social no depende del énfasis que pongamos en la idea de libertad, sino en la idea de igualdad. La igualdad ha de presidir todas las instancias por las que nos socializamos y si no hay igualdad la cohesion social no será posible y la libertad será cosa de muy pocos" (13; The institutional change that facilitates social cohesion does not depend on the emphasis we place on the idea of liberty but on the idea of equality. Equality must precede in all instances for which we socialize, and if there is not equality, social cohesion is not possible, and liberty will pertain to a very few).

In order to achieve the integration of liberty and equality, Miyares relies on the concept of "sexual consciousness" (*conciencia de sexo*), an alternative to "gender," which she believes is a depoliticized term. In sexual consciousness, both men and women understand that reality cannot be determined by sexual categories, thus dissolving any link between liberty and stereotypical roles. In this way, equality is freed from normativity; and sex is eliminated from discussions of relations between women and men, the resources for obtaining work, and the ways in which intimacy or religiosity are carried out (Miyares 2003, 171). For Miyares, sexual consciousness politicizes discussion of the sexes with respect to equality; it is as essential to feminism as class struggle is to Marxism or individualism to liberalism. She avers that sexual consciousness derives from individualism in that sex is no longer a differentiating trait for men and women; and it also derives from equality because it allows the process of recognition between individuals to take place (171). Sexual consciousness operates at different levels of reality, allowing for the recognition of both individuality and equality.

The principles of sexual consciousness and recognition move Miyares towards her "third way" feminist democracy, which is more inclusive than liberalism or Marxism. A feminist democracy would reduce the private sphere to intimacy and beliefs, and it would not allow media entertainment to use women as sexual objects, nor would it allow religious motivations to enter the public sphere and exacerbate conflicts between the sexes. Feminist democracy would give absolute parity to both sexes, and women would have access to the political power denied them because of their family responsibilities. Miyares's solution to women's submission to the cultural normativity and inequality of private family life is to make private life public. Echoing some of Empar Pineda's arguments from1980, in Miyares's version of political feminism, equality should change everyone's position, both that of men and women. No one particular measure can be directed only towards modifying women's attitudes; men must always be part of the equation. She argues that the aura of privacy surrounding the family and the dependence of women's subjectivity on emotional relationships leads women to put up with domestic violence (Miyares 2003). Despite her attempts to incorporate the difference feminist emphasis on the interior realm into her theory via "sexual consciousness," her aversion to difference feminism is nonetheless evident. In an overt jab at difference feminism, which had so triumphantly announced the end of patriarchy in 1996, she sardonically observes that the burial of an ideology does not imply the death of the hierarchical family (2003, 161–209).

The Spanish feminist polemic over equality and difference is far from over. Books that address gender equality and difference continue to appear. In her *Rebeldes: Hacia la paridad* (2000; Rebels: Towards parity), Amelia Valcárcel maintains that equality goals have not been achieved. Victoria Sendón de León's *Marcar las diferencias* (2002; Marking differences) continues vigorously to defend difference feminism, although she now complicates her arguments and modulates her tone with Sartrean notions of the *en soi* and the *pour soi*. Carlos Lomas's *Los chicos también lloran: Identidades masculinas, igualdad entre los sexos y coeducación* (2004; Boys also cry: Masculine identities, equality between the sexes, and coeducation) brings a male perspective to the polemic. Also focusing on education is Ylanda Herranz Gómez's *Igualdad bajo sospecha: El poder transformador de la educación* (2006; Equality under suspicion: The transformative power of education). And María Elena Simón Rodríguez's *Hijas de la igualdad, herederas de injusticias* (2008; Daughters of equality, inheritors of injustice) considers the second generation of constitutional-era women who have lived under legal parity. Carlos Lomas again takes a male viewpoint in *¿El otoño del patriarcado? Luces y sombras de la igualdad entre mujeres y hombres* (2008; The autumn of the patriarchy? Pluses and minuses of equality between women and men).

Equality feminists might seem to have gained an official victory in 2008 with the establishment of the Ministerio de Igualdad (Ministry of Equality). However, in 2010, under the conservative Partido Popular leadership, that government ministry was abolished, and in 2011 its work was integrated into the Ministerio de Sanidad, Política e Igualdad de España (Ministry of Health, Politics, and Equality in Spain). The new ministry seems to focus on matters related to health rather than gender equality; thus the official and theoretical work regarding equality begun several years before the 1978 Constitution and ratified by the document is not yet complete. It is perhaps safe to say that the debate over equality and difference will be a subject of interest to Spanish-feminist theorists for some years to come, although future debates will doubtless take into consideration immigrant women and other dimensions of the subject.

33 Catalan Feminisms from 1996 to the Present

Mª ÁNGELES CABRÉ

Although the actual situation continues to be difficult to assess, the last two decades in Catalonia seem to have had a happy conclusion in the public sector, since the Catalonian Parliament approved the Law of Equality for Men and Women in July 2015, a law that comes a little late compared to that of 2007 approved by the Spanish Parliament. However, it is good news, because it demonstrates that the feminist impulse has been kept alive in Catalonia; without it, the law would not exist. It also indicates another reality: that the strong push for women's rights in the 1970s, which culminated in the Jornadas Catalanas de la Dona (Catalan Women's Meetings) and in publications like *Vindicación Femenista* (Feminist vindication; 1976–9), has not been muffled. Thus, although the 1980s were years of agitation, above all in the area of cultural feminism, with personalities of the stature of Maria Aurèlia Capmany and Montserrat Roig, the 1990s that brought Olympic euphoria was not propitious for women's cause, because a false sense of equality dominated, obliging feminism to reformulate itself. Feminism is now besieged by urgent matters such as the perpetuation of sexist roles and the growing threat of a return to the mysticism of femininity that Betty Friedan combated in the 1960s.

Fortunately the new paradigm generated a plural feminism, the sum of diverse tendencies. The great enemy is the 23% salary gap, while scarcely 2% of the population considers itself feminist. In this postfeminist period, the struggle for women's visibility and the exploration of new paths to finding their identity coexist not only because of the man-woman dichotomy but also because of the wide range of possibilities proposed by queer theory.

We find ourselves in an age that writes itself with a new calligraphy that is going in two different directions – one destined definitively to achieve real equality and the other to defend difference/differences. The different feminisms, in practice, perfectly complement each other. The first is underwritten primarily by institutional, associationist feminism; the second is cultivated in essays and university centres. In basic feminism (both difference feminism and equality feminism), there is a dichotomy whose gap today's feminist pluralism is able to bridge.

As the sociologist Marina Subirats (who was director of the Women's Institute) writes in *Con diferencia: Las mujeres frente al reto de la autonomía* (1998; With difference: Women in the face of the challenge of autonomy), all social movements, sooner or later, undergo fragmentation, and feminism is no exception. In fact, it would be odd if it had not happened, given the vertiginous rhythm with which women's situation has changed. However, it is not a "puzzle de piezas contradictorias" (Subirats 2012, 602; a puzzle with contradictory pieces) but, as Nuria Varela states in *Feminismo para principantes* (2008, 115; Feminism for beginners), the consequence of feminism having opened the dam's gates and emptying out all the water. In what follows, I briefly outline what has happened in the last two decades in four different feminist arenas – the institutional, the academic, the associative, and the base – to which I add a new element: the observatories of gender.

In regard to institutional feminism, modelled after the Instituto de la Mujer (The Women's Institute) at the state level, the Catalonian government created the Institut Català de la Dona (Catalan Women's Institute) in 1989; thus it has been in existence for a quarter of a century. It promotes a politics in favour of equal opportunities between women and men, and ultimately is dedicating itself to signing agreements for collaboration with different organizations within the Strategic Plan for Women's Politics 2012/2015, which is designed to incorporate a gender perspective into all governmental policies and actions. It lacks the ability to intervene in the sociopolitical order. Also, the town halls of provincial capitals and medium-sized cities now have Concejalías de la Mujer (Women's Offices) devoted to fomenting policies in favour of women. It is also noteworthy that with the arrival in 2015 of the first woman mayor of Barcelona, activist Ana Colau (b. 1947), the Concejalía de Mujer y Derechos Civiles del Ayuntamiento de Barcelona (Registry of Women and Civil Rights of the Barcelona City Hall) was baptized as Regiduría de Feminismos y LGTBI (Registry of Feminisms and LGTBI).

Pertinent to academic feminism, the last few years have seen a substantial change in women's studies, above all in terms of viewpoint, so that they have progressively been substituted for gender studies. This is evident in the University of Vic's Centre d'Estudis Interdisciplinaris de Gènere (CEIG; Centre of Gender Interdisciplinary Studies), in line with the name change of the aforementioned registry. In Catalonia since 2000, academic feminism can rely on the Institut Interuniversitari d'Estudis de Dones i Gènere (IIEDG; Interuniversities Institute in Women and Gender Studies), created by the collaboration of groups of researchers from seven Catalonian universities. It serves as an umbrella for feminist thought whose objectives are interdisciplinarity and the recognition of gender studies. The aforementioned CEIG and several other groups are active at the Autonomous University of Barcelona, such as the Grup Dona i Dret-Antígona (Antigone Women and Law Group), the Seminari d'Estudis de la Dona (SED; Seminar in Women's Studies) in the Sociology Department, and Cos i Textualitat (Body and Textuality), an intrepid research group in the Department of Philology.

During this time, several groups at the University of Barcelona like Centre Dona i Literatura: Género, Sexualidades, Crítica de la Cultura (Women and Literature Centre: Gender, Sexualities, Cultural Criticism), the Seminario Filosofía i Gènere (Philosophy and Genre Seminar), and Tàcita Muta: Grup d'Estudis de Dones i Gènere a l'Antiguitat (Tacita Muta: Study Group on Women and Gender in Antiquity) collaborate with the above-mentioned groups. At the core of all of these groups is the Centre Dona i Literatura: Género, Sexualidades, Crítica de la Cultura , which in the 1990s began its activity under another name. Since 2004, it has been, in collaboration with the University of Vic, the seat of the UNESCO Chair of Women, Development, and Cultures. The seminar Filosofía i Genere (Philosophy and Gender) has been in existence for twenty-five years under the direction of Fina Birulés, the author of the epilogue to this volume, focused on studying women's philosophical production so that it does not fall into oblivion. *Duoda,* founded in 1982 out of its relation with the Librería de Mujeres de Milán (Milan Women's Book Store) and the philosophical community Diótima at the University of Verona, deserves a special mention as a centre for research on women at the University of Barcelona that has resisted as a bulwark of difference feminism. The sum of all these intellectual pathways allows students to pursue specialized PhD and MA programs that did not exist before.

Associative feminism also occupies an important space with diverse women's associations centred in Catalonia, which recently have celebrated significant anniversaries. The Associació de Dones Periodistes de Catalunya (ADPC; Association of Catalonian Women Journalists), whose statutes were approved in 1992, is the first association of women reporters of the Spanish state and recently celebrated its twentieth anniversary. In addition, the Dones Juristes (Women Jurists), instituted in 1989, just celebrated its twenty-fifth anniversary. All of these celebrations are taking place, despite the fact that in Spain there are few women's professional organizations, except for those mentioned in audio-visual media and that organize the Mostra Internacional de Films de Dones (International Women's Film Festival) – a film festival, which in 2013 had existed for twenty years – and the association of scenic creators Projecte Vaca (Cow Project), created in 1998.

However, in the Catalonian cultural sector, one finds lacking more associationist initiatives. In the capital, Madrid, there have been associations, such as the Asociación de Mujeres Cineastas y de Medios Audiovisuales (CIMA; Association of Women Film-Makers and Audio-Visual Specialists) and Mujeres en las Artes Visuales (MAV; Women in the Visual Arts), founded in 2006 and 2009, respectively, to defend the interests of professionals in these sectors (see chapter 34 for such alliances in Galicia).

The contestatory spirit of base feminism has searched for other avenues by which to enlarge and renovate the feminist ranks and has become affiliated with new struggles, such as the one culminating in 15M (15 May Movement), one of whose epicentres was the Plaza de Cataluña in Barcelona. But feminism is resilient and continues to stay alive in Barcelona in places like Ca la Dona (House of Women) and the women's book store Pròleg. Ca la Dona, established in 1988, is a meeting place for women that has been changing meeting sites until it came to its present location, as has occurred with Pròleg, which heroically has resisted the attacks of the economic crisis. Both Pròleg and Ca la Dona have inherited the old spirit of sisterhood of La Sal Editions and are the engine behind diverse activities. In addition, since 2010, Ca la Dona promotes the Escuela Feminista de Verano (Feminist Summer School).

Espai Francesca Bonnemaison (Francesca Bonnemaison Space), which is a dependency of the Diputación de Barcelona (Barcelona Congress) and for many years has been a place for reflection and exchange of ideas, is also an essential part of the necessary intergenerational dialogue and the updating of matters that affect women. Today it is the principal place for fomenting the participation of women in culture; feminists can meet there without worrying about the conflicts of the various feminist orientations.

Factual journalism has become a useful instrument for denouncing problems, and hence the essential function of the observatories. The Observatori de les Dones en els Mitjans de Comunicación (Women's Observatory in Communication Media) is an example of citizen participation underwritten by several Catalonian town halls. In addition, the teams of Catalonian university researchers that are devoted to gender have for some time been serving as observatories, such as, for example, the aforementioned Seminari d'Estudis de la Dona (SED) in the Sociology Department where equality policies are tracked. Moreover, new observatories are being created to serve feminist causes.

Such is the case of the Observatori Dona, Empresa i Economía (Woman, Enterprise, and Economy), of the Observatorio IQ, Vida cotidiana (IQ Daily Life Observatory) and of the Observatorio Cultural de Género (Cultural Observatory of Gender). The first, managed by the Cámara de Comercio (Chamber of Commerce), is a forum for reflection, study, and action with relation to women in today's economic world. For its part, the IQ, or Instituto para el Estudio y la Transformación de la Vida Cotidiana (Institute for the Study and Transformation of Everyday Life) uses statistical indicators to approach Catalonian reality from a non-androcentric perspective, while the main objective of the Observatorio Cultural de Género is to give more voice to women engaged in cultural production and to produce reports about inequality in various cultural sectors. The Equality Law approved in Catalonia in July 2015 echoes this new system of mediation and at the request of some feminist groups has included the creation of an institutional observatory that would centralize all the data gathered until now and generate new data.

Collective Thought and Transgressive Philosophy

If earlier thinkers who favoured feminism did it alone (e.g., Simone de Beauvoir or Betty Friedan) and then wrote their texts as a group, in recent times in Catalonia, efforts have been focused on the collective enterprise, and it has been in that arena that new thought paradigms have been generated. A rich web of knowledge has emerged from the numerous proposals set forth. In this "melting pot," one finds collections like that of the Centre d'Estudis Interdisciplinaris de Gènere (CEIG; Centre of Gender Interdisciplinary Studies); in the publishing house Eumo, the Cos i Textualitat (Body and Textuality) line of publications, with titles that open new perspectives such as, among others, the volumes *El cuerpo en mente: Versiones del ser desde el pensamiento contemporáneo* (2011; The body in mind: Versions of being in contemporary thought), coedited by Mireia Calafell and Aina Pérez and *Cuerpos sexuados, cuerpos de (re)producción* (2012; Sexual bodies, [re]productive bodies) by Patricia Mayayo Bost; and the series Mujeres y Cultura (Women and culture) of the publishing house Icaria, directed by the Centre Dona i Literatura, which also publishes the journals *Lectora* and also *Duoda* devoted to studies of sexual difference.

Without forgetting that fundamental piece that is the revision of canons through genealogy, as I proposed in *Leer y escribir en femenino* (Cabré 2013; Feminine reading and writing), I myself suggested constructing a new literary canon. Under Anna Caballé's direction, *La vida escrita por las mujeres* (2004; Life written by women) gathers together the most significant literary texts from the Middle Ages to the twentieth century; see also *Pensadoras del siglo XX: Aportaciones al pensamiento filosófico femenino* (2011, Twentieth-century women thinkers: Contributions to female philosophical thought), edited by Fina Birulés and Rosa Rius; or *Vivir en femenino: Estudios de mujeres en la antigüedad* (2008; To live in the feminine: Studies on women in antiquity), coordinated by M. Dolors Molas.

And, of course, there are individual women to consider. While Amelia Valcárcel and Celia Amorós are Spanish feminist philosophers par excellence, in Catalonia we also have philosopher Victoria Camps, who has published *El siglo de las mujeres* (1998; The century of women), although she does not fully subscribe to a feminist position, and Fina Birulés, who does. Also in the area of sociology is Marina Subirats, and in the circle of *Duoda*, María-Milagros Rivera Garreta, one of its cofounders, who has published works such as *La diferencia sexual en la historia* (2005; Sexual difference in history).

However, it has been Paul B. Preciado (previously Beatriz), a non-Catalonian philosopher associated with Barcelona, who has given a real turn to feminist thought. His area of expertise is the politics of the body and queer theory, which the aforementioned group Cos i Textualitat led by Meri Torras also cultivates. In recent years, Preciado has collaborated with the Museo de Arte Contemporáneo de Barcelona (MACBA; Barcelona's Museum of Contemporary Art). Preciado has published pathfinding essays such as *Manifiesto contrasexual* (2011; Countersexual manifesto). To Preciado's work we should add that of

Gerard Coll-Planas, the current director of Centre d'Estudis Interdisciplinaris de Gènere (CEIG), also in this transgressive tendency.

Empowering Narrative

As for narrative fiction, it appears that currently there are no titles that have the symbolic power of Carmen Laforet's *Nada* (1945) in its day, or Carme Riera's early books. In 1994, poet Maria Mercè Marçal (1952–1998) was awarded the Premi Carlemany (Carlemany Prize) for her only novel *La passió segons Renée Vivien* (1994; The passion according to Renée Vivien), a work centred on lesbian love and for which she was also conferred the Crítica Serra d'Or (1995) and the Institució de les Lletres Catalanes (Institution of Catalan Letters; 1996). Her premature death in 1998 makes her the Catalan Virginia Woolf. In these last two decades, women writers have received more and more media attention, as is evidenced by Rosa Regàs receiving the fiftieth Planeta Prize in 2001 for *La Canción de Dorotea* (2001; Dorotea's Song). Publishers have discovered that the majority of readers are female and that readers are interested in the female world, which they have ignored. Thus, those who award prizes have seen the explosion of female voices as a threat and thus have decided to bury it under the umbrella of "women's literature," a label that refuses to disappear.

Among these writers, there are few (with some exceptions) who wave the purple flag, while the majority rejects the feminist label. At the same time, women have gained greater visibility; the new narrative devotes itself to exploring the female condition and empowers its protagonists. The result has been the normalization of the female voice in literary creation. Going one step further, now that we are well into the twenty-first century, we find even greater emphasis on the short autobiographical narrative of some writers like Llucia Ramis (b. 1977) and Najat El Hachmi (b. 1979), which delves deeply into female identity with renewed ambition and good prospects for the future.[17]

34 Galician Feminisms Post-1996

MARÍA DO CEBREIRO RÁBADE VILLAR

Dominant preoccupations of the 1990s in the field of literary production are sexualities and the body, as attested by Edicións Xerais's explicit attempt to cultivate erotic narrative by both male and female authors in the early and mid-1990s. Since then, sexuality has acquired a noticeable presence in poetry to the point that it became the main characteristic of a new generation of women writers whose most outstanding representative is Yolanda Castaño (b. 1977) – poet, video artist, television personality, translator, and cultural activist.

The body became central to critical discourse and is a distinctive element in the poetry written by women who began producing in the 1990s. Scholars such as Teresa Seara (2000) and Chus Nogueira (2008), and especially Helena González Fernández (2000, 2003, 2004), have devoted much critical effort to illuminating the way female voices function in the Galician literary field, contributing to making visible the growing incorporation of women in the literary and editorial world. However, by making eroticism a key to accessing poetry by women, feminist criticism in fact became a two-edged sword, since every time the body continues to be the principal mechanism by which to assess women's production, we operate within the patriarchal discourses that try to reduce women to their biological condition. Thus the celebration of eroticism by the 1990s poets, once processed and widely circulated, ended up conveying complex and even contradictory messages (Rábade Villar).

In 2005, Helena González examined this process in her *Elas e o paraugas totalizador* (Women and the totalizing umbrella), as well as in some essays on what she retrospectively called "a moda violeta" (González Fernández 2006, 2007, 2013; the violet mode, in which she assigned a value to women's (although not necessarily feminist) poetics. González, as the anthologist of the new millennium with the trilingual *A tribo das baleas* (2001; The tribe of whales), went against the indisputable media success of Yolanda Castaño's work by explicitly excluding Castaño's poetry from the anthology, one of the principal volumes of this generation. In the years immediately prior, Castaño converted the practice and discourse of physical beauty into one of her poetics' marks of identity and into the mainstay of her publishing and public success.

Given González's position as a feminist critic and her statements in the anthology's prologue, Castaño's exclusion is explained by the difficulty of accommodating her earlier work to the cultural agenda of literary feminism in Galicia. The poet had debuted in the artistic scene as a performer and audiovisual artist, showcasing a number of gender roles that were firmly implanted in the public imagination – the female vampire, the princess, and the pin-up, which, far from being seen as transgressive within feminist circles, could be perceived as a means to seal the most herteronormative aspects of femininity. The issue became further complicated when considering Yolanda Castaño's evolution as an author, whose understanding of beauty and eroticism evolved considerably, in large part as a result of reactions to her use of her body as an object of artistic practices during the prior decade (Rodríguez García 2011). This process is evident in her book of poetry *O libro da egoísta* (2003; The egotist's book), an interesting deconstruction of her previous poetics, but perhaps also a tentative construction of an authorial position from a place of greater "respectability" than that socially conceded to physical beauty. The same play of tensions that often arises when considering women's literary production is also evident in the well-publicized polemic between the poet and the group of comedians and graphic artists Aduaneiros sen Fronteiras (Customs Officers without Borders), whose most visible leader was the cultural activist Berto Yáñez (b. 1976). The group was forced to close its blog after protests from Castaño, who initiated actions against an entry in which she was treated as a cut-out doll surrounded by a parodic set of clothes.

Castaño's case illustrates many of the tensions that affect women's cultural production: from reactions from certain feminist thinking to the artistic and media use of sexuality, and even the intent on the part of authors themselves to reorient their literary trajectory by means of a public recantation of public reactions to treatments of the female body, even when it is problematized by the authors themselves. However, the exemplary nature of this case should not make us forget that the literary approach to the body was in fact very different in other poets from this generation. As an example, we can point to the three different positions represented by Lupe Gómez (b. 1972), Estíbalez Espinosa (b. 1974), and Olga Novo (b. 1975).

In her poetic manifesto *Pornografía* (1995; Pornography), Lupe Gómez's literary debut, the author is already displaying a grotesque and deliberately pro-ugly emphasis, further accentuated in later projects such as *Os teus dedos na miña braga con regra* (1999; Your fingers in my menstruated panties). Her literary position is situated between postporn and a romantic kitsch, in line with Portuguese Adília Lopes (Simões de Almeida, Bela, and Baltrusch 2007). The telluric eroticism of Olga Novo, displayed in books like *A teta sobre o sol* (The tit on the sun; 1996) and *Nós nus* (Us naked; 1997), has been read as ecofeminist (Fernández-Rodríguez 2009; Palacios 2009). However, perhaps its place in Galician literature belongs more to a landscape aesthetic that has been present in lyric discourse since the medieval troubadours and that was echoed in the naturalist and pantheist poetics of Rosalía de Castro. Finally, it is important to note the constant allusions in Estíbaliz Espinosa's poetry to queer and cyborg aesthetics, years before Teresa Moure introduced some of these questions in her *Queer-emos un mundo novo* (2012; We want a new queer world).

This discursive confrontation of models, which is more attentive to the plurality of actual practices than the search for thematic constants between authors, became the topic of a university course titled Demasiados Zapatos para una Cenicienta (Too many shoes for one Cinderella; 2007), organized by professors Germán Labrador and Pedro Serra in a summer session at the University of Salamanca. Through the importation of Galician literature into a prestigious Spanish university, the course legitimized the so-called *poetas de los noventa* (poets of the 1990s) more than a decade after the appearance of their first books. However, the experience, which also meant the coexistence and joint creation of the writers invited to participate in the course, actually constituted a swansong of their work. In the face of the tendency to write erotic poetry, a hallmark of women's literature, Demasiados Zapatos para una Cenicienta is a critical attempt to create means of escape and internal dialogue, underlining the plurality and even discrepancy of the active literary voices at the end of the century.

The reincorporation of the theme of maternity into contemporary Galician literature is only apparently unconnected to the cultural treatment of eroticism and therefore shares with it the ability to create a polemic beyond a strictly literary arena. Confined primarily to children's literature throughout the twentieth century,[18] in the mid 1990s poet Xela Arias (1962–2003) reintroduced motherhood in a highly innovative way in her book *Darío a diario* (1996; Darío daily). The author, who was also a literary translator (her premature death came as she was translating Jean Rhys's *The Wide Sargasso Sea* into Galician), was one of the salient voices in the Galician poetic underground of the 1980s and thus anticipated the explosion of female poetic eroticism in the 1990s in her transgressive poetic-photographic *Tigres como cabalos* (1990; Tigers like horses). In the first poem of her literary testament *Intempériome* (2003), she deals explicitly with AIDS in a similar way to her generational companion Lois Pereiro (1958–1996) – although importantly in a way that did not exclude gender – with many fewer repercussions in the media. Both Pereiro and Arias make Germán Labrador's (2009) hypothesis that contemporary Spanish poetry brilliantly conveys the poetic underground with intense proposals to rewrite the canonical culture of the Transition into a reality for Galician literature.

Well into the twenty-first century, maternity has become a locus of debate with antagonistic positions that bring once more to the fore the opposition between equality and difference feminisms, which were believed to have been overcome.[19] The point of departure can be found in Moure's essay *A palabra das fillas de Eva* (2004; The word of Eve's daughters), which begins with a passage in which the experience of giving birth is compared to erotic experience. It formulates questions such as:

> ¿Cantas descricións dun parto podemos atopar na literatura? ¿Cantas veces aparece a lactancia baixo a figura da nai-nutricia ou baixo a percepción, moi íntima, desa experiencia de pracer nas mulleres (unha experiencia, por certo, que é erótica tamén, aínda que a ollada masculina non a contemple como tal)? ¿Cantas veces a menstruación se converte nun motivo literario?" (2004, 24)

> (How many descriptions of a birth do we find in literature? How many times does breastfeeding under the figure of the mother-nurturer or under the very intimate perception of this pleasurable experience for women – an experience, certainly, that is also erotic, even though it is not perceived as such by the masculine eye? How often does menstruation become a literary motif?)

The book, then, was an attempt to undiscursify distinctly female experiences, especially those related to maternity, understood as a social and symbolically repressed practice. It is not surprising that a theoretical trip is not without contradictions and even dangers, but the affirmation that birth is discursive arises from the return to the biological,[20] especially by means of the defence of practices like nonmedicalized birth, cosleeping (where babies sleep in their parents' bed), and breastfeeding on demand. Thus, positions like these were openly challenged years later in the book *Maternosofía* (2014; Maternosophy) by the novelist and essayist Inma López Silva (b. 1978), object of an unfavourable review published in the blog of the feminist collective *A Sega*, where Susana Sánchez Aríns considers that "a autora para em conflitos superficiais que mantenhem ocultos os substanciais, os que afectam à configuração da identidade das mulheres e ao mantemento da ordem social no seu conjunto" (2014; the author emphasizes superficial conflicts that cover up the substantial ones, those that affect the configuration of women's identity and in general the maintenance of the social order).

Social discourses like lactation and new ways of caring for babies (above all, the so-called attachment method) have pervaded, with much force, all feminist debates in recent years. Often, however, the exchange of ideas is bound up with a series of presuppositions that tend to equate gender egalitarianism with a liberal-bourgeois, heterocentric, and institutionalized social orientation, in which difference feminism (here allied with the practice of breastfeeding) would be considered subversive. Once more, it is important to keep two premises in mind: (1) as Joan Scott (1992) would have it, the opposite of equality is not difference but inequality; and (2) that there is no woman but women, or as Rosi Braidotti says, "El sujeto 'mujer' no es una esencia monolítica definida de una vez y para siempre, sino que es más bien el sitio de un conjunto de experiencias múltiples, complejas y potencialmente contradictorias, definido por variables que se superponen tales como la clase, la raza, la edad, el estilo de vida, la preferencia sexual y otras" (Braidotti 2004, 30; The subject "woman" is not a monolithic essence defined once and for all, but is rather a site of a constellation of complex and potentially contradictory, multiple experiences defined by variables such as class, race, age, lifestyle, and sexual preferences, which are superimposed).

Examples like these emphasize that, as with all social movements, the history of feminism is the history of oppositions, of missed encounters, of struggles between positions adopted by their parties at specific times. Up to this moment, we have considered the discursive battlefields in regard to eroticism and maternity with the potential to reopen the old dialectic between equality and difference feminism. However, it is also important to take into account here the relationship between feminist practices and other discourses and social movements that, as we know, have not always been harmonious – except, perhaps, in the case of Begoña Caamaño Rascado (1964–2014), feminist, syndicalist, journalist, and author of the novels *Circe ou o pracer do azul* (Circe and the pleasure of the colour blue; 2009) and the multiawarded *Morgana en Esmelle* (Morgana in Esmelle; 2012). Along with feminist writer and radio personality Ana Romaní (b. 1962) and a group of women in media and communications, Caamaño Rascado was one of the driving forces behind the constitution of the Asociación de Mulleres Galegas na Comunicación (MUGACOM; Association of Galician Women in Communications), officially launched on 8 March, 1997. She is considered "unha voz imprescindible no feminismo galego" ("Begoña Caamaño Rascado") for her fierce antimilitarism, her commitment to social justice, and her activism against gender violence and in favour of women's right to choose (i.e., abortion).

In recent years, the influence of digital culture on these polemics has introduced interesting variables; social media constitute a privileged means of discussion, although other characteristics associated with them, such as immediacy or brevity, do not always make them ideal for the exchange of ideas. The Internet in general and Twitter in particular have become powerful mechanisms for denouncing micromachismo and as tools for making known those *machista* agressions that are not characterized as illegal and often socially unpunished or uncensored; the *piropo* (flattering remark made in public by a man to a woman), which is still a relatively common tradition in Iberian cultures, would be an example.

In this context, a polemic in 2015 confronted some well-known members of two kinds of Galician sociopolitical activism: feminists tied to a women's collective in the San Pedro neighbourhood of Santiago de Compostela and the reintegrationists, a type of political and cultural group that for decades advocated the linguistic unification of Galician and Portuguese. The polemic originated in an anonymous woman's accusation directed at the group Mulheres Feministas de Compostela (Feminist Women of Compostela), which was publicly disseminated in successive versions.[21] It referred to an episode of supposed intimidation on the part of the leader of Associaçom Galega da Língua (AGAL; Galician Association of the Language), who had initiated physical contact without the accuser's consent. The object of the accusation placed on her own personal blog, found on the official website of AGAL, a manifesto titled "Sobre as desculpas que (nom) me pedem"[22] (On the apologies that I have not received), where she gave her own version of what happened and announced that she would take legal action for slander.

In the ensuing days, the feminist movements linked to the first public denunciation painted the old section of the city with the slogan "Basta de agressons nos movementos sociais!" (Stop the aggressions on social media!). The sympathizers of the reintegrationist leader undertook a campaign on social media (especially on Facebook) employing the hashtag #susosacameabailar, with which they tried to defend the honour of the accused and vindicate a ludic attitude towards the body and relations between men and women in public space, under the assumption (implicit or explicit, depending on the viewpoint) that denouncing micromachismo could be considered a kind of puritanism.

What is interesting about this case were the reactions of those participants affected by double militancy. From the reintegrationist position, Xurxo Nóvoa Martins drafted a "Carta aberta ao macho militante" (Open letter to the militant macho), in which he evoked the well-known sentence of Emma Goldman, "Si no puedo bailar no es mi revolución" (If I cannot dance, it is not my revolution), in order to give it a twist and conclude: "Até aí tod@s de acordo. Mas depois é cada mulher a que decide com quem (ela ou ele) dançar ou se preferir dançar em roda, ou sozinha. Uma cousa nom exclui a outra. Junt@s na diversidade com alegria, respeito e consciência, eis o lindo caminho que muit@s querem/os construir" (2015; Up to that point, we are in agreement. However afterwards it is each woman who decides with whom – her or him – to dance or to prefer to dance in a circle or a line. One thing does not exclude another. Together in diversity with joy, respect, and conscience is the beauty of the road that together we want to construct). In the opposite direction, Teresa Moure traced a defence in accordance with her ties to feminism and as a significant member of AGAL. On 24 July 2015, the writer placed the following declaration on her Facebook page:

> Sou feminista. Quero um mundo de mulheres livres. Mas acho que mulheres e homens podem tocar-se o braço para convidarem-se a bailar, que não há nisso agressão nenhuma. Talvez cumpra repensarmos muitos assuntos mas nunca nunca nunca tornar o feminismo, que nasceu para libertar, numa intimidação, numa ameaça que vigie e puna, numa procura

de cabeça de turco. E sinto muito ter que levantar a voz para significar-me mas o bom nome das pessoas merece respeito e cuidados. (Moure 2015)

(I am a feminist. I want a world of free women. But I find that women and men can touch the arm to invite [someone] to dance, that there is no aggression on that [action]. Maybe we should rethink many issues, but never, never, never turn feminism, which was born to free [us], into an intimidation, a threat that patrols and penalizes, seeking a Turk's head. And I am sorry to have to raise my voice to signify me, but the good name of the people deserves respect and care.)

Beyond the anecdotal value of these and other positions, the incident constitutes proof of the difficulties feminism has had in finding a comfortable, stable space within social movements, as well as a way in which to reconcile the double militancies – in Galicia, fundamentally, the feminist and nationalist, which cannot always coexist in a harmonious way in the public space. From the point of view of constructing a social and cultural history, the case just narrated illustrates the importance of taking into consideration new platforms and mechanisms of construction for a social dialogue, which is more and more decisive in the symbolic articulation of the contemporary world.

To conclude, I call attention to the several pivotal contributions that have sought to participate in the social dialogue by historicizing Galician feminism on diverse fronts. In 2005, Editorial Trymar published volumes 1 and 2 of the series Mulleres Galegas Ilustres (Famous Galician Women), respectively titled *Mulleres mais que mitos* (2005a; Women more than myths) and *Ousadas e valentes* (2005b; Daring and brave), both authored by Ana María Castro y Antonio. In 2006, Castro y Antonio also published with Editorial Trymar, a two set CD; *A Historia do Feminismo en Galicia: 1* (2006a; The history of Galician feminism: 1) and *A Historia do Feminismo en Galicia: As protagonistas* (2006b; The history of Galician feminism: The protagonists). Lastly in 2007, and once again with Trymar, Castro y Antonio came out with *Mulleres revolucionarias* (Revolutionary women). In 2009, the Fundación Galiza Sempre (Galicia Always Foundation) was behind the itinerant 2009–10 exhibition titled *Feminismo Galego: Cambios Sociais e Dereito das Mulleres* (Galician Feminism: Social Changes and Women's Rights), delineating the trajectory of Galician feminisms from the 1800s to the present (see www.galizasempre.org.microsites/feminismo-galego).[23] In the summer of 2010, the foundation also published the reproduction of 22 *documentos do Feminismo Galego* (Twenty-two documents of Galician feminism), which includes pamphlets and manifestos from 1975 to 2003 (www.galizasempre.org/biblioteca/22-documentos-do-feminismo-galego). Also in 2010, Monica Bar Cendón, member of the editorial board of the journal *Festa da Palabra Silenciada* (Festival of the silenced word), published her monumental *Feministas galegas: Claves dunha revolución en marcha* (Galician feminists: Keys of an ongoing revolution), which was presented in Vigo on 17 March 2010 by María Xosé Queizán, a leading feminist in Galician letters, and Manuel Bragado, the general director of Edicións Xerais (for feminism and nationalism in Queizán, see Thompson 2011).

The Comisión de Igualdade do Consello da Cultura Galega (Galician Cultural Council Commission on Equality) similarly contributed to chronicling the history of Galician feminism by publishing *Recuperación da documentación e memoria do Movemento Feminista Organizado en Galicia* (2013; Recovery of the documents and memory of the Organized Feminist Movement in Galicia), coordinated by Carmen Pérez Pais and Mariam Mariño Costales, both affiliated with the Galician Council of Culture's Commission on Equality. The project, divided into three periods – 2005–8, 2008–10, and 2011–12 – focuses on the identification of organizations, groups, women's book stores, journals, fliers, posters, newspaper clippings, banners, recordings, and interviews in order to unify under one umbrella documents and information that are scattered or missing. Also in 2013, Marisol Rodríguez Rodríguez and Helena Miguélez-Carballeira called attention to feminist positions in the narratives of Xohana Torres, María Xosé Queizán, Carmen Blanco y Teresa Moure (Rodríguez Rodríguez and Miguélez-Carballeira 2013). All of these projects attest to the need for recovering and preserving diverse bodies of feminist documents to further social dialogue.

35 Multifaceted Feminism: Promoting Diversity in the Twenty-First-Century Basque Country

JONE M. HERNÁNDEZ GARCÍA

Proclaiming a feminist crisis has become a commonplace in some sectors of feminist writing culture. In a large part of the West, including the Basque Country, the feminist movement is having trouble attracting participants. As has been noted in chapter 29 above, the advances made in achieving feminist goals may have caused recent generations to believe that feminist activism is no longer necessary. María Martínez (2007) analyses the debate that arose over the existence of a younger generation of feminists, an innovative third wave, which will advance alongside so-called postfeminism. Is this "third wave" reinventing feminism by adding "new" perspectives to those already in existence? Many of the analyses of the history of feminism point out its plural nature, an aspect that has tended to be considered an obstacle to the advance of its agenda instead of an opportunity to decolonize feminism (Gandarias and Pujol 2013) and recognize the richness that a variety of agencies, themes, discourses, visions, practices, and experiences imply.

The present chapter addresses this historic diversity and suggests that confronting and promoting it will be one of the future challenges of feminism. The aims of this chapter are: first, to detail the multifaceted nature of feminism by understanding its different motivations and dimensions as elements integrated into its development; second, to undertake a brief overview of the different dimensions of Basque feminism, citing some of its salient and documented aspects; and third, to point out some ideas oriented towards confronting the aforementioned challenge of diversity. The focus is on different practical aspects of Basque feminism in the most recent decades, grouped together in two sections; the first deals with rights, mobilizations, and militancies and the second with the knowledge and articulation of the proposals.

The fight for equal rights has been a common goal of feminism since its origins. In the case of the Basque Country, as in other areas of the West, the rights that feminism seeks have been many and varied; but in the period covered by this part of the volume (1996 to the present), those measures tied to the labour world, sexual violence, homosexuality, and abortion have been prioritized. The important incorporation of women into the working world during the years from 1970 to 1990 is reflected in the agenda of the incipient Basque feminist movement. In fact, during these decades issues related to work are at the centre of Basque feminism. Basque feminists' claims are similar to those in other geographical contexts – employing women within the economic system (their incorporation during times of plenty and their expulsion in periods of crisis), salary discrimination, the segregation in work or lack of recognition for work performed by women. These problems are the basis for many present demands. Special attention is given to the movements initiated by women in certain companies in the Basque industrial complex[24] – women demanding their rights as workers or denouncing their husbands' or other family members' working conditions.[25] For example, protests occurred in the arena of public service entities (sanitation, geriatric care, household service, school cafeterias, etc.), asking for improvements in the working environment and recognition of work carried out by women in sectors that are clearly feminized. Also, one should mention the cases of rural women, whose unions' and associations' demands have recently received attention in 2012 via a law that regulates 50% of the distribution of economic benefits and title to their husbands' agrarian resources. Special mention is due to the collective of female domestic workers, a union that, in the Basque case, has been closely tied to feminism since its beginnings. The association of workers has posed a challenge to the sector and played a key role in the gains that have been made. Today the recognition of the political and economic nature of domestic work continues to form part of the feminist agenda (Epelde, Aranguren, and Retolaza 2015, 505). Finally, I note the debates taking place in the heart of the feminist movement about prostitution – the search for new approaches and proposals for action; for example, in the 1980s, several associations sought an improvement in sex workers' quality of life.

Combating sexual violence has been a key part of the Basque feminist agenda.[26] All groups and assemblies had some system or organ charged with initiating protests and mobilizations whenever an act of sexual violence occurred. In the 1970s and 1980s, the priority was action rather than theory. Already in the 1980s, different state groups joined together to demand changes in the penal code. Besides the legal vindications, another of the urgent tasks was to publicize beatings and other mistreatment, the majority of which remained invisible within the domestic realm. Cases of violence against women are especially pernicious, because women interiorize a deep sense of guilt and are reluctant to denounce their situation. Thus, feminism has decided to call special attention to this problem, employing various strategies – holding special days about the topic, demanding services to attend to victims (like refuge homes), street demonstrations, and denouncing all types of violence. In recent years, one could say that the response to violence has increased (more attendance at protest rallies), diversified (the formation of new ways to eradicate the problem), and has even been institutionalized, as in the actions taken in connection with the events each 25 November, the International Day for the Elimination of Violence Against Women, as designated by the United Nations General Assembly. In recent years, the Basque Country has actively participated in events focused on denouncing gender-based violence, with multiple initiatives geared to raise public awareness on the many aspects of violence against women.

Basque feminism has made two proposals regarding domestic violence. On the one hand Basque feminists emphasize the importance of self-defence[27] as a means of confronting violence, and since the 1980s, there have been a number of self-defence courses for women throughout Euskal Herria. On the other hand, analyses of violence have gained in sophistication, which is more and more understood as a problem with many faces and expressions, an approach to which would require the deconstruction of the heteronormative model (Epelde, Aranguren, and Retolaza 2015, 482–3) and the participation of several agents.

Denouncing the limits imposed on female sexuality, its ties to reproduction, and a challenge to the heterosexual model have been some of the proposals that feminism has laid out throughout its development and that have also echoed in the Basque realm.[28] Also, since the 1980s, lesbianism and its political dimension have been the subject of a number of campaigns.[29] The creation of spaces of their own for lesbians (Elpelde, Aranguren, and Retolaza 2015, 493) and even the use itself of the concept *lesbian* has given rise to different perspectives. These could be placed in two groups: (1) those who view lesbianism as a sexual option and who demand recognition of lesbian rights; and 2) those who see lesbianism as a political position from which to combat heteronormativity. This second type of proposal has found helpful support in queer theory and the so-called transfeminism, positions within Basque feminism since the beginning of the 2000s. Since then, different groups have been developing initiatives centred on the vindication of what they consider issues that have been marginalized by feminism – pornography, transsexuality, and prostitution (Epelde, Aranguren, and Retolaza 2015, 497). The transexual movement and transfeminism are today active within the Basque feminist movement.

Free and open-access abortion is a demand that has been present in Basque feminism up to the present time and that, in practice, gathers together other equally paradigmatic demands for feminism, such as the right to decide and to govern one's own body. Abortion has also contributed to uncovering other struggles, such as those of class, since in reality the need for an abortion does not play out in the same way in the different social classes. The motivation, reflection, and debate generated by the abortion issue are reflected in the legal proceedings against the "Eleven of Basauri" (Las 11 de Basauri), a turning point in Basque feminism – and documented in the introduction to part 6 and in other chapters of this volume[30] – that in its day served as a motivator for feminist activism. As a result of feminist pressure, in 1985 a legal reform decriminalized abortion in three cases. This reform did not please feminists, who, since then, have continued the tension surrounding this issue. As an example of this situation are the 1987 protests in Pamplona about public health personnel's refusal to perform abortions, and the successful protests in 2014 over the proposal by Rajoy's conservative government to curtail abortion rights (also discussed in the introduction to part 6). Lastly, and relevant to abortion issues, we need to note the family-planning centres fomented by Basque feminism,[31] resources that have been integrated into the public health system with the primary objective to inform, counsel, and help women become knowledgeable in their sexual rights. Because of their feminist commitment, these spaces have acquired a political character (Elpede, Aranguren, and Retolaza 2015, 447).

How has Basque feminist militancy developed in the last few years? Mari Luz Esteban states that "a partir de finales de los años ochenta del siglo pasado, las asociaciones se van adelgazando y el feminismo deja de estar tan presente en la calle" (Esteban 2015, 64; as of the end of the 1980s, the associations became smaller, and feminism stopped being a public presence). The histories of Spanish feminism talk about fragmentation and segmentation, and the end of collective action (Martínez

2008). All of this, as Martínez points out, was fundamentally influenced by (1) the development of public and/or private organizations linked to equal opportunities, (2) the increase in women's groups that substituted the vindicative approach with a desire for participation, and (3) the consolidation of an academic feminism that interacted with the feminist movement. There was a sense that feminism was dissolving, but when faced with achieving rights, it revived and took to the streets. The public space evoked women's struggles and has an important presence in the public consciousness, not only as the scene of mobilizations but also as an object of feminist demands (Epelde, Aranguren, and Retolaza 2015, 545–82). The feminist Okupation (*okupación*, with k to indicate its connection to the Okupa Movement), the participation in local festivals, the right to enjoy an evening out, and the growing protagonism of women artists and creators are examples of the feminist transformation of the public arena, a line of action that both the queer movement and transfeminism especially emphasize.

Thus, the street becomes one of the central spaces for the coming together of feminism. And along with the street, the body emerges as an articulating nucleus of mobilization and militancy – the body as a central theme in feminism – abortion, sexuality, violence, prostitution; the body as a motor of action and resistence; the body as material to work and mould in becoming a woman, feminist, or any other option.[32] The mobilization and militancy of the past and present of Basque feminism could also be narrated from its bodies.

In 1994, the trajectory of the Seminario de Estudios de la Mujer/Emakumeari Buruzko Ikerketarako Mintegia (SEM/EBIM; Seminary of the Study of Women) ended, which had been created in 1981 to encourage the study of the situation and reality of Basque women, a commitment that Basque academic feminism had been developing in different phases (Hernández and Imaz 2010) in order to form a clearly expanding sector. Over the years, a great deal of research and publications have been generated, and also different resources have arisen to support research and education.[33] It is also important to point to the increasing presence of feminist and gender studies at the postgraduate level. The first masters degree program in Women's and Men's Equality at the Universidad del País Vasco (UPV/EHU; University of the Basque Country) was launched in 2001, and since the 2009/2010 academic year, this degree has been offered online. The University of Deusto has offered a masters in Intervention in Violence against Women since 2003; in the 2008/2009 academic year, the UPV/EHU initiated the university masters in Feminist and Gender Studies and a doctorate with the same title.[34] In addition, the Public University of Navarre (UPNA) offers a degree Experto/a en Género (Expert in Gender).

From the philosophy of self-consciousness (Esteban 2014, 66) to the special feminist days, with all the lectures, informal conversations, round tables, and forums, knowledge and feminist theories have become notably enriched and diversified, which has also generated distrust and tensions. The increasing specialization, professionalization, and hierarchization of knowledge, along with the growth of a "culture of experts" and a hegemonic academic culture, have imposed forms of management and dissemination of knowledge that do not always coincide with the premises espoused by feminism as a locus committed to the production of knowledge. Esteban (2015, 70) emphasizes the role acquired recently by the Casas de Mujeres (Women's Houses), particularly by the empowerment schools in the sphere of knowledge and education. This kind of initiative – of a local nature – was set in motion at the beginning of the 2000s. In them, different types of feminism and women of all strata attended courses and activities with varied content, a type of experience that meant "un salto cualitativo en la formación feminista" (Esteban 2015, 72; a qualitative leap in feminist education).

One important aspect in the development of feminism was the dissemination of feminist thought and proposals. A number of different media contributed to this dissemination – publications as well as pamphlets, posters, fanzines, and more recently the Internet: magazines such as *Leioa* (the name of a municipality in Biscay where many feminist meetings have taken place), which began publication in 1977; *Geu Emakumeok* (We women; 1985–95), linked to the Asamblea de Mujeres de Bizkaia (Assembly of Women of Biscay); *Sorginak* (Witches), journal of the Colectivo de Lesbianas Feministas de Euskadi (Feminist Lesbian Collective of the Basque Country); and *Lanbroa* (Mist), publication of the group with the same name. In 2002, the collective Bilgune Feminista (Feminist Meeting Spaces) published the journal *Emaraun* (Women's network), now an online informational bulletin. The appearance of *Andra* (Woman) in 2001 was an important event, but this journal is no longer published. *Frida*, another feminist communication project published initially in 2005, suffered the same fate. The gap left by both initiatives was covered by *Pikara magazine* (Clever magazine), an online journal created in 2010 that had a large social impact.

By way of conclusion, I call attention to the way in which Basque feminism faces the task of articulating its different proposals and initiatives, a dimension of feminist work that says a great deal about its nature and peculiarities. Again we face the notion of fragmentation and the absence of a consistent network of relations among collectives (Sobrado and Aierdi 1997). A difficulty overcome in part by (1) the existence of provincial assemblies,[35] (2) the importance of personal relations as a bridge between people and collectives, and (3) the creation of ad hoc platforms for the organization of demonstrations and concrete events. An interesting topic of debate would be the existence of a common Basque-feminist identity. Also remaining to be determined is how the emerging feminist tendencies – such as queer and transfeminist[36] – encompass and engage with already-existing proposals of a more traditional nature.

At the beginning of the twenty-first century, it seems as though the fragmentation would have disappeared, not only for internal reasons but also because of global changes that affect social movements. As has occurred with other issues (e.g., ecology), the generalization of feminist discourse would have carried with it a transfer of feminist practice to individual space obliging us to rethink the feminist subject and the weight of the group on its identity. Martínez asks if it is possible to construct a collective identity that embraces the plurality (Martínez 2008). Judith Butler (2007) suggests a feminism based on a coalition, which would abandon the goal of unity as an expression of a political identity based on essentialism, an identity that ends up provoking resistances and ruptures in the interior of the movements (Alves de Atayde 2011, 145). It is probably time to put new notions of identity into practice, or perhaps reformulate the idea of identity itself. Basque feminism could be advancing this trend; an example would be Martínez's proposal (2008) of an archipelago identity in which different feminist groups are not independent of each other but are interrelated by diverse means. It would be a model similar to that proposed by the theory of the Community of Practices (CoP), a suggestion that feminism is employing in contexts such as that linked to feminist linguistics of the Third Wave (Mills and Mullany 2011, 70). Penelope Eckert and Sally McConell-Ginet define the CoP as "an aggregate of people who come together around mutual engagement in some common endeavor. Ways of doing things, ways of talking, beliefs, values, power relations – in short, practices – emerge in the course of their joint activity around that endeavor" (1992, 464).

In this view of the collective, the emphasis is on practices, charged with socially structuring the group and helping to shape concrete aspects or abstract ideas such as *gender identity*. The objective would be to observe the way in which feminism – beyond theory – takes shape today in day-to-day activities, paying special attention to the elements that contribute to creating the business (or community) of Basque feminism in the twenty-first century, not so much from the definition of the feminist as from doing – something that has influenced the analysis of identities. This type of proposal opens up a different way to foment the diversity of feminism, prioritizing the practical aspects implied in its adherence to a group. This suggestion obliges us to respond to new questions that will surely occupy the Basque feminist agenda in the twenty-first century: what do we talk about when we talk about feminist practice?

36 Bodies and Feminist Politics in Basque Society

MARI LUZ ESTEBAN

The new century confirmed the continuity of Basque feminism; in the last decades, the associative movement has experienced a decrease and less impact on the streets, if we compare it to that of the 1980s, but it has continued to be an important reference point that reinvents itself. In addition, institutional, academic, and professional feminism has grown significantly. The fourth (and last) Jornadas Feministas de Euskal Herria (Basque Feminist Meetings), which took place in Portugalete (Biscay) in April 2008, began with the drum rolls of the Lesbianbanda de Valencia (see figure 5). In a context like ours of legal equality and changes for women and feminists, although the future is uncertain, opening a meeting with the beating of drums is a great idea; the music and the meetings help conjure up phantoms and convince us that, in spite of differences and difficulties, harmony and the future are possible.[37] This experience is also a perfect example of how a social movement like feminism is constructed by means of group activities of all kinds that mobilize and put individual feminist bodies into contact to form a collective body, in the sense of unfolding, renovating, and articulating an emotion and a shared energy completely imbued with ideology. This is best summarized in the words of Argentine Silvia Palumbo, founder of the Lavender Band project: "espacio expresivo, creativo y reflexivo" (Palumbo n.d.; an expressive, creative, and reflexive space). In its wake, feminist percussion bands have cropped up in both Latin America and Spain in recent years.

The reference to the event and these practices are also a good introduction to this chapter, whose principal objective is to offer a brief history of recent Basque feminism, with special attention to the relations between bodies and politics, and to feminist political bodies. This is the

Figure 5. Feminist bands playing in the end of the year festivity of the Schools of Empowerment of Biscay, Ondarroa (Biscay), June 2011 (copyright Iñaki Delgado Iriondo, with permission).

axis of analysis that many authors such as Mari Luz Esteban consider central to studying social movements in general and that has identity, lifestyle, and political implications. The concept of body that underlies this chapter is not biomedical but pertains, rather, to social-science proposals that take into account the symbolic, phenomenological, material, and agency dimensions.[38]

Feminist Body Politics and Feminist Political Bodies

By body politics, I refer to the actions carried out by a movement (in this case the feminist movement), which directly, explicitly takes bodies as prioritized or privileged elements of denouncing, vindication, resignification, and action.[39] However, in a wider sense, all politics are corporal, in that they always act "with" and "from" bodies. From the social theory of the body, developed at the end of the 1980s, we can affirm that all significant transformations in social or political praxis necessarily imply a reconceptualization of the corporeal; and the reverse, that all reconfiguration of the corporeal also carries with it an alternative to formulating subjectivity and individual and collective action.[40]

And what is more, we could say that to become a feminist is no more than to configure and reconfigure, consciously or unconsciously, our corporality, our subjectivity and intersubjectivity, our "being-in-the-world" (Merleau-Ponty 1962), our individual and collective action in a way that casts a critical eye on cultural mandates. Although it can provoke tensions and contradictions, feminism teaches us to privilege practising freedom over submission, action over passivity, revealing over covering up, strength over fragility, exercising pleasure in the face of danger, just to give a few examples (Esteban 2011, 52).

In relation to the foregoing, the notion of a political body (Esteban 2011) can recall those representations, images, ideas, attitudes, techniques, and conducts incarnated in and consciously or unconsciously promoted by a social movement (in this case, feminism) that individually or collectively takes specific form. A body politic always carries with it concrete ways to understand the person, gender, social relations, and looking, knowing, and interacting with the world, and at the same time supposes ways (or at least attempts) to resist, answer, and/or modify reality.

There has not been, nor is there, nor will there be a single feminist body politic, even if we take into consideration our analysis of the last decades in the Basque Country, in which we have identified different ideological and strategic positions, as well as concrete geographic and cultural specifics of feminism. One of the dominant political bodies in Basque society is the plural reproductive body, including the self-help body, the body of contraception and abortion laws, and the sexual and maternal bodies, just to name a few bodies with different characteristics and meanings – some current, others not. Other political bodies that are relevant within diverse collective actions, topics, and activities are those that refer to aesthetics/image,[41] art,[42] lesbianism,[43] queer theory,[44] and actions against gender violence, war,[45] or discrimination in employment and job insecurity.[46] The principal characteristics of political bodies is that, by means of attitudes, techniques, and diverse activities (appearing nude, painting or adornment, wearing costumes, different ways of occupying public space, of interacting, etc.), they denounce a whole range of situations of oppression and inequality while simultaneously defending a number of vindications – always from an affirmation of the existence and social presence of women and feminists. Feminist bodies appear in the public arena, and when they resignify themselves and the spaces they occupy, they resignify the world; that is to say, they are agents of response, transgression, and questioning stereotypes, values, and differential assignations of spaces, powers, and times. In the following pages, I will comment on the principal traits of the political bodies of Basque feminism that I consider most significant, while also identifying some of these bodies' limitations – restrictions and boundaries of feminist policies – as well as their theoretical and practical potential.

As mentioned earlier, reproductive political bodies have been an identity marker and a principal feminist action, a standard of vindication, a primordial political lever, subject and object of actions whose meaning has gone beyond the reproductive sphere. In the Basque case, the campaigns in favour of the right to abortion initiated at the end of the 1970s and early 1980s in response to the trial of the eleven women of Basauri (Biscay) are crucial to second-wave feminism, with repercussions for the entire Spanish state.[47] During the period from 1976 to 1985, the year in which those trials came to an end and the moment in which the first Spanish abortion law was passed, the streets of the principal Basque (and Spanish) cities filled with women demonstrating in favour of control of their own bodies.[48]

In 2013 during the world financial crisis, the Spanish government under the control of the conservative, right-wing Partido Popular (PP; Popular Party) attempted to reform the abortion law to make it more restrictive. This provoked a reaction in all segments of the feminist movement and in a broad sector of social and professional circles, since the majority of the population was against such reform. Although the attempts by Mariano Rajoy's government to curtail abortion rights ended in failure, the process made clear that feminist gains are not definitive and signalled the collusion of capitalism and patriarchy. Silvia Federici stressed that "quieren conquistar el cuerpo de la mujer porque el capitalismo depende de él … Si no está el control sobre el cuerpo de la mujer, no hay control de la fuerza de trabajo" (they want to conquer women's bodies because capitalism depends on it [said body] ... If there is no control over the body of a woman, there is no control of the workforce).[49]

Likewise, feminism has been compelled to renew and adapt itself by putting into practice diverse protests and passive resistance actions. One of the actions from the Basque Country that impacts the media is the activity called *encerrona* (to lock oneself inside a location) organized by Plataforma Abortatzeko Eskubidea (Right to Abortion) on 27 December 2014. In this instance, women locked themselves inside the Hospital de Cruces (Barakaldo, Biscay), one of the most important within the Basque Health Network.[50] In contrast to what has occurred before on similar occasions, the Ertzaintza (Basque Police) ousted the participants, who were resisting passively, by dragging them one by one. Since a crew from the state television channel La Sexta (The Sixth) was there, the process was broadcast live on television and social networks. This situation had a national impact because the cameras showed public performances by the activists from the group Femen, naked from the waist up and with slogans in favour of abortion written in their bodies. The performance with the most widespread impact was conducted in the Spanish Parliament on 9 October 2013.[51]

In addition to the campaigns related to abortion, at the end of the 1970s and early 1980s, when attention to public health was very deficient, Basque feminism (along with feminism in Madrid and Catalonia) was a pioneer in establishing family-planning centres. On this issue, feminists were operating from a philosophy that defended sexual pleasure and the right to birth control. However, despite the vindicative and transforming dimension of all these actions, feminist reproductive policies have had to be much more circumscribed within the epistemological borders of biomedical discourse that medicalizes and naturalizes women's being and constructs the female body in a completely homogeneous way in clear opposition to the masculine. Even so, feminists have been critical of Western scientific representations and have known how to reappropriate biomedical technologies, making way for proposals with a significant theoretical-conceptual and revulsive potential. One such example is found in the political and artistic actions focused on menstruation that have been gaining traction in the Basque context in the decade 2000–10, above all among young women. One of the fundamental axes of this camp, besides the defence of an ecological movement and an alternative to menstrual blood, has to do with the equation woman-reproduction-impurity within the framework of very different initiatives – workshops, books, fanzines, graffiti, expositions.[52]

Another important dimension of feminist corporality is that sexuality is central to how European and North American feminism is configured within perfectly delimited cultural biopolitics. Consequently, sexuality has been and is a crucial factor in pleasure, agency, transgression, and subversion, and occupies a preferred place. Basque feminists have participated in the debates of recent decades on sexuality and maternity – sexuality as pleasure and danger, lesbianism, and pornography.[53]

However, one of the events that marks a before and an after in the field of sexuality in the Basque sphere was the meetings of Porno Punk Feminism in Arteleku, an alternative art space in Donostia (Gipuzkoa) in July 2008. The meetings were organized by Beatriz (Paul) Preciado and the Medeak group as a way to explore "la pornografía como una de las tecnologías biopolíticas de producción y normalización del cuerpo, del género, de la sexualidad y del placer en las sociedades postindustriales" (http://old.arteleku.net/programa-es/archivo/feminismopornopunk; pornography as one of the biopolitical technologies for the production and normalization of the body, gender, sexuality, and pleasure in postindustrial societies).

One topic that has been acquiring importance in the last years, both in the Basque and Spanish context, has been violence against women, which has become a major problem and one that institutional measures are clearly insufficient to curb.[54] One of the principal strategies developed by Basque feminists has been the organization of courses and workshops on self-defence, directed mostly at young women for the purpose of consciousness raising about the roots of violence and training in physical and emotional techniques that allow women to confront a situation of mistreatment or aggression.[55] However, if reproduction and sexuality and, to a lesser degree, violence against women are privileged dimensions in feminist body politics, there are other aspects that remain hidden – especially regarding social class and precarious labour markets. However, this does not mean that they are not central to the generation of gender inequality (especially in times of crisis) or to aging in a society that privileges youth.[56] For feminists, who are also influenced by hegemonic culture, some topics are more glamorous than others, more or less subversive. The danger is not only that these other matters remain in second place, but they can unconsciously be fomenting ways of life and identity and practical configurations that do not completely break the dominant ideologies.

Caregiving is another important feminist theme today and historically in the Basque context. In this realm, there is a certain lack of consistency between theory and its practical application. In the last few years, images have circulated of famous men caring for people of various ages, as a way of vindicating the need to share domestic responsibilities. Strangely, in contradiction to other feminist political bodies it is the masculine body that allows the projection of feminist vindications.

By way of conclusion, I underline that the most current feminist theories invite us to challenge various dichotomies – I/body, feminine/masculine, reason/emotion – and to understand ourselves as incarnated agents, which allows us to invent and put into practice alternative modes of diagnosis, reflection, and action. We are invited to think *as* bodies, bodies that are objects and subjects at the same time and that can open for us – are in fact already opening for us now – new possibilities to revise, integrate, and/or reformulate ideas, experiences, and debates that have been there since feminism was feminism.

Epilogue. Some Remarks on *Gender Indifference* and the Eulogy of the *Margins*

FINA BIRULÉS[1]

In recent years it has been constantly repeated that the victorious, non-violent revolution of the twentieth century has been that of women; and it is true that far-reaching changes have flowed from this notion, ranging from the critique of androcentric science to women's rights to sexual freedom; from the integration of women into almost every sphere of culture and the labour market to their public pursuit of leisure; from changes in everyday customs to the increased presence of women at the summits of economic, institutional, and political power.[2] Some have talked of the "death of patriarchy," asserting that men's power is only real while women accept seeing themselves as inferior (Librería de Mujeres de Milán 1996). However, this should not allow us to forget that many inequalities still persist, and that the end of a tradition does not necessarily mean that traditional ideas have lost their power over individual minds; on the contrary, it sometimes seems that the power of outworn categories and ideas becomes more tyrannical as tradition loses its vitality.[3] Historically and within Spain, nowhere was this more evident than in December 2013, when the Spanish government ruled by the People's Party (PP) sought to present sweeping reforms to the 2010 abortion laws to fulfil 2011 election promises. The reforms – to allow abortion only in cases of rape or risk to a mother's health – were immediately questioned and contested as setting back women's rights to Francisco Franco's times. One of the most vocal and emblematic protests was carried out by a collective movement of feminist women from Gijón and Barredos (both in Asturias) who bought train tickets to arrive in Madrid on 1 February 2014, in order to show up on the steps of Congress and request a withdrawal of the proposals, thus launching El Tren de la Libertad (The Freedom Train). This action led antiabortion law opponents, including thousands of men, to do the same from other locations across the country. The Freedom Train achieved its objective when, in September 2014, Prime Minister Mariano Rajoy announced the tabling of the reforms to the 2010 abortion laws until further notice.

These shifts in women's lives are the results of many historic moments of feminist struggle, but they originate particularly in what we now call the second wave of feminism. Contemporary feminism is largely the fruit of a generation that, we could say, discovered for themselves the experience of politics and felt the enthusiasm and power that came from collectively taking the initiative in the public realm, in such a way that (as some of those involved have commented) political action even turned out to be fun:[4] a courageous generation with a powerful will to action and remarkable confidence in their ability to redesign the public sphere. In fact, second-wave feminism was a creative insurrection aspiring to respond to events and give rise to new relationships and ways of seeing the world without reference to sacred texts, so that it became embodied as practice, as a form of action without models.[5] And, in fact, there was no global vision of a future society but rather the will constantly to engage in and accept the risks of action, with the result that feminism was never easily reducible to any formula or banner (Collin 1986, 10; 2010–11, 9). This defining feature, alien to modern revolutionary movements, gave birth to a whole range of different lines of action, a wide variety of currents and tendencies often in conflict with each other. Rather than a protest movement, feminism is an explosion of freedom. But however we understand it, freedom always involves at the very least the autonomy to dissent: to be free, to say "yes" or "no" is one of the basic liberties of the person. In other words, and as Hannah Arendt observed, before Stalin and Hitler no other leader had argued against the freedom to say "yes": Hitler excluded the Jews and the gypsies from the right to assent, and Stalin eliminated his most enthusiastic supporters, "perhaps because he thought that whoever said yes could also say no" (Arendt 1972, 221). The feminists of the 1970s put all of the stress on their freedom to say "no" to the dominant forms of femininity inherited from the androcentric tradition and on their decision to take up new ways of speaking "the feminine." Now, it is worth remarking that, in contrast, many current postfeminists say "yes" to pornography, to prostitution, and to playing the role of a hyperbolic femininity, opposing what they consider to be the conservatism or puritanism of the femininity inherited from second-wave feminism. Also, they appear to have decided to take up new ways of speaking "the masculine." What does this mean?

Here I will limit myself to making a few comments on this question, but before that, in order to approach this phenomenon, we should bear in mind some of the major shifts of the last three decades. First, women as a group have gained active access to the erotic, a change that seems to have been accompanied by the desacralization and/or technification of eroticism. Second, we have seen changes in parenting, especially maternity – we could even say that the French women's slogan from the beginning of the 1970s, "A child if I want and when I want,"[6] has been surpassed with astonishing efficiency by technical-scientific advances: we have gone from "a child if I want" to "the child that I want," not to speak of surrogate motherhood (the only reproductive option not included in the laws on assisted reproduction in Spain). Third, the associative networks of feminism have diminished in strength, visibility, and the ability to innovate, and in some variants and locations, feminist discourse has ceased to be revolutionary and has become institutionalized. One such example at the national level is the 1983 founding of the Instituto de la Mujer (Institute for Women) with the express purpose of promoting women's equality thoroughly questioned by difference feminists (see Brooksbank Jones 1995). In Catalonia, L'Institut Català de les Dones (ICD; The Catalan Institute for Women) is the body of the government (Generalitat) that formulates, promotes, coordinates, and evaluates policies for gender equality. Both agencies emblematize forms of state feminism.

Thus, for some time now it has been said that feminism has been civilized, domesticated, and that the cutting-edge protest movement, heir to nineteenth-century projects of emancipation and twentieth-century insurrectionary movements, has gradually been turned into a form of state feminism, so that, as institutions often do, it seems to manage the ideal of a homogeneous society where everyone is interchangeable, as if politics could be reduced to the language of statistics and figures. In addition, the system of parties and elections in which institutional feminism is embedded, although it may represent the interests of voters, does not place the latter participants in the public sphere but instead expels them from it; this has meant that the new generation has not been attracted to what they see as outcomes of the "old" feminism.[7] Also, with the reconciliation between one wing of the feminist movement and the institutions, it seems that directly or indirectly it has granted the state – an institution of patriarchal origin – the power to regulate the normal representation of sexuality and gender.

These changes have emerged contemporaneously with new feminist discourses stressing the key role of challenging heteronormativity, the denaturalization of gender, and forms of critical thinking and activism that do not exclude people on the basis of gender, race, or class. This new emphasis shows that we are dealing with the idea of embracing all differences – without privileging any, not even sexual difference – or the endeavour to be everywhere, not neglecting any form of difference;[8] we are dealing with the endeavour to subvert the conformism of the feminist movement reconciled with national and international institutions, along with gay and lesbian struggles that have pursued security through campaigning for the right to marriage. To go beyond these "respectable," "conservative," identities, in 1990 Teresa de Lauretis organized an encounter titled "Queer Theory," aiming to initiate "a critical dialogue between lesbians and gay men on sexuality and on our respective sexual histories ... around sexuality and its interrelations with sex and race," and to "construct another discursive horizon, another way of thinking the sexual."[9] None of this can be separated from the fact that already since the end of the 1980s the political subject of feminism, "women," had been called into question because, although it was supposed to represent all women, it seemed more to universalize white, Western, heterosexual women, and because it had ignored its own historicity (Riley 1988; Scott 2011, 53). At the same time, the category of "women" was being questioned by theorists, with writers such as Chantal Mouffe, Ernesto Laclau, and Judith Butler herself showing that politics is possible without a previously specified and unified subject.

For years now, and as if they were linked to these changes, prefixes such as *post-*, *de-*, *trans-*, *re-*, etc. have proliferated, appearing, first, to indicate the expectation of a transition towards a new paradigm in all spheres of experience, a new era, and second, to evidence the repeated realization that these new times have never actually arrived, so that after each successive frustration a new formula had to be invented.[10] And I should also remark that, in this context, *de-* does not only allude to negation but also often to an inversion of meaning; *trans-* indicates a change of form; *post-* expresses not only the feeling of being an epigone but also some kind of break, with clear difficulties in finding a new name; and while *re-* indicates repeating, differing, among its various meanings we also find that of intensity or excess (also, of course, resistance and refusal) – and so we talk of reinventing, rewriting, rearticulating, resignifying, representing. And along with this proliferation of prefixes, we also see the constant use of the forward slash, as for example in *in/visibility* or *sex/textual*, making explicit both the endeavour to avoid and at the same time the difficulty of avoiding the language we have at hand. Perhaps all of these prefixes and slashes are like traces, like sites where subjectivity is inscribed.

As a backdrop to this, I believe we can discern that despite many legal and social changes in women's lives, our freedom and the yearned-for changes in the dominant symbolic realm have not arrived. Perhaps, more than thirty years after the irruption of separatist feminism, we should admit that there is still much to do in this area, and that their attempt to find words to speak "the feminine" (going beyond the stereotype that sees it only as a lack or excess) – both to the mirror and in exchanges with other women – has become bogged down and has not managed to free itself from this impasse.[11] Thus we can understand both the current criticisms and concerns on the part of some involved in the second wave in response to the "post" turn of new generations who have neither continued the struggle for women's liberation nor followed the path opened up in the 1970s when addressing this new turn, which now bases itself on a gender revolution, as we can read in manifestos concerning the political centrality of "expropriating the codes of masculinity" (Preciado 2008).

To begin with, we could say that the older-generation feminists seem not to take into account that no one can foresee the fate of their legacy, and that we may need to undertake a critical analysis of the path taken up to now, not in order to retract it but rather to detect the obstacles to women's liberation and symbolic independence. The new generation, in its attempt to change society (which seems to remain intact despite the quotas for the representation of the various differences in public institutions), eagerly chooses to exclude itself from the "dutiful daughter" market and instead to occupy the "masculine" sphere, while in the same gesture rejecting the "victim" identity and practising forms of resistance – other than complaining and demanding – through a satirical exaggeration of stereotypes. The renunciation of female conditioning and the move towards "occupying" the masculine or towards a playful and overstated parody of gender stereotypes can also be understood as suggesting that being a woman often comes back repeatedly to a tiresome particularity that we constantly feel forced to justify, forget, or make others forget. However, it is impossible to parody convincingly a position with which we have no ties; a certain capacity for self-identification is needed, and this means that the parody is doubly encoded in political terms: it subverts and at the same time legitimizes what is parodied. It is a peculiar style of authorized transgression that does not guarantee complete liberation or large-scale planned changes, although in some of its forms it may play an important role in subverting dominant models.

This "borderline" feminism has brought to the surface an unforeseen form of subversion aiming to change women's condition by calling attention to the construction and the "performativity" of masculinity; this form of feminism powerfully stresses the male violence that both women and minority-excluded groups have to put up with. It represents the insubordination of those who, instead of keeping a "low profile," would perhaps rather wreck everything, and who wonder how long we will have to wait for masculine emancipation. This questioning of masculinity may complete the Beauvoirian analysis of "second sex" status, reminding us that "one is not born, but rather becomes, a man – vir."[12] With the introduction of the category of "gender," we may be able to overcome the limits of some feminist analyses and at the same time go beyond the hated binarism.[13] The aspiration is to embrace all differences and to escape from the regulatory heteropatriarchal forms by which they exclude people or declare their lives to be socially and culturally "unliveable." As a corollary to debates on the subjection of women and the language articulating this, it is not strange that the issues of pornography and prostitution should quickly emerge. Thus, for example, Beatriz Preciado wrote in 2007 that

> este nuevo feminismo posporno, punk y transcultural nos enseña que la mejor protección contra la violencia de género no es la prohibición de la prostitución sino la toma del poder económico y político de las mujeres y de las minorías migrantes. Del mismo modo, el mejor antídoto contra la pornografía dominante no es la censura, sino la producción de representaciones alternativas de la sexualidad, hechas desde miradas divergentes de la mirada normativa. Así, el objetivo de estos proyectos feministas no sería tanto liberar a las mujeres o conseguir su igualdad legal como desmantelar los dispositivos políticos que producen las diferencias de clase, de raza, de género y de sexualidad haciendo así del feminismo una plataforma artística y política de invención de un futuro común. (Preciado 2007)

(this new postporn, punk and transcultural feminism shows us that the best protection against gender violence is not the prohibition of prostitution but the capture of economic and political power by women and migrant minorities. In the same way, the most effective antidote to the dominant form of pornography is not censorship but the production of alternative representations of sexuality, created from points of view other than the normative gaze. Thus, the goal of these feminist projects would be not so much to liberate women or achieve legal equality but to dismantle the political apparatuses that generate differences in class, race, gender, and sexuality, thus making feminism an artistic and political platform for the invention of a common future.)

Thus, still setting out from the fact that affirming abjection does not necessarily mean yielding to the ideological and material conditions that make it possible, these feminists seem to suggest that devoting oneself to pornography or prostitution would not be so much doing "a job like any other" – a criticism often leveled against those who defend regulating prostitution – but situating oneself within a site and practice of resistance.

Currently we are witnessing many young women and artists whose words and works evidence a desire to enact for themselves the drama of subjection, to inhabit the margins, to abandon the well-trodden ideological paths, to join the community of exiles.[14] Thus in their self-naming ("poofs, tomboys, queens, whores, dykes, bags, gigolos, gender fuckers, bears, inverts, vicious, precarious, etc. ... we survive in the margins of gender, class, the geographies of the normal, the sewers of sex" [ZIGA 2009b]), we see attempts to reappropiate or resignify insults. In this way, young feminists challenge regulatory norms from the margins, which is why Itziar Ziga, author of the fascinating *Devenir perra* (Becoming a bitch), sees herself as a Tamagotchi: each everyday rebellion makes her life longer (Ziga 2009a, 73).

The strident stir that has accompanied this new turn reproaching 1960s feminism for its integration into the political-constitutional sphere indicates that it represents not only the determination to embrace all excluded forms of difference and to bring to the foreground the monstrous and the abject in order to defuse sexual violence, but also a new commitment to gender indifference, or a provocative "sexual mixing" that creates a certain social unease and points towards some kind of symbolic disorder.[15] Thus, understood as a utopian ideal, gender indifference, or sexual mixing, could be a good terrain from which to criticize and/or call into question the shortcomings and deficits of the present.[16] Undoubtedly, not only are these different movements fruit of a sustained critique of feminism, but, as we have seen, they also respond to the ethically and politically important changes the world has gone through in recent decades; and to those that I have already noted, we should add shifts in the relationship between the natural and the artificial (I am thinking of our hybrid condition as cyborgs, or of genetically modified organisms that compel us to rethink the limits between technology and culture, humankind and nature, science and social responsibility) and changes in parenting habits and relationships. All of this reminds us that the meaning of the nature-culture opposition is no longer clear – if it ever was – and that both social and cultural constructivism and the view of femininity and masculinity as organic or natural attributes are insufficient tools for analysing the new subjectivities. The site of analysis, therefore, is to be found at the crossroads of many paths rather than in simple "binary" nature-culture polarity (Haraway 1991; 2000; 2004).

Also, and as we have already seen, behind these moves towards embracing all differences there lies the will to escape from the norms of the masculine and feminine as social and sexual assignations, a will that implies a challenge to the terms of what we regard as human: this involves, then, an ontological rebellion. Now, reviewing the interventions and proclamations of the new feminism, we see that this subversion of the normal seems to be embodied in a paradoxical search for sexual identity, since it is played out between sexual indeterminism and the definition of a sexuality, between the positive construction of the subject and its provocative deconstruction, such that in these practices the key question is that relating to the identity (criticized or peripheral) of the subject (Fraisse 2010b, 461).

And if the nub of the question takes us back to identity, then it may also be a good idea to ask ourselves if this goes any further than a justified aspiration to the individual liberty of the diverse subjectivities – especially those often dubbed as unliveable, to use Butler's expression (2007) – and if it points towards issues relating not only to the subject but also to the world, to public freedom. In fact, in considering these movements, we often have the impression that they embrace only a limited notion of power, apparently understood only as that power which forces obedience to rules, and that we are being offered forms of resistance for a society of atomized individuals, such as ours. And this can lead us to pose questions, such as: To what extent is it enough to limit ourselves to seeing the issues from an aesthetic, performative, or merely individual-liberties point of view? Can the exclusion of ontology be immediately turned into a common denominator of resistance? Behind this parodic exaggeration of learned forms of femininity, does there lie only the will to subvert or is there also a political project? Is it enough to proclaim that, as of today, we can raise the anchors of gender?[17] With these questions, I wish to say that in every era some women have been able to transgress their allotted role and achieve a degree of freedom individually, without waiting for collective liberation; but the question is whether, in this case, there is something more than the will to "occupy" a space; whether there exists the possibility or the determination to widen or reconfigure the visible public sphere.

In other words, at a time like the present, when the centre – although fragmented and dispersed – continues to be a centre, is it enough to substitute a supposedly normalizing nucleus with its marginalized fragments? This form of postfeminism seems to be developing, in its main lines, in an ambivalent and pragmatic relationship with the powers that be, between yes and no, between the challenge to the status quo and the fashionable margins – well received in contemporary art museums – between the criticism of institutional structures and subsidies from them. Perhaps all of the above points once more towards the lack, both in today's 70s-style feminism and in the "borderline" or "post" varieties, of an attention to political freedom, since today – and I am aware of simplifying the issues – we find some women focusing on the social question and others on seeking out defiant, antitraditional heroines.

Notes

Introduction

1 We follow Douglas L. Wheeler's assertion that "although there are distinct regional and provincial differences between Minho and Algarve, tiny Portugal did not have the severe cleavages and centrifugal forces found in neighboring Spain. In Portugal, with the exception of Lisbon, and in some cases, Oporto, no separatist regional movements – such as those in the Basque provinces and Catalonia in Spain – developed (Wheeler 1978, 5–6).
2 All English translations for titles and quotations throughout the volume have been provided by the authors unless otherwise noted.

Part I. Iberian Feminism in the Age of Enlightenment

1 Translated by Catherine M. Jaffe.
2 Translated by Elizabeth Franklin Lewis.
3 These two views of women's place in Enlightenment reforms are thoroughly discussed in Mónica Bolufer's contribution to this volume, ch. 2.
4 Among recent book-length studies of the contributions of Spanish Enlightenment women and their sociopolitical roles are those by the aforementioned Bolufer (1998) and Smith (2006), as well as López-Cordón (2005c), Lewis (2004), and Jaffe and Lewis (2009).
5 For analyses of Amar's essay and its impact see McClendon (1980), Lewis (1989 and 2004), Sullivan (1993), Baum (1994), Bolufer (1998), López-Cordón (2005c), and Smith (2006).
6 See López-Cordón's edition and introduction to Amar's book (1994), as well as her study of Amar's life and works (2005c). See also Lewis (2002) for analysis of Amar's proposal for women's physical education as mothers.

7 I argue elsewhere that one of these statements regarding a woman's choice of marriage or the convent is a subtle commentary on larger questions of personal liberty and rebellion (Lewis 2004, 55).

8 The members of the Junta de Damas – although most of them resided at court at least part of the year – came from noble families whose origins spread across Spain. One such member of the *junta* was the Basque author Rita de Barrenechea, the Condesa del Carpio, studied in this volume by Barkarne Altornaga. See Demerson (1975) and Martín-Valdepeñas (2010) for more on the Junta de Damas.

9 See ch. 4 below for a discussion of more of Gálvez's plays that deal with marriage and love.

10 Fernando Doménech includes this historical reference in his edition of the play (Gálvez de Cabrera 1995, 80). See also Bordiga (2003). For more on Gálvez, see also Establier (2005 and 2006).

11 The text for Hickey has not been modernized throughout this chapter. English translations are my own, unless otherwise indicated.

12 The *seguidilla* is a traditional Castilian folk song.

13 The author, ironically, is misidentified as "Marly Wollstonecraft" and referred to as masculine in the articles. *Diario de Madrid* 250 (6 September 1792), 252 (8 September 1752), 282 (8 October 1792), 283 (9 October 1792).

14 Such policy changes might be the case of the legal legitimation of marriage without fatherly consent (1768), the legal determinations on the duration and form of the manifestations of mourning in the case of widowed women (1772), and the legal determinations to create public schools for young girls in Lisbon (1790). See Figueiredo Marcos (1990) and Adão (2014).

15 Relevant religious authors of the period are Soror Maria do Céu (1658–1753) and Soror Madalena da Gloria (1672–1760), who had their allegorical novels printed; other nuns also published works in different genres, such as Soror Maria Benta do Céu (b. 1702) who published a collection of biographies of virtuous women, or Tomásia Caetana de Aquino and Tomásia Caetana de Santa Maria (b. 1719), who managed to publish occasional literature, composed for a specific occasion.

16 The quotations that follow are translated from the critical edition prepared by Maria da Santa Cruz (Silva e Orta 2002).

17 Translated from Spanish by Elizabeth Franklin Lewis. This article has been written with the help of a predoctoral contract given by the UPV/EHU (Universidad del País Vasco/Euskal Herriko Unibertsitatea; 2013) and is part of the University Research Group of the UPV/EHU titled "La experiencia de la sociedad moderna en España, 1870–1990" ("Experience

of Modern Society in Spain 1870–1990"), GIU14/04, UFI 11/27 and the project of MINECO (Ministerio de Economía, Industria, y Competitividad) code: HAR2012-37959-C02-01. I would like to thank Nerea Aresti Esteban for reading this work.

18 From here on I will refer to this entity as the Basque Society (*la Bascongada*) or the "RSBAP."

19 The speech was presented by Montehermoso in 1765 and collected in a text entitled *Historia de la Real Sociedad Bascongada de los Amigos del País*. Its first publication date is from 1931. This text was attributed to the Count of Peñaflorida by Julio de Urquijo. Cécile Mary Trojani believes that it was Miguel José de Olaso y Zumalabe, the secretary of the society, who wrote it (Trojani 2007, 151).

20 With a different interpretation, Trojani has held that in the education praised by the RSBAP the weight of tradition was overwhelming since, upon presenting a femininity tied to maternity and domesticity, they would agree to "modernizar el papel tradicional de la mujer" (Trojani 2007, 154; modernize the traditional role of women). I consider, however, that in line with the view sustained by Lola Valverde (1988, 39) the sentimental view of femininity as lovers, mothers, and housewives constituted an authentic novelty introduced at the end of the eighteenth century, which would be intensified in the nineteenth.

21 In Euskara: "Cémbat contrario tuén necazáriac? Chinúrriac cámpoan, ságuac granéroan ta despénsan, ta ságu gaistoéna dá emacúme tripa gaisto ta orz ona duéna."

Part II. The Long Nineteenth Century (1808–1920)

1 She had previously written, under the pseudonym Cil, "Um Raríssimo Tipo de Mulher," dedicated to Concepción Arenal (Pestana 1898b); and "Congresso Feminista," about the congress in London that was being prepared by the International Council of Women (Pestana 1899a).

2 See, among others, Kirkpatrick (1991, 69–99), Jiménez (1992), Perinat and Marrades (1980), Sánchez Llama (2000), and Segura and Selva (1984).

3 On Silva, see Criado (1889, 48–51), Sánchez Hita (2009), and Carmen Silva (1811).

4 During the *trienio*, women disguised themselves as men to enter parliament and political meetings (Cantizano 2004, 284).

5 For the subversive potential of flower imagery, see Kirkpatrick (1991, 202–7). See also Robustiana Armiño's "Cantos de otoño" [Autumn Songs], *El Vergel de Andalucía* (30 November 1845): 53–4 and Coronado's "A Claudia"

[To Claudia], *El Vergel de Andalucía* (11 December 1845): 68–70. For a later example, see Concepción Gimeno de Flaquer's delicious "Historia de una flor, contada por ella misma" (History of a flower, told by herself), whose narrative voice pays tribute to her "gardener," Carolina Coronado.

6 See Satorres, "Estudios filosóficos sobre la mujer" [Philosophical studies on woman], *El Pensil del Bello Sexo* 6 (1845): 49–50 and no. 9, 74, respectively. Opposing views, however, are evident in Encarnación Calero de los Ríos's and Coronado's mutually dedicated poetic exchanges (see no. 8, 67 and no. 10, 86, respectively). Regarding the Madrid *El Pensil del Bello Sexo* and its Barcelona counterpart, see Burguera (2011, 62–3).

7 See "Cuatro palabras," *Ellas* 1 (1 September 1851): 1, and "Otra palabrita" (2). Other female contributors were Carolina Coronado, Luisa Núñez de C., Ángela Grassi, Emilia Pallares, Matilde López, Josefa Maestre, E. de Olavarria, Robustiana Armiño, La Huérfana Numantina, and Emilia de Tamarit.

8 See also Vicenta García Miranda's poem, "A las Españolas" [To Spanish women], *Gaceta del Bello Sexo* 2 (15 December 1851): 10–12.

9 From 30 January 1852, the *Gaceta del Bello Sexo* became *Álbum de Señoritas: Periódico de Literatura, Educación, Música, Teatro y Modas* (A young ladies' album: Periodical of literature, education, music, theatre, and fashion), in which many female contributors to the *Gaceta* and *La Mujer* published.

10 Contributors were Natalia B. de Ferrant, Ángela Grassi, Vicenta Villaluenga y García, Robustiana Armiño de Cuesta, Cecilia González, La Ciega de Manzanares (María Francisca Díaz Carralero), Gertrudis Gómez de Avellaneda, Ana María, Ángela Morejón de Masas, Rosa Butler, Venancia López Villabrillo, Josefa Moreno Nartes, Enriqueta Lozano, María Verdejo y Durán, Rogelia León, Elisa Gutiérrez Soriano, Eloisa G. de Santa Coloma, María de Mar Salas y P., Elena Cánovas de Freyre, and Clara del Valle.

11 Other scholars, however, have seen *La Mujer* as anachronistic (Sánchez Llama 2000, 161), more concerned with destabilizing a former social order than defending women's rights (Jiménez 1992, 95), only advocating an improved, not equal, education for women (Perinat and Marrades 1980, 321, 354) and offering a conservative pseudofeminism (Elorza 1975, 53).

12 Issues 32 and 34 of *La Mujer* authorize the female writer and critic through reviews of Coronado's work by North American Anita George and of Grassi's poetry by Ana María, who deem both authors superior to male poets. Most of issue 34 praises contemporary female poets and intellectuals, while the lead essay in issue 49 centres on La Ciega de

Manzanares (The Blind Woman from Manzanares), reputedly the rival of the most learned grammatician (1).

13 Later, María del Pilar Sinués would also use famous historical women to vindicate feminist claims in *Galería de mujeres célebres* (1864–9) (Sánchez Llama 2000, 347–65; Gallery of famous women).

14 On this essay, see Burguera (2011, 66–8) and Jiménez (1992, 61–3).

15 In *El Vergel de Andalucía,* La Adalia also advocates marriage based on love, comparing the alternative to prostitution (10 [21 December 1845]: 76–7).

16 On the *Pensiles* and their editors, María Josefa Zapata and Margarita Pérez de Celis, see Espigado (2008). On Zapata, see also Perinat and Marrades (1980, 24n22).

17 On women's education in the long nineteenth century, see Flecha (2010, 77–87) and Scanlon (1986, 15–50).

18 Quoted and translated by Blanco (1998, 87). Nelken's work was first published in 1918 by the Barcelona publisher, Minerva.

19 Czinski's translation, together with another pamphlet, *Una palabra a las Españolas, dirigida por una compatricia* (A word to Spanish women, by a female compatriot), was reputedly by Joaquina de Morla de Virués (Jérez), who moved in the Cádiz circle of Fourierist women (Espigado Tocino, Pérez Sánchez, and Sánchez Álvarez 1996, 60–2). Burguera (2011, 78n47) indicates that the translation had also previously appeared in *La Ilustración: Álbum de las damas* (18 [11 January 1846]: 1–3 and 20 [25 January 1846]: 1–3; Enlightened education: Album for ladies).

20 Elorza considers that Marina may be Zapata (1975, 58), while Jiménez Morell suggests that she is Pérez de Celis (1992, 106n8). I believe that Marina existed in her own right, as she is among the four female contributors to *El Pensil de Iberia* listed on each issue's front page, together with Pérez de Celis, Zapata, and Butler. Moreover, in Zapata's poem "La jardinera a mi querido Pensil" (From the [woman] gardener to my beloved garden), she pays homage to each female contributor, with Marina alluded to as "la *marina rosa,* tan hermosa" (the *marine rose,* so beautiful) and Pérez de Celis described as "la vistosa *margarita,* la que incita" (*El Nuevo Pensil de Iberia* 32 [20 August 1858]: 3; the showy *daisy* that encourages). On Marina, see also Ramírez (2009).

21 See Pérez de Celis's "Mi retrato" (*La Buena Nueva* [30 January 1866]: 6–8; My portrait), a self-portrait and declaration of principles.

22 References to suspensions of publication due to censorship are apparent from 28 February 1866 onward. Authorities found especially worrying the periodical's links with Fourierist socialism, spiritism, and feminism (Elorza 1975, 63).

23 See Zapata's poem, "El jardín de Flora" (*La Buena Nueva* 6 [28 February 1866]: 3; Flora's garden) and Pérez de Celis's "¡Guerra!!! ..." (10 [15 April 1866]: 4–6; War!). The periodical's alignment with freethinking is evident in articles on a Masonic baptism in New York and the Quakers (see 4 [8 February 1866]: 7–8; 9 [8 April 1866]: 7–8).

24 Here Zapata foreshadows Rosario de Acuña's 1888 essay "Consecuencias de la degeneración femenina," discussed in ch. 11.

25 Caterina Albert i Paradís, an author from Catalonia who barely overlapped with Böhl, published novels in Catalan under her male-sounding penname "Víctor Català." See ch. 6.

26 All translations into English are my own.

27 In her recent "feminist translation" of Castro's poems into English, *On the Edge of the River Sar,* Michelle Geoffrion-Vinci strives "to make the feminine – i.e., women – visible in the text" (Castro 2014, 9).

28 Regarding Castro, Miguélez-Carballeira asserts "the multi-layered nature of her feminist message" (2014, 186).

29 Spain's largest bourgeois population and its highest percentage of literate citizens – and hence its principal reading public – resided in Madrid and Barcelona.

30 The number of women authors who separated from their husbands or encountered marital opposition to their writing careers is significant. This is an economic incentive for a feminist vindication for women who could support themselves by writing and publishing.

31 In *La mujer de su casa* (1883) Arenal poses a key question. Since the entrenched belief in male superiority permits society to declare women intellectually inferior, "*¿a qué edad empieza* la superioridad intelectual del hombre?" ([1883] 1974a, 121–2; [emphasis in original] *at what age* does a man's intellectual superiority *commence*?).

32 On the Catalan legal system, see Enríquez (1998, 238–9).

33 In 1873 Concepción Gimeno and Sofía Tartilán founded the Madrid fortnightly, *La Ilustración de la Mujer* (The enlightenment of woman). Although in extant issues (31 May 1875–30 December 1876) Tartilán figured as the director and wrote most lead articles, aimed at improving the lot of the working classes, overall there were few female contributors and little content dedicated to women's education in a progressive sense.

34 See "Nuestro programa," *La Ilustración* 1 (June 1883): 2.

35 See "O votos o rejas," *La Ilustración* 2 (15 June 1883): 10. Similarly, "No tan malos" (Men aren't so bad) states that contemporary women are not goddesses but mortals who need to be able to live independently and with dignity (*La Ilustración* 9 [1 October 1883]: 66).

36 See "La inteligencia y el corazón," *La Ilustración* 21 (1 April 1884): 162.
37 See "La mano izquierda," *La Ilustración* 13 (1 December 1883): 98.
38 See "Las preocupaciones," *La Ilustración* 22 (15 April 1884): 170.
39 See "Mujeres hacendosas," *La Ilustración* 16 (15 January 1884): 122.
40 See "Puerilidades," *La Ilustración* 23 (1 May 1884): 178. "Influencias" (Influences) asserts that confining women's education to domestic matters is selfish for society; *La Ilustración* 24 (15 May 1884): 180.
41 See "El santo matrimonio," *La Ilustración* 17 (1 February 1884): 140.
42 See "¡La compañera!," *La Ilustración* 19 (1 March 1884): 146. "Su majestad el vulgo" (His Majesty, the common people) looks to the high numbers of single, working women in perceivedly civilized countries to claim that marriage should not be women's only option; *La Ilustración* 12 (15 November 1883): 90.
43 See "El justo medio," *La Ilustración* 14 (15 December 1883): 106. The critique of education in Spain looks to North America as a model ("El primer paso" [The First Step], *La Ilustración* 10 [15 October 18830]: 71), while London's female telegraphists feature in another piece ("Estación telefónica de Londres" [London's Telephone Exchange], *La Ilustración* 16 [15 January 1884]: 122–3). There is even an article on Polish women: "La mujer en Polonia," *La Ilustración* 23 (1 May 1884): 184.
44 See "¡Adelante!," *La Ilustración* 7 (1 September 1883): 50.
45 See "Doña María de la Paz Borbón," *La Ilustración* 1 (1 June 1883): 2; and "Carmen Silva," *La Ilustración* 6 (15 August 1883): 42, respectively.
46 See Manuel Escudé Bartolí, "Josefa Pujol de Collado," *La Ilustración* 24 (15 May 1884): 180. The eleven issues of the fortnightly *El Parthenón: Revista de literatura, ciencias y artes* (The Parthenon: Magazine for literature, the sciences, and arts; 1879–80) carried articles on political theory, geology, geography, and mythology. Many contributions were by male freethinkers, while few pieces from female writers dealt with feminist concerns.
47 See "María Josefa Massanés," *La Ilustración* 12 (15 November 1883): 91; "María Mendoza de Vives," *La Ilustración* 15 (1 January 1884): 114; and "Una escritora portuguesa" [A Portuguese writer], *La Ilustración* 22 (15 April 1884): 174, respectively.
48 For an excellent overview of many of these writers, see Ramos (2011).
49 On *La Luz del Porvenir* and aspects of Domingo Soler's life, see Arkinstall (2014b, 23–59).
50 See "Paralelo entre el claustro y el hogar," *La Luz* 2 (4 June 1884): 13–16. Carmen Piferrer likewise critiques the traditional belief that feeling is incompatible with thinking; "La mujer católica" [The Catholic woman], *La Luz* 42 (10 March 1887): 333.

51 "La misión de la mujer," *La Luz* 32 (29 December 1887): 254–6.
52 See "Carta a un amigo" [Letter to a male friend], *La Luz* 44 (23 March 1888): 353–6.
53 See "Necesidad apremiante," *La Luz* 15 (4 September 1884): 113–17.
54 See "La mujer," *La Luz* 24 (6 November 1884): 190–2.
55 See "La mujer en los tiempos modernos," *La Luz* 31 (24 December 1885): 245–6.
56 "Ayer y hoy" [Today and yesterday], *Las Dominicales del Libre Pensamiento* 715, Year 14 (24 April 1896): 2.
57 For López de Ayala, see Arkinstall (2014b, 60–136), and Clemente (2015). For *La Conciencia Libre* and Sárraga's writings, see Arkinstall (2014b, 139–87).
58 Mañé directed and published with Juan Montseny ("Federico Urales") the anarchist periodical *La Revista Blanca* (The white magazine; Madrid, 1898–1906; Barcelona, 1923–36), which had substantial feminist content. Mañé represented *La Revista Blanca* at the 1899 Second International Women's Convention in London, as did members of López de Ayala's Sociedad Progresiva Femenina; see Greene (1998) and Ackelsberg (1991).
59 For the Sociedad Progresiva Femenina's international reach, see "Victoria notable" [A noteworthy victory], *Las Dominicales del Libre Pensamiento* 714, Year 14 (17 April 1896): 1; and "Congreso Feminista Internacional" [International Women's Conference], *Las Dominicales del Libre Pensamiento* 887, Year 17 (30 June 1899): 3, respectively.
60 Regarding the ANME and its links with Catalan and Valencian feminisms, see Arkinstall (2014a, 65).
61 See "La mujer ante el progreso social," *La Luz* 10 (18 July 1895): 77–86.
62 For a fuller discussion of this essay, see Arkinstall (2014b, 177–80).
63 On the 1910 demonstration, see "Mitin femenino" (Women's Meeting), *El Gladiador del Librepensamiento* 104, Year 7, Second Epoch (19 May 1917): 1. For Acuña's speech, see Acuña ([1917] 2008a, 890).
64 On *El Gladiador del Librepensamiento*, see Arkinstall (2014a).
65 On Acuña's life, see Bolado (2007a, 33–432) and Hernández (2012).
66 For Acuña's essays, see Díaz Marcos (2012, 261–360).
67 However, in 1885 Acuña refers to women's situation as comparable to slavery; see Álvarez Lázaro 1985, 340). See Scanlon (1986, 126–37) for a critique of women's legal slavery.
68 In a 1920 essay in honour of a prominent socialist feminist, Acuña states that the only emancipation possible is through work; Acuña (2007b, 1783).
69 Acuña's constant interpellation of women as privileged addressees parallels María Martínez Sierra's similar use in feminist essays between 1916 and

1932, which Alda Blanco sees as a "feminist political strategy that promotes the association by and for women as an organizational form" (1998, 82).

70 For Díaz Marcos, Acuña thus forges a feminine prototype both traditional and revolutionary, and deploys discursive strategies that permit her texts to appear inoffensive while at the same time generating an alternative space (2012, 292, 338).

71 In mid-nineteenth-century Spain, female illiteracy levels stood at 85.9%, and in 1900 at 71% (Capel 1986, 116, 144).

72 Arenal partook of all three forms of Spanish feminism, being at times a radical individualist and always Catholic and moderate.

73 See ch. 11 for a discussion of Rosario de Acuña's feminist thought.

74 In ch. 11, Arkinstall cites the historian Rosa María Capel as specifying 71% illiteracy among Spanish women in 1900.

75 For a discussion of Pardo Bazán's networking with other Spanish women, see Bieder (2015). She nevertheless revelled in repeating that, if given a choice, most Spanish women would vote to lynch her (*El Caballero Audaz* 1914, 8).

76 Pardo Bazán's two daughters did not attend the university, although her son did, as had his father.

77 Gimeno figures as owner, director, publisher, and lead editorial writer of *El Álbum de la Mujer* and owner-editor of *El Álbum Ibero Americano*. Starting in 1886 in Mexico, her husband, Flaquer, edited a publication for men, *La Crónica: Periódico político, mercantil, de noticias y avisos* (The chronicle: Political, mercantile magazine with news and advertisements), which accompanied his wife's magazine as a free gift to readers.

78 Similarly, she modelled *Mujeres: Vidas paralelas* (Women: Parallel lives; 1893) on Plutarch.

79 Margarita Pintos's 2016 biography evinces her research in Mexico, Spain, and Argentina to fill in the long-standing lacunae in Gimeno's life and writings.

80 In 1902 Burgos's estranged husband published in his satirical magazine, *Almería Alegre* (Light-Hearted Almería), a bitter, self-serving attack on feminists in "El feminismo" (Núñez Rey 2005, 84; Feminism).

81 Burgos herself lost three infants under the age of one year.

82 Concepción Gimeno attended the lecture (Núñez Rey 2005, 151).

83 In her response to the survey, Pardo Bazán somewhat disingenuously claimed to have no opinion and stated she lacked time to reflect on the issue (Burgos 1904a, 71).

84 The proposed law enfranchised only single women over twenty-three and solely for municipal elections (Castañeda 1994, 121).

85 Although literary works by female writers exist before the nineteenth century, such as improvised medieval oral works or Maria Estibaliz de Sasiola's written poems (Deba 1550–1611), *Ipui onak* is the first work by a woman printed in the Basque language.

86 In the eighteenth and nineteenth centuries, literate women were few and far between. According to Dávila, Eizagirre, and Fernández (1994, 76), between 1816 and 1820 only 13% of women in Ipar Euskal Herria (Northern Basque Country) could sign their name, and in Hego Euskal Herria (Southern Basque Country), between 1835 and 1860, most women could read but not write. Only 15% of Basque women were completely literate.

87 We thank the journalist and researcher, Marta Brancas, for her generosity on providing material for writing this section.

88 As Montserrat Duch affirms (2012, 35), in national narratives the family stands for the nation and the mother, an allegorical figure for the nation, becomes the guardian of national tradition.

89 This situation also characterizes the beginning of the nineteenth century, as Bizenta Mogel's activity demonstrates. It is not coincidental that *Ipui onak* is a work with a clear pedagogical and moralistic intention. Moreover, Mogel participated in various groups that met in Abando to strengthen and normalize education in the Basque language.

90 I would like to thank Christopher L. Anderson for his careful translation of my original version in Spanish, project FEM2013-42699 (Fernández 2015b).

Part III. The Iberian Feminist Movements Gain Strength under Republics (1910–1939)

1 João Esteves provides a comprehensive study of this organization in *A Liga Republicana das Mulheres Portuguesas: uma organização política e feminista (1909-1919)* (Lisbon: Esteves, 1991).

2 Anja Louis (2005, 15) outlines the tenets of The School of Natural Law that informed Enlightenment thinkers and subsequently Burgos's approach to the law.

3 Indicating her openmindedness, Burgos translated Moebius's *La inferioridad mental de la mujer* (Women's mental inferiority).

Part IV. The Dictatorships of António de Oliveira Salazar (1926–1974) and Francisco Franco (1939–1975)

1 *Catálogo da Exposição de Livros Escritos por Mulheres organizada pelo Conselho Nacional das Mulheres Portuguesas na Sociedade Nacional de Belas Artes* (Lisbon: Gráfica Santelmo, 1947).

2 Associação Feminina Portuguesa para a Paz, Estatutos, Lisbon, s.a.
3 Women who remained loyal to their ideals were demonized as "deviants" and were even disowned by their own families for neglecting their duties as mothers and wives (Martins Rodríguez 2011, 93–4).
4 In "Cárceles y mujeres en Galicia durante el franquismo" (2011; Prisons and women in Galicia during Franco's regime), Martins Rodríguez calls attention to the stigmatization of the Communist woman as "combativa, peligrosa, descarada y grosera" (95; combative, dangerous, shameless, and rude).
5 The publication of *Letras armadas: As vidas de Enriqueta Otero Blanco* is one more example of the recovery of the historical memory of Galician Republican women taking place in Galicia since the 1980s. The book was published as a joint project by the Concello de Lugo (Lugo Council) and the Fundación 10 de marzo (The 10 March Foundation).
6 The Real Academia Galega (RAG) was founded in 1906 under the presidency of Rosalía de Castro's husband, the prestigious historian and leading Rexurdimento figure Manuel Murguía (1833–1923).
7 Among the women poets publishing in Galician during the period under consideration are also María do Carme Kruckenberg (1926–2015) with *Carnaval de ouro* (Carnival of gold; 1962); and two exophonic authors: Portuguese María Manuela Couto Viana (1919–83) with her 1964 *Frauta lonxana* (Distant flute) and United States writer Anne Marie Morris (1916–99) with *Voz fuxitiva* (Fugitive voice; 1965). For more on these exophonic writers, see García-Liñeira 2015, 208–11.
8 Olga Gallego Domínguez, historian and archivist, was the first Galician woman officially to join the Royal Galician Academy in 1986. Pozo Garza, in the above-mentioned interview, specifies that she was the first Galician woman literary writer to become a member. Her pertinent clarification served to remind everyone that in 1945 the Royal Galician Academy had elected author Francisca Herrera Garrido (1869–1950), who wrote narrative and poetry primarily in Galician, to become a member. However, by the time of her passing in 1950, the antifeminist Herrera Garrido had not being allowed to join the academy.
9 Although the movement known as Euskal Pizkundea would also have repercussions in the Basque area of France, its activity was basically centred in the southern provinces of Euskal Herria, Araba, Biscay, Gipuzkoa, and Nafarroa.
10 As a young woman, Arantxa Gurmendi's mother performed theatre in *euskera* with Toribio Alzaga (López Aguirre 2015, 11). Thus Gurmendi's biography exemplifies the link between the cultural projects of the prewar era and the vanguard cultural movements in the 1960s.

11 Elena López defines it as "la rokera rebelde de Ez Dok Amairu (López Aguirre 1015, 10; the rebellious rocker of Ez Doc Amairu).

12 This expression refers to a popular poem by Gabriel Aresti titled "Nir aitaren etxea defendatuko dut" (I will defend my father's house), in which the house really means Euskal Herria. The poem was published in the book *Harri eta Herri* (1964; Stone and people).

13 One of the principal characteristics of the *ikastolas* or Basque schools was teaching entirely in *euskera,* in addition to the goal of spreading Basque culture. This kind of school began to function in the second half of the 1960s and the first years of the 1970s.

14 International Women's Day is celebrated on 8 March.

15 The Burgos trial was a war tribunal initiated in 1970 against sixteen members of ETA. Among those indicted were three women: Itziar Aizpurua, Arantxa Arruti, and Jone Dorronsoro.

16 José Antonio Garmendia's death sentence was commuted to life in prison. Ángel Otaegi and Juan Paredes Manot ("Txiki") were shot on 27 September 1975. The three were members of ETA. Besides Txiki and Otaegi, three members of the Frente Revolucionaria Antifascista y Patriota (FRAP; Revolutionary Anti-Fascist Patriotic Front) – Ramón Garcia Sanz, José Humberto Baena, and José Sánchez Bravo – were also shot. These five executions were the last of the Franco regime.

Part V. A New Beginning: The Transition to Democracy and Iberian Second-Wave Feminism (1974/1975–1994/1996)

1 "Jardim da Europa 'a beira-mar plantado" (Europe's garden planted by the sea) was a verse in the preface of a patriotic work published in 1862 by ultraromantic writer and politician, Tomás Ribeiro (1831–1901). It became a metaphor for Portugal during the latter part of dictator António de Oliveira Salazar's regime and, after 1968, used by Marcello Caetano to assert the peace-loving character of the Portuguese against the criticism by the international community of the colonial wars waged in three African fronts between 1961 and 1974. It continues to be used, mostly with irony, as it is here.

2 Arnedo was in charge of the publication of the volume titled *El gran libro de la mujer* (The great book of women; 1997), a reference work to address women's issues in the areas of health, psychology, nutrition, sexology, and law. She also authored *Desbordadas: La agitada vida de la 'elastic woman'* (Overwhelmed: The restless life of the elastic woman; 2000); and *La picadura del tábano: La mujer frente a los cambios de edad* (The sting of the

horsefly: Women and age-related changes; 2003) on the considerable misinformation on menopause.

3 The abortion issue continued to mobilize several groups, not necessarily identified with feminist struggle. Abortion in Portugal was only legalized in 2007.

4 The Mouvement de Libération des Femmes was founded in 1968, six years after Algeria gained independence and the former colonials and their descendants migrated to France.

5 In 1979, Maria de Lurdes Pintasilgo became the third woman prime minister in Europe. She was a major national and international leader not only of issues related to women but also of social justice. Her works will be analysed in the section dedicated to postdictatorial Portugal.

6 The Spanish Divorce Law of 1981 was the second of its kind in Spanish legal history. The first was the Divorce Law of 1932, which remained in force during the Second Republic, lapsing in 1939 after Franco's rise to power (Glos 1983, 667).

7 Based on the research of Célia Valiente about state feminism in Portugal, Tavares (2011, 347) notes the greater distance and conflict between government and nongovernment feminist activities in Spain compared to Portugal.

8 Red carnations adorned the war tanks and the guns of the military responsible for the coup d'état, calling for an end to the wars that, still in the mid-1970s, sustained Portuguese colonialism in Africa.

9 All translations are mine unless noted otherwise.

10 Natália Correia became famous among the greater public for her contributions to the periodical press and appearances on television. Her program *Mátria*, a series of documentaries running throughout 1986, unabashedly celebrated women's passion and eroticism as sources of life, markedly distancing herself from equal-rights feminism.

11 Until its reissue in 2002 by Editorial Caminho, this book was impossible to find in bookstores and even in most libraries.

12 Founded in 1914, the National Council of Portuguese Women was the national branch of the International Council of Women. Maria Lamas became its president in 1946, resulting in a marked increase in membership from all over the country. In retaliation, Salazar's government outlawed the council and had Maria Lamas fired from her job as editor-in-chief of the weekly women's supplement of a major Lisbon newspaper where she had worked since 1928; see Fiadeiro (1993, 13–14); Fiadeiro (2003); and Ferreira (2008).

13 This is how Maria de Lurdes Pintasilgo describes this conflation: "When the military coup of April 25, 1974 bursted out, people's power became, to a large extent, women's power. Or so it seemed until two years later, when it became apparent that 'old attitudes' kept coming up and shaping behavior at all levels" (Pintasilgo 1984, 573).

14 Barreno's thought clearly resonates with what Judith Butler argued in such important works as *Gender Trouble* (1990) and *Bodies That Matter* (1993). More importantly, however, is what appears to be Barreno and Butler's common inspiration in the thought of Luce Irigaray, for example, in *Ce sexe qui n'en est pas un* (1977; trans. *This Sex Which Is Not One*, 1985).

15 In her contribution to *Sisterhood Is Global*, Pintasilgo evokes a telling scene when she was running for president: "I will never forget the undisguised loss of control of most members of the conservative parties when, in the Parliament, I denounced the lies they had used to attach to the program of my government" (Pintasilgo 1984, 572).

16 During this period, Pintasilgo held different posts in committees of the United Nations, serving also on the Board of Directors of the United Nations University between 1983 and 1993, and as special adviser to its rector between 1990 and 1992. Mention should be made of her book, *Les nouveux feminismes: quéstions pour les chrétiens?* (1980), translated into Portuguese and published the following year as *Os novos feminismos: Interrogação para os cristãos* (1981).

17 For logical reasons, given Pintasilgo's affiliation with the Christian organization Graal, she did not take a stand on women's right to abortion.

18 Tellingly, Elena Laurenzi's annotated anthology of Zambrano's writings on women is titled *Nacer de sí misma* (Born from oneself), hinting at affinities between Zambrano and Italian feminist theory. Her analyses of Zambrano's essays also draw parallels with French difference-feminist thinkers such as Luce Irigaray.

19 "The two main tendencies that had appeared since 1975 (double and single militancy feminism) turned out to be irreconcilable. ... Besides the dichotomy of double and single militancy, the debate on 'equality' v. 'difference' feminism was sour and intense" (Durán and Gallego 1986, 213). Both Brooksbank Jones and de Grado note that difference feminism arose in part from the disillusion Spanish feminists experienced after the first exhilaration of the democratically sanctioned feminist movement wore off and the movement fragmented into various factions.

20 Mercedes de Grado defines the schism as between "feminismo socialista y el radical" (2004, 29).

21 See Brooksbank Jones 1997, 1–6 for a summary of the origins of post-Civil War Spanish feminism in oppositional activities to the Franco regime.

22 The "absence of a strong feminist tradition" is not quite accurate, since, as Geraldine Scanlon has amply demonstrated, there was a major Spanish feminist movement in the 1920s that had an important role in promulgating the Second Spanish Republic in 1931 and in women receiving the vote in 1932. Underground feminist activity tied to clandestine opposition parties during the Franco era continued some feminist presence during the dictatorship.

23 Italian difference feminist Carla Lonzi's *Escupamos sobre Hegel* was available in Spanish translation (published in Buenos Aires) in 1975, and Luce Irigaray's *Speculum* was published in Spanish in Madrid in 1978.

24 Rosa Chacel made a similar point in her 1931 essay "Esquema" and again in *Saturnal* (1972).

25 This *dependencia* is recent; the Instituto began as a *dependencia* of the Ministerio de Asuntos Sociales (Ministry of Social Issues) and was later moved to Asuntos Sociales y Trabajo (Social Issues and Labour) when these were consolidated in 1997; the Ministerio de Igualdad (Ministry of Equality) was created in 2008.

26 Even though the Instituto was conceived as an autonomous agency, as Anny Brooksbank Jones notes, the Instituto's "critics represented the Institute as a channel for the implementation of PSOE government policy on women and questioned its assumption that new institutional structures and priorities would win more supporters for women's causes (1995, 262). Many difference feminists feel the Instituto attempts "to speak on behalf of women who do not share its priorities, and for colluding with capitalism through measures that are themselves potentially oppressive" (1995, 262). Difference feminists believe the Instituto's "point of reference remains the hegemonic masculine model'" (1995, 265).

27 However, the judge retracted the decision, and in 1983 the Supreme Court annulled the Bilbao Audience's decision, sentencing five people. The case finally reached the Constitutional Court, which ratified the Supreme Court's decision in 1985.

28 We should point out that the relation with academic feminism has been fluid, of give and take, so that the academy has in a way invigorated activist feminism. The Feminist Meetings of 2009 celebrated in Granada attest to this phenomenon.

29 Largely influenced by global movements of decolonization, Galician nationalism also experienced a strong internationalist profile during those

years as attested by Galicia's participation in the signing of the so-called Letter of Brest. Said letter was also endorsed by representatives of separatist organizations in Ireland, Brittany, Galicia, the Basque Country, and Wales. The letter is a manifesto against colonialism in Western Europe and cannot be understood without taking into account the context of anticolonial thought, very influential at that time in the social and political structuring of peripheral cultural movements. At that time, also relevant in Galicia was the concept of "internal colonialism" linked to the regionalism of Robert Lafont (1967) and mediated through the influence of Frantz Fanon on Albert Memmi. All of this activity permeated *O atraso económico da Galiza* (1972; Galicia's economic backwardness) by Xosé Manuel Beiras, signalling the beginning of Galician postcolonial theory in economic thought.

30 The board was established in 1976, with organizations throughout major Galician cities. In addition to the above-mentioned campaigns, these groups were involved in promoting the decriminalization of abortion and amnesty for imprisoned women because of abortion issues. They also developed training activities related to biopolitical issues such as contraception and family matters.

31 As per the proliferation of groups such as the Asociación de Amas de Casa de Hogar, Zona Centro (Association of Housewives Home, Downtown), the Asociación de Amas de Casa, As Travesas (Association of Housewives, As Travesas), or the Asociación de Mujeres de Barrio del Calvario y Santa Cristina de Lavadores (Association of Women of Barrio del Calvario and Santa Cristina de Lavadores), all incorporated in the 1970s.

32 In 2009, the Popular Party took over the Xunta de Galicia, leading to the establishment of a Decreto del Plurilingüismo (Decree of Multilingualism) that, in practice reduced the political action of the government in regard to linguistic policy and translation. For example, there was a drastic cut in the governmental subsidies devoted to translation, whose impact on women's collections such as As letras das mulleres (Women's writings) by the publishing house Sotelo Blanco needs to be studied. Before the taking over of the Popular Party, feminist literary translation had experienced much momentum both in the Xerais section dedicated to the literary classics by women authors (directed by Maria Xosé Queizán) and in editorial houses specialized in translation, such as Rinoceronte. Precisely in the latter publishing house, a feminist publication by Maria Reimóndez created a high-profile controversy in the early millennium (Reimóndez 2009).

33 As per the creation of a Gender Section within the portal of Consello da Cultura Galega (Galician Culture Council), which among other

outstanding actions such as the publication of the *Álbum de mulleres* (Women's album) promoted, in collaboration with the Centre Dona i Literatura (Woman and Literature Centre) of the University of Barcelona, the initiative to digitalize the historical magazines from Galician feminism such as the above-mentioned *A Festa da Palabra Silenciada*, and *A Saia* or *Andaina*. See *Hemeroteca Feminista Galega A Saia* (Feminist Galician library [newspapers] A Saia), http://consellodacultura.gal/fondos_documentais/hemeroteca_feminista_galega/.

34 Pornography, as an audiovisual product, would have to wait more than a decade to be represented in Galicia. In fact, it was not until 2012 when Totó García, director and porn actor, presented the film *O divino ferrete* (The divine stinger). The title of the film was inspired by Manuel Curros Enríquez's *O divino sainete* (The divine comedy-sketch). The reference to Curros Enríquez, one of the most canonical writers of the nineteenth century in Galicia, clearly illustrates the weight still given to literature in shaping cultural products with Galician identity markers. It is no accident that Diego Ameixeiras, one of the star writers of the editorial house Xerais, collaborated in the writing of the script, thus indicating the link between cultural production and social aspiration for normalization.

Part VI. Iberian Feminisms' Diversity (1996 to the Present)

1 By the early 1990s, allegations of corruption and the beginning of an economic slowdown discredited the government of Aníbal Cavaco Silva, a Social Democrat who had shepherded the country into the European Union as prime minister between 1985 and 1996. He would go on to become president elect between 2010 and 2016.

2 Estádio do Sport Lisboa Benfica, more commonly known as Estádio da Luz, was founded in 1954, under the ownership of the famous soccer team Benfica. Throughout the years, it underwent several changes and expansions, the last of which included a complete renovation to host the World Cup in 2003.

3 The reference here is to the title of Expo '98, "The Oceans: A Heritage for the Future." Expo '92 was held in Seville, honouring "The Era of Discovery."

4 The survey responded to one of the items included in the Platform for Action in the aforementioned United Nations Fourth World Conference on Women.

5 Since the year 2002, scholar Pilar López Díez has conducted research, with the support of the Radio Televisión Española (RTVE; Spanish Radio

and Television) on how to discuss gender violence properly on television news. Another important contribution is the study by Asunción Bernárdez Rodal et al. on gender violence in Spanish cinema (Bernárdez, García, and González 2008).

6 On 14 July 2008, the Ministry of Equality of the Government of Spain, in collaboration with the Autonomous Communities, published the Evaluation Report on the implementation of the Organic Law. The report consists of a "Presentación" (Presentation) and three sections divided as follows: I. Prevención de la violencia de género: Sensibilización, concienciación, educación y formación (Prevention of violence: Sensitize, awareness raising, education, and training); II. Protección y asistencia social a las víctimas (Social protection and assistance to victims); III. Evolución de la violencia de género y análisis del impacto de la Ley Integral (Evolution of gender violence and impact analysis of the Comprehensive Law). The presentation offers the following assessment: "Three years is too short a time to make an assessment of the impact of the law because of the complexity of the problem which it intends to face" (1).

7 See Luna's personal reflections in "The Train That Gave Women a Voice" in the forthcoming *Cartographies of Madrid: Contesting Urban Space at the Crossroads of the Global South and Global North* by Silvia Bermúdez and Anthony L. Geist.

8 One of the many web sources supporting this protest and all feminist issues from the array of feminist positions in the Spanish state is the Federación Estatal de Organizaciones Feministas, Coordinadora Feminista (Federation of Feminist Organizations of the Spanish State, Feminist Coordinator), a network of women's groups that functions as an assembly (see www.feministas.org).

9 The trials in 2001, in the northern city of Maia, of seventeen women who had clandestine abortions captured national and international attention. Journalist Paula Moura Pinheiro captured the prochoice arguments in the book *Pela dignidade e saúde das mulheres portuguesas: Depoimentos pela despenalização do aborto no contexto do julgamento da Maia* (2002; For the dignity and health of Portuguese women: Testimonies on the decriminalization of abortion in the context of the Maia trial).

10 Interestingly so, even though the Spanish Clínica Arcos opened in Portugal after the decriminalization of abortion in 2007, those who could afford it still opted to get abortions in Badajoz or other locations of the famous clinic across the border (Gomes 2008).

11 In a provocative article titled, "O Clube Safo não é um grupo de lésbicas!" (Club Sappho is not a group of lesbians!), activist and scholar Eduarda

Ferreira argues for the struggle of lesbian rights to include those who do not identify as lesbian but defend the rights of freedom of sexuality and sexual expression within a more just society (Ferreira 2015, 43).

12 Pérez (2010) argues that Spanish LGTB communities have made pivotal contributions to queer theory.

13 The Feminist University is physically located in the Centre of Feminist Culture and Information, in Lisbon, an organ of the União de Mulheres Alternativa e Resposta [Alternative and Reply Womens's Union], known by the acronym, UMAR. This was the name given in the second half of the 1990 to a feminist group founded in 1976 and pointedly called until 1989, União de Mulheres Antifascistas e Revolucionárias (Antifacist and Revolutionary Women's Union). For more information on the long history of the group, see: http://www.umarfeminismos.org/index.php/quemsomos.

14 In contrast, there is also a tradition of motherless daughters in mid- to late-twentieth century novels by women. See, among others, Arkinstall 2002.

15 Much earlier, María Martínez Sierra argued for women as human beings: "¿No soy un ser humano, mundo dentro del mundo. Compendio de humilde pero firme grandeza? ... ¿Por qué no he de lograr, si únicamente de mí depende, esa eminencia impasionable?" (1920, 42). This concept is akin to the notion of "persona" that María Zambrano developed in the 1950s. See Juan Fernando Ortega Muñoz (1999) for a discussion of Zambrano's "persona" as a philosophical category.

16 Surprisingly, Miyares does not invoke Lidia Falcón who has meticulously argued for women as a social class.

17 See, among others, Ramis's *Coses que et passen a Barcelona quan tens 30 anys* (2008; Things that happen to you when you are 30 years old in Barcelona) and *Egosurfing* (2010), for which she was given the Premio Josep Pla (The Josep Pla Award). In 2007, Najat El Hachmi was awarded the Ramon Llull Prize for her novel *L'últim patriarca* (2008; The Last Patriarch). Her essay *Jo també sóc catalana* (2004; I am also Catalan) addresses migrant integration in Catalonia; she herself was born in Nador, Morocco.

18 Maternity as a literary discourse first arises in Rosalía de Castro's work, which shifts between a more traditional treatment in *A mi madre* (To my mother; 1863) and *En las orillas del Sar* (On the banks of the Sar river; 1884; Castro 2014) – for editorial reasons, the two books were subjected to her husband Manuel Murguía's guiding hand – to the heterodoxy of some poems in *Follas Novas* (New leaves; 1881), where the poetic voice narrates nocturnal adventures in which a woman leaves her children alone.

19 The presence of maternity in contemporary Galician literature is the subject of María Comesaña Amado's doctoral thesis (2016), which to date has not been published.

20 The prolific trajectory that Moure traces offers various examples of fertile, changing, and even problematic evolution. If in her first essay the author's position seems close to difference feminism, conceding special emphasis to the way in which biological identity could strengthen gender activism, in *Queer-emos un mundo novo* (2012), she articulates an adamant defence of queer theory as a tool to invalidate the continuum sex-gender.

21 The denunciation and the previous letter to the woman who was supposedly harassed are accessible on the following blog: http://sexualidademedular.blogspot.com.es/2015/06/feminismos-fwd-comunicado-final.html, accessed 22 February 2016, referring to the latest version of the communication dated 18 June 2015. The polemic unleashed on social media obliged the activists to rewrite successive editions of the denunciation. Other pages tied to feminism entered into the polemic. See, for example, the following blog, in which in contrast to the anonymity of the actions described, a manifesto signed by 150 Galician feminists was placed: https://ascandongasdoquirombo.wordpress.com/2015/07/21/pelo-fim-da-invisibilizac%CC%A7om-de-agressons-machistas-nos-movimentos-sociais/.

22 In her reply, the activist made explicit reference to the letter by Xurxo Nóvoa, that I comment on here. See the blog, or http://agal-gz.org/blogues/index.php/suso/.

23 Inaugurated on 20 October 2009 at the Centro Sociocultural O Ensanche (Ensanche Sociocultural Centre) in Santiago de Compostela, the exhibition remained in Galicia's capital city for ten days before it was shown throughout the rest of Galicia. Historian Encarna Otero, Nanina Santos Castroviejo, the founder of the feminist journal *Andaina* (discussed in ch. 30), and María Xosé Agra Romero, professor of philosophy, expert on feminist theory, and coordinator of the Comisión de Igualdade do Consello da Cultura Galega (Galician Council of Culture's Commission on Equality), supervised the project.

24 Some of these companies include Suchard, Molinex, Artiach, Hifraus, and Europunto.

25 As in the case of companies like Olarra, Michelin, Euskalduna, and Contenimar.

26 See ch. 29 above.

27 See ch. 29.

28 Self-defence is discussed in ch. 36.

29 Some of these campaigns were "Lesbianak edonon!" (Lesbians everywhere!), "Ez duzu lesbiana Izateko arrazoirik behar" (You don't need a reason to be a lesbian), "Sexualitateari mugarik ez!" (Sexuality without restrictions!), and "Zergatik zara heterosexuala?" (Why are you heterosexual?).

30 See ch. 29 and 36.

31 The first of these was created in Baiona in the 1960s. In 1988, there were thirty-six centres in all the Basque Country and Navarre.

32 See ch. 36.

33 For example, resources such as the Centro de Documentación y Estudios de la Mujer Maite Albiz de Bilbao (Centre for Documentation and Study of Women Maite Albiz of Bilbao; created in 1982) and the library and documentation centre of the Instituto de Promoción de Estudios Sociales (IPES; Institute for the Promotion of Social Studies) of Navarre (created in 1985).

34 Initiatives sponsored by Ekimen Feminista (Feminist Initiative) and Red de Estudios Feministas y de Género (Network of Feminist and Gender Studies), established in 2006 and bringing together professors and researchers from different fields.

35 Although presently there are assemblies in each one of the provinces of the Basque Country, only the Asamblea de Bizkaia has remained active.

36 At least in the Basque case, the new groups are small, have great autonomy, and appear to be linked to new means of communication such as the Internet; they also have a presence in special days and even in performances and festivals.

37 In the Basque Country, there are feminist bands in Basauri, Bilbao, Durango, Ermua, Gasteiz, Getxo, and Ondarroa, some of which spring up around the so-called Schools of Empowerment. These schools are spaces of feminist education, encounter, reflection, and stimulation for women's social and political participation, and function within the Equality Offices of various Basque townships.

38 An approach to the social theory of the body can be found in the first chapter of my *Antropología del cuerpo: Género, itinerarios corporales, identidad y cambio* (Esteban 2004; Anthropology of the body: Gender, corporal itineraries, identity, and change). Also see Blackman 2008.

39 In Hannah Arendt's sense, politics is understood as an ambience for human fulfilment, a collective action that engenders power. In a more restrictive way, politics would be a process oriented towards achieving group objectives. Here I include both dimensions.

40 See Connell 1995.

41 From the burning of bras in the 1970s and 1980s to current actions against major clothing companies, with chants such as "Abajo las barbies, arriba las barriguitas" (Down with Barbies, up with bellies) or "La talla 38 me oprime el chocho" (Size 38 busts my cunt) that are habitually sung in feminist marches. For those not familiar with Spanish clothing sizes, 38 is equivalent to a small.

42 The relationships between art, body, and feminism have been central themes of artistic works and exhibitions held in different Basque art centres like Arteleku (Donostia, Gipuzkoa) (http://www.arteleku.net/), the cultural centre Montehermoso (Vitoria-Gasteiz, Alava), during the time it was directed by Xabier Arakistain, or the Corn Exchange (Bilbao, Biscay). The Faculty of Fine Arts at the University of the Basque Country (UPV/EHU) has played a key role in the formation of various feminist artists such as Estibaliz Sadaba and Azucena Vieitez, who belong to the group Erreakzioa-Reaction. A specialist in this field is the Basque anthropologist Lourdes Mendez.

43 Here we underscore the so-called *besadas* (kissing) as actions where women kiss other women and/or men kiss other men publicly on 28 June, International Pride LGTB Day.

44 The feminist group Medeak (https://medeak.wordpress.com/), from Donostia (Gipuzkoa), autoidentifies itself as transfeminist and has carried out multiple activities that question the boundaries of gender and sexuality.

45 It is important to note some of the actions taken by associations close to the international group Mujeres de Negro (Women in Black) (http://mujeresdenegromadrid.blogspot.com.es/). In the Basque Country, María Seco and May Serrano have been promoting, since 2013, a performance called "Women in Black Acción (Action)" in memory of women killed by their partners or ex-partners. The action consists in forming a circle of women dressed in black that, suddenly, fall onto the floor where their silhouette is designed in chalk. Then, very slowly, each woman gets up in silence. Images of one of these performances can be seen at the following link; http://ecuadoretxea.blogspot.com.es/2015/10/women-in-black-accion-marcha-mundial.html.

46 This particular area of activism is the less creative of them all since, in general, what we find are protests or marches denouncing women's labour conditions.

47 See ch. 29 and 35.

48 This first law allowed for abortions in three cases: (1) danger to the health of the pregnant woman or (2) to the fetus, or (3) rape. In 2010, the law was expanded to permit the free cessation of a pregnancy before the fourteenth week, while keeping the earlier restrictions after that time.

49 See http://www.eldiario.es/norte/euskadi/cuerpo-mujer-ultima-frontera-capitalismo_0_260374735.html.

50 See http://www.feministas.org/plataforma-abortatzeko-eskubidea-818.html.

51 See, for example, http://politica.elpais.com/politica/2013/10/09/actualidad/1381304240_913874.html.

52 See the work of Basque anthropologist Miren Guilló Arakistain (2013, 2014). She is completing doctoral research on menstrual politics carried out by women and feminists in the Basque Country and throughout the Spanish state.

53 See ch. 35.

54 Catalan anthropologist Dolors Comas d'Argemir (2008) has pointed out that one of the distinctive elements of the Spanish state in this regard is the active involvement of the media in publicizing aggression against women, which heightens public awareness. This phenomenon is not occurring in other European countries or in the United States. For an analysis of the campaigns against violence against women in the Basque Countries, see ch. 35.

55 Maitena Monroy is one of the specialists in self-defence workshops. See http://www.feministas.org/IMG/pdf/curso_de_autodefensa_feminista_de_maitena_monroy.pdf.

56 See ch. 35.

Epilogue

1 Translated by Steve Roberts. This article would have not been possible without help from and many fruitful discussions with my many colleagues on the research project "The transmission of knowledge in female philosophical thought," supported by FFI2015–63828-P, Ministerio de Economía, Industria y Competitividad (MINECO; Ministry of Economy, Industry, and Competitiveness, Spanish Government) and the Fondo Europeo de Desarrollo Regional (FEDER; European Regional Development Fund, 2016–18); and in the Consolidated Research Group "Women's Creation and Thought," sponsored by SGR 44, Agència de Gestió d'Ajuts Universitaris i de Recerca (AGAUR; Agency for Administration of University and Research of the Generalitat of Catalonia).

2 See, for example, how a woman born in 1969 describes the "feminist revolution" (Despentes 2007, 16–17).

3 As Hannah Arendt says in "Tradition and the Modern Age" (1968, 26).

4 "Yo me muevo en el terreno de los hechos consumados, en la creación de zonas no-patriarcales, no-heterosexistas. Las compañeras que optan por la vía de la participación en instituciones patriarcales, necesitan de estos hechos consumados para poder avanzar en el terreno ... Y es a la necesidad de crear esos hechos a la que hemos de dedicar nuestras pasiones. Parece que últimamente no damos demasiado miedo a los patriarcas ... Volvamos a asustarlos un poco. Resulta muy divertido" (Amman 2000, 59; I move in the terrain of the fait accompli, in the creation of non-patriarchal, non-heterosexist areas. Colleagues who choose the path of participation in patriarchal institutions need these fait accompli in order to gain ground … And it is the need to create these to which we should devote our passions. It seems that lately we're not inspiring so much fear in the patriarchs … Let's frighten them a bit again. It's a lot of fun).

5 *The Second Sex* cannot be seen as the feminist equivalent of a Marxist theoretical text, and neither can it be represented as a set of commandments, as Françoise Collin (1986, 10) has pointed out.

6 "Un enfant si je veux, quand je veux!"

7 When I speak of a new generation, this is not because I believe that its youth is the source of a free and authentic standpoint, but because it is their first experience in the world of political participation: as Arendt says, in Stephen Spender's words, what for us are "problems" are issues "embodied in the flesh and blood of youth" (Arendt 1972, 119).

8 A character in a short story by Isabel Franc "leafs through the programs of various organizations: feminist centers and LGBTIQR [Lesbian, Gay, Bisexual, Trans, Intersexual, Queer], etc. associations (we keep adding more and more initials, wouldn't it be better just to call ourselves the alphabet collective?)"(Torras 2011, 206).

9 In fact, it was then that the expression "queer theory" was coined (De Lauretis 1991; and the talk "Identidad de género, teoría queer y la mala educación" [Gender identity, queer theory and the bad education] given at the Universidad Complutense de Madrid in May 2011).

10 José Luís Pardo, "La vieja historia de los nuevos tiempos (o algunas reflexiones sobre la fenomenología del tiempo como propedéutica para la filosofía de la historia)" (in Birulés, Roldán, and Gómez Ramos 2012, 123).

11 In 2006, Françoise Collin stated that the world still represents itself as masculine even after the spaces where women can intervene have changed a little. In fact, "the quantitative extension of women's creativity still has

not qualitatively remodeled the whole field." Proof of this is that women's creativity is still seen as something "particular," as a supplement to be added to the "universal" (and feminism itself has contributed in a certain measure to this perverse and paradoxical effect, as I noted at the outset); as if the actions and creations of women were never considered as capable of producing structural changes in our shared world, for the whole of humankind (Collin 2006, 189).

12 This is a play on the famous sentence by Simone de Beauvoir, "One is not born but becomes, a woman." Book 2 of her book *The Second Sex* begins with such a statement.

13 Thus we can read gestures appropriating masculinity as attempts to stop men from believing that they possess it.

14 See Françoise Collin's "La salida de la inocencia" (in Collin 2006, 165).

15 In some way, the fear that democracy will progressively advance towards the sameness of all human beings until it abolishes the difference between the sexes is not new, as Geneviève Fraisse has noted, but is in fact deeply rooted: it was one of the key arguments for the exclusion of women from political representation in the aftermath of the French Revolution. Thus in 1806, Étienne Pivert de Senancour expressed his apprehension that equality between the sexes would do away with love (Fraisse 2010b, 12–13).

16 Aina Pérez Fontdevila speaks of the "right to indifference," "un dret desitjable només en la seva consecució utòpica, és a dir, si aquesta indiferència fos el resultat d'una multiplicació i d'una desjerarquització de la diferència; si la visibilització aixequés el peatge de relegar sempre a algú a la invisibilitat" (Torras 2011, 146; a right desirable only in its utopian fulfilment, that is, if this indifference results from a multiplication and a dehierarchization of difference; if visibilization raises the barrier that always condemns someone to invisibility).

17 Françoise Collin has said in an interview that she would have no faith in a premature elimination of the difference between the sexes, of a supposed "indifference" that would only benefit the dominant position (Rochefort and Haase-Dubosc 2001, 195–210); and perhaps she was pointing towards what we noted previously: it seems that being a woman is a condition that we feel continually obliged to forget or to make others forget.

Works Cited

I Encuentro de Lesbianas de Euskadi, May 21–2, 1983.

AA.VV. 2004. *Elina Guimarães. "Pequenina mas constante": Uma feminista portuguesa, vida e obra (1904–1991)*. Lisbon: Comissão para a Igualdade e para os Direitos das Mulheres.

Ackelsberg, Martha. 1991. *Free Women of Spain: Anarchism and the Struggle for the Emancipation of Women*. Bloomington: Indiana University Press.

Acuña, Rosario de. [1887] 2007a. "A las mujeres del siglo XIX." In Bolado 2007b, 1225–40.

___. [1920] 2007b. "A Virginia González." In Bolado 2007b, 1781–83.

___. [1917] 2008a. "A Jaime Febré y Vicente Delgado." In Bolado 2008, 875–97.

___. [1881] 2008b. "Algo sobre la mujer (apuntes)." In Bolado 2008, 165–84.

___. [1888] 2008c. "Consecuencias de la degeneración femenina." In Bolado 2008, 505–33.

___. [1888] 2008d. "Discurso pronunciado en el acto de la instalación de la logia femenina Hijas del Progreso." In Bolado 2008, 555–82.

Adão, Áurea. 2014. "A necessidade de um ensino público para as meninas, no início de oitocentos: Das decisões políticas à instalação das primeiras escolas." Interacções 28: 55–67.

Aguado, Ana. 2007. "Mujeres y participación política entre la transición y la democracia en España." *Estudios de derecho judicial* 142: 165–80.

Aguado, Ana and Teresa María Ortega, eds. 2011. *Feminismos y antifeminismos: Culturas políticas e identidades de género en la España del siglo* XX. Valencia: Publicacions de la Universitat de València-Universidad de Granada.

Aguilar Fernández, Paloma. 1997. "La amnesia y la memoria: las movilizaciones por la amnistía en la transición a la democracia." In *Cultura y movilización en la España contemporánea*, edited by Rafael Cruz and Manuel Pérez Ledesma, 327–57. Madrid: Alianza.

Aguirre, Juan. 2006. "El teatro independiente en Vasconia, 1969–1984." *Revista de Estudios Vascos* 51 (2): 335–83.

Ahmed, Sara. 2004. *The Cultural Politics of Emotion*. New York: Routledge.
Aires, Matias. 2005. *Reflexões sobre a vaidade dos homens*. 2nd ed. Edited by Violeta Crespo de Figueiredo. Lisbon: Imprensa Nacional.
Albin, María C. 2007. "El costumbrismo feminista de Gertrudis Gómez de Avellaneda." *Anales de Literatura Hispanoamericana* 36: 150–70.
Aldekoa, Iñaki. 2004. *Historia de la literatura vasca*. San Sebastián: Erein.
Alemany García, Macario. 2005. *El concepto y la justificación del paternalismo*. Alicante: Biblioteca Virtual Miguel de Cervantes.
Almeida, São José. 2014. "Retornados: Uma história de sucesso por contar." *Público: Temas*. 20/04/2014. Accessed 13 September 2015. http://www.publico.pt/temas/jornal/retornados-uma-historia-de-sucesso-por-contar-28145408.
Almeida Portugal, Leonor de. [Marquesa de Alorna]. 1844. *Obras poeticas de D. Leonor d'Almeida Portugal Lorena e Lencastre, Marqueza d'Alorna, Condessa d'Assumar e d'Oeynhausen, conhecida entre os poetas portuguezes pello nome de Alcipe*. 6 vols. Lisbon: Na Imprensa Nacional.
Almeida Rodrigues, Graça. 1980. *Breve História da Censura Literária em Portugal*. Lisbon: ICALP, Biblioteca Breve.
Altamirano, Carlos, and Jorge Myers, eds. 2008. *Historia de los intelectuales en América Latina: I. La ciudad letrada, de la conquista al modernismo*. Buenos Aires: Katz.
Altuna, Belen. 2003. *Euskaldun fededun: Euskaldun ona izateko modu baten historia*. Zarautz: Alberdania.
___. 2015. "Género, obediencia y sociabilidad en el trabajo durante el primer franquismo." In *VIII Congreso de Historia Social: Sociabilidades en la historia*, edited by Santiago Castillo and Montserrat Duch. CD-ROM. Tarragona: Universitat Rovira i Virgili.
Álvarez Bustos, Arturo. 1902. "Feminismo." *Almería Alegre* 9 February.
Álvarez Lázaro, Pedro. 1985. *Masonería y librepensamiento en la España de la Restauración (Aproximación histórica)*. Madrid: Publicaciones de la Universidad Pontificia Comillas.
Álvarez-Uria, Amaia. 2011. *Genero eta nazio identitateak Katalina Eleizegiren antzezlanetan*. Bilbao: Universidad del País Vasco.
Alves de Atayde, Franke. 2011. "Eikasia." *Revista de Filosofía* 39: 113–51.
Amar y Borbón, Josefa. [1786] 2012. "Discurso en defensa del talento de las mugeres, y de su aptitud para el gobierno y otros cargos en que se emplean los hombres." In Johnson and Zubiaurre 2012, 47–51.
____. [Original work published 1790] 1994. *Discurso sobre la educación física y moral de las mujeres*. Edited by M. Victoria López-Cordón. Madrid: Cátedra.
Amaral, Ana Luísa. 2013. *Ara*. Lisbon: Sextante.

Amaral, Ana Luísa and Ana Gabriela Macedo. 2005. *Dicionário da crítica feminista*. Porto: Edições Afrontamento.
Amman, Gretel. 2000. *Escritos*. Barcelona: Associació de 20 Anys de Feminisme a Catalunya.
Amorós, Celia. 1998. "Feminismo y perversión." In *Sexo y esencia: De esencialismos encubiertos y esencialismos heredados: Desde un feminismo nominalista*, edited by Luisa Posada Kubissa, 130–41. Madrid: Horas y Horas.
Amorós i Pons, Anna. 2012. "Unha homenaxe as mulleres das nosas vidas." *Andaina: Revista do Movimento Feminista Galego* 61–2: 49.
Anastácio, Vanda. 2010. "Women and Literary Sociability in Eighteenth-Century Lisbon." In *Women Writing Back/Writing Women Back: Transnational Perspectives from the Late Middle Ages to the Dawn of the Modern Era*, edited by Alicia Montoya, Anke Gilleir, and Suzan van Dijk, 93–110. Leiden: Brill.
___. 2015. "Notes on the *Querelle des femmes* in Eighteenth-Century Portugal." *Portuguese Studies* 31 (1): 49–61.
Andrade, Paiva de. 1630. "Que se guardem de estar ociosas." In *Casamento perfeito, em que se contem advertências muito importantes pera viverem os casados em quietação e contentamento*, 174–86. Lisbon: Jorge Rodrigues.
Andrieu, Rosa. 1988. "Emakumea frankismo garaian." In *Emakumea Euskal Herriko historian: La mujer en la historia de Euskal Herria*, 90–1.
"Anticonceptivos y aborto." 1977. In *Jornadas de la Mujer de Euskadi* 26.
Apalategi, Ur. 2005. "Iparraldeko azken aldiko literatura euskal literatura sistemaren argitan (eta vice versa)." *Lapurdum* 10 (10): 1–18. https://doi.org/10.4000/lapurdum.32.
Aranda Pérez, Francisco José, ed. 2000. *Sociedad y élites eclesiásticas en la España Moderna*. Cuenca: Universidad de Castilla-La Mancha.
Arantza, et al., and AMV. 1986. "Reflexiones sobre el movimiento feminista de Euskadi." In *II Jornadas feministas de Euskadi*, edited by Asamblea de Mujeres de Euskadi and Aizan, 253–76. Bilbao: Asambleas de Mujeres de Euskadi.
Arbaiza, Mercedes. 1996. *Familia, trabajo y reproducción social: Una perspectiva microhistórica de la sociedad vizcaína a finales del Antiguo Régimen*. Leioa: Universidad del País Vasco.
Arenal, Concepción. 1895. "Estado actual de la mujer en España." *La España Moderna* 81: 62–90.
___. 1974a. *La emancipación de la mujer en España*. Edited by and prologue by Mauro Armiño. Madrid: Júcar.
___. [1868] 1974b. *La mujer del porvenir*. In Arenal 1974a, 97–188.
___. [1883] 1974c. *La mujer de su casa*. In Arenal 1974a, 189–284.
Arendt, Hannah. 1972. *Crisis of the Republic*. New York: Harcourt, Brace, and Company.

Aresti, Nerea, Miren Llona, and Javier Díaz Freire. 1994. "La mujer hablada: El discurso feminista y su crisis actual." *Viento Sur* 14: 73–82.

Aretxaga, Begoña. 1988. *Los funerales en el nacionalismo radical vasco*. Donostia: Casa Baroja.

Arias, Xela. 1990. *Tigres como cabalos*. Vigo: Xerais.

___. 1996. *Darío a diario*. Vigo: Xerais.

___. 2003. *Intempériome*. A Coruña: Espiral Maior.

Arkinstall, Christine. 2002. "Towards a Female Symbolic: Re-presenting Mothers and Daughters in Contemporary Spanish Narrative by Women." In *Writing Mothers and Daughters: Renegotiating the Mother in Western European Narratives by Women*, edited by Adalgisa Giorgio, 47–84. Providence: Berghahn.

___. 2014a. "An Overlooked Chapter in Spanish Feminist Histories: Ángeles López de Ayala's *El Gladiador del Librepensamiento* (1914–1920)." *Revista de Estudios Hispánicos* 48 (1): 49–74. https://doi.org/10.1353/rvs.2014.0010.

___. 2014b. *Spanish Female Writers and the Freethinking Press, 1879–1926*. Toronto: University of Toronto Press.

Arrien, Gregorio. 1987. *Educación y escuelas de barriada de Bizkaia (Escuela y autonomía, 1898–1936)*. Bilbao: Diputación Foral de Bizkaia.

Artola Renedo, Andoni. 2013. *De Madrid a Roma: La fidelidad del episcopado en España (1760–1833)*. Gijón: Trea.

Asamblea de Mujeres de Bizkaia. 1978. "Dña. Consti." *Leihoa* 2:5–6.

Asamblea de Mujeres de Euskadi and Aizan, ed. 1986. *II Jornadas feministas de Euskadi*. Bilbao: Asambleas de Mujeres de Euskadi.

Asociación "Mujeres en la Transición Democrática." 1999. *Españolas en la Transición: De excluidas a protagonistas (1973–1982)*. Madrid: Biblioteca Nueva.

Associação Feminina Portuguesa para a Paz. Estatutos. Lisbon, s.a.

Astigarraga, Jesús, ed. 2014. *The Spanish Enlightenment Revisited*. Oxford: Voltaire Foundation.

Astigarraga, Jesús, M. Victoria López-Cordón Cortezo, and José María Urquia, eds. 2009. *Ilustración, ilustraciones*. 2 vols. San Sebastián: Real Sociedad Bascongada de Amigos del País, Sociedad Estatal de Conmemoraciones Culturales.

Atienza López, Ángela. 2008. *Tiempos de conventos: Una historia social de las fundaciones en la España moderna*. Madrid: Marcial Pons.

Augustín Puerta, Mercedes. 2003. *Feminismo: Identidad personal y lucha colectiva (Análisis del movimiento feminista español en los años 1975 a 1985)*. Granada: Universidad de Granada, Colección Feminae.

Auzmendi, Lurdes. 2002. *Mª Dolores Agirre (1903–1997)*. Vitoria-Gasteiz: Eusko jaurlaritzaren argitalpen zerbitzu nagusia [Servicio Central de Publicaciones del Gobierno Vasco].

Bagüés Erriondo, Jon. 1990. *Ilustración musical en el País Vasco*. San Sebastián: Real Sociedad Bascongada de los Amigos del País.

Balaguer, Javier. 2001. *Solo mía*. Prod. Star Line Production/Televisión Española (TVE), film.

Ballesteros, Isolina. 2005. "Embracing the Other: The Feminization of Spanish Immigration Cinema." *Studies in Hispanic Cinemas* 2 (1): 3–14. https://doi.org/10.1386/shci.2.1.3/1.

Bar Cendón, Mónica. 2010. *Feministas galegas: Claves dunha revolución en marcha*. Vigo: Xerais.

Barreno, Maria Isabel. 1989. *A morte da mãe*. Lisbon: Caminho.

Barreno, Maria Isabel, Maria Teresa Horta, and Maria Velho da Costa. 1974. *Novas cartas portuguesas*. Lisbon: Futura.

___. [1972] 1980. *Novas cartas portuguesas*. 3rd ed. Lisbon: Moraes Editora.

___ [The Three Marias]. 1994. *New Portuguese Letters*. Translated by Helen R. Lane and Faith Gillespie. Columbia, LA: Readers International.

Barrio Gozalo, Maximiliano. 2010. *El clero en la España moderna*. Córdoba: Caja Sur.

Baum, Michael, and Ana Espírito-Santo. 2012. "Portugal's Quota-Parity Law: An Analysis of its Adoption." *West European Politics* 35 (2): 319–42. https://doi.org/10.1080/01402382.2011.648009.

Baum III, Robert. 1994. "The Counter-Discourse of Josepha Amar y Borbón's Discurso." *Dieciocho* 17 (1): 7–15.

"Begoña Caamaño Rascado." n.d. Álbum de mulleres. http//www.culturagalega.org.

Beiras Torrado, Xosé Manuel. 1972. *O atraso económico da Galiza*. Vigo: Galaxia.

Belo, Maria. 1989. "A Hero of Portuguese Women." In *Women and Counter Power*, edited by Yolande Cohen, 163–77. Montreal: Black Rose Books.

Bello Vazquez, Raquel. 2005. *Mulher, nobre, ilustrada, dramaturga: Osmia de Teresa de Mello Breyner no sistema literário português (1788–1795)*. Santiago: Laiovento.

Bento, Almerinda. 1998. "Feminismo: O espaço para além da institucionalização." In *Movimento Feminista em Portugal*, Seminário organizado pela UMAR 5–6 de Dezembro de 1998, 84–6. Accessed 10 September 2015. http://www.umarfeminismos.org/images/stories/pdf/seminariomovfeminista.pdf.

Bermúdez, Silvia. 2001. "Rocking the Boat: The Black Atlantic in Spanish Pop Music from the 1980s and the '90s." *Arizona Journal of Hispanic Cultural Studies* 5 (1): 177–93. https://doi.org/10.1353/hcs.2011.0034.

___. 2002. "De *La ansiedad de la influencia* a *Los diálogos con Rosalía*: Hablemos de relaciones intrapoéticas en la literatura gallega." In *Sexualidad y escritura (1850–2000)*, edited by Raquel Medina and Barbara Zecchi, 281–94. Barcelona: Anthropos.

___. 2015. "Feminismo y responsabilidad social en el siglo XXI." *Letras femeninas* 41 (1): 147– 62.

Bernárdez Rodal, Asunción, Irene García Rubio, and Soraya González Guerrero, eds. 2008. *Violencia de género en le cine español: Análisis de los años 1998 a 2002*. Madrid: Editorial Complutense.

Bettaglio, Marina. 2015. "(Post) Feminist Maternal Chronicles and Their Discontents." *Letras femeninas* 41 (1): 228–45.

Bhabha, Homi K., ed. 2010. *Nación y narración: Entre la ilusión de una identidad y las dificultades*. Translated by M.G. Ubaldini. Buenos Aires: Siglo XXI.

Bieder, Maryellen. 1990. "Feminine Discourse/Feminist Discourse: Concepción Gimeno de Flaquer." *Romance Quarterly* 37 (4): 459–77. https://doi.org/10.1080/08831157.1990.9925881.

___. 1994a. "Caterina Albert i Paradis." In McNerney and Enríquez de Salamanca 1994, 31–5.

___. 1994b. "Dolors Monserdà i Vidal de Macià." In McNerney and Enríquez de Salamanca 1994, 245–8.

___. 2015. "'Eminencias hembras': Emilia Pardo Bazán y las redes literarias, sociales e intelectuales de mujeres de letras." In Fernández 2015a, 167–90.

Bilbao, Begoña, Gurutze Ezkurdia, Karmele Pérez, and Josu Chueca, eds. 2012. *Emakumeak, hitza eta bizitza*. Bilbao: Universidad del País Vasco.

Birulés, Fina, and Rosa Rius, eds. 2011. *Pensadoras del siglo X: Aportaciones al pensamiento filosófico femenino*. Madrid: Instituto de la Mujer.

Birulés, Fina, Concha Roldán, and Antonio Gómez Ramos, eds. 2012. *Vivir para pensar: Ensayos en homenaje a Manuel Cruz*. Barcelona: Herder.

Blackbourn, David. 2012. "'The Horlogue of Time': Periodization in History." *PMLA* 127 (2): 301–7. https://doi.org/10.1632/pmla.2012.127.2.301.

Blackman, Lisa. 2008. *The Body: The Key Concepts*. New York: Berg.

Blanco, Alda. 1998. "A las mujeres de España: The Feminist Essays of María Martínez Sierra." In Glenn and Mazquiarán de Rodríguez 1998, 75–99.

Blanco, Carmen. 1986. "O antisufraxismo e a condición feminina en 'A muller galega' de Francisca Herrera Garrido." *Grial* 92 (April, May, June): 147–62.

___. 1995a. *Nais, damas, prostitutas e feirantas*. Vigo: Xerais.

___. 1995b. *Mulleres e independencia*. A Coruña: Ediciós do Castro.

___. 1995c. *O contradiscurso das mulleres*. Vigo: Nigra.

___. 2006. *Sexo e lugar*. Vigo: Xerais.

Blanco, Oliva. 2010. *La polémica feminista en la España ilustrada: La "Defensa de las mujeres" de Feijoo y sus detractores*. Ciudad Real: Almud.

Blasco, Inmaculada. 2010. *Paradojas de la ortodoxia: Política de masas y militancia católica femenina en España (1919–1939)*. Saragossa: Prensas Universitarias de Zaragoza.

Bock, Gisela, and Margarete Zimmermann, eds. 1997. *Die europäische Querelle des Femme: Geschlecterdebatten seit dem 15. Jahrhundert*. Querelles, Jahrbuch für Frauenforschung, series 2. Stuttgart: Meztler.

Bolado, José, ed. 2007a. *Artículos (1881–1884)*. Vol. 1 of *Rosario de Acuña y Villanueva: Obras reunidas*, edited by José Bolado. Oviedo: KRK.

___. 2007b. *Artículos (1885–1923)*. Vol. 2 of *Rosario de Acuña y Villanueva: Obras reunidas*, edited by José Bolado. Oviedo: KRK.

___. 2008. *Prosa*. Vol. 3 of *Rosario de Acuña y Villanueva: Obras reunidas*, edited by José Bolado. Oviedo: KRK.

Bollaín, Icíar. 2003. *Te doy mis ojos*. Prod. Alta Producción/Producciones La Iguana S.L., film.

Bolufer, Mónica. 1998. *Mujeres e Ilustración: La construcción de la feminidad en la España del siglo XVIII*. Valencia: Institució Alfons el Magnànim.

___. 2005a. *"Neither Male, Nor Female:* Rational Equality in the Spanish Enlightenment." In *Women, Gender and Enlightenment*, edited by Sarah Knott and Barbara Taylor, 389–409. London: Palgrave.

___. 2005b. "Transformaciones culturales: Luces y sombras." In *Historia de las mujeres en España y América Latina*, vol. 2: El mundo moderno: España y América colonial, edited by Isabel Morant, 479–510. Madrid: Cátedra.

___. 2007. "'Hombres de bien': Modelos de masculinidad y expectativas femeninas, entre la ficción y la realidad." *Cuadernos de Ilustración y Romanticismo* 15: 7–31.

___. 2008. *La vida y la escritura en siglo XVIII: Inés Joyes: Apología de las mujeres*. Valencia: Publicacions de la Universitat de València.

___. 2009a. "Debate de los sexos y discursos de progreso en la Ilustración española." In *Modernidad iberoamericana: Cultura, política y cambio social*, edited by Francisco Colom, 321–49. Madrid: Iberoamericana/Vervuert.

___. 2009b. "Las relaciones entre los sexos en el discurso ilustrado del progreso: España y Europa." In Astigarraga, López-Cordón, and Urquia, 2:793–10. San Sebastián: Real Sociedad Bascongada de los Amigos del País.

___. 2009c. "Women of Letters in Eighteenth-Century Spain: Between Tradition and Modernity." In *Eve's Enlightenment: Women's Experience in Spain and Spanish America, 1726–1839*, edited by Catherine Jaffe and Elizabeth Franklin Lewis, 17–32. Baton Rouge: Louisiana State University Press.

___. 2011. "Conversations from a Distance: Spanish and French Eighteenth-Century Women Writers." In Ros and Hazbun 2011, 175–88.

Bolufer, Mónica, and Mónica Burguera, eds. 2010. "Dossier: Género y modernidad en España: De la Ilustración al liberalismo." *Ayer* 78: 13–168.

Bolufer Peruga, Mónica, and Isabel Morant Deusa. 1998. "On Women's Reason, Education and Love: Women and Men of the Enlightenment in Spain and France." *Gender & History* 10 (2): 183–216. https://doi.org/10.1111/1468-0424.00097.

Bolufer Peruga, Mónica. 2014. "Traducción, cultura y política en el mundo hispánico del siglo XVIII: Reescribir las *Lettres d'une péruvienne* de Françoise de Graffigny." *Studia historica: Historia Moderna* 36 (0): 293–325. https://doi.org/10.14201/shhmo201436293325.

___. 2016a. "En torno a la sensibilidad dieciochesca: Discursos, prácticas, paradojas." In *Las mujeres y las emociones en Europa y América: Discursos, representaciones, prácticas: Siglos XVII–X IX*, edited by María Luisa Candau Chacón, 29–56. Santander: Editorial de la Universidad de Cantabria.

___. 2016b. "Reasonable Sentiments: Sensibility and Balance in Eighteenth-Century Spain." In *Engaging the Emotions in Spanish Culture and History*, edited by Luisa E. Delgado, Pura Fernández, and Jo Labanyi, 21–38. Nashville: Vanderbilt University Press.

Bordiga Grinstein, Julia. 2002. "Panorama de la dramaturgia femenina española en la segunda mitad del siglo XVIII y principios del XIX." *Dieciocho* 25 (2): 195–218.

___. 2003. "La rosa trágica de Málaga: Vida y obra de María Rosa de Gálvez." *Dieciocho anejos* 26 (3): 1–223.

Bosé, Bimba. 2013. *Y de repente soy madre*. Madrid: Temas de Hoy.

Botrel, Jean-François. 1987. "L'aptitude à communiquer: alphabétisation et scolarisation en Espagne de 1860 à 1920." In *De l'alphabétisation aux circuits du libre en Espagne: XVIe–XIXe siècles: ouvrage collectif*, 105–40. Paris: Centre National de la Recherche Scientifique.

Braidotti, Rosi. 2004. *Feminismo, diferencia sexual y subjetividad nómade*. Barcelona: Gedisa.

Brancas, Marta. 1998. *Guía de mujeres de Bilbao: 700 años de historia*. Bilbao: Ayuntamiento de Bilbao/Servicio Municipal de la Mujer.

Brandenberger, Tobias. 1997. "*Malas hembras* und *virtuosas mujeres*: *Querelles* in der spätmittelalterlichen und frühneuzeitlichen Iberoromania." In Bock and Zimmermann 1997, 183–202. Stuttgart: J.B. Metzler. https://doi.org/10.1007/978-3-476-03690-2_6.

Bretz, Mary Lee. 1998. "Nelken's *La condición social de la mujer en España*: Between the Pedagogic and the Performative." In Glenn and Mazquarian de Rodríguez 1998b, 100–26.

Brooksbank Jones, Anny. 1995. "Spain's Institute for Women." *European Journal of Women's Studies* 2 (2): 261–9. https://doi.org/10.1177/135050689500200209.

____. 1997. *Women in Contemporary Spain*. Manchester: Manchester University Press.

Burdiel, Isabel, ed. 2012. *Los borbones en pelota*. Saragossa: Institución Fernando el Católico.

Burgos, Carmen de, 1900. *Ensayos literarios*. Almería: n.p.

___. 1904. *La protección y la higiene de los niños*. Valencia: El Campeón del Magisterio.

___. 1904b. *El divorcio en España*. Madrid: Teléfono.

___. 1908. "El voto de la mujer." *El Heraldo de Madrid*, 19 March, 1.

___. 1911a. "La Condesa de Pardo Bazán [interview]." *El Liberal*, 9 February, 2.

___. 1911b. *Misión social de la mujer*. Bilbao: n.p.

___. 1914. *Impresiones de Argentina*. Almería: H. Navarro de Vera.

___. 1917. *Mis viajes por Europa*. 2 vols. Madrid: Sanz Calleja.

___. 1927. *La mujer moderna y sus derechos*. Valencia: Sempere.

___. 2007. *La mujer moderna y sus derechos*. Edited by Pilar Ballarín. Madrid: Biblioteca Nueva.

Burguera, Mónica. 2011. "Historia e identidad: Los lenguajes sociales del feminismo romántico en España (1844–1846)." *Arenal* 18 (1): 53–83.

___. 2012. *Las damas del liberalismo respetable: Los imaginarios sociales del feminismo liberal en España (1834–1850)*. Madrid: Cátedra.

____. 2016. "Mujeres y revolución liberal en perspectiva: Esfera pública y ciudadanía femenina en la primera mitad del siglo XIX en España." In *Cuando todo era posible: Liberalismo y antiliberalismo en España e Hispanoamérica (1740–1842)*, edited by Encarnación García Monerris, Ivana Frasquet, and Carmen García Monerris, 257–96. Madrid: Sílex.

Busquests, Milena. 2015. *També això passarà*. Barcelona: Ara Llibres.

Butler, Judith. 2007. *El género en disputa: El feminismo y la subversión de la identidad*. Barcelona: Paidós.

Caballé, Anna, ed. 2004. *La vida escrita por las mujeres*. Barcelona: Lumen.

___. 2013. *El feminismo en España: La lenta conquista de un derecho*. Madrid: Cátedra.

Cabañas, Mariana. 2007. "Las mujeres solas." In *Antología del teatro breve español del siglo XVIII*, edited Fernando Doménech, 205–26. Madrid: Biblioteca Nueva. [1757?]

Cabarrús, Francisco. 1786. "Discurso." *Memorial literario* 8 (May): 74–85.

Cabezas, Juan Antonio. 1942. Concepción Arenal o el sentido romántico de la justicia. Madrid: Espasa-Calpe.

Cabré, María Ángeles. 2013. *Leer y escribir en femenino*. Barcelona: Aresta.

Cabrera Bosch, María Isabel. 1988. "Las mujeres que lucharon solas: Concepción Arenal y Emilia Pardo Bazán." In Folguera 1988b, 29–50.

Cabezas, Juan Antonio. *Concepción Arenal o el sentido romántico de la justicia*. Madrid: Espasa-Calpe, 1942.

Caiel. 1892. *O que deve ser a instrução secundária da mulher?* Lisbon: Typographia e Stereotypia Moderna.

___. 1900. *Comentários à vida.* Lisbon: Parceria de António Maria Pereira.

Caine, Barbara, and Glenda Sluga. 2000. *Gendering European History: 1780–1920.* London: Continuum.

Calafell, Mireia, and Aina Pérez, eds. 2011. *El cuerpo en mente: Versiones del ser desde el pensamiento contemporáneo.* Barcelona: Universitat Oberta de Catalunya.

Callahan, William James. 1989. *Iglesia, poder y sociedad en España, 1750–1874.* Madrid: Nerea.

Calleja, Mariano. 2009. "La Comisión de Igualdad se aburre." *ABC* (20 September) 20.

Campoamor, Clara. 2006. *El voto femenino y yo: Mi pecado mortal.* Madrid: horas y Horas.

Camps, Victoria. 1998. *El siglo de las mujeres.* Madrid: Cátedra.

Candau Chacón, María Luisa. 1994. *La carrera eclesiástica en el siglo XVIII.* Sevilla: Universidad de Sevilla.

Cano, Harkaitz. 1997. *Emakumeak euskal antzerkian.* Colección Bidegileak 9. Vitoria: Eusko Jaurlaritza.

Cantizano Márquez, Blasina. 2004. "La mujer en la prensa femenina del XIX." *Ámbitos* 11–12: 281–98.

Capdevila-Argúelles, Nuria. 2008. *Autoras inciertas: Voces olvidadas de nuestro feminismo.* Madrid: horas y Horas.

Capel Martínez, Rosa María. 1986. *El trabajo y la educación de la mujer en España (1900–1930).* Madrid: Ministerio de Cultura/Instituto de la Mujer.

Capmany, María Aurèlia. 1973. *El feminisme à Catalunya.* Barcelona: Nova Terra.

___. 2008. *La dona a Catalunya: Consciència i situació.* Madrid: horas y Horas.

Carbonell, Neus. 1997. "Feminisme, modernitat i narrativa en Dolors Monserdà." *Lectora: Revista de dones i textualitat* 3: 19–26.

Cardoso, Dulce Maria. 2011. *O retorno.* Lisbon: Tinta da China.

"Carme Karr i Alfonsetti." 2015. http://www.escriptors.cat/autors/karrc/pagina.php?id_sec=1631.

Carr, Raymond. 1980. *Modern Spain 1875–1980.* Oxford: Oxford University Press.

___. 1982. *Spain 1808–1975.* 2nd ed. Oxford: Clarendon.

Caruncho, Cristina, and Purificación Mayobre, eds. 1998. *Entre a igualdad e a diferencia.* Vigo: Universidad de Vigo.

Caso, Ángeles. 2010. *Contra el viento.* Barcelona: Planeta.

Castañeda, Paloma. 1994. *Carmen de Burgos, Colombine.* Madrid: Horas y Horas.

Castaño, Yolanda. 2003. *O libro da egoísta*. Vigo: Galaxia.

Castro, João Baptista de. 1752. *Confortaçam para os queixosos em que se queixa hum estudante pobre, hum soldado humilde, huma freira descontente, do casado, da cazada, e o pay do filho indocil e perverso; a que responde e conforta hum sabio e catholico politico em tudo experimentado. Que consagra dedica, e offerece ao senhor doutor Manoel Dias Ortigam*. Lisbon: José da Sylva Natividade. Republished 1818 as *A affliccção confortada dirigida á Virtude da Paciência*. Lisbon: Typographia Rollandiana.

Castro, Olga. 2011. "Feminismo nacionalista nunha nación patriarcal: Análise da proposta e recepción crítica da obra de Queizán." In *Cara a unha poética feminista: Homenaxe a María Xosé Queizán*, edited by Camiño Noia and Manuel Forcadela, 81–101. Vigo: Servizo de Publicacións da Universidade de Vigo.

Castro, Rosalía de. [1858] 1996a. "Lieders." In *Álbum del Miño* [Vigo]: *Obra completa*. Padron: Fundación Rosalía de Castro.

___. [1865] 1996b. "Las literatas: Carta a Eduarda." In *Water Lilies / Flores del Agua*, edited by Amy Kaminsky, 471–7. Minneapolis: University of Minnesota Press.

___. 2014. *On the Edge of the River Sar: A Feminist Translation*. Edited and translated by Michelle Geoffrion-Vinci. London: Farleigh Dickinson University Press / Rowan and Littlefield.

Castro e Almeida, Virgínia de. 1913. *A mulher: História da mulher, a mulher moderna – Educação*. Lisbon: Livraria Clássica de A.M. Teixeira.

Castro Osório, Ana de. 19–. *Mundo nuevo*. Porto: Tipografía Companhia Portuguesa Editora.

___. 1905. *Às mulheres portuguesas*. Lisbon: Livraria Editora Viúva Tavares Cardoso.

___. 1907. "Galeria feminina: Louise Ey." *Vanguarda* (18 March): 2, col. 4.

___. 1911. *A mulher no casamento e no divórcio*. Lisbon: Guimarães.

___. 1913. "Carta a D. Felismina Torrezão." In *Almanaque das senhoras para 1913*, 253. Lisbon: Parceria A. Maria Pereira.

___. 1925. *O direito da mãe: Novela*. Porto: Civilizaçao.

Castro y Antonio, Ana María. 2005a. *Mulleres mais que mitos*. Vigo: Trymar.

___. 2005b. *Ousadas e valentes*. Vigo: Trymar.

___. 2006a. *A historia do feminismo en Galicia: 1*. Vigo: Trymar. Compact Disc.

___. 2006b. *A historia do feminismo en Galicia: As protagonistas*. Vigo: Trymar. Compact Disc.

___. 2007. *Mulleres revolucionarias*. Vigo: Trymar.

Cerezales, Cristina. 2000. *De oca a oca*. Barcelona: Destino.

___. 2006. *Por el camino de las grullas*. Barcelona: Destino.

___. 2009. *Música blanca*. Barcelona: Destino.

Chacel, Rosa. 1931. "Esquema de los problemas prácticos y actuales del amor." *Revista de Occidente (Madrid, Spain)* 92: 129–80.

___. 1972. *Saturnal*. Barcelona: Seix Barral.

Chacón, Dulce. 2002. *La voz dormida*. Madrid: Santillana.

Chacón Jiménez, Francisco, ed. 1990. *Historia social de la familia en España: Aproximación a los problemas de familia, tierra y sociedad en Castilla (ss. XV–XIX)*. Alicante: Gil-Albert.

___. 2009. "Familia y hogar en la sociedad española." In *La familia en la historia*, edited by Javier Lorenzo Pinar Francisco, 121–34. Salamanca: Universidad de Salamanca.

Charnon-Deutsch, Lou. 2011. "What They Saw: Women's Exposure to and in Visual Culture in Nineteenth-Century Spain." In Ros and Hazbun 2011, 189–209. Woodbridge, Suffolk: Tamesis.

Chartier, Roger. 1992. *L'ordre des livres: lecteurs, auteurs, bibliothèques en Europe entre le XIVe et le XVIIIe siècle*. Aix-en-Provence: Alinéa.

Chueca Intxusta, Josu. 2012. "Emakumeak erresistentziaren haziak." In Bilbao et al. 2012, 123–40.

Cienfuegos, Beatriz. [1763] 2005. *La pensadora gaditana*. Edition, introduction, and notes by Scott Dale. Newark, Delaware: Juan de la Cuesta.

Clemente Palacios, María Victoria. 2015. "Ángeles López de Ayala (1858–1926): Ícono del librepensamiento en la España de entre siglos." PhD dissertation, Universidad Complutense de Madrid.

Colaizzi, Giulia, ed. 1990. *Feminismo y teoría del discurso*. Madrid: Cátedra.

Collin, Françoise. 1986. "Le féminisme et la crise du moderne." In *Fragments et collages*, edited by Diane Lamoureux, 7–16. Montreal: Remue-ménage.

___. 2006. *Praxis de la diferencia: Liberación y libertad*. Barcelona: Icaria.

___. 2010–11. "Penser/agir, la différence des sexes: entre insurrection et institution avec et autour de Françoise Collin." *Transmissio(s) feministe(s)* 1: 6–15.

Comas d'Argemir, Dolors. 2008. "Construyendo imaginarios, identidades, comunidades: El papel de los medios de comunicación." In *Retos teóricos y nuevas prácticas: Actas del XI Congreso de Antropología de la FAAEE*, edited by Margaret Bullen and María Carmen Díez Mintegui, 179–208. Donostia: Ankulegi.

Comella Gutiérrez, Beatriz. 2012. "Los Reales Colegios de Santa Isabel y Loreto de Madrid según sus Constituciones de 1715 y 1718." *Historia de la Educación: Revista Interuniversitaria* 31: 167–87.

Comesaña Amado, María. 2016. "De Darío a Sofía (1996–2014): A representación da maternidade nas autoras galegas actuais." PhD dissertation, Universidad de Vigo.

Comisión Antiagresiones, 1991. "Jueces, cómplices, acusados." *Geu Emakumeok* 13: 4.

Comisiones y Colectivos de Lesbianas de Euskadi. 1986. "El amor existe entre mujeres." *Sorginak* 1: preludio.

"Concepción Arenal, nuevo 'doodle' de Google." 2015. *La Vanguardia* (31 January). http://www.lavanguardia.com/cultura/20150131/54426698362/concepcion-arenal.html.

Connell, Robert W. 1995. "Men's Bodies." In *Masculinities*, edited by Raewyn Connell, 45–67. Oxford: Polity.

Conselho Nacional das Mulheres Portuguesas na Sociedade Nacional de Belas Artes. 1947. *Catálogo da Exposição de Livros Escritos por Mulheres.* Lisbon: Gráfica Santelmo.

Constituciones y códigos políticos españoles 1808–1978. 1998. Edited by Julio Montero. Barcelona: Ariel.

Coordinadora Feminista de Barcelona. 1978. *Mujer y constitución: Dona, la constitució no recull els nostres drets.* Barcelona.

Coordinadora Feminista. Federación Estatal de Organizaciones Feministas. 2012. "Galicia: memoria histórica de las mujeres con las que el franquismo no pudo." Accessed 16 June 2016. http://feministas.org/galicia-memoria-historica-de-las.html.

Cordeiro, Célia Carmen. 2012. *Ana de Castro Osório e a mulher republicana portuguesa: Veículo de regeneração da nação e da preservação da identidade nacional.* Lisbon: Fonte da Palavra.

Cornell, Drucilla, ed. 2007. *Feminism and Pornography.* New York: Oxford University Press.

Coronado, Carolina. 1991. *Poesías.* Edited by Noël Valis. Madrid: Castalia/Instituto de la Mujer.

Correia, Natália. 2003. *Breve história da mulher e outros escritos.* Lisbon: Parceria A.M. Pereira.

Costa, Marie. 2007. "Conflictos matrimoniales y divorcio en Cataluña: 1775–1833." PhD dissertation, Institut Universitari d'Història Jaume Vicens Vives, Universitat Pompeu Fabra.

Costa Lopes, Ana Maria. 2005. *Imagens da mulher na imprensa feminina de oitocentos: Percursos de modernidade.* Lisbon: Quimera.

———. 2013. "Francisca de Assis Martins Wood." In Esteves and Osório de Castro 2013, 316.

Council of Europe. 2016. "Chart of Signatures and Ratifications of Treaty 210." Treaty Office. http://www.coe.int/en/web/conventions/full-list/-/conventions/treaty/210/signatures.

Couto-Potache, Dejanirah. 1982. "Les origines du féminisme au Portugal." In *Actes du Colloque Utopie et Socialisme au Portugal au XIX siècle*, 449–78. Paris: Centre Culturel Portugais/Fondation Calouste Gulbenkian.

Cova, Anne. 2014. "The National Councils of Women in France, Italy and Portugal: Comparisons and Entanglements 1888–1939." In *Gender History in a Transnational Perspective: Networks, Biographies, Gender Orders*, 46–76. Oxford: Berghahn Books.

Cova, Anne, and António Costa Pinto. 1997. "Le Salazarisme." In *Encyclopédie politique et historique des femmes*, edited by Christine Fauré, 685–99. Paris: Presses Universitaires de France.

Criado y Domínguez, D. Juan P. 1889. *Literatas españolas del siglo XIX: Apuntes bibliográficos*. Madrid: Imprenta de Antonio Pérez Dubrull.

d'Armada, Fina. 2008. *O Livro feminista de 1715: O Primeiro Grito Revolucionário*. Rio Tinto: Evolua.

Davies, Catherine. 1991. "Feminist Writers in Spain Since 1900: From Political Strategy to Personal Inquiry." In *Textual Liberation: European Feminist Writing in the Twentieth Century*, edited by Helena Forsås, 192–226. London: Routledge.

___. 1998. *Spanish Women's Writing, 1849–1996*. London: Athlone.

___. 1999. "Feminism." In *Encyclopedia of Contemporary Spanish Culture*, edited by Eamonn Rodgers, 177–8. London: Routledge.

Davies, Rebecca. 2014. *Written Maternal Authority and Eighteenth-Century Education in Britain: Educating by the Book*. Aldershot, Hants: Ashgate.

Dávila, Paulí, Ana Eizagirre, and Idoia Fernández. 1992. "Los procesos de alfabetización y euskaldunización en Euskal Herria, 1860–1990." *Ikastaria: Coadernos de educación* 7: 63–99.

Davis, Rhian. 2012. "'La cuestión femenina' and *La España moderna* (1889–1914)." *Bulletin of Spanish Studies* 89 (1): 61–85. https://doi.org/10.1080/14753820.2012.646811.

Dedieu, Jean-Pierre. 2010. *Après le roi: essai sur l'effondrement de la monarchie espagnole*. Madrid: Casa de Velázquez.

Delgado, Luisa Elena, Pura Fernández, and Jo Labanyi. 2016. *Engaging the Emotions in Spanish Culture and History*. Nashville: Vanderbilt University Press.

De Lauretis, Teresa. 1991. "Queer Theory: Lesbian and Gay Sexualities, Differences." *Journal of Feminist and Cultural Studies* 3 (2): iii–xviii.

Delille, Maria Manuela. 2001. "Carolina Michäelis de Vasconcelos (1851–1925): 'Intermediária nata entre a cultura neolatina e a germânica..'" *Revista da Faculdade de Letras, Línguas e Literaturas* 18: 33–48.

Dellinger, Mary Ann. 2013. "The Mythopoeia of Dolores Ibárruri, Pasionaria." In *Memory and Cultural History of the Spanish Civil War: Realms of Oblivion*, edited by Aurora Morcillo, 285–316. Leiden: Brill. https://doi.org/10.1163/9789004259966_010.

Demerson, Paula. 1975. *María Francisca de Sales y Portocarrero, condesa de Montijo: Una figura de la Ilustración*. Madrid: Nacional.

Despentes, Virginie. 2007. *Teoría King Kong*. Madrid: Melusina.

[Dias, Baltasar?]. 1659. *Malicia das Mulheres: Obra novamente feita, e chamada Malicia das mulheres, porque nella se tratão muytas sentenças, & autoridades acerca da malicia, q' há em algumas dellas; & assim trata, como duas mulheres enganarão seus maridos graciosamente*. Lisbon: Domingos Carneyro.

Díaz Freire, José Javier. 2001. "El cuerpo de Aitor: Emoción y discurso en la creación de la comunidad nacional vasca." *Historia y Sociedad* (Rio Piedras, San Juan, PR) 40: 79–96.

Díaz Marcos, Ana María. 2012. *Salirse del tiesto: Ensayistas españolas, feminismo y emancipación (1861–1923)*. Oviedo: KRK.

Díaz Noci, Javier. 1992. *Euskal prentsaren sorrera eta garapena (1834–1939)*. Bilbao: Universidad del País Vasco-Euskal Herriko Unibertsitatea.

Di Febo, Giuliana. 2003. "'Nuevo Estado,' nacionalcatolicismo y género." In *Mujeres y hombres en la España franquista: Sociedad, economía, política, cultura*, edited by Gloria Nielfa Cristóbal, 19–44. Madrid: Universidad Complutense de Madrid.

Domènech, Xavier. 2008. *Clase obrera, antifranquismo y cambio político*. Madrid: La Catarata.

Domínguez Ortiz, Antonio. 1983. *Sociedad y estado en el siglo XVIII español*. Barcelona: Ariel.

Dopico, Montse, and A. R. López. 2010. "Historia do feminismo galego." *Revista das Letras* (suplemento cultural de *El Correo Gallego*) 806 (28 January): 1–8.

Duch, Montserrat. 2012. "Tot pensant històricament el sexe de les nacions." In *In/dependents: Dones i projectes nacionals*, edited by Montserrat Palau and Agnès Toda, 33–50. Valencia: Tres i Quatre.

Dueñas, María. 2010. *El tiempo entre costuras*. Madrid: Planeta.

Durán, María-Ángeles. 1993. "Introducción: La formación del pensamiento igualitario." In *Mujeres y hombres: La formación del pensamiento igualitario*, edited by María-Ángeles Durán, 11–50. Madrid: Castalia/Instituto de la Mujer.

Durán, María Ángeles, and María Teresa Gallego. 1986. "The Women's Movement in Spain and the New Spanish Democracy." In *The New Women's*

Movement: Feminism and Political Power in Europe and the USA, edited by Drude Dahlerup, 200–16. London: Sage.

E. 1901. Review of *Evangelios de la mujer*, 2nd ed., by Concepción Gimeno de Flaquer. *Revista Contemporánea* 27 (121): 445–7.

Eckert, Penelope, and Sally McConnell-Ginet. 1992. "Think Practically and Look Locally: Language and Gender as Community-Based Practice." *Annual Review of Anthropology* 21 (1): 461–88. https://doi.org/10.1146/annurev.an.21.100192.002333.

El Abate, 1905. "A la luz de la lámpara." *La Última Moda* 26: 7.

El Caballero Audaz [José María Carretero Novillo]. 1914. "Nuestras visitas: La condesa de Pardo Bazán" [interview]. *La Esfera* 1 (7): 8–9.

El Hachmi, Najat. 2004. *Jo també sóc catalana*. Barcelona: Columna.

___. 2008. *L'últim patriarca*. Barcelona: Planeta.

Elorza, Antonio. 1975. "Feminismo y socialismo en España (1840–1868)." *Tiempo de Historia* 3: 46–63.

Emakumea Euskal Herriko historian: La mujer en la historia de Euskal Herria. 1992. Bilbao: GITE-IPES.

"Emilia Pardo Bazán en el Ateneo. 1897." 1897. *El Liberal* 27: 1.

Ena Bordonada, Ángela. 2013. "*Revista Crítica*, una revista literaria fundada por Carmen de Burgos *Colombine*." In Servén and Rota 2013, 95–116.

Enríquez de Salamanca, Cristina. 1998. "La mujer en el discurso legal del liberalismo español." In Jagoe, Blanco, and Enríquez de Salamanca 1998, 219–52.

Epelde Pagola, Edurne, Miren Aranguren Etxarte, and Iratxe Retolaza. 2015. *Gure genealogia feministak: Euskal Herriko Mugimendu Feministaren kronika bat*. n.p.: Emagin Dokumentazio eta Ikerkuntza Zentro Feminista.

Escolano Benito, Agustín. 1982. "Las normales, siglo y medio de perspectiva histórica." *Revista de Eeducación* 269: 55–76.

Eskisabel, Jon. 2012. *Euskal kantagintza: Pop, rock, folk /La canción vasca: Pop, rock, folk /Basque Songwriting: Pop, Rock, Folk*. San Sebastián: Etxepare Institutua.

Espelho Crítico no qual claramente se vem alguns das Mulheres fabricado na loja da Verdade pelo irmão Amador do Dezengano, que pode servir de estimulo para a reforma dos mesmos defeitos. 1761. Lisbon: Off. de Antonio Vicente da Silva.

Espigado Tocino, Gloria. 2008. "La buena nueva de la mujer profeta: Identidad y cultura política en las fourieristas Mª Josefa Zapata y Margarita Pérez de Celis." *Revista de Historia Contemporánea* 7 (7): 15–33. https://doi.org/10.14198/PASADO2008.7.02.

___. 2016. "En la estela de las Luces: La marquesa de Villafranca, una ilustrada del siglo XIX." In *El siglo XVIII en femenino*, edited by Manuel-Reyes García Hurtado, 251–75. Madrid: Síntesis.

Espigado Tocino, Gloria, Isabel Pérez Sánchez, and Ana Sánchez Álvarez. 1996. *Fuentes bibliográficas para la historia de la mujer en los fondos antiguos de las bibliotecas gaditanas*. Madrid: Ministerio de Asuntos Sociales/Instituto de la Mujer.

Espín López, Rosa María. 2010. "'Hacer Divorcio' en Castilla, siglos XVI, XVII y XVIII." PhD dissertation, Universidad Complutense de Madrid.

Esselink, Jean Ann. 2016. "Portugal's Parliament Overrides Presidential Veto of Gay Adoption." *New Civil Rights Movement*, 11 February 2016. Accessed 24 April 2016. http://www.thenewcivilrightsmovement.com/uncucumbered/portugal_s_parliament_overrides_presidential_veto_of_gay_adoption_law.

Establier Pérez, Helena. 2005. "El teatro trágico de María Rosa Gálvez de Cabrera en el tránsito de la Ilustración al Romanticismo: Una utopía femenina y feminista." *Anales de Literatura Española* 18 (18): 143–61. https://doi.org/10.14198/ALEUA.2005.18.11.

___. 2006. "Una dramaturgia feminista para el siglo XVIII: Las obras de María Rosa Gálvez de Cabrera en la comedia de costumbres ilustrada." *Dieciocho* 29 (2): 179–203.

___. 2015. "María Martínez Abello y la 'Comedia Nueva' de entresiglos en clave femenina: Entre los riesgos de amor, sostenerse con honor: *La Laureta* (1800)." *Dieciocho* 38 (1): 125–51.

Esteban, Mari Luz. 2004. *Antropología del cuerpo: Género, itinerarios corporales, identidad y cambio*. Barcelona: Bellaterra.

___. 2011. "Cuerpos y políticas feministas: El feminismo como cuerpo." In *Cuerpos políticos y agencia: Reflexiones feministas sobre cuerpo, trabajo y colonialidad*, edited by Cristina Villalba Augusto and Ignacio (Nacho) Álvarez Lucena, 45–84. Colección Periferias, vol. 12. Granada: Universidad de Granada.

___. 2015. "El feminismo vasco y los circuitos del conocimiento: El movimiento, la universidad y la casa de las mujeres." In Mendia Azkue et al. 2015, 61–76.

Esteves, João. 1991. *A Liga Portuguesa das Mulheres Republicanas: Uma organização política e feminista (1909–1919)*. Lisbon: Comissão para Igualdade e para os Direitos das Mulheres.

___. 1998. *As origens do sufragismo português: A primeira organização sufragista portuguesa-a "Associação de Propaganda Feminista" (1911–1918)*. Lisbon: Editorial Bizâncio.

___. 2001. "A intervenção cívica e política na 1.ª década do século XX: Dos salões literários ao associativismo pacifista, feminista, maçónico, republicano e socialista." Paper presented at the International Colloquium

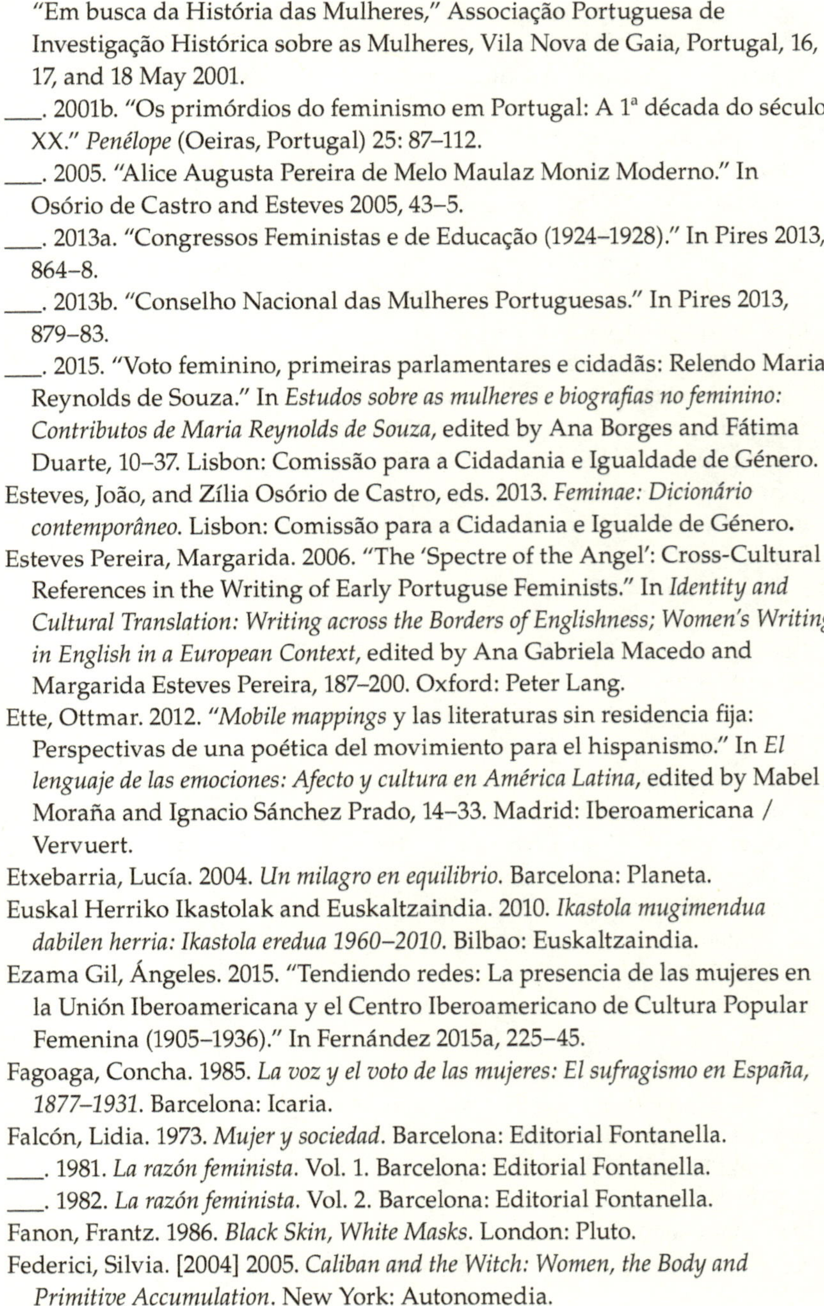

"Em busca da História das Mulheres," Associação Portuguesa de Investigação Histórica sobre as Mulheres, Vila Nova de Gaia, Portugal, 16, 17, and 18 May 2001.

___. 2001b. "Os primórdios do feminismo em Portugal: A 1ª década do século XX." *Penélope* (Oeiras, Portugal) 25: 87–112.

___. 2005. "Alice Augusta Pereira de Melo Maulaz Moniz Moderno." In Osório de Castro and Esteves 2005, 43–5.

___. 2013a. "Congressos Feministas e de Educação (1924–1928)." In Pires 2013, 864–8.

___. 2013b. "Conselho Nacional das Mulheres Portuguesas." In Pires 2013, 879–83.

___. 2015. "Voto feminino, primeiras parlamentares e cidadãs: Relendo Maria Reynolds de Souza." In *Estudos sobre as mulheres e biografias no feminino: Contributos de Maria Reynolds de Souza*, edited by Ana Borges and Fátima Duarte, 10–37. Lisbon: Comissão para a Cidadania e Igualdade de Género.

Esteves, João, and Zília Osório de Castro, eds. 2013. *Feminae: Dicionário contemporâneo.* Lisbon: Comissão para a Cidadania e Igualde de Género.

Esteves Pereira, Margarida. 2006. "The 'Spectre of the Angel': Cross-Cultural References in the Writing of Early Portuguse Feminists." In *Identity and Cultural Translation: Writing across the Borders of Englishness; Women's Writing in English in a European Context*, edited by Ana Gabriela Macedo and Margarida Esteves Pereira, 187–200. Oxford: Peter Lang.

Ette, Ottmar. 2012. "*Mobile mappings* y las literaturas sin residencia fija: Perspectivas de una poética del movimiento para el hispanismo." In *El lenguaje de las emociones: Afecto y cultura en América Latina*, edited by Mabel Moraña and Ignacio Sánchez Prado, 14–33. Madrid: Iberoamericana / Vervuert.

Etxebarria, Lucía. 2004. *Un milagro en equilibrio.* Barcelona: Planeta.

Euskal Herriko Ikastolak and Euskaltzaindia. 2010. *Ikastola mugimendua dabilen herria: Ikastola eredua 1960–2010.* Bilbao: Euskaltzaindia.

Ezama Gil, Ángeles. 2015. "Tendiendo redes: La presencia de las mujeres en la Unión Iberoamericana y el Centro Iberoamericano de Cultura Popular Femenina (1905–1936)." In Fernández 2015a, 225–45.

Fagoaga, Concha. 1985. *La voz y el voto de las mujeres: El sufragismo en España, 1877–1931.* Barcelona: Icaria.

Falcón, Lidia. 1973. *Mujer y sociedad.* Barcelona: Editorial Fontanella.

___. 1981. *La razón feminista.* Vol. 1. Barcelona: Editorial Fontanella.

___. 1982. *La razón feminista.* Vol. 2. Barcelona: Editorial Fontanella.

Fanon, Frantz. 1986. *Black Skin, White Masks.* London: Pluto.

Federici, Silvia. [2004] 2005. *Caliban and the Witch: Women, the Body and Primitive Accumulation.* New York: Autonomedia.

Feijoo, Benito Jerónimo. 1726–39. *Theatro crítico universal, o discursos varios, en todo género de materias, para desengaño de errores comunes*. Madrid: Lorenzo Francisco Mojados.

Felices de la Fuente, María del Mar. 2013. *La nueva nobleza titulada de España y América (1700–1746): Entre el mérito y la venalidad*. Almería: Universidad de Almería.

"Feminismo galego: Cambios sociais e dereito das mulleres." 2009–10. www.galizasempre.org/microsites/feminismo-galego. Exhibition.

Fernández, Idoia. 1994. *Oroimenaren hitza*. Bilbao: Udako Euskal Unibertsitatea.

Fernández, Pura. 2011. "Geografías culturales: Miradas, espacios y redes de las escritoras hispanoamericanas en el siglo XIX." In *Miradas sobre España*, edited by Facundo Tomás, Isabel Justo, and Sofía Barrón, 153–70. Madrid: Anthropos.

___, ed. 2015a. *La Re(d)pública transatlántica de las Letras: Escritoras españolas y latinoamericanas (1824–1936)*. Madrid: Iberoamericana/Vervuert.

___. 2015b. "'No hay nación para este sexo': Redes culturales de mujeres de letras españolas y latinoamericanas (1824–1936)." In Fernández 2015a, 9–57.

Fernández, Pura, and Marie-Linda Ortega, eds. 2008. *La mujer de letras o la letraherida: Textos y representaciones sobre la mujer escritora en el siglo XIX*. Madrid: Consejo Superior de Investigaciones Científicas.

Fernández Díaz, Roberto. 1993. *Manual de historia de España*. Vol 4, *Siglo XVIII*. Madrid: Historia 16.

Fernández Freixanes, Víctor, ed. 1992. *Contos eróticos: Eles/Contos eróticos: Elas*. 2 vols. Vigo: Xerais.

Fernández-Rodríguez, Manuel. 2009. "Primitive Alchemy: Alienness in Olga Novo." In *Writing Bonds: Irish and Galician Contemporary Women Poets*, edited by Manuela Palacios and Laura Lojo, 57–76. Oxford: Peter Lang.

Ferreira, Ana Paula. 2011. "*Os Sensos Incomuns*, de Maria Isabel Barreno, Ou duma séria brincadeira do contra." In *O Grande Prémio do Conto Camilo Castelo Branco*, edited by Petar Petrov, 27–33. Lisbon: Editora Roma.

Ferreira, Eduarda. 2014. "Lesbian Activism in Portugal: Facts, Experiences and Critical Reflections." *Lambda Nordica* 2: 53–82.

___. 2015. "Movimento Lésbico em Portugal." *Faces de Eva* 34: 35–50.

Ferreira, Eduarda, et al., eds. 2015. *Percursos feministas: Desafiar os tempos*. Lisbon: Uniao de Mulheres Alternativa e Resposta / Universidade Feminista. E-book.

Fiadeiro, Maria Antónia. 2003. *Maria Lamas*. Lisbon: Quetzal.

Figueiredo, Isabela. 2009. *Caderno de memórias coloniais*. Lisbon: Angelus Novus.

Figueiredo Marcos, Manuel de Rui. 1990. *A Legislação Pombalina: Alguns aspectos fundamentais*. Coimbra: Universidade de Coimbra.

Fish, Stanley. 1980. *Is There a Text in this Class? The Authority of Interpretive Communities*. Cambridge: Harvard University Press.

Flecha García, Consuelo. 1996. *Las primeras universitarias en España, 1872–1910*. Madrid: Narcea.

___. 2010. "Between Modernization and Conservatism: Spain." In *Girls' Secondary Education in the Western World: From the 18th to the 20th Century*, edited by Joyce Goodman, Rebecca Rogers, and James C. Albisetti, 77–91. New York: Palgrave Macmillan.

Flores, Conceição, Constância Lima Duarte, and Zenóbia Collares Moreira. 2009. *Dicionário de escritoras portuguesas: Das origens à atualidade*. Florianópolis, SC: Editora Mulheres.

Flunser Pimentel, Irene. 2000. *História das organizações femininas no Estado Novo*. Lisbon: Círculo de Leitores.

Folguera, Pilar. 1988a. "De la transición política a la democracia: La evolución del feminismo en España durante el periodo 1975–1988." In Folguera 1988b, 111–31.

___, ed. 1988b. *El feminismo en España: Dos siglos de historia*. Madrid: Pablo Iglesias.

Foronda, Valentín de. [1787] 1996. *Miscelánea o colección de varios discursos*. Madrid: Marcial Pons.

___. [1820] 1998. *Cartas sobre la policía por D. Valentín de Foronda: Segunda edición*. Vitoria: Ararteko.

Foucault, Michel. 1984. *Historia de la sexualidad*. Translated by Ulises Giñazu. Madrid: Siglo XXI.

Fraisse, Geneviève. 2003. *Los dos gobiernos: La familia y la ciudad*. Madrid: Cátedra.

___. 2010a. *À côté du genre: Un vade-mecum*. Lormont: Le Bord de l'Eau.

___. 2010b. *Les femmes et leur histoire*. Paris: Gallimard.

Franco, Gloria. 2005. "Bárbara de Braganza, la querella de las mujeres y la educación femenina." In *La reina Isabel y las reinas de España: Realidad, modelos e imagen historiográfica*, vol. 1, edited by M. Victoria López-Cordón and Gloria Franco, 497–522. Madrid: Fundación Española de Historia Moderna.

Franco Rubio, Gloria. 1994. "Patronato regio y preocupación pedagógica en la España del siglo XVIII: El Real Monasterio de la Visitación de Madrid." *Espacio, Tiempo y Forma, serie IV: Historia moderna* 7: 227–44.

___. 1997. "Educación femenina y posopografía: Las alumnas del colegio de las Salesas Reales en el siglo XVIII." *Cuadernos de Historia Moderna* 19: 171–82.

___. 2000. "Formas de sociabilidad y estrategias de poder en la España del siglo XVIII." In *Poder y mentalidad en España e Iberoamérica*, edited by Enrique Martínez Ruiz, 389–416. Madrid: Universidad Complutense de Madrid / Universidad Zulia.

___. 2009. "Las Sociedades Económicas de Amigos del País: Un observatorio privilegiado para la práctica política y el nacimiento de la ciudadanía a finales del antiguo régimen." In Astigarraga, López-Cordón, and Urquia 1: 351–68.

Frandsen, Dorothea. 1974. *Helene Lange*. Hannover: Niedersächsischen Landeszentrale für politische Bildung.

Freira Álvarez, Marta. 2007. *La desamortización de la tierra en el tránsito del Antiguo Régimen al liberalismo*. Gijón: Caja Rural.

Fuerte-Híjar, Marquesa de [María Lorenza de los Ríos y Loyo]. 1800a *"El Eugenio": Comedia en tres actos*. Madrid: Biblioteca Nacional. Mss. 17422.

___. [1800?b] 2000. "La sabia indiscreta." In *La Marquesa de Fuerte-Híjar: Una dramaturga de la Ilustración (Estudio y edición de* La sabia indiscreta*)*, edited by Alberto Acereda, 215–43. Cádiz: Universidad de Cádiz.

Gallagher, Tom. 1983. *Portugal: A Twentieth-Century Interpretation*. Manchester: Manchester University Press.

Gálvez de Cabrera, María Rosa. 1804a. *Obras poéticas*. 3 vols. Madrid: Imprenta Real.

___. 1804b. "La beneficencia." In Gálvez de Cabrera 1804a, 1: 9–13.

___. 1804c. "*Zinda*." In Gálvez de Cabrera 1804a, 3: 100–68.

___. 1995. *Safo: Zinda; La familia a la moda*. Edited by Fernando Doménech. Madrid: Asociación de Directores de Escena de España.

Gálvez y Valenzuela, María Josefa [Condesa de Castroterreño]. 1801. *Elogio de la Reyna Nuestra Señora, formado por la Excelentísima Señora Condesa de Castroterreño, Socia de Honor y Mérito de la Real Sociedad Económica de Madrid Leído en la Junta Pública de Distribución en Premios en 7 de Febrero de 1801*. Madrid: Imprenta Real.

Gandarias, Itziar and Joan Pujol. 2013. "De las Otras al No(s)otras: Encuentros, tensiones y retos en el tejido de articulaciones entre colectivos de mujeres migradas y feministas locales en el País Vasco." *Encrucijadas: Revista Crítica de Ciencias Sociales* 5: 71–99.

García Garrosa, María Jesús. 1990. *La retórica de las lágrimas: La comedia sentimental española, 1751–1802*. Valladolid: Universidad de Valladolid.

___. 2004. "En los inicios de la comedia neoclásica: La aya, de María Rita de Barrenenchea (1750–1795); Estudio y edición." *Cuadernos de Estudios del Siglo XVIII* 14: 25–66.

___. 2007a. "La creación literaria femenina en España en el siglo XVIII: Un estado de la cuestión." *Cuadernos de Historia Moderna: Anejos* 6: 203–19.

___. 2007b. "'Unión de voluntades' y 'Ajuste de intereses': El matrimonio en el teatro sentimental del siglo XVIII." *Boletin de la Biblioteca de Menendez Pelayo* 83: 129–51.

García-Liñeira, María. 2015. "Literary Citizenship and the Politics of Language: The Galician Literary Field between 1939 and 1965." PhD dissertation, University of Oxford.

García López, Emilia. n.d. "Isabel Ríos: O compromiso de toda unha vida." Accessed 24 June 2016. *Álbum de Mulleres*. www.culturagalega.org.

___. n.d. "María Araujo: Dúas patrias unha loita; María a Guerrilleira." Accessed 22 June 2016. *Álbum de Mulleres*. www.culturagalega.org.

García Negro, Pilar. 1986. "Rosalía á luz de Mara." In *Actas do Congreso Internacional de Estudios sobre Rosalía de Castro e o Seu Tempo*, 73–80. Santiago de Compostela: Consello da Cultura Galega.

García-Zarza, Isabel. 2010. *Diario de una madre imperfecta*. Barcelona: Viceversa.

Gatens, Moira. 1991. *Feminism and Philosophy: Perspectives on Difference and Equality*. Cambridge: Polity.

Gilaberte Asín, Inmaculada. 2009. *Equilibristas: Entre la maternidad y la profesión*. Barcelona: Alienta.

Gimeno, Beatriz. 2014. "Construyendo un discurso antimaternal." *Píkara*. Accessed 22 March 2016. http://www.pikaramagazine.com/2014/02/construyendo-un-discurso-antimaternal/

Gimeno de Flaquer, M. Concepción. 1877. *La mujer española: Estudios acerca de su educación y sus facultades intelectuales*. Madrid: Guijarro.

___. 1880. "Historia de una flor, contada por ella misma." *El Parthenón* 10 (15 March): 152–7.

___. 1900. *Evangelios de la mujer*. 2nd ed. Madrid: Fernando Fe.

___. 1901. Review of *Evangelios de la mujer*, 2nd ed. *Revista Contemporánea* 27 (121): 445–7.

___. 1909. *Una Eva moderna*. El Cuento Semanal 152. Madrid: El Cuento Semanal.

___. [1903] 1998. "El problema feminista." In Jagoe, Blanco, and Enríquez de Salamanca 1998, 530–5. Original paper presented at the conference of the Ateneo de Madrid.

Glenn, Kathleen M., and Mercedes Mazquiarán de Rodríguez. 1998a. "Introduction." In Glenn and Mazquiarán de Rodríguez 1998b, 1–5.

___, eds. 1998b. *Spanish Women Writers and the Essay: Gender, Politics, and the Self*. Columbia: University of Missouri Press.

Glos, George E. 1983. "The Spanish Divorce Law of 1981." *International and Comparative Law Quarterly* 32 (3): 667–88. https://doi.org/10.1093/iclqaj/32.3.667.

Gobierno representativo y constitucional del bello sexo español. 1841. Madrid: Compañía Tipográfica.

Gomes, Catarina. 2008. "Quase 500 mulheres portuguesas já foram abortar a Espanha este ano." Público. 15 July 2008. Accessed 19 March 2016. http://www.publico.pt/portugal/jornal//quase-500-mulheres-portuguesas-ja--foram-abortar-a-espanha-este-ano-268873.

Gómez, Lupe. 1995. *Pornografía*. Santiago de Compostela: author's edition.

___. 1999. *Os teus dedos na miña braga con regra*. Vigo: Xerais.

Gómez de Avellaneda, Gertrudis. 1845. "Capacidad de las mujeres para el gobierno." *La Ilustración: Álbum de Damas* (2 November): 1–2.

Gonçalves, Ruy. 1557. *Dos privilégios & praerogativas q ho genero feminine të por dereito comum & ordenações do Reyno mais que ho género Masculino*. Lisbon: João de Barreira.

González, Corona. 1927. "Pr'os pais que tein fillas." *A Nosa Terra* 235 (1–4): 9–10.

González Calbet, María Teresa. 1988. "El surgimiento del movimiento feminista, 1900–1930." In Folguera 1988b, 81–8.

González Enciso, Agustín. 1980. *Estado e industria en el siglo XVIII: La fábrica de Guadalajara*. Madrid: Fundación Universitaria Española.

___. 2000. "La política industrial en el siglo XVIII." In *Pensamiento y política económica en la época moderna*, edited by Luis Antonio Ribot and Luigi Da Rosa, 137–72. Madrid: Actas.

González Fernández, Helena. 2000. "Las poetas y las poéticas desde la postguerra hasta hoy: ¡YO TAMBIÉN NAVEGAR!" In *Breve historia feminista de la literatura española (en lengua catalana, gallega y vasca)*, edited by Iris M. Zavala, 196–218. Barcelona: Anthropos.

___. 2001. *A tribo das baleas: Poetas galegos de arestora; Antoloxía da poesía galega última*. Vigo: Xerais.

___. 2003. "Mulleres e ficción en Galicia ou a necesidade de superar os estados carenciais." In *Escrita e mulleres: Doce ensaios arredor de Virginia Woolf*, edited by Belén Fortes, 45–60. Santiago de Compostela: Sotelo Blanco.

___. 2004. "Las poetas gallegas, la nueva gramática del canon." *Zurgai* (July): 68–71.

___. 2005. *Elas e o paraugas totalizador*. Vigo: Xerais.

___. 2006. "Anatomía de 'tanta visibilidade' das mulleres na literatura." *Madrygal* 9: 69–72.

___. 2007. "A resistencia é proceso de creación." *Grial* 175: 123–4.

___. 2013. "Complicidades y silencios: Literatura y crítica feminista en Galicia." *Sociocriticism* 28: 53–89.

González Fernández, Helena, and María do Cebreiro Rábade. 2012. "Una rueca en los brazos de un atleta." In *Canon y subversión: La obra narrativa de Rosalía de Castro*, edited by Helena González Fernández and María do Cebreiro Rábade, 9–24. Barcelona: Icaria.

González Herrán, José Manuel. 2008. "La emancipación de una mujer de letras: Emilia Pardo Bazán, 1889–1892." In Fernández and Ortega 2008, 345–63.

González Posada, Adolfo. 1899. *Feminismo*. Madrid: Ricardo Fe.

Gorjão, Vanda. 1994. *A Reivindicação do voto no programa do Conselho Nacional das Mulheres Portuguesas (1914–1947)*. Lisbon: Comissão para a Igualdade e para os Direitos das Mulheres.

Graça, Paula da. [1715] 1741. *Bondade das Mulheres vendicada e malícia dos Homens manifesta: Papel métrico, e apologético, em que se defende a femenina innocencia, contra outro em que injustamente se argüe a sua maldade, com o título de Malícia das Mulheres; Composto pelo zelo de PAULA DA GRAÇA, natural da Villa de Cabanas, e assistente nesta Corte*. Lisbon: Na Officina de Pedro Ferreira, Impressor da Augustíssima Rainha N.S.

Grado, Mercedes de. 2004. "Encrucijada del feminismo español: Disyuntiva entre igualdad y diferencia." In *La mujer en la España actual: ¿Evolución o involución?* edited by Jacqueline Cruz and Barbara Zecchi, 25–58. Barcelona: Icaria.

Graffigny, Françoise de. 1792. *"Cartas de una peruana": Escritas en francés por Mad. de Griffigni y traducidas al castellano con algunas correcciones y aumentada con notas, y una carta para su mayor complemento*. Translated by María Romero Masegosa y Cancelada. Valladolid: Viuda de Santander.

Greene, Patricia V. 1998. "Prensa y praxis feminista en *La Revista Blanca* (1898-1905)." In vol. 4 of *Actas del XIII Congreso AIH, Madrid, 6–11 July 1998*, 4 vols., Centro Virtual Cervantes, 105–10. 10 October 2013. http://cvc.cervantes.es/literatura/aih/pdf/13/aih_13_4_012.pdf.

Gruber, Helmut, and Pamela Graves. 1998. *Women and Socialism: Socialism and Women; Europe Between the World Wars*. New York: Berghahn.

Grupo de Mujeres Jóvenes de la AMV. 1985. "Seguimos avanzando." In *10 años de historia feminista*, edited by Asamblea de Mujeres de Bizkaia, 15–16. Bilbao: Asambleas de Mujeres de Euskadi.

Grupo "Mujer y violencia" [Asamblea de Mujeres de Bizkaia]. 1986. "Mujer y violencia." In *II Jornadas feministas de Euskadi*, edited by Asamblea de Mujeres de Euskadi and Aizan, 81–9. Bilbao: Asambleas de Mujeres de Euskadi.

Guallart, Arturo. 2011. *Carmen de Burgos, la Colombine: Libre y luchadora*. Málaga: C & T.

Guillo Arakistain, Miren. 2014. "Mujeres jóvenes y menstruación: Contracultura y resignificación del ciclo menstrual en el País Vasco." In *Jóvenes, desigualdades y salud: Vulnerabilidad y políticas públicas*, edited by Oriol Romaní and Lina Casadó, 143–65. Tarragona: Publicacions Universitat Rovira i Virgil/Antropologia Mèdica.

Guimarães, Elina. 1975. *Coisas de mulheres*. Porto: Promoção.

___. 1987. *Portuguese Women Past and Present*. 2nd ed. Lisbon: Comission on the Status of Women.

___. 1989. *Mulheres portuguesas, ontem e hoje*. Lisbon: Comissão da Condição Feminina.

Haidt, Rebecca. 1998. *Embodying Enlightenment: Knowing the Body in Eighteenth-Century Spanish Literature and Culture*. New York: St. Martin's.

Haraway, Donna Jeanne. 1991. *Simians, Cyborgs and Women*. New York: Routledge.

___. 2000. "The Birth of the Kennel: Cyborgs, Dogs and Companion Species." Lecture given at the European Graduate School on 1 September 2000. http://www.youtube.com/watch?v=-yxHIKmMI70.

___. 2004. *Testigo modesto; Segundo milenio: HombreHembra; Conoce oncoratón: Feminismo y tecnociencia*. Barcelona: Universitat Oberta de Catalunya.

Hartzenbusch, Eugenio. 1894. *Apuntes para un catálogo de periódicos madrileños desde el año 1661 hasta 1870*. Madrid: Sucesores de Rivadeneyra.

Hernández, Jone M., and Elixabete Imaz. 2010. In *Demythicizing, Unveiling, Challenging: A Review of Twenty-Five Years of Feminist Academic Production; Feminist Challenges in the Social Sciences*, edited by Mari Luz Esteban and Mila Amurrio, 55–70. Reno: Center for Basque Studies, University of Nevada.

Hernández Sandoica, Elena. 2012. "Rosario de Acuña: La escritura y la vida." In *Política y escritura de mujeres*, edited by Hernández Sandoica, 171–328. Madrid: Abada.

Herr, Richard. 1991. *La hacienda real y los cambios en la España rural a finales del Antiguo Régimen*. Madrid: Instituto de Estudios Fiscales.

Herranz Gómez, Yolanda. 2006. *Igualdad bajo sospecha: El poder transformador de la educación*. Madrid: Narcea.

Herrero Figueroa, Araceli. 2010–11. "Emilia Pardo Bazán. 'Feminista': Desigualdad. intergenérica y maltrato doméstico." *La Tribuna: Cadernos de Estudos da Casa-Museo Emilia PardoBazán* 8: 57–70.

Herrmann, Gina. 1998. "'The Hermetic Goddess': Dolores Ibárruri as Text." *Letras Peninsulares* 11 (1): 181–206.

Hesse, Carla. 2001. *The Other Enlightenment: How French Women Became Modern*. Princeton: Princeton University Press.

Hibbs-Lissorgues, Solange. 2006. "Itinerario de una filósofa y creadora del siglo XIX: Concepción Jimeno de Flaquer." In *Regards sur les espagnoles créatrices (XVIIIe–XXe siécles)*, edited by François Étienvre, 119–35. Paris: Presses Sorbonne Nouvelle.

___. 2008. "Escritoras españolas entre el deber y el deseo: Faustina Sáez de Melgar (1834–1895), Pilar Sinués de Marco (1835–1893) y Antonia Rodríguez de Utrera." In Fernández and Ortega 2008, 325–43.

Hickey y Pellizzoni, Margarita. 1789. *Poesías varias sagradas, morales y profanes o amorosas: Con dos poemas épicos en honor del Capitán General D. Pedro Cevallos; Obras todas de una dama de esta Corte.* Madrid: Imprenta Real.

Hooper, Kirsty. 2008. *A Stranger in My Own Land: Sofía Casanova, a Spanish Writer in the European Fin de Siècle.* Nashville: Vanderbilt University Press.

Hooper, Kirsty, and Manuel Puga Moruxa. 2011. "Introduction: Galician Geographies." In *Contemporary Galician Cultural Studies: Between the Local and the Global,* edited by Kirsty Hooper and Manuel Puga Moruxa, 1–16. New York: Modern Language Association.

Horta, Maria Teresa. 1977. *Mulheres de abril.* Lisbon: Editorial Caminho.

Hunt, Lynn. 2009. *La invención de los derechos humanos.* Barcelona: Tusquets.

Ibárruri, Dolores. 1936. "Tres alocuciones." Archivo del PCE.

Ilie, Paul. 1980. *Literature and Inner Exile: Authoritarian Spain, 1939–1975.* Baltimore: Johns Hopkins University Press.

Imízcoz, José María, ed. 2001. *Redes familiares y patronazgo: Aproximación al entramado social del País Vasco y Navarra en el Antiguo Régimen (siglos XV–XIX).* Vitoria: Universidad del País Vasco.

Imízcoz, José María, and Rafael Guerrero. 2004. "Familias en la monarquía: La política familiar de las élites vascas y navarras en el Imperio de los Borbones." In *Casa, familia y sociedad (País Vasco, España y América siglos XV–XIX),* 177–238. Bilbao: Universidad del País Vasco, Servicio de Publicaciones.

Inverno, Catarina Raquel Costa. 2010. Mulher no país *de Maria Lamas: A questão sem nome na obra* Para além do amor. Masters thesis, Faculdade de Ciências Sociais e Humanas, Universidade Nova de Lisboa.

Irizarry, Estelle. 1998. "Concepción Arenal and the Essay of Advocacy: 'The Medium Is the Message.'" In Glenn and Mazquiarán de Rodríguez 1998b, 6–24.

Izagirre, Koldo. 2012. *Emakumeak trena hartu zuenekoa.* Ea: HEA kultur elkartea.

Jaffe, Catherine M. 2004. "Of Women's Love, Learning, and (In)Discretion: María Lorenza de los Ríos's *La sabia indiscreta* (1803)." *Modern Language Notes* 119 (2): 270–89.

___. 2009. "*El Eugenio* de la marquesa de Fuerte-Híjar: Ilustración y experiencia femenina." In *La época de Carlos IV (1788–1808),* edited by Elena de Lorenzo Álvarez, 653–60. Oviedo: Instituto Feijoo de Estudios del Siglo XVIIII/Sociedad Española de Estudios del Siglo XVIIII.

Jaffe, Catherine M., and Elizabeth F. Lewis, eds. 2009. *Eve's Enlightenment: Women's Experience in Spain and Spanish America, 1726–1839.* Baton Rouge: Louisiana State University Press.

Jaffe, Catherine M., and Elisa Martín-Valdepeñas Yagüe. 2013. "Sociabilidad, filantropía, y escritura: María Lorenza de los Ríos y Loyo, Marquesa de Fuerte-Híjar (1761–1821)." In *Mujeres y culturas políticas en España, 1808–1845*, edited by Ana Yetano Laguna, 85–126. Barcelona: Universitat Autònoma de Barcelona.

Jaffe, Catherine M., and Elisa Martín-Valdepeñas Yagüe. 2015. "Gender, Translation, and Eighteenth-Century Women Dramatists: Elizabeth Griffith's *The School for Rakes* (1769) and María Lorenza de los Ríos y Loyo's *El Eugenio* (1801)." *Eighteenth Century* (Lubbock, TX) 56 (1): 41–57. https://doi.org/10.1353/ecy.2015.0006.

Jagoe, Catherine, Alda Blanco, and Cristina Enríquez de Salamanca, eds. 1998. *La mujer en los discursos de género*. Barcelona: Icaria.

Jesus, Gertrudes Margarida de. 1761a. *Primeira carta Apologética em favor, e defensa das Mulheres, escrita por Dona Gertrudes Margarida de Jesus, ao irmão amador do dezengano, com a qual destroe toda a fabrica do seu espelho critico*. Lisbon: Officina de Francisco Borges de Sousa.

———. 1761b. *Segunda Carta Apologetica, em favor, e defensa das mulheres, escrita por dona Gertrudes Margarida de Jesus, ao Irmão Amador do Dezengano, Com a qual destroe toda a fabrica do seu Espelho Critico: E se responde ao terceiro defeito, que nelle contemplou*. Lisbon: Na Officina de Francisco Borges de Sousa.

Jiménez Morell, Inmaculada. 1992. *La prensa femenina en España (desde sus orígenes a 1868)*. Madrid: Ediciones de la Torre.

Joaquim, Teresa. 2010. "Maria de Lurdes Pintasilgo ou os caminhos de cuidar o futuro." *Investigaciones Feministas* 1: 77–85.

Johnson, Roberta, and Maite Zubiaurre, eds. 2012. *Antología del pensamiento feminista español (1726–2011)*. Madrid: Cátedra.

Jones, Wendy S. 2005. *Consensual Fictions: Women, Liberalism, and the English Novel*. Toronto: University of Toronto Press.

Jorge, Lídia. 1997. *O belo adormecido*. Lisbon: Dom Quixote.

———. 2002. *O vento assobiando nas gruas*. Lisbon: Dom Quixote.

———. 2011. *O marido e outros contos*. Lisbon: Dom Quixote.

Joyes y Blake, Inés. 1798. "Apología de las mugeres en carta original de la traductora dirigida a sus hijas." In *"El príncipe de Abisinia", novela traducida del inglés*, translated by Inés Joyes y Blake, 177–204. Madrid: Sancha.

Kelly, Joan. 1982. "Early Feminist Theory and the *Querelle des femmes*, 1400–1789." *Signs* (Chicago, IL) 8 (1): 4–28. https://doi.org/10.1086/493940.

Kirkpatrick, Susan. 1989. *Las Románticas: Women Writers and Subjectivity in Spain, 1835–1850*. Berkeley: University of California Press.

———. 1990. "La 'hermandad lírica' de la década de 1840." In *Escritoras románticas españolas*, edited by Marina Mayoral, 25–41. Madrid: Fundación Banco Exterior.

___. 1991. *Las románticas: Escritoras y subjetividad en España, 1835–1850.* Madrid: Cátedra.

___. 2011. "Women as Cultural Agents in Spanish Modernity." In Ros and Hazbun 2011, 227–41.

Kitts, Sally Ann. 1995. *The Debate on the Nature, Role and Influence of Woman in Eighteenth-Century Spain*. Lewiston, NY: Edwin Mellen.

Knott, Sarah. 2009. *Sensibility and the American Revolution*. Chapel Hill: University of North Carolina Press.

Kriegel, Blandine. 2002. "The Rule of the State and Natural Law." In *Natural Law and Civil Sovereignty: Moral Right and State Authority in Early Modern Political Thought*, edited by Ian Hunter and David Saunders, 13–26. Houndmills: Palgrave Macmillan. https://doi.org/10.1057/9781403919533_2.

Labrador, Germán. 2009. *Letras arrebatadas: Poesía y química en la Transición española*. Madrid: Devenir.

Lacalzada de Mateo, María José. 2005. "Concepción Gimeno de Flaquer en la emancipación de las mujeres." In *Redes intelectuales y formación de naciones en España y América Latina 1890–1940*, edited by Marta E. Casaús Arzú and Manual Pérez Ledesma, 369–86. Madrid: Universidad Autónoma de Madrid.

___. 2012. *Concepción Arenal: Mentalidad y proyección social*. Saragossa: Prensas Universitarias de Zaragoza.

Laffitte, María [Condesa de Campo Alange]. 1948. *La secreta guerra de los sexos*. Madrid: Revista de Occidente.

Lafont, Robert. 1967. *La révolution régionaliste*. Paris: Gallimard.

Laforet, Carmen. 1945. *Nada*. Barcelona: Destino.

Laina Gallego, José María. 1993. "Licencia paterna y real permiso en la Prágmatica sanción de 1776." *Revista de Derecho Privado* 77: 355–78.

"La Ley Moyano de Instrucción Pública." http://personal.us.es/alporu/historia/leymoyano.htm.

Lamas, Maria. 1948. *As mulheres do meu país*. Lisbon: Actuális.

Larrañaga, Carmen. 2000. "Teatralidad y poética alternativas: El bertsolarismo y las mujeres." In Breve historia feminista de la literatura española (en lengua catalana, gallega y vasca), edited by Iris M. Zavala, 399–424. Barcelona: Anthropos.

"La señora Pardo Bazán socia de número del Ateneo de Madrid." 1905. *La Época* (15 February): 1.

Leal, Ivone. 1992a. "A Assembleia Literária." In Leal 1992c, 55–64.

___. 1992b. "*A Voz Feminina*." In Leal 1992c, 65–71.

___. 1992c. *Um século de periódicos femininos: Arrolamentos de periódicos entre 1807 e 1926*. Lisbon: CIDM.

Leandro, Sandra. 2005. "*O Progresso*." In Osório de Castro and Esteves 2005, 824.
Ledo, Margarita. 1982. "A prensa nacionalista e a muller." *A Saia* 0: 3.
Lerner, Gerda. 1993. *The Creation of Feminist Consciousness: From the Middle Ages to Eighty-Seven*. New York: Oxford University Press.
"Lesbianismo." 1983a. *Andaina* 0: 3.
Levine, Linda Gould and Gloria Feiman Waldman. 1979. *El feminismo ante el Franquismo*. Miami: Ediciones Universal.
Lewis, Elizabeth Franklin. 1989. "Feijoo, Josefa Amar y Borbón and the 'Feminist' Debate in Eighteenth-Century Spain." *Dieciocho* 12 (2): 188–203.
___. 1997. "Breaking Chains: Language and Slavery in María Rosa Gálvez's *Zinda* (1804)." *Dieciocho* 20 (2): 263–72.
___. 2002. "The Sensibility of Motherhood in Josefa Amar y Borbón's *Discurso sobre la educación física y moral de las mujeres* (1790)." *Eighteenth-Century Women* 2: 209–42.
___. 2004. *Women Writers in the Spanish Enlightenment: The Pursuit of Happiness*. Aldershot: Ashgate.
___. 2008. "Actos de caridad: Women's Charitable Work in Eighteenth-Century Spain." *Dieciocho* 31 (2): 269–84.
___. 2009. "A su reina benéfica: Representaciones de María Luisa de Parma." In *La época de Carlos IV (1788–1808:) Actas del IV Congreso Internacional de la Sociedad Española del Siglo XVIII*, edited by Elena de Lorenza Álvarez, 697–705. Oviedo: Instituto Feijoo de Estudios del Siglo XVIII.
___. 2010. "Economía doméstica: Caridad y trabajo femenino en el discurso reformista de las mujer." *Ayer* 78 (2): 93–115.
___. 2017. "Hispano-Irish Women Writers of Spain's Late Enlightenment Period." In *The Routledge Companion to Iberian Studies*, edited by Javier Muñoz-Basols, Laura Lonsdale, and Manuel Delgado, 269–81. Abingdon: Routledge.
Librería de Mujeres de Milán. 1996. *El final del patriarcado*. Barcelona: Llibreria Pròleg.
Lizarraga, Joakin. [1780] 2004. "Lizarragaren sermoiak-1." In *Bonaparte ondareko eskuizkribuak*, edited by Rosa Miren Pagola, 1–445. Bilbao: Universidad de Deusto. Compact disc.
Llona, Miren. 2002. *Entre señorita y garçonne: Historia oral de las mujeres bilbaínas de clase media (1919–1939)*. Málaga: Universidad de Málaga.
___. 2013. "From Militia Women to Emakume: Myths Regarding Femininity during the Civil War in the Basque Country." In *Memory and Cultural History of the Spanish Civil War: Realms of Oblivion*, edited by Aurora Morcillo, 179–213. Leiden: Brill.
___. 2016. "La imagen viril de Pasionaria: Los significados simbólicos de Dolores Ibárruri en la II República y la Guerra Civil." *Historia y Política* 36 (July–December): 263–87.

Lomas, Carlos. 2004. *Los chicos también lloran: Identidades masculinas, igualdad entre los sexos y coeducación*. Barcelona: Paidós.

___. 2008. *El otoño del patriarcado? Luces y sombras de la igualdad entre mujeres y hombres*. Barcelona: Península.

Lopes, Maria Antónia. 1989. *Mulheres, espaço e sociabilidade: A transformação dos papéis femininos em Portugal à luz de fontes literárias (segundamente do século XVIII)*. Lisbon: Horizonte.

López de Ayala, Ignacio. 1786. "Papel sobre si las señoras deben admitirse como individuos de las Sociedades." In Negrín Fajardo 1984, 178–9.

López Aguirre, Elena. 2015. *Neskatxa maite: 25 mujeres que la música vasca no debería olvidar*. Bilbao: Aianai.

López Atxurra, Rafael. 1995. "Cultura, educación y estudios vascos: Hitos para la recuperación de nuestra memoria histórica." In *XXI Congreso de Estudios Vascos: Estudios vascos en el sistema educativo; Eusko Ikaskuntzak hezkuntza sarean*, edited by Eusko Ikaskuntza, 55–81. Donostia: Eusko Ikaskuntza.

López-Cordón Cortezo, María Victoria. 1986. "La situación de la mujer a fínales del Antiguo Régimen." In *Mujer y sociedad en España (1700–1975)*, edited by María Ángeles Durán Heras and Rosa María Capel Martínez, 47–108. Madrid: Ministerio de Cultura.

___. 1994. "Esponsales, dote y gananciales en los pleitos civiles castellanos." In *Fallstudien zur spanischen und portugiesische Justiz: 15. bis 20. Jahrhundert*, edited by J.-M. Scholz, 33–58. Frankfurt am Main: Vittorio Klostermann.

___. 1996a. "Cambio social y poder administrativo en la España del siglo XVIII: Los secretarios de Estado y del Despacho." In *Administración y poder en la España del Antiguo Régimen*, edited by Juan Luis Castellano, 109–30. Granada: Universidad de Granada.

___. 1996b. "Oficiales y caballeros: La carrera administrativa en la España del siglo XVIII." In *El mundo hispánico en el siglo de las Luces*, 843–53. Madrid: Sociedad Española de Estudios del Siglo XVIII.

___. 1998. "Familia, sexo y género en la Edad moderna" In *Studia histórica: Historia moderna* 18: 105–34.

___. 2000. "Instauración dinástica y reformismo administrativo: La implantación del sistema ministerial." *Manuscrits* 18: 93–111.

___. 2005a. "La construcción de una reina en la edad moderna: Entre el paradigma y los modelos." In *Actas de la VIII Reunión Científica de la F.E.H.M.: La reina Isabel y las reinas de España*, vol. 1, edited by Gloria Franco and María Victoria López-Cordón, 309–38. Madrid: Fundación Española de la Historia Moderna.

___. 2005b. "La fortuna de escribir: Escritoras de los siglos XVII y XVIII." In *Historia de las mujeres en España y América latina*, vol. 2, edited by Isabel Morant, 193–234. Madrid: Cátedra.

___. 2005c. *Condición femenina y razón ilustrada: Josefa Amar y Borbón.* Saragossa: Prensas Universitarias.

___. 2007a. "Mujeres en familia y familia de mujeres en las sociedades del Antiguo Régimen." In *Maternidad, familia y trabajo: De la invisibilidad histórica de las mujeres a la igualdad contemporánea*, edited by Josefina Méndez Vázquez, 99–125. Madrid: Fundación Sánchez-Albornoz.

___. 2007b. "Ved a Minerva que del alto cielo desciende presurosa ..." *Cuadernos de Historia Moderna Anejos* 6: 309–38.

___. 2009. "Women in Society in Eighteenth-Century Spain: Models of Sociability." In Jaffe and Lewis 2009, 103–14.

___. 2011. "Servicios y favores en la casa de la reina." In *El poder del dinero: Ventas de cargos y honores en el Antiguo Régimen*, edited by Francisco Andujar and María del Mar Felices, 223–44. Madrid: Biblioteca Nueva.

___. 2013a. "En las redes palatinas: De damas intrigantes a señoras políticas." In *La corte de los borbones: Crisis del modelo cortesano*, vol. 2, edited by José Martínez Millán and Marcelo Luzzi Traficante, 941–74. Madrid: Polifemo.

___. 2013b. "Un ilustrado en la encrucijada: Mariano Luís de Urquijo (Discursos pronunciados con motivo del Acto de Ingreso de María Victoria López-Cordón Cortezo." Nuevos extractos de la Real Sociedad Bascongada de Amigos del País 20-G: 10–70.

López Penedo, Susana. 2008. *El laberinto queer: La identidad en tiempos de neoliberalismo.* Barcelona: Egales.

López Sánchez, Oliva. 2010. "Los mensajes con contenidos emocionales dirigidos a las mujeres en dos revistas femeninas progresistas de la segunda mitad del siglo XIX en México." *Revista Latinoamericana de Estudios sobre Cuerpos, Emociones y Sociedad* 2 (4; December): 6–17. http://www.relaces.com.ar/fullissue/RELACES-N4.pdf.

López Silva, Inma. 2014. *Maternosofía ou o embarazo da escritora primípara.* Vigo: Galaxia.

Louis, Anja. 2005. *Women and the Law: Carmen de Burgos, An Early Feminist.* Woodbridge: Tamesis.

Lousada, Maria Alexandre. 1995. "Espaços de sociabilidade em Lisboa: Finais do século XVIII a 1834." 2 vols. PhD dissertation, University of Lisbon.

___. 1997. "Public Space and Popular Sociability in Lisbon in the Early 19th Century." *Santa Barbara Portuguese Studies* 4: 220–32.

Lousada, Maria Alexandre, and Eduardo Brito Henriques. 2007. "Viver nos escombros: Lisboa durante a reconstrução." In *O Terramoto de 1755: Impactos históricos*, edited by Ana Cristina Araújo, José Luís Cardoso, Nuno Gonçalo Monteiro, Walter Rossa, and José Vicente Serrão, 183–97. Lisbon: Livros Horizonte.

Luna, Alicia. Forthcoming. "The Train that Gave Women a Voice." In *Cartographies of Madrid: Contesting Urban Space at the Crossroads of the Global*

South and Global North, edited by Silvia Bermúdez and Anthony L. Geist. Nashville: Vanderbilt University Press.

Machado Rosa, Elzira Dantas. 2013. "Cruzada das Mulheres Portuguesas." In Esteves and Osório de Castro 2013, 213–15.

Madariaga Orbea, Juan. 2014. *Sociedad y lengua vasca en los siglos XVII y XVIII*. Bilbao: Euskaltzaindia.

Maldonado, Tere. 1994. "Zorioneko aniztasuna." *Geu Emakumeok* 20: 52–3.

Mangini González, Shirley. 1995. *Memories of Resistance: Women's Voices from the Spanish Civil War*. New Haven: Yale University Press.

___. 2001. *Las modernas de Madrid: Las grandes intelectuales españolas de la vanguardia*. Madrid: Península.

Manzano Garías, Antonio. 1969. "De una década extremeña y romántica." *Revista de Estudios Extremenos* 24: 1–29.

Marco, Aurora. 1993. *As precursoras: Achegas para o estudo da escrita feminina (Galiza 1800–1936)*. A Coruña: Biblioteca Gallega and La Voz.

Marçal, Maria Mercè. 1994. *La passió segons Renée Vivien*. Barcelona: Columna.

Marçal, Maria Mercè and Joan Brossa. 1977. *Cau de llunes*. Els Llibres de l'Óssa Menor 92. Barcelona: Proa.

Mariano, Fátima. 2011. *As mulheres e a I República*. Lisbon: Caleidoscópio.

Marín, José María, Carme Molinero, and Pere Ysàs. 2001. *Historia política de España 1939–2000*. Madrid: Istmo.

Marina, Rosa. 1857. *La mujer y la sociedad*. Cádiz: La Paz.

Mariño, María. 1963. *Palabra no tempo*. Lugo: Editorial Celta.

Marques de Almeida, Joana. 2006. *A figura feminina em Fernanda Botelho*. Lisbon: Acontecimento.

Martín Gaite, Carmen. [1972] 1987. *Usos amorosos del dieciocho en España*. Barcelona: Anagrama.

Martin-Márquez, Susan. 2002. "A World of Difference in Home-Making: The Films of Icíar Bollaín." In *Women's Narrative and Film in Twentieth-Century Spain*, edited by Ofelia Ferrán and Kathleen Mary Glenn, 256–72. New York: Routledge.

___. 2007. "Jovenes y feminismo: ¿Hacía un feminismo de la subversión?" *Inguruak* 43: 97–116.

___. 2008. "La movilización feminista en el País Vasco: Modalidades identitarias de la praxis feminista." In *Feminismo e interculturalidad: V Congreso Internacional AUDEM*, edited by Ángeles Cruzado Rodríguez and A. Ortiz de Zárate, 251–74. Seville: Arcibel Editores.

Martinez, María. 2007. "Jovenes y feminismo: ¿Hacia un feminismo de la subversión?" *Inguruak* 43: 97–116.

___. 2008. "La movilización feminista en el País Vasco: Modalidades identitarias de la praxis feminista". In *Feminismo e interculturalidad: V Congreso Internacional AUDEM* [Asociación Universitaria de Estudios de las

Mujeres], edited by Ángeles Cruzado Rodríguez and A. Ortiz de Zárate, 251–74. Seville: Arcibel Editores.

Martínez Abello, María. [1800?]. *Comedia nueva: Entre los riesgos de amor, sostenerse con honor; "La Laureta"*. Barcelona: Antonio Sastres.

Martínez Sierra, Gregorio. 1920. *Cartas a las mujeres de España*. Madrid: Renacimiento.

___. 1920. *Feminismo, feminidad, españolismo*. Madrid: Calleja.

Martins, Maria Teresa Valadão Caldeira. 2004. "'Novas cartas portuguesas': Denúncia da condição feminina em temo de censura." Masters thesis, Universidade Aberta, Lisbon.

Martins Rodríguez, María Victoria. 2010. "A muller baixo o franquismo: Apuntalando mentalidades." *Andaina: Revista Galega de Pemsamento Feminista* 56: 44–6.

___. 2011. ""Cárceles y mujeres en Galicia durante el franquismo." *Studia histórica." Historia Contemporánea* 29: 87–117.

___. 2012. "Sección Femenina: Modelos de mujer bajo el franquismo." In *Mujeres bajo sospecha: Memoria y sexualidad, 1930–1980*, edited by Raquel Osborne Verdugo, 275–92. Madrid: Fundamentos.

Matto de Turner, Clorinda. 1909. *Viaje de recreo: España, Francia, Inglaterra, Italia, Suiza y Alemania*. Valencia: F. Sempere.

Mayayo Bost, Patricia. 2012. *Cuerpos sexuados, cuerpos de (re)producción*. Barcelona: Publicacions de la Universitat de Barcelona.

McClendon, Carmen Chaves. 1980. "Josefa Amar y Borbón: Essayist." *Dieciocho* 3 (2): 138–43.

McNerney, Kathleen, and Cristina Enríquez de Salamanca, eds. 1994. *Double Minorities of Spain: A Bio-Bibliographic Guide to Women Writers of the Catalan, Galician, and Basque Countries*. New York: Modern Language Association of America.

Mello Breyner, Teresa de. 1781. *Idea de um Elogio Historico de Maria Thereza Arquiduquesa de Áustria, Imperatriz Viuva, Rainha Apostólica da Hungria e da Bohemia, Princeza Soberana dos Paises Baixos, escripta em francez por M.M.* Translated by Marie-Caroline Murray. Lisbon: Francisco Luiz Ameno.

Méndez Bejarano, Mario D. 1922. "López de Ayala y Molero (Ángeles)." In *Diccionario de escritores, maestros y oradores naturales de Sevilla y su actual provincia* 1: 388–9. Seville: Tipografía Gironés.

Mendia Azkue, Irantxu, Marta Luxán, Matxalen Legarreta, Gloria Guzmán, Iker Zirion, and Jokin Azpiazu Carballo, eds. 2015. *Otras formas de (re)conocer: Reflexiones, herramientas y aplicaciones desde la investigación feminista*. Bilbao: Hegoa- Universidad del País Vasco/Euskal Herriko Unibertsitatea (UPV/EHU)-Seminario Interdisciplinar de Metodología de Investigación Feminista (SIMReF).

Merleau-Ponty, Maurice. 1962. *Fenomenología de la percepción*. México City: Fondo de Cultura Económica.

Michaëlis de Vasconcelos, Carolina. 1896. "O congresso feminista de Berlim." *Comércio do Porto*, 19–27 November.

___. 1901. "Die Frauenbewegung in Spanien und Portugal." *Handbuch der Frauenbewegung*, edited by Helene Lange and Gertrude Bäumer, 1: 424–55. Berlin: Moeser.

___. 2002. *O movimento feminista em Portugal*. Paio Pires: Editorial Seis-Filetes.

Miguélez-Carballeira, Helena. 2013. *Galicia, A Sentimental Nation: Gender, Culture, and Politics*. Bangor: University of Wales.

___. 2014. "Rosalía de Castro: Life, Text and Afterlife." In *A Companion to Galician Culture*, edited by Helena Miguélez-Carballeira, 175–93. Woodbridge: Tamesis.

Mills, Sara, and Louise Mullany. 2011. *Language, Gender and Feminism*. New York:. Routledge.

Miyares, Alicia. 2003. *Democracia feminista*. Madrid: Cátedra.

Mohanti, Chandra. [1984] 2003. "Under Western Eyes." In *Feminism Without Borders: Decolonizing Theory, Practicing Solidarity*, 17–42. Raleigh, NC: Duke University Press.

Mo Romero, Esperanza, and Margarita Eva Rodríguez García. 2005. "Educar: ¿A quién y para qué?" In Morant 2005, 729–56.

Mogel, Bizenta. 1963. *Ipui onak*. San Sebastián: Auspoa.

Molas, M. Dolors, ed. 2008. *Vivir en femenino: Estudios de mujeres en la antigüedad*. Barcelona: Universidad de Barcelona.

Molina, Álvaro. 2013. *Mujeres y hombres en la España del siglo XVIII: Identidad, género y visualidad*. Madrid: Cátedra.

Molinero, Carme and Pere Ysàs. 2015. "Un proceso policéntrico: La transición de la dictadura a la democracia en España." *Avances del Cesor* 12: 189–207.

Monteiro, Rosa. 2012. "A descriminalização do aborto em Portugal: Estado, movimentos de mulheres e partidos políticos." *Analise Social* 204 (48): 586–605.

Montejo, Julia. 2011. *Violetas para Olivia*. Barcelona: Martínez Roca.

Montero, Justa. 1994. "Igualdad y diferencia: Encrucijada del movimiento." *El Viejo Topo* 73:39–44.

Montero, Manuel. 2008. *Historia general del País Vasco*. San Sebastián: Txertoa.

Montero, Rosa. 2011. *El corazón del Tártaro*. Madrid: Espasa.

Moral Vargas, Marta del. 2007. "Acción colectiva femenina republicana: Las *Damas Rojas* de Madrid (1909–1911), una breve experiencia política." *Hispania: Revista Española de Historia* 67 (226): 541–66. 10 October 2013. http://hispania.revistas.csic.es/index.php/hispania/article/viewArticle/53.

Morand, Fréderique. 2004. *Doña María Gertrudis Hore (1742–1801), vivencia de una poetisa gaditana entre el siglo y la clausura*. Alcalá de Henares: Ayuntamiento de Alcalá de Henares.

___. 2009. "Enlightenment Experience in the Life and Poetry of Sor María Gertrudis de la Cruz Hore." In Jaffe and Lewis 2009, 33–50.

Morant, Isabel, ed. 2005. "El mundo moderno en la América colonial." Part 5 in *Historia de las mujeres en España y América Latina 3: El mundo moderno*. Madrid: Cátedra.

Morant Deusa, Isabel, and Mónica Bolufer. 1998. *Amor, matrimonio y familia*. Madrid: Síntesis.

Moraña, Mabel. 2012. "Postscríptum: El afecto en la caja de herramientas." In *El lenguaje de las emociones: Afecto y cultura en América Latina*, edited by Mabel Moraña and Ignacio Sánchez Prado, 313–37. Madrid: Iberoamericana/Vervuert.

Moreno Sardá, Amparo. 1988. "La réplica de las mujeres al franquismo." In Folguera 1988, 85–110.

Moreno Seco, Mónica. 2012. "Feministas y ciudadanas: Las aportaciones del feminismo español a la construcción del estado democrático." *Alcores* 13: 85–100.

Moura Pinheiro, Paula. 2002. *Pela dignidade e saúde das mulheres portuguesas: Depoimentos pela despenalização do aborto no contexto do julgamento da Maia*. Lisbon: Plataforma pelo Direito de Optar.

Moure Pereiro, Teresa. 2004. *A palabra das fillas de Eva*. Vigo: Galaxia.

___. 2012. *Queer-emos un mundo novo: Sobre cápsulas, xéneros e falsas clasificacións*. Vigo: Galaxia.

___. 2015. Teresa Moure's Facebook page. http://www.facebook.com/teresa.mourepereiro.

Moutinho dos Santos, Maria José. 1987. *O folheto de cordel: Mulher, família e sociedade no Portugal do século XVIII (1750–1800)*. Masters thesis, Faculdade de Letras da Universidade do Porto.

"Muerte de la señora Gimeno de Flaquer." 1919. *La Época* 6: 4.

Mujeres del EMK de la AMV. 1977. "Doble militancia." In *Jornadas de la Mujer de Euskadi* 68.

Mujika, Tene. 1923. *Miren Itziarri idazkiak eta olerkiak*. Amorebieta: Jaungoikozaleren irarkola.

Munibe e Idiáquez, Francisco Xavier María de. 1775. *Reflexiones sobre el Informe pedido por el Consejo a la Sociedad acerca de la fundación de Enseñanza para Niñas que se quiere hacer en Vergara*. Archivo del Territorio Histórico de Álava (ATHA), Fondo Prestamero, Caja 8, n. 16.3.

—. 1931. "Historia de la Real Sociedad Bascongada de los Amigos del País por el Conde de Peñaflorida: Fin." *Revista Internacional de Estudios Vascos* 22 (3): 443–82.

Muñoz de Bustillo, Carmen. 1995. "Encuentros y desencuentros en la historia: Los territorios del norte peninsular en la coyuntura del setecientos." *Historia Contemporánea* 12: 135–74.

Murray, Marie-Caroline. 1781. *Essai d'un Eloge historique de Marie Therèse archiduchesse d'Autriche, Imperatrice-Douairiere, Reine Apostolique d'Hongrie et Boheme, Princesse Souveraine des Pays-Bas*. Brussels: J. Vanden Berghen.

Nash, Mary. 1994. "Experiencia y aprendizaje: La formación histórica de los feminismos en España." *Historia y Sociedad* (Rio Piedras, San Juan, PR) 20: 151–72.

—. 1999. *Rojas: Las mujeres republicanas en la Guerra Civil*. Madrid: Taurus.

—. 2007. *Dones en transició: De la resistència política a la legitimitat feminista, les dones a la Barcelona de la Transició*. Barcelona: Ajuntament de Barcelona.

—. 2011. "La construcción de una cultura política desde la legitimidad feminista durante la Transición política a la democracia." In Aguado and Ortega 2011, 283–306.

—. 2012. "Feminismos de la Transición: Políticas identitarias, cultura política y disidencia cultural como resignificación de los valores de género." In *Entre dos orillas: Las mujeres en la historia de España y América Latina*, edited by Pilar Pérez-Fuentes Hernández, 355–80. Barcelona: Icaria.

Nava Rodríguez, María Teresa. 1995. "La mujer en las aulas (siglos XVI–XVIII): Una historia en construcción." *Cuadernos de Historia Moderna* 16: 377–90.

Negrín Fajardo, Olegario. 1984. *Ilustración y educación: La Sociedad Económica Matritense*. Madrid: Nacional.

Nelken, Margarita. 1922. *La condición social de la mujer en España*. Barcelona: Minerva.

Nogueira, Carlos. 2013. "Emília de Sousa Costa: Educação e literatura." *Revista Lusófona de Educação* 23: 159–78.

Nogueira, Chus. 2008. "Voces femeninas en la poesía gallega actual." *Revista de Erudición y Crítica* 5: 90–9.

___. 2013. "Emília de Sousa Costa: Educação e literatura." *Revista Lusófona de Educação* 23: 159–78.

Nogueira, María Xesús. 2009a. "Dolls, Princesses and Cinderellas: New Feminine Representations in Contemporary Galician Women's Poetry." In Palacios and Lojo, 97– 122.

—. 2009b. "Most Faithful Stories: An Interview with Luz Pozo-Garza." In Palacios and Lojo, 205–17.

Nóvoa Martins, Xurxo. 2015. "Carta aberta ao macho militante." *Diario Liberdade*. http://www.diarioliberdade.org/opiniom/opiniom-propia/57595-carta-aberta-ao-macho-limitante.html.

Nunes Ribeiro Sanches, António. 1760. Cartas sobre a Educação da Mocidade. Colónia: n.p.

Núñez Betelu, Maite. 2001. "Género y construcción nacional en las escritoras vascas." PhD dissertation, University of Missouri-Columbia.

Núñez Paredes, Juan. 1992. "El feminismo de Emilia Pardo Bazán." *Cuadernos de Estudios Gallegos* 40 (105): 303–13. https://doi.org/10.3989/ceg.1992.v40.i105.312.

Núñez Rey, Concepción. 2005. *Carmen de Burgos, "Colombine," en la Edad de Plata de la literatura española*. Seville: Fundación José Manuel Lara.

Nye, Joseph S., Jr. 2004. *Soft Power: The Means to Success in World Politics*. New York: Public Affairs.

Offen, Karen. 1988. "Defining Feminism: A Comparative Historical Approach." *Signs* (Chicago, IL) 14 (1): 119–57. https://doi.org/10.1086/494494.

___. 2000. *European Feminisms, 1700–1950: A Political History*. Stanford: Stanford University Press.

Okin, Susan Moller. 1998. "Gender, the Public, and the Private." In Phillips 1998, 116–41.

Olaziregi, Mari Jose. 2003. "Bizenta Mogel (1782–1854), edo euskal tradizio literario androzentrikoa pitzatu zenekoa." In *Euskal gramatikari eta euskal literaturari buruzko jardunaldiak XXI. mendearen atarian*, edited by Euskaltzaindia, 2:203–21. Bilbao: Euskaltzaindia.

Oliveira Martins, Joaquim Pedro de. 1924. *Dispersos*, 2:159–66. Lisbon: Biblioteca Nacional.

Oronoz, Belen. 2012. *JosAnton Artze "Harzabal": Inguruaren eragina poesiagintzan*. Bilbao: Universidad del País Vasco.

Ortbals, Candice D. 2008. "Subnational Politics in Spain: New Avenues for Feminist Policymaking and Activism." *Politics & Gender* 4 (01): 93–119. https://doi.org/10.1017/S1743923X08000044.

Ortega, Margarita. 1999. "La práctica judicial en las causas matrimoniales de la sociedad española del siglo XVIII: *Espácio, tiempo y forma, serie IV*." *Historia Moderna* 12: 275–96.

Osório de Castro, Zília, and João Esteves, dir. 2005. *Dicionário no feminino, séculos XIX–XX*. Edited by António Ferreia de Sousa, Ilda Soares de Abreu, and Maria Emília Stone. Lisbon: Horizonte.

Palacios, Manuela. 2009. "The Course of Nature: An Eco-Feminist Reading of Contemporary Irish and Galician Women Poets." In Palacios and Lojo 2009, 77–96.

Palacios, Manuela, and Laura Lojo, eds. 2009. *Writing Bonds: Irish and Galician Contemporary Women Poets*. Bern: Peter Lang.

Palacios Fernández, Emilio. 2002. *La mujer y las letras en el siglo XVIII*. Madrid: Laberinto.

Palomo, Ana. 1993. "Feminismo 2000." *Geu Emakumeok* 18: 14.

Palumbo, Silvia. n.d. https://pruebasilviap.wordpress.com/proyectos-2/lesbianbanda/.

Pàmies, Teresa. 1976. *Maig de les dones: Crònica d'unes Jornades*. Barcelona: Laia.

Paniagua, Javier. 2009. *La transición democrática: De la dictadura a la democracia en España (1973–1986)*. Madrid: Anaya.

Pardo, Rosa. 1988. "El feminismo en España: Breve resumen 1953–1985." In Folguera 1988, 133–40.

Pardo Bazán, Emilia. 1886. "Apuntes autobiográficos." In *Los pazos de Ulloa: Novela original, precedido de unos apuntes autobiográficos*, 5–92. Barcelona: Daniel Cortezo y C[a].

___. 1890. "Dos palabras." In Carolina Valencia, *Poesías*, vii–xi. Palencia: Alonso y Menéndez.

___. 1891. "La cuestión académica." *Nuevo Teatro Crítico* 1 (3): 61–73.

___. 1892. "La educación del hombre y la de la mujer: Sus relaciones y diferencias." *Nuevo Teatro Crítico* 2 (22): 14–64.

___. 1893. "Doña Concepción Arenal y sus ideas sobre la mujer." *Nuevo Teatro Crítico* 3 (26): 269–304.

___. 1900. Review of *Evangelios de la mujer*, 2nd ed., edited by Concepción Gimeno de Flaquer. *Revista Contemporánea* 27 (121): 445–7.

___. 1915. "Don Francisco Giner." *La Lectura* (March): 269–74.

___. 1917. "Los tiempos de Isabel." *El Día* (11 February): 1.

___. [1913] 1962. "Letter to don Alejandro Barreiro." In Carmen Bravo-Villasante, *Vida y obra de Emilia Pardo Bazán*, 279–81. Madrid: Revista de Occidente.

___. [1893] 1981a. "Concepción Arenal y sus ideas acerca de la mujer." *Nuevo Teatro Crítico* 3 (26): 269–304. Also in Pardo Bazán 1981d, 173–95.

___. [1892] 1981b. "La educación del hombre y la de la mujer." In Pardo Bazán 1981d, 71–102.

___. [1890] 1981c. "La mujer española." In Pardo Bazán 1981d, 25–97.

___. [1890] 1981d. *La mujer española*. Edited by Leda Schiavo. Madrid: Nacional.

___. [1892] 1981e. "Una opinión sobre la mujer." *Nuevo Teatro Crítico* 15. In Pardo Bazán 1981d, 155–62.

___. [1901] 1999. ""Sobre los derechos de la mujer: *La Ilustración Artística* 1015." In *La mujer española y otros escritos*, edited by Guadalupe Gómez Ferrer, 258–62. Madrid: Cátedra.

___. [1902] 2010a. "*De siglo a siglo (1896–1901)*." In Pardo Bazán 2010c, 227–66.

___. [1901] 2010b. *Discurso pronunciado en los Juegos Florales de Orense la noche del 7 de junio de 1901*. In Pardo Bazán 2010c, 305–39.

___. 2010c. *Obra crítica (1888–1908)*. Edited by Íñigo Sánchez Llama. Madrid: Cátedra.

___. 2013. *"Miquiño mío": Cartas a Galdós*. Edited by Isabel Parreño and Juan Manuel Hernández. Madrid: Turner.

___. 2016a. *Cartas de buena amistad: Epistolario de Emilia Pardo Bazán a Blanca de los Ríos (1893–1919)*. Edited by Ana Mª Freire López and Dolores Thion Soriano Molla. Madrid: Iberoamericana/Vervuert.

___. [1905] 2016b. "Letter to Blanca de los Ríos de Lampérez." 3 November 1905. In Pardo Bazán 2016a, 133.

___. [1905] 2016c. "Letter to Blanca de los Ríos de Lampérez." 18 November 1905. In Pardo Bazán 2016a, 133.

Pascua, María José de. 1998. *Mujeres solas: Historias de amor y de abandono en el mundo hispánico*. Málaga: Centro de Ediciones de la Diputación de Málaga.

Pateman, Carole. 1989. *The Disorder of Women*. Stanford: Stanford University Press.

Pau Janer, María de la. 2002. *Las mujeres que hay en mí*. Barcelona: Planeta.

Pereira Martínez, Carlos. 1998. "Mulleres e República: Aproximación ás asociacións de mulleres progresistas na Coruña republicana." *Anuario Brigantino* 21: 255–90.

Pérez, Jorge. 2010. "Pensamiento y no solo acción: Sobre la valiosa aportación peninsular a la teoría queer." *Revista Canadiense de Estudios Hispánicos* 35 (1): 141–61.

Pérez, Karmele, Gurutze Ezkurdia, and Begoña Bilbao. 2012. "Euzko ikastolen andereñoen formazioa eta eskola-praktikak." In Bilbao et al. 2012, 45–76.

Pérez Cantó, Pilar, and Rocío de la Nogal. 2005. "Las mujeres en la arena pública." In Morant 2005, 757–89.

Pérez de Celis, Margarita de. 1857. "Prólogo." In Marina, 1857, iii–xvi.

Pérez Pais, Carmen, and Mariam Mariño, eds. 2013. *Recuperación da documentación e memoria do Movemento Feminista Organizado en Galicia*. Santiago de Compostela: Consello da Cultura Galega.

Pérez Sarrión, Guillermo. 2003. "Casual Poverty in the Spanish Enlightenment: Josefa Amar y Borbón and the Real Sociedad Económica Aragonesa de Amigos del País." *Dieciocho* 26 (2): 265–93.

Perinat, Adolfo, and María Isabel Marrades. 1980. *Mujer, prensa y sociedad en España, 1800–1939*. Madrid: Centro de Investigaciones Sociológicas.

Pestana, Alice. 1888. "Relatório da viagem de estudo a estabelecimentos de instrução secundária do sexo feminino na Inglaterra, Suíça e França." *Diário do Governo*, appendix 17, 25 January 1888.

___. 1893. *Relatório de uma visita de estudo a estabelecimentos de ensino profissional do sexo feminino no estrangeiro*. Lisbon: Imprensa Nacional.

___. 1898a. *La femme et la paix: Appel aux mères portugaises*. Lisbon: Imprensa Nacional.

___. 1898b. "Um raríssimo tipo de mulher." *Vanguarda* (2 November): 1, cols. 5–6 and (7 November): 1, col. 6.

___. 1899a. "Congresso Feminista." *Vanguarda* (22 April): 1, cols. 1–2.

___. 1899b. "Feminismo." *Vanguarda* (27 May): 1, cols. 1–2; (3 June): 1, cols. 1–2; (10 June): 1, cols. 1–2; and (12 July): 1, cols. 1–2.

Peyrou, Florencia, and Darina Martykánová. 2014. "Presentación." In *Dosier: La historia transnacional,* edited by Florencia Peyrou and Darina Martykánová. *Ayer* 94 (2): 13–22.

Phillips, Anne, ed. 1998. *Feminism and Politics.* Oxford: Oxford University Press.

Phillips, Roderick. 1991. *Untying the Knot: A Short History of Divorce.* Cambridge: Cambridge University Press.

Pina, Luís de. 1968. "Plano para a educação de uma menina portuguesa no século XVIII: No II Centenario da Publicação do *Método* de Ribeiro Sanches." *Cale: Revista da Faculdade de Letras do Porto* 1: 5–46.

Pineda, Empar. 1980. "¿El mito de la feminidad cabalga de nuevo?" *El Viejo Topo.* Extra 10: 16–24.

Pinheiro, Beatriz. 1899a. "Crónica" *Ave Azul* 8 (15 August 1899): 321–7; 10 (15 October 1899): 433–41; 11 (15 November 1899): 497–506; 1/2 (25 February 1900): 1–11; and "A emancipação da mulher" 6 (June 1900): 390–400.

___. 1899b. "Crónica." *Ave Azul* 8 (15 August): 324.

___. 1899c. "Crónica." *Ave Azul* 11 (15 November): 500.

Pintasilgo, Maria de Lurdes. 1984. "Portugal: Daring to be Different." In *Sisterhood is Global: The International Women's Movement Anthology,* edited by Robin Morgan, 571–5. Garden City, NY: Anchor Press/Doubleday.

___. 1986. "Candidata à Presidência da Républica." *Manifesto Eleitoral.* Ms.

Pintos, Margarita. 2016. *Concepción Gimeno de Flaquer: Del sí de las niñas al yo de las mujeres.* Madrid: Plaza y Valdés.

Piñeiro, Ramón. 2007. *Olladas no futuro.* Vigo: Galaxia.

Pires, Ana Paula, ed. 2013. *Dicionário de história da I República e do republicanismo.* Vol. 1. Lisbon: Assembleia da República.

"¿Por qué esta revista?" 1983b. *Andaina* 0: 3.

Portillo, J.M. 1991. *Monarquía y gobierno provincial: Poder y Constitución en las provincias vascas (1760–1808).* Madrid: Centro de Estudios Constitucionales.

Pozo Garza, Luz. 1949. *Ánfora.* n.p.: n.p.

___. 1952. *O paxaro na boca.* Montforte de Lemos: Xistral.

___. 1986. *Códice calixtino.* Santiago de Compostela: Sotelo Blanco.

___. 1992. *Prometo a flor de loto.* A Coruña: Diputación Provincial.

Preciado, Beatriz. 2007. "Mújeres en los márgenes." *El País,* Babelia (13 January 2008): 2. Also available at http://elpais.com/diario/2007/01/13/babelia/1168648750_850215.html. Accessed 26 June 2017.

___. 2008. *Testo yonqui.* Madrid: Espasa Calpe.

___. 2011. *Manifiesto contrasexual.* Barcelona: Anagrama.

Presbit, J.A. 1785. "Dedicatória, prólogo." In *Dos Privilégios e prerrogativas que o sexo feminino tem por direito comum e ordenações do Reino mais que o sexo masculino*. Lisbon: Off. Filipe da Silva e Azevedo.

Puértolas, Soledad. 2001. *Con mi madre*. Barcelona: Anagrama.

___. 2005. *Historia de un abrigo*. Barcelona: Anagrama.

Puleo, Alicia H. 2011. *Ecofeminismo para otro mundo posible*. Madrid: Cátedra.

Puleo, Alicia H., María Luisa P. Cavana, and Cristina Segura. 2004. *Mujeres y ecología: Historia, pensamiento, sociedad*. Madrid: Asociación Cultural Al-Mudayna.

Pusich, Antónia Gertrudes. 1848. *Galeria das Senhoras na Câmara dos Senhores Deputados, ou as minhas observações*. Lisbon: Tip. de Borges.

___. 1849. "Educação." *A Assembleia Literária* 4 (25 August): 25, col. 2.

___. 1850. "A Assembleia Literária." *A Assembleia Literária* 22 (12 January): 169, col. 1.

Queizán, María Xosé. 1977. *A muller en Galicia: A muller na sociedade galega, a lingua galega e a muller (Análise estructural de dous métodos represivos)*. A Coruña: Edicións do Castro.

___. 1998. *Misoxinia e racismo na poesía de Pondal*. Santiago de Compostela: Laiovento.

Quintás Pérez, Leticia. 2015. "As edicións facsimilares no Castro, un exemplo de recuperación da memoria histórica." *Madrygal* 18: 517–28.

Rábade Villar, María do Cebreiro. 2008. "Nuestro cuerpo es un campo de batalla: El sentido político de la poesía escrita por mujeres." In *Palabras extremas: Escritoras gallegas e irlandesas de hoy*, edited by M. Palacios González and H. González Fernández, 99–108. A Coruña: Netbiblo.

Radcliff, Pamela. 2007. "La ciudadanía y la transición a la democracia." In *De súbditos a ciudadanos: Una historia de la ciudadanía de España*, edited by Manuel Pérez Ledesma, 343–71. Madrid: Centro de Estudios Políticos y Constitucionales.

Rama, Ángel. 1984. *La ciudad letrada*. Hanover, NH: Ediciones del Norte.

Ramírez Almazán, María Dolores. 2009. "Las fourieristas gaditanas y la reivindicación de los derechos de la mujer: *La mujer y la sociedad* de Rosa Marina." In *Las revolucionarias: Literatura e insumisión femenina*, edited by Estela González de Sande and Ángeles Cruzado Rodríguez, 513–29. Seville: Arcibel.

Ramiro Moya, Francisco. 2012. *Mujeres y trabajo en la Zaragoza del siglo XVIII*. Saragossa: Prensas Universitarias de Zaragoza.

Ramis, Llucia. 2008. *Coses que et passen a Barcelona quan tens 30 anys*. Barcelona: Columna.

___. 2010. *Egosurfing*. Barcelona: Destino.

Ramos, María Dolores. 1999. "La construcción de la ciudadanía femenina: Las librepensadoras (1898–1909)." In *1898–1998: Un siglo avanzando hacia la igualdad de las mujeres*, edited by Concha Fagoaga, 91–111. Madrid: Dirección General de la Mujer/Consejería de Sanidad y Servicios Sociales/ Comunidad de Madrid.

___. 2011. "Feminismo laicista: Voces de autoridad, mediaciones y genealogías en el marco cultural del modernismo." In Aguado and Ortega 2011, 21–44.

Rebelo, Dulce. 2008. "Feminismo e movimentos de mulheres ao tempo de Maria Lamas." In *A memória, a obra e o pensamento de Maria Lamas*, edited by Regina Marques, 43–56. Lisbon: Colibri.Top of FormBottom of Form

Reboredo Marques, Pedro Miguel. 2005. "Não são fêmeas, ou machos as almas com distinção: Estratégias de valorização da mulher em papéis volantes setecentistas." *Portuguese Studies Review* (Trent University, 2007) 13 (1–2): 305–29.

Recarte Barriola, María Teresa. 1990. *Ilustración vasca y renovación educativa: La Real Sociedad Bascongada de los Amigos del País*. Salamanca: Universidad Pontificia de Salamanca.

Reddy, William. 2000. "Sentimentalism and Its Erasure: The Role of Emotions in the Era of French Revolution." *Journal of Modern History* 72 (1): 109–52. https://doi.org/10.1086/315931.

Regàs, Rosa. 2001. *La canción de Dorotea*. Barcelona: Planeta.

Rego, Paco, and Begoña Pérez. 2004. "La frontera del aborto." Suplemento Crónica 471, Elmundo.es. 24 October. 5 pages. Accessed 10 March 2016. http://www.elmundo.es/cronica/2004/471/1098717829.html.

Rego, Raul. 1982. *Os índices expurgatórios e a cultura portuguesa*. Lisbon: ICALP, Biblioteca Breve.

Reher, David-Sven. 1994. "Ciudades, procesos de urbanización y sistemas urbanos en la península ibérica, 1550–1991." In *Atlas histórico de las ciudades europeas: Península ibérica*, edited by M. Guàrdia, F.J. Monclús, and J.L. Oyón, 1–30. Barcelona: Salvat-Centre de Cultura Contemporània de Barcelona.

___. 1996. *La familia en España: Pasado y presente*. Madrid: Alianza.

Reimóndez, María. 2009. "The Curious Incident of Feminist Translation in Galicia: Courtcases, Lies and Gendern@tions." *Galicia 21* A: 68–89.

Rekalde Rodríguez, Itziar. 2012. "Emakume Abertzale Batza: Bere ibilbidea aztergai." In Bilbao et al. 2012, 21–42.

"Report Beijing + 20 Portugal." [April] 2014. Lisbon: Comissão para a Cidadania e Igualdade de Género. Accessed 3 October 2017. https://sustainabledevelopment.un.org/content/documents/13169Portugal_review_Beijing20.pdf.

Retolaza, Iratxe. 2012. "Emakume Abertzale Batza eta emakume idazleak." In Bilbao et al. 2012, 103–19.

Reyes, Alfonso. 1944. *"El deslinde": Prolegómenos a la teoría literaria*. México: Colegio de México.

Reynolds de Souza, Maria. 1986. "As primeiras deputadas portuguesas." In *A mulher na sociedade portuguesa: Visão histórico e perspectivas atuais*, vol. 2, 427–44. Coimbra: Instituto de História Económica e Social/Faculdade de Letras da Universidade de Coimbra.

___. 2013. *A concessão do voto às mulheres*. Lisbon: Comissão para a Cidadania e a Igualdade de Género.

[R.F.C.]. 1822. *Dedução filosófica da desigualdade dos sexos, e de seus direitos políticos por natureza*. Lisbon: na Impressão de M. P. de Lacerda.

Ribeiro, Olga, Isabel Campos, Maria José Geraldes, Helena Campos, and Madalena Barbosa, eds. 2004. *Elina Guimarães: Uma feminista portuguesa, vida e obra (1904–1991)*. Lisbon: Comissão para a Igualdade e para os Direitos das Mulheres, D.L.

Riera, Carme. 2003. *La mitad del alma*. Translated by Carme Riera. Barcelona: Alfaguara.

Rigaudias, Marie-Claude. 1980. "Feminism & Spain's Political Revival." *Off Our Backs* 10 (4): 22–3.

___. 2009. *La transición democrática: De la dictadura a la democracia en España (1973–1986)*. Madrid: Anaya.

Riley, Denise. 1988. *Am I That Name? Feminism and the Category of "Women" in History*. London: Macmillan.

Ringrose, David R. 1996. *Spain, Europe, and the "Spanish Miracle," 1700–1900*. Cambridge: Cambridge University Press.

Rios Bergantinhos, Noa. 2001. *A mulher no nacionalismo galego (1900–1936)*. Santiago de Compostela: Laiovento.

Ríos Lazcano, Isabel. 1986. *Testimonio de la Guerra Civil*. A Coruña: Ediciós do Castro.

Rivera, María-Milagros. 1994. "Partir de sí." *El Viejo Topo* 73: 31–5.

___. 1997. *El fraude de la igualdad*. Barcelona: Planeta.

Rivera Garreta, María-Milagros. 2005. *La diferencia sexual en la historia*. Valencia: Publicaciones de la Universidad de Valencia.

Robinson, Richard Alan. 1979. *Contemporary Portugal: A History*. London: Allen and Unwin.

Roca i Girona, Jordi. 2003. "Esposa y madre a la vez: Construcción y negociación del modelo ideal de mujer bajo el (primer) franquismo." In *Mujeres y hombres en la España franquista: Sociedad, economía, política, cultura*, edited by Gloria Nielfa Cristóbal, 45–66. Madrid: Universidad Complutense de Madrid.

Rochefort, Florence, and Danielle Haase-Dubosc. 2001. "Entretien avec Françoise Collin: Philosophe et intellectuelle féministe." *Clio: Histoire, femmes et sociétés* 13: 195–210.

Rodrigo, Antonina. 1994. *María Lejárraga, una mujer en la sombra*. Madrid: Vosa.

Rodrigues, Catarina Marques. 2015. "Fez-se história: Um terço dos lugares no Parlamento vai ser ocupado por mulheres." Observador. 5 October 2015. http://observador.pt/2015/10/05/mulheres-no-parlamento/.

Rodríguez, Isabel, and Andrea Bila. 1993. "Ahora te dejan entrar al WC, pero no bajarte las bragas." *Geu Emakumeok* 16: 41–2.

Rodríguez Gallardo, Ángel. n.d. "Enriqueta Otero: Mestra e guerrilleira antifranquista, presa vinte anos nos cárceres franquistas." Accessed 22 June 2016. .álbum de mulleres. www.culturagalega.org.

___. 2005. *Letras armadas: As vidas de Enriqueta Otero Blanco*. Lugo: Concello de Lugo; Santiago de Compostela: Fundación 10 de Marzo.

Rodríguez García, José María. 2011. "Yolanda Castaño: Fashionista and Floating Poet." *Discourse* 33 (4): 101–27.

Rodríguez Mate, Isabel, ed. 2010. *22 documentos do feminismo galego*. Santiago de Compostela: Fundación Galiza Sempre.

Rodríguez Rodríguez, Marisol, and Helena Miguélez-Carballeira. 2013. *Feminismo e innovación literaria en la narrativa gallega de autoría femenina: Xohana Torres, María Xosé Queizán, Carmen Blanco y Teresa Moure*. Lewiston, NY: Edwin Mellen Press.

Rodríguez Sánchez, Ángel. 1990. "El poder familiar: La Patria Potestad en el Antiguo Régimen." *Chronica Nova: Revista de Historia Moderna de la Universidad de Granada* 18: 365–80.

Romeu Alfaro, Fernanda. 2002. *El silencio roto: Mujeres contra el franquismo*. Madrid: El Viejo Topo.

Ros, Xon de, and Geraldine Hazbun, eds. 2011. *A Companion to Spanish Women's Studies*. Woodbridge, Suffolk: Tamesis.

Roseman, Sharon R. 1997. "Celebrating Silenced Words: The 'Reimagining' of a Feminist Nation in Late-Twentieth-Century Galicia." *Feminist Studies* 23 (1): 43–71. https://doi.org/10.2307/3178297.

RSBAP [Real Sociedad Bascongada de los Amigos del País]. 1784. *Plan y Ordenanzas de un Seminario para señoritas en la ciudad de Vitoria bajo la dirección de la Real Sociedad Bascongada*. Archivo del Territorio Histórico de Álava (ATHA), Fondo Prestamero, Caja 8, n.18.

___. 1985a. *Extractos de las juntas generales celebradas por la Real Sociedad Bascongada de los Amigos del País, (1783–1785)*. San Sebastián: Sociedad Guipuzcoana de ediciones y publicaciones.

———. 1985b. *Extractos de las juntas generales celebradas por la Real Sociedad Bascongada de los Amigos del País (1789–1791)*. San Sebastián: Sociedad Guipuzcoana de ediciones y publicaciones.

Rubio, Coro. 1996. *Revolución y tradición: El País Vasco ante la revolución liberal y la construcción del estado español, 1808–1868*. Madrid: Siglo XXI.

Ruiz Franco, Rosario. 2007. *Eternas menores*. Madrid: Biblioteca Nueva.

Saavedra, Luisa. 2010. "Psicologia feminista em Portugal: Dificultades e conquistas." In *Investigaciones actuales de las mujeres y del género*, edited by Rita Maria Radl Philipp, 59–77. Santiago de Compostela: Universidade de Santiago de Compostela.

Saavedra Fernández, Pegerto. 1994. *La vida cotidiana en la Galicia del Antiguo Regimen*. Barcelona: Crítica.

Sadlier, Darlene J. 1989. *The Question of How: Women Writers and New Portuguese Literature*. Contributions to Women's Studies Series 109. New York: Greenwood Press.

Sáiz de Otero, Concepción. 1998. "El feminismo en España." In Jagoe, Blanco, and Enríquez de Salamanca 1998, 515–22. Original in *La Escuela Moderna* 13.2 (1897): 248–60 and 13.5 (1897): 321–34.

Salgado, María A. 2009. "Margarita Hickey's Guide to the Traps of Love." In Jaffe and Lewis 2009, 62–83.

Samara, Maria Alice. 2007. *Operárias e burguesas: As mulheres no tempo da república*. Lisbon: A Esfera dos Livros.

Sanches, Andreia. 2015. "Direitos das mulheres, 20 anos depois: Salários e chefias são 'pontos críticos.'" *Público*. 4 September 2015. Accessed 24 March 2016. https://www.publico.pt/2015/09/04/sociedade/noticia/direitos-das-mulheres-20-anos-depois-salarios-e-chefias-sao-pontos-criticos-1706813.

Sánchez Aríns, Susana. 2014. "Maternosofía: Suficiência racional vs. instinto maternal." A Sega: Plataforma de crítica literaria. http://www.asega-critica.net/2014/04/maternosofia-suficiencia-racional-vs.html.

Sánchez Dueñas, Blas. 2013. "Preocupación patriótica y compromiso nacional en las escritoras españolas finiseculares a través de la prensa." In Servén edited by Carmen and Ivana Rota 2013, 237–66.

———. 2014. "Carmen Karr D'Alaforetto (1865–1943)." Escritores en la prensa. http://www.escritorasenlaprensa.es/carmen-serven-diez/.

Sánchez Ferré, Pere. 1998. "Els orígens del feminisme a Catalunya: 1870–1926 (2)." *L'Avenç* 223 (March): 6–11.

Sánchez Hita, Beatriz. 2009. "María del Carmen Silva, la Robespierre española: Una heroína y periodista en la Guerra de la Independencia." In *Heroínas y patriotas: Mujeres de 1808*, edited by Irene Castells, Gloria Espigado Tocino, and María Cruz Romeo, 399–425. Madrid: Cátedra.

Sánchez Llama, Íñigo. 1999. "María del Pilar Sinués de Marco y la cultura oficial peninsular del siglo XIX: Del neocatolicismo a la estética realista." In *Revista Canadiense de Estudios Hispánicos* 23 (2): 271–88.

___. 2000. *Galería de escritoras isabelinas: La prensa periódica entre 1883 y 1895.* Madrid: Cátedra.

Sancho, José Luis. 2008. "Retratos de familia de los Borbones 1700–1801." In *Arte, poder y sociedad en la España de los siglos XV a XX*, edited by Miguel Cabañas Bravo, Amelia López-Yarto, and Wilfredo Rincón García, 123–8. Madrid: Consejo Superior de Investigaciones Científicas.

Santos, Care. 2009. *Supermami: Mil maneras de ser una mamá feliz.* Barcelona: Grijalbo.

Santos, Zulmira. 2002. *Literatura e espiritualidade na obra de Teodoro de Almeida (1722–1804).* Lisbon: Fundação Calouste Gulbenkian.

Sarasúa, Carmen. 2002. "Aprendiendo a ser mujeres: Las escuelas de niñas en la España del siglo XIX." *Cuadernos de Historia Contemporánea* 24: 281–97.

Sarazin, Marie-Paule. 1995. "Introducción." In Félix Dupanloup, *La mujer estudiosa*, 9–23. Translated by Marie-Paule Sarazin. Cádiz: University of Cádiz.

Saugnieux, Joël. 1975. *Le jansenisme espagnol du XVIIIe siècle, ses composans et ses sources.* Oviedo: Cátedra Feijoo.

Scanlon, Geraldine M. 1986. *La polémica feminista en la España contemporánea, 1868–1974.* 2nd ed. Translated by Rafael Mazarrasa. Madrid: Akal.

Schiavo, Leda. 1981. "Introducción." In Pardo Bazán 1981d, 7–23.

Sciuti Russo, Vittorio. 2009. *Inquisizione spagnola e riformismo borbonico fra sette e ottocento, il diabattito europeo sulla soppressione del "terrible monstre."* Firenze: Olschki.

Schumm, Sandra J. 2015. "Female Revalorization in Twenty-First Century Spanish Novels." *Letras femeninas* 41 (1): 245–64.

Scott, Joan. 1992. "Igualdad versus diferencia: Los usos de la teoría posestructuralista." *Debate feminista* 3 (5): 85–104.

___. 1996. *Only Paradoxes to Offer: French Feminists and the Rights of Man.* Cambridge: Harvard University Press.

___. 2011. *The Fantasy of Feminist History.* Durham and London: Duke University Press.

Seara, Teresa. 2000. "A poesía galega na fin de milenio." *Revista de Lenguas y Literaturas Gallega, Catalana y Vasca* 7: 125–34.

Segura, Isabel, and Marta Selva. 1984. *Revistes de dones (1846–1935).* Barcelona: Edhasa.

Seixo, Vicente del. 1801. *Discurso filosófico y económico-político sobre la capacidad o incapacidad natural de las mujeres para las Ciencias y las Artes….* Madrid: Repullés.

Sendón de León, Victoria. 2002. *Marcar las diferencias: Discursos feministas ante un nuevo siglo.* Barcelona: Icaria.

Serralheiro, Lúcia. 2011. *Mulheres em grupo contra a corrente*. Rio Tinto: Evolua.
Serrano de Wilson, Emilia. 1890. *América y sus mujeres*. Barcelona: Establecimiento Tipográfico de Javier Giró.
Servén, Carmen, and Ivana Rota. 2013. *Escritoras españolas en los medios de prensa, 1868–1936*. Seville: Renacimiento.
Servén Díez, Carmen. 2013. "El 'feminismo moderado' de Concepción Gimeno de Flaquer en su contexto histórico." *Revista de Estudios Hispánicos* 47 (3): 397–415. https://doi.org/10.1353/rvs.2013.0052.
Sierra, María. 2015. "Entre emociones y política: La historia cruzada de la virilidad romántica." *Rúbrica Contemporánea* 4 (7): 11–25.
Silva, María del Carmen. 1811. *El Robespierre Español: Amigo de las leyes o Questiones atrevidas sobre la España*. Isla de León, Cádiz: Imprenta de Periu.
Silva, Maria Regina Tavares da. 1982. *Feminismo em Portugal na voz de mulheres escritoras do início do século XX*. Lisbon: Comissão da Condição Feminina.
——. 1983. "Feminismo em Portugal na voz de mulheres escritoras do início do século XX." *Análise Social* 19:77–9; [3°, 4°, 5°]: 875–907.
——. 1986. "O tema 'Mulher' em folhetos volantes portugueses." In *A mulher na sociedade portuguesa: Visão histórico e perspectivas atuais*, vol. 2, 39–54. Coimbra: Instituto de História Económica e Social, Faculdade de Letras da Universidade de Coimbra.
——. 198? "Carolina Michaëlis de Vasconcelos." In *Mulheres portuguesas: Vidas e obras celebradas, vidas e obras ignoradas*, edited by Maria Regina Tavares da Silva and Ana Vicente, 44–58. Lisbon: CIDM.
——. 1998. "História no feminino: Os movimentos feministas em Portugal." In *História de Portugal dos tempos pré-históricos aos nossos dias*, vol. 15, edited by João Medina, 283–97. Lisbon: Ediclube.
——. 1999. *A mulher: Bibliografia portuguesa anotada (monografias, 1518–1998)*. Lisbon: Cosmos.
——. 2005. "Alice Evelina Pestana Coelho." In Osório de Castro and Esteves 2005, 46–50.
——. n.d. "História da CIG décadas de 70 a 90." Accessed 20 March 2016. https://www.cig.gov.pt/a-cig/historia-da-cig/.
Silva e Orta, Teresa Margarida da. 2002. *Aventuras de Diófanes*. Edited by Maria da Santa Cruz. Lisbon: Caminho.
Simões de Almeida, Ana Bela, and Burghard Baltrusch. 2007. "Entre o essencialismo rural de Fisteus e o Pós-modernismo urbano de Lisboa: Uma comparação (im)possível entre Lupe Gómez e Adília Lopes." In *Actas do VII Congreso Internacional de Estudios Galegos*, edited by Helena González and María Xesús Lama, 299–311. A Coruña: Castro.

Simón Palmer, María del Carmen. 1991. "Introducción." In *Escritoras españolas del siglo XIX: Manual bio-bibliográfico*, edited by María del Carmen Simón Palmer, ix–xvii. Madrid: Castalia.

___. 2013. "Escritoras en la prensa catalanista." In Servén and Rota 2013, 290–317.

___. 2014. "La mirada social en la prensa: Concepción Arenal." *Arbor: Ciencia, Pensamiento y Cultura* 190 (767): 1–8.

Simón Rodríguez, María Elena. 2008. *Hijas de la igualdad, herederas de injusticias*. Madrid: Narcea.

Smith, Jennifer. 2009. "La violencia de género en dos cuentos de Emilia Pardo Bazán." In *La literatura de Emilia Pardo Bazán*, edited by José Manuel González Herrán, Cristina Patiño Eirín, and Ermitas Penas Varela, 697–705. A Coruña: Fundación CaixaGalicia.

Smith, Theresa Ann. 2006. *The Emerging Female Citizen: Gender and Enlightenment in Spain*. Berkeley: University of California Press.

Soares de Abreu, Ilda. 2005. "Almanaque das Senhoras." In Osório de Castro and Esteves 2005, 54–62.

___. 2005. "Guiomar Delfina de Noronha Torrezão." In Osório de Castro and Esteves 2005, 379–83.

Sobrado, José Manuel, and Xabier Aierdi. 1997. "Entramado organizativo del movimiento feminista en el País Vasco." *Reis: Revista Española de Investigaciones Sociológicas* 80 (80): 183–201. https://doi.org/10.2307/40183922.

Solé, Belén, and Beatriz Díaz. 2014. *"Era más la miseria que el miedo." Mujeres y franquismo en el Gran Bilbao: Represión y resistencia*. Bilbao: Asociación Elkasko de Investigación Histórica.

Soria Mesa, Enrique. 2007. *La nobleza en la España moderna, cambio y continuidad*. Madrid: Marcial Pons.

Sousa, Antónia de, Bruno da Ponte, Dórdio Guimarães, and Edite Soeiro. 2004. *Entrevistas a Natália Correia*. Lisbon: Parceria A.M. Pereira.

Sousa Costa, Emília de. 1914 (trans). *Aos profesores e às professoras*. Lisbon: A.M. Teixeira; Porto: Sequeira.

___. 1923. *Ideais antigas de mulher moderna*. Braga: Cruz.

___. 1934. *Maria Amália Vaz de Carvalho*. Lisbon: Sociedade Nacional de Tipografia.

Starcevic, Elizabeth. 1976. *Carmen de Burgos: Defensora de la mujer*. Almería: Cajal.

Stone, Maria Emília. 2005a. "A Assembleia Literária." In Osório de Castro and Esteves 2005, 139–40.

___. 2005b. "Antónia Gertrudes Pusich." In Osório de Castro and Esteves 2005, 127–29.

Sturkenboom, Dorothée. 2000. "Historicizing the Gender of Emotions: Changing Perceptions in Dutch Enlightenment Thought." *Journal of Social History* 34 (1): 55–75. https://doi.org/10.1353/jsh.2000.0125.

Suárez Briones, Beatriz. 1998. "Sobre hombres y márgenes: Relaciones entre el feminismo y la teoría queer." *Lectora: Revista de Dones i Textualitat* 4: 83–91.

___. 2003. *Sextualidades: Teorías literarias feministas*. Alcalá de Henares: Ayuntamiento de Alcalá de Henares/Centro Asesor de la Mujer.

___, ed. 2014. *Feminismos lesbianos y queer: Representación, visibilidad y política*. Madrid: Plaza y Valdés.

Subirats, Marina. 1998. *Con diferencia: Las mujeres frente al reto de la autonomía*. Barcelona: Icaria.

___. 2012. "Somos iguales, somos diferentes." In Johnson and Zubiaurre 2012, 599–612.

Sudupe, Pako. 2011. *50eko hamarkadako euskal literatura: III. Antzerkia eta hamarkadaren ikuspegi orokorra*. San Sebastián: Utriusque Vasconiae.

Sullivan, Constance A. 1992. "Josefa Amar y Borbón and the Royal Aragonese Economic Society (with documents)." *Dieciocho* 15 (1): 95–148.

___. 1993. "The Quiet Feminism of Josefa Amar y Borbón's 1790 Book on the Education of Women." *Indiana Journal of Hispanic Literatures* 2 (1): 50–73.

Tavareda Dalmira, Dorotheia Engrassia [Teresa Margarida da Silva e Orta]. 1752. *Máximas da virtude, e fermosura com que Diofanes, Clyminea, e Hemirena Principes de Thebas venceraõ os mais apertados lances da desgraça*. Lisbon: Officina Miguel Manescal da Costa.

Tavares, Manuela. 2000. *Movimentos de mulheres em Portugal: Décadas de 70 e 80*. Lisbon: Horizonte.

___. 2011. *Feminismos: Percursos e desafios (1947–2007)*. Lisbon: Texto, 23.

___. 2013. "Associações de Mulheres nas décadas de 70 e 80 do século XX." In Esteves and Osório de Castro 2013, 113–19.

Tavares, Manuela, and Maria José Magalhães. 2015. "Correntes Feministas." In *Percursos feministas: Desafiar os tempos*, edited by Eduarda Ferreira et al., 92–117. Lisbon: UMAR/Universidade Feminista.

Taylor, Barbara. 2005. "Feminists versus Gallants: Manners and Morals in Enlightenment Britain." In *Women, Gender and Enlightenment*, edited by Sarah Knott and Barbara Taylor, 30–52. Hampshire: Palgrave. https://doi.org/10.1057/9780230554801_3.

___. 2012. "Enlightenment and the Uses of Woman." *History Workshop Journal* 74 (1): 79–87. https://doi.org/10.1093/hwj/dbr063.

Téllez Alarcia, Diego. 2010. *Absolutismo e ilustración en la España del siglo XVIII: El despotismo ilustrado de D. Ricardo Wall*. Madrid: Fundación Española de Historia Moderna.

Thomson, J.K.J. 1990. *La indústria d'indianes a la Barcelona del segle XVIII.* Barcelona: L'Avenç.

___. 1994. *Els orígens de la industrialització a Catalunya: El cotó a Barcelona 1728–1832.* Barcelona: Edicions 62.

Thompson, John. 2011. "Feminismo e nacionalismo: As perspectivas teóricas de María Xosé Queizán." In *Cara a unha poética feminista: Homenaxe a María Xosé Queizán*, edited by Camino Noia and Manuel Forcadela, 229–42 Vigo: Edicións Xerais de Galicia.

Threlfall, Monica. 1985. "The Women's Movement in Spain." *New Left Review* 151: 44–73.

Threlfall, Monica, Christine Cousins, and Celia Valiente. 2005. *Gendering Spanish Democracy.* New York: Routledge.

Threlfall, Mónica. 2009. "El papel transformador del movimiento de mujeres en la transición política española". In *El movimiento feminista en España en los años 70*, edited by Purificación Martínez Ten, Carmen Gutiérrez López, and Pilar González Ruiz, 17–52. Madrid: Cátedra.

Tomsich, María Giovanna. 1972. *El jansenismo en España.* Madrid: Siglo XXI.

Topa, Francisco. 2000. *Um caso do século XVIII: Isabel Clesse a Parca Cristaleira, poemas inéditos sobre o tema.* Porto: Edição de Autor.

Torras, Meri, ed. 2011. *Accions I reinvencions: Cultures lèsbiques a la Catalunya del tombant de segle XX–XXI.* Barcelona: Universitat Oberta de Catalunya-Universitat Autònoma de Barcelona.

Torrealdai, Joan Mari. 1997. *Euskal kultura, gaur.* San Sebastián: Jakin.

Torres, Xohana. 1957. *Do sulco.* Vigo: Galaxia.

___. 1980. *Estacións ao mar.* Vigo: Galaxia.

___. 1992. *Tempo de ría.* A Coruña: Edicións Espiral Maior.

Torres Feijó, Elias. 2005. "Cartas apologéticas, cartas polemistas: As Cartas apologéticas de Gertrudes Margarida de Jesus; Argumentaçom e inovaçom." In *Correspondências: Usos da Carta no século XVIII*, edited by Vanda Anastácio, 223–53. Lisbon: Colibri.

Torrezão, Guiomar. 1894. *Educação moderna.* Lisbon: José Bastos, Tip. Universal.

Trabudúa de Mandaluniz, Polixene. 1997. *Polixene: Crónicas de amama.* Bilbao: Fundación Sabino Arana.

Tratado sobre a Igualdade dos Sexos, ou Elogio do Merecimento das Mulheres oferecido, e Dedicado às Ilustres Senhoras de Portugal por um Amigo da Razão. 1790. Lisbon: Na Off. Patriarcal De Francisco Luiz Ameno.

Trevor-Roper, H.R., Conrad Russell, and Christopher Thompson. 1972. "*Stone* and *Anti-Stone*: A Discussion." *Economic History Review*, 2nd series, 25 (1): 114–36.

Trojani, Cécile Mary. 2007. "Privacidad nobiliaria y condición de la mujer en el siglo XVIII (La Real Sociedad Bascongada de los Amigos del País)." In *Historia social y literatura: Familia y nobleza en España (siglos XVIII–XIX)*, edited by Solange Hibbs, Cécile Trojani, Roberto Fernández, and María José Vilalta, 149–83. Lleida: Milenio.

Trujillo Barbadillo, Gracia. 2009. *Deseo y resistencia (1977–2007): Treinta años de movilización lesbiana en el estado español*. Barcelona: Egales.

Tubert, Silvia. 2001. *Deseo y representación: Convergencias de psicoanálisis y teoría feminista*. Madrid: Síntesis.

___. 2003. *Del sexo al género: Los equívocos de un concepto*. Madrid: Cátedra.

Tuñón, Amparo. 1977. "Carmen Alcalde: Ser mujer en España." *Cuadernos de Pedagogía* 31–2 (July): 23–5.

Tusquets, Esther. 2001. *Correspondencia privada*. Barcelona: Anagrama.

Ugalde, Mercedes. 1993. *Mujeres y nacionalismo vasco: Génesis y desarrollo de Emakume Abertzale Batza (1906–1936)*. Bilbao: Universidad del País Vasco.

Ugarte, Michael. 1998. "Carmen de Burgos ('Colombine'): Feminist *avant la lettre*." In Glenn and Mazquiarán 1998, 55–74.

Umerez Goribargoitia, Manuel. [1805] 2013. *Osaba baten instruccinuac bere Illoba Ezcondu eta Necazari batentzat bere eta bere Familiaren gobiernu oneraco Jaungoicoaren Legue Santubagaz conforme*. Transcribed by Jerardo Elortza. Oñati: Oñatiko Udal Euskaltegia. Accessed 24 June 2015. http://www.xn--oati-gqa.eus/eu/udal-zerbitzuak/euskara-eta-hezkuntza/bedita-larrakoetxea-udal-euskaltegia/argitalpenak/umerez-goribargoitia-1805-_eskuizkribua.pdf/view.

United Nations. 1995. "Beijing Declaration and Platform for Action." http://www.un.org/womenwatch/daw/beijing/pdf/BDPfA%20E.pdf.

"UN World Conferences on Women." 2015. United Nations System Chief Executive Boards for Coordination. http://www.unsceb.org/content/un-world-conferences-women.

Urkizu, Patri. 2000. *Historia de la literatura vasca*. Madrid: Universidad Nacional de Educación a Distancia.

Urra Olazabal, Manuela. 2007. "La Compañía de María Nuestra Señora de Lestonnac –ODN-." *Educadores: Revista de Renovación Pedagógica* 221–2: 77–84.

Urzainqui, Inmaculada. 2006. *"Catalin" de Rita de Barrenechea y otras voces de mujeres en el siglo XVIII: Estudio introductorio de Inmaculada Urzainqui*. Vitoria: Ararteko.

Valcárcel, Amelia. 1980. "El derecho al mal." *El Viejo Topo Extra* 10: 25–9.

___. 2000. *Rebeldes: Hacia la paridad*. Barcelona: Plaza y Janés.

Valiente Fernández, Celia. 1998. "La liberalización del régimen franquista: La Ley de 22 de julio de 1961 sobre derechos políticos, profesionales y de trabajo de la mujer." *Historia y Sociedad* (Rio Piedras, San Juan, PR) 31: 45–65.

___. 2003. "The Feminist Movement and the Reconfigured State in Spain (1970–2000)." In *Women's Movements Facing the Reconfigured State*, edited by Lee Ann Banaszak, Karen Beckwith, and Dieter Rucht, 30–47. New York: Cambridge University Press.

Valis, Noël. 1991a. *Carolina Coronado: Poesías*. Madrid: Castalia.

___. 1991b. "Introduction." In Valis 1991a, 7–41.

Valverde, Lola. 1988. "Contexto social y situación de la mujer vasca en el Antiguo Régimen." In *Emakumea Euskal Herriko historian: La mujer en la historia de Euskal Herria*, 35–45.

___. 1994. *Entre el deshonor y la miseria: Infancia abandonada en Guipúzcoa y Navarra siglos XVIII y XIX*. Bilbao: Universidad del País Vasco.

Valverde, Lola, and Ángel García-Sanz. 1989. "La Ilustración." In *Los vascos a través de la historia: Comportamientos, mentalidades y vida cotidiana*, edited by José Luis Orella, 190–222. San Sebastián: Gipuzkoako Kutxa.

Varela, Nuria. [2005] 2008. *Feminismo para principiantes*. Barcelona: Ediciones B.

Vaz de Carvalho, Maria Amália. 1904. *As nossas filhas: Cartas ás mães*. Lisbon: Parceria Antonio Maria Pereira.

___. 1913. *Coisas d'agora*. Lisbon: Parceria Antonio Maria Pereira.

Vázquez, Pura. 1943. *Peregrino de amor*. Lareche: n.p.

___. 1948. *En torno a la voz: Poemas*. Orense: Otero.

___. 1952. *Íntimas*. Lugo: Xistral.

___. 1963. *A saudade i outros poemas*. Vigo: Galaxia.

Vázquez Montalbán, Manuel. 2002. *Pasionaria y los siete enanitos*. Barcelona: Debolsillo.

Ventura Franch, Asunción. 1999. *Las mujeres y la Constitución Española de 1978: Madrid; Ministerio de Trabajo y Asuntos Sociales*. Madrid: Instituto de la Mujer.

Verdugo Martí, Vicenta. 2010. "Desmontando el patriarcado: Prácticas políticas y lemas del movimiento feminista español en la transición democrática." *Feminismos* 16 (16): 259–80. https://doi.org/10.14198/fem.2010.16.12.

Verney, Luís António. 1746. *O Verdadeiro Método de Estudar para ser util à Republica e à Igreja proporcionado ao Estilo e Necessidade e Portugal exposto em varias cartas escritas pelo R.P. Barbadinho da Congregasam de Itália*. Valensa: Antonio Balle.

Vialette, Aurélie. 2015. "Vidas paralelas e historias conectadas: Concepción Gimeno de Flaquer (1850–1919) y sus redes transatlánticas." In Fernández 2015a, 147–67.

Viennot, Élianne, and Nicole Pellegrin. 2012. *Revisiter la "querelle des femmes": Discours sur l'égalité/inégalité des sexes, de 1750 aux lendemains de la Révolution*. Saint Étienne: Publications de l'Université de Saint-Étienne.

Viera y Clavijo, María Joaquina. 2006. *La obra poética de María Joaquina de Viera y Clavijo*. Edited by Victoria Galván González. Las Palmas de Gran Canaria: Cabildo de Gran Canaria.

Vilas-Boas e Alvim, Maria Helena. 1990. "Da educação da mulher no Portugal oitocentista: Notas de um estudo." *Revista de Ciências Históricas Universidade Portucalense* 5: 334–7.

___. 2005. "Angelina Casimira do Carmo Vidal." In Osório de Castro and Esteves 2005, 114.

Vilhena, Maria da Conceição. 1987. *Alice Moderno: A mulher e a obra*. Angra do Heroísmo: Secretaria Regional da Educação e Cultura.

___. 1988. *Alice Moderno e a Inovação*. Ilha Nova.

Vollendorf, Lisa. 2001a. "Introduction." In *Recovering Spain's Feminist Tradition*, edited by Lisa Vollendorf, 1–27. New York: Modern Languages Association.

___. 2001b. *Reclaiming the Body: María de Zayas's Early Modern Feminism*. Chapel Hill: The University of North Carolina.

Walker, Lesley H. 2008. *A Mother's Love: Crafting Feminine Virtue in Enlightenment France*. Lewisburg: Bucknell University Press.

Wank-Nolasco Lamas, Rosmarie. 1995. *Mulheres para além do seu tempo*. Lisbon: Bertrand.

Wheeler, Douglas A. 1978. *Republican Portugal: A Political History 1910–1926*. Madison, WI: University of Wisconsin Press.

"Who are we." n.d. Women on Waves. Accessed 25 April 2016. http://womenonwaves.org/en/page/650/who-are-we.

Yebes, Condesa de. 1955. *La condesa duquesa de Benavente: Una vida en unas cartas (1752–1834)*. Madrid: Espasa-Calpe.

Young, Iris Marion. 1998. "Polity and Group Difference: A Critique of the Ideal of Universal Citizenship." In Phillips 1998, 401–29.

Zabala, Begoña. 2008. *Movimiento de mujeres, mujeres en movimiento*. Tafalla: Txalaparta.

Zambrano, Maria. 1995. "Eloísa o la existencia." In *María Zambrano: Nacer por sí misma*, edited by Elena Lauarenzi, 90–113. Madrid: horas y Horas.

Zanatti, Ana. 2016. *O sexo inútil*. Lisbon: Sextante.

Zavala, Iris M., ed. 2000b. *Feminismos, cuerpos, escrituras*. Santa Cruz de Tenerife: La Página Ediciones.

Zavala, Iris M. and Myriam Díaz-Diocaretz. 1993. *Breve historia feminista de la literatura española (en lengua castellana)*. Madrid: Anthropos.

Zavala, Iris M., Cristina Dupláa, Mari Jose Olaziregi, María Jesús Farina, and Beatriz Suárez Briones. 2000a. *Breve historia feminista de la literatura española (en lengua catalana, gallega y vasca)*. Vol. 6. Barcelona: Anthropos.

Ziga, Itziar. 2009a. *Devenir perra*. Barcelona: Melusina.

___. 2009b. "Confesiones sentimentales de la doctora Ziga: Experta en putología y perróloga ¡QUEER ES COMPARTIR!" Parole de Queer. 15 April–15 July. Accessed 26 June 2017. http://paroledequeer.blogspot.com.es/2012_02_01_archive.html.

Zorrilla, José. 2002. *Don Juan Tenorio*. Edited by Juan Francisco Peña, prologue by Francisco Nieva. Madrid: Espasa Calpe.

Contributors

Bakarne Altonaga Begoña: Doctoral candidate at the University of the Basque Country (UPV/EHU). Her doctoral thesis "Feminidades decimonónicas: La construcción de la diferencia sexual por el fuerismo vasco" analyses the construction of a vision of gender and feminine ideals elaborated by defenders of special Basque statutes from the middle of the eighteenth century to the end of the nineteenth century. Recently she edited the book *Diskurtsoak, eraikuntzak, gorputzak: Gorputzen eta binarismo sexualaren eraikuntzaz* (2014) with Alaitz Aizpuru, and she has also collaborated with him on a chapter on the historical construction of difference.

Amaia Alvarez-Uria: Lecturer at the Department of Language and Literature Pedagogy of the University of the Basque Country (UPV/EHU). She received her doctorate in 2011 with the thesis "Genero eta nazio identitateak Katalina Eleizegiren antzezlanetan" (Gender and nation identities in Katalina Eleizegi's plays). She gives seminars and workshops on "Discourse and gender" and on children's theatre. She is a member of the feminist literary group Sareinak (Las rederas; sareinak.net) and writes literary criticism for the journal *Argia*. Her research focuses on gender in Basque literature and multimodal analysis of discourse.

Vanda Anastácio: Professor of Portuguese literature and culture at the University of Lisbon. She is the author of *Marquesa de Alorna 1750–1839* and *Sonatas da Marquesa de Alorna*, and has edited the works of numerous Portuguese authors. She has also edited or coedited several volumes of critical essays, including *Correspondências (usos da carta no século XVIII).*

Maialen Aranguren: Predoctoral researcher and fellow at the University of the Basque Country (UPV/EHU). Her doctoral thesis "La anatomía política del cuerpo feminista: El movimiento autónomo de mujeres en el País Vasco (1975–1994)" analyses the Basque feminism that arose towards the end of the Franco dictatorship. She has recently published (along with Ana Peña and Antonio Prada) *La Guerra Civil y el Franquismo en Zumarraga: Gerra Zibila eta Frankismoa Zumarragan* (2014).

Nerea Aresti: Tenured researcher at the University of the Basque Country (UPV/EHU). Specialist in history of gender in the nineteenth and twentieth centuries, she is author of the following books: *Médicos, donjuanes y mujeres modernas: Los ideales de feminidad y masculinidad en el primer tercio del siglo XX* (2001) and *Masculinidades en tela de juicio: Hombres y género en el primer tercio del siglo XX* (2010). Some of her recent articles are "Los argumentos de la exclusión: Mujeres y liberalismo en la España contemporánea," *Historia Constitucional* 13 (2012); and "De heroínas viriles a madres de la patria: Las mujeres y el nacionalismo vasco (1893–1937)," *Historia y Política* 31 (2014).

Christine Arkinstall: Professor in Spanish at the University of Auckland. She obtained her master's degree from the University of Oviedo, Spain, and her PhD from the University of Auckland. A specialist in Spain's late nineteenth- and twentieth-century literatures and cultures, she has a particular interest in the Spanish Civil War and dissident writing under the Franco dictatorship, and has published widely on issues of gender, genre, and nation. Her 2014 book *Spanish Female Writers and the Freethinking Press, 1879–1926* (University of Toronto Press) foregrounds the exceptional contributions made by female freethinking writers in the fin de siècle to the beginnings of democracy in Spain. Previous books include *Histories, Cultures, and National Identities: Women Writing Spain, 1877–1984* (2009) and *Gender, Class and Nation: Mercè Rodoreda and the Subjects of Modernism* (2004), both published by Bucknell UP.

Silvia Bermúdez: Professor of Spanish at the University of California at Santa Barbara. Her areas of research and teaching are contemporary Iberian studies, with particular emphasis on women writers, Galician literatures and cultures, and Spanish popular culture, as per her *Rocking the Boat: Migration and Race in Contemporary Spanish Music* (2018). She is also interested in transatlantic studies and Peruvian women poets, having published *La esfinge de la escritura: La poesía ética de Blanca Varela* (2005). The volume *Cartographies of Madrid: Contesting Urban Space at the Crossroads of the Global South and Global North*, coedited with Anthony L. Geist, is forthcoming with Vanderbilt University Press.

Asunción Bernárdez Rodal: Professor of communication and gender, mass media semiotics and information theory in the School of Information Sciences at the Universidad Complutense de Madrid. She is the director of the Instituto de Investigaciones Feministas (Institute for Feminist Research). An expert on women in/and media, as well as on gender violence and cinema, she has published, among other works, the coedited volume *Violencia de género en el cine español: Análisis de los años 1998 a 2002, Guía didáctica* (2008) and *Mujeres en medio(s): Propuestas para analizar la comunicación masiva con perspectiva de género* (2015). Currently she is researching the topic "Museums and Women's Art within the Research Group of the Institute" in conjunction with the European project DIVERCITY: Diversity in Museums and in the City.

Maryellen Bieder: Professor emerita of Spanish at Indiana University, Bloomington. She publishes on Carmen de Burgos, Emilia Pardo Bazán – especially the friendships between Pardo Bazán and women authors Gabirela Cunninghame Graham and Blanca de los Ríos – and Catalan authors Mercè Rodoreda and Carme Riera. She continues to research nineteenth-century visual culture. With Roberta Johnson, she has coedited the critical anthology *Spanish Women Authors and Spain's Civil War* (Taylor & Francis/Routledge, 2017).

Fina Birulés: Professor of philosophy at the University of Barcelona. Her research centres on political subjectivity, feminist theory, and women's philosophical production. She founded the seminar Philosophy and Gender in 1990. She is the author of *Una herencia sin testimento: Hannah Arendt* and numerous scholarly articles. In addition, she has edited the volumes *Filosofía y género*; *El género de la memoria*; *El torno a Hannah Arendt*; *Hannah Arendt: El orgullo de pensar*; *Pensadoras del siglo XX*; *Aportaciones al pensamiento filosófico y político*; and *Lectoras de Simon Weil*.

Mónica Bolufer Peruga: Associate professor of early modern history at the University of Valencia, Spain. As a historian, she works within the theoretical framework of cultural history and gender history, with a particular interest in historiographical orientations (*histoire des représentations,* cultural history, *microstoria*) that link collective perceptions and values to individual appropriation and agency. Her research covers a wide array of subjects in the field of eighteenth-century Spanish and European cultural history: women's writing and translating; travel narratives and the construction of European identity; concepts of politeness and ideas of progress; the history of the family; and the dissemination of medical knowledge.

She has published four books and many essays in academic journals and essay collections, and has also coedited the multivolume collective work *Historia de las mujeres en España y América Latina*, 4 vols. (Cátedra, 2005–6). Her books include: *Mujeres e Ilustración: La construcción de la feminidad en la España del siglo XVIII* (Institució Alfons el Magnànim, 1998); in collaboration with Isabel Morant, *Amor, matrimonio y familia: La construcción histórica de la familia moderna* (Síntesis, 1998); a critical edition of Antonio Ponz's *Viaje fuera de España, 1785* (Universidad de Alicante, 2007); *La vida y la escritura en el siglo XVIII: Inés Joyes: "Apología de las mujeres"* (Universidade de València, 2008); and she is coauthor of *Mujeres y modernización: Estrategias culturales y prácticas sociales (siglos XVIII–XX)* (Instituto de la Mujer, Colección Estudios, 2008).

Mª Ángeles Cabré: Writer, literary critic, and director of the Observatorio Cultural de Género (Cultural Observatory of Gender) dedicated to promoting culture produced by women. Among other books, she is the author of the novel *Silence* (2008), made into the film *The Love of Silence* (2016). She is also a poet, with the collections *Gran amor* (2011) and *Si se calla el cantor* (2012). Her scholarly works are *Leer y escribir en femenino* (2013); *A contracorriente: Escritoras a la intemperie del siglo XX* (2015); and *Wonderwomen: 35 retratos de mujeres fascinantes* (2016). Her writings have been collected in volumes and anthologies. She is also active in press and all media.

Olga Castro: Lecturer in translation studies and Spanish at Aston University, Birmingham, UK. Her research areas include feminist translation studies, Galician literature in English translation, and gender and media. She has coauthored *Feminismos* (Xerais, 2013) and edited a special issue on feminism and translation for the journal *Gender and Language* (2013). She has also coedited a special issue on Galician literature for the journal *Abriu: Textuality Studies on Brazil, Galicia and Portugal* (2015), as well as the collections *Trama e urda: Contribucións multidisciplinares desde os estudos galegos* (Consello da Cultura Galega, 2015),

Feminist Translation Studies (Routledge, 2017), and *Self-Translation and Power* (Palgrave Macmillan, 2017). Between 2009 and 2015 she was secretary and vice-president of the International Association for Galician Studies. She is a corresponding member of the Royal Galician Academy.

Mari Luz Esteban: Holds a bachelor of arts in medicine and surgery from the University of the Basque Country (UPV/EHU, 1983) and a doctorate in social anthropology from the University of Barcelona (1993). She is senior lecturer in social anthropology at UPV/EHU, where she is also in charge of the doctoral program in feminism and gender studies. Her research focuses on feminist anthropology and anthropology of the body and the emotions. Her best-known books are: *Antropología del cuerpo: Género, itinerarios corporales, identidad y cambio* (Edicions Bellaterra, 2004) and *Crítica del pensamiento amoroso* (Edicions Bellaterra, 2011).

João Esteves: Doctoral candidate in modern and contemporary history at the Instituo Universitário de Lisboa (ISCTE). Since 1985, his research has focused on the female and feminist associations in Portugal from the nineteenth century until 1952. He has published extensively on women's organizations in Portugal, including: *A Liga Republicana das Mulheres Portuguesas: Uma organização política e feminista, 1909–1919* (1992), winner of the Carolina Michaëlis de Vasconcelos prize in 1991; *As origens do sufragismo português* (1998), winner of the CMV prize in 1998; *Mulheres e republicanismo, 1908–1928* (2008); and *Ana de Castro Osório, 1872–1935* (2014). He has also collaborated on *Dicionário dos educadores portugueses* (2003), directed by Antonio Nóvoa, and *Dicionário de história da I República e do republicanismo* (2013–14). Along with Zília Osório de Castro, he coedited the *Dicionário no feminino (séculos XIX–XX)* (2005) and *Feminae: Dicionário contemporâneo* (2013). He is the scientific commissioner of the exhibition *Carolina Beatriz Ângelo – Interseção dos sentidos: Palavras, Atos e Imagens* organized by the Museum of the Guarda (2010); winner of the Associação Portuguesa de Museologia (APOM) prize in 2011; and the scientific adviser of the exhibition *Percursos, Conquistas e Derrotas das Mulheres na 1.ª República*, organized by the Biblioteca-Museu República e Resistência (BMRR; 2010).

Pura Fernández: Research professor at the Centre for the Humanities and Social Sciences at Spain's National Research Council (CSIC), of which she was deputy director 2010–12. She has directed various group research projects on the modern history of publishing and reading; the professionalization of women writers; transatlantic cultural and publishing networks; and the intersections of literature, scientific discourse, and public policy. The results have been published in numerous edited volumes and academic journals (*Bulletin Hispanique; Journal of Spanish Cultural Studies; Studi Ispanici; Bulletin of Spanish Studies; Revista de Occidente; Journal of the History of Sexuality*). She has authored, edited, or coedited: *Eduardo López Bago y el naturalismo radica: Literatura y mercado editorial en el siglo XIX* (1995); *Mujer pública y vida privada: Del arte eunuco a la novela lupanaria* (2008); *La mujer de letras o la letra herida: Discursos y representaciones sobre la mujer escritora en el siglo XIX* (2008); *Redes públicas, relaciones trasatlánticas: Escritores, editores y lectores en el entresiglos hispánico (XIX–XX)* (2012; monographic issue of *Revista de Estudios Hispánicos*); *No hay nación para este sexo: La Re(d)pública transatlántica de las Letras; Escritoras españolas y latinoamericanas (1824–1936)* (Iberoamericana/Vervuert, 2015); "'Por ser mujer y autora ...': Identidades autoriales de escritoras y artistas en la cultura contemporánea" (2017; monographic issue of *Ínsula: Revista de letras y ciencias humanas*) ; and in collaboration with Jo Labanyi and Elena Delgado, *Engaging the Emotions in Spanish Culture and History (18th Century to the Present)* (Vanderbilt University Press, 2015; Spanish translation, Cátedra, forthcoming, 2018). She has also coordinated the edition of the *Obras completas* of Ramón Gómez de la Serna (1996–2014, 20 vols.) and has edited the volume *Total de Greguerías* (2014).

Ana Paula Ferreira: Professor of Portuguese literature at the University of Minnesota. She specializes in Race and Postcolonial Studies and on Women Writers, feminisms, and Empire. She reintroduced the forgotten women writers from Salazar's New State in the volume *A urgência de contar: Contos de mulheres, anos 40*. Her work on the fiction of Lídia Jorge has been published widely and includes the edited collection *Para um leitor ignorado: Ensaios sobre O Vale da Paixão e outras ficções de Lídia Jorge*. Recently she has coedited with Ana Luísa Amaral and Marilena Freitas *New Portuguese Letters to the World: International Reception*.

Elizabeth Franklin Lewis: Professor of Spanish at the University of Mary Washington. Author of *Women Writers in the Spanish Enlightenment: The Pursuit of Happiness* (2004) and coeditor with Catherine Jaffe of *Eve's Enlightenment: Women's Experience in Spain and Spanish America 1726–1839* (2009). She has authored numerous articles on eighteenth-century

Spain, including "Hispano-Irish Women of Spain's Late Enlightenment Period"; "La 'verdadera' Ilustración en 'Fernando en Zaragoza, Una visión' de Frasquita Larrea (1814)"; "Enlightenment Politics and Catholic Charity in Spain: Bernardo Ward's *Obra pia* (1750) and *Proyecto económico* (1762)"; "La caridad de una mujer: Modernización y ambivalencia sentimental en la escritura femenina decimonónica"; "Economía doméstica: Caridad y trabajo femenino en el discurso reformista de las mujeres ilustradas"; "A su reina benéfica: Representaciones de María Luisa de Parma"; "*Actos de caridad*: Women's Charitable Work in Eighteenth-Century Spain"; "The Sensibility of Motherhood in Josefa Amar y Borbón's *Discurso sobre la educación física y moral de las mujeres* (1790)"; "Breaking Chains: Language and Slavery in María Rosa Gálvez's *Zinda* (1804)"; "The Tearful Reunion of Divided Femininity in María Rosa Gálvez's Neoclassic Theater"; and "Feijoo, Josefa Amar y Borbón and the 'Feminist' Debate in Eighteenth-Century Spain."

Jone M. Hernández García: Received her doctorate from the University of the Basque Country (UPV/EHU) and is a lecturer in social anthropology at UPV/EHU. She has researched topics related to the Basque language (Euskara) and Basque culture, youth, free time, and sports, mainly from a feminist and gender perspective. Her latest publications have to do with *bertsolarismo*, or oral improvization characteristics of Euskal Herria.

Miren Llona: Lecturer in contemporary history at the University of the Basque Country (UPV/EHU). Between 2010 and 2012, she was vice-president of the International Oral History Association (IOHA). Her publications and articles include: *Entre señorita y garçonne: Historia oral de las mujeres bilbainas de clase media, 1919–1939* (2002); and "From Militia Women to *Emakume*: Myths Regarding Femininity during the Civil War in the Basque Country," in *Memory and Cultural History of the Spanish Civil War* (2013).

Catherine M. Jaffe: Professor of Spanish at Texas State University at San Marcos. Editor with Elizabeth Franklin Lewis of *Eve's Enlightenment: Women's Experience in Spain and Spanish America, 1726–1839* (2009), and author of numerous articles including: "Sociabilidad, filantropía, y escritura: María Lorenza de los Ríos y Loyo, Marquesa de Fuerte-Híjar (1761–1821) (with Elisa Martín Valdepeñas); "Female Quixotism and National Identity in *Contigo, pan y cebolla* (1833)"; "Doña Leonora's

Library: Women's Reading from *The Spectator* (1711) to the *Semanario de Salamanca* (1795)"; "El Quijotismo femenino: Mujer y lectura al fin de la Ilustración"; "Gender, Translation, and Eighteenth-Century Women Dramatists: Elizabeth Griffith's *The School for Rakes* (1769) and María Lorenza de los Ríos y Loyo's *El Eugenio* (1801)" (with Elisa Martín-Valdepeñas Yagüe); "Lectora y lectura femenina en la modernidad: El *Semanario de Salamanca* (1793–1798)"; "*Noticia de la vida y obras del Conde de Rumford* (1802) by María Lorenza de los Ríos, Marquesa de Fuerte-Híjar: Authorizing a Space for Female Charity"; "Of Women's Love, Learning, and (In)Discretion: María Lorenza de los Ríos's *La sabia indiscreta* (1803)"; "From *Les précieuses ridicules* to *Las preciosas ridículas*: Ramón de la Cruz's Translation of Molière and the Problems of Cultural Adaptation"; "Suspect Pleasure: Writing the Woman Reader in Eighteenth-Century Spain."

Roberta Johnson: Professor emerita at the University of Kansas and adjunct professor at the University of California, Los Angeles. She is the author of *Carmen Laforet* (Twayne, 1981); *El ser y la palabra en Gabriel Miró* (Fundamentos, 1985); *Crossfire: Philosophy and the Novel in Spain 1900–1934* (University of Kentucky Press, 1993); *Las bibliotecas de Azorín* (Caja de Ahorros del Mediterráneo, 1996); and *Gender and Nation in the Spanish Modernist Novel* (Vanderbilt University Press, 2003). She coedited the *Antología del pensamiento feminista español 1726–2011* (Cátedra, 2013) with Maite Zubiaurre and is currently completing a book on "Major Concepts in Spanish Feminist Theory."

María Victoria López-Cordón Cortezo: Professor emerita of modern history at the Universidad Complutense, Madrid. She is author of *El pensamiento político-internacional del federalismo español, 1868–1874* (Planeta, 1975); *La Revolución de 1868 y la I República* (Siglo Veintiuno de España, 1976); *Realidad e imagen de Europa en la España Ilustrada* (Aguirre, 1992); and of a study of Josefa Amar y Borbón, *Condición femenina y razón ilustrada* (Saragossa, 2005). Prof. López-Cordón edited *La casa de Borbón, familia, corte y política*, vol. 1 (Alianza, 2000); the works of Sofía Casanova, *La revolución bolchevista: Diario de un testigo* (Instituto de la Mujer, 1990); Josefa Amar y Borbón's *Discurso sobre la educación física y moral de las mujeres* (Cátedra, 1994); and Germaine de Stäel's *Reflexiones sobre el proceso de la reina* (Abada, 2006). Prof. López-Cordón is also coeditor of several volumes, including *La España de Fernando VII: La posición europea y la emancipación americana* (Espasa-Calpe, 1996–2001) and *Gobernar en tiempos de crisis: Las quiebras dinásticas en el ámbito hispánico 1250–1808* (Sílex, 2008).

Deborah Madden: Doctoral researcher in the School of Languages and Cultures at the University of Sheffield, and a White Rose College of the Arts and Humanities Research Council award holder. Her research seeks to identify left-of-centre Spanish and Portuguese women writers from the early decades of the twentieth century whose works have been excluded from the literary canon. By focusing on novels by politically progressive women in early twentieth-century Iberia, her thesis aims to examine how a selection of female authors used literature as a means of political expression, while uncovering the shared experiences of Iberian women. Madden's other research interests include the history of feminism in the Iberian Peninsula, the political development of women in Spain and Portugal, and questions of gender and sexuality more broadly in Hispanic and Lusophone contexts.

Fátima Mariano: Doctoral candidate and researcher at the Instituto de História Contemporânea Faculdade de Ciências Sociais e Humanas (Institute of Contemporary History at the School of Humanities and Social Sciences), Universidade Nova de Lisboa (New University of Lisbon). Her areas of expertise are the Portuguese First Republic (1910–26), women studies, and First-World-War history.

Josune Muñoz: Specialist in the Basque language, whose research focuses on the geographical and historical recovery and analysis of literature and comics created by women. Since 2003, she has directed the bilingual literary project SKOLASTIKA in Bilbao (www.skolastika.net), through which she gives courses, methodological seminars in feminist literary criticism, lectures, and organizes cultural activities centred on literature and culture produced by women.

Mary Nash: Chaired professor of history at the University of Barcelona, specializing in women's history and Spanish feminism. Her books include: *Mujeres libres: España 1936–1939* (1996); *Mujer y movimiento obrero en España* (1981); *Mujer, familia y trabajo en España (1895–1936)* (1983); *Presencia y protagonismo: Aspectos de la presencia de la mujer* (1984); *Las mujeres en la guerra civil* (1989); *Defying Male Civilization: Women in the Spanish Civil War* (1995; Spanish version, *Rojas: Las mujeres republicanas en la guerra civil* [1999]). In addition, she edited with Rosa Ballester

Mulheres, trabalho e reprodução: Atitudes sociáis e políticas de protecção à vida (1996).

María do Cebreiro Rábade Villar: Award-winning poet and professor in the Department of Literary Theory and Comparative Literature at the Universidad de Santiago de Compostela (University of Santiago of Compostela, Galicia). She published her first poetic collection *O estadio do espello* in 1988, followed by *Nós, as inadaptadas* (2002), which was awarded the runner-up of the XXI Esquío Award in Galician Language Poetry, followed by *Non queres que o poema te coñeza* (2004), awarded the II Poetry Prize Caixanova; *O barrio das chinesas* (2005); *Os hemisferios* (2006); *Cuarto de outono* (2008); *Non son de aquí* (2008); *Os inocentes* (2014); and *O deserto* (2015), awarded the 2016 Fundación Premios da Crítica Galicia (Foundation Critics' Awards Galicia). From 2016 to 2020, she is serving as associate dean in the School of Philology at the University of Santiago of Compostela.

Iratxe Retolaza: Lecturer in social sciences and communications at the University of the Basque Country (UPV/EHU). Her research is focused on contemporary Basque literature from a feminist-theory perspective. In this vein, she has published the book *Malkoen mintzoa: Arantxa Urretabizkaia eta eleberrigintza* (2002); she collaborated with Edurne Epelde and Miren Aranguren in *Gure Genealogia Feministak: Euskal Herriko Mugimendu Feministaren kronika bat* (2015); and she has edited with Isa Castillo *Genero-ariketak: Feminismoaren subjektuak* (EDO!, 2014). She is member of Emagin, Feminist Research and Documentation Centre.

María Ruiz Torrado: Doctoral candidate in feminist and gender studies at the University of the Basque Country (UPV/EHU). She has published in the journal *Kondaira* and has collaborated in team research, investigating the social difficulties and disadvantages of women who have been in prison. Her dissertation focuses on prison as a gendered institution.

Index

TORONTO IBERIC

1 Anthony J. Cascardi, *Cervantes, Literature, and the Discourse of Politics*
2 Jessica A. Boon, *The Mystical Science of the Soul: Medieval Cognition in Bernardino de Laredo's Recollection Method*
3 Susan Byrne, *Law and History in Cervantes' Don Quixote*
4 Mary E. Barnard and Frederick A. de Armas (eds), *Objects of Culture in the Literature of Imperial Spain*
5 Nil Santiáñez, *Topographies of Fascism: Habitus, Space, and Writing in Twentieth-Century Spain*
6 Nelson Orringer, *Lorca in Tune with Falla: Literary and Musical Interludes*
7 Ana M. Gómez-Bravo, *Textual Agency: Writing Culture and Social Networks in Fifteenth-Century Spain*
8 Javier Irigoyen-García, *The Spanish Arcadia: Sheep Herding, Pastoral Discourse, and Ethnicity in Early Modern Spain*
9 Stephanie Sieburth, *Survival Songs: Conchita Piquer's* Coplas *and Franco's Regime of Terror*
10 Christine Arkinstall, *Spanish Female Writers and the Freethinking Press, 1879–1926*
11 Margaret Boyle, *Unruly Women: Performance, Penitence, and Punishment in Early Modern Spain*
12 Evelina Gužauskytė, *Christopher Columbus's Naming in the* diarios *of the Four Voyages (1492–1504): A Discourse of Negotiation*
13 Mary E. Barnard, *Garcilaso de la Vega and the Material Culture of Renaissance Europe*
14 William Viestenz, *By the Grace of God: Francoist Spain and the Sacred Roots of Political Imagination*
15 Michael Scham, Lector Ludens*: The Representation of Games and Play in Cervantes*
16 Stephen Rupp, *Heroic Forms: Cervantes and the Literature of War*
17 Enrique Fernández, *Anxieties of Interiority and Dissection in Early Modern Spain*

18 Susan Byrne, *Ficino in Spain*
19 Patricia M. Keller, *Ghostly Landscapes: Film, Photography, and the Aesthetics of Haunting in Contemporary Spanish Culture*
20 Carolyn A. Nadeau, *Food Matters: Alonso Quijano's Diet and the Discourse of Food in Early Modern Spain*
21 Cristian Berco, *From Body to Community: Venereal Disease and Society in Baroque Spain*
22 Elizabeth R. Wright, *The Epic of Juan Latino: Dilemmas of Race and Religion in Renaissance Spain*
23 Ryan D. Giles, *Inscribed Power: Amulets and Magic in Early Spanish Literature*
24 Jorge Pérez, *Confessional Cinema: Religion, Film, and Modernity in Spain's Development Years (1960–1975)*
25 Joan Ramon Resina, *Josep Pla: Seeing the World in the Form of Articles*
26 Javier Irigoyen-García, *"Moors Dressed as Moors": Clothing, Social Distinction, and Ethnicity in Early Modern Iberia*
27 Jean Dangler, *Edging Toward Iberia*
28 Ryan D. Giles and Steven Wagschal (eds): *Beyond Sight: Engaging the Senses in Iberian Literatures and Cultures, 1200–1750*
29 Silvia Bermúdez, *Rocking the Boat: Migration and Race in Contemporary Spanish Music*
30 Hilaire Kallendorf, *Ambiguous Antidotes: Virtue as Vaccine for Vice in Early Modern Spain*
31 Leslie Harkema, *Spanish Modernism and the Poetics of Youth: From Miguel de Unamuno to* La Joven Literatura
32 Benjamin Fraser, *Cognitive Disability Aesthetics: Visual Culture, Disability Representations, and the (In)Visibility of Cognitive Difference*
33 Robert Patrick Newcomb, *Iberianism and Crisis: Spain and Portugal at the Turn of the Twentieth Century*
34 Sara J. Brenneis, *Spaniards in Mauthausen: Representations of a Nazi Concentration Camp, 1940–2015*
35 Silvia Bermúdez and Roberta Johnson (eds): *A New History of Iberian Feminisms*

www.ingramcontent.com/pod-product-compliance
Lightning Source LLC
LaVergne TN
LVHW090757070826
844660LV00022B/1006

* 9 7 8 1 4 8 7 5 2 0 0 8 3 *